THE MEDIEVAL WORLD AND

ITS TRANSFORMATIONS

800–1650

Western Society: Institutions and Ideals

McGRAW-HILL BOOK COMPANY New York St. Louis San Francisco
Toronto London Sydney

Gerald M. Straka

Associate Professor of History, University of Delaware

VOLUME II

THE MEDIEVAL WORLD AND ITS TRANSFORMATIONS

800—1650

THE MEDIEVAL WORLD AND ITS TRANSFORMATIONS
800–1650, Volume II

Library of Congress Catalog Card Number 67-10883

1 2 3 4 5 6 7 8 9 0   HD   7 4 3 2 1 0 6 9 8 7

The following articles or selections have been reprinted in this volume with the permission of the publishers:

Glanville, "Concerning the Laws and Customs of the Kingdom of England," from ENGLISH HISTORICAL DOCUMENTS, 1042–1189, edited by D. C. Douglas and G. W. Greenaway. Eyre and Spottiswoode, London, 1953. U. S. permission from Oxford University Press, New York.

Selection from THE SONG OF WILLIAM, translated by E. N. Stone. University of Washington Press, Seattle, Wash., 1951.

Selection from THE ART OF COURTLY LOVE by Andreas Capellanus, translated by J. J. Parry, Columbia University Press, 1941.

"Charter of the Garment Cutters of Stendal," from A SOURCE BOOK FOR MEDIEVAL ECONOMIC HISTORY, edited by R. C. Cave and H. H. Coulson. The Bruce Publishing Co., Milwaukee, Wis., 1936.

"The Life of St. Godric," from SOCIAL LIFE IN BRITAIN FROM THE CONQUEST TO THE REFORMATION by G. G. Coulton. Cambridge University Press, New York, 1918.

Selection from THE STATEMAN'S BOOK OF JOHN OF SALISBURY, translated and edited by John Dickinson. Copyright 1927 by Alfred A. Knopf, Inc. Copyright renewed 1955 by Lindsay Rogers. Reprinted by permission of Appleton-Century-Crofts.

Selection from PIERS THE PLOUGHMAN by William Langland, translated by J. F. Goodridge. Penguin Books, 1964.

Selection from THE GOLDEN LEGEND OF JACOBUS DE VORAGINE, translated by G. Ryan and H. Ripperger. New York, 1941. Used by permission of David McKay Co., Inc.

Selection from THE LETTERS OF POPE GREGORY VII, translated and edited by E. Emerton. Columbia University Press, 1932.

Various selections from MEDIEVAL POLITICAL IDEAS, edited by Ewart Lewis. Alfred A. Knopf, Inc., 1954.

Selection from UNIVERSITY RECORDS AND LIFE IN THE MIDDLE AGES, translated and edited by L. Thorndike. Columbia University Press, 1944.

Selection from THE OPUS MAJUS of ROGER BACON, translated by R. B. Burke. New York: Russell & Russell, Inc., 1962.

Selection from INTRODUCTION TO ST. THOMAS AQUINAS, edited by Anton C. Pegis. Random House Inc., 1948. Canada permission from Burns & Oates Ltd., London.

Selection from A FLORENTINE DIARY by Luca Landucci, edited by I. del Badia. Published by E. P. Dutton & Co., Inc., and reprinted with their permission. Canada permission from J. M. Dent & Sons Ltd., London.

Selection from ON EDUCATION by Juan Luis Vives, translated and edited by F. Watson. Cambridge University Press, New York, 1913.

Selection from MENNO SIMONS' LIFE AND WRITINGS, edited and translated by H. S. Bender and J. Horsch. Mennonite Publishing House, Scottsdale, Penn., 1944.

To MARIAN WILSON, friend, critic, and secretary extraordinary

Preface

This anthology grew out of a college freshman course in Western
Institutions and Social Ideas taught by a staff that used original sources
as materials for discussion and analysis. To keep a discussion course stimulating and exciting to teacher and student alike, we found ourselves
supplementing existing anthologies with new documents. This anthology
is the logical end product of these efforts. On the basis of our experience in
discussing original documents in an introductory course, we determined
that three principles should characterize our anthology.

First, we asked that an anthology have a range sufficient to allow real
flexibility. A useful anthology should permit the revamping of a course
from year to year, if only to prevent the instructors from going stale.
In theory, our four volumes at well over one million words could
include enough selections to suppy a two-year discussion course meeting
four days a week. Attractive as some of us might find such a prospect,
most Western civilization courses meet for a single academic year
and, at that, for one or two weekly discussion sessions. We would expect
most courses to use less than half of the anthologized documents in any
one year. Consequently, this anthology should provide every instructor
(or staff) with ample leeway to assign material to fit his particular students.

Our arrangement of the readings within each of the four volumes is
topical as well as chronological. Although we have grouped together
documents that are likely to be discussed together (or that provide a
common pool from which to choose one reading) and have put them in
what seems to us a sensible sequence, our organization in no way impinges
upon the freedom of the instructor to rearrange as he sees fit.

Second, we felt that a useful anthology should have definite limits and
a point of view; otherwise flexibility might dissolve into chaos. Our
limits are explicit: we selected documents either to portray ideas about
Western society or to illustrate Western political, economic, religious,
or other institutions. We did not seek to present historical events as such,
leaving this task to a text or to the discretion of the instructor. By focusing on institutions and social ideas, we excluded "pure" philosophy (such
as linguistic analysis) and "pure" science (such as the Quantum Theory)
on the one hand and literature and art for their own sakes on the other.
Selections from Chaucer's *Canterbury Tales* and Dostoevski's *The Brothers
Karamazov* appear in this collection because in our judgment they illustrate certain values and institutions better than other available documents. It is in any case obvious that with the availability of primary
works in paperback, an instructor who so wishes can easily pick supplementary literary works. By focusing on the West, we have deliberately

excluded documents from cultures like the Byzantine or Islamic that are related, yet raise complex questions of affiliations best handled in text or lecture.

Third, we relied on our classroom experience for selecting documents that by their content and format lend themselves to fruitful and interesting discussion. By choosing selections of from ten to twenty pages, we have been able to include many documents in full and others in excerpts substantial enough to permit the author's line of argument and point of view to emerge. Athough almost every conceivable type of document—from philosophical treatise to personal diary—is represented, we have been sparing in the use of legal and constitutional texts that tend to appeal to professional historians, but are too technical for undergraduate discussion. In making our selections, we have tried neither to draw up a catalogue of familiar names nor to stock a museum of esoterica. We have tried to find and edit the most interesting and significant documents that illustrate major ideological and institutional trends. Some two dozen documents have been specially translated into English for this anthology. Our guidelines throughout have been significance, intrinsic interest, and discussability.

Our introductions preceding the documents attempt to provide just enough background to permit intelligent reading, without prejudging issues by means of capsule summaries or leading questions. They make no claim to provide continuity or depth. We consider it more constructive to suggest to the student—in the short introductory essay following the Table of Contents—the kinds of questions by which he can learn to come to grips with original sources for himself.

From its half-conscious inception to its final form, this four-volume anthology has been a collective venture on the part of three historians and one philosopher. Not only did all the editors participate in the detailed planning of each volume, but each of us has contributed selections and introductions to each of the four volumes. Our overriding concern has been to produce a collection of readings that would be interesting, unhackneyed, and enjoyable to use. We can only hope that we have succeeded.

For accuracy of expression, for tedious counting of words and pages, for the indispensable flash of insight, the general editor of Volume II wishes to express his indebtedness to his wife, Lois Straka.

Gerald M. Straka

Peter H. Amann
Richard J. Burke, Jr.
Melvin Cherno

Contents

III MEDIEVAL INTELLECTUAL LIFE

IV AN IMPRESSION OF THE AGE

V RENAISSANCE AND REFORMATION

On Reading
Original Sources

A generation ago the historian Carl Becker shocked an after-dinner audience with a speech entitled, "Every Man His Own Historian." His audience was made up of members of the American Historical Association who had come to honor and hear their newly elected president. Yet Becker upset their mental equilibrium—and their digestion—by suggesting that history was not some secret art to be passed on to a cloistered initiate who would emerge years later from behind ivy walls with eyesight impaired and a Ph.D. to his name. Becker's point was that man's attempt to make sense of his own past was a natural and universal concern; that since no two men were alike, every man had to deal with the past—to be his own historian—in terms meaningful to himself. Yet Becker did not imply that all men were equally qualified for the task. Though the past is always seen through human eyes—by someone with interests, predilections, prejudices, and blind spots—there is nonetheless something like 20/20 vision in history as opposed to the myopia that results from lack of training. There are *some* tricks to the trade, and they can be learned.

One of the aims of any course using an anthology such as this is to provide you with some critical insight into the unavoidable job of being your own historian. All your life you will have to come to terms with the past, whether it be yesterday's personal encounter or the international roulette wheel stopping at your number. Even most family arguments boil down to historical controversy.

In dealing with the readings in this anthology, your first objective should be to master the technique of being your own *competent* historian. Here you are asked to make sense of a cultural tradition by analyzing documents illustrating different aspects of that tradition. The variety of documents that you will face is enormous. They may be roughly classified as follows:

1 History, biography, autobiography
2 Letters, journals, memoirs
3 Philosophical and scientific treatises
4 Speeches, sermons, manifestoes, public debates
5 Articles in periodicals
6 Essays, dialogues, poetry
7 Legal and constitutional documents
8 Diplomatic reports

You may best begin your analysis by following some rather basic considerations. Every one of these documents may be studied from various perspectives: each will have (1) an author, (2) a social and cultural context, (3) a purpose or function, (4) a subject matter, (5) a structure and method, and (6) relationship with and affiliations to other documents. You can make each of these "dimensions" of a document a focus for analysis, either by yourself or in class discussion. Each is a *direction* in which you can strike out; each suggests a *question* or a cluster of questions that you can raise about the document. If you learn to ask these questions habitually while reading, you are well on your way toward a critical understanding of history, even in its more difficult social and intellectual aspects.

Dimension 1: The Author. You may read a document as an expression of the author's point of view. A presidential message to Congress, for instance, is an expression of presidential policy on a given problem or problems. You may raise the question of the author's background, of his values and biases. In most cases this is a straightforward enough question. Sometimes this may be a crucial question, although at other times it is of minor importance or even altogether irrelevant.

Dimension 2: The Historical Context. You may read a document as reflecting the social and cultural milieu out of which it comes. When a Chinese leader makes a statement of national policy, for example, to what extent do his ideas and the way in which he puts them reflect the historical experience of China on the one hand, of the Chinese Communist movement on the other? This kind of question is related to the previous one, yet it is broader: it involves the ideas and values held during whole historical eras. You should learn to move back and forth between textbook and documents, evaluating the textbook interpretations of the Protestant Reformation or of the Industrial Revolution in terms of generalizations you have drawn from your original readings for each period.

Dimension 3: The Purpose. Not all documents aim simply to tell the truth, the whole truth, and nothing but the truth. Many of them, through the use of rhetorical devices, are designed to win a case, whether in an actual court, in formal debate, or in a wider forum of opinion. Many are pitched to a special audience to get some particular point across, for instance, a speech of Adolf Hitler's addressing a Nazi party rally. Some are justifications of actions already taken, others exhortations for the future. Clearly, all written documents are intelligible only in terms of the purpose or function they intended to serve and of the audience they attempted to reach.

Dimension 4: The Subject Matter. This may be the obvious question, yet it may not always be easy to answer. What is the reading about? You should practice summarizing documents in your own words and as briefly as possible, particularly when this is difficult to do. You may have to summarize ideas that have been advanced or to characterize institutions that have been described or exemplified. In historical or biographical narratives, subject matter is normally central. What were the ancient Germans like? What sort of man was Leonardo da Vinci? What was the structure of the ancient Roman Republic? What was life like at the court of Louis XIV of France?

Dimension 5: Structure and Method. This is the *internal* dimension. How does a document hang together? What is the relation of the parts to the whole? *How* does the President present his case for certain legislation to Congress? In a straightforward historical narrative or a list of grievances, these internal relationships may be very simple; in a philosophical treatise or in a tragedy the internal structure may be very complex and artful. If a document presents an *argument,* then the question of its validity is perfectly in order, as is the question of the truth of its premises.

Dimension 6: Relationships to Other Documents. In this broad category fall all the questions about the influence of earlier writers on later ones and about similarities, contrasts, "climates of opinion," and traditions. How does the foreign policy statement of our Chinese Communist leader compare with earlier such announcements? With announced Russian Communist aims, recent and in Lenin's day? With the way non-Communist countries justify and announce their policy? Does our Chinese Communist seem to follow the guidelines for holding on to power suggested by Machiavelli in the sixteenth century? You may consider a given document as an effect of earlier developments and as a cause of subsequent ones. It may be combined with others of its own period to form a trend. It may be grouped in countless ways. As editors, we have already done some grouping by dividing the readings into four volumes and by choosing an arrangement within the volumes that is partly topical. Your instructor, by assigning some readings and not others, will have made yet another such grouping.

All this may seem very abstract and remote, until you really get down to cases. Take, as an example, the Declaration of Independence of July 4, 1776 (see Vol. III, pages 327–330). This document is at least vaguely familiar to most Americans, yet it reveals its full significance—as well as a nest of controversial issues—only when analyzed in terms of the six dimensions that have been suggested.

The Declaration of Independence was drafted chiefly by Thomas Jefferson, revised by a committee that included Benjamin Franklin and John Adams, and signed by all fifty-six delegates to the Second Continental Congress, the representatives of the "Thirteen" United States of America. Who, then, was its *author?* Does it really represent the views of all the inhabitants of those thirteen states? A majority of them? How were the delegates elected?

The social and cultural *context* of the document was the eighteenth-century Enlightenment, with its appeal to "self-evident truths" characteristic of that period's buoyant confidence in the power of human reason to apprehend objective fact. Could such an appeal carry any force today, after modern psychology has revealed the numberless ways in which we all deceive ourselves and after the history of modern wars and totalitarian regimes has demonstrated the folly of calling man the "rational animal"?

The *purpose* of the Declaration, as we are told explicitly, is to justify the revolution of the thirteen colonies against their mother country. But what is "justification"? Is it only a convenient cover-up for what they had undertaken? Was it an attempt to win support from other countries, perhaps from France?

As for its *subject matter,* most of it seems to be about the actions of "the present

King of Great Britain." (This is puzzling in itself, for did not the Glorious Revolution of 1688–1689 establish the supremacy of Parliament over the King?) On closer examination, however, these actions all have one thing in common: they are allegedly violations of the "rights" of the colonists. With this as a clue, we see that the opening and closing sections of the document also deal with the concept of rights.

This leads to a consideration of the *structure* of the Declaration of Independence, which proves to be that of a "hypothetical syllogism": *if* any government fails to protect the rights of its citizens to life, liberty, and the pursuit of happiness, *then* such a government forfeits all claim to their allegiance; the English government *has* failed to protect our rights (the long list of grievances is intended to prove this); *therefore* we owe the English government no allegiance. This is Jefferson's argument reduced to its essentials. In form it is a logical argument: if x is true, then y is true; but x *is* true: therefore y is true. If its premises are also true—and this is quite another question—then its conclusion must be accepted. But what are these premises? How can we tell whether they are true?

Finally, the Declaration of Independence reveals the strong *influence* of John Locke's Second Treatise of Civil Government (see Vol. III, pages 44–64), and in turn the Declaration of Independence had an undoubted *effect* on the great French Revolution that broke out only thirteen years later. Did the Declaration also serve as the basis for the United States Constitution, or was that latter document founded on different philosophical premises? Did the Declaration establish political democracy? Did it have anything to say about capitalism? Have the principles set forth in the Declaration played any part in the current wave of colonial wars of independence in Africa and Asia?

Not all these dimensions are equally important in every document. Even so, you would do well to cultivate the habit of asking yourself all six questions about every document you encounter, before deciding which are the most significant in each particular case. In time this becomes second nature, yet to do this is to cultivate the critical faculty that is an essential part of an educated man.

THE MEDIEVAL WORLD AND
ITS TRANSFORMATIONS
800–1650

Part One

Medieval Society

The Manor

Forerunners of the medieval manorial system appeared in earlier Germanic and late Roman arrangements. The breakdown of the economic unity of the Roman Empire and the fierce disruptions caused by the invasions of non-Christian people, which lasted at least until the days of Charlemagne, hastened its development. Despite wide regional differences, by the eleventh century the basic functions of manorialism had clearly emerged: economic self-sufficiency necessitated by isolation, the system of bondage in varying degrees, the contractual relationships regulating both the peasants' rights to their own portions of manorial land and their labor on the portions reserved for the lord's use (i.e., the demesne lands), the social and economic dominance of the lord. The following documents give an idea of the complexity and compactness of the economic and social arrangements on a particular manor.

Seneschaucie, *or* The Book of the Office of Seneschal, *is a statement of the duties of the various members of the manor. It is particularly interesting because it depicts an ideal rather than an actual situation. It takes us into the day-by-day operation of the manor, particularly its division of labor, which accommodated the complexities of agricultural production. Thus the title is misleading; in addition to the seneschal (an important supervisory assistant to the lord), the whole range of agrarian positions—from the lord himself down to the lowly dairymaid —is discussed, together with the functions and relationships. The original manuscript, probably from the late thirteenth century, is in French and is unsigned. Although it may have been written in England,* Seneschaucie *reflects a system widely established throughout Western Europe. The following is a glossary of unfamiliar agricultural terms:*

amerciament   an unfixed fine, set at the mercy of the inflicter; usually lighter than a fixed fine
aver   draft horse
bedel   an under-officer of justice
boon and custom   obligations of the tenants
byre   cow-house
conygarth   rabbit warren
draft   a selection from a large number
dredge   a mixture of grain, usually oats and barley
escheat   the right of appropriating lands left without an owner
fold *n.,*   an enclosure for domestic animals; *v.,* to enclose animals in a fold
frank   a freeman
heriot   inheritance tax paid by serf
marl *n.,*   a kind of soil used as fertilizer; *v.,* to fertilize with marl

merchet   payment of serf to lord on marriage of his daughter
perch   a measure of land (usually 1/160 of an acre)
vaccary   a place where cows are kept
wether   ram (male sheep)

*The second selection is a thirteenth-century description of the manor of
Alwalton in the county of Huntingdon, England. The lord happens
to have been a churchman, the Abbot of Petersborough. The medieval
abbot or bishop was often a great landholder, not only lording
over great estates, but also frequently appearing—mace and shield in
hand—on the field of battle. This abbot's manor held three kinds of
tenants, whose obligations and holdings are described in detail.*

↝ SENESCHAUCIE

HERE BEGINS THE BOOK OF THE OFFICE OF SENESCHAL

The seneschal of lands ought to be prudent and faithful and profitable, and he ought
to know the law of the realm, to protect his lord's business and to instruct and give
assurance to the bailiffs who are beneath him in their difficulties. He ought two or
three times a year to make his rounds and visit the manors of his stewardship, and
then he ought to inquire about the rents, services, and customs, hidden or withdrawn,
and about franchises of courts, lands, woods, meadows, pastures, waters, mills, and
other things which belong to the manor and are done away with without warrant, by
whom, and how: and if he be able let him amend these things in the right way without doing wrong to any, and if he be not, let him show it to his lord, that he may deal
with it if he wish to maintain his right.

The seneschal ought, at his first coming to the manors, to cause all the demesne
lands of each to be measured by true men, and he ought to know by the perch of the
country how many acres there are in each field, and thereby he can know how much
wheat, rye, barley, oats, peas, beans, and dredge one ought by right to sow in each
acre, and thereby can one see if the provost or the hayward account for more seed
than is right, and thereby can he see how many ploughs are required on the manor,
for each plough ought by right to plough nine score acres, that is to say: sixty for
winter seed, sixty for spring seed, and sixty in fallow. Also he can see how many acres
ought to be ploughed yearly by boon or custom, and how many acres remain to be tilled
by the ploughs of the manor. And further he can see how many acres ought to be
reaped by boon and custom, and how many for money. And if there be any cheating in
the sowing, or ploughing, or reaping, he shall easily see it. And he must cause all the
meadows and several pastures to be measured by acres, and thereby can one know the

Walter of Henley's Husbandry, together with . . . Seneschaucie . . . (London: Longmans,
Green & Co., Ltd., 1890), pp. 85–91, 97–99, 103–107, 111–119.

cost, and how much hay is necessary every year for the sustenance of the manor, and how much stock can be kept on the several pasture, and how much on the common.

The seneschal has no power to remove a bailiff or servant who is with the lord, and clothed and kept by him, without the special order of the lord, for so he would make of the head the tail; but if the bailiff be less capable or less profitable than he ought to be, or if he have committed trespass or offence in his office, let it be shown to the lord and to his council, and he shall do as he shall think good.

The seneschal should not have power to sell wardship, or marriage, or escheat, nor to dower any lady or woman, nor to take homage or suit, nor to sell or make free a villein without special warrant from his lord. And the seneschal ought not to be chief accountant for the things of his office, for he ought on the account of each manor to answer for his doings and commands and improvements, and for fines and amercia-ments of the courts where he has held pleas as another, because no man can or ought to be judge or justice of his own doings.

The seneschal ought, on his coming to each manor, to see and inquire how they are tilled, and in what crops they are, and how the cart-horses and avers, oxen, cows, sheep, and swine are kept and improved. And if there be loss or damage from want of guard, he ought to take fines from those who are to blame, so that the lord may not lose. The seneschal ought to see that each manor is properly stocked, and if there be overcharge on any manor more than the pasture can bear, let the overcharge be moved to another manor where there is less stock. And if the lord be in want of money to pay debts due, or to make a purchase at a particular term, the seneschal ought before the term, and before the time that need arises, to look to the manors from which he can have money at the greatest advantage and smallest loss, for if he will not provide, he will often lose.

The seneschal ought, on his coming to the manors, to inquire how the bailiff bears himself within and without, what care he takes, what improvement he makes, and what increase and profit there is in the manor in his office, because of his being there. And also of the provost, and hayward, and keeper of cattle, and all other offices, how each bears himself towards him, and thereby he can be more sure who makes profit and who harm. Also he ought to provide that there should be no waste or destruction on any manor, or overcharge of anything belonging to the manor. He ought to re-move all those that are not necessary for the lord, and all the servants who do noth-ing, and all overcharge in the dairy, and other profitless and unreasonable offices which are called wrong outlays, without profit.

The seneschal ought, on his coming to the manors, to inquire about wrong-doings and trespasses done in parks, ponds, warrens, conygarths, and dove-houses, and of all other things which are done to the loss of the lord in his office.

THE OFFICE OF BAILIFF

The bailiff ought to be faithful and profitable, and a good husbandman, and also pru-dent, that he need not send to his lord or superior seneschal to have advice and instruc-tion about everything connected with his baillie, unless it be an extraordinary matter, or of great danger; for a bailiff is worth little in time of need who knows nothing, and has nothing in himself without the instruction of another. The bailiff ought to rise every morning and survey the woods, corn, meadows, and pastures, and see what damage may have been done. And he ought to see that the ploughs are yoked in the morning, and unyoked at the right time, so that they may do their proper ploughing every day, as much as they can and ought to do by the measured perch. And he must cause the land to be marled, folded, manured, improved, and amended as his knowledge may approve, for the good and bettering of the manor. He ought to see how many measured acres the boon-tenants and customary-tenants ought to plough yearly, and how many the ploughs of the manor ought to till, and so he may lessen the surplus of the cost. And he ought to see and know how many acres of meadow the customary-tenants ought to mow and make, and how many acres of corn the boon-tenants and customary-tenants ought to reap and carry, and thereby he can see how many acres of meadow remain to be mowed, and how many acres of corn remain to be reaped for money, so that nothing shall be wrongfully paid for. And he ought to forbid any provost or bedel or hayward or any other servant of the manor to ride on, or lend, or ill-treat the cart-horses or others. And he ought to see that the horses and oxen and all the stock are well kept, and that no other animals graze in, or eat their pasture.

The bailiff ought to be just in all points and in all his doings, and he ought not, without warrant, to take fines or relief from the land, nor enfranchise a woman without the seneschal, nor hold pleas touching fees or freehold or franchise which turn to the loss of the lord. . . .

THE OFFICE OF PROVOST

The provost ought to be elected and presented by the common consent of the township, as the best husbandman and the best approver among them. And he must see that all the servants of the court rise in the morning to do their work, and that the ploughs be yoked in time, and the lands well ploughed and cropped, and turned over, and sown with good and clean seed, as much as they can stand. And he ought to see that there be a good fold of wooden hurdles on the demesne, strewed within every night to improve the land.

And he ought to see that he have a good fold for wethers, and another for ewes, and a third for hogs, according as there are sheep. And the keeper of the wethers ought to have in his keeping four hundred wethers if the pasture be large, or more, if it is narrow, fewer; the keeper of the ewes ought to have three hundred in large pasture; the keeper of the hogs two hundred. And the provost ought to see that they be well kept, in the pasture, in the fold, and in houses. The provost ought to see that the corn is well and cleanly threshed, so that nothing is left in the straw to grow in thatches, nor in manure to sprout. The husks, and the trampled corn, and the refuse of the winnowing, may be put together and threshed, and then winnowed and put with the other. And the provost must take care that no thresher or winnower shall take corn [grain] to carry it away in his bosom, or in tunic, or boots, or pockets, or sacks or sacklets hidden near the grange. . . .

THE OFFICE OF HAYWARD

The hayward ought to be an active and sharp man, for he must, early and late, look after and go round and keep the woods, corn, and meadows and other things belonging to his office, and he ought to make attachments and approvements faithfully, and make the delivery by pledge before the provost, and deliver them to the bailiff to be heard. And he ought to sow the lands, and be over the ploughers and harrowers at the time of each sowing. And he ought to make all the boon-tenants and customary-tenants who are bound and accustomed to come, do so, to do the work they ought to do. And in haytime he ought to be over the mowers, the making, the carrying, and in August assemble the reapers and the boon-tenants and the labourers and see that the corn be properly and cleanly gathered; and early and late watch so that nothing be stolen or eaten by beasts or spoilt. And he ought to tally with the provost all the seed, and boon-work, and customs, and labour, which ought to be done in the manor throughout the year, and what it amounts to the bailiff tallies and accounts for, and they ought to answer on the account for the rest.

THE OFFICE OF THE LORD

The lord ought to love God and justice, and be faithful and true in his sayings and doings, and he ought to hate sin and injustice, and evil-doing. The lord ought not to take counsel with young men full of young blood, and ready courage, who know little or nothing of business, nor of any juggler, flatterer, or idle talker, nor of such as bear witness by present, but he ought to take counsel with worthy and faithful men, ripe in years, who have seen much, and know much, and who are known to be of good fame, and who never were caught or convicted for treachery or any wrong-doing; nor for love, nor for hate, nor for fear, nor for menace, nor for gain, nor for loss, will turn aside from truth, and knowingly counsel their lord to do him harm.

The lord ought to command and ordain that the accounts be heard every year, but not in one place but on all the manors, for so can one quickly know everything, and understand the profit and loss. And he ought to command and ordain that no bailiff have his food in the manors except at a fixed price in money, so that he take nothing from the manors but hay, firewood, and straw; and that no friend, stranger, nor anyone from the lord's hostel or elsewhere be received at the manors at the lord's expense, nor shall anything be given or delivered to them without warrant of writ, unless the bailiff or provost wish to acquit it from their own purses for the great expense one is unnecessarily put to, as can be seen above in another chapter.

The lord ought to inquire by his own men and others on his manors as many as there are, about his seneschal and his doings, and the approvements he has made since his coming; in the same way he ought to inquire about profits and losses from the bailiff and provost, and how much he will have to seek from both. He ought to ask for his auditors and rolls of account, then he ought to see who has done well and who not, and who has made improvement and who not, and who has made profit and who not, but loss, and those he has then found good and faithful and profitable, let him keep on this account. And if anyone be found who has done harm and is by no means profitable, let him answer for his doing and take farewell. And if the lord observe these said forms, then will each lord live a good man and honestly, and be as he will rich and powerful without sin, and will do injustice to no one.

The lord ought to command the auditors on the manors to hear the plaints and wrongs of everybody who complains of the seneschal, or provost, or hayward, or any other who is of the manor, and that full justice be done to franks and villeins, customary-tenants, and other plaintiffs, such as by inquest can be had; and that the auditors do right at their peril. . . .

THE OFFICE OF PLOUGHMEN

The ploughmen ought to be men of intelligence, and ought to know how to sow, and how to repair and mend broken ploughs and harrows, and to till the land well, and crop it rightly; and they ought to know also how to yoke and drive the oxen, without beating or hurting them, and they ought to forage them well, and look well after the forage that it be not stolen nor carried off; and they ought to keep them safely in meadows and several pastures, and other beasts which are found therein they ought to impound. And they and the keepers must make ditches and build and remove the earth, and ditch it so that the ground may dry and the water be drained. And they must not flay any beast until some one has inspected it, and inquired by what default it died. And they must not carry fire into the byres for light, or to warm themselves, and have no candle there, or light unless it be in a lantern, and for great need and peril.

THE OFFICE OF WAGGONERS

The waggoner ought to know his trade, to keep the horses and curry them, and to load and carry without danger to his horses, that they may not be overloaded or over-worked, or overdriven, or hurt, and he must know how to mend his harness and the gear of the waggon. And the bailiff and provost ought to see and know how many times the waggoners can go in a day to carry marl or manure, or hay or corn, or timber or firewood, without great stress; and as many times as they can go in a day, the waggoners must answer for each day at the end of the week. No waggoner or other shall cause a cart-horse or aver to be flayn without inspection and the command of his superior, until it be known why and for what default it died, as is said above. And no waggoner shall carry fire or candle into the stables, unless the candle be in a lantern, and this for great need, and then it must be carried and watched by another than himself. Each waggoner shall sleep every night with his horses, and keep such guard as he shall wish to answer for without damage; and so shall the oxherds sleep in the same way with their oxen.

THE OFFICE OF COWHERD

The cowherd ought to be skilful, knowing his business and keeping his cows well, and foster the calves well from time of weaning. And he must see that he has fine bulls and large and of good breed pastured with the cows, to mate when they will. And that no cow be milked or suckle her calf after Michaelmas, to make cheese of rewain; for this milking and this rewain make the cows lose flesh and become weak, and will make them mate later another year, and the milk is better and the cow poorer. And he ought to see that the avers be well supplied with forage, and well kept in winter and summer, as he shall wish to answer, and that no cow or aver by flayn before his superior has seen it and known by what default it died. And no fire or candle shall be carried into the cowhouse, except in the manner aforesaid. And every year, from each vaccary, cause the old cows with bad teeth, and the barren, and the draft of the young avers that do not grow well to be sorted out that they may be sold in the way aforesaid. And every night the cowherd shall put the cows and other beasts in the fold during the season, and let the fold be well strewed with litter or fern, as is said above, and he himself shall lie each night with his cows.

THE OFFICE OF SWINEHERD

The swineherd ought to be on those manors where swine can be sustained and kept in the forest, or in woods, or waste, or in marshes, without sustenance from the grange; and if the swine can be kept with little sustenance from the grange during hard frost, then must a pigsty be made in a marsh or wood, where the swine may be night and day. And then when the sows have farrowed, let them be driven with the feeble swine to the manors and kept with leavings as long as the hard frost and the bad weather last, and then driven back to the others. And if there is no wood or marsh or waste where the swine may be sustained without being altogether kept on the grange, no swineherd or swine shall be on the manor, except only such as can be kept in August on the stubble and leavings of the grange, and when the corn is threshed for sale, and as soon as they are in good condition and well, let them be sold. For whoever will keep swine for a year from the cost of the grange alone, and count the cost and the allowance for the swine and swineherd, together with the damage they do yearly to the corn, he shall lose twice as much as he shall gain, and this will soon be seen by whoever keeps account.

THE OFFICE OF SHEPHERD

Each shepherd ought to find good pledges to answer for his doings and for good and faithful service, although he be companion to the miller. And he must cover his fold and enclose it with hurdles and mend it within and without, and repair the hurdles and make them. And he ought to sleep in the fold, he and his dog; and he ought to pasture his sheep well, and keep them in forage, and watch them well, so that they be not killed or destroyed by dogs or stolen or lost or changed, nor let them pasture in moors or dry places or bogs, to get sickness and disease for lack of guard. No shepherd ought to leave his sleep to go to fairs, or markets, or wrestling matches, or wakes, or to the tavern, without taking leave or asking it, or without putting a good keeper in his place to keep the sheep, that no harm may arise from his fault.

Let all the lord's sheep be marked with one mark, and let no ewes be milked after the feast of our Lady [December 8], for they will mate more tardily another year, and the lambs shall be worth less; and let no sheep be flayn before it be seen and known for what fault it died, for if the ewe die before shearing then must the skin be worth a fleece, and if it die after shearing then the shepherd must answer for the lamb and the fleece and the fresh carcase with the skin. And if a wether die before shearing, he must answer for a good skin and for the carcase, if it be fresh; and if it be after shearing he must answer for the fleece and for the fresh carcase and the skin and the hog. Let no lamb be given or marked, nor any wool or skin be given, unless before the bailiff. Let good gelded sheep with good wool be with the ewes at the time of mating. Let the ewes and the wethers and the hogs be inspected three times a year by men who know their business, and the draft picked out and sold in the way aforesaid.

THE OFFICE OF DAIRYMAID

The dairymaid ought to be faithful and of good repute, and keep herself clean, and ought to know her business and all that belongs to it. She ought not to allow any under-dairymaid or another to take or carry away milk, or butter, or cream, by which the cheese shall be less and the dairy impoverished. And she ought to know well how to make cheese and salt cheese, and she ought to save and keep the vessels of the dairy, that it need not be necessary to buy new ones every year. And she ought to know the day when she begins to make cheese and of what weight, and when she begins to make two cheeses a day, of how much and of what weight, and then the bailiff and the provost ought to inspect the dairy often and the cheeses, when they increase and decrease in weight, and that no harm be done in the dairy, nor any robbery by which the weight shall be lessened. And they ought to know and prove and see when the cows make a stone of cheese and butter, and when the ewes make a stone of the same, that they may be able the more surely to answer in the account. No cow shall be milked or suckled after Michaelmas, and no ewe after the feast of our Lady, for the reason aforesaid.

The dairymaid ought to help to winnow the corn when she can be present, and she ought to take care of the geese and hens and answer for the returns and keep and cover the fire, that no harm arise from lack of guard.

HERE ENDS THE BOOK OF THE OFFICE OF SENESCHAL

❧ THE MANOR OF ALWALTON

The abbot of Peterborough holds the manor of Alwalton and vill from the lord king directly; which manor and vill with its appurtenances the lord Edward, formerly king of England gave to the said abbot and convent of that place in free, pure, and perpetual alms. And the court of the said manor with its garden contains one half an acre. And to the whole of the said vill of Alwalton belong 5 hides and a half and 1 virgate of land and a half; of which each hide contains 5 virgates of land each virgate contains 25 acres. Of these hides the said abbot has in demesne 1 hide and a half of land and half a virgate, which contain as above. Likewise he has there 8 acres of meadow. Also he has there separable pasture which contains 1 acre. Likewise he has there 3 water mills. Likewise he has there a common fish pond with a fish-weir on the bank of the Nene, which begins at Wildlake and extends to the mill of Newton and contains in length 2 leagues. Likewise he has there a ferry with a boat.

Free Tenants Thomas le Boteler holds a messuage with a court yard which contains 1 rood, and 3 acres of land, by charter, paying thence yearly to the said abbot 14s.

Likewise the rector of the church of Alwalton holds 1 virgate of land with its appurtenances, with which the said church was anciently endowed. Likewise the said rector has a holding the tenant of which holds 1 rood of ground by paying to the said rector yearly 1d.

And the abbot of Peterborough is patron of the church.

Villeins Hugh Miller holds 1 virgate of land in villenage by paying thence to the said abbot 3s. 1d. Likewise the same Hugh works through the whole year except 1 week at Christmas, 1 week at Easter, and 1 at Whitsuntide, that is in each week 3 days, each day with 1 man, and in autumn each day with 2 men, performing the said works at the will of the said abbot as in plowing and other work. Likewise he gives 1 bushel of wheat for benseed and 18 sheaves of oats for foddercorn. Likewise he gives 3 hens and 1 cock yearly and 5 eggs at Easter. Likewise he does carrying to Peterborough and to Jakele and no where else, at the will of the said abbot. Likewise if he sells a brood mare in his court yard for 10s. or more, he shall give to the said abbot 4d., and if for less he shall give nothing to the aforesaid. He gives also merchet and heriot, and is tallaged at the feast of St. Michael, at the will of the said abbot. There are also there 17 other villeins, viz. John of Ganesoupe, Robert son of Walter, Ralph son of the reeve, Emma at Pertre, William son of Reginald, Thomas son of Gunnilda, Eda widow of Ralph, Ralph Reeve, William Reeve, William son of William Reeve, Thomas Flegg, Henry Abbot, William Hereward, Serle son of William Reeve, Walter Palmer, William Abbot, Henry Serle; each of whom holds 1 virgate of land in villenage, paying and doing in all things, each for himself, to the said abbot yearly just as the said Hugh Miller. There are also 5 other villeins, viz. Simon Mariot, Robert of Hastone, Thomas Smith, John Mustard, and William Carter, each of whom holds half a virgate of land

English Manorial Documents, Translations and Reprints from the Original Sources of European History (Philadelphia: University of Pennsylvania Press, 1912), Vol. III, No. 5, 4–7.

by paying and doing in all things half of the whole service which Hugh Miller pays and does.

Cotters   Henry, son of the miller, holds a cottage with a croft which contains 1 rood, paying thence yearly to the said abbot 2s. Likewise he works for 3 days in carrying hay and in other works at the will of the said abbot, each day with 1 man and in autumn 1 day in cutting grain with 1 man.

Likewise Ralph Miller holds a cottage with a croft which contains a rood, paying to the said abbot 2s.; and he works just as the said Henry.

Likewise William Arnold holds a cottage with a croft which contains half a rood, paying to the abbot 2d.; and he works just as the said Henry.

Likewise Hugh Day holds a cottage with a croft which contains 1 rood, paying to the abbot 8d.; and he works just as the said Henry.

Likewise Sara, widow of Matthew Miller, holds a cottage and a croft which contains half a rood, paying to the said abbot 4d.; and she works just as the said Henry.

Likewise Sara, widow of William Miller, holds a cottage and a croft which contains half a rood, paying to the abbot 4d.; and she works just as the said Henry.

Likewise William Kendale holds a cottage and a croft which contains 1 rood, paying to the abbot 8d.; and he works just as the said Henry. . . .

Likewise William Drake holds a cottage with a croft which contains half a rood, paying to the abbot 6d.; and he works just as the said Henry.

There are there also 6 other cotters, viz. William Drake Jr., Amycia the widow, Alice the widow, Robert son of Eda, William Pepper, William Coleman, each of whom holds a cottage with a croft which contains half a rood, paying and doing in all things, each for himself, just as the said William Drake.

Likewise William Russel holds a cottage with a croft which contains half a rood, paying to the abbot 8d.; and he works in all things just as the said Henry Miller.

There are moreover there 5 other cotters, viz. Walter Pestel, Ralph Shepherd, Henry Abbot, Matilda Tut, Jordan Mustard, each of whom holds a cottage with a croft which contains half a rood, paying thence and doing in all things to the said abbot just as the said William Russel.

Likewise Beatrice of Hampton holds a cottage and a croft which contains 1 rood, paying to the abbot 12d.; and she works in all things just as the said Henry.

Likewise Hugh Miller holds 3 acres of land, paying to the abbot 42d.

Likewise Thomas, son of Richard, holds a cottage with a croft which contains half a rood, and 3 acres of land, paying to the abbot 4s.; and he works just as the said Henry.

Likewise Ralph Reeve holds a cottage with a croft which contains 1 rood, and 1 acre of land, paying to the abbot 2s.; and he works just as the said Henry.

Likewise each of the said cottagers, except the widows, gives yearly after Christmas a penny which is called head-penny.

Feudal Laws
and Customs

By the end of the sixth century, the European countryside had fallen under the control of the wielders of the axe and sword. Gone was the security of Roman law; the manorial system arose when those who survived traded liberty for the protection of the local chieftain. Initially, military service was exacted from the warrior by the king, in return for which the warrior was given land holdings commensurate with his prowess. The obligation was thus reciprocal, and each party took a solemn religious oath to uphold it. But lacking the permanence of law, these holdings were shaky; it was from such simple considerations that the feudal system (from feudum, "land") was conceived. Later the warrior might have to supply men, equipment, horses, or money. With enlarged obligations came status; with increasing wealth from the land came complications, as relatives claimed their share, families died out or became too numerous, or new kings denied recognition of their predecessors' grants.

Concerning the Laws and Customs of the Kingdom of England, *dates from about 1190. It is a manual specifying the conditions of feudal tenure, designed to bring order to an increasingly complex society. Ranulff Glanville, its probable author, had been justiciar in England from 1180 to 1189, and in that office he had been responsible for settling the disputed claims and titles resulting from twenty years of anarchy. The aim of this document is legal precision, but this should not obscure the fact that feudalism aroused deep feelings of personal loyalty and religious obligation.*

Administration of the law occupied men far more than abstract speculation about it. The usual problem was to arrest the criminal or to convince the litigant to appear in court. Considering the grim choice open to a defendant, it is surprising that the forests of medieval Europe were not overrun with outlaws preferring to be fugitives rather than risk trial by combat or worse. When fugitives were apprehended, a standard procedure for proving guilt or innocence was the elaborate and horrendous ordeal of torture in which it was believed God would establish innocence by preventing pain or maiming or establish guilt by allowing nature to take its course. The ordeals described below represent the typical forms used from the sixth to the thirteenth centuries.

ꙮ CONCERNING THE LAWS AND CUSTOMS OF THE KINGDOM OF ENGLAND

Ranulff Glanville

Book IX

Chap. I It remains to continue upon the subject of performing homage and receiving reliefs. Upon the death of the father or any other ancestor, the lord of the fee is bound from the first to receive the homage of the true heir, whether the heir has attained full age or not, provided always that he be male. For females cannot by law perform any homage, although, generally speaking, they are wont to do fealty to their lords. But if they are married their husbands ought to do homage to their lords for their fee; if, I mean, homage be due in respect of such fees. If, however, the heir be male and a minor, the lord of the fee is not entitled by law to the wardship of the heir or of his holding until he has received the homage of the heir; because it is a general principle that no one can exact from an heir, whether he is of age or not, any service, whether a relief or otherwise, until he has received the homage of the heir in respect of that holding for which the service is claimed. But a person may perform homage to several lords on account of different fees, but of these homages one should be the chief and should be liege homage, and this must be performed to the lord from whom the person performing homage holds his chief tenement. Homage ought to be done in this manner, namely, that he who performs it shall so become the man of his lord that he shall bear faith to him for the tenement in respect of which he performs homage, and shall preserve the earthly honour of his lord in all things save the faith due to the king and to his heirs. From this it is evident that a vassal cannot injure his lord without breaking the faith involved in homage, unless perhaps in his own defence, or unless on the order of the king he joins the king's army when it goes against his lord. Generally speaking, the law holds that no one can, without breaking the faith implied in homage, do anything which tends to deprive his lord of his inheritance, or do anything to the dishonour of his body. If then a tenant has, in respect of several fees, done homage to different lords who afterwards make war upon each other, and the chief lord should command the tenant to go in person with him against another of his lords, he ought to obey this command saving, however, the service due to the other lord in respect of the fee held from him. From what has been said it therefore follows that if a tenant should do anything contributing to the disinheritance of his lord, and should be convicted of it, he and his heirs shall according to the law lose for ever the fee held of this lord. The same consequence will follow if the tenant lays violent hands on his lord to hurt him, or puts him to shame, and this be lawfully proved in court against the tenant. But it may be asked whether anyone can be compelled to defend himself against the lord in the lord's court against such charges; and whether his lord can, by the judgment of his own court, distrain the tenant so to do, without the precept of the king or of his justices or without the king's

Ranulff Glanville, "Concerning the Laws and Customs of the Kingdom of England," *English Historical Documents, 1042–1189*, ed. David C. Douglas and George W. Greenaway (London: Eyre and Spottiswoode (Publishers), Ltd., 1953), pp. 937–943.

writ or that of his chief justice. The law indeed permits a lord by the judgment of his court to summon and distrain one who has paid him homage to appear in court, and unless such a one can purge himself against the charge of his lord by three persons, or as many as the court shall decide, he shall be amerced to the lord to the extent of the whole fee that he holds from this lord. It may also be inquired whether a lord can distrain one who has paid him homage to appear in his court to answer for a service which the lord claims has not been rendered, or of which some part has been withheld. The answer is that the lord may by law well do so, and this even without the precept of the king or his justices. And in such a controversy the lord and the man who has paid him homage may submit their dispute to the duel, or to the Grand Assize by means of one of the tenant's peers who duly witnesses to the fact that he has seen the tenant himself or his ancestors perform such service for the fee to the lord or his ancestors, and is prepared to prove the fact. And if the tenant be convicted of this charge, he shall by law be disinherited of the whole fee which he holds of his lord. If, however, anyone is unable to constrain his tenants, it then becomes necessary to have recourse to the [king's] court. Every free male person may perform homage, whether of full age or otherwise, whether clerk or layman. But consecrated bishops are not accustomed to perform homage to the king even for their baronies; but merely fealty accompanied by an oath. But bishops-elect are wont to do homage previous to their consecration.

Chap. II   Homage is only due for lands, free tenements, services, and dues, either of money or in kind, which have been precisely determined. Only in respect of demesne should homage be rendered to no one except to the king. Yet homage ought not always to be performed for every kind of land. Thus it is not due for land in dower or for a marriage portion freely bestowed, nor from the fee of younger sisters holding from the eldest, within the third descent on both sides; nor is it due from a fee given in frankalmoign, nor for any tenement given in any way as a marriage portion, so far as concerns the person of the husband of the woman to whom the property belongs as her marriage portion.

Chap. III   Homage may, however, be done to any free person whether male or female, whether of full age or otherwise, and whether clerk or lay. But it should be understood that if a person has done homage for a tenement to a woman who afterwards marries, then he shall be compelled to repeat it to her husband for the same tenement. If, however, anyone has by agreement made in court recovered a tenement against another who had previously paid a relief for it to the chief lord, it may be questioned whether the person so recovering the tenement ought to pay any further relief for it.

Chap. IV   There ought to be a reciprocal obligation of fidelity between lordship and homage. Nor does the tenant owe more to his lord in respect of homage than the lord owes to the tenant on account of lordship, reverence alone excepted. Hence if one person gives to another any land in return for service and homage, which land is afterwards recovered against the tenant by a third party, the lord shall be bound to warrant such land to him or to return him an adequate equivalent. It is otherwise, however, in the case of a man who holds a fee from another as his inheritance and in this character has done homage, because in this instance although he lose his land the lord shall not be bound to give him an equivalent. In the case we have previously mentioned of the death of the father or ancestor leaving an heir who is a minor, the lord of the fee has no right to the wardship of the heir or of his inheritance unless he has first received the homage of the heir. But after homage has been received, the heir with his inheritance shall remain, as mentioned earlier, in the wardship of his lord until he has attained full age. Having at last arrived at such age and received restitution of his inheritance, he shall by reason of his having been in ward be exempt from the payment of relief. But a female heir, whether she has attained full age or not, shall remain in the wardship of her lord until with his consent she is married. If, however, she was below age when the lord received her into wardship, then upon her marriage the inheritance shall be quit from the relief so far as it concerns herself and her husband. But if she was of full age at that time, although she may continue for a space in the wardship of her lord before she is married, her husband shall pay a relief. When, however, the relief has been once paid by the husband of a woman, it shall exempt both the husband and the wife during their several lives from the payment of another relief for the inheritance, because neither the woman, nor her second husband should he survive her ought again to pay relief for the same land. But when a male heir is left of full age, and known to be such, he shall hold his inheritance as we have noted above, even though his lord be unwilling, provided that he offers to his lord, as he ought, in the presence of worthy persons, his homage and a reasonable relief. According to the custom of the realm a reasonable relief for a knight's fee is said to be 100 shillings, whilst that of land held in socage is said to be one year's value. But as to baronies, nothing definite is fixed, because barons holding of the king in chief are wont to pay their reliefs to the king according to his will and pleasure. The same rule applies to serjeanties. If, however, the lord will neither receive the homage nor a reasonable relief from the heir, then the latter should keep the relief in safety and frequently offer it to his lord by the hands of reputable persons. If the lord will even so not receive it, then the heir shall make complaint to the king or to his justices; and he shall receive the following writ:

Chap. V

> The king to the sheriff greeting. Order *N.* that justly and without delay he receive the homage and the reasonable relief of *R.* concerning the free tenement which he holds in such-and-such a village, and that he claims to hold of him. And if he fails to do this, summon him by good summoners to attend before me or my justices on such-and-such a day to show why he has not done it. And you shall have there the summoners, etc.

Chap. VI   As to the procedure to be followed in case the lord should not obey this summons, and the means by which he shall be distrained to appear in court, they may be collected from the former part of this treatise. When at last he appears in court he will either acknowledge that the tenant is the right heir, or deny that he is the heir, or express doubt on this point. If he acknowledges him to be the right heir, he will then either deny that the tenant has offered him homage and reasonable relief or he will admit it. If he confess both the one and the other, then he shall either accept forthwith the tenant's homage and reasonable relief, or he shall appoint a suitable day for doing this. And provided that he admits the tenant to be the heir, the same course should be adopted even if he denies that the tenant has offered him homage and relief. But if in clear terms he denies the tenant to be the heir, then the latter, if out of possession, may claim against his lord an assize of *Mort d'Ancestor.* Should the tenant, however, be in possession, he may retain it and patiently wait until the lord is pleased to accept his homage, because no one is bound to pay relief to his lord before the lord has received his homage for the fee for which homage is due. But if the lord doubts whether the person offering homage is the right heir or not, being for example, unknown as such to the lord himself or even to the neighbourhood, then the lord of the fee may take the land into his own hands, and retain it until the matter be fully elucidated. This, moreover, is the course which the king usually adopts in the case of all baronies held of him in chief. For upon the death of a baron holding in chief, the king immediately retains the barony in his own hands until the heir has given security for the relief, even though the heir be of full age. But for a reasonable cause lords may sometimes postpone receiving homage and relief for their fees. Suppose, for example, another person than the one who asserts himself to be the heir claims a right to the inheritance: then while this suit is pending homage ought not to be received nor a relief given. Or, if the lord think that he has himself a right to hold the inheritance as part of his own demesne, and if in such case he should by means of the king's writ or that of his justices, sue the person in possession: then the tenant may put himself upon the Grand Assize. . . .

Chap. VIII   After it has been settled between the lord and the heir of the tenant concerning the giving and receiving of a reasonable relief, the heir may exact reasonable aids in respect of this from his own men. This, however, must be done with moderation in accordance with the number and resources of their fees lest they should be too much oppressed or should lose their contenement. But nothing certain is fixed concerning the giving and exacting of aids of this kind except that the conditions we have noted must be always observed. There are also other cases in which a lord can exact from his men similar aids, always observing the prescribed form: as when his son and heir is made a knight, and when he gives his eldest daughter in marriage. But whether lords can exact aids to maintain private war is doubtful. The opinion which prevails is that they cannot lawfully distrain their tenants for such a purpose except in so far as the tenants agree. But with respect to the payment of reasonable aids, lords may of their own right, without the king's precept or that of his justices, but by the judgment of their own court, distrain their tenants by such of their chattels as may be found within their fees or if necessary by their fees themselves; provided always that the tenants are dealt with according to the judgment of the lord's court and consistently with its reasonable custom. If therefore a lord may thus distrain his tenants to pay such reasonable aids, much stronger is the argument that he may lawfully distrain in the same manner for a relief, or for any other service necessarily due to him in respect of the fee. If, however, a lord is unable by judgment to compel his tenant to render his due and customary services, then recourse must be had to the king or to his chief justice, and he shall obtain the following writ:

Chap. IX

The king to the sheriff greeting. I order you to compel *N.* justly and without delay to render to *R.* the due and customary services which he ought to render in respect of the tenement he holds of him in such-and-such a village, as can be reasonably shown to be due to the lord, lest complaint be made again in respect of default of justice. Witness, etc.

Chap. X   When the plea proceeds by virtue of this writ, the plaintiff shall in the shire court and before the sheriff demand his dues, whether they consist of reliefs or other things, according to the custom of the shire court. And if the plaintiff shall prove his case, then the tenant shall render the reasonable relief to his lord, and shall in addition be amerced to the sheriff, it being a recognized principle that the amercement which results from any suit dealt with and decided in the shire court belongs to the sheriff. The amount of such amercement has, it is true, been determined by no general assize, but is regulated by the custom of the different shires, in one shire more, in another less.

ORDEALS

Let the priest go to the church with the prosecutors and with him who is about to be tried. And while the rest wait in the vestibule of the church let the priest enter and put on the sacred garments except the chasuble and, taking the Gospel and the chrismarium and the relics of the saints and the chalice, let him go to the altar and speak thus to all the people standing near: Behold, brethren, the offices of the Christian religion. Behold the law in which is hope and remission of sins, the holy oil of the chrisma, the consecration of the body and blood of our Lord. Look that ye be not deprived of the heritage of such great blessing and of participation in it by implicating yourselves in the crime of another, for it is written, not only are they worthy of death who do these things, but they that have pleasure in them that do them.

Then let him thus address the one who is to undertake the ordeal: I command thee, N., in the presence of all, by the Father, the Son, and the Holy Ghost, by the tremendous day of judgment, by the ministry of baptism, by thy veneration for the saints, that, if thou art guilty of this matter charged against thee, if thou hast done it, or consented to it, or hast knowingly seen the perpetrators of this crime, thou enter not into the church nor mingle in the company of Christians unless thou wilt confess and admit thy guilt before thou art examined in public judgment.

"Ordeals," *Translations and Reprints from Original Sources of European History,* ed. Arthur C. Howland (New York: Longmans, Green & Co., 1897), Vol. IV, No. 4, 7–15.

Then he shall designate a spot in the vestibule where the fire is to be made for the water, and shall first sprinkle the place with holy water, and shall also sprinkle the kettle when it is ready to be hung and the water in it, to guard against the illusions of the devil. Then, entering the church with the others, he shall celebrate the ordeal mass. After the celebration let the priest go with the people to the place of the ordeal, the Gospel in his left hand, the cross, censer and relics of the saints being carried ahead, and let him chant seven penitential psalms with a litany.

Prayer over the boiling water: O God, just Judge, firm and patient, who art the Author of peace, and judgest truly, determine what is right, O Lord, and make known Thy righteous judgment. O Omnipotent God, Thou that lookest upon the earth and makest it to tremble, Thou that by the gift of Thy Son, our Lord Jesus Christ, didst save the world and by His most holy passion didst redeem the human race, sanctify, O Lord, this water being heated by fire. Thou that didst save the three youths, Sidrac, Misac, and Abednago, cast into the fiery furnace at the command of Nebuchadnezzar, and didst lead them forth unharmed by the hand of Thy angel, do Thou O clement and most holy Ruler, give aid if he shall plunge his hand into the boiling water, being innocent, and, as Thou didst liberate the three youths from the fiery furnace and didst free Susanna from the false charge, so, O Lord, bring forth his hand safe and unharmed from this water. But if he be guilty and presume to plunge in his hand, the devil hardening his heart, let Thy holy justice deign to declare it, that Thy virtue may be manifest in his body and his soul be saved by penitence and confession. And if the guilty man shall try to hide his sins by the use of herbs or any magic, let Thy right hand deign to bring it to no account. Through Thy only begotten Son, our Lord Jesus Christ, who dwelleth with Thee.

Benediction of the water: I bless thee, O creature of water, boiling above the fire, in the name of the Father, and of the Son, and of the Holy Ghost, from whom all things proceed; I adjure thee by Him who ordered thee to water the whole earth from the four rivers, and who summoned thee forth from the rock, and who changed thee into wine, that no wiles of the devil or magic of men be able to separate thee from thy virtues as a medium of judgment; but mayest thou punish the vile and the wicked, and purify the innocent. Through Him whom hidden things do not escape and who sent thee in the flood over the whole earth to destroy the wicked and who will yet come to judge the quick and the dead and the world by fire. Amen.

Prayer: Omnipotent, Eternal God, we humbly beseech Thee in behalf of this investigation which we are about to undertake here amongst us that iniquity may not overcome justice but that falsehood may be subjected to truth. And if any one seek to hinder or obscure this examination by any magic or by herbs of the earth, deign to bring it to naught by Thy right hand, O upright Judge.

Then let the man who is to be tried, as well as the kettle or pot in which is the boiling water, be fumed with the incense of myrrh, and let this prayer be spoken: O God, Thou who within this substance of water hast hidden Thy most solemn sacraments, be graciously present with us who invoke Thee, and upon this element made ready by much purification pour down the virtue of Thy benediction that this creature, obedient to Thy mysteries, may be endued with Thy grace to detect diabolical and human fallacies, to confute their inventions and arguments, and to overcome their multiform arts. May all the wiles of the hidden enemy be brought to naught that we may clearly perceive the truth regarding those things which we with finite senses and simple hearts are seeking from Thy judgment through invocation of Thy holy name. Let not the innocent, we beseech Thee, be unjustly condemned, or the guilty be able to delude with safety those who seek the truth from Thee, who art the true Light, who seest in the shadowy darkness, and who makest our darkness light. O Thou who perceivest hidden things and knowest what is secret, show and declare this by Thy grace and make the knowledge of the truth manifest to us who believe in Thee.

Then let the hand that is to be placed in the water be washed with soap and let it be carefully examined whether it be sound; and before it is thrust in let the priest say: I adjure thee, O vessel, by the Father, and the Son, and the Holy Ghost, and by the holy resurrection, and by the tremendous day of judgment, and by the four Evangelists, that if this man be guilty of this crime either by deed or by consent, let the water boil violently, and do thou, O vessel, turn and swing.

After this let the man who is to be tried plunge in his hand, and afterwards let it be immediately sealed up. After the ordeal let him take a drink of holy water. Up to the time of the decision regarding the ordeal [1] it is a good thing to mix salt and holy water with all his food and drink.

ORDEAL OF HOT WATER UNDERTAKEN BY A PRIEST TO CONFUTE A HERETIC

An Arian presbyter disputing with a deacon of our religion made venemous assertions against the Son of God and the Holy Ghost, as is the habit of that sect. But when the deacon had discoursed a long time concerning the reasonableness of our faith, and the heretic blinded by the fog of unbelief continued to reject the truth, according as it is written, "Wisdom shall not enter the mind of the wicked," the former said: "Why weary ourselves with long discussions? Let acts approve the truth; let a kettle be heated over the fire and some one's ring be thrown into the boiling water. Let him who shall take it from the heated liquid be approved as a follower of the truth, and afterwards let the other party be converted to the knowledge of this truth. And do thou also understand, O heretic, that this our party will fulfil the conditions with the aid of the Holy Ghost; thou shalt confess that there is no discordance, no dissimilarity in the Holy Trinity." The heretic consented to the proposition and they separated after appointing the next morning for the trial. But the fervor of faith in which the deacon had first made this suggestion began to cool through the instigation of the enemy. Rising with the dawn he bathed his arm in oil and smeared it with ointment. But nevertheless he made the round of the sacred places and called in prayer on the Lord. What more shall I say? About the third hour they met in the market place. The people came together to see the show. A fire was lighted, the kettle was placed upon it, and when it grew very hot the ring was thrown into the boiling water. The deacon invited the heretic to take it out of the water first. But he promptly refused, saying, "Thou who didst propose this trial art the one to take it out." The deacon all of a tremble bared his arm. And when the heretic presbyter saw it besmeared with

---

[1] *A period of three days was allowed to elapse before the hand was examined.*

ointment he cried out: "With magic arts thou hast thought to protect thyself, that thou hast made use of these salves, but what thou hast done will not avail." While they were thus quarreling there came up a deacon from Ravenna named Iacinthus and inquired what the trouble was about. When he learned the truth he drew his arm out from under his robe at once and plunged his right hand into the kettle. Now the ring that had been thrown in was a little thing and very light so that it was thrown about by the water as chaff would be blown about by the wind; and searching for it a long time he found it after about an hour. Meanwhile the flame beneath the kettle blazed up mightily so that the greater heat might make it difficult for the ring to be followed by the hand; but the deacon extracted it at length and suffered no harm, protesting rather that at the bottom the kettle was cold while at the top it was just pleasantly warm. When the heretic beheld this he was greatly confused and audaciously thrust his hand into the kettle saying, "My faith will aid me." As soon as his hand had been thrust in all the flesh was boiled off the bones clear up to the elbow. And so the dispute ended.

DOOM OF KING AETHELSTAN REGARDING THE ORDEAL OF RED-HOT IRON

If any one shall have given pledge to undergo the ordeal of iron . . . , let him go three days beforehand to the priest whose duty it is to bless him with the sign of the cross; and let him live upon bread, water, salt and herbs, and hear mass each one of the three days; and let him make his offering and go to the holy communion on the day when he is to be examined by the ordeal; and before he is examined let him swear that by the law of the realm he is innocent of the charge. . . . Concerning the ordeal we enjoin in the name of God and by the command of the archbishop and of all our bishops that no one enter the church after the fire has been brought in with which the ordeal is to be heated except the priest and him who is to undergo judgment. And let nine feet be measured off from the stake to the mark, by the feet of him who is to be tried. . . . And when the ordeal is ready let two men from each side go in and certify that it is as hot as we have directed it to be. Then let an equal number from both sides enter and stand on either side of the judgment place along the church, and let them all be fasting and abstinent from their wives on the preceding night. And let the priest sprinkle them all with water and let them bow themselves every one to the holy water and let the holy Gospel and the cross be given them all to kiss. And no one shall mend the fire any longer than the beginning of the hallowing, but let the iron lie on the coals until the last collect. Afterwards let it be placed on a frame, and let no one speak except to pray diligently to God, the Father Omnipotent, to deign to manifest His truth in the matter. And let the accused drink of the holy water and then let the hand with which he is about to carry the iron be sprinkled, and so let him go [to the ordeal]. Let the nine feet that were measured off be divided into three sections. In the first division let him hold his right foot, close to the stake. Then let him move his right foot across the second into the third division, where he shall cast the iron in front of him and hasten to the holy altar. Then let his hand be sealed up, and on the third day let examination be made whether it is clean or foul within the wrapper. And whoever shall transgress these laws, be the ordeal of no worth in his case, but let him pay the king a fine of twenty shillings.

ORDEAL OF GLOWING PLOUGHSHARES UNDERGONE BY QUEEN EMMA

The queen was brought at the king's command from Whewell to Winchester and throughout all the night preceding her trial she kept her vigil at the shrine of St. Swithin. . . . On the appointed day the clergy and the people came to the church and the king himself sat on the tribunal. The queen was brought before her son and questioned whether she was willing to go through with what she had undertaken. . . . Nine glowing ploughshares were placed on the carefully swept pavement of the church. After these had been consecrated by a short ceremony the queen's shoes and stockings were taken off; then her robe was removed and her cloak thrown aside, and, supported by two bishops, one on either side, she was led to the torture. The bishops who led her were weeping and those who were much more afraid than she were encouraging her not to fear. Uncontrollable weeping broke out all over the church and all voices were united in the cry "St. Swithin, O St. Swithin, help her!" If the thunder had pealed forth at this time the people could not have heard it, with such strength, with such a concourse of voices did the shout go up to Heaven that St. Swithin should now or never hasten to her aid. God suffers violence and St. Swithin is dragged by force from Heaven. In a low voice the queen offered this prayer as she undertook the ordeal: "O God, who didst free Susanna from the wicked elders and the three youths from the fiery furnace, from the fire prepared for me deign to preserve me through the merits of St. Swithin."

Behold the miracle! With the bishops directing her feet, in nine steps she walked upon the nine ploughshares, pressing each one of them with the full weight of her whole body; and though she thus passed over them all, she neither saw the iron nor felt the heat. Therefore she said to the bishops: "Am I not to obtain that which I especially sought? Why do you lead me out of the church when I ought to be tried within it?" For she was going out and yet did not realize that she had gone through the ordeal. To which the bishops replied as well as they could through their sobs: "O lady, behold, you have already done it; the deed is now accomplished which you think must yet be done." She gazed and her eyes were opened; then for the first time she looked about and understood the miracle. "Lead me," she said, "to my son, that he may see my feet and know that I have suffered no ill."

ORDEAL OF FIRE

. . . All these things were pleasing to us, and having enjoined on him [Peter Bartholomew]* a fast, we declared that a fire should be prepared upon the day on which the

* [A crusader who returned from the Holy Land with what he claimed was the lance which had pierced Christ's side. (*Ed.*)]

Lord was beaten with stripes and put upon the cross for our salvation. And the fourth day thereafter was the day before the Sabbath. So when the appointed day came round a fire was prepared after the noon hour. The leaders and the people to the number of 60,000 came together; the priests were there also with bare feet, clothed in ecclesiastical garments. The fire was made of dry olive branches, covering a space thirteen feet long; and there were two piles with a space about a foot wide between them. The height of these piles was four feet. Now when the fire had been kindled so that it burned fiercely, I, Raimond, in presence of the whole multitude, spoke: "If Omnipotent God has spoken to this man face to face, and the blessed Andrew has shown him our Lord's lance while he was keeping his vigil, let him go through the fire unharmed. But if it is false let him be burned together with the lance which he is to carry in his hand." And all responded on bended knees, "Amen." The fire was growing so hot that the flames shot up thirty cubits high into the air and scarcely any one dared approach it. Then Peter Bartholomew clothed only in his tunic and kneeling before the bishop of Albar called to God to witness "that he had seen Him face to face on the cross, and that he had heard from Him those things above written. . . ." Then when the bishop had placed the lance in his hand, he knelt and made the sign of the cross and entered the fire with the lance, firm and unterrified. For an instant's time he paused in the midst of the flames, and then by the grace of God passed through. . . . But when Peter emerged from the fire so that neither his tunic was burned nor even the thin cloth with which the lance was wrapped up had shown any sign of damage, the whole people received him after that he had made over them the sign of the cross with the lance in his hand and had cried, "God aid us!" All the people, I say, threw themselves upon him and dragged him to the ground and trampled on him, each one wishing to touch him or to get a piece of his garment, and each thinking him near some one else. And so he received three or four wounds in the legs where the flesh was torn away, his back was injured and his sides bruised. Peter had died on the spot, as we believe, had not Raimond Pelet, a brave and noble soldier, broken through the wild crowd with a band of friends and rescued him at the peril of their lives. . . . [Twelve days later] Peter died in peace at the hour appointed to him by God, and journeyed to the Lord; and he was buried in the place where he had carried the lance of the Lord through the fire.

MAGNA CARTA

Although the supposedly reciprocal feudal obligations between lords and vassals were sometimes broken by the vassals, they were more often breached by the lords. It is true that great kings—Alfred, Canute, Henry I, St. Louis—personalized their reigns with touches of wisdom and humanity for which they were well loved, respected, and obeyed. But what of the ruler who exploited the tie between lord and vassal, tak-

*ing but seldom giving? William Rufus, as an instance, was murdered,
thus forestalling a bloody rebellion. His successor, Henry, was
forced at his coronation to swear that there would be no repetition of
Rufus's gouging and stealing.*

*A hundred years later, vassals suffered far more thoroughly and sys-
tematically under a king, so tyrannical that no English sovereign since
has dared to take his name. There has been only one King John. Magna
Carta was forced on John by his barons in 1215, on the field of Runnymede near the town of Staines. The sixty-three clauses, intended as
cures for specific violations, could well be subtitled "The Crimes of
the Tyrant." There was no one whom John had not offended: the
nobles, the freemen, the Jews, the Church, the merchants. Even foreigners sought redress. Yet, surprisingly, this is not a progressive document. John, who may have intended some good (and this is debatable)
in trying to modernize and streamline the feudal system into a lord-vassal
corporation yielding high personal financial dividends, had offended
by innovation. Magna Carta demands a return to what had been, freez-
ing the feudal contract in rigid clauses. Such fixed definition robbed
feudalism of needed flexibility; consequently, the system began to degen-
erate.*

*Yet modern Anglo-American law has adopted some of the Charter's
adamant clauses with as much determination as did the barons, though
for very different reasons. Many of the articles dealt with purely feudal
problems but have come to be interpreted as referring to primary civil
liberties. Through precedent, implications of the principles of "no
taxation without representation," representative government, and equality
before the law were read into the medieval phraseology.*

John, by the grace of God, king of England, lord of Ireland, duke of Normandy and
Aquitaine, count of Anjou, to the archbishops, bishops, abbots, earls, barons, justiciars,
foresters, sheriffs, reeves, servants, and all bailiffs and his faithful people greeting.
Know that by the suggestion of God and for the good of our soul and those of all our
predecessors and of our heirs, to the honor of God and the exaltation of holy church,
and the improvement of our kingdom, by the advice of our venerable fathers Stephen,
archbishop of Canterbury, primate of all England and Cardinal of the Holy Roman
Church, Henry, archbishop of Dublin, William of London, Peter of Winchester,
Joscelyn of Bath and Glastonbury, Hugh of Lincoln, Walter of Worcester, William of

"Great Charter of Liberties," *Select Documents of English Constitutional History*, ed. George
Burton Adams (New York: The Macmillan Company, 1901), pp. 42–52.

Coventry, and Benedict of Rochester, bishops; of Master Pandulf, subdeacon and member of the household of the lord Pope, of Brother Aymeric, master of the Knights of the Temple in England; and of the noblemen William Marshall, earl of Pembroke, William, earl of Salisbury, William, earl Warren, William, earl of Arundel, Alan of Galloway, constable of Scotland, Warren Fitz-Gerald, Peter Fitz-Herbert, Huber de Burgh, seneschal of Poitou, Hugh de Nevil, Matthew Fitz-Herbert, Thomas Bassett, Alan Bassett, Philip d'Albini, Robert de Ropesle, John Marshall, John Fitz-Hugh, and others of our faithful.

1 In the first place we have granted to God, and by this our present charter confirmed, for us and our heirs forever, that the English church shall be free, and shall hold its rights entire and its liberties uninjured; and we will that it thus be observed; which is shown by this, that the freedom of elections, which is considered to be most important and especially necessary to the English church, we, of our pure and spontaneous will, granted, and by our charter confirmed, before the contest between us and our barons had arisen; and obtained a confirmation of it by the lord Pope Innocent III.; which we will observe and which we will shall be observed in good faith by our heirs forever.

We have granted moreover to all free men of our kingdom for us and our heirs forever all the liberties written below, to be had and holden by themselves and their heirs from us and our heirs.

2 If any of our earls or barons, or others holding from us in chief by military service shall have died, and when he has died his heir shall be of full age and owe relief, he shall have his inheritance by the ancient relief; that is to say, the heir or heirs of an earl for the whole barony of an earl a hundred pounds; the heir or heirs of a baron for a whole barony a hundred pounds; the heir or heirs of a knight, for a whole knight's fee, a hundred shillings at most; and who owes less let him give less according to the ancient custom of fiefs.

3 If moreover the heir of any one of such shall be under age, and shall be in wardship, when he comes of age he shall have his inheritance without relief and without a fine.

4 The custodian of the land of such a minor heir shall not take from the land of the heir any except reasonable products, reasonable customary payments, and reasonable services, and this without destruction or waste of men or of property; and if we shall have committed the custody of the land of any such a one to the sheriff or to any other who is to be responsible to us for its proceeds, and that man shall have caused destruction or waste from his custody we will recover damages from him, and the land shall be committed to two legal and discreet men of that fief, who shall be responsible for its proceeds to us or to him to whom we have assigned them; and if we shall have given or sold to any one the custody of any such land, and he has caused destruction or waste there, he shall lose that custody, and it shall be handed over to two legal and discreet men of that fief who shall be in like manner responsible to us as is said above.

5 The custodian moreover, so long as he shall have the custody of the land, must keep up the houses, parks, warrens, fish ponds, mills, and other things pertaining to the land, from the proceeds of the land itself; and he must return to the heir, when

he has come to full age, all his land, furnished with ploughs and implements of husbandry according as the time of wainage requires and as the proceeds of the land are able reasonably to sustain.

6   Heirs shall be married without disparity, so nevertheless that before the marriage is contracted, it shall be announced to the relatives by blood of the heir himself.

7   A widow, after the death of her husband, shall have her marriage portion and her inheritance immediately and without obstruction, nor shall she give anything for her dowry or for her marriage portion, or for her inheritance which inheritance her husband and she held on the day of the death of her husband; and she may remain in the house of her husband for forty days after his death, within which time her dowry shall be assigned to her.

8   No widow shall be compelled to marry so long as she prefers to live without a husband, provided she gives security that she will not marry without our consent, if she holds from us, or without the consent of her lord from whom she holds, if she holds from another.

9   Neither we nor our bailiffs will seise any land or rent, for any debt, so long as the chattels of the debtor are sufficient for the payment of the debt; nor shall the pledges of a debtor be distrained so long as the principal debtor himself has enough for the payment of the debt; and if the principal debtor fails in the payment of the debt, not having the wherewithal to pay it, the pledges shall be responsible for the debt; and if they wish, they shall have the lands and the rents of the debtor until they shall have been satisfied for the debt which they have before paid for him, unless the principal debtor shall have shown himself to be quit in that respect towards those pledges.

10   If any one has taken anything from the Jews, by way of a loan, more or less, and dies before that debt is paid, the debt shall not draw interest so long as the heir is under age, from whomsoever he holds; and if that debt falls into our hands, we will take nothing except the chattel contained in the agreement.

11   And if any one dies leaving a debt owing to the Jews, his wife shall have her dowry, and shall pay nothing of that debt; and if there remain minor children of the dead man, necessaries shall be provided for them corresponding to the holding of the dead man; and from the remainder shall be paid the debt, saving the service of the lords. In the same way debts are to be treated which are owed to others than the Jews.

12   No scutage or aid shall be imposed in our kingdom except by the common council of our kingdom, except for the ransoming of our body, for the making of our oldest son a knight, and for once marrying our oldest daughter, and for these purposes it shall be only a reasonable aid; in the same way it shall be done concerning the aids of the city of London.

13   And the city of London shall have all its ancient liberties and free customs, as well by land as by water. Moreover, we will and grant that all other cities and boroughs and villages and ports shall have all their liberties and free customs.

14   And for holding a common council of the kingdom concerning the assessment of an aid otherwise than in the three cases mentioned above, or concerning the assessment of a scutage we shall cause to be summoned the archbishops, bishops, abbots,

earls, and greater barons by our letters individually; and besides we shall cause to be summoned generally, by our sheriffs and bailiffs all those who hold from us in chief, for a certain day, that is at the end of forty days at least, and for a certain place; and in all the letters of that summons, we will express the cause of the summons, and when the summons has thus been given the business shall proceed on the appointed day, on the advice of those who shall be present, even if not all of those who were summoned have come.

15 We will not grant to any one, moreover, that he shall take an aid from his free men, except for ransoming his body, for making his oldest son a knight, and for once marrying his oldest daughter; and for these purposes only a reasonable aid shall be taken.

16 No one shall be compelled to perform any greater service for a knight's fee, or for any other free tenement than is owed from it.

17 The common pleas shall not follow our court, but shall be held in some certain place. . . .

20 A free man shall not be fined for a small offence, except in proportion to the measure of the offence; and for a great offence he shall be fined in proportion to the magnitude of the offence, saving his freehold; and a merchant in the same way, saving his merchandise; and the villain shall be fined in the same way, saving his wainage, if he shall be at our mercy; and none of the above fines shall be imposed except by the oaths of honest men of the neighborhood.

21 Earls and barons shall only be fined by their peers, and only in proportion to their offence.

22 A clergyman shall be fined, like those before mentioned, only in proportion to his lay holding, and not according to the extent of his ecclesiastical benefice.

23 No vill or man shall be compelled to make bridges over the rivers except those which ought to do it of old and rightfully.

24 No sheriff, constable, coroners, or other bailiffs of ours shall hold pleas of our crown.

25 All counties, hundreds, wapentakes, and trithings shall be at the ancient rents and without any increase, excepting our demesne manors.

26 If any person holding a lay fief from us shall die, and our sheriff or bailiff shall show our letters-patent of our summons concerning a debt which the deceased owed to us, it shall be lawful for our sheriff or bailiff to attach and levy on the chattels of the deceased found on his lay fief, to the value of that debt, in the view of legal men, so nevertheless that nothing be removed thence until the clear debt to us shall be paid; and the remainder shall be left to the executors for the fulfilment of the will of the deceased; and if nothing is owed to us by him, all the chattels shall go to the deceased, saving to his wife and children their reasonable shares.

27 If any free man dies intestate, his chattels shall be distributed by the hands of his near relatives and friends, under the oversight of the church, saving to each one the debts which the deceased owed to him.

28 No constable or other bailiff of ours shall take any one's grain or other chattels, without immediately paying for them in money, unless he is able to obtain a postponement at the good-will of the seller.

29 No constable shall require any knight to give money in place of his ward of a castle if he is willing to furnish that ward in his own person or through another honest man, if he himself is not able to do it for a reasonable cause; and if we shall lead or send him into the army he shall be free from ward in proportion to the amount of time during which he has been in the army through us.

30 No sheriff or bailiff of ours or any one else shall take horses or wagons of any free man for carrying purposes except on the permission of that free man.

31 Neither we nor our bailiffs will take the wood of another man for castles, or for anything else which we are doing, except by the permission of him to whom the wood belongs.

32 We will not hold the lands of those convicted of a felony for more than a year and a day, after which the lands shall be returned to the lords of the fiefs.

33 All the fish-weirs in the Thames and the Medway, and throughout all England shall be done away with, except those on the coast. . . .

35 There shall be one measure of wine throughout our whole kingdom, and one measure of ale, and one measure of grain, that is the London quarter, and one width of dyed cloth and of russets and of halbergets, that is two ells within the selvages; of weights, moreover it shall be as of measures. . . .

38 No bailiff for the future shall put any one to his law on his simple affirmation, without credible witnesses brought for this purpose.

39 No free man shall be taken or imprisoned or dispossessed, or outlawed, or banished, or in any way destroyed, nor will we go upon him, nor send upon him, except by the legal judgment of his peers or by the law of the land.

40 To no one will we sell, to no one will we deny, or delay right or justice.

41 All merchants shall be safe and secure in going out from England and coming into England and in remaining and going through England, as well by land as by water, for buying and selling, free from all evil tolls, by the ancient and rightful customs, except in time of war, and if they are of a land at war with us; and if such are found in our land at the beginning of war, they shall be attached without injury to their bodies or goods, until it shall be known from us or from our principal justiciar in what way the merchants of our land are treated who shall be then found in the country which is at war with us; and if ours are safe there, the others shall be safe in our land.

42 It is allowed henceforth to any one to go out from our kingdom, and to return, safely and securely, by land and by water, saving their fidelity to us, except in time of war for some short time, for the common good of the kingdom; excepting persons imprisoned and outlawed according to the law of the realm, and people of a land at war with us, and merchants, of whom it shall be done as is before said. . . .

45 We will not make justiciars, constables, sheriffs or bailiffs except of such as know the law of the realm and are well inclined to observe it.

46 All barons who have founded abbeys for which they have charters of kings of England, or ancient tenure, shall have their custody when they have become vacant, as they ought to have.

47 All forests which have been afforested in our time shall be disafforested immediately; and so it shall be concerning river banks which in our time have been fenced in.

48 All the bad customs concerning forests and warrens and concerning foresters and warreners, sheriffs and their servants, river banks and their guardians shall be inquired into immediately in each county by twelve sworn knights of the same county, who shall be elected by the honest men of the same county, and within forty days after the inquisition has been made, they shall be entirely destroyed by them, never to be restored, provided that we be first informed of it, or our justiciar, if we are not in England.

49 We will give back immediately all hostages and charters which have been liberated to us by Englishmen as security for peace or for faithful service. . . .

51 And immediately after the reëstablishment of peace we will remove from the kingdom all foreign-born soldiers, cross-bow men, serjeants, and mercenaries who have come with horses and arms for the injury of the realm.

52 If any one shall have been dispossessed or removed by us without legal judgment of his peers, from his lands, castles, franchises, or his right we will restore them to him immediately; and if contention arises about this, then it shall be done according to the judgment of the twenty-five barons, of whom mention is made below concerning the security of the peace. Concerning all those things, however, from which any one has been removed or of which he has been deprived without legal judgment of his peers by King Henry our father, or by King Richard our brother, which we have in our hand, or which others hold, and which it is our duty to guarantee, we shall have respite till the usual term of crusaders; excepting those things about which the suit has been begun or the inquisition made by our writ before our assumption of the cross; when, however, we shall return from our journey or if by chance we desist from the journey, we will immediately show full justice in regard to them.

53 We shall, moreover, have the same respite and in the same manner about showing justice in regard to the forests which are to be disafforested or to remain forests, which Henry our father or Richard our brother made into forests; and concerning the custody of lands which are in the fief of another, custody of which we have until now had on account of a fief which any one has held from us by military service; and concerning the abbeys which have been founded in fiefs of others than ourselves, in which the lord of the fee has asserted for himself a right; and when we return or if we should desist from our journey we will immediately show full justice to those complaining in regard to them.

54 No one shall be seised nor imprisoned on the appeal of a woman concerning the death of any one except her husband.

55 All fines which have been imposed unjustly and against the law of the land, and all penalties imposed unjustly and against the law of the land are altogether excused, or will be on the judgment of the twenty-five barons of whom mention is made below in connection with the security of the peace, or on the judgment of the majority of them, along with the aforesaid Stephen, archbishop of Canterbury, if he is able to be present, and others whom he may wish to call for this purpose along with him. And if he should not be able to be present, nevertheless the business shall go on without him, provided that if any one or more of the aforesaid twenty-five barons are in a similar suit they should be removed as far as this particular judgment goes, and others who shall be chosen and put upon oath, by the remainder of the twenty-five shall be substituted for them for this purpose.

56   If we have dispossessed or removed any Welshmen from their lands, or franchises, or other things, without legal judgment of their peers, in England, or in Wales, they shall be immediately returned to them; and if a dispute shall have arisen over this, then it shall be settled in the borderland by judgment of their peers, concerning holdings of England according to the law of England, concerning holdings of Wales according to the law of Wales, and concerning holdings of the borderland according to the law of the borderland. The Welsh shall do the same to us and ours.

57   Concerning all those things, however, from which any one of the Welsh shall have been removed or dispossessed without legal judgment of his peers, by King Henry our father, or King Richard our brother, which we hold in our hands, or which others hold, and we are bound to warrant to them, we shall have respite till the usual period of crusaders, those being excepted about which suit was begun or inquisition made by our command before our assumption of the cross. When, however, we shall return or if by chance we shall desist from our journey, we will show full justice to them immediately, according to the laws of the Welsh and the aforesaid parts.

58   We will give back the son of Lewellyn immediately, and all the hostages from Wales and the charters which had been liberated to us as a security for peace.

59   We will act toward Alexander, king of the Scots, concerning the return of his sisters and his hostages, and concerning his franchises and his right, according to the manner in which we shall act toward our other barons of England, unless it ought to be otherwise by the charters which we hold from William his father, formerly king of the Scots, and this shall be by the judgment of his peers in our court.

60   Moreover, all those customs and franchises mentioned above which we have conceded in our kingdom, and which are to be fulfilled, as far as pertains to us, in respect to our men; all men of our kingdom as well clergy as laymen, shall observe as far as pertains to them, in respect to their men.

61   Since, moreover, for the sake of God, and for the improvement of our kingdom, and for the better quieting of the hostility sprung up lately between us and our barons, we have made all these concessions; wishing them to enjoy these in a complete and firm stability forever, we make and concede to them the security described below; that is to say, that they shall elect twenty-five barons of the kingdom, whom they will, who ought with all their power to observe, hold, and cause to be observed, the peace and liberties which we have conceded to them, and by this our present charter confirmed to them; in this manner, that if we or our justiciar, or our bailiffs, or any one of our servants shall have done wrong in any way toward any one, or shall have transgressed any of the articles of peace or security; and the wrong shall have been shown to four barons of the aforesaid twenty-five barons, let those four barons come to us or to our justiciar, if we are out of the kingdom, laying before us the transgression, and let them ask that we cause that transgression to be corrected without delay. And if we shall not have corrected the transgression or, if we shall be out of the kingdom, if our justiciar shall not have corrected it within a period of forty days, counting from the time in which it has been shown to us or to our justiciar, if we are out of the kingdom; the aforesaid four barons shall refer the matter to the remainder of the twenty-five barons, and let these twenty-five barons with the whole community of the country distress and injure us in every way they can; that is to say by the seizure of our castles, lands, possessions, and in such other ways as they can until it shall have been corrected according to their judgment, saving our person and that of our queen, and those of our children; and when the correction has been made, let them devote themselves to us as they did before. And let whoever in the country wishes take an oath that in all the above-mentioned measures he will obey the orders of the aforesaid twenty-five barons, and that he will injure us as far as he is able with them, and we give permission to swear publicly and freely to each one who wishes to swear, and no one will we ever forbid to swear. All those, moreover, in the country who of themselves and their own will are unwilling to take an oath to the twenty-five barons as to distressing and injuring us along with them, we will compel to take the oath by our mandate, as before said. And if any one of the twenty-five barons shall have died or departed from the land or shall in any other way be prevented from taking the above-mentioned action, let the remainder of the aforesaid twenty-five barons choose another in his place, according to their judgment, who shall take an oath in the same way as the others. In all those things, moreover, which are committed to those five and twenty barons to carry out, if perhaps the twenty-five are present, and some disagreement arises among them about something, or if any of them when they have been summoned are not willing or are not able to be present, let that be considered valid and firm which the greater part of those who are present arrange or command, just as if the whole twenty-five had agreed in this; and let the aforesaid twenty-five swear that they will observe faithfully all the things which are said above, and with all their ability cause them to be observed. And we will obtain nothing from any one, either by ourselves or by another by which any of these concessions and liberties shall be revoked or diminished; and if any such thing shall have been obtained, let it be invalid and void, and we will never use it by ourselves or by another.

62   And all ill-will, grudges, and anger sprung up between us and our men, clergy and laymen, from the time of the dispute, we have fully renounced and pardoned to all. Moreover, all transgressions committed on account of this dispute, from Easter in the sixteenth year of our reign till the restoration of peace, we have fully remitted to all, clergy and laymen, and as far as pertains to us, fully pardoned. And moreover we have caused to be made for them testimonial letters-patent of lord Stephen, archbishop of Canterbury, lord Henry, archbishop of Dublin, and of the aforesaid bishops and of Master Pandulf, in respect to that security and the concessions named above.

63   Wherefore we will and firmly command that the Church of England shall be free, and that the men in our kingdom shall have and hold all the aforesaid liberties, rights and concessions, well and peacefully, freely and quietly, fully and completely, for themselves and their heirs, from us and our heirs, in all things and places, forever, as before said. It has been sworn, moreover, as well on our part as on the part of the barons, that all these things spoken of above shall be observed in good faith and without any evil intent. Witness the above named and many others. Given by our hand in the meadow which is called Runnymede, between Windsor and Staines, on the fifteenth day of June, in the seventeenth year of our reign.

Feudal Monarchies:
Louis IX and Edward I

Criminal and civil law became increasingly complex from as early as the settlements of the Franks and the Saxons, yet it was not until the nineteenth century that truly effective judicial administration and law enforcement appeared. No matter how many crimes might come to be punishable by medieval kings, no matter how expansive their court systems might become, obedience to the law was hardly more than voluntary. Uniform enforcement was first attempted in the eleventh century; but the true age of administrative reform began in the thirteenth century, when the salaried administrator, forerunner of the bureaucrat, made his humble appearance. Since noblemen could use their royal offices as fronts for rebellion, kings preferred to put this trust in the merchants and nonfeudal landowners, who were personally less dangerous.

Philip Augustus created the office of bailiff—a royal superintendent paid by the treasury—to supervise tax, law, and military enforcements. When, fifty years later, Saint Louis returned from the Holy Land to France (1254) and ushered in a period of peace and stability, he strengthened the office and, as will be seen in the accompanying documents, set a rigid standard for his officials. Thus the process of governmental centralization was early in coming to France; and the new royal officials were commoners, fully dependent on and answerable to the king—unlike the older aristocratic crown agents, who had answered to none but themselves. It is to Louis' credit that he tried to protect his subjects from the abuses of officialdom by prohibiting his agents from capitalizing on their local power.

In Western Europe generally, and particularly in France, Spain, and England, commoners were being drawn into positions of trust and responsibility, and not only on the local level. The sovereign's reliance on their participation forced the town and country people to develop a conception of responsible citizenship.

Since in England the tax sums that were derived from the nobles—and these were the major taxes the kings then claimed—were fixed by Magna Carta, Edward I found that by law he could assess no more than had his grandfather. Inflation made this amount painfully inadequate. To broaden the tax base, Edward expanded the old feudal Great Council of the bishops and barons (the forerunner of Parliament), inviting two untitled knights from each shire and two merchants from each of the larger towns to participate, in a limited way, in the law-making. By their representation in Parliament, commoners were made liable to royal taxation. Kings, faced with increasing problems of a business nature, found a genuine need for the advice of the merchant class on fiscal matters; but even more, they needed the money that could be obtained from the merchants. Although the monied commoners at first gave grudgingly of their advice and wealth, they were soon flattered by the royal attention and found themselves enjoying the benefits of this new power based on royal need. By 1360 the House of Commons, as it came to be called, was already finding that the larger a king's need was for increased taxes, the more rights and privileges could be wrung from him in return: trading concessions, business monopolies, civil liberties—including free speech and freedom from arbitrary arrest for members of Parliament—and such political prerogatives as the control of royal expenditures and even the removal of unpopular court favorites—even of kings themselves.

The following writs were issued by Edward I for his Parliament of 1295. They display a number of innovations in political ideas: the clause that reads, "what affects all, by all should be approved," is the seed of representative government. Note too, the urgency conveyed concerning an imminent French invasion. Here is an early use of propaganda appealing to national pride. The final writ is interesting, for those things to which the lords agreed could generally be relied upon, as the lords were not expected to speak for any but themselves, but the king had learned, and in a very short space of time, that the knights and merchants must be representative of their constituents for their promises to be binding.

❧ ORDINANCE FOR THE ADMINISTRATION OF THE KINGDOM (1256)

Louis IX

1   We order that all our seneschals, bailiffs and all others, whatever their office, shall swear that as long as they shall hold said offices, they shall deal justly with all, making no exceptions, with poor as with rich, with stranger as with friend, and that they shall keep the good and tested customs of the region. And should it happen that they [break] their oath and are caught, we want them to be punished by fine and imprisonment, in accordance with their misdeeds.

Ordonnances des rois de France de la troisième race (Paris, 1723–1849), Vol. I, 77–83. Translated by Norman Susskind for this volume.

2 The above-mentioned seneschals and bailiffs shall swear that they will loyally preserve our rights and revenues, and that they will not knowingly permit these to be taken from us, suspended or diminished.

3 They will swear not to accept, either directly or through others, any gift, gold or silver, or any material or spiritual benefit or anything else, unless it be fruit or wine or other gifts valued at no more than 10 sols in any one week.

4 They will swear that they will not have their wives, children, relatives, associates, friends or servants accept any [gifts]; nor will they offer any to those who keep the accounts, nor to any [roving] investigator or examiner whom we send to the places where they have held appointive office from us, in order to seek evidence against them.

5 All our officials will swear that they [the bailiffs and seneschals] will not seek to profit by selling or marketing any of our revenues, provostships, bailiwicks, [control] over our waters, forests, mints, nor of any other of our holdings, nor of anything belonging to us; and they will faithfully turn over to us the amount of taxes they collect in our name, and when they sell our property or lease other of our sources of revenue, they will sell or lease them at the best possible price, as faithfully, suitably and profitably as they can.

6 They will swear that if they know of any officials or sergeants under their authority who are disloyal, robbers, usurers, or having other vices which should result in their dismissal from our service, they [the higher officials] will not aid and abet them by way of gifts, promises, personal intervention, nor by any other means, but rather will they force them to make reparation for their misdeeds.

7 Our minor officials, such as provosts, lieutenants, viscounts, mayors, gamekeepers, sergeants and other such, will swear that they will not offer gifts to their superiors, nor to the latter's wives, children, friends, or other familiars.

8 And in order that these oaths be more firmly kept, we want them to be sworn in the public square before all clerics and laymen, even if such oaths have already been taken before ourselves, so that the oath-taker may fear to incur the vice of perjury not only before God and ourselves, but for fear of being shamed before the people.

9 We further desire and order that all our seneschals, bailiffs, and all our other officials and servants, of whatever estate or condition they may be, refrain from uttering words disrespectful of God, of our Blessed Lady Mary, and of all the saints, and stay away from dice games, brothels, and taverns.

10 Let the making of dice be forbidden and outlawed throughout our kingdom. Any man who will be found playing at dice or who is known to be a habitual frequenter of taverns and brothels, shall be reputed infamous and disqualified from bearing witness.

11 Let all tarts and common whores be expelled from all of our good towns and cities. In particular, let them be kept off the streets of said good towns, to be forced to dwell outside the city walls, as well as far away from any holy places such as churches and cemeteries. And whosoever in such cities, good towns and other chartered municipalities should rent any house to prostitutes, or receive them in his own house, shall have to pay one year's rent to the municipality by our order.

12 Let no one go drink in a tavern, unless he be a transient or one who owns no house in the town.

13 We forbid all our seneschals, bailiffs, and other high officials to purchase or acquire without our special leave, personally or through the connivance of others, for their own or others' gain, any possessions or lands that are within their administrative jurisdiction, or any debt that we may owe there or elsewhere, as long as they hold their official positions. And if it happens that such purchases or acquisitions be made, we declare them to be null and void and order the said possessions and debts thus purchased to revert to us according to our pleasure.

14 We forbid any of our aforementioned officials, unless on leave, to give their sons or daughters or any of their people in marriage to anyone residing within their seneschalship, bailiwick, or other administrative jurisdiction unless we have granted them special permission. Nor are they to place them in Holy Orders, or invest them with any benefice or possession of Holy Mother Church; nor are they to accept hospitality from religious houses at the latter's expense, nor accept garments and board from anyone who has dealings with us.

15 We do not wish to extend this ban on marriage and the acquisition of goods and offices to officials of lesser degree than those named above, nor to petty provosts and others who purchase the right to collect our revenues.

16 No seneschals, bailiffs, or other officials in our service are to retain an excessive number of sergeants or peace officers, but no more than the execution of our commands and those of our courts require. The peace officers and sergeants are to be appointed in open session of the court, otherwise they should not be recognized as such. And if it happens that our peace officers or sergeants are sent to distant or foreign places, they are not to be recognized unless they show letters from their superiors. If they fail to comply with this, let it be reported to their local superior whom we order to punish them suitably.

17 We forbid any senescal, bailiff, or other officer in our service, whoever he may be, to oppress our subjects unjustly or to imprison them for any outstanding debt, unless the debt [owed] be to ourselves.

18 And if it should happen that someone under indictment should not wish to await the judgment of the court, but rather offer to pay a certain sum of money, if [the latter seems] appropriate, let it be accepted [by our official]. If not, let him set the fine, even if the accused now wishes to accept the jurisdiction of the court.

19 We do not want those who shall hold our provostships, vicarships, viscounties, mayoralties, bailiwicks, or other offices, to be enabled to sell them to others without our leave. And if several people join together to purchase in common any of the above-mentioned offices, only one among the buyers shall perform the duties of the office and be entitled to the privileges and exemptions pertaining to [feudal] levies, taxes, collections and other common charges, as is our custom.

20 We forbid them to sell the said offices to relatives, brothers, cousins, nephews, or to intimates of their cousins and friends, or to any nobleman. Nor can a nobleman collect debts for them, unless it be debts for things appertaining to their office. Let them rather have their personal debts collected by authority of the seneschal, bailiff, or other sovereign judge of the place, as though they were not in our service.

21 We forbid the bailiffs, seneschals, and other officials named above to force our subjects secretly or publicly, by threat, by fear or by chicanery, to pay fines; nor are they to accuse them without reasonable cause.

22 We forbid our above-named officials to harass our subjects in a case under their jurisdiction by a change of venue without reasonable cause. Let them rather hear the cases before them in the places where they are customarily heard and let them not fail to protect the rights of their subjects regardless of effort or expense.

23 We forbid them to deprive any person of any possession without just cause or without special orders from us. Nor are they to oppress our subjects by new exactions of the *taille* [the basic tax on property held by commoners] and by novel taxes; nor are they to order anyone to call a [feudal] levy for monetary gain [by means of exemption payments]. No one should be obliged to appear in person with the host [the feudal army] unless there be a reasonable and necessary cause. Those who do appear in person should not be constrained to buy their way out with money.

24 None of our officials may prohibit without good reason the transport of wine, wheat or other merchandise within or beyond the kingdom. When such a prohibition is appropriate, we want it to be enacted by the Council of Notables without fraud or deceit. Once the decision is reached, the Council may not reverse it on its own initiative, nor grant special dispensation to anyone as long as [the prohibition] is in force.

25 After they leave office, we want all our seneschals, bailiffs, and other officials to remain for a period of forty days within the region which they had administered either personally or through delegates, so that they are answerable to those whom they may have wronged and who may want to bring suit against them before the new seneschals, bailiffs, or other officials in charge.

26 And in all these things that we have ordained for the peace and tranquillity of our subjects and our kingdom, in behalf of our [royal] prerogative we retain the power to proclaim, to add, to amend, and to diminish as we see fit. Proclaimed in Paris in the year 1256.

ORDINANCE CONCERNING THE MAYORALTY IN ALL THE GOOD CITIES OF THE KINGDOM (*ca.* 1256)

1 We order that all the mayors in France assume office on the day following Saint Simon and Saint Jude's Day [October 28].

2 Moreover, we order also that the new as well as the former mayor, together with four notables of the town, among whom shall be one or two who have been in charge of the town's revenues and expenditures the year before, shall come to Paris a week after Saint Martin's Day [November 11] to meet with our officials and render account of their receipts and outlays.

3 Moreover, on penalty of imprisonment and fine, we forbid our chartered towns and our good cities to extend any manner of loan or gift without our permission, with the exception of wine in pots or barrels.

4 Moreover, no one but the mayor or the vice-mayor, accompanied by no more than two companions, by the town clerk and one spokesman, if needed, may come to court on town business, regardless of the size of their city. The mayor, the vice-mayor, and their companions shall have with them no more horses and servants than are required for their personal needs.

5   Moreover, those responsible for the city's finances shall not keep the municipal funds [in their personal possession] with the exception of the disbursing official, who shall be permitted to retain up to twenty livres. City funds are to be kept in the municipal treasury.

ৰঌ WRITS OF SUMMONS TO PARLIAMENT, 1295

Edward I

Summons of the Clergy

The King to the venerable father in Christ Robert, by the same grace archbishop of Canterbury, primate of all England, greeting. As a most just law, established by the careful providence of sacred princes, exhorts and decrees that what affects all, by all should be approved, so also, very evidently should common danger be met by means provided in common. You know sufficiently well, and it is now, as we believe, divulged through all regions of the world, how the king of France fraudulently and craftily deprives us of our land of Gascony, by withholding it unjustly from us. Now, however, not satisfied with the before-mentioned fraud and injustice, having gathered together for the conquest of our kingdom a very great fleet, and an abounding multitude of warriors, with which he has made a hostile attack on our kingdom and the inhabitants of the same kingdom, he now proposes to destroy the English language altogether from the earth, if his power should correspond to the detestable proposition of the contemplated injustice, which God forbid. Because, therefore, darts seen beforehand do less injury, and your interest especially, as that of the rest of the citizens of the same realm, is concerned in this affair, we command you, strictly enjoining you in the fidelity and love in which you are bound to us, that on the Lord's day next after the feast of St. Martin, in the approaching winter, you be present in person at Westminster; citing beforehand the dean and chapter of your church, the archdeacons and all the clergy of your diocese, causing the same dean and archdeacons in their own persons, and the said chapter by one suitable proctor, and the said clergy by two, to be present along with you, having full and sufficient power from the same chapter and clergy, to consider, ordain and provide, along with us and with the rest of the prelates and principal men and other inhabitants of our kingdom, how the dangers and threatened evils of this kind are to be met. Witness the king at Wangham, the thirtieth day of September.

"Writs of Summons to Parliament," *Select Documents of English Constitutional History,* ed. George Burton Adams (New York: The Macmillan Company, 1901), pp. 82–84.

[Identical summons were sent out to the two archbishops and eighteen bishops, and, with the omission of the last paragraph, to seventy abbots.]

Summons of the Barons

The king to his beloved and faithful relative, Edmund, Earl of Cornwall, greeting. Because we wish to have a consultation and meeting with you and with the rest of the principal men of our kingdom, as to provision for remedies against the dangers which in these days are threatening our whole kingdom; we command you, strictly enjoining you in the fidelity and love in which you are bound to us, that on the Lord's day next after the feast of St. Martin, in the approaching winter, you be present in person at Westminster, for considering, ordaining and doing along with us and with the prelates, and the rest of the principal men and other inhabitants of our kingdom, as may be necessary for meeting dangers of this kind.

Witness the king at Canterbury, the first of October.

[Similar summons were sent to seven earls and forty-one barons.]

Summons of Representatives of the Counties and Boroughs

The king to the sheriff of Northamptonshire. Since we intend to have a consultation and meeting with the earls, barons and other principal men of our kingdom with regard to providing remedies against the dangers which are in these days threatening the same kingdom; and on that account have commanded them to be with us on the Lord's day next after the feast of St. Martin in the approaching winter, at Westminster, to consider, ordain, and do as may be necessary for the avoidance of these dangers; we strictly require you to cause two knights from the aforesaid county, two citizens from each city in the same county, and two burgesses from each borough, of those who are especially discreet and capable of laboring, to be elected without delay, and to cause them to come to us at the aforesaid time and place.

Moreover, the said knights are to have full and sufficient power for themselves and for the community of the aforesaid county, and the said citizens and burgesses for themselves and the communities of the aforesaid cities and boroughs separately, then and there for doing what shall then be ordained according to the common counsel in the premises; so that the aforesaid business shall not remain unfinished in any way for defect of this power. And you shall have there the names of the knights, citizens and burgesses and this writ.

Witness the king at Canterbury on the third day of October.

⋙ THE SONG OF WILLIAM

While we may look for the institutions of feudalism in legal documents such as the Magna Carta *(see page 23), for the personal and social ideals of the ruling caste we must, as in the case of the Homeric Greeks, turn*

to epic poetry. The Song of William, *dating from about 1100, is one
of the earliest surviving French narrative poems known as* chansons de geste
*("songs of deeds"). These were popular throughout the twelfth and into
the thirteenth century. Some eighty such epics have survived.* The Song of
William *may be the oldest of what came to be a cycle, or group of
twenty-four poems dealing with three generations of the Counts of
Toulouse in southwestern France.*

These chansons de geste *share certain common features: all of them
focus on the heroic deeds of a nobleman, usually a little-known historic
figure of the eighth or ninth century. An armed clash between Islam and
Christianity, described in lovingly detailed battle scenes, is generally central
in these poems. Almost invariably they are also concerned with problems
of feudal loyalty. Though contemporaries accepted these narratives
as fact, they are almost wholly works of fiction.*

In the case of The Song of William, *the poem, as well as the whole related
cycle of poems, rests on an extremely slender historical foundation. We
know that in 804 William, Count of Toulouse, who had fought bravely
against the Moslems in Spain, retired to a Benedictine monastery near
Montpellier in southern France. A few years later he founded and endowed
a monastery of his own in the same vicinity. It is likely that the unknown
eleventh- or twelfth-century poet who composed the epic had not much
more information about William than we do.*

The most plausible theory about the origin of the chansons de geste
*relates them to the needs of certain religious shrines and monastic hostels
along competing routes to Saint James of Compostella in northwestern
Spain, the most popular place of pilgrimage in western Europe. According
to this theory, in order to advertise their particular establishment monks
would turn over the meager information about their sainted patron
to a* jongleur *(itinerant minstrel), who would then compose a narrative
poem around the secular deeds of the saint, a variant on the tradition of
saints' lives. As these songs became widely known, pilgrims on the way
to Compostella would, for example, make the short detour to stop off
at Saint-Guilhem-le-Desert to view the relics of Saint William, now
an epic hero as well as a saint.*

Whether or not some of these jongleurs *were themselves nobles, as*
The Song of William *affirms (page 45), the poems were clearly meant
to be sung or recited before an aristocratic audience. Though the monks
who furnished the occasion for the poems may have succeeded in
christianizing their content, in the final analysis it was the taste of the
warlike audience that prevailed. Thus if* The Song of William *cannot serve*

as realistic portrayal of the twelfth-century feudal class, it gives us a
good idea of how that class liked to view itself. However fantastic the
plot of the epic, its values are authentic.

Would ye listen, my lords, to a goodly lay,
   Of fightings fell and of battles sore,
Of a Saracen chief King Deramé,
   Of the war that he waged on our Emperor?
But Dan William waged fiercer war on him,
Till in Archamp he slew him in combat grim.

Oft did he joust with the paynim men;
   There he lost of his knights the flower,
And his nephew, bold Count Viviën.
   Sad was his heart for him that hour,
On Monday, when Vespertide is near.
THE SONG OF WILLIAM beginneth here. . . .

At Barcelona Count William lay,
Thither returned from a long drawn fray.
   At Bordeaux on Gironde was the battle fought,
And a host of his men had he lost that day.
   And lo, Girart hath his tidings brought!

Back from his Vespers, Sir William went
   And stood in a balcony window wide;
Dame Guiburc on his right arm leant.
   Then he gazed at a hillside and there descried
Girart, from Archamp thitherward bent.
A bloody sword in his right hand he bare,
With its point to the ground he braced him there.

"Sister, sweet friend," thus William spake,
Happy the hour when I took thee as make,
And the hour thou gat'st Christendom happier still.
A man do I see descending yon hill;
A bloody sword in his hand bears he,
And I'll tell thee this of a verity:
That in battle fierce he late hath been
And cometh to me my succour to win.
   Come, go we to meet him, his tidings to get!"
Then together Guiburc and the crook-nosed one

The Song of William, trans. E. Noble Stone (Seattle: University of Washington Press, 1951),
pp. 3, 39–44, 51–67, 69–76.

Adown the steps of the stairway run.
　　And when they were down, Girart they met.
William beholds him and knows him well;
Then calls he upon him his tidings to tell.

"Forward, Girart, and thy tidings say!"
Quoth Girart: "Ill tidings in sooth are they!

From Córdova cometh King Deramé,
To the high sea sent he his fleet away,
France hath he entered and waste doth lay.
The Marches he harries, the farmsteads lights.
　　Through all the land he worketh his will.
Where'er he finds them, he seizes thy knights,
　　Angry and grieving, his ships to fill.
　　Think, help thy folk that suffer such ill!

Forth from his own land is Deramé bent,
　　In our land he worketh evil untold.
Tedbald and Esturmi against him went,
　　And together with them Vivien the bold.
The one is fighting, the twain have fled."
　　"God!" cried William. "My nephew is he!"
Quoth Girart: "A true word now hast thou said.
　　This message he sends, and I tell it to thee:
　　That thou succour him now in dire jeopardy!

Know'st the word noble Vivien sendeth to thee?
　　And thou mind'st thee of Límenes city grand,
Of Breher, the haven that lies by the sea,
Of Fleury town, taken by his own hand,
　　Come, help him in Archamp above the strand.

Know'st what word he sends thee, Vivien the true?
Mind'st thou the battle with King Turleu,
Where fights three and thirty for thee he fought,
And an hundred and fifty to thee he brought
Of the mightiest men of heathenry?
In a rout, where Lewis himself did flee,
He came to the hill with his company,
Ten score, cried 'Monjoie!' and gained thee the fight.
That day lost he Rahel, his faithful knight.
(Not a day, not an hour but he mourns him, alas!)
Go, bring him help in this dolorous pass!

Dost know what he asks thee, Vivien the bold,
An thou mindest the battle whereof he told,
'Neath Orange, where Tedbald the Steersman fought?

In that fight, where the Franks the victory got,
With Bernard of Bruban to the hill did he ride;
As companion, Count Bertram rode at his side—
   One of the best of all thy kin.
'God help!'—the Normans' war cry—he cried;
   Therewith he caused thee that field to win.
There Tedbald the Steersman did he slay.
Come, bring him aid in Archamp today
And succour him there in the dolorous fray. . . .

"Ah, God! Can I find him alive?" William cried.
"In vain thou askest," Guiburc replied.
"Save him! Not thine to question and plod.
An thou lose him thou'st not a friend save God!"
When William heard her his head he shook,
Tenderly, gently to weeping he took.
Warm flows the water along his nose,
Down his white beard to his baldric it goes.
Guiburc he calleth, and seeketh to find
In what wise her heart to him is inclined
   And how greatly she loveth both him and his kin.
   With cunning purpose doth he begin:
"Sister, sweet friend, give heed in God's name!
   Three days' space hath it not yet been
Since hither from a great battle I came
   That late I fought at Bordeaux by the sea.
   There lost I my noble chivalry.
Far are the marches where I have to command,
Hardy the men I there should needs band.
Moreover, all this could I never bear—
Iron and steel might be handled there!
Well fighteth Vivien, the far-famed knight;
This time I cannot regard his plight.
Without me, well can he finish this fight!"
Then no more could Guiburc her tears resist.
She bowed her low and his shoe she kissed;
To William she spake, and began to plead:
"Save him! To tarry thou hast no need!
My nephew Guischart I trust to thee,
Whom of late, of thy goodness, thou dubbedst for me! . . .

When night came down on the goodly town
   William the Crook-nosed rode away,
With thirty thousand arm'd horsemen boune
   To Archamp, seeking King Deramé.
All night through the chill and the damp they rode,

Till the morrow came and the bright day shewed.
But when to Archamp they came, by the main,
    Already the battle had Deramé won,
And taken the booty and stripped the slain,
    And the Saracens into their ships were gone,
Their galleys, their huge craft iron-braced.
    But the wind had failed them, to stay were they fain.
So the lords and nobles and peers in haste
Went forth to visit the solid land,
Full a league away by the salt sea strand.
And now behold William on counsel intent
    With thirty thousand armèd knights.
Fifteen thousand on battle are bent,
    As behooveth to strike in well-pitched fights.
"Monjoie!" they cry and to charge are fain.
But that charge the heathen cannot sustain,
For armour to fend their bodies they've none.
    They turn and they flee toward the shore of the deep.
    To the barges, the galleys, the ships they leap;
They seize their weapons, their armour they don.

These Saracens coming from Saragosse' shore,
    An hundred thousand, in warfare bold;
Not one but hauberk and helmet wore,
    With flowered frontals and clasps of gold;
Swords girt, with the bright blades hanging free,
    Their goodly shields by the bands they hold,
    Their hands keen darts and spearshafts enfold;
'Neath their saddles, swift coursers of Araby—
So sallied they forth on the pebbled sand,
Seeking the shore and the solid land.
'Gainst William the Count to battle they steer.
Doleful the tale thereof ye'll hear.

This battle lasted a Monday through,
And all the morrow, and Wednesday too,
Withouten respite at any time,
E'en until Thursday at coming of prime.
Nor ever the Franks forbore to attack,
Nor ceased the Arabs to strike them back,
Till of William's host neither man nor shield
Was left—save three only—to hold the field.
    (*On Thursday, when evening's light grows less.*)
With three shields left alone in the press!
With three shields left in the press alone—
Girart, the valiant swordsman, was one;

The other, Guischart, Guiburc's brother's son.
And now of the noble knights will ye hear,
How each took his leave of the royal fere?

Of the noble vassals now shall I tell,
How each bade the king's own fere farewell?
Girart his course to the leftward bent.
His horse in a sand bank headlong went,
Up over his shoulders his hauberk goes.
Down upon him come thirty foes;
In thirty places they wound Girart,
Thrusting him through with spear and dart.
He calls and he cries as death draws nigh.
Then cometh William to answer his cry.
Ten foemen he slew, then fled the rest.
He came to Girart, whom he softly addressed.

"Friend Girart, if hence one could thee bear
And make shift for the wounds of thy body to care,
Say, couldst thou be healed again? For well knowest thou
In heaven thou oughtst to be long ere now!"
And Girart made answer: "Nay, lord, let be!
I would not that hence one should carry me,
Or his art on the wounds of my body should ply.
I'll be healed not, for all that mortal can try.
But if one would help me to mount once more—
My helmet green laced fast as before,
At my neck my mighty buckler hung,
In my hand the shaft of my sharp lance swung—
And would give me one draught of the wine so red,
Or, if need be, one draught from the brook instead,
Then I would not give o'er, by the faith I owe Heaven!
Dear would I sell them each wound they have given,
Whence in great streams my blood flows away."
And William made answer: "Here alone thou'lt not stay."
    (*Thursday, at eventide!*)
Then the count gat him down by his nephew's side.

Down on the ground by his nephew he got,
Girart's right hand with his own he sought;
He raised him, sitting the grass upon.
His visage was troubled, his cheeks were wan,
Backward his eyes in their sockets were bent
And all his head to the leftward leant.
Down to his chin his helmet rolled,
Nor his passing soul could his head uphold.

Quoth the count: "Nought else could be, Girart!"
Ah, God! What grief when such brave men part!
Needs must William weep for his nephew bold. . . .

Dame Guiburc forgot not the crook-nosed knight:
Well she knew how in Archamp he stood in the fight,
Battling 'gainst paynim Deramé.
   She calls her messengers, summons her men,
Till thirty thousand she's brought in array;
   Ready were fifteen thousand then,
Who to fight in well-pitched battle were fain.
She withdrew all the vassals of high domain
And up in the palace she set them to dine,
   And lays and fables she caused them to hear.
Herself she served them and bare round the wine.
   Then she leant 'gainst a marble pillar near.
Forth of a window she gazed at will:
Then spied she William descending a hill
Bearing a dead man in front as he came;
Then she minded herself of Vivien's name.
Had she erewhile been glad, now began she to cry.
   And they asked her: "What cause have ye, lady, to weep?"
"In God's name, reason enow have I!
   I behold my lord descending yon steep,
A dead man before him bearing, and lo,
He hath turned the corse o'er his saddlebow.
'Tis Vivien! That right well do I know!"
"Peace, lady! Give to him not that name!"
So spake the lords of the realm to the dame.

"Who might it be, then, in God's name I pray,
Whom William would bring from the battle away,
An it were not Lewis, his liege forsooth,
Or Vivien his nephew, the stout-hearted youth?"
"Peace, lady! No mention of these let us make!"
'Twas thus one of William's nobles spake:
"Howbeit, a jongleur hath William my lord;
   In all France no singer so good will ye find,
Nor a hardier dealer of blows with the sword.
   All the songs of history hath he in mind:
Of Clovis, first of the Frankish kings
   Who in God our Lord and Ruler believed,
Of Flovent his son, the fighter, he sings,
   Who from him the rule of sweet France received,
Of all the kings of warlike renown
Clean to Pepin, the short but valiant, down;

Of Charlemagne, Roland his nephew dear,
Of Girart and of Oliver the peer:
My lord's kinsmen these and his forbears.
Right worthily my lord's love he shares.
Since in him he'th a singer so prized by us
And in combat a vassal victorious,
He bringeth him back from the battle thus."

"My lords, free men, for God's love, I pray
That ye give me your leave to get me away.
   'Tis my lord, and to serve him behooves me to go."
   Down the staircase she hied to the gateway below.
She came to the gate and unbarred it straightway,
She opened it up and let the count in.
He gazed upon her and thus did begin:

"Dame Guiburc, how long hast thou kept my gate?"
"By my faith, lord, I do it only of late.
Sir William, thou art in but feeble state!"

"Sister, sweet friend, hast thou tended my door
For long?" "Faith, lord, newly but not of yore.
Sir William, thou'rt hardly a warrior more!"

"Take him, Guiburc; 'tis thy nephew Guischart.
   Thou'lt never behold Count Vivien again."
The noble Guiburc spread her arms apart,
   Therein laid William the warrior slain.
Heavy the corse, her arms gave way;
   She was but a woman, and had little strength.
   Down to the ground fell the body full length.
All his tongue thrust forth to one side, he lay.
   (*Thursday, at eventide!*)
Forth to the left his tongue did glide.

Guiburc regards him as lowly he lies:
   Troubled his visage, his cheek all cold;
Back in their sockets are turned his eyes;
   Full length, his tongue to the leftward lolled;
To his chin his helmet parts fallen were.
Then wept Guiburc. William comforted her.

" 'Fore God, Guiburc, thou'st reason and right
   To weep. In the court of my liege did they say
That thou wert wife to a puissant knight,
   To a valiant count and bold in the fray.
But now art thou wife to a craven undone,
   To a coward count, a runaway base,

Who brings back of his men, from the battle, not one.
    Now with cooks and with scullions thou'lt find thy place,
No more thou'lt be ranked with the nobles proud;
    Thou'lt ne'er see my nephew Vivien again;
Whomsoever it grieve, my valour is bowed.
    Ne'er again on earth I'll have honour of men."
William wept, and Guiburc shed her own tears thereat.
    The lady heard the plaint of her lord,
And a part of her own grief she forgat.
    When she spake, right lovingly said she this word:
"Marquis William, in God's name now listen to me!
    That a man must weep is most grievous and sad,
    And a pity great that he act as one mad.
'Twas the custom amongst thine ancestry,
    What time they went forth other lands for to gain—
    Dead on the field did they always remain.
I'd liever thou died in Archamp by the sea
    Than that through thee thy kinsmen were brought to shame,
    Or thine heirs gat nought but reproach from thy name."
When William heard this his head he shook;
Tenderly, gently to weeping he took.
Guiburc he addressed, his wife and make;
To her in his own Romance he spake:
"Sister, sweet friend, my word now receive.
I've good reason to weep, whomsoever it grieve.
An hundred and fifty years and more
Have passed since the day when my mother me bore.
I am old and feeble, nor weapons can wield.
It is gone—what God erst in trust did yield—
Glorious youth, that can never return!
And the paynim hold me now in such scorn
That before me they've neither faltered nor fled.
    King Deramé the battle hath won,
Hath taken the booty and stripped the dead,
    And back to their ships are the Saracens gone.
Far are the marches where I have to command,
Hardy the men I should there needs band,
And when I should come to Archamp by the sea
The Saracens all would departed be.
Whomsoever it grieve, all alone I remain.
Ne'er on earth I'll have honour of men again."
William wept, and him Guiburc comforted.
"Ah, marquis, my lord, in God's name," she said,
"Now let me lie with thy full consent!
    I'll have thirty thousand ready for thee;

Fifteen thousand all armed shall be
As beseems those on well-pitched battle bent."
"Where are they, Guiburc? Thou'lt not hide this from me?
    Sister, sweet friend, now tell me the truth!"
    "Up in the palace, a-dining forsooth."
Then William laughed, nor longer wept he.
"Go, Guiburc! Lie freely with my consent!"
Then up the steps of the stairway she went;
Erewhile she wept, but now did she sing.
They gazed upon her, all questioning.
"Dame Guiburc, pray tell what without thou hast found."
    "In God's name, lordings, good tidings I've learned.
    William the Crook-nosed hath returned,
By the mercy of God all safe and sound.
The mighty battle hath William won
And Deramé to death hath he done.
But this gain hath been at a woeful cost:
The pride of his knighthood hath he lost,
The flower of sweet France and her beauty bright—
They have slain Vivien, the blameless knight!
In heathen lands or on Christian ground
Never could better warrior be found
Holy Christendom to extend
And true religion uphold and fend.
For God's sake, haste you to Archamp, I pray!
    Their ships are shattered, their barges stove;
The wind hath failed them, they cannot away.
    On a rock by the sea, at the head of a cove,
Ten thousand paynim are gone ashore.
    The gold and the silver with them they've ta'en,
    The booty they've gathered, and stripped the slain
My lord was alone, nor could tarry there more.
But an one were to go to Archamp by the sea
    To take these spoils whereof I have told,
    Many vast heirdoms my lord doth hold,
And he'll give you thereof right gladly and free.

But an one be not fain to take lands without wife—
    Yet an hundred and sixty maidens have I,
    King's daughters, none fairer under the sky;
Thanks to William, bred to the courtly life;
Working mine orfrays and silks wheel-decked—
Let him come to me and the fairest elect.
I'll give him a wife and my lord give him lands,
If he fight with such valour as honour demands."

Then many a one vied the fairest to choose
(*On Thursday, when fall the evening dews!*)
Who after in Archamp his head did lose.

To serve her lord Guiburc hath sped,
Brought water, a towel before him spread,
Then seated him at a table low;
For pain, to the high board he could not go.
Then a wild boar's shoulder before him she placed,
And the knight fell to eating thereof in haste,
As 'twere tender and pleasant to the taste.

She brought a great loaf of the manchet fine,
   And eke two great cakes well baked to a toast;
And she brought a great slice of the brawn of a swine,
   And thereafter a mighty peacock roast;
Then she brought a great beaker filled with wine:
   With both her arms 'twas all she could bear.
The loaf of manchet did William eat,
   Nor the two great cakes did he stint nor spare;
The brawn of the swine he devoured complete;
The roasted peacock—he ate it all,
And drained in two draughts the beaker tall.

*   *   *

Nor once to Guiburc did he offer the cup,
Nor lifted his head, nor his face raised up.
Guiburc beheld, then nodding laughed she;
   Natheless with both of her eyes she wept.
   Then him in her own Romance she clept:
"By the glorious God, who converted me,
To whom this sinful soul I shall pay
When cometh the awful Judgment Day:
He who a great manchet loaf doth eat,
   Nor spareth thereby the two baked cakes,
And devours the brawn of a swine complete,
   And the whole of a roasted peacock takes,
And at two draughts a beaker of wine doth gage—
Grim war in sooth on his neighbour he'll wage,
Nor basely flee from the battle in haste,
Nor his kindred will be through him abased!"
"Sister," quoth William, "sweet friend, list to me!
   An I were to die, who would then hold my lands?
   Heir have I none, could hold these with his hands."
From the hearth rose one of his nephews, Dan Gui:

Son of the marquis Bueve Cornebut he,
And born of the daughter of Count Aimeri;
Nephew to William, the crook-nosed knight,
And brother to Vivien, bold in the fight.
He was but fifteen, and in stature right small.
Beard had he none, nor hair had he at all
Save that of his head, which at birth he possessed.
    To his feet he rose, to his uncle drew near.
    In what wise he accosted him now shall ye hear.
"By my faith!" thus young Gui his uncle addressed,
"By me, shouldst thou die, would thy lands holden be!
    My lady Guiburc right fain would I serve;
    She'll suffer no ill from which I can preserve,
Because so gently she nurtured me."
William heard the child, then began he to scold;
    To his nephew made he ungracious reply:
    "Better 'seemeth thee, rogue, in the ashes to lie
Than becomes thee my county ever to hold!

In the ashes to rest is more seemly for thee,
Thou rogue, than to hold my county in fee.
Guiburc my wife thou'lt not have to guard."
    When Gui heard this he made answer most sage:
"Faith, uncle! The like I never have heard!"
    "Whereof dost accuse me?" quoth he in a rage.
"I'll tell thee, but I will bethink me first,
Since one in wisdom not deeply versed
Doth rashly o'errun his goal withal.
    My littleness wherefore dost thou decry?
There is no one great who was not born small;
    And—by the rood of God Most High!—
In all of Christendom is there none,
    Well I wot, nor in all God's fighting band,
    If after thy death he should take thy land
(Now that Vivien is dead, the blameless one),
    Whom I'd not slay in battle, with mine own hand.
Then all thine heritage would I seize,
And my lady Guiburc would I guard at mine ease."
When William heard this his head he shook;
Tenderly, gently to weeping he took.
Then he called the child, to embrace him began;
    Thrice did he kiss him, and then avowed he:
    "Faith, nephew, thou'st spoken right cannily!
Thou hast a child's body, but the mind of a man.
After my death let my fief be thine.

To thy lodging, Guiburc, lead him now by the hand!"
(*On Thursday, when evening's star doth shine!*)
He was but fifteen, and he gave him much land.

Count William then from table arose;
The bed is ready, and thither he goes.
Guiburc softly kneaded his flesh with her hand:
None like her in any Christian land,
 Were it to serve and honour her lord,
Or holy Christendom to expand,
 Or true religion uphold and ward.
She stayed with him till he softly slept,
 Then commended him to God Most High.
To speak with her knights toward the hall she stepped.
 But William slept until evening was nigh;
Then from bed like a fierce wild boar did he spring.
 Straightway made he ready to ride,
 "Monjoie! To horse, free knights!" he cried.
Armour he seeks, and his armour they bring.

Then an hauberk fair on his body they placed
And an helmet green to his head they laced;
 His sword he girded, the blade hung bright.
His mighty shield by the band he clasped,
His lance so keen in his right hand grasped.
 A steed of Castile Guiburc brought the knight,
 By the left stirrup he mounted light,
 Dame Guiburc was holding for him the right;
His foot she kisses, full low she bends,
And him to heaven's Glorious One commends.

When night came down on the goodly town
 William the Crook-nosed rode away
With thirty thousand arm'd horsemen boune
 To Archamp, seeking King Deramé.
In the goodly town did Guiburc abide;
 With Gui to a balcony she trod,
And so long as William the Crook-nosed they spied
 The twain commended him unto God.
When they saw him no more, then began Gui to cry.
 Guiburc beholds him and asks him now:
 "Friend Gui, what reason to weep hast thou?"
"Faith, my lady, reason enough have I!
 I am but fifteen, and so worthless a one
I am kept back from the battle field!
Who to me would fief or heritage yield

An I earn them not with my sword girt on?
On yonder hillside my lord do I see
   To battle riding in fashion most base:
Not one of his kindred with him hath he
   But the God of glory, who saved our race."
Quoth Guiburc: "Now attend, little Gui, I pray.
   Thou'rt too much a child, thine age is too small
   The toil and the travail to thole withal,
The watching by night and the fasting by day,
Or to dree and to suffer the battle's fierce fray.
Thee, then, did the count commit to my ward.
   I'll not let thee go, whate'er trick thou may'st use,
   For I fear me his friendship and favour I'd lose."
Answered Gui: "The like I never have heard!
I know how to lie, and to him I will say
That by force I gat me from thee away.
And this do I promise, God helping me:
An I go not to Archamp beside the sea
Nevermore thou'lt see William, the crook-nosed knight;
An I go, I'll bring him back from the fight."
   "Then I'll let thee go." Thus answerèd she. . . .

Then a little hauberk about him they placed,
And a little helmet above it they laced;
A small sword, but good, in his belt they hung,
And a small double targe from his neck they slung.

Then brought they a little lance so light,
But good was the steel, the shaft seasoned aright;
From the point to his hands swung the ensign white.

Guiburc brought her palfrey, Balçan was he hight.
   Good was the sell, but the stirrups hung high;
Never yet had she lent him to any knight.
   Gui mounted; she aided him, standing by,
   And commended to Him who created the sky. . . .

The whole night long with the squires he rode,
Till the morrow came and the bright day shewed.
And when they were come to Archamp by the sea,
   Then would William address his chivalry.
   All the high barons aside he sent;
   To a council apart by themselves they went,
And to them in his own Romance spake he:

"Barons and lords, ye must help me today!
Your boar hounds, your greyhounds I take not away;

Nay I'd give to you dogs of mine own, an't you please
Goshawk or sparhawk of yours I'll not seize,
Nor ever let cause for discord appear.
The dead father's son I have aye held so dear
That to mother no reason for wrath have I given.
No sergeant by me from his holding is driven,
But his sons have I nourished right willingly
Until they were all dubbed knight by me.
All his land I restored him, without relief;
Was it small, from mine own I increased his fief.
A nithing be William an a penny kept he!
    Help, then, your gonfalonier * today!"
And they answered: "That do we right willingly.
    We'll not fail thee whilst yet on our feet we can stay;
    With such a lord one must keep faith alway
(*On Monday, when evening darkens the sky!*)
And, if need be, in the battle must die."

The high lords he leaves when they've pledged him their troth,
And to speak with the vavasors † William go'th
To a council the vavasors all hath he led
And these words in his own Romance he said:
"Lords and barons, vavasors grand,
Deramé comes a-seeking us in our own land!
This pride of his no further must go;
We must not endure or suffer it so.
Therefore tell I you this, ye knights tried and free:
They have killed one bitterly mourned by me—
    Yea, Vivien they've slain, the widely renowned!
This side the Strait or beyond the sea,
    In heathendom or on Christian ground,
    Can never a better vassal be found
Holy Christendom to extend
And true religion uphold and fend.
To you, then, free knights and wise, do I say
In all Christendom is there none other today
Could assemble so many vavasors—nay,
None save Lewis, who holdeth all France in ward,
The noble, the honoured, her lawful lord.
'Gainst him behooveth me not to boast.
Now hear me, free knights, well proved in the host:
Ne'er will pitched battle be rightly fought
    An therein the vavasors hold not their ground,

* [Overlord. (*Ed.*)]
† [The vassals of his vassals. (*Ed.*)]

And the bachelors nimble uphold them not—
　　The stout ones that bold and prudent are found."
Amongst them he looked—and of Gui gat a sight!
Asked he: "Who is yonder wee, armour-clad wight
That I see on yon horse, your own selves among?
He sore needed man that brought him along!"
Quoth they: "And wherefore ask us to tell?
Thine own nephew thou oughtest to know right well."

When William heard this his head he shook,
Tenderly, gently to weeping he took.
Then began he Guiburc most roundly to blame:
"God's displeasure today bring my wife to great shame!
No longer thou seemest to be in her thrall!"
Gui heard and made answer, but wisely withal:
"Faith, lord, thou blam'st her most wrongfully;
A woman thou settest on guard over me,
And from her by sheer force I gat myself free!"
"Rogue, wherewith dost thou charge me? Come, tell me it."
"I'll tell thee, an thou wilt hearken a bit.
In their barges and ships yon paynim folk see!
They have killed one for whom thou must grieve bitterly:
Vivien, the warrior renowned, have they slain.
Upon them ought we to avenge us again!"
"Faith, nephew, thou'st spoken right cannily.
　　Thou hast a child's body, a grown man's mind.
After my death let my fief go to thee.
　　But one thing that troubleth me sore do I find:
Thou art far too young, thine age is too small
The toil and the travail to thole withal—
The watchings by night and the fastings by day—
Or to dree and to suffer the battle's fierce fray.
But I'll have thee to yonder hilltop led
　　And a score of my men mount guard over thee.
So many I'll lose, nor aught gain in their stead.
　　In the battle these might well have holpen me."
Answered Gui: "Of the like I have never heard tell!"
　　"Nephew," quoth he, "for what blam'st thou me now?"
"Since thou hast asked me, I'll tell thee right well.
　　Is God so forgetful (so thinkest thou?),
Who can guard and uphold the great men all,
That He doth not the same for the small ones withal?
There is no one great who was not born small.
This day will I strike with this sword at my side
　　And well will I prove my valour to thee.

Safe, with me, will honour and heritage be."
"Wise words have I heard from thee." William replied,
"But now, spur forward! Let the horse go!
How thine arms thou canst bear, that fain would I know.". . .

Deramé had won the battle again
   Over Count William, the crook-nosed one,
Had taken the booty and stripped the slain,
   And the Saracens back to their ships were gone.
But the wind it fails them, they cannot away.
   So the lords and the peers of the paynim band,
Twenty thousand men of King Deramé,
   Went forth to visit the solid land
   A long league away from the pebbled strand.
With them they carried their victual fine,
And in ranks had they sat themselves down for to dine.
Then, lo, cometh William, eke on dining intent,
   Thirty thousand armed knights in his company!
Cold cheer in sooth to the feasters served he!
"Monjoie!" cried the French, and to jousting they went.
"To horse, free knights!" is the paynims' cry.
   From their tables, fain to join battle, they leap.
Then that only remained that could not fly:
   Bread, wine, flesh in plenty and many an heap
Of carpets and curtains and golden ware.
   But this onset the heathen could not withstand;
   In flight they betake them back to the strand
And enter their ships and their barges there.
Their weapons they seize, their armour they don,
And the solid land sees them give battle anon. . . .

The French are all ta'en or in combat have died
Save William only, the battle-tried
And his nephew, who rideth aye at his side. . . .

"O Uncle William, what can I do?
Mine heart it fails me, I swear that is true!
My weapons I can neither handle nor wield,
Neither spur nor curb my horse in the field.
God! An I die, what peril, what pain!
Of my lineage then will scarce any remain."
"Nephew," quoth William, "that irks me in truth.
   Couldst make thy way to yon barn again
   Where on Monday we found the Saracen
Sitting them down for to dine forsooth?
   What could not flee, that remained there then."

"And what was that, uncle?" "Meat, wine, and bread.
Go thither, nephew," the marquis said,
"Eat of the bread, but drink little wine,
Help me then in this dolorous danger that's mine,
Nor forget me, for greatly I trust in thee!"
On this wise parted William and Gui.
(*All this befell on a Wednesday now.*)
And the lad Gui passed round a hillock's brow. . . .

When the heathen had hemmed him round about
They hurled at him spear and javelin stout
And pointed pike and piercing dart.
Dead, twixt his thighs, have they stretched Liart.
And lo, on his feet stands the noble knight,
Draws his sword, and knightly beginneth to fight.

When the heathen all have compassed him so
Their lances they hurl and their sharp spears throw.
In his quartered shield so many cling fast
To his head he cannot lift it at last.
Low on the ground the knight they laid,
All his form in the sand displayed.
With lance and with spear they thrust and they hack,
But the stout linkèd hauberk they cannot crack.

  Forth from his throat the blood flows free;
  He cries, "Gui, fair nephew! Come, Gui! Come, Gui!
  Help me, an ever a knight wert thou!"
  Then appeared the lad, who had eaten now.
Well heard he the cry, and came hastening back.

When the lad Gui came down, the hillside along,
And heard William cry in the midst of the throng,
A paynim he smote on his buckler new,
Brake it and clave it and tare it in two;
Rent his hauberk good and the links unbound,
Struck him down from his horse, stretched him dead on the ground
Cried: "Monjoie! Uncle William, where mayest thou be?"
Then another upon his new buckler smote he,
Brake it and clave it and tare it apart;
His hauberk he rent, made the stout links to start,
  Pierced his breast, all under his ample gown;
  Dead, from the saddlebow, struck he him down.
"Monjoie!" cried he. "Uncle, where is it thou art?"

Then he smiteth a third on the double shield,
  Cleaves it asunder clean down to the boss,

That 'gainst his gullet the splinters toss;
Drives his great lance through him into the field,
That the neck bone is shattered, the marrow forth flows.
Behind his shoulders the ensign shows.
When falleth the knave the lance shaft breaks.
After this stroke to his sword he takes.

Gui drew the sword that had made him a knight,
The pointed blade hath he raised upright.
Then smote he an heathen helmeted,
Clean to the nasal cleft his head,
Through skull and through chine, dividing both.
Mighty the stroke, but Gui was wroth:
He split his foemen down through the belt,
Cleaving saddle and steed with the blow that he dealt;
Of the twain, in the field four parts he made.
At this blow were the Saracens sore affrayed.
Quoth one to another: " 'Tis a levin-brand!
    The warrior Vivien is come back to life!"
    They turn them in flight and give over the strife.
To his feet riseth William and on them doth stand.
Count William is now of the footmen's band.

'Twas a miracle that Our Lord wrought then:
Before one, fled twenty thousand men.
    On toward the sea the Saracen reel.
Then William stood up on his feet again,
    And they pressed them hard with their spears of steel.

As the paynim fled away toward the sea
William lifted him up, to his feet rose he,
And they pressed the foe hard with the swords that they bare.
    Then Gui spied his uncle afoot on the plain,
Pricked his steed, and hasted to meet him there.
    "Sire," quoth he, "mount thou this palfrey amain!
My Lady Guiburc lent him freely to me."
    Gui lighteth down, William mounts in his stead,
    And when he was set to his nephew he said:
"Thou hast fooled me, Gui, of a verity!
Late saidst thou that from her thou rannest away;
    Now say'st thou she lent thee the horse for to use!
    Who bade thee my lady wife accuse?"
Quoth Gui: "Ne'er heard I the like ere this day!
    Prick forward! Prick forward, straight to the sea!
    Gone, gone already the heathen will be!"
With these words, his good sword doth he display.

Sir William he rideth the battlefield through,
His good sword drawn, his helm all askew.
Below the boy's stirrups his feet hung free,
The irons a-beating the back of each knee.
Held 'twixt point and pommel his sword he bore,
Flat on the saddlebow him before.
    Balçan went ambling peacefully
    And after his uncle, on foot, followed Gui
Hour after hour, knee-deep in gore.
In the midst of the field lay King Deramé,
    Besmeared and befouled with blood and with dirt.
When William espied him he knew him straightway,
    But from dart-thrusts (thought he) he had taken such hurt
No enemy could he longer withstand.
    But the king had in mind a deed most bold:
To his feet he rose, on his horse laid his hand,
    From the right fore foot the rein he unrolled,
Stoutly he grasped his goodly brand,
    To his courser's back he sprang from the plain,
    And on he came spurring against the twain. . . .

William smiteth the heathen upon the helm,
The right half thereof doth the stroke o'erwhelm.
From the mighty blow, to the ground he bent,
Grasping neck and reins of his horse as he leant.
As William passed him, the marquis brave,
Deramé's thigh on the saddle he clave;
The trunk, on the other side, fell to the sand.
Then good Marquis William put forth his hand,
Seized from behind, as he ran, the rein,
Came to Gui, and accosted his nephew again.

In the midst of the meadow the Saracen lay
And watched William leading his good steed away.
Then began he to mourn him, bitter and sore:
    "Alas, Balçan! So lovèd I thee
I brought thee here from the far sea shore.
    He that now hath thee—little knows he
How to groom thee and deck thee, to shoe and to bleed."
    "Knave!" quote William. "Give over such speech
    And rather take counsel thy thigh for to leech.
For the good horse's care myself will give heed."
Then came he to Gui and gave him the steed.

In the Saracen's heart found great bitterness place:
    "Alas, Balçan! Good steed that thou wast!

Ah, thy noble body! Thy stately pace!
   Thou hast brought me here, where my leg I have lost.
So many a fight on thy back have I won!
No better horse is there under the sun.
Sore will they mourn thee, the paynim folk."
Quoth the count: "Naught care I for the words thou hast spoke.". . .

Whilst his uncle to shift the saddles was bound
Gui spied the king as he writhed on the ground.
His sword he drew, and struck off his head.
Then William, exceeding angry, said:

"Thou wretch! Thou nithing! How wast thou so bold
   That thou durst a maimèd man to strike?
In high court 'gainst thee will this be told."
   Quoth Gui: "I never have heard the like!
If feet, wherewith he might walk, lacked he,
Yet had he eyes wherewith he could see,
And organs he had wherewith sons to beget.
To his own land he'd have himself carried yet.
Thence an heir of Deramé yet would spring
Who would seek on our realm great evil to bring.
Forthwith, from such, must deliverance be wrought."
   "Nephew," quoth William, "Thou'st spoke like a sage.
A child's is thy body, a man's thy thought.
   Thine be, on my death, all mine heritage!"
   (*Now was it Wednesday, at set of sun.*)
And now had William his battle won.

ᴥ THE ART OF COURTLY LOVE

Andreas Capellanus

*Until the twelfth century, love had had a generally bad press in the West-
ern world. The classical and Christian traditions agreed in condemning
it as a corrupting and weakening influence. How much attention people
paid to the strictures of philosophers and theologians is another question. In any case, even among ancient writers there were two notable,
though very different, dissenters: Plato considered love the road to
philosophical wisdom; and Ovid, a widely read Roman poet, celebrated
"merry sensuality" without cares or responsibility. The Spanish Arabs
combined Plato's and Ovid's attitudes into an amalgam of licentiousness*

*and idealism which as "courtly love" came to captivate the medieval
ruling classes.*

*In twelfth-century France, courtly love was more than simply a synthesis
of Plato and Ovid: it was very much a medieval phenomenon, centered
in the lavish courts (hence the name) of kings, queens, or barons. The
etiquette of courtly love was modelled after the feudal vassal's relationship to his overlord. The lover was captured by Cupid and enlisted in
his lady's retinue; he was expected to be prepared to perform any service
for her. And the measure of his own honor was the extent of the lady's
fame—a far cry from the quarrel of Achilles and Agamemnon!*

*The author of this text, Andreas, was chaplain (capellanus) at the court
of Marie de France at Troyes. He probably wrote it at her request in
1185. Very little is known about him apart from what can be gathered
here: that he was a clergyman for whom spiritual matters were not
always the first consideration. About Marie, however, and her even more
illustrious mother, Eleanor of Aquitaine (ca. 1122–1204), we know a
great deal. It was probably Eleanor's father, Duke William of Aquitaine ("the Troubadour"), who first brought courtly love across the
Pyrenees into southern France. After the annulment of a brief marriage
to Louis VII of France, Eleanor married Henry, Duke of Normandy,
who subsequently became Henry II of England, bringing vast areas of
France under the English crown. Eleanor was not only wife to two
kings, but mother of two more: Richard I (" the Lionhearted"), troubadour and hero of the Third Crusade, and John, signer of the Magna
Carta (see page 23). Her court at Poitiers was the epitome of the cult
of courtly love: while her husband fought battles and ruled nations,
she herself ruled a remarkable collection of lovers of all sorts, who im-
mortalized her name in magnificent love poetry. (According to legend,
Eleanor is the queen of hearts in the modern card deck.) It is this
court that her daughter Marie was imitating at Troyes, and that Andreas
is describing in this treatise.*

BOOK ONE: INTRODUCTION TO THE TREATISE ON LOVE

We must first consider what love is, whence it gets its name, what the effect of love
is, between what persons love may exist, how it may be acquired, retained, increased,
decreased, and ended, what are the signs that one's love is returned, and what one of
the lovers ought to do if the other is unfaithful.

Andreas Capellanus, *The Art of Courtly Love*, trans. John Jay Parry (New York: Columbia
University Press, 1941), pp. 28–30, 31–36, 44–47, 58–61, 98–101, 149–150, 161–163.

Chapter I. What Love Is

Love is a certain inborn suffering derived from the sight of and excessive meditation upon the beauty of the opposite sex, which causes each one to wish above all things the embraces of the other and by common desire to carry out all of love's precepts in the other's embrace.

That love is suffering is easy to see, for before the love becomes equally balanced on both sides there is no torment greater, since the lover is always in fear that his love may not gain its desire and that he is wasting his efforts. He fears, too, that rumors of it may get abroad, and he fears everything that might harm it in any way, for before things are perfected a slight disturbance often spoils them. If he is a poor man, he also fears that the woman may scorn his poverty; if he is ugly, he fears that she may despise his lack of beauty or may give her love to a more handsome man; if he is rich, he fears that his parsimony in the past may stand in his way. To tell the truth, no one can number the fears of one single lover. This kind of love, then, is a suffering which is felt by only one of the persons and may be called "single love." But even after both are in love the fears that arise are just as great, for each of the lovers fears that what he has acquired with so much effort may be lost through the effort of someone else, which is certainly much worse for a man than if, having no hope, he sees that his efforts are accomplishing nothing, for it is worse to lose the things you are seeking than to be deprived of a gain you merely hope for. The lover fears, too, that he may offend his loved one in some way; indeed he fears so many things that it would be difficult to tell them.

That this suffering is inborn I shall show you clearly, because if you will look at the truth and distinguish carefully you will see that it does not arise out of any action; only from the reflection of the mind upon what it sees does this suffering come. For when a man sees some woman fit for love and shaped according to his taste, he begins at once to lust after her in his heart; then the more he thinks about her the more he burns with love, until he comes to a fuller meditation. Presently he begins to think about the fashioning of the woman and to differentiate her limbs, to think about what she does, and to pry into the secrets of her body, and he desires to put each part of it to the fullest use. Then after he has come to this complete meditation, love cannot hold the reins, but he proceeds at once to action; straightway he strives to get a helper and to find an intermediary. He begins to plan how he may find favor with her, and he begins to seek a place and a time opportune for talking; he looks upon a brief hour as a very long year, because he cannot do anything fast enough to suit his eager mind. It is well known that many things happen to him in this manner. This inborn suffering comes, therefore, from seeing and meditating. Not every kind of meditation can be the cause of love, an excessive one is required; for a restrained thought does not, as a rule, return to the mind, and so love cannot arise from it.

Chapter II. Between What Persons Love May Exist

Now, in love you should note first of all that love cannot exist except between persons of opposite sexes. Between two men or two women love can find no place, for we see that two persons of the same sex are not at all fitted for giving each other the exchanges of love or for practicing the acts natural to it. Whatever nature forbids, love is ashamed to accept. . . .

Chapter IV. What The Effect of Love Is

Now it is the effect of love that a true lover cannot be degraded with any avarice. Love causes a rough and uncouth man to be distinguished for his handsomeness; it can endow a man even of the humblest birth with nobility of character; it blesses the proud with humility; and the man in love becomes accustomed to performing many services gracefully for everyone. O what a wonderful thing is love, which makes a man shine with so many virtues and teaches everyone, no matter who he is, so many good traits of character! There is another thing about love that we should not praise in few words: it adorns a man, so to speak, with the virtue of chastity, because he who shines with the light of one love can hardly think of embracing another woman, even a beautiful one. For when he thinks deeply of his beloved the sight of any other woman seems to his mind rough and rude. . . .

Chapter V. What Persons Are Fit for Love

We must now see what persons are fit to bear the arms of love. You should know that everyone of sound mind who is capable of doing the work of Venus may be wounded by one of Love's arrows unless prevented by age, or blindness, or excess of passion. Age is a bar, because after the sixtieth year in a man and the fiftieth in a woman, although one may have intercourse his passion cannot develop into love; because at that age the natural heat begins to lose its force, and the natural moisture is greatly increased, which leads a man into various difficulties and troubles him with various ailments, and there are no consolations in the world for him except food and drink. Similarly, a girl under the age of twelve and a boy before the fourteenth year do not serve in love's army. However, I say and insist that before his eighteenth year a man cannot be a true lover, because up to that age he is overcome with embarrassment over any little thing, which not only interferes with the perfecting of love, but even destroys it if it is well perfected. But we find another even more powerful reason, which is that before this age a man has no constancy, but is changeable in every way, for such a tender age cannot think about the mysteries of love's realm. Why love should kindle in a woman at an earlier age than in a man I shall perhaps show you elsewhere.

Blindness is a bar to love, because a blind man cannot see anything upon which his mind can reflect immoderately, and so love cannot arise in him, as I have already fully shown. But I admit that this is true only of the acquiring of love, for I do not deny that a love which a man acquires before his blindness may last after he becomes blind.

An excess of passion is a bar to love, because there are men who are slaves to such passionate desire that they cannot be held in the bonds of love—men who, after they have thought long about some woman or even enjoyed her, when they see another woman straightway desire her embraces, and they forget about the services they have received from their first love and they feel no gratitude for them. Men of this kind lust after every woman they see; their love is like that of a shameless dog. They should rather, I believe, be compared to asses, for they are moved only by that low nature which shows that men are on the level of the other animals rather than by that true nature which sets us apart from all the other animals by the difference of reason. Of such lovers I shall speak elsewhere.

Chapter VI. In What Manner Love May Be Acquired, and in How Many Ways

It remains next to be seen in what ways love may be acquired. The teaching of some people is said to be that there are five means by which it may be acquired: a beautiful figure, excellence of character, extreme readiness of speech, great wealth, and the readiness with which one grants that which is sought. But we hold that love may be acquired only by the first three, and we think that the last two ought to be banished completely from Love's court, as I shall show you when I come to the proper place in my system.

A beautiful figure wins love with very little effort, especially when the lover who is sought is simple, for a simple lover thinks that there is nothing to look for in one's beloved besides a beautiful figure and face and a body well cared for. I do not particularly blame the love of such people, but neither do I have much approval for it, because love between uncautious and unskilled lovers cannot long be concealed, and so from the first it fails to increase. For when love is revealed, it does not help the lover's worth, but brands his reputation with evil rumors and often causes him grief. Love between such lovers seldom lasts; but if sometimes it should endure it cannot indulge in its former solaces, because when the girl's chaperone hears the rumors, she becomes suspicious and watches her more carefully and gives her no opportunities to talk, and it makes the man's relatives more careful and watchful, and so serious unfriendliness arises. In such cases, when love cannot have its solaces, it increases beyond all measure and drives the lovers to lamenting their terrible torments, because "we strive for what is forbidden and always want what is denied us."

A wise woman will therefore seek as a lover a man of praiseworthy character—not one who anoints himself all over like a woman or makes a rite of the care of the body, for it does not go with a masculine figure to adorn oneself in womanly fashion or to be devoted to the care of the body. It was people like this the admirable Ovid meant when he said,

> Let young men who are decked out like women stay far away from me,
> A manly form wants to be cared for within moderate limits.

Likewise, if you see a woman too heavily rouged you will not be taken in by her beauty unless you have already discovered that she is good company besides, since a woman who puts all her reliance on her rouge usually doesn't have any particular gifts of character. As I said about men, so with women—I believe you should not seek for beauty so much as for excellence of character. Be careful therefore, Walter, not to be taken in by the empty beauty of women, because a woman is apt to be so clever and such a ready talker that after you have begun to enjoy the gifts you get from her you will not find it easy to escape loving her. A person of good character draws the love of another person of the same kind, for a well-instructed lover, man or woman, does not reject an ugly lover if the character within is good. A man who proves to be honorable and prudent cannot easily go astray in love's path or cause distress to his beloved. If a wise woman selects as her lover a wise man, she can very easily keep her love hidden forever; she can teach a wise lover to be even wiser, and if he isn't so wise she can restrain him and make him careful. A woman, like a man, should not seek for beauty or care of the person or high birth, for "beauty never pleases if it lacks goodness," and it is excellence of character alone which blesses a man with true nobility and makes him flourish in ruddy beauty. For since all of us human beings are derived originally from the same stock and all naturally claim the same ancestor, it was not beauty or care of the body or even abundance of possessions, but excellence of character alone which first made a distinction of nobility among men and led to the difference of class. Many there are, however, who trace their descent from these same first nobles, but have degenerated and gone in the other direction. The converse of this proposition is likewise true.

Character alone, then, is worthy of the crown of love. Many times fluency of speech will incline to love the hearts of those who do not love, for an elaborate line of talk on the part of the lover usually sets love's arrows a-flying and creates a presumption in favor of the excellent character of the speaker. How this may be I shall try to show you as briefly as I can.

To this end I shall first explain to you that one woman belongs to the middle class, a second to the simple nobility, and a third to the higher nobility. So it is with men: one is of the middle class, another of the nobility, a third of the higher nobility, and a fourth of the very highest nobility. What I mean by a woman of the middle class is clear enough to you; a noblewoman is one descended from a vavasor or a lord, or is the wife of one of these, while a woman of the higher nobility is descended from great lords. The same rules apply to men, except that a man married to a woman of higher or lower rank than himself does not change his rank. A married woman changes her status to match that of her husband, but a man can never change his nobility by marriage. In addition, among men we find one rank more than among women, since there is a man more noble than any of these, that is, the clerk. . . .

Second Dialogue: A man of the middle class speaks with a woman of the nobility If a man of the middle class should seek the love of a noblewoman, he may follow this plan. If he finds that the woman, although noble, is not sophisticated, all the things will serve which were given in the dialogue between the man and the woman of the middle class, except that here commendation of the nobility of her family may claim a place. But if the woman should be wise and shrewd, he ought to be careful not to overdo the praise of her beauty. For if he should praise a noble and prudent woman beyond all measure, she will think that he isn't very good at the art of conversation or that he is making up all this flattery and thinks her a fool. So after he has begun the conversation in the usual way, let him come down to words of love in this manner. "If I could shut up my heart within the bounds of my will, I would, perhaps, pass over in silence many things which I am urgently driven to say. But my heart drives on my will with sharp spurs, diverting it from its natural path and causing it to wander and to seek things too great for me to express. So if love compels me to say anything aimless or foolish, I ask Your Nobility to endure it patiently and to reprove me gently. I know well that Love is not in the habit of differentiating men with titles of distinction, but that he obligates all equally to serve in his (that is, Love's) army, making no exceptions for beauty or birth and making no distinctions of sex or of inequality of family, considering only this, whether anybody is fit to bear Love's armor. Love is a thing that copies Nature herself, and so lovers ought to make no more distinction between classes of men than Love himself does. Just as love inflames men of all classes, so lovers should draw no distinctions of rank, but consider only whether the man who asks for love has been wounded by Love. Supported by this unanswerable argument, I may select for my beloved any woman I choose so long as I have no depravity of character to debase me.

"So if you will give me a patient hearing, I shall try to ask only what you can have no good reason for denying me, and if my remarks offend you in any way and you use harsh words in defending yourself, that will be an unbearable misfortune to me and the cause of all sorts of grief.

"You must know, then, that many days ago I was smitten with the arrow of your love, and that I have tried with all my might to conceal the wound, not because I consider myself an incompetent soldier of Love, but because I am afraid of Your Highness's wisdom. The sight of your face so terrifies my spirit and disturbs my mind that I completely forget even those things I have carefully thought out in my mind. With reason, therefore, I tried to hide my grief, but the more I sought to cover up my wound, the more the pain of it increased. Yet the wound did remain hidden so long as the pain of it was not too much for me; but after I was overcome by the strength of it, by its mighty power it forced me to ask for great things and to seek for a cure for my ever-present pain. You are the cause of my suffering and the cure for my mortal pain, for you hold both my life and my death shut up in your hand. If you grant what I ask, you will give me back the life I have lost and much solace in living, but if you deny me, my life will be a torment to me, and that is worse than if I met with sudden death; for a quick death would be preferable to suffering continually such terrible torture. I cannot tell you all the things my soul thinks should be told, but God knows the words that the dumb man wishes to speak."

The woman says: "I am very much surprised—it is enough to surprise anyone—that in such a great upsetting of things the elements do not come to an end and the world itself fall into ruin. If I were not determined to ignore the shame you cast on my nobility, I would rebuke you very bitterly; but since it is too unladylike for a noble-woman to speak harsh and discourteous words to anyone, no matter who he is, my soul endures with patience your crazy remarks and gives you a soft answer. Who are you that you ask for such great gifts? I know well enough what you look like, and the family you come from is obvious. But where can one find greater effrontery than in a man who for the space of a whole week devotes all his efforts to the various gains of business and then on the seventh day, his day of rest, tries to enjoy the gifts of love and to dishonor Love's commands and confound the distinctions of classes established among men from of old? It is not without cause or reason that this distinction of rank has been found among men from the very beginning; it is so that every man will stay within the bounds of his own class and be content with all things therein and never presume to arrogate to himself the things that were naturally set aside as belonging to a higher class, but will leave them severely alone. Who are you, then, to try to defile such ancient statutes and under the pretense of love to attempt to subvert the precepts of our ancestors and so presumptuously go beyond the limits of your own class? If I should so far forget my senses as to be induced to assent to what you say, your heart would not be able to endure such great things. Did a buzzard ever overcome a partridge or a pheasant by its courage? It is for falcons and hawks to capture this prey, which should not be annoyed by cowardly kites. Your folly needs to be sharply checked, because you seek a love from the upper class, although you are not worthy of her.

Third Dialogue: A man of the middle class speaks with a woman of the higher nobility . . . The woman says: "You seem to be upsetting the natural order and course of things, since first you ask for love and then you show yourself in every way unworthy of it by asking like a raw recruit to be trained in the science of love. But since it would seem to set a shameful precedent, one prompted by avarice, if those who have experience were to deny their lessons to those who have not and ask to be taught, you will without a doubt obtain the grant of our instruction; and if you will pay careful attention to our words, before you leave you will be fully informed on the subjects you ask about.

"Well then, the man who would be considerd worthy to serve in Love's army must not be in the least avaricious, but very generous; he must, in fact, give generously to as many people as he can. When he sees that money is needed, especially by noblemen and men of character, and when he thinks that his gifts would be helpful to anybody, he ought not wait to be urged, for a gift made in answer to a request seems dearly bought. But if he cannot find a pressing opportunity of giving something under these circumstances, let him give something helpful to the man who does ask, and give it with such a spirit that it may seem more pleasing and acceptable to his feelings to give the thing to his friend than to keep possession of it himself. And also if he sees that the poor are hungry and gives them nourishment, that is considered very courteous and generous. And if he has a lord, he should offer him due respect. He should utter no word of blasphemy against God and His saints; he should show himself humble to all and should stand ready to serve everybody. He ought never speak a word in disparagement of any man, since those who speak evil may not remain within the threshold of courtesy. He ought not utter falsehood in praise of the wicked, but he should if possible make them better by secret reproofs. If he finds that they remain wholly incorrigible, he should consider them stiff-necked and banish them from his company lest he be considered, and rightly, a promoter and a sharer of the error. He ought never mock anyone, especially the wretched, and he should not be quarrelsome or ready to take part in disputes; but he should be, so far as possible, a composer of differences. In the presence of women he should be moderate about his laughter, because, according to Solomon's saying, too much laughter is a sign of foolishness; and clever women are in the habit of turning away fools and unwise men in contempt or of eluding them beautifully. Great prudence is necessary in the management of a love affair and diligence in all one does. He ought to frequent assemblies of great men and to visit great courts. He should be moderate about indulging in games of dice. He should gladly call to mind and take to heart the great deeds of the men of old. He ought to be courageous in battle and hardy against his enemies, wise, cautious, and clever. He should not be a lover of several women at the same time, but for the sake of one he should be a devoted servant of all. He should devote only a moderate amount of care to the adornment of his person and should show himself wise and tractable and pleasant to everybody, although some men have the idea that women like it very much if they utter foolish, almost crazy, remarks and act like madmen. He should be careful, too, not to utter falsehoods and should take care not to talk too much or to keep silent too much. He should not be too quick and sudden about making promises, because the man who is good-natured about making promises will be slow to keep them, and the man who is too ready to make them gets little credit. If any worthy man wants to give him some money, he should accept it with a look of joy and by no means refuse it unless the giver had the idea that he needed it, when he didn't. In that case he may decline it in this way: 'Since I have no need for this at present, I consider it as given to me, and I return it to you that you may make use of it in my name in any way you please.' He should never utter foul words and should avoid serious crimes, especially ones that are notorious. He should never cheat anyone with a false promise, because anybody can be rich in promises. If anybody has deceived him with a false promise or has been rude to him, he should never say anything to disparage the man, but on the contrary he should do good to him in return and serve him in every way, and thus prudently compel him to acknowledge his fault. He should offer hospitality freely to everybody. He should not utter harmful or shameful or mocking words against God's clergy or monks or any person connected with a religious house, but he should always and everywhere render them due honor with all his strength and with all his mind, for the sake of Him whose service they perform. He ought to go to church frequently and there listen gladly to those who are constantly celebrating the divine service, although some men very foolishly believe that the women like it if they despise everything connected with the Church. He ought to be truthful in everything he says and never envy any man's renown. I have presented to you briefly the main points. If you have listened attentively to them and will be careful to practice them, you will be found worthy to plead in the court of Love."

Seventh Dialogue: A man of the higher nobility speaks to a woman of the simple nobility . . . The woman says: "Even though I found you in every respect worthy of love, still we are separated by too wide and too rough an expanse of country to be able to offer each other love's solaces or to find proper opportunities for meeting. Lovers who live near together can cure each other of the torments that come from love, can help each other in their common sufferings, and can nourish their love by mutual exchanges and efforts; those, however, who are far apart cannot perceive each other's pains, but each one has to relieve his own trouble and cure his own torments. So it seems that our love should go no further, because Love's rule teaches us that the daily sight of each other makes lovers love more ardently, while I can see on the other hand that by reason of distance love decreases and fails, and therefore everybody should try to find a lover who lives near by."

The man says: "You are troubling yourself to say what seems to be against all reason, for all men know that if one gets easily what he desires he holds it cheap and what formerly he longed for with his whole heart he now considers worthless. On the other hand, whenever the possession of some good thing is postponed by the difficulty of getting it, we desire it more eagerly and put forth a greater effort to keep it. Therefore if one has difficulty in obtaining the embraces of one's lover and obtains them rarely, the lovers are bound to each other in more ardent chains of love and their souls are linked together in heavier and closer bonds of affection. For constancy is made perfect amid the waves that buffet it, and perseverance is clearly seen in adversities. Rest seems sweeter to a man who is wearied by many labors than to one who lives in continual idleness, and a new-found shade seems to offer more to one who is burdened by the heat than to one who has been constantly in air of a moderate temperature. It is not one of Love's rules, as you said it was, that when lovers seldom meet the strength of their love is weakened, since we find it false and misleading. Therefore you cannot properly refuse me your love with the excuse of the long and difficult distance between us, but you should gratify me rather than someone who lives near by; besides it is easier to conceal a love affair when the lovers do not meet than when they converse frequently with each other."

The woman says: "So far as hiding one's love goes, I do not think there is any choice between a distant lover and one who is present. If the lover proves to be wise and clever it doesn't matter whether he is far from his beloved or near her, he will so govern his actions and his will that no one can guess the secrets of their love; on the other hand a foolish lover, whether far or near, can never conceal the secrets of his love. Your argument must therefore fall before this most obvious one on the other side. Besides there is another fact, by no means trivial, which keeps me from loving you. I have a husband who is greatly distinguished by his nobility, his good breeding, and his good character, and it would be wicked for me to violate his bed or submit to the embraces of any other man, since I know that he loves me with his whole heart and I am bound to him with all the devotion of mine. The laws themselves bid me refrain from loving another man when I am blessed with such a reward for my love."

The man says: "I admit it is true that your husband is a very worthy man and that he is more blest than any man in the world because he has been worthy to have the joy of embracing Your Highness. But I am greatly surprised that you wish to misapply the term 'love' to that marital affection which husband and wife are expected to feel for each other after marriage, since everybody knows that love can have no place between husband and wife. They may be bound to each other by a great and immoderate affection, but their feeling cannot take the place of love, because it cannot fit under the true definition of love. For what is love but an inordinate desire to receive passionately a furtive and hidden embrace? But what embrace between husband and wife can be furtive, I ask you, since they may be said to belong to each other and may satisfy all of each other's desires without fear that anybody will object? Besides, that most excellent doctrine of princes shows that nobody can make furtive use of what belongs to him. Do not let what I have said seem absurd to you, for husband and wife may be joined together by every sort of affection, but this feeling cannot take the place of love. In friendship we see the same thing. Father and son may feel every sort of affection for each other, but there is no true friendship between them, because, as Cicero tells us, the feeling that offspring of the blood have for each other is affection. It is clear then that there is just as much difference between every kind of affection of husband and wife and the obligation of lovers as there is between the mutual affection of father and son and the strongest friendship between two men, so that in the one case we say there is no love, just as in the other we say friendship is lacking. So then you see clearly that love can by no means exercise its functions between husband and wife, but has wished to withdraw its privileges completely.

"But there is another reason why husband and wife cannot love each other and that is that the very substance of love, without which true love cannot exist—I mean jealousy—is in such a case very much frowned upon and they should avoid it like the pestilence; but lovers should always welcome it as the mother and the nurse of love. From this you may see clearly that love cannot possibly flourish between you and your husband. Therefore, since every woman of character ought to love, prudently, you can without doing yourself any harm accept the prayers of a suppliant and endow your suitor with your love.". . .

Chapter XI. The Love of Peasants

But lest you should consider that what we have already said about the love of the middle class applies also to farmers, we will add a little about their love. We say that it rarely happens that we find farmers serving in Love's court, but naturally, like a horse or a mule, they give themselves up to the work of Venus, as nature's urging teaches them to do. For a farmer hard labor and the uninterrupted solaces of plough and mattock are sufficient. And even if it should happen at times, though rarely, that contrary to their nature they are stirred up by Cupid's arrows, it is not expedient that they should be instructed in the theory of love, lest while they are devoting themselves to conduct which is not natural to them the kindly farms which are usually made fruitful by their efforts may through lack of cultivation prove useless to us. And if you should, by some chance, fall in love with some of their women, be careful to puff them up with lots of praise and then, when you find a convenient place, do not hesitate to take what you seek and to embrace them by force. For you can hardly soften their outward inflexibility so far that they will grant you their embraces quietly or permit you to have the solaces you desire unless first you use a little compulsion as a convenient cure for their shyness. We do not say these things, however, because we want to persuade you to love such women, but only so that, if through lack of caution you should be driven to love them, you may know, in brief compass, what to do.

Chapter XII. The Love of Prostitutes

Now in case anybody should ask how we feel about the love of prostitutes we say that they are all to be shunned absolutely, because it is most shameful to have dealings with them, and with them one almost always falls into the sin of lewdness. Besides, a prostitute seldom gives herself to anyone until she has been given a present that pleases her. Even if it should happen once in a while that a woman of this kind does fall in love, all agree that her love is harmful to men, because all wise men frown upon having familiar intercourse with prostitutes, and to do so spoils anybody's good name. Therefore we have no desire to explain to you the way to gain their love, because whatever the feeling that makes them give themselves to a suitor they always do so without much urging, so you don't need to ask for instructions on this point.

BOOK TWO: HOW LOVE MAY BE RETAINED

Chapter VI. If One of The Lovers Is Unfaithful

. . . But what if the man should be unfaithful to his beloved—not with the idea of finding a new love, but because he has been driven to it by an irresistible passion for another woman? What, for instance, if chance should present to him an unknown woman in a convenient place or what if at a time when Venus is urging him on to that which I am talking about he should meet with a little strumpet or somebody's servant girl? Should he, just because he played with her in the grass, lose the love of his beloved? We can say without fear of contradiction that just for this a lover is not considered unworthy of the love of his beloved unless he indulges in so many excesses with a number of women that we may conclude that he is overpassionate. But if whenever he becomes acquainted with a woman he pesters her to gain his end, or if he attains his object as a result of his efforts, then rightly he does deserve to be deprived of his former love, because there is a strong presumption that he has acted in this way with an eye toward a new one, especially where he has strayed with a woman of the nobility or otherwise of an honorable estate.

But perhaps you will ask what a woman is to do if her adored lover asks for permission to leave her in favor of some other woman. We are bound to say emphatically that a woman ought by no means to give her lover permission to enjoy the embraces of another woman; instead she should in very plain words forbid him the other woman's embraces. But if she has granted him such permission and he has taken advantage of this, it is just as useless for him to go back to his former love as if he had left her without receiving permission. For although by granting such a request the woman has clearly committed a sin against love, still her error cannot excuse the bad faith of the lover or cover up his offense. On the other hand, if the lover tried to take advantage of the permission she gave him but his attempt was unsuccessful, the woman cannot on this account deny him the regular solaces, since she, too, is at fault and one misdeed may balance the other.

But now let us discuss the old mistake and see what should be done if it is the woman who is unfaithful to her lover. The old opinion, held by some, is that when the woman is at fault the same rule should be followed as in the case of the man just mentioned. But this rule, although old, should not be respected on that account, since it would lead us into great error. God forbid that we should ever declare that a woman who is not ashamed to wanton with two men should go unpunished. Although in the case of men such a thing is tolerated because it is so common and because the sex has a privilege by which all things in this world which are by their nature immodest are more readily allowed to men, in the case of a woman they are, because of the decency of the modest sex, considered so disgraceful that after a woman has indulged the passions of several men everybody looks upon her as an unclean strumpet unfit to associate with other ladies. Therefore if a woman goes back to her former lover after enjoying the embraces of someone else, it is a disgrace to him, for he can see perfectly well that she no longer has any love for him. Why, therefore, should he place his affection on her? . . .

The Medieval Town

Early medieval Europe was almost entirely agrarian. Farming villages had always dotted the plains and hills; peasant cottages clustered near castles and abbeys for protection. Between the tenth and twelfth centuries, this agricultural world was disturbed by the appearance of towns that usually grew up along the increasingly busy trade routes. What distinguished these proliferating towns was that their inhabitants gained their livelihood from commerce and manufacture rather than from the land. Guilds of affluent craftsmen and merchants came to sell their merchandise over wide territories. The towns sought out great lords, kings, and bishops for patronage, and in return for protection guaranteed payment of annual sums, goods, or services, as required by the lord. The larger cities in time became "communes," purchasing charters which secured self-government of internal affairs and monopoly rights over trading areas. In such charters are seen the origins of urban independence as well as the idea of constitutionalism.

The Charter of Rouen, reprinted here in entirety, was a standard constitutional formula granted throughout France. It shows the diversity of medieval town organization, and—of greater importance—indirectly reveals the desires and vexations of the aspiring middle classes. The Charter was granted by King Henry II of England for his Norman subjects about 1165; its primary concern is political and legal order. The second document, the "Customs of Newcastle-upon-Tyne," of the same period, exemplifies commercial regulations and is typical of medieval protectionist policies, which resulted in the creation of hundreds of exclusive monopolistic trade districts. The guild regulations of Stendal, those of the town's garment cutters, illustrate internal control over production.

The next reading is a rare portrait of the medieval merchant; since Godric was canonized for his piety, his biographer is understandably an admirer.

Godric bestowed his entire wealth upon the Church; this was an exceptional act, but medieval businessmen were expected to endow charitable institutions with large portions of their profits, even if they did not follow Godric's saintly example to its extreme.

In Fitz Stephen's day—around 1200—London, long a great European trade center, boasted a population of forty thousand. It was over four times the size of any other medieval English city, though less than half that of Paris. Fitz Stephen's complimentary portrait would have been applauded by any chamber of commerce: he makes no mention of such unpleasant aspects of the city's life as crime, plague, fires, the crowded quarters, and the heavy smoke that hung over the city. Yet it is one of the few vivid pictures we have of medieval man in his urban setting.

৶§ THE CHARTER OF ROUEN

1   When it becomes necessary to select a mayor in Rouen, the one hundred peers will elect three men of the city whom they will present to the king, who will name as mayor the one he chooses from the list.

2   From among the one hundred peers, twenty-four will be elected by the consent of the one hundred peers; these twenty-four will be changed each year; twelve of them will be named as aldermen [*échevin*] and the other twelve as counsellors. These twenty-four, at the beginning of their term, will swear to maintain the rights of the Holy Church, to preserve loyalty to the king, and to maintain his justice; they will also swear to judge well themselves according to their conscience, and if the mayor confides a secret to them, they will keep it; and if one of them reveals it, he will be removed from his office and placed at the mercy of the commune.

3   The mayor and the twelve aldermen will meet twice a week to take care of town business, and if they are uncertain about some matter they will call those they wish from among the twelve counsellors, to have their advice. The twelve counsellors will meet each Saturday with the mayor and the twelve aldermen, and all one hundred peers will meet every other Saturday.

4   Whichever of the above-mentioned persons fails without prior notice to come to the meetings with the other peers on the above-mentioned days, before Prime is sung, will pay, if he is an alderman, five sous to the profit of the town of Rouen. A counsellor who is absent will pay three sous and one of the other peers two sous, unless the mayor has received a valid excuse. Whoever of the above-mentioned leaves

Les etablissements de Rouen: etudes sur l'histoire des institutions municipales . . . , ed. and trans. A. Giry, Vol. II (published as Vol. LIX of *Bibliotheque de l'Ecole des Hautes Etudes: Sciences philologiques et historiques* [Paris, 1885]), 3–55. Translated by Peter Amann for this volume.

the assembly without the mayor's permission will pay the same fine as if he had not arrived by the hour of Prime. And if at times the mayor needs some of them, if one of them does not come at his order and notice, he will pay the established fine unless he produces a valid excuse.

5   If one of the twelve aldermen wishes to go to England or to a distant land or on a pilgrimage, he will ask the authorization of the mayor and the other aldermen on Saturday, when they are assembled, and they will choose by common agreement someone to replace him until his return.

6   When the mayor and the aldermen sit in council and the mayor speaks, if someone interrupts him or disturbs the one to whom the mayor has given the floor, the mayor will order him to remain silent, and if subsequently he again disturbs the speaker's ideas, he will pay, if he is one of the members [jurés] of the commune, twelve deniers, of which eight will go to the profit of the town of Rouen and four to the clerks and sergeants.

7   If one of the aldermen, counsellors, or peers sitting with the others on the established days to legislate leaves his seat for the purpose of consultation without the authorization of the mayor, he will pay twelve deniers of which eight will be given to the town of Rouen and four to the clerks and sergeants.

8   If the mayor and the aldermen are sitting as a body of magistrates and someone insults another publicly, he will be at the mercy of the mayor and the aldermen, who will determine the gravity of the offense and whether he has previously committed the act.

9   If the mayor violates the Charter [les Etablissements] of the commune, his fine will be double that of an alderman, because he ought to set an example in observing the law and equity and in maintaining the Charter.

10   If someone finds something belonging to him on a thief or a swindler arrested and convicted at Rouen, and if he can prove by loyal testimony of his neighbors that he is the owner of what he claims, it will be restored to him and the thief or swindler will be judged by the commune and put in the pillory so that all may see and recognize him, and if he ought to be marked, let him be marked; if his punishment entails loss of limb or life, the accused and his property will be turned over to men responsible for the king's justice to see that justice is done to him.

11   If one commune member kills another, and if he has subsequently become a fugitive or has been convicted [of the crime], his house will be torn down, and if he can be captured he will be turned over with his property to the king's justice.

12   If one commune member cripples a fellow member's limb, the case and the fine will be up to the king, and the accused himself will be at the mercy of the commune, because it is his fellow member whom he has crippled.

13   If someone commits an act of sedition in the town of Rouen and if two of the twenty-four members have witnessed it, when accused of the crime he will be convicted on the basis of their testimony alone, because when they took office they swore to tell the truth about what they might hear and see. If two of the other peers have seen it, the accused will be convicted by their testimony under oath. He will be at the mercy of the mayor and the aldermen and will make amends for his crime at their appraisal, according to its gravity and whether he has previously committed the act.

14   If someone injures someone else in the town, whether in a street or in a house, he will be convicted by the testimony without oath of two of the one hundred peers,* and will make amends for the injury at the mercy of the mayor and the aldermen, according to the gravity of the crime and his previous record of injury. If the damaged party can find no witnesses from among the peers, the matter will be judged according to the law of the land.

15   If someone has been placed in the pillory, not for theft but for an infraction of the Charter of the commune, and if someone reproaches him for it to shame him before his fellow members, the latter will pay twenty sous, of which the injured party will have five sous and fifteen will be given to the town. And if the one who has committed the injury does not wish to, or cannot, pay the twenty sous, he will be put into the pillory.

16   A woman convicted of being quarrelsome or a slanderer will be tied by a cord under the armpits and three times plunged into the water; if a man reproaches her for it, he will pay ten sous; if a woman does it, she will pay ten sous or will be plunged into the water.

17   If someone not a member of the commune commits an offense against a member of the commune, he will be summoned to make amends for the fault; if he refuses, the members will be forbidden to have any dealings with him—with regard to sale, loan, purchase, lodging—except when the king or his son or an assize court is in Rouen. And if in this case he refuses to make amends for his crime, the commune will denounce him before the royal justice and will aid its member to pursue his rights. If one of the members contravenes this ban, he will be at the mercy of the mayor and the aldermen.

18   If someone has filed a complaint against a man who has committed a misdeed against him and subsequently refuses the justice granted him by the judgment of the mayor and the aldermen, he will be arrested and will have to furnish a pledge and a guarantee and swear that for this misdeed he will do no more injury to the one of whom he complained. If subsequently he does some injury to him for the same misdeed, he will be judged as a perjurer.

19   If one of the members of the commune placed at the mercy [of the commune] for a crime committed by him has someone intervene on his behalf, except when this is done by the king's order his sentence will be doubled, for we do not wish to incur the ill will of the powerful townspeople [when their intervention is rejected].

20   If someone claims to be a member of the commune and we are uncertain about it, he will prove the truth of his allegation by the testimony of two members.

21   If a cleric or a knight in debt to someone of the city of Rouen rejects the jurisdiction of the mayor and the peers, it will be forbidden for anyone to have dealings with him of sale, purchase, or lodging, unless the king or his son or an assize court is in Rouen. If someone contravenes this ban he will pay the creditor and will be at the mercy of the mayor and the commune. If the debtor rejects all jurisdiction, the commune will aid the member to pursue his rights.

22   If there is a dispute in the commune over a matter of a debt, contract, or

* [In the medieval French version, the figures read twelve peers not bound by oath and two upon oath. (*Ed.*)]

business dealing, it will be decided by the testimony and the record of two of the twenty-four members who will be believed on their word alone, because they have taken an oath at the beginning of their magistracy. And if, when they have ended their year of magistracy and have been removed from office, there is a dispute about a debt, a loan, a contract, or some other act done before them, this dispute will be decided by their oath; if only one of the twenty-four bears witness with one or more of the other peers, this witness under oath will decide the dispute. If there is not one of the one hundred peers to serve as a witness, the matter will be judged according to the law of the land. If the matter does not exceed ten sous in value, the testimony of the peers without oath will suffice to decide it.

23   If someone asserts the right to some land held by another, the one who demands it must offer a pledge and a bond to pursue the action, and if, later, by the investigation the plaintiff is convicted of false action, he will owe the mayor and the aldermen fifty-nine angevin sous.

24   If a justiciary calls for an investigation of a matter having to do with land, it will be granted, but if justice is not done within four weeks, unless there is a legitimate excuse known to the mayor and the aldermen the commune will judge [the matter].

25   If a justiciary calls for an investigation of a matter having to do with a debt, it will be granted, and justice must be done to the plaintiff within two weeks, or else the commune will judge [the matter], unless the one in charge of the court has a legitimate excuse known to the mayor and the aldermen.

26   If someone has contracted with another a debt which he cannot or does not wish to pay, the creditor will be given the property to satisfy the debt, if the property is sufficient for this. If the debtor has nothing with which to pay, he will be banished from the town of Rouen until he gives satisfaction to the mayor and to his creditor. And if he is found in the town of Rouen before having given satisfaction, he will be held in custody in the prison of the commune until he has paid, by his own means or those of his friends, one hundred sous for his liberation and has sworn not to re-enter the town without having previously given satisfaction to the mayor and his creditor.

27   If a stranger begins an action in the commune with regard to a debt owed him by a member [of the commune], the lord of the plaintiff will have an investigation if he demands it, but if he [the lord] does not provide justice for the plaintiff within three days, the commune will take up the matter.

28   If the commune, by order of the king or of his justice, must take to the field, the mayor and the aldermen will see about designating those who must remain to protect the town of Rouen. Anyone who, after the hour indicated for the departure, is found in the town, will be convicted by those who have stayed to protect the town and will be at the mercy of the king; furthermore, the commune will make a decision as to the destruction of his house or [the imposition of] a fine of one hundred sous if he has no house. If, when the commune is on the march, someone leaves it to find lodging or for another reason, without permission of the mayor and without a personal excuse, he will be at the mercy [of the commune].

29   The mayor, on the king's order, will convoke the commune and lead it to the host [the feudal army raised by the king]; whoever stays behind must stay behind at his order. If someone stays behind without his permission, the mayor must punish him according to what has taken place, unless he has a reasonable excuse which authorizes him to stay behind.

30 No one must reside in the town longer than a year and a day unless he is a member of the commune. During this time and before he becomes a member, he cannot enjoy any of the liberties of the town. He cannot be received in the commune and swear allegiance to it unless previously the mayor and the aldermen are seated in council. The oath taken, he will have all the privileges of the town.

31 Whoever wishes to make a complaint against a member of the commune will come to the mayor; the mayor will be in charge of doing justice with regard to any complaint up to the point when the battle pledges are made, because from the moment the duel has begun the king's bailiff is in charge.

32 Apprehended adulterers are not judged by us but by the hand of the Holy Church.

33 If the mayor and the members [of the commune] wish to make an expenditure, they can do it by themselves without asking permission of the council.

34 A thief apprehended and arrested in Rouen, or in the outskirts, will be led to the mayor and judged by him and the king's bailiff; the execution of the sentence will be made by the bailiff's officers at the king's expense. All the objects found in the thief's possession will belong to the king unless someone can prove within reason that they belong to him, in which case they will be returned to him immediately. In case the thief has houses in Rouen or in the outskirts, the one in which he resided will be, immediately after his being sentenced, pulled down by the commune's justice; then the king will enjoy for a year and a day the condemned man's lands and holdings and their income. After this period they will be taken over, in the presence of the king or his bailiffs, by the lords to whom they appertain; the latter will have them to keep in perpetuity.

35 The same principle applies to homicides and to those who after some misdeed are fugitives from the king's territory.

36 If a member is placed in the pillory for a crime he has committed and later someone reproaches him for the crime and the punishment he has undergone, the calumniator will be punished at the will of the mayor and the peers, either by the pillory, the destruction of his house, or a fine of one hundred sous.

37 A perjurer will be at the mercy of the mayor and the peers who, according to the [nature of the] case, will be able at their will to demolish his house or seize his property; if the guilty person has no house or insufficient property, he will be banished from the town for a year and a day, at the mercy of the mayor and the peers.

38 If a member wishes to leave the commune and says that he no longer wishes to be a part of it, he must leave the town, and from that time he will not enjoy the privileges of the commune and will not be able to re-enter it until he has stayed outside it for a year and a day and has again sworn loyalty to the commune in full magistracy before the mayor and the peers.

39 If the mayor has turned over to the creditor the house and holdings of a debtor in payment of his debt, the creditor will take them as acquittal of what is due him; and if later the debtor is in possession of property, the mayor will have the property seized and turned over to the creditor as the balance of his debt, because it is the property of his debtor.

40 The mayor must safeguard the keys of the town and may turn them over into safe hands only with the consent of the peers.

41 If someone absents himself from the watch, he will be at the mercy of the mayor, who will take into account the greater or lesser utility of the watch under the circumstances.

42 If a member refuses to serve under the orders of the mayor, he must be punished by the penalty specified in the convocation, at the will of the mayor and the peers.

43 It is to be noted that all the fines and all the pledges that come into the hands of the mayor must be used for the affairs of the town, according to the decisions of the mayor and the peers.

44 If a member demands justice of another member anywhere else but before the mayor, unless there has been a default of justice on the part of the mayor, he will be at the mercy of the mayor and the peers.

45 If the provost or the viscount of the king our sire wishes to begin an action against a member [of the commune], he must present himself before the mayor and there, in the presence of the mayor, he must have justice done him.

46 It is to be known, furthermore, that it is established in the commune of Rouen that if someone speaks evil of the commune or breaks his word to it in some way and two aldermen hear it, he will be condemned on their simple statement; if two commune members have heard it, he is condemned on their testimony with an oath; if there is only one witness, the accused can rid himself of the charge by his oath and that of six men.

47 Whoever among the inhabitants of the town refuses the oath of the commune and is convicted of this must be arrested, chained, and imprisoned until he gives satisfaction to the commune.

48 The viscount of the town cannot because of an offense touch a member, except in a case of homicide. One who is convicted of homicide is, with all his property, in the hands of the king our sire; if he possesses a house or an orchard, these immovables are in the hands of the mayor and the commune to do justice with.

49 If a stranger to the commune commits a crime to the prejudice of a member of the commune and if he can be arrested, he must be chained and put in prison until he gives satisfaction to the commune. If he cannot be arrested, the commune must demand justice of the lord of the felon; and if justice cannot be obtained from the said lord, those of the commune who can apprehend him will do justice.

50 The commune member, whoever he may be, who draws a knife, sword, or sharpened weapon upon a man, must be arrested and put in prison until he gives satisfaction to the commune.

51 If it is necessary to make a trip on the town's business, it will be supervised by the mayor and the peers. Whoever is asked to do it and refuses to go will be at the mercy of the mayor and the peers.

52 No one may refuse to lend his horse for the town's service; one who refuses will be at the mercy of the mayor and the commune.

53   The mayor, at the beginning of his year of service, will swear not to ask the lord of the land or the barons to allow him to remain mayor beyond his year, except by the common consent of the town.

54   The mayor, the aldermen, and the peers, at the beginning of their magistracy, will swear to judge with equity and not to allow themselves to be led into injustice by either hostility or friendship. They will swear not to accept money or gifts and to judge in equity according to their conscience.

55   If it can be proved that one of the twenty-four members has received a gift for a matter which has brought someone else before the magistracy, his house (that is to say, that of the mayor or whoever received the gift) will be unquestionably pulled down, and neither the guilty one in this matter nor his heir can from that time exercise any function in the commune.

THE CUSTOMS OF NEWCASTLE-UPON-TYNE

These are the laws and customs which the burgesses of Newcastle-upon-Tyne had in the time of Henry [I], king of England. . . . :

The burgesses may distrain foreigners within their market and without, and within their houses and without, and within their borough and without, and they may do this without the permission of the reeve, unless the courts are being held within the borough, or unless they are in the field on army service, or are doing castle-guard. But a burgess may not distrain on another burgess without the permission of the reeve.

If a burgess shall lend anything in the borough to someone dwelling outside, the debtor shall pay back the debt if he admit it, or otherwise do right in the court of the borough.

Pleas which arise in the borough shall there be held and concluded except those which belong to the king's crown.

If a burgess shall be sued in respect of any plaint he shall not plead outside the borough except for defect of court; nor need he answer, except at a stated time and place, unless he has already made a foolish answer, or unless the case concerns matters pertaining to the crown.

If a ship comes to the Tyne and wishes to unload, it shall be permitted to the burgesses to purchase what they please. And if a dispute arises between a burgess and a merchant, it shall be settled before the third tide.

Whatever merchandise a ship brings by sea must be brought to the land; except salt and herring which must be sold on board ship.

If anyone has held land in burgage for a year and a day justly and without challenge, he need not answer any claimant, unless the claimant is outside the kingdom of England, or unless he be a boy not having the power of pleading.

"The Customs of Newcastle-upon-Tyne in the Time of Henry I," *English Historical Documents, 1042–1189*, ed. David C. Douglas and George W. Greenaway (London: Eyre and Spottiswoode (Publishers), Ltd., 1953), Vol. II, 970–971.

If a burgess have a son in his house and at his table, his son shall have the same liberty as his father.

If a villein come to reside in the borough, and shall remain as a burgess in the borough for a year and a day, he shall thereafter always remain there, unless there was a previous agreement between him and his lord for him to remain there for a certain time.

If a burgess sues anyone concerning anything, he cannot force the burgess to trial by battle, but the burgess must defend himself by his oath, except in a charge of treason when the burgess must defend himself by battle. Nor shall a burgess offer battle against a villein unless he has first quitted his burgage.

No merchant except a burgess can buy wool or hides or other merchandise outside the town, nor shall he buy them within the town except from burgesses.

If a burgess incurs forfeiture he shall give 6 oras to the reeve.

In the borough there is no 'merchet' nor 'heriot' nor 'bloodwite' nor 'stengesdint' [fines imposed for drawing blood and for striking another].

Any burgess may have his own oven and handmill if he wishes, saving always the rights of the king's oven.

If a woman incur a forfeiture concerning bread or ale, none shall concern himself with it except the reeve. If she offend twice she shall be punished by the forfeiture. If she offend thrice justice shall take its course.

No one except a burgess may buy cloth for dyeing or make or cut it.

A burgess can give or sell his land as he wishes, and go where he will, freely and quietly unless his claim to the land is challenged.

⊰§ GUILD REGULATIONS OF THE GARMENT CUTTERS OF STENDAL

. . . John and Otto, by the grace of God, margraves of Brandenburg. . . . We make known . . . that we . . . desiring to provide properly for our city of Stendal, have changed, and do change, for the better, the laws of the gild brethren, and of those who are called cloth-cutters, so that they might have the same laws in this craft as their gild brethren the garment-cutters in Magdeburg have been accustomed to observe in the past.

These are the laws:

1   No one shall presume to cut cloth, except he be of our craft; those who break this rule will amend to the gild with three talents.

2   Thrice a year there ought to be a meeting of the brethren, and whoever does not come to it will amend according to justice.

3   Whoever wishes to enter the fraternity whose father was a brother and cut cloth

"Charter of the Garment Cutters of Stendal," *Source Book for Medieval Economic History*, ed. R. C. Cave and H. H. Coulson (Milwaukee: The Bruce Publishing Company, 1936), pp. 246–247.

will come with his friends to the meeting of the brethren, and if he conduct himself honestly, he will be able to join the gild at the first request on payment of five solidi, and he will give six denarii to the master. And if he be dishonest and should not conduct himself well, he should be put off until the second or third meeting. But any of our citizens who wish to enter the gild, if he be an honest man, and worthy, will give a talent to the brethern on entry into the gild, and will present a solidus to the master. But if a guest who is an honest man should decide to join our fraternity, he he will give thirty solidi to the gild on his entry, and eighteen denarii to the master.

4   But in the time of the fairs, that is of the annual fair, any guest, even if he be not of the craft, will be able to cut cloth during the whole fair.

5   If any of our burgesses holding office wish to enter the crafts he will abjure his office, and, on entrance to the gild, will present one mark of gold freely to the brethren, and to the master eighteen denarii.

6   If any brother has been accustomed to prepare cloth in his house and is wont to cut or sell it at the wish of others, he will either cease or have no part in his fraternity.

7   Whatever two parts of the brethren have decreed to do the third part ought to consent to do; but if that third be unwilling, each will amend with three solidi, and will pay them at the next meeting.

8   Every year a master and four other good men who shall preside over the affairs of the gild will be faithfully chosen.

9   Moreover whoever goes contrary to these decrees and is unwilling to obey the master and brethren according to justice, his contumacy ought to be referred to the judgment of his superior. . . .

⊰ᶘ LIFE OF ST. GODRIC

Reginald of Durham

This holy man's father was named Ailward, and his mother Edwenna; both of slender rank and wealth, but abundant in righteousness and virtue. They were born in Norfolk, and had long lived in the township called Walpole. . . . When the boy had passed his childish years quietly at home; then, as he began to grow to manhood, he began to follow more prudent ways of life, and to learn carefully and persistently the teachings of worldly forethought. Wherefore he chose not to follow the life of a husbandman, but rather to study, learn and exercise the rudiments of more subtle conceptions. For this reason, aspiring to the merchant's trade, he began to follow the chapman's way of life, first learning how to gain in small bargains and things of insignificant price; and

Reginald of Durham, "Life of St. Godric," *Social Life in Britain from the Conquest to the Reformation*, ed. and trans. G. G. Coulton (London: Cambridge University Press, 1918), pp. 415–420.

thence, while yet a youth, his mind advanced little by little to buy and sell and gain from things of greater expense. For, in his beginnings, he was wont to wander with small wares around the villages and farmsteads of his own neighbourhood; but, in process of time, he gradually associated himself by compact with city merchants. Hence, within a brief space of time, the youth who had trudged for many weary hours from village to village, from farm to farm, did so profit by his increase of age and wisdom as to travel with associates of his own age through towns and boroughs, fortresses and cities, to fairs and to all the various booths of the market-place, in pursuit of his public chaffer. He went along the high-way, neither puffed up by the good testimony of his conscience nor downcast in the nobler part of his soul by the reproach of poverty. . . .

Seeing that he then dwelt by the sea-shore, he went down one day to the strand to seek for some means of livelihood. . . . The place is called Wellstream, hard by the town of Spalding; there, when the tide was out, the country-folk were wont to scour and explore the stretches of sand, discovering and converting to their own use whatever wreckage or drift the sea might have brought to shore; for hence they sometimes get wealth, since they are free to seize there upon whatsoever goods or commodities they may find by the shore. The saint, then, inspired by such hopes, roamed one day over these stretches of foreshore; and, finding nothing at first, he followed on and on to a distance of three miles, where he found three porpoises lying high and dry, either cast upon the sands by the waves or left there by the ebb-tide. Two were still alive and struggling: the third, in the midst, was dead or dying. Moved with pity, he left the living untouched, cut a portion from the dead fish, and began carrying this away upon his back. But the tide soon began to flow; and Godric, halting under his burden, was overtaken by the waves; first they wet his feet, then his legs; then his upper body was compassed about by the deep; at length the waters went even over his head; yet Godric, strong in faith, bare his burden onwards even under the waves, until, by God's help, he struggled out upon the very shore from which he had gone forth. Then, bringing the fish to his parents, he told them the whole tale, and exhorted them to declare the glory of God.

Yet in all things he walked with simplicity; and, in so far as he yet knew how, it was ever his pleasure to follow in the footsteps of the truth. For, having learned the Lord's Prayer and the Creed from his very cradle, he oftentimes turned them over in his mind, even as he went alone on his longer journeys; and, in so far as the truth was revealed to his mind, he clung thereunto most devoutly in all his thoughts concerning God. At first, he lived as a chapman for four years in Lincolnshire, going on foot and carrying the smallest wares; then he travelled abroad, first to St Andrews in Scotland and then for the first time to Rome. On his return, having formed a familiar friendship with certain other young men who were eager for merchandise, he began to launch upon bolder courses, and to coast frequently by sea to the foreign lands that lay around him. Thus, sailing often to and fro between Scotland and Britain, he traded in many divers wares and, amid these occupations, learned much worldly wisdom. . . . He fell into many perils of the sea, yet by God's mercy he was never wrecked; for He who had upheld St Peter as he walked upon the waves, by that same strong right arm kept this His chosen vessel from all misfortune amid these perils. Thus, having learned by frequent experience his wretchedness amid such dangers, he began to worship certain of the Saints with more ardent zeal, venerating and calling upon their shrines, and giving himself up by wholehearted service to those holy names. In such invocations his prayers were oftentimes answered by prompt consolation; some of which prayers he learned from his fellows with whom he shared these frequent perils; others he collected from faithful hearsay; others again from the custom of the place, for he saw and visited such holy places with frequent assiduity. Thus aspiring ever higher and higher, and yearning upward with his whole heart, at length his great labours and cares bore much fruit of wordly gain. For he laboured not only as a merchant but also as a shipman . . . to Denmark and Flanders and Scotland; in all which lands he found certain rare, and therefore more precious, wares, which he carried to other parts wherein he knew them to be least familiar, and coveted by the inhabitants beyond the price of gold itself; wherefore he exchanged these wares for others coveted by men of other lands; and thus he chaffered most freely and assiduously. Hence he made great profit in all his bargains, and gathered much wealth in the sweat of his brow; for he sold dear in one place the wares which he had bought elsewhere at a small price.

Then he purchased the half of a merchant-ship with certain of his partners in the trade; and again by his prudence he bought the fourth part of another ship. At length, by his skill in navigation, wherein he excelled all his fellows, he earned promotion to the post of steersman. . . .

For he was vigorous and strenuous in mind, whole of limb and strong in body. He was of middle stature, broad-shouldered and deep-chested, with a long face, grey eyes most clear and piercing, bushy brows, a broad forehead, long and open nostrils, a nose of comely curve, and a pointed chin. His beard was thick, and longer than the ordinary, his mouth well-shaped, with lips of moderate thickness; in youth his hair was black, in age as white as snow; his neck was short and thick, knotted with veins and sinews; his legs were somewhat slender, his instep high, his knees hardened and horny with frequent kneeling; his whole skin rough beyond the ordinary, until all this roughness was softened by old age. . . . In labour he was strenuous, assiduous above all men; and, when by chance his bodily strength proved insufficient, he compassed his ends with great ease by the skill which his daily labours had given, and by a prudence born of long experience. . . . He knew, from the aspect of sea and stars, how to foretell fair or foul weather. In his various voyages he visited many saints' shrines, to whose protection he was wont most devoutly to commend himself; more especially the church of St Andrew in Scotland, where he most frequently made and paid his vows. On the way thither, he oftentimes touched at the island of Lindisfarne, wherein St Cuthbert had been bishop, and at the isle of Farne, where that Saint had lived as an anchoret, and where St Godric (as he himself would tell afterwards) would meditate on the Saint's life with abundant tears. Thence he began to yearn for solitude, and to hold his merchandise in less esteem than heretofore. . . .

And now he had lived sixteen years as a merchant, and began to think of spending on charity, to God's honour and service, the goods which he had so laboriously acquired. He therefore took the cross as a pilgrim to Jerusalem, and, having visited the Holy Sepulchre, came back to England by way of St James [of Compostella]. Not long afterwards he became steward to a certain rich man of his own country, with the care of his whole house and household. But certain of the younger household were men of iniquity, who stole their neighbours' cattle and thus held luxurious feasts, whereat Godric, in his ignorance, was sometimes present. Afterwards, discovering the truth, he rebuked and admonished them to cease; but they made no account of his warnings; wherefore he concealed not their iniquity, but disclosed it to the lord of the household, who, however, slighted his advice. Wherefore he begged to be dismissed and went on a pilgrimage, first to St Gilles and thence to Rome the abode of the Apostles, that thus he might knowingly pay the penalty for those misdeeds wherein he had ignorantly partaken. I have often seen him, even in his old age, weeping for this unknowing transgression. . . .

On his return from Rome, he abode awhile in his father's house; until, inflamed again with holy zeal, he purposed to revisit the abode of the Apostle and made his desire known unto his parents. Not only did they approve his purpose, but his mother besought his leave to bear him company on this pilgrimage; which he gladly granted, and willingly paid her every filial service that was her due. They came therefore to London; and they had scarcely departed from thence when his mother took off her shoes, going thus barefooted to Rome and back to London. Godric, humbly serving his parent, was wont to bear her on his shoulders. . . .

Godric, when he had restored his mother safe to his father's arms, abode but a brief while at home; for he was now already firmly purposed to give himself entirely to God's service. Wherefore, that he might follow Christ the more freely, he sold all his possessions and distributed them among the poor. Then, telling his parents of this purpose and receiving their blessing, he went forth to no certain abode, but whithersoever the Lord should deign to lead him; for above all things he coveted the life of a hermit.

⊷§ DESCRIPTION OF THE MOST NOBLE CITY OF LONDON
William Fitz Stephen

Amongst the noble and celebrated cities of the world, that of London, the capital of the kingdom of England, is one of the most renowned, possessing above all others abundant wealth, extensive commerce, great grandeur and magnificence. It is happy in the salubrity of its climate, in the profession of the Christian religion, in the strength of its fortresses, the nature of its situation, the honour of its citizens, and the chastity of its matrons; in its sports too it is most pleasant, and in the production of illustrous men most fortunate. All which things I wish separately to consider.

There then

"Men's minds are soft'ned by a temp'rate clime,"

William Fitz Stephen, "A Description of the Most Noble City of London," *The Survey of London by John Stow* (London: Everyman's Library, 1912), pp. 501–509.

not so however that they are addicted to licentiousness, but so that they are not savage and brutal, but rather kind and generous.

There is in St. Paul's church an episcopal see: it was formerly metropolitan, and, it is thought, will be so again, should the citizens return to the island: unless perhaps the archiepiscopal title of St. Thomas, and his bodily presence there, should always retain that dignity at Canterbury, where it now is. But as St. Thomas has ennobled both these cities, London by his birth, and Canterbury by his death, each of them, with respect to the saint, has much to allege against the other, and with justice too. As regards divine worship, there are also in London and in the suburbs thirteen larger conventual churches, besides one hundred and thirty-six lesser parochial ones.

On the east stands the Palatine tower, a fortress of great size and strength, the court and walls of which are erected upon a very deep foundation, the mortar used in the building being tempered with the blood of beasts. On the west are two castles strongly fortified; the wall of the city is high and thick, with seven double gates, having on the north side towers placed at proper intervals. London formerly had walls and towers in like manner on the south, but that most excellent river the Thames, which abounds with fish, and in which the tide ebbs and flows, runs on that side, and has in a long space of time washed down, undermined, and subverted the walls in that part. On the west also, higher up on the bank of the river, the royal palace rears its head, an incomparable structure, furnished with a breastwork and bastions, situated in a populous suburb, at a distance of two miles from the city.

Adjoining to the houses on all sides lie the gardens of those citizens that dwell in the suburbs, which are well furnished with trees, spacious and beautiful.

On the north side too are fields for pasture, and a delightful plain of meadow land, interspersed with flowing streams, on which stand mills, whose clack is very pleasing to the ear. Close by lies an immense forest, in which are densely wooded thickets, the coverts of game, stags, fallow-deer, boars, and wild bulls. The tillage lands of the city are not barren gravelly soils, but like the fertile plains of Asia, which produce abundant crops, and fill the barns of their cultivators with

"Ceres' plenteous sheaf."

There are also round London, on the northern side, in the suburbs, excellent springs; the water of which is sweet, clear, and salubrious,

"Mid glistening pebbles gliding playfully:"

amongst which, Holywell, Clerkenwell, and St. Clement's well, are of most note, and most frequently visited, as well by the scholars from the schools, as by the youth of the city when they go out to take the air in the summer evenings. The city is delightful indeed, when it has a good governor.

This city is ennobled by her men, graced by her arms, and peopled by a multitude of inhabitants; so that in the wars under King Stephen there went out to a muster, of armed horsemen, esteemed fit for war, twenty thousand, and of infantry sixty thousand. The citizens of London are respected and noted above all other citizens for the elegance of their manners, dress, table, and discourse.

The matrons of the city are perfect Sabines.

The three principal churches possess, by privilege and ancient dignity, celebrated schools; yet often, by the favour of some person of note, or of some learned men eminently distinguished for their philosophy, other schools are permitted upon sufferance. On festival days the masters assemble their pupils at those churches where the feast of the patron saint is solemnised; and there the scholars dispute, some in the demonstrative way, and others logically; some again recite enthymemes, while others use the more perfect syllogism. Some, to show their abilities, engage in such disputation as is practised among persons contending for victory alone; others dispute upon a truth, which is the grace of perfection. The sophisters, who argue upon feigned topics, are deemed clever according to their fluency of speech and command of language. Others endeavour to impose by false conclusions. Sometimes certain orators in their rhetorical harangues employ all the powers of persuasion, taking care to observe the precepts of the art, and to omit nothing apposite to the subject. The boys of the different schools wrangle with each other in verse, and contend about the principles of grammar or the rules of the perfect and future tenses. There are some who in epigrams, rhymes, and verses, use that trivial raillery so much practised amongst the ancients, freely attacking their companions with Fescennine licence, but suppressing the names, discharging their scoffs and sarcasms against them, touching with Socratic wit the failings of their schoolfellows, or perhaps of greater personages, or biting them more keenly with a Theonine tooth. The audience,

> "well disposed to laugh,
> With curling nose double the quivering peals."

The artizans of the several crafts, the vendors of the various commodities, and the labourers of every kind, have each their separate station, which they take every morning. There is also in London, on the bank of the river, amongst the wine-shops which are kept in ships and cellars, a public eating-house: there every day, according to the season, may be found viands of all kinds, roast, fried, and boiled, fish large and small, coarser meat for the poor, and more delicate for the rich, such as venison, fowls, and small birds. If friends, wearied with their journey, should unexpectedly come to a citizen's house, and, being hungry, should not like to wait till fresh meat be bought and cooked:

> "The canisters with bread are heap'd on high;
> The attendants water for their hands supply:"

Meanwhile some run to the river side, and there every thing that they could wish for is instantly procured. However great the number of soldiers or strangers that enters or leaves the city at any hour of the day or night, they may turn in there if they please, and refresh themselves according to their inclination; so that the former have no occasion to fast too long, or the latter to leave the city without dining. Those who wish to indulge themselves would not desire a sturgeon, or the bird of Africa, or the godwit of Ionia, when the delicacies that are to be found there are set before them. This indeed is the public cookery, and is very convenient to the city, and a distinguishing mark of civilisation. . . . There is, without one of the gates, immediately in the suburb, a certain smooth field in name and in reality. There every Friday, unless it be one of the more solemn festivals, is a noted show of well-bred horses exposed for sale. The earls, barons, and knights, who are at the time resident in the city, as well as most of the citizens, flock thither either to look on or buy. It is pleasant to see the nags, with their sleek and shining coats, smoothly ambling along, raising and setting down alternately, as it were, their feet on either side: in one part are horses better adapted to esquires; these, whose pace is rougher but yet expeditious, lift up and set down, as it were, the two opposite fore and hind feet together; in another the young blood colts, not yet accustomed to the bridle,

> "Which upright walk on pasterns firm and straight,
>   Their motions easy, prancing in their gait."

In a third are the horses for burden, strong and stout-limbed; and in a fourth, the more valuable chargers, of an elegant shape and noble height, with nimbly moving ears, erect necks, and plump haunches. In the movements of these the purchasers observe first their easy pace, and then their gallop, which is when the fore-feet are raised from the ground and set down together, and the hind ones in like manner, alternately. When a race is to be run by such horses as these, and perhaps by others, which in like manner, according to their breed, are strong for carriage, and vigorous for the course, the people raise a shout, and order the common horses to be withdrawn to another part of the field. The jockeys, who are boys expert in the management of horses, which they regulate by means of curb-bridles, sometimes by threes, and sometimes by twos, according as the match is made, prepare themselves for the contest. Their chief aim is to prevent a competitor getting before them. The horses, too, after their manner, are eager for the race; their limbs tremble, and, impatient of delay, they cannot stand still; upon the signal being given, they stretch out their limbs, hurry over the course, and are borne along with unremitting speed. The riders, inspired with the love of praise and the hope of victory, clap spurs to their flying horses, lashing them with their whips, and inciting them by their shouts. You would think with Heraclitus, that all things were in motion, and that Zeno's opinion was altogether erroneous, when he said, that there was no such thing as motion, and that it was impossible to reach the goal. In another quarter, apart from the rest, stand the goods of the peasants, implements of husbandry, swine with their long sides, cows with distended udders,

> "Oxen of bulk immense, and woolly flocks."

There, too, stand the mares fitted for the plough, the dray, and the cart, of which some are big with foal, others have their frolicsome colts running close by their sides. To this city, from every nation under heaven, merchants bring their commodities by sea,

> "Arabia's gold, Sabaea's spice and incense,
>   Scythia's keen weapons, and the oil of palms
>   From Babylon's rich soil, Nile's precious gems,
>   Norway's warm peltries, Russia's costly sables,
>   Sera's rich vestures, and the wines of Gaul,
>   Hither are sent."

According to the evidence of chroniclers London is more ancient than Rome: for, as both derive their origin from the same Trojan ancestors, this was founded by Brutus before that by Romulus and Remus. Hence it is that, even to this day, both cities use the same ancient laws and ordinances. This, like Rome, is divided into wards; it has annual sheriffs instead of consuls; it has an order of senators and inferior magistrates, and also sewers and aqueducts in its streets; each class of suits, whether of the deliberative, demonstrative, or judicial kind, has its appropriate place and proper court; on stated days it has its assemblies. I think that there is no city in which more approved customs are observed—in attending churches, honouring God's ordinances, keeping festivals, giving alms, receiving strangers, confirming espousals, contracting marriages, celebrating weddings, preparing entertainments, welcoming guests, and also in the arrangement of the funeral ceremonies and the burial of the dead. The only inconveniences of London are, the immoderate drinking of foolish persons, and the frequent fires. Moreover, almost all the bishops, abbots, and great men of England, are, in a manner, citizens and freemen of London; as they have magnificent houses there, to which they resort, spending large sums of money, whenever they are summoned thither to councils and assemblies by the king or their metropolitan, or are compelled to go there by their own business.

Let us now proceed to the sports of the city; since it is expedient that a city be not only an object of utility and importance, but also a source of pleasure and diversion. Hence even in the seals of the chief pontiffs, up to the time of Pope Leo, there was engraved on one side of the Bull the figure of St. Peter as a fisherman, and above him a key stretched out to him, as it were, from heaven by the hand of God, and around him this verse—

"For me thou left'st thy ship, receive the key."

On the obverse side was represented a city, with this inscription, GOLDEN ROME. It was also said in praise of Augustus Caesar and the city of Rome,

"All night it rains, the shows return with day.
Caesar, thou bear'st with Jove alternate sway."

London, instead of theatrical shows and scenic entertainments, has dramatic performances of a more sacred kind, either representations of the miracles which holy confessors have wrought, or of the passions and sufferings in which the constancy of martyrs was signally displayed. Moreover, to begin with the sports of the boys (for we have all been boys), annually on the day which is called Shrovetide, the boys of the respective schools bring each a fighting cock to their master, and the whole of that forenoon is spent by the boys in seeing their cocks fight in the school-room. After dinner, all the young men of the city go out into the fields to play at the well-known game of foot-ball. The scholars belonging to the several schools have each their ball; and the city tradesmen, according to their respective crafts, have theirs. The more aged men, the fathers of the players, and the wealthy citizens, come on horseback to see the contests of the young men, with whom, after their manner, they participate, their natural heat seeming to be aroused by the sight of so much agility, and by their participation in the amusements of unrestrained youth. Every Sunday in Lent, after dinner, a company of young men enter the fields, mounted on warlike horses—

"On coursers always foremost in the race;"

of which

"Each steed's well-train'd to gallop in a ring."

The lay-sons of the citizens rush out of the gates in crowds, equipped with lances and shields, the younger sort with pikes from which the iron head has been taken off, and there they get up sham fights, and exercise themselves in military combat. When the king happens to be near the city, most of the courtiers attend, and the young men who form the households of the earls and barons, and have not yet attained the honour of knighthood, resort thither for the purpose of trying their skill. The hope of victory animates every one. The spirited horses neigh, their limbs tremble, they champ their bits, and, impatient of delay, cannot endure standing still. When at length

"The charger's hoof seizes upon the course,"

the young riders having been divided into companies, some pursue those that go before without being able to overtake them, whilst others throw their companions out of their course, and gallop beyond them. In the Easter holidays they play at a game resembling a naval engagement. A target is firmly fastened to the trunk of a tree which is fixed in the middle of the river, and in the prow of a boat driven along by oars and the current stands a young man who is to strike the target with his lance; if, in hitting it, he break his lance, and keep his position unmoved, he gains his point, and attains his desire: but if his lance be not shivered by the blow, he is tumbled into the river, and his boat passes by, driven along by its own motion. Two boats, however, are placed there, one on each side of the target, and in them a number of young men to take up the striker, when he first emerges from the stream, or when

"A second time he rises from the wave."

On the bridge, and in balconies on the banks of the river, stand the spectators,

"well disposed to laugh."

During the holydays in summer the young men exercise themselves in the sports of leaping, archery, wrestling, stone-throwing, slinging javelins beyond a mark, and also fighting with bucklers. Cytherea leads the dances of the maidens, who merrily trip along the ground beneath the uprisen moon. Almost on every holyday in winter, before dinner, foaming boars, and huge-tusked hogs, intended for bacon, fight for their lives, or fat bulls or immense boars are baited with dogs. When that great marsh which washes the walls of the city on the north side is frozen over, the young men go out in crowds to divert themselves upon the ice. Some, having increased their velocity by a run, placing their feet apart, and turning their bodies sideways, slide a great way: others make a seat of large pieces of ice like mill-stones, and a great number of them running before, and holding each other by the hand, draw one of their companions who is seated on the ice: if at any time they slip in moving so swiftly, all fall down headlong together. Others are more expert in their sports upon the ice; for fitting to, and binding under their feet the shinbones of some animal, and taking in their hands poles shod with iron, which at times they strike against the ice, they are carried along with as great rapidity as a bird flying or a bolt discharged from a cross-bow. Sometimes two of the skaters having placed themselves a great distance apart by mutual agreement, come together from opposite sides; they meet, raise their poles, and strike each other; either one or both of them fall, not without some bodily hurt: even after their fall they are carried along to a great distance from each other by the velocity of the motion; and whatever part of their heads comes in contact with the ice is laid bare to the very skull. Very frequently the leg or arm of the falling party, if he chance to light upon either of them, is broken. But youth is an age eager for glory and desirous of victory, and so young men engage in counterfeit battles, that they may conduct themselves more valiantly in real ones. Most of the citizens amuse themselves in sporting with merlins, hawks, and other birds of a like kind, and also with dogs that hunt in the woods. The citizens have the right of hunting in Middlesex, Hertfordshire, all the Chilterns, and Kent, as far as the river Cray. The Londoners, then called Trinovantes, repulsed Caius Julius Caesar, a man who delighted to mark his path with blood. Whence Lucan says,

"Britain he sought, but turn'd his back dismay'd."

The city of London has produced some men, who have subdued many kingdoms, and even the Roman empire; and very many others, whose virtue has exalted them to the skies, as was promised to Brutus by the oracle of Apollo:

"Brutus, there lies beyond the Gallic bounds
An island which the western sea surrounds:

. . .

To reach this happy shore thy sails employ:
There fate decrees to raise a second Troy,
And found an empire in thy royal line
Which time shall ne'er destroy, nor bounds confine."

Since the planting of the Christian religion there, London has given birth to the noble emperor Constantine, who gave the city of Rome and all the insignia of the empire to God and St. Peter, and Pope Sylvester, whose stirrup he held, and chose rather to be called defender of the holy Roman church, than emperor: and that the peace of our lord the Pope might not, by reason of his presence, be disturbed by the turmoils consequent on secular business, he withdrew from the city which he had bestowed upon our lord the Pope, and built for himself the city of Byzantium. London also in modern times has produced illustrious and august princes, the empress Matilda, King Henry the Third, and St. Thomas, the archbishop and glorious martyr of Christ, than whom no man was more guileless or more devoted to all good men throughout the whole Roman world.

THE STATESMAN'S BOOK OF JOHN OF SALISBURY

An English bishop, John of Salisbury (ca. 1110–1180), is a good example of how a medieval clergyman could combine piety with worldliness and culture. Like the Renaissance humanists of 300 years later, he preferred the grace and eloquence of the pagan Cicero to the elaborate dialectics of the scholastic philosophers or the turgid fulminations of the preachers of hellfire and brimstone. From his two books, Policraticus *and* Metalogicon *(his use of these Greek words reveals the influence of the ancient classics), we learn a good deal about medieval life and thought.*

John had studied under the leading teachers of his day, including the brilliant Peter Abélard (see page 227); his Metalogicon, *a treatise on education, sets forth the humanistic ideals of the school of Chartres in opposition to the "logic-choppers." Perhaps even more important, however, was the* Policraticus *(or "Statesman's Manual"), for which he drew on his years of diplomatic service for popes, archbishops, and kings. In particular, he had been secretary to Thomas à Becket when Becket was Archbishop of Canterbury, and he knew King Henry II of England well. At first the* Policraticus *seems a string of anachronisms, in which feudal knights and barons are confused with ancient Roman soldiers and senators. Gradually, however, we detect the art of a master of diplomacy who was using neutral language to steer a careful line down the middle of every major controversy of his day. In the end he achieved a kind of minor miracle for the twelfth century: he had written a book on church, state, and society that was original without seeming to be and that offended nobody.*

These selections illustrate a theme that dominates medieval thought about society: the analogy between the individual man, made up of the soul and the body with its various parts, and the "body social" with its various orders or classes. Sometimes the analogy was carried further, to compare the "microcosm" (man) and the "macrocosm" (the universe), with God as its "head," the heavenly bodies as its "ministers," etc.

WHAT A COMMONWEALTH IS

Book V

Chapter ii . . . A commonwealth, according to Plutarch, is a certain body which is endowed with life by the benefit of divine favor, which acts at the prompting of the

The Statesman's Book of John of Salisbury, *trans. John Dickinson (New York: Alfred A. Knopf, Inc., Political Science Classics, 1927), pp. 3–4, 6–8, 9, 10–11, 64–65, 108, 109, 112–113, 173–174, 180, 199–200, 243–244, 323–324, 335–336, 370–371, 372–373.*

highest equity, and is ruled by what may be called the moderating power of reason. Those things which establish and implant in us the practice of religion, and transmit to us the worship of God (here I do not follow Plutarch, who says "of the Gods") fill the place of the soul in the body of the commonwealth. And therefore those who preside over the practice of religion should be looked up to and venerated as the soul of the body. For who doubts that the ministers of God's holiness are His representatives? Furthermore, since the soul is, as it were, the prince of the body, and has rulership over the whole thereof, so those whom our author calls the prefects of religion preside over the entire body. Augustus Caesar was to such a degree subject to the priestly power of the pontiffs that in order to set himself free from this subjection and have no one at all over him, he caused himself to be created a pontiff of Vesta, and thereafter had himself promoted to be one of the gods during his own life-time. The place of the head in the body of the commonwealth is filled by the prince, who is subject only to God and to those who exercise His Office and represent Him on earth, even as in the human body the head is quickened and governed by the soul. The place of the heart is filled by the Senate, from which proceeds the initiation of good works and ill. The duties of eyes, ears, and tongue are claimed by the judges and the governors of provinces. Officials and soldiers correspond to the hands. Those who always attend upon the prince are likened to the sides. Financial officers and keepers (I speak now not of those who are in charge of the prisons, but of those who are keepers of the privy chest) may be compared with the stomach and intestines, which, if they become congested through excessive avidity, and retain too tenaciously their accumulations, generate innumerable and incurable diseases, so that through their ailment the whole body is threatened with destruction. The husbandmen correspond to the feet, which always cleave to the soil, and need the more especially the care and foresight of the head, since while they walk upon the earth doing service with their bodies, they meet the more often with stones of stumbling, and therefore deserve aid and protection all the more justly since it is they who raise, sustain, and move forward the weight of the entire body. Take away the support of the feet from the strongest body, and it cannot move forward by its own power, but must creep painfully and shamefully on its hands, or else be moved by means of brute animals. . . .

THE "ORGANS" OF THE BODY POLITIC

Book IV

Chapters i, ii, iii: The "head"   Between a tyrant and a prince there is this single or chief difference, that the latter obeys the law and rules the people by its dictates, accounting himself as but their servant. It is by virtue of the law that he makes good his claim to the foremost and chief place in the management of the affairs of the commonwealth and in the bearing of its burdens; and his elevation over others consists in this, that whereas private men are held responsible only for their private affairs, on the prince fall the burdens of the whole community. Wherefore deservedly there is conferred on him, and gathered together in his hands, the power of all his subjects, to the end that he may be sufficient unto himself in seeking and bringing about the advantage of each individually, and of all; and to the end that the state of the human commonwealth may be ordered in the best possible manner, seeing that each and all are members one of another. Wherein we indeed but follow nature, the best guide of life; for nature has gathered together all the senses of her microcosm or little world, which is man, into the head, and has subjected all the members in obedience to it in such wise that they will all function properly so long as they follow the guidance of the head, and the head remains sane. Therefore the prince stands on a pinnacle which is exalted and made splendid with all the great and high privileges which he deems necessary for himself. And rightly so, because nothing is more advantageous to the people than that the needs of the prince should be fully satisfied; since it is impossible that his will should be found opposed to justice. Therefore, according to the usual definition, the prince is the public power, and a kind of likeness on earth of the divine majesty. Beyond doubt a large share of the divine power is shown to be in princes by the fact that at their nod men bow their necks and for the most part offer up their heads to the axe to be struck off, and, as by a divine impulse, the prince is feared by each of those over whom he is set as an object of fear. And this I do not think could be, except as a result of the will of God. For all power is from the Lord God, and has been with Him always, and is from everlasting. The power which the prince has is therefore from God, for the power of God is never lost, nor severed from Him, but He merely exercises it through a subordinate hand, making all things teach His mercy or justice. "Who, therefore, resists the ruling power, resists the ordinance of God," in whose hand is the authority of conferring that power, and when He so desires, of withdrawing it again, or diminishing it. For it is not the ruler's own act when his will is turned to cruelty against his subjects, but it is rather the dispensation of God for His good pleasure to punish or chasten them. . . .

Princes should not deem that it detracts from their princely dignity to believe that the enactments of their own justice are not to be preferred to the justice of God, whose justice is an everlasting justice, and His law is equity. Now equity, as the learned jurists define it, is a certain fitness of things which compares all things rationally, and seeks to apply like rules of right and wrong to like cases, being impartially disposed toward all persons, and allotting to each that which belongs to him. Of this equity the interpreter is the law, to which the will and intention of equity and justice are known. Therefore Crisippus asserted that the power of the law extends over all things, both divine and human, and that it accordingly presides over all goods and ills, and is the ruler and guide of material things as well as of human beings. To which Papinian, a man most learned in the law, and Demosthenes, the great orator, seem to assent, subjecting all men to its obedience because all law is, as it were, a discovery, and a gift from God, a precept of wise men, the corrector of excesses of the will, the bond which knits together the fabric of the state, and the banisher of crime; and it is therefore fitting that all men should live according to it who lead their lives in a corporate political body. All are accordingly bound by the necessity of keeping the law, unless perchance there is any who can be thought to have been given the license of wrong-doing. However, it is said that the prince is absolved from the obligations of the law; but this is not true in the sense that it is lawful for him to do unjust acts, but only in the sense that his character should be such as to cause him to practice equity not through fear of the penalties of the law but through love of justice; and should also be such as to cause him from the same motive to promote the advantage of the commonwealth, and in all things to prefer the good of others before his own private will. Who, indeed, in respect of public matters can properly speak of the will of the prince at all, since therein he may not lawfully have any will of his own apart from that which the law or equity enjoins, or the calculation of the common interest requires? For in these matters his will is to have the force of a judgment; and most properly that which pleases him therein has the force of law, because his decision may not be at variance with the intention of equity. "From thy countenance," says the Lord, "let my judgment go forth, let thine eyes look upon equity"; for the uncorrupted judge is one whose decision, from assiduous contemplation of equity, is the very likeness thereof. The prince accordingly is the minister of the common interest and the bond-servant of equity, and he bears the public person in the sense that he punishes the wrongs and injuries of all, and all crimes, with evenhanded equity. His rod and staff also, administered with wise moderation, restore irregularities and false departures to the straight path of equity, so that deservedly may the Spirit congratulate the power of the prince with the words, "Thy rod and thy staff, they have comforted me." His shield, too, is strong, but it is a shield for the protection of the weak, and one which wards off powerfully the darts of the wicked from the innocent. Those who derive the greatest advantage from his performance of the duties of his office are those who can do least for themselves, and his power is chiefly exercised against those who desire to do harm. Therefore not without reason he bears a sword, wherewith he sheds blood blamelessly, without becoming thereby a man of blood, and frequently puts men to death without incurring the name or guilt of homicide. . . .

This sword, then, the prince receives from the hand of the Church, although she herself has no sword of blood at all. Nevertheless she has this sword, but she uses it by the hand of the prince, upon whom she confers the power of bodily coercion, retaining to herself authority over spiritual things in the person of the pontiffs. The prince is, then, as it were, a minister of the priestly power, and one who exercises that side of the sacred offices which seems unworthy of the hands of the priesthood. For every office existing under, and concerned with the execution of, the sacred laws is really a religious office, but that is inferior which consists in punishing crimes, and which therefore seems to be typified in the person of the hangman. . . . But if one who has been appointed prince has performed duly and faithfully the ministry which he has undertaken, as great honor and reverence are to be shown to him as the head excels in honor all the members of the body. Now he performs his ministry faithfully when he is mindful of his true status, and remembers that he bears the person of the *universitas* of those subject to him; and when he is fully conscious that he owes his life not to himself and his own private ends, but to others, and allots it to them accordingly, with duly ordered charity and affection. Therefore he owes the whole of himself to God, most of himself to his country, much to his relatives and friends, very little to foreigners, but still somewhat. He has duties to the very wise and the very foolish, to little children and to the aged. Supervision over these classes of persons is common to all in authority, both those who have care over spiritual things and those who exercise temporal jurisdiction. . . . And so let him be both father and husband to his subjects, or, if he has known some affection more tender still, let him employ that; let him desire to be loved rather than feared, and show himself to them as such a man that they will out of devotion prefer his life to their own, and regard his preservation and safety as a kind of public life; and then all things will prosper well for him, and a small bodyguard will, in case of need, prevail by their loyalty against innumerable adversaries. For love is strong as death; and the wedge which is held together by strands of love is not easily broken. . . .

Book V

Chapter ix: The "heart"   The place of the heart, on the authority of Plutarch, is filled by the senate. Now "senate," according to the opinion of the ancients, is the name of an office, and its distinguishing mark is old age; the word senate is itself derived from "senectus," which means old age. . . .

For age of mind is the wisdom which consists in properly apportioning all duties and in practising the whole art of life. For the art of right living, as the Stoics thought, is the art of arts. To say that there is no art of the greatest of all things, although everyone admits that the minor things have each their respective art, is an opinion of those who speak with too little reflection, and who in respect to the largest things fall into the error of thinking that everything is a matter of the arbitrary will and discretion of those who make decisions, instead of being rather a matter of truth and science. But there is, as the ancient philosophers knew, a supreme guiding principle of things divine and human, namely wisdom, and a science of things to be done and to be left undone. To apply one's self to this is to philosophize, for philosophy is the study of wisdom. . . .

Unjust men are therefore to be excluded, and men who are overbearing and avaricious, and all such manner of human plagues. Nought, indeed, is more deadly than the unrighteous counsellor of a rich man. "With all watchfulness," it is written, "guard thy heart, for it is the source of life." Therefore the ruler should provide that his counsellors be not needy, lest they covet immoderately the things of others. The same principle extends to all whose duties touch the inner parts of the body of the commonwealth, and whom we called above financial officials and bailiffs and overseers of private property. For all these must have subsistence in sufficient quantity, and this should be interpreted on the basis of necessity and usage, having due regard to distinction between persons. For if it is absorbed too greedily and not sufficiently distributed, distempers will be produced which are incurable, or difficult to cure. Certainly it is impossible to seek justice and money at one and the same time; either a man will cleave to the one and despise the other, or else he will be perverted by the worse and lose the better. For according to the testimony of Wisdom, "there is nought more wicked than a covetous man, and nought more unjust than love of money; for such a one setteth even his soul to sale and while he liveth, he hath cast away his bowels." And perchance it is for this reason that mother nature, the most loving of parents, has prudently protected the inner parts of the body with the crating of the chest and the solid structure of the ribs and the barrier of the outer flesh, to the end that they may be the more safe against all violence from without; and then proceeds to supply them with their several necessities; nor are they ever exposed to external contacts without injury to their health. So in the commonwealth it behooves us to follow this pattern of nature's craftsmanship and from the public store supply these officials with a sufficiency for their needs. . . .

Book VI

Chapters i, ii, viii: The "hands"   The hand of the commonwealth is either armed or unarmed. The armed hand is that which performs the soldiering of camps and blood; the unarmed is that which administers justice and, keeping holiday from arms, is enlisted in the service of the law. For not those alone do military service for the commonwealth who, protected by helmets and cuirasses, ply their swords or what other weapons you please against the foe, but also the advocates and pleaders of causes who, trusting to the bulwark of their glorious voice, lift up the fallen, refresh the weary; nor do they less serve mankind, than if they were preserving from the foe by the use of weapons the life, hope and posterity of those who are hard-pressed. Publicans, apparitors, and all officers of the law courts may also be said to perform military service. For as some offices are of peace and others of war, so it is necessary that the ones should be performed by one set of officials, the others by another.

The armed hand is employed only against the enemy, the unarmed is stretched out against the citizen also. It is needful that both should be subject to discipline, because both have a noteworthy tendency to viciousness. Besides, the way in which the hands are used bears witness to the character of the head, because, as Wisdom says, an unjust king has none but ungodly ministers; and as is the ruler of a state, so are those who inhabit therein. A magistrate, said Perides, blaming his colleague Soffocles, should not only have continent hands, but continent eyes as well. And the continence of rulers is praiseworthy when it is such that they not merely refrain their own hands from extortion and wrong, but restrain the hands of others as well.

The hand of each militia, to wit both the armed and the unarmed, is the hand of the prince himself; and unless he restrains both, he is not continent. And in truth the unarmed hand is to be curbed the more tightly for the reason that while the soldiery of arms are enjoined to abstain from extortion and rapine, the unarmed hand is debarred even from taking gifts. But if a lawful penalty is demanded of anyone, if it is a question in other words of exacting or receiving that which is fixed or allowed by law, then there is no ground for punishment or blame. Whatever it is, it cannot properly be called an exaction; nor does it fall into the class of gifts which officials are forbidden to receive. . . .

There remains the armed hand, which, as has been said, performs the service of camps and blood. The control exercised over it is the principal test of the wisdom and justice of the prince. For, as Vegetius Renatus says, there is no one who should have more knowledge or better knowledge than a prince, whose learning ought to be of advantage to all his subjects. For since works of both peace and war require to be regulated, he ought to be learned both in the law and in military science. Something has already been said above concerning the pursuits of peace, and we now proceed to discuss the armed hand, which is never fit and vigorous without selection, science, and training. . . .

The sacred Gospel narrative bears witness that two swords are enough for the Christian *imperium;* all others belong to those who with swords and cudgels draw nigh to take Christ captive and seek to destroy His name. For wherein do they partake of the character of the true soldier who, although they may have been called, yet do not obey the law according to their oath, but deem the glory of their military service to consist in bringing contempt upon the priesthood, in cheapening the authority of the Church, in so extending the kingdom of man as to narrow the empire of Christ, and in proclaiming their own praises and flattering and extolling themselves with false commendations, thus imitating the braggart soldier to the amusement of all who hear them? Their valor shines forth chiefly in stabbing with swords or tongues the clergy and the unarmed solidery. But what is the office of the duly ordained soldiery? To defend the Church, to assail infidelity, to venerate the priesthood, to protect the poor from injuries, to pacify the province, to pour out their blood for their brothers (as the formula of their oath instructs them), and, if need be, to lay down their lives. The high praises of God are in their throat, and two-edged swords are in their hands to execute punishment on the nations and rebuke upon the peoples, and to bind their kings in chains and their nobles in links of iron. But to what end? To the end that they may serve madness, vanity, avarice, or their own private self-will? By no means. Rather to the end that they may execute the judgment that is committed to them to execute; wherein each follows not his own will but the deliberate decision of God, the angels, and men, in accordance with equity and the public utility. I say "to the end that they may *execute*"; for as it is for judges to pronounce judgment, so it is for these to perform their office by executing it. Verily, "This honor have all His saints." For soldiers that do these things are "saints," and are the more loyal to their prince in proportion as they more zealously keep the faith of God; and they advance the more successfully the honor of their own valor as they seek the more faithfully in all things the glory of their God. . . .

Book VI

Chapter xx: The "feet"   Those are called the feet who discharge the humbler offices, and by whose services the members of the whole commonwealth walk upon solid earth. Among these are to be counted the husbandmen, who always cleave to the soil, busied about their plough-lands or vineyards or pastures or flower-gardens. To these must be added the many species of cloth-making, and the mechanic arts, which work in wood, iron, bronze and the different metals; also the menial occupations, and the manifold forms of getting a livelihood and sustaining life, or increasing household property, all of which, while they do not pertain to the authority of the governing power, are yet in the highest degree useful and profitable to the corporate whole of the commonwealth. All these different occupations are so numerous that the commonwealth in the number of its feet exceeds not only the eight-footed crab but even the centipede, and because of their very multitude they cannot be enumerated; for while they are not infinite by nature, they are yet of so many different varieties that no writer on the subject of offices or duties has ever laid down particular precepts for each special variety. But it applies generally to each and all of them that in their exercise they should not transgress the limits of the law, and should in all things observe constant reference to the public utility. For inferiors owe it to their superiors to provide them with service, just as the superiors in their turn owe it to their inferiors to provide them with all things needful for their protection and succor. Therefore Plutarch says that course is to be pursued in all things which is of advantage to the humbler classes, that is to say to the multitude; for small numbers always yield to great. Indeed the reason for the institution of magistrates was to the end that subjects might be protected from wrongs, and that the commonwealth itself might be "shod," so to speak, by means of their services. For it is as it were "unshod" when it is exposed to wrong,—than which there can be no more disgraceful pass of affairs to those who fill the magistracies. For an afflicted people is a sign and proof of the goutiness, so to speak, of the prince. Then and then only will the health of the commonwealth be sound and flourishing when the higher members shield the lower, and the lower respond faithfully and fully in like measure to the just demands of their superiors, so that each and all are as it were members one of another by a sort of reciprocity, and each regards his own interest as best served by that which he knows to be most advantageous for the others. . . .

LIBERTY AND TYRANNY

Book VII

Chapter xxv   Liberty means judging everything freely in accordance with one's individual judgment, and does not hesitate to reprove what it sees opposed to good morals. Nothing but virtue is more splendid than liberty, if indeed liberty can ever properly be severed from virtue. For to all right-thinking men it is clear that true liberty issues from no other source. Wherefore, since all agree that virtue is the highest good in life, and that it alone can strike off the heavy and hateful yoke of slavery, it has been the opinion of philosophers that men should die, if need arose, for the sake of virtue, which is the only reason for living. But virtue can never be fully attained without liberty, and the absence of liberty proves that virtue in its full perfection is wanting. Therefore a man is free in proportion to the measure of his virtues, and the extent to which he is free determines what his virtues can accomplish; while, on the other hand, it is the vices alone which bring about slavery, and subject a man to persons and things in unmeet obedience; and though slavery of the person may seem at times the more to be pitied, in reality slavery to the vices is ever far the more wretched. And so what is more lovely than liberty? And what more agreeable to a man who has any reverence for virtue? We read that it has been the impelling motive of all good princes; and that none ever trod liberty under foot save the open foes of virtue. The jurists know what good laws were introduced for the sake of liberty, and the testimony of historians has made famous the great deeds done for love of it. Cato drank poison, pierced himself with his sword, and that no delay might prolong life on terms which he deemed ignoble, he thrust in his hand to widen the wound, and poured out his noble blood, that he might not see Caesar reigning. Brutus set on foot civil wars to save the city from slavery; and that seat of empire preferred rather to bear the wretched afflictions of perpetual war than to endure a lord, though of the mildest character. I pass on to the weaker sex. The wives of the Teutons, because of the value they set upon their chastity, besought Marius after his victory that they might be presented as a gift to the Vestal Virgins, promising that they would abstain from all unchastity; and when their prayers were not heeded, on the following night they ended their lives by strangling themselves in order not to become slaves or suffer loss of their chastity. If I wished to recall individual instances of this kind, time would run out before the examples were exhausted. The practice of liberty is a notable thing and displeasing only to those who have the character of slaves.

Things which are done or spoken freely avoid the fault of timidity on the one hand and of rashness on the other, and so long as the straight and narrow path is followed, merit praise and win affection. But when under the pretext of liberty rashness unleashes the violence of its spirit, it properly incurs reproach, although, as a thing more pleasing in the ears of the vulgar than convincing to the mind of the wise man, it often finds in the indulgence of others the safety which it does not owe to its own prudence. Nevertheless, it is the part of a good and wise man to give a free rein to the liberty of others and to accept with patience the words of free speaking, whatever they may be. Nor does he oppose himself to its works so long as these do no involve the casting away of virtue. For since each virtue shines by its own proper light, the merit of tolerance is resplendent with a very special glory. . . .

Book VIII

Chapters xvii, xx Wherein the prince differs from the tyrant has already been set forth above when we were reviewing Plutarch's "Instruction of Trajan"; and the duties of the prince and of the different members of the commonwealth were also carefully explained at that point. Wherefore it will be easier to make known here, and in fewer words, the opposite characteristics of the tyrant. A tyrant, then, as the philosophers have described him, is one who oppresses the people by rulership based upon force, while he who rules in accordance with the laws is a prince. Law is the gift of God, the model of equity, a standard of justice, a likeness of the divine will, the guardian of well-being, a bond of union and solidarity between peoples, a rule defining duties, a barrier against the vices and the destroyer thereof, a punishment of violence and all wrong-doing. The law is assailed by force or by fraud, and, as it were, either wrecked by the fury of the lion or undermined by the wiles of the serpent. In whatever way this comes to pass, it is plain that it is the grace of God which is being assailed, and that it is God himself who in a sense is challenged to battle. The prince fights for the laws and the liberty of the people; the tyrant thinks nothing done unless he brings the laws to nought and reduces the people to slavery. Hence the prince is a kind of likeness of divinity; and the tyrant, on the contrary, a likeness of the boldness of the Adversary, even of the wickedness of Lucifer, imitating him that sought to build his throne to the north and make himself like unto the Most High, with the exception of His goodness. For had he desired to be like unto Him in goodness, he would never have striven to tear from Him the glory of His power and wisdom. What he more likely did aspire to was to be equal with him in authority to dispense rewards. The prince, as the likeness of the Deity, is to be loved, worshipped and cherished; the tyrant, the likeness of wickedness, is generally to be even killed. The origin of tyranny is iniquity, and springing from a poisonous root, it is a tree which grows and sprouts into a baleful pestilent growth, and to which the axe must by all means be laid. For if iniquity and injustice, banishing charity, had not brought about tyranny, firm concord and perpetual peace would have possessed the peoples of the earth forever, and no one would think of enlarging his boundaries. Then kingdoms would be as friendly and peaceful, according to the authority of the great father Augustine, and would enjoy as undisturbed repose, as the separate families in a well-ordered state, or as different persons in the same family; or perhaps, which is even more credible, there would be no kingdoms at all, since it is clear from the ancient historians that in the beginning these were founded by iniquity as presumptuous encroachments against the Lord, or else were extorted from Him. . . .

Let me prove by another story that it is just for public tyrants to be killed and the people thus set free for the service of God. This story shows that even priests of God repute the killing of tyrants as a pious act, and if it appears to wear the semblance of treachery, they say that it is consecrated to the Lord by a holy mystery. Thus Holofernes fell a victim not to the valor of the enemy but to his own vices by means of a sword in the hands of a woman; and he who had been terrible to strong men was vanquished by luxury and drink, and slain by a woman. Nor would the woman have gained access to the tyrant had she not piously dissimulated her hostile intention. For that is not treachery which serves the cause of the faith and fights in behalf of charity. For verily it was due to the woman's faith that she upbraided the priests because they had set a time-limit upon the divine mercy by agreeing with the enemy that they would surrender themselves and deliver up the city if the Lord should not come to their aid within five days. Likewise it was because of her charity that she shrank from no perils so long as she might deliver her brethren and the people of the Lord from the enemy. . . .

The histories teach, however, that none should undertake the death of a tyrant who is bound to him by an oath or by the obligation of fealty. For we read that Sedechias, because he disregarded the sacred obligation of fealty, was led into captivity; and that in the case of another of the kings of Juda whose name escapes my memory, his eyes were plucked out because, falling into faithlessness, he did not keep before his sight God, to whom the oath is taken; since sureties for good behavior are justly given even to a tyrant.

But as for the use of poison, although I see it sometimes wrongfully adopted by infidels, I do not read that it is ever permitted by any law. Not that I do not believe that tyrants ought to be removed from our midst, but it should be done without loss of religion and honor. For David, the best of all kings that I have read of, and who, save in the incident of Urias Etheus, walked blamelessly in all things, although he had to endure the most grievous tyrant, and although he often had an opportunity of destroying him, yet preferred to spare him, trusting in the mercy of God, within whose power it was to set him free without sin. He therefore determined to abide in patience until the tyrant should either suffer a change of heart and be visited by God with return of charity, or else should fall in battle, or otherwise meet his end by the just judgment of God. How great was his patience can be discerned from the fact that when he had cut off the edge of Saul's robe in the cave, and again when, having entered the camp by night, he rebuked the negligence of the sentinels, in both cases he compelled the king to confess that David was acting the juster part. And surely the method of destroying tyrants which is the most useful and the safest, is for those who are oppressed to take refuge humbly in the protection of God's mercy, and lifting up undefiled hands to the Lord, to pray devoutly that the scourge wherewith they are afflicted may be turned aside from them. For the sins of transgressors are the strength of tyrants.

⅋ PIERS THE PLOUGHMAN

William Langland

The last half of the fourteenth century was a time of woe for the common man: in 1348 the bubonic plague ravaged the agricultural population in its first and strongest wave, and after that it appeared sporadically as a chilling reminder of the evanescence of life. In 1337 England began a war against France. The pillage and plunder dragged through a hundred years and across hundreds of farms and villages. Where there was no warfare, landlords began increasing rents or evicting tenants in order to use their lands for sheep raising, which was more profitable than mere subsistence farming. The Church, sapped of the charitable zeal and piety of the thirteenth century, tithed its parishioners mercilessly to support its magnificently endowed episcopal princes; and the state, engulfed in debts to pay for mercenaries, also taxed more relentlessly than ever. When a head tax was levied in June, 1381, on all persons over the age of fifteen (the first universal tax to be imposed), noticeable evasions—in some areas only half the exasperated populace bothered to pay—brought royal action. With arrests came insurrection. The Peasants' Revolt in England— concentrated in one month's time and in two counties near London— failed, for its leaders were untrained in military or political coordination. Reprisals were restrained; this had not been the case in France, where an earlier and larger peasants' rebellion had ended in mass slaughter.

What had the serfs and landless workers hoped to gain? Repeal of the head tax, of course, but also much more. On their way to London, intending to remonstrate with the king, they burned manor houses and—with particular glee—the manor rolls where the names and duties of the estate's serfs were inscribed. Their program, if so it can be called, was summarized by their leader, the "mad priest," John Ball: "Ah, ye good people, the matters goeth not well to pass in England, nor shall not do till everything be common, and that there be no villains [serfs] nor gentlemen, but that we may be all united together, and that the lords be no greater masters then we be."

In the midst of this unrest, a masterpiece of social criticism was composed by a lowly cleric who had shared a life of poverty and labor with the poor. Piers the Ploughman, *by William Langland, begun in 1370 and completed in 1395, is a long allegorical poem steeped in medieval piety. It is largely a didactic sermon, though imaginatively filled with dreamlike images, summoning mankind back to simplicity of faith and charitable humaneness. Portrayals of the humble people as crudely virtuous contrast with depictions of the sophisticated dishonesty of the wealthy and lordly. The passage in which the rats talk of the cat is a criticism of Parliament's attempt to control the king, though the allegory, as can be seen, has other far-reaching implications.*

PROLOGUE: THE PLAIN FULL OF PEOPLE

One summer season, when the sun was warm, I rigged myself out in shaggy woollen clothes, as if I were a shepherd; and in the garb of an easy-living hermit I set out to roam far and wide through the world, hoping to hear of marvels. But on a morning in May, among the Malvern Hills, a strange thing happened to me, as though by magic. For I was tired out by my wanderings, and as I lay down to rest under a broad bank by the side of a stream, and leaned over gazing into the water, it sounded so pleasant that I fell asleep.

And I dreamt a marvellous dream: I was in a wilderness, I could not tell where, and looking Eastwards I saw a tower high up against the sun, and splendidly built on top of a hill; and far beneath it was a great gulf, with a dungeon in it, surrounded by deep, dark pits, dreadful to see. But between the tower and the gulf I saw a smooth plain, thronged with all kinds of people, high and low together, moving busily about their worldly affairs.

Some laboured at ploughing and sowing, with no time for pleasure, sweating to produce food for the gluttons to waste. Others spent their lives in vanity, parading themselves in a show of fine clothes. But many, out of love for our Lord and in the hope of Heaven, led strict lives devoted to prayer and penance—for such are the hermits and anchorites who stay in their cells, and are not forever hankering to roam about, and pamper their bodies with sensual pleasures.

Others chose to live by trade, and were much better off—for in our worldly eyes such men seem to thrive. Then there were the professional entertainers, some of whom,

William Langland, *Piers the Ploughman*, trans. J. F. Goodridge (Baltimore: Penguin Books, Inc., 1964), pp. 63–69, 83–92, 298.

I think, are harmless minstrels, making an honest living by their music; but others, babblers and vulgar jesters, are true Judas' children! They invent fantastic tales about themselves, and pose as half-wits, yet they show wits enough whenever it suits them, and could easily work for a living if they had to! I will not say all that St Paul says about them; it is enough to quote, 'He who talks filth is a servant of the Devil.'

And there were tramps and beggars hastening on their rounds, with their bellies and their packs crammed full of bread. They lived by their wits, and fought over their ale—for God knows, they go to bed glutted with food and drink, these brigands, and get up with foul language and filthy talk; and all day long, Sleep and shabby Sloth are at their heels.

And I saw pilgrims and palmers banding together to visit the shrines at Rome and Compostella. They went on their way full of clever talk, and took leave to tell fibs about it for the rest of their lives. And some I heard spinning such yarns of the shrines they had visited, you could tell by the way they talked that their tongues were more tuned to lying than telling the truth, no matter what tale they told.

Troops of hermits with their hooked staves were on their way to Walsingham, with their wenches following after. These great, long lubbers, who hated work, were got up in clerical gowns to distinguish them from laymen, and paraded as hermits for the sake of an easy life.

I saw the Friars there too—all four Orders of them—preaching to the people for what they could get. In their greed for fine clothes, they interpreted the Scriptures to suit themselves and their patrons. Many of these Doctors of Divinity can dress as handsomely as they please, for as their trade advances, so their profits increase. And now that Charity has gone into business, and become confessor-in-chief to wealthy lords, many strange things have happened in the last few years; unless the Friars and Holy Church mend their quarrel, the worst evil in the world will soon be upon us.

There was also a Pardoner, preaching like a priest. He produced a document covered with Bishops' seals, and claimed to have power to absolve all the people from broken fasts and vows of every kind. The ignorant folk believed him and were delighted. They came up and knelt to kiss his documents, while he, blinding them with letters of indulgence thrust in their faces, raked in their rings and jewellery with his roll of parchment!—So the people give their gold to support these gluttons, and put their trust in dirty-minded scoundrels. If the Bishop were worthy of the name, if he kept his ears open to what went on around him, his seal would not be sent out like this to deceive the people. But it is not by the Bishop's leave that this rogue preaches; for the parish priest is in league with the Pardoner, and they divide the proceeds between them—money which, but for them, would go to the poor of the parish.

Then I heard parish priests complaining to the Bishop that since the Plague their parishes were too poor to live in; so they asked permission to live in London, where they could traffic in Masses, and chime their voices to the sweet jingling of silver. Bishops and novices, Doctors of Divinity and other great divines—to whom Christ has given the charge of men's souls, and whose heads are tonsured to show that they must absolve, teach, and pray for their parishioners, and feed the poor—I saw them all living in London, even in Lent. Some took posts at Court counting the king's money, or in the Courts of Exchequer and Chancery, where they claimed his dues from the wards of the City and his right to unclaimed property. Others went into the service of lords and ladies, sitting like stewards managing household affairs—and gabbled their daily Mass and Office without devotion. Indeed, I fear that there are many whom Christ, in His great Consistory Court, will curse for ever.

Then I understood something of that power which was entrusted to Peter, to 'bind and unbind' as the Scripture puts it. Peter, by our Lord's command, left it in the hands of Love, sharing it out among the four greatest virtues, which are called Cardinal. For these are the hinges on which swing the gates of Christ's kingdom, closing against some, and opening on the bliss of Heaven to others. But as to those other Cardinals at Rome who have assumed the same name, taking upon themselves the appointment of a Pope to possess the power of St Peter, I will not call them in question. The election of a Pope requires both love and learning. There is much more I could say about the Papal Court, but it is not for me to say it.

*   *   *

Then there came into the field a king, guided by the knights. The powers of the Commons gave him his throne, and Common Sense provided men of learning to counsel him and to protect the people.

The king, with his nobles and counsellors, decided that the common people should provide them with resources; so the people devised different trades, and engaged ploughmen to labour and till the soil for the good of the whole community, as honest ploughmen should. Then the king and the people, helped by Common Sense, established law and order, so that every man might know his rights and duties.

Whereupon a long, lean, crazy fellow knelt before the king and said gravely: 'God save you, your majesty, and protect your kingdom. May He grant you grace to be so just a ruler, that you may win the love of your loyal subjects, and the reward of Heaven hereafter.'

And then from the air on high an angel of Heaven stooped down and spoke something in Latin—for the ignorant folk could not speak for themselves, they could only suffer and serve; so the angel said:

'You say, "I am a king; I am a prince,"—but in time you may be neither. It is your duty to administer the laws of Christ the King; the better to do this, be as mild as you are just. You should clothe naked justice with mercy, and sow those crops which you hope to reap. Strip justice of mercy, and you shall be judged by justice alone: sow mercy, and you shall reap mercy.'

A garrulous fellow, with his head full of quotations, took offence at these words, and retorted to the angel:

'Since a king is entitled to be a king only by the act of ruling, he is a king only in name if he does not maintain the laws.'

Whereupon all the common people, wishing to add their own piece of advice to the king, shouted out a line of Latin—let him make what he could of it—

'The king's decrees are as binding to us as the Law.'

Then all at once there ran out a horde of rats, and with them more than a thousand little mice, all coming to hold a Council to discuss their common safety. For a cat from a certain court used to come when he chose, to pounce on them and paw them, toss them about and play with them in the most alarming manner. 'We're surrounded with so many dangers,' they said, 'that we scarcely dare to move. And if we complain of his games, he'll plague us all the more and never let us alone—he'll scratch and claw us and trap us between his paws, till our lives are not worth living! If we could only think of some scheme to stop him, we could be lords in our own domain and live at ease.'

Then a certain rat, well known as an eloquent speaker, put forward an excellent plan of his own invention: 'I have noticed,' he said, 'certain liveried men in the City, who wear bright gold chains around their necks, and fancy collars. They behave like dogs off the leash, straying about wherever they like over warrens and commons; and I'm told that they sometimes go wandering off and cause trouble elsewhere. Now it has often occurred to me, that if they had bells attached to their collars, people could hear them coming and run away!

'So,' continued the rat, 'I have thought of a good scheme like that for us. We must buy a bell of brass or shining silver, attach it to a collar and hang it round the cat's neck! Then we shall be able to hear what he's up to—whether he's stirring abroad or having a rest or running out to play; and if he's in a pleasant, frisky mood, we can peep out of our holes and just put in an appearance, but if he's in a bad temper, we can take care and keep out of his way.'

The whole rat-assembly applauded this scheme. But when the bell was bought and attached to the collar, there was not a rat in the whole company who dared to fix it round the cat's neck—not for the whole realm of England! So they were disgusted with themselves and ashamed of their feeble plan, and felt that all their long labour and planning had been wasted.

Then a mouse who looked very shrewd pushed himself boldly forward, and, standing before them all, spoke like this: 'Even if we killed the cat, another like him would come to scratch us—and it would be no use our creeping under the benches! So I advise all commoners to leave him alone: and let's not be so rash as even to show him the bell.

'I heard my father say, several years ago, that when the cat is a kitten the court is a sorry place. And so it says in Holy Scripture: "Woe to that land whose king is a child." For then no one can rest for the rats at night. In any case, the cat is not after our blood while he's off catching rabbits; let us give him his due—he's content with his "venison". So surely a little trouble now is better than long years of misery and confusion. True, we should be rid of a tyrant, but what would happen?—We mice would be eating up men's malt, and you rats would tear their clothes to shreds. So thank God the cat can outrun you! For if you had your own way, you could never govern yourselves.

'Therefore my counsel is, don't offend the cat or the kitten in any way; for I can foresee all the trouble it would lead to. And let us have no more talk of this collar.— Not that I ever gave any money for it myself—though if I had, I must say I should have kept quiet about it. So let them both go, cat and kitten, leashed or unleashed, and catch what they can. Be sensible and mark my words—and let us keep out of what doesn't concern us!'

Now what this dream means you folk must guess for yourselves, for I haven't the courage to tell you—and that's God's truth!

*   *   *

Besides all this, a hundred men in silk gowns stood swaying from side to side and making speeches. These were the lawyers who served at the bar, pleading their cases for as much money as they could get. Never once did they open their mouths out of love for our Lord; indeed you could sooner measure the mist on the Malvern Hills, than get a sound out of them without first producing some cash!

I saw many more in this great concourse of people, as you shall hear presently: barons, burgesses, and peasants; bakers, brewers, and butchers; linen-weavers and tailors, tinkers and toll-collectors, masons and miners and many other tradesfolk. And all kinds of labourers suddenly appeared—shoddy workmen, who would while away their hours with bawdy songs—like 'God help you, Mistress Emma!'—while cooks with their boys cried, 'Hot pies! Hot pies! Fat pigs and geese! Come and eat!' and inn-keepers were bawling, 'White wine! Red wine! Gascon and Spanish! Wash down your meat with the finest Rhenish!'—

All this I saw in my dream, and a great deal more besides. . . .

BOOK III: LADY LUCRE AT WESTMINSTER

Lady Lucre, deserted by all her companions, was brought before the king by the beadles and bailiffs. And the king, calling one of his counsellors (I need not mention his name), told him to take her and see that she was properly looked after. 'I shall examine her myself,' the king said, 'and ask her outright which man she would really prefer. If she proves amenable and is willing to do as I tell her, I intend, God willing to pardon her for this offence.'

Then, as the king commanded, this counsellor politely put his arm round Lucre and guided her to her chamber, where music and other entertainments were provided for her amusement.

All those who resided at Westminster treated Lucre with the greatest respect. Some of the judges, with the Clergy's permission, hastened along full of gallantry and good humour, to console her as she sat in her boudoir. 'Do not lose heart, Lady Lucre,' they said. 'You have no cause for distress. We will speak to the king and smooth the way for you. And we can promise you that you will be able to marry whom you wish, in spite of Conscience and all his tricks!'

Lucre thanked them graciously for their great kindness, giving everyone presents of gold and silver vessels, with rings, rubies, and valuables of all kinds, not forgetting a gold piece even for the lowest of their retainers. Then the judges took their leave of her.

Whereupon the Clergy and Counsellors came to comfort her in the same way, saying,

'Take heart, Lady, for we will always be at your disposal, for as long as there's life left in you; don't hesitate to make full use of us.' Lucre politely returned the compliment, and said that for her part she would always be faithful to them, get them titles, and obtain seats for them in the Bishop's Court. 'You needn't worry about your education,' she said, 'as long as you're friends of mine; I'm well known in places where learning gets you nowhere.'

Her next visitor was a Friar, come to hear her confession. Speaking in the dulcet undertones of the confession-box, he said to Lucre, 'Don't worry how many men you have had to do with, clerics or laymen, or if Falsehood has hung at your heels for half a century, I will still give you absolution—for a small offering, of course—shall we say one horse-load of wheat? For that I will undertake to be your own beadsman, and spread your influence among the gentry and clergy, undermining Conscience wherever I go.'

So Lucre knelt before him and made her confession, shamelessly; and when she had told him a suitable tale or two, she gave him a coin accepting him as her beadsman and personal agent. Then, after gabbling through the form of absolution, he added, 'We are having a stained-glass window made for us, and it's proving rather expensive. If you would care to pay for the glazing yourself, and have your name engraved in the window, you may have no doubts of your eternal salvation.'

'Ah! If I can be sure of that,' the woman said, 'I will do anything for you, Father. You can count me your unfailing friend—but never be hard on those lords and ladies who give way to their lusts. Do not blame them for it, for lechery is a frailty of the flesh, a natural instinct, Father—that's what all the books say. We all began that way, so there can't be much harm in it, as long as one avoids a scandal. And it's quite the easiest to forgive of all the Seven Deadlies. So you be kind to them, and then I will roof your church, build you a cloister, whitewash your walls, glaze your windows, have paintings and images made, and pay for everything. People will all be saying I am a lay-sister of your Order.'

*   *   *

But God forbids us to blazon our good deeds on walls and windows, lest they become mere monuments of pride and worldly pomp. For all your motives and purposes lie open to God; He sees your natural greed, and knows where the money really belongs.

Therefore I advise you, lords and ladies, have done with such inscriptions, and do not cry out for the notice of men of God when you want to give alms, lest you have your reward on earth, and your Heaven too. And 'Let not thy left hand know what thy right hand doeth,' for so the Gospel bids men do good deeds.

And you Mayors and Officers who uphold the Law, and are the chief link between king and people, be sure that you punish all fraudulent tradesmen, the brewers, the bakers, the butchers, and the cooks, in your pillories and ducking-stools. For these are the men who do most harm to the poor, poisoning them with adulterated food, at extortionate prices. They grow rich by selling at retail prices, and invest in properties by robbing the bellies of the poor. For how could they build themselves such tall houses, and buy up lands and tenements, if they were honest dealers? But Lucre has begged the Mayor to accept money from them—or if not money, plate, and gold rings and other valuables—to let them stay in business undisturbed. 'For my sake,' she says, 'leave them all alone, and let them overcharge just a wee bit.'

Now hear what Solomon said for the benefit of such Mayors and officials: 'Fire shall consume the tabernacles of those who freely take bribes'—that is, all who expect gratuities or New Year boxes because they hold office will have their houses and homes burned to ashes.

*   *   *

The king, coming from his Council, sent for Lucre at once, and a band of his officers, in great high spirits, escorted her to his private chamber.

Then the king spoke graciously to her and said, 'This is not the first time, Lady, that you have acted unwisely, but you never did worse than when you accepted Fraud! However, I will forgive you this time—but never do such a thing again, as long as you live.

'Now I have a knight called Conscience, who has recently come from overseas. If he is willing to make you his wife, will you have him?'

'Certainly, my liege,' answered the Lady. 'God forbid that I should refuse! Why, I'd rather be hanged than shirk any wish of yours.'

So Sir Conscience was summoned to appear before the king and Council. He made a low obeisance to the king, and knelt to hear his wishes.

'Are you willing to marry this woman, if I give my consent?' said the king. 'She would gladly accept you as a husband.'

'God forbid!' said Conscience, 'I'd rather be damned than marry such a wife! She is fickle and faithless, and has led countless men into sin. Thousands already have been betrayed by trusting in her riches. She makes wantons of wives and widows, using presents as baits to lure them into sin. She has poisoned Popes and corrupted Holy Church, and your own father she ruined by her false promises. I swear to God you won't find a greater bawd between Heaven and hell, though you search the whole earth! She's as lecherous as a monkey—a talebearer too!—and as common as a cart-track to every wayfaring wretch—monks and minstrels and the lepers that lie under the hedges. The only men who treat her with respect are jurors and summoners and suchlike, and County Sheriffs who would be ruined without her; for by bribing them she causes men to lose their lands and their lives. She gives gold to the gaolers to let prisoners loose, and lets criminals wander at large, while honest men, who have done no harm, are seized, cast into irons, and hanged, to satisfy her spite.

'What does she care about threats of excommunication? She keeps the Bishop's men in clothes, and can get absolution whenever she likes. Her purse can do more in a single month than the king's privy seal can do in six. Even the Pope confides in her —as is well known to those who buy livings in Rome; for it is she and Simony who seal her Papal mandates.

'She makes bishops of men who can scarcely read. She provides livings for parsons and for lawless priests to spend their lives with mistresses and concubines, and rear families. Heaven help that land where she wins the king's favour! For she will always smile on falsehood and trample on the truth.

'Christ! How her jewels mow down the magistrates! How she perjures herself in the law-courts, and chokes up the course of justice! Her florins fly so thick, that truth is smothered with them. She bends the Law as she likes, chooses her own days for settling disputes, and makes men lose for her sake what the Law might have won them. A poor man is bewildered and confused: he may plead in the courts for ever, but the Law will not move an inch; it hates to reach a verdict, and without bribes or presents Lucre will satisfy no one.

'So she brings disaster upon barons and burgesses, and all commoners who try to lead honest lives. This, my liege, is her way of life—and may God confound her and all her supporters! For she has coupled Education with Avarice, and she holds such sway over men of property that, no matter how the poor are wronged, there is nothing they can do about it.'

Then Lucre looked aggrieved, and whined to the king for a chance to speak and defend herself; and the king willingly allowed her. 'Excuse yourself if you can, by all means,' he said, 'for with all these accusations of Conscience, you are like to be packed off for good.'

'Ah, my good lord,' said the Lady, 'when you know the truth of the matter you will credit him less. In times of trouble, Lucre is very useful.—And you know well enough, Conscience, that I did not come here in pride, to quarrel, or slander you. You know too, you liar, unless you try to gloss it over, that you have come crawling to me many times in the past, and laid your hands on my gold and doled it out as you liked. So why you should be so angry with me now, I can't imagine. For I can still honour you with my favours, if I choose, and bolster up your courage in ways that you never dreamt of.

'But you have foully slandered me before the king here. For I never killed, or planned the death of a king, nor did any of the things that you say—as the king himself will bear me witness. And in the French Wars, I did him no wrong at all—unlike you, who shamed him again and again, creeping into hovels to keep your fingers warm, fearing the winter would last for ever, frightened to death of a few storm-clouds—and then rushing home because your belly was empty!

'And you robbed the poor men without pity, you thief, and carried their money away on your back, to sell at Calais. And meanwhile, I stayed behind with my lord, to protect his life. I cheered his men up and made them forget their miseries, and slapped them on the back to liven up their spirits, till they fairly danced for joy, hoping to have me all to themselves. By God, if I had been Commander of his men, I wager my life I'd have made him master of that whole land, from end to end—and king, too, and what an honour that would have been for his family—the smallest brat among them would now be as good as a baron!

'But then you, Conscience, stepped in with your coward's advice—to give it all up, the richest realm under the sun, for a handful of silver!

'Why, a king, as guardian of the realm, is bound to give lucre to those who serve him, and show courtesy to all men, especially to foreigners, with handsome gifts. Such openhandedness makes people love and respect him. And without me, how could the nobles, or even emperors, retain young men to ride about for them? Even the Pope and the prelates accept offerings, and reward those who uphold their laws. Servants all get fixed wages for services rendered; beggars demand a reward for their begging, and minstrels for entertaining. The king receives money from his men, to keep peace in the land. Schoolmasters get paid for their pupils; skilled workmen take fees for their apprentices; and even priests expect a wage, of food or Mass-offerings, for teaching people virtue; and surely merchants must make a profit, to carry on their trade. There's not a man on earth that can live without lucre!'

'By Heaven!' said the king to Conscience, 'Lucre has certainly won her point, it seems to me.'

'No,' said Conscience, and he knelt down on the ground. 'By your leave, my lord, there are two different kinds of payment. The one is the gift of Heaven which God, of His grace, gives to those who do their work well on earth. The Psalmist speaks of this: "Lord, who shall dwell in thy tabernacle, with thy saints? Who shall dwell in thy holy hill?" And King David answers the question too: "He that walketh uprightly, and worketh righteousness"—that is, he who is unspotted from the world, and single-minded, who has acted with reason and justice, and sought after truth; who has taught the poor, and has not lived by usury—"Who putteth not out his money to usury, nor taketh rewards against the innocent." So all who help the innocent and side with the righteous, doing good to them without reward, and maintaining truth, shall have this payment from God in their time of greatest need, when they leave this world.

'But there is another kind of payment, a lucre without measure, which men in authority grasp at—the bribes they get for supporting evil-doers. And of them the Psalter also speaks:

"In whose hands is wickedness:
    and their right hand is full of gifts."

And even the man who receives money from them shall pay a bitter price for it, unless the Scripture lies! And priests who seek their own pleasure, exacting money for the Masses they sing, gain all their reward on earth, as we read in St Matthew: "Verily I say unto you, they have their reward."

'The money, my liege, which labourers receive from their master, is not lucre at all, but a fair wage. Nor is there any lucre in trading with goods: it is simply an exchange, one pennyworth for another.

'Tell me, you shameless Lucre, did you never read the Book of Samuel, nor notice why vengeance fell on Saul and his children? For God sent a message to Saul, by his prophet Samuel, that Agag, king of the Amalekites, and all his people, must die for a deed done by their ancestors. "Therefore," said Samuel to Saul, "God himself commands you to obey Him and do His will, to go with thy host to the land of the Amalekites, and slay all that you find there—men and beasts alike, burn them to death; wives, widows, and children, all their estates and belongings, and everything you find, burn it, and carry nothing away, no matter how valuable. Take no booty; destroy it all; spare nothing, and it will be better for you."

'And because Saul coveted the booty, and spared the life of the king and of his beasts, against the prophet's warning, God told Samuel that Saul and all his seed should die, and come to a shameful end. This was what lucre did for Saul—such harm that

God hated him for evermore, and all his heirs after him. But I had better draw no conclusions from this, lest anyone should be offended. For this world is so changed now, that the man who tells the truth to those in power is condemned first.

'Yet I am certain of one thing, for Common Sense has taught me to believe it: that Reason shall reign supreme and rule over the nations. And there are many who shall share the fate of Agag; for once more Samuel shall slay him, and Saul shall be condemned, and David shall be crowned king and subdue all kingdoms. Then one Christian king shall rule over the whole world.

'And no more shall Lucre prevail, as she does now; but Love and Meekness and Honesty shall be the rulers of the earth, and the guardians of truth.

'And if any man commits a sin against truth, or takes a bribe to permit a falsehood, he shall have but one judge, and that is Honesty. Lawyers shall no longer plead at the bar with their hoods of silk and cloaks of ermine. For as it is now, Lucre is a law unto herself: she makes lords of criminals, and rules kingdoms over the heads of judges.

'But Natural Love and Conscience shall come together, and turn Law into an honest workman.—Such love shall arise, and such peace and perfect truth among the people, that the Jews, amazed that men should be so truthful, will be filled with joy, thinking that Moses or the Messiah has come to earth.

'And any man who carries a sword, a lance, an axe, a dagger, or any kind of weapon, shall be put to death, unless he sends it to the smithy to be turned into a scythe, a sickle, or a ploughshare.—"They shall beat their swords into ploughshares, and their spears into pruning hooks." And men will pass their time in digging or ploughing, spinning yarn or spreading dung, or else there will be nothing for them to do.

'And the only kind of hunting left to priests will be for the souls of the dead; and they will hammer at their Psalms from morn till night. For if any of them hunt with hawks and hounds, they shall lose their boasted livings.

'No king or knight or officer or Mayor shall tyrannize over the people, or summon them to serve on juries and compel them to take oaths. But each criminal will be punished according to his crime, heavily or lightly as Truth shall decide. And the King's Court, the Common Court, the Church Court, and the Chapter shall all be one Court, with a single judge, one True-tongue, an honest man who never opposed me. There shall be no more battles, and any blacksmith who forges a weapon shall perish by it.

> "Nation shall not lift up sword against nation,
>   neither shall they learn war any more."

'But before this comes to pass, men shall see the worst; and the sign of its coming will be six suns in the sky, with a ship and half a sheaf of arrows. And then an Easter full moon shall convert the Jews; and when they see these things, the Saracens shall sing the *Gloria in Excelsis*. But to you, Lucre, and to Mahomet, will come disaster; for it is written,

> "A good name is rather to be chosen than great riches,
>   and loving favour rather than silver or gold." '

Then Lucre suddenly grew as furious as the wind. 'I don't know any Latin,' she said,—'I leave that to the scholars. But you should read what Solomon says in the Book of Proverbs: "He that giveth gifts winneth the victory, and hath much honour withal." '

'Your quotation is quite correct, Madam,' said Conscience. 'But you are like a certain lady reading the Scriptures, who, when she came to the words "Prove all things," was highly delighted. However, the text broke off at the end of a page, and if she had turned over, she would have found the rest of it—"Hold fast to that which is good."

'You, my Lady, have done the same as she did. You've discovered half the text, but you could never find the rest, not if you pored over Proverbs all day long: you need a scholar to turn the pages for you! Your version would suit the lords of this world very well, but the sequel is bitter medicine for those who take bribes. For this is the text complete—

"He that giveth gifts winneth the victory, and hath much honour withal, *but he taketh away the soul of him that receiveth them." '. . .*

"THE POOREST FOLK ARE OUR NEIGHBOURS"

The poorest folk are our neighbours, if we look about us—the prisoners in dungeons and the poor in their hovels, overburdened with children, and rack-rented by land-lords. For whatever they save by spinning they spend on rent, or on milk and oatmeal to make gruel and fill the bellies of their children who clamour for food. And they themselves are often famished with hunger, and wretched with the miseries of winter —cold, sleepless nights, when they get up to rock the cradle cramped in a corner, and rise before dawn to card and comb the wool, to wash and scrub and mend, and wind yarn and peel rushes for their rushlights.—The miseries of these women who dwell in hovels are too pitiful to read, or describe in verse.

Yet there are many more who suffer like them—men who go hungry and thirsty all day long, and strive their utmost to hide it—ashamed to beg, or tell their neigh-bours of their need. I've seen enough of the world to know how they suffer, these men who have many children, and no means but their trade to clothe and feed them. For many hands are waiting to grasp the few pence they earn, and while the Friars feast on roast venison, they have bread and thin ale, with perhaps a scrap of cold meat or stale fish. And on Fridays and fast-days a farthing's worth of cockles or a few mussels would be a feast for such folk. I tell you, it would be a real charity to help men so burdened, and comfort these cottagers along with the blind and the lame.

ح§ *Part Two*

Medieval Christianity

The Saints

In the Middle Ages, Christianity was primarily not a system of ideas but
a way of life. It was the "imitation of Christ," to quote the title of an
influential fifteenth-century work. This way of life was described in the
Gospels, of course, but it was also to be seen in the lives of the saints,
those paragons of virtue who demonstrated the power of God's grace
in overcoming temptations of all kinds. Just as the ancient Greeks had
thrilled to the exploits of Achilles and Odysseus, medieval people never
tired of the achievements of their own heroes in the never-ending
struggle against the forces of evil. The signs and wonders that filled the
legends about these holy men were a constant reassurance that God
was indeed with them in this struggle.

One of the favorite collections of such legends, and a work of considerable historical merit, was The Ecclesiastical History of the English
Nation by Baeda, a Benedictine monk who is usually called the Venerable Bede (ca. 673–735). In this, his best-known book, Bede tells
the story of the coming of Christianity to England; he includes capsule
biographies of many of the men and women who brought it there.
The vision of the man from Cuningham, as described by Bede in the
third selection below, was an important source of medieval ideas about
the afterlife and probably inspired Dante's Divine Comedy.

A much later collection of saints' lives, lacking the narrative unity of
Bede's book but equally popular, was The Golden Legend of Jacobus
de Voragine (ca. 1230–1298). The organizing principle of Voragine's
work is the calendar: each day of the year is sacred to the memory of
some saint, and his life story is accordingly given for the convenience
of daily worshippers. Voragine is much less critical than Bede in his
use of sources, and many of his "saints" are clearly pagan gods or heroes
in disguise. Others like Saint Christopher in the selection below, show a
wonderful blend of pagan and Christian virtues. William Caxton's
translation of The Golden Legend was one of the first books printed
in English and went through many editions, indicating that this sort
of spirituality met the needs of the common man in those times.

THE ECCLESIASTICAL HISTORY OF THE ENGLISH NATION

Bede

HOW CHAD WAS MADE BISHOP OF THE MERCIANS; OF HIS LIFE, DEATH, AND BURIAL [A.D. 669]

At that time, the Mercians were governed by King Wulfhere, who, on the death of Jaruman, desired of Theodore to supply him and his people with a bishop; but Theodore would not obtain a new one for them, but requested of King Oswy that Chad might be their bishop. He then lived retired at his monastery, which is at Lestingau, Wilfrid filling the bishopric of York, and of all the Northumbrians, and likewise of the Picts, as far as the dominions of King Oswy extended. And, seeing that it was the custom of that most reverend prelate to go about the work of the Gospel to several places rather on foot than on horseback, Theodore commanded him to ride whenever he had a long journey to undertake; and finding him very unwilling to omit his former pious labour, he himself, with his hands, lifted him on the horse; for he thought him a holy man, and therefore obliged him to ride wherever he had need to go. Chad, having received the bishopric of the Mercians and Lindisfarne, took care to administer the same with great rectitude of life, according to the example of the ancients. King Wulfhere also gave him land of fifty families, to build a monastery, at the place called Ad Barve, or "At the Wood," in the province of Lindsey, wherein marks of the regular life instituted by him continue to this day.

He had his episcopal see in the place called Lichfield, in which he also died, and was buried, and where the see of the succeeding bishops of that province still continues. He had built himself a habitation not far from the church, wherein he was wont to pray and read with seven or eight of the brethren, as often as he had any spare time from the labour and ministry of the word. When he had most gloriously governed the church in that province two years and a half, the Divine Providence so ordaining, there came round a season like that of which Ecclesiastes says, "That there is a time to cast stones, and a time to gather them;" for there happened a mortality sent from heaven, which, by means of the death of the flesh, translated the stones of the church from their earthly places to the heavenly building. And when, after many of the church of that most reverend prelate had been taken out of the flesh, his hour also drew near wherein he was to pass out of this world to our Lord, it happened one day that he was in the aforesaid dwelling, with only one brother, called Owini, his other companions being upon some reasonable occasion returned to the church. Now Owini was a monk of great merit, having forsaken the world with the pure intention of obtaining the heavenly reward; worthy in all respects to have the secrets of our Lord revealed to him, and worthy to have credit given by his hearers to what he said, for he came with Queen Etheldrid from the province of the East Angles, and was her prime minister, and governor of her family. As the fervour of his faith increased, resolving to

Bede, *The Ecclesiastical History of the English Nation* (New York: E. P. Dutton & Co., Inc., 1910), pp. 165–170, 194–197, 241–246.

renounce the world, he did not go about it slothfully, but so fully forsook the things of this world, that, quitting all he had, clad in a plain garment, and carrying an axe and hatchet in his hand, he came to the monastery of that most reverend prelate, called Lestingau; denoting, that he did not go to the monastery to live idle, as some do, but to labour, which he also confirmed by practice; for as he was less capable of meditating on the Holy Scriptures, he the more earnestly applied himself to the labour of his hands. In short, he was received by the bishop into the house aforesaid, and there entertained with the brethren, and whilst they were engaged within in reading, he was without, doing such things as were necessary.

One day when he was thus employed abroad, and his companions were gone to the church, as I began to state, the bishop was alone reading or praying in the oratory of that place, when on a sudden, as he afterwards said, he heard the voice of persons singing most sweetly and rejoicing, and appearing to descend from heaven. Which voice he said he first heard coming from the south-east, and that afterwards it drew near him, till it came to the roof of the oratory where the bishop was, and entering therein, filled the same and all about it. He listened attentively to what he heard, and after about half an hour, perceived the same song of joy to ascend from the roof of the said oratory, and to return to heaven the same way it came, with inexpressible sweetness. When he had stood some time astonished, and seriously revolving in his mind what it might be, the bishop opened the window of the oratory, and making a noise with his hand, as he was often wont to do, ordered him to come in to him. He accordingly went hastily in, and the bishop said to him, "Make haste to the church and cause the seven brothers to come hither, and do you come with them." When they were come, he first admonished them to preserve the virtue of peace among themselves, and towards all others; and indefatigably to practise the rules of regular discipline, which they had either been taught by him, or seen him observe or had noticed in the words or actions of the former fathers. Then he added, that the day of his death was at hand; for, said he, "that amiable guest, who was wont to visit our brethren, has vouchsafed also to come to me this day, and to call me out of this world. Return, therefore, to the church, and speak to the brethren, that they in their prayers recommend my passage to our Lord, and that they be careful to provide for their own, the hour whereof is uncertain, by watching, prayer, and good works."

When he had spoken thus much and more, and they, having received his blessing, had gone away in sorrow, he who had heard the heavenly song returned alone, and prostrating himself on the ground, said, "I beseech you, father, may I be permitted to ask a question?"—"Ask what you will," answered the bishop. Then he added, "I entreat you to tell me what song of joy was that which I heard coming upon this oratory, and after some time returning to heaven?" The bishop answered, "If you heard the singing, and know of the coming of the heavenly company, I command you, in the name of our Lord, that you do not tell the same to any before my death. They were angelic spirits, who came to call me to my heavenly reward, which I have always longed after, and they promised they would return seven days hence, and take me away with them." Which was accordingly fulfilled, as had been said to him; for being presently seized with a languishing distemper, and the same daily increasing, on the seventh day, as had been promised to him, when he had prepared for death by receiving the body and blood of our Lord, his soul being delivered from the prison of the body, the angels, as may justly be believed, attending him, he departed to the joys of heaven.

It is no wonder that he joyfully beheld the day of his death, or rather the day of our Lord, which he had always carefully expected till it came; for notwithstanding his many merits of continence, humility, teaching, prayer, voluntary poverty, and other virtues, he was so full of the fear of God, so mindful of his last end in all his actions, that, as I was informed by one of the brothers who instructed me in Divinity, and who had been bred in his monastery, and under his direction, whose name was Trumhere, if it happened that there blew a strong gust of wind when he was reading or doing any other thing, he immediately called upon God for mercy, and begged it might be extended to all mankind. If the wind grew stronger, he closed his book, and prostrating himself on the ground, prayed still more earnestly. But, if it proved a violent storm of wind or rain, or else that the earth and air were filled with thunder and lightning, he would repair to the church, and devote himself to prayers and repeating of psalms till the weather became calm. Being asked by his followers why he did so, he answered, "Have not you read—'The Lord also thundered in the heavens, and the Highest gave forth his voice. Yea, he sent out his arrows and scattered them; and he shot out lightnings, and discomfited them.' For the Lord moves the air, raises the winds, darts lightning, and thunders from heaven, to excite the inhabitants of the earth to fear Him; to put them in mind of the future judgment; to dispel their pride, and vanquish their boldness, by bringing into their thoughts that dreadful time, when the heavens and the earth being in a flame, He will come in the clouds, with great power and majesty, to judge the quick and the dead. Wherefore," said he, "it behoves us to answer his heavenly admonition with due fear and love; that, as often as He lifts his hand through the trembling sky, as it were to strike, but does not yet let it fall, we may immediately implore his mercy; and searching the recesses of our hearts, and cleansing the filth of our vices, we may carefully behave ourselves so as never to be struck."

With this revelation and account of the aforesaid brother, concerning the death of this prelate, agrees the discourse of the most reverend Father Egbert, above spoken of, who long led a monastic life with the same Chad, when both were youths, in Ireland, praying, observing continency, and meditating on the Holy Scriptures. But when he afterwards returned into his own country, the other continued in a strange country for our Lord's sake till the end of his life. A long time after, Hygbald, a most holy and continent man, who was an abbot in the province of Lindsey, came out of Britain to visit him, and whilst these holy men were discoursing of the life of the former fathers, and rejoicing to imitate the same, mention was made of the most reverend prelate, Chad, whereupon Egbert said, "I know a man in this island, still in the flesh, who, when that prelate passed out of this world, saw the soul of his brother Cedd, with a company of angels, descending from heaven, who, having taken his soul along with them, returned thither again." Whether he said this of himself, or some other, we do not certainly know; but the same being said by so great a man, there can be no doubt of the truth thereof.

Chad died on the 2nd of March, and was first buried by St. Mary's Church, but afterwards, when the church of the most holy prince of the apostles, Peter, was built, his bones were translated into it. In both which places, as a testimony of his virtue, frequent miraculous cures are wont to be wrought. And of late, a certain distracted person, who had been wandering about everywhere, arrived there in the evening, unknown or unregarded by the keepers of the place, and having rested there all the night, went out in his perfect senses the next morning, to the surprise and delight of all; thus showing that a cure had been performed on him through the goodness of God. The place of the sepulchre is a wooden monument, made like a little house, covered, having a hole in the wall, through which those that go thither for devotion usually put in their hand and take out some of the dust, which they put into water and give to sick cattle or men to drink, upon which they are presently eased of their infirmity, and restored to health. In his place, Theodore ordained Winfrid, a good and modest man, to preside, as his predecessors had done, over the bishoprics of the Mercians, the Midland Angles, and the Lindisfarnes, of all which, Wulfhere, who was still living, was king. Winfrid was one of the clergy of the prelate he had succeeded, and had for a considerable time filled the office of deacon under him.

HOW QUEEN ETHELDRIDA ALWAYS PRESERVED HER VIRGINITY, AND HER BODY SUFFERED NO CORRUPTION IN THE GRAVE [A.D. 660]

King Egfrid took to wife, Etheldrida, the daughter of Anna, king of the East Angles, of whom mention has been often made; a man very religious, and in all respects renowned for his inward disposition and actions. She had before been given in marriage to another, viz. to Tonbert, chief of the Southern Girvii; but he died soon after he had received her, and she was given to the aforesaid king. Though she lived with him twelve years, yet she preserved the glory of perfect virginity, as I was informed by Bishop Wilfrid, of blessed memory, of whom I inquired, because some questioned the truth thereof; and he told me that he was an undoubted witness of her virginity, forasmuch as Egfrid promised he would give many lands and much money, if he could persuade the queen to consent to pay the marriage duty, for he knew the queen loved no man so much as himself; and it is not to be doubted that the same might in one instance take place in our age, which true histories tell us happened several times in former ages, through the assistance of the same Lord who has promised to continue with us unto the end of the world; for the miraculous circumstance that her flesh, being buried, could not suffer corruption, is a token that she had not been defiled by familiarity with man.

She had long requested the king that he would permit her to lay aside worldly cares, and to serve only the true King, Christ, in a monastery; and having at length with difficulty prevailed, she went as a nun into the monastery of the Abbess Ebba, who was aunt to King Egfrid, at the place called the city Coludi, having taken the veil from the hands of the aforesaid Bishop Wilfrid; but a year after she was herself made abbess in the country called Ely, where, having built a monastery, she began, by works and examples of a heavenly life, to be the virgin mother of very many virgins dedicated to God. It is reported of her, that from the time of her entering into the monastery, she never wore any linen but only woollen garments, and would rarely wash in a hot bath, unless just before any of the great festivals, as Easter, Whitsuntide, and the Epiphany, and then she did it last of all, after having, with the assistance of those about her, first washed the other servants of God there present; besides, she seldom did eat above once a day, excepting on the great solemnities, or some other urgent occasion, unless some considerable distemper obliged her. From the time of matins she continued in the church at prayer till it was day; some also say, that by the spirit of prophecy, she, in the presence of all, not only foretold the pestilence of which she was to die, but also the number of those that should be then snatched away out of her monastery. She was taken to our Lord, in the midst of her flock, seven years after she had been made abbess; and, as she had ordered, was buried among them, in such a manner as she had died, in a wooden coffin.

She was succeeded in the office of abbess by her sister Sexberga, who had been wife to Erconbert, king of Kent; who, when her sister had been buried sixteen years, thought fit to take up her bones, and, putting them into a new coffin, to translate them into the church. Accordingly she ordered some of the brothers to provide a stone to make a coffin of; they accordingly went on board ship, because the country of Ely is on every side encompassed with the sea or marshes, and has no large stones, and came to a small abandoned city, not far from thence, which, in the language of the English, is called Grantchester, and presently, near the city walls, they found a white marble coffin, most beautifully wrought, and neatly covered with a lid of the same sort of stone. Concluding therefore that God had prospered their journey, they returned thanks to Him, and carried it to the monastery.

The body of the holy virgin and spouse of Christ, when her grave was opened, being brought into sight, was found as free from corruption as if she had died and been buried on that very day; as the aforesaid Bishop Wilfrid, and many others that know it, can testify. But the physician, Cynefrid, who was present at her death, and when she was taken up out of the grave, was wont of more certain knowledge to relate, that in her sickness she had a very great swelling under her jaw. "And I was ordered," said he, "to lay open that swelling, to let out the noxious matter in it, which I did, and she seemed to be somewhat more easy for two days, so that many thought she might recover from her distemper; but the third day the former pains returning, she was soon snatched out of the world, and exchanged all pain and death for everlasting life and health. And when so many years after her bones were to be taken out of the grave, a pavilion being spread over it, all the congregation of brothers were on the one side, and of sisters on the other, standing about it singing, and the abbess, with a few being gone to take up and wash the bones, on a sudden we heard the abbess within loudly cry out, 'Glory be to the name of the Lord.' Not long after they called me in, opening the door of the pavilion, where I found the body of the holy virgin taken out of the grave and laid on a bed, as if it had been asleep; then taking off the veil from the face, they also showed the incision which I had made, healed up; so that, to my great astonishment, instead of the open gaping wound with which she had been buried, there then appeared only an extraordinary slender scar.

"Besides, all the linen cloths in which the body had been buried, appeared entire and as fresh as if they had been that very day wrapped about her chaste limbs." It is reported, that when she was much troubled with the aforesaid swelling and pain in her jaw, she was much pleased with that sort of distemper, and wont to say, "I know that I deservedly bear the weight of my sickness on my neck, for I remember, when I was very young, I bore there the needless weight of jewels; and therefore I believe the Divine goodness would have me endure the pain in my neck, that I may be absolved from the guilt of my needless levity, having now, instead of gold and precious stones, a red swelling and burning on my neck." It happened also that by the touch of that linen, devils were expelled from bodies possessed, and other distempers were sometimes cured; and the coffin she was first buried in is reported to have cured some of distempers in the eyes, who, praying with their heads touching that coffin, presently were delivered from the pain or dimness in their eyes. They washed the virgin's body, and having clothed it in new garments, brought it into the church, and laid it in the coffin that had been brought, where it is held in great veneration to this day. The coffin was found in a wonderful manner, as fit for the virgin's body as if it had been made purposely for her, and the place for the head particularly cut, exactly fit for her head, and shaped to a nicety.

Ely is in the province of the East Angles, a country of about six hundred families, in the nature of an island, enclosed, as has been said, either with marshes or waters, and therefore it has its name from the great plenty of eels taken in those marshes; there the aforesaid servant of Christ desired to have a monastery, because, as we have before observed, she was descended from that same province of the East Angles.

OF ONE AMONG THE NORTHUMBRIANS, WHO ROSE FROM THE DEAD, AND RELATED THE THINGS WHICH HE HAD SEEN, SOME EXCITING TERROR AND OTHERS DELIGHT [A.D. 696]

At this time a memorable miracle, and like to those of former days, was wrought in Britain; for, to the end that the living might be saved from the death of the soul, a certain person, who had been some time dead, rose again to life, and related many remarkable things he had seen; some of which I have thought fit here briefly to take notice of. There was a master of a family in that district of the Northumbrians which is called Cuningham, who led a religious life, as did also all that belonged to him. This man fell sick, and his distemper daily increasing, being brought to extremity, he died in the beginning of the night; but in the morning early, he suddenly came to life again, and sat up, upon which all those that sat about the body weeping, fled away in a great fright, only his wife, who loved him best, though in a great consternation and trembling, remained with him. He, comforting her, said, "Fear not, for I am now truly risen from death, and permitted again to live among men; however, I am not to live hereafter as I was wont, but from henceforward after a very different manner." Then rising immediately, he repaired to the oratory of the little town, and continuing in prayer till day, immediately divided all his substance into three parts; one whereof he gave to his wife, another to his children, and the third, belonging to himself, he instantly distributed among the poor. Not long after, he repaired to the monastery of Melrose, which is almost enclosed by the winding of the river Tweed, and having been shaven, went into a private dwelling, which the abbot had provided, where he continued till the day of his death, in such extraordinary contrition of mind and body, that though his tongue had been silent, his life declared that he had seen many things either to be dreaded or coveted, which others knew nothing of.

Thus he related what he had seen. "He that led me had a shining countenance and a bright garment, and we went on silently, as I thought, towards the north-east. Walking on, we came to a vale of great breadth and depth, but of infinite length; on the left it appeared full of dreadful flames, the other side was no less horrid for violent hail and cold snow flying in all directions; both places were full of men's souls, which seemed by turns to be tossed from one side to the other, as it were by a violent storm; for when the wretches could no longer endure the excess of heat, they leaped into the middle of the cutting cold; and finding no rest there, they leaped back again into the middle of the unquenchable flames. Now whereas an innumerable multitude of deformed spirits were thus alternately tormented far and near, as far as could be seen, without any intermission, I began to think that this perhaps might be hell, of whose intolerable flames I had often heard talk. My guide, who went before me, answered to my thought, saying, 'Do not believe so, for this is not the hell you imagine.'

"When he had conducted me, much frightened with that horrid spectacle, by degrees, to the farther end, on a sudden I saw the place begin to grow dusk and filled with darkness. When I came into it, the darkness, by degrees, grew so thick, that I could see nothing besides it and the shape and garment of him that led me. As we went on through the shades of night, on a sudden there appeared before us frequent globes of black flames, rising as it were out of a great pit, and falling back again into the same. When I had been conducted thither, my leader suddenly vanished, and left me alone in the midst of darkness and this horrid vision, whilst those same globes of fire, without intermission, at one time flew up and at another fell back into the bottom of the abyss; and I observed that all the flames, as they ascended, were full of human souls, which, like sparks flying up with smoke, were sometimes thrown on high, and again, when the vapour of the fire ceased, dropped down into the depth below. Moreover, an insufferable stench came forth with the vapours, and filled all those dark places.

"Having stood there a long time in much dread, not knowing what to do, which way to turn, or what end I might expect, on a sudden I heard behind me the noise of a most hideous and wretched lamentation, and at the same time a loud laughing, as of a rude multitude insulting captured enemies. When that noise, growing plainer, came up to me, I observed a gang of evil spirits dragging the howling and lamenting souls of men into the midst of the darkness, whilst they themselves laughed and rejoiced. Among those men, as I could discern, there was one shorn like a clergyman, a layman, and a woman. The evil spirits that dragged them went down into the midst of the burning pit; and as they went down deeper, I could no longer distinguish between the lamentation of the men and the laughing of the devils, yet I still had a confused sound in my ears. In the meantime, some of the dark spirits ascended from that flaming abyss, and running forward, beset me on all sides, and much perplexed me with their glaring eyes and the stinking fire which proceeded from their mouths and nostrils; and threatened to lay hold on me with burning tongs, which they had in their hands, yet they durst not touch me, though they frightened me. Being thus on all sides enclosed with enemies and darkness, and looking about on every side for assistance, there appeared behind me, on the way that I came, as it were, the brightness of a star shining amidst the darkness; which increased by degrees, and came rapidly towards me: when it drew near, all those evil spirits, that sought to carry me away with their tongs, dispersed and fled.

"He, whose approach put them to flight, was the same that led me before; who, then turning towards the right, began to lead me, as it were, towards the south-east, and having soon brought me out of the darkness, conducted me into an atmosphere of clear light. While he thus led me in open light, I saw a vast wall before us, the length and height of which, in every direction, seemed to be altogether boundless. I began to wonder why we went up to the wall, seeing no door, window, or path through it. When we came to the wall, we were presently, I know not by what means, on the top of it, and within it was a vast and delightful field, so full of fragrant flowers that the odour of its delightful sweetness immediately dispelled the stink of the dark furnace, which had pierced me through and through. So great was the light in this place, that it seemed to exceed the brightness of the day, or the sun in its meridian height. In this field were innumerable assemblies of men in white, and many companies seated together rejoicing. As he led me through the midst of those happy inhabitants, I began to think that this might, perhaps, be the kingdom of heaven, of which I had often heard so much. He answered to my thought, saying, 'This is not the kingdom of heaven, as you imagine.'

"When we had passed those mansions of blessed souls and gone farther on, I discovered before me a much more beautiful light, and therein heard sweet voices of persons singing, and so wonderful a fragrancy proceeded from the place, that the other which I had before thought most delicious, then seemed to me but very indifferent; even as that extraordinary brightness of the flowery field, compared with this, appeared mean and inconsiderable. When I began to hope we should enter that delightful place, my guide on a sudden stood still; and then turning back, led me back by the way we came.

"When we returned to those joyful mansions of the souls in white, he said to me, 'Do you know what all these things are which you have seen?' I answered, I did not; and then he replied, 'That vale you saw so dreadful for consuming flames and cutting cold, is the place in which the souls of those are tried and punished, who, delaying to confess and amend their crimes, at length have recourse to repentance at the point of death, and so depart this life; but nevertheless because they, even at their death, confessed and repented, they shall all be received into the kingdom of heaven at the day of judgment; but many are relieved before the day of judgment, by the prayers, alms, and fasting, of the living, and more especially by masses. That fiery and stinking pit, which you saw, is the mouth of hell, into which whosoever falls shall never be delivered to all eternity. This flowery place, in which you see these most beautiful young people, so bright and merry, is that into which the souls of those are received who depart the body in good works, but who are not so perfect as to deserve to be immediately admitted into the kingdom of heaven; yet they shall all, at the day of judgment, see Christ, and partake of the joys of his kingdom; for whoever are perfect in thought, word and deed, as soon as they depart the body, immediately enter into the kingdom of heaven; in the neighbourhood, whereof that place is, where you heard the sound of sweet singing, with the fragrant odour and bright light. As for you, who are now to return to your body, and live among men again, if you will endeavour nicely to examine your actions, and direct your speech and behaviour in righteousness and simplicity, you shall, after death, have a place or residence among these joyful troops of blessed souls; for when I left you for a while, it was to know how you were to be disposed of.' When he had said this to me, I much abhorred returning to my body, being delighted with the sweetness and beauty of the place I beheld, and with the company of those I saw in it. However, I durst not ask him any questions; but in the meantime, on a sudden, I found myself alive among men."

Now these and other things which this man of God saw, he would not relate to slothful persons and such as lived negligently; but only to those who, being terrified with the dread of torments, or delighted with the hopes of heavenly joys, would make use of his words to advance in piety. In the neighbourhood of his cell lived one Hemgils, a monk, eminent in the priesthood, which he honoured by his good works: he is still living, and leading a solitary life in Ireland, supporting his declining age with coarse bread and cold water. He often went to that man, and asking several questions, heard of him all the particulars of what he had seen when separated from his body; by whose relation we also came to the knowledge of those few particulars which we have briefly set down. He also related his visions to King Alfrid, a man most learned in all respects, and was by him so willingly and attentively heard, that at his request he was admitted into the monastery above-mentioned, and received the monastic tonsure; and the said king, when he happened to be in those parts, very often went to hear him. At that time the religious and humble abbot and priest, Ethelwald, presided over the monastery, and now with worthy conduct possesses the episcopal see of the church of Lindisfarne.

He had a more private place of residence assigned him in that monastery, where he might apply himself to the service of his Creator in continual prayer. And as that place lay on the bank of the river, he was wont often to go into the same to do penance in his body, and many times to dip quite under the water, and to continue saying psalms or prayers in the same as long as he could endure it, standing still sometimes up to the middle, and sometimes to the neck in water; and when he went out from thence ashore, he never took off his cold and frozen garments till they grew warm and dry on his body. And when in the winter the half-broken pieces of ice were swimming about him, which he had himself broken, to make room to stand or dip himself in the river, those who beheld it would say, "It is wonderful, brother Drithelm (for so he was called), that you are able to endure such violent cold"; he simply answered, for he was a man of much simplicity and indifferent wit, "I have seen greater cold." And when they said, "It is strange that you will endure such austerity"; he replied, "I have seen more austerity." Thus he continued, through an indefatigable desire of heavenly bliss, to subdue his aged body with daily fasting, till the day of his being called away; and thus he forwarded the salvation of many by his words and example.

THE GOLDEN LEGEND

Jacobus de Voragine

SAINT CHRISTOPHER

Before his baptism, Christopher was called Reprobus, but after his baptism he was called Christopher, which means Christ-bearer, because he bore Christ in four ways: upon his shoulders when he carried Him, in his body by his mortifications, in his mind by his devotion, and in his mouth by professing and preaching Him.

Christopher, a Canaanite, was a man of prodigious size, being twelve cubits in height, and fearful of aspect. According to certain authors who have written down his deeds, he was in the service of the king of the Canaanites, when the idea came to him that he should go in search of the most powerful king on earth, and should enter his service. Thus he went to a certain very great king, of whom it was commonly said that no other king on earth equalled him in power. And when the king saw him, he gladly received him, and gave him lodgings in his palace. But one day, in the presence of the king, a minstrel sang a song in which the Devil was named several times. And the king, who was a Christian, made the sign of the cross each time that the Devil's name was mentioned. Christopher was astonished thereat, and wondered why the king did this, and what the sign meant. But the king refused to tell him, until he said: 'Unless thou tell me, I shall no longer remain with thee!' Then the king said: 'Each time that I hear the Devil's name, I make this sign as a safeguard, lest he gain power over me and do me harm!' Then Christopher replied: 'If thou fearest that the Devil harm thee, he must be more puissant than thou! Therefore am I thwarted in my hope, for I thought to be in the service of the most powerful king on earth. So now farewell, for I shall seek out the Devil, and take him for my lord and give myself into his service!' Then he left the king and hurried off in search of the Devil. And in the desert he came face to face with a great host, whose leader, a soldier fierce and terrible of visage, came to him and asked whither he was going. And Christopher answered: 'I am in search of my lord the Devil, that I may take service with him.' And the soldier answered: 'I am he whom thou seekest!' Christopher rejoiced, and bound himself forever to the Devil. But as they marched along a common road, they came upon a cross, and the Devil, terrified, took flight, and leaving the road, led Christopher through a wild desert, and returned to the road at some distance. He asked the reason thereof, and when the Devil refused to answer, said: 'Then shall I quit thy service, unless thou tell me!' And the Devil was forced to reply: 'A certain man named Christ was once nailed to a cross, and since that time, at the sight of the cross, I take fright and flee!' 'This Christ,' answered Christopher, 'must therefore be greater and more puissant than thou; and once more I have laboured in vain, for I have not yet found the most powerful king on earth! Farewell then, for I go to seek Christ!'

The "Golden Legend" of Jacobus de Voragine, trans. G. Ryan and H. Ripperger (New York: Longmans, Green & Co., Inc., 2 vols., 1941), Part II, 377–382.

Long he sought for someone who could give him word of Christ, until at last he found a hermit who preached Christ to him and diligently instructed him in the faith. And the hermit said to him: 'The King whom thou desirest to serve demands of thee that thou fast oftentimes in His honour!' And Christopher answered: 'Let him demand somewhat else, for to fast I am not able!' 'Then He demands,' said the hermit, 'that thou offer Him many prayers!' 'Nor can I do this service,' answered Christopher, 'for I know not how to pray!' Then the hermit said: 'Knowest thou a certain river, into which many who attempt to cross tumble and are drowned?' 'I know it,' replied Christopher. 'Since thou art mighty of stature and strong of arm,' responded the hermit, 'thou couldst dwell beside the river, and carry over all who wished to cross. This would be most pleasing to Christ, the King Whom thou desirest to serve; and I hope that He may show Himself to thee there!' 'This at last is a thing that I can do,' said Christopher, 'and I promise to do it for the service of Christ!' He betook himself therefore to the river, built a hut upon its bank, and using a great pole as a staff to steady himself in the water, he bore across all who sought his aid.

When many days had passed, he lay asleep one night in his hut, when he heard a child's voice calling him and saying: 'Christopher, come out and carry me across the river!' Swiftly he hurried out of his hut, but found no one. And when he went back indoors, the same voice called to him a second time; but going out again, he found no one. But at the third call he went out, and found a child standing on the river bank, who earnestly besought him to carry him across. Christopher took the child upon his shoulders, and taking up his staff, set out through the water. But little by little the water rose, and the child became heavier than a leaden weight; and the farther he went, the higher rose the water, and the heavier grew the child, until Christopher was so sorely tried that he thought he would founder in the waves. But at last he made his way to the other bank, and set the child down, saying: 'Child, thou hast put me in dire peril, and hast weighed so heavy upon me that if I had borne the whole world upon my shoulders, it could not have burdened me more heavily!' And the child answered: 'Wonder not, Christopher, for not only hast thou borne the whole world upon thy shoulders, but Him Who created the world. For I am Christ thy King, Whom thou servest in this work! And as a sign that I say the truth, when thou shalt have returned to the other side of the river, plant thy staff in the earth near thy hut, and in the morning thou shalt see it laden with flowers and fruits!' And straightway He disappeared. And Christopher planted his staff in the earth, and rising in the morning he saw that it had borne leaves and fruits, like to a palm tree.

After this he came into Samos, a city of Lycia; and not understanding the language of this place, he prayed the Lord to give him understanding thereof. And as he prayed, the judges, thinking him mad, left him alone; and having obtained his request, he covered his face, and went to the circus, and there comforted the Christians who were being tortured for the faith. Then one of the judges struck him a blow in the face. And Christopher uncovered his face, and said: 'Were I not a Christian, I should quickly avenge this blow!' Then he planted his staff in the earth, and prayed to the Lord to make it to bloom, in order that the people might be converted. And straightway this was done, and eight thousand men were converted. Then the king sent two hundred men to seize him; but when the soldiers came and found him in prayer, they dared not molest him. The king sent as many more; and they, likewise finding him in prayer, prayed with him. Then Christopher arose and said to them: 'Whom seek ye?' And the soldiers answered: 'The king has sent us to bind thee and bring thee to him!' And Christopher replied: 'If I so will, ye shall not be able either to bind me or to lead me away!' 'If thou art unwilling to come with us,' they said, 'take thy freedom and go where thou wilt, and we shall say to the king that we could not find thee!' 'Not so,' said Christopher, 'I am ready to go with you!' But first he converted them to the faith of Christ: then he made them to bind his hands behind his back, and they led him to the king. And at the sight of him the king was terror-stricken, and fell from his seat. Then his servitors lifted him up again, and he questioned Christopher about his name and his place of origin. 'Before I was baptized,' said Christopher, 'I was called Reprobus, the outcast; but now I am called Christopher, the Christ-bearer!' And the king said: 'A fool's name hast thou taken, calling thyself after the crucified Christ, who could do naught for Himself and can do naught for thee! Mischief-doer, wherefore dost thou not offer sacrifice to our gods?' And Christopher replied: 'Well art thou called Dagnus, for thou art the death of the world and the fellow of the Devil, and thy gods are the works of the hands of men!' And the king said: 'Thou art reared among the wild beasts, and speakest wild things, not to be understood by men. Now, however, if thou offerest sacrifice, thou shalt have great honours of me; else thou shalt perish in torment!' And when the saint refused to sacrifice, he commanded him to be thrown into prison; and the soldiers who had been sent to Christopher and had been converted by him were beheaded. Then the king sent into his cell two young women fair of form but of abandoned life, called Nicaea and Aquilina, promising them rich rewards if they would entice Christopher to sin with them. But when the saint saw them, he gave himself up to prayer. And when the women sought to arouse him by gently stroking and embracing him, he arose and said to them: 'Whom seek ye, my children, and for what end have they sent you here?' And they, overcome with the brightness of his countenance, replied: 'Saint of God, have pity on us, and help us to believe in the God Whom thou preachest!' Learning of this, the king had them brought before him and said: 'You too have allowed yourselves to be led astray! I swear by the gods, if ye do not offer sacrifice, ye shall die an evil death!' Then they made answer: 'If thou wilt have us offer sacrifice, command that the streets be cleared, and that the folk gather in the temple!' Then, entering the temple, they threw their girdles about the necks of the idols and pulled them to earth, and they crumbled to dust. Then they said to the people: 'Go now, and bring physicians to heal your gods!' Then, at the king's order, Aquilina was hanged, a great stone was attached to her feet, and all her bones were broken. And when she had breathed forth her soul to the Lord, her sister Nicaea was thrown into the fire, but emerged unscathed; whereupon the king had her beheaded.

Christopher was then brought before the king, who ordered him to be beaten with iron rods, and an iron casque, heated in the fire, to be placed upon his head; and he had an iron seat made, and Christopher bound thereon, and a fire lighted underneath, and pitch thrown upon the flames. But the seat fell to pieces like wax, and Christopher arose unharmed. Then the king had him tied to a pillar, and ordered four thousand soldiers to shoot arrows at him. But the arrows hung in mid-air, nor could a single one of them touch Christopher. And when the king, thinking that he was already transfixed with arrows, shouted invectives at him, suddenly an arrow fell from the air, turned upon him, struck him in the eye, and blinded him. Then Christopher said: 'I know, O king, that I shall be dead on the morrow. When I am dead, do thou, tyrant, make a paste of my blood, rub it upon thine eyes, and thou shalt recover thy sight!' Then at the king's order he was beheaded; and the king took a little of his blood, and placed upon his eyes, saying: 'In the name of God and Saint Christopher!' And at once he was made whole. Then the king was baptized, and decreed that whoever should blaspheme against God or Saint Christopher should at once be beheaded.

ᴇᔆ JOHN THORESBY'S SERMON

> *It is inaccurate to think of the medieval parish priests and their parishioners as uniformly living in benighted ignorance. That there was a decided effort made to instruct the people systematically in church teachings, at least at some times and in some places, is illustrated by the following sermon, published in the common man's English sometime in the fourteenth century. It is a translation of a Latin sermon written by John Thoresby, Archbishop of York (died 1373), at the request of the York Convocation. As the early part of the piece itself indicates, Thoresby ordered the document to be "Englished" by a cleric named Dan John Gaytrigg so that it might be used as a manual of instruction among the people. Parts of Gaytrigg's version were written (although not printed) in alliterative verse; this accounts for the repetitive and sometimes awkward phrasing. All in all, the document is a brief but comprehensive compendium of Christian obligations.*

Here begins a sermon . . . , which teaches how confession is to be made and whereof, and in confession how many things should be considered. . . .

As a great doctor shows in his book, of all the creatures that God made in Heaven and on earth and in air or in aught else, the sovereign cause and the reason why He made them was His own good will and His goodness, through which goodness (as He is all good) He wished that some creatures of those that He made might be sharers of that bliss that lasts forever. And since no creature can come to that bliss without knowledge of God, as that cleric teaches, He made reasonable creatures—angels

Religious Pieces in Prose and Verse, George G. Perry, ed. (London: Printed for the Early English Text Society by Kegan Paul, Trench, Trubner & Co., Ltd., 1867), pp. 1–14. Rendered into modern English by Melvin Cherno.

and man—of intelligence and wisdom to know God Almighty, and through their knowledge to love Him and serve Him, and so come to that bliss that they were made for. This manner of knowing our forefathers had in the innocent state they were made in; and we should have had it also if they had not sinned; not so much as holy souls now have in Heaven, but much more than man now has on earth. For our forefathers sinned, says the prophet, and we bear the wickedness of their misdeeds; for the knowledge that they had about God Almighty was theirs through God's gift from their beginning, without travail or pain [on their part] or passing of time. And all the knowledge that we have in this world about Him comes through hearing and learning and the teaching of another, from Holy Church's law and learning, which all creatures who love God Almighty ought to know and to imitate, and so come to that bliss that never ends. And since many people now in this world are neither sufficiently learned to know God Almighty nor to love Him and serve Him as they ought to do, and (as their deeds openly show) [are] in great peril to their life and soul, and perhaps the fault may be in those who have charge of their souls and should teach them, such as prelates and parsons, vicars and priests, who have an obligation to teach them: therefore our Father the Bishop—may God Almighty save him—who (as St. Paul says in his epistle) wishes that all men be saved and know God Almighty, and especially His subjects, has arranged and ordained for the common profit in council with his clergy, that each one who under him has the care of souls preach and teach in English on Sundays, publicly, to those in their care, the law and the knowledge of God Almighty, which principally may be shown in these six things: the fourteen points that make up the Creed, the ten commandments that God has given us, the seven sacraments of Holy Church, the seven works of mercy toward our fellow Christian, the seven virtues that each man is to practice, and the seven deadly sins that each man is to reject. And he bids and commands as strongly as he can that all who have care or keeping [of souls] under him enjoin their parishioners and their subjects that they hear and learn these very six things and often rehearse them until they know them and so teach them to their children, if they have any, as soon as they are old enough to learn them. And that parsons and vicars and all parish priests inquire diligently of their subjects in the Lenten period, when they come to confession, whether they know and are acquainted with these six things; and if it be found that they do not know them that they enjoin them upon his behalf, and upon pain of penance, to know them. And since no one is to use ignorance as an excuse, our holy Father the Bishop of his goodness has ordained and bidden that they be demonstrated openly in English among the people. Wherefore now to the first of these things, that is, to know the articles which make up the Creed. As great clerics teach and show in their books, there are in the Creed fourteen points, of which seven concern God's Godhood and the other seven Christ's manhood. The first point that we are to believe of the Godhood is to believe steadfastly in a true God and that there is no other to believe in. The second is that the High Father of Heaven is steadfastly and truly God Almighty. The third is that Jesus Christ, God's Son of Heaven, is truly God equal to the Father. The fourth is that the Holy Ghost, which jointly comes of both the Father and the Son, is truly God equal to them both; and there are not two Gods, the Father and the Son, nor three Gods, the Father and the Son and the Holy Ghost, but three separate persons and only one God. The fifth article is that the Trinity—the Father and the Son and the Holy Ghost, three persons and one God—is the maker of Heaven and earth and of all things. The sixth article is that Holy Church our Mother is wholly one throughout the world, that is, a community and fellowship of all Christian people who come together in the sacraments and in other holy things that pertain to Holy Church, without which no soul is saved. The seventh article that we ought to believe is the resurrection of the flesh and life without end. For death will sunder our bodies and our souls for a certain time, as our nature demands, until God judges the quick and the dead; then our souls are to return again to our bodies, and we, the same and no other than we are now, truly are to rise up in body and soul that never again are to be separated from that time forth, but together, if we do well while we are here, turn toward God to that bliss that lasts forever. And if we do evil, to endless pain. There are seven other points of Christ's manhood that must be believed by all who are Christian. The first is that Jesus Christ, God's Son of Heaven, was truly conceived of the maiden Mary and took flesh and blood and became man through the might and the strength of the Holy Ghost, without any marring of her motherhood, without any demeaning of her maidenhood. The second article is that we are to believe that He, God and man both in one person, came truly of that blessed maiden, a God begotten of His Father before any time and a man born of his mother and brought forth in time. The third point that we are to believe is Christ's passion that He suffered bodily for sinful mankind—how He was betrayed by his disciple and taken by the Jews, beaten with scourges so that [His] skin was not whole, nailed on the Cross and crowned with thorns, and many other hard pains—and died at the last. The fourth article is that when He was dead and His body taken down and shrouded and buried, yet, while His body lay in the grave, the spirit with the Godhood went to Hell and harrowed it and took out those who were there, such as Adam and Eve and other forefathers who He in his providence wished might be saved. The fifth point is that on the third day after He died He rose from death to life, truly God and man in body and in soul. For as He died because of the weakness of our manhood, so He rose through the strength of His Godhood, and so destroyed our death through His dying and quickened us unto life through His rising. The sixth article is that we are to believe that on the fourth day after He rose through His own strength, He ascended into Heaven, where in His blessed person, our nature, which before was less than the nature of angels, is now not only equal in status to the angels, but supreme crowned king above all His angels. The seventh article is that just as He died and afterwards rose and ascended into Heaven, just so is He to come upon the last day, to judge both the quick and the dead, when all the people who ever were or are or will be are truly to be shown and seen before Him, and each man answer of his own deeds and be saved or damned as he deserves; for as His righteousness now is mingled with mercy so then is it to be without mercy.

II *The Ten Commandments* [*Notice that the numbering differs from the traditional Protestant practice.*]

The second thing of the six [by which] to know God Almighty is the ten commandments which He has given us. Of which ten, the three first we are wholly obligated to hold toward our God, and the latter seven toward our fellow Christian. The first commandment charges us and teaches us that we love not people or false gods; and in this commandment is forbidden us all misbeliefs and all idolatries, all false enchantments and all sorceries, all false charms and all witchcrafts, which men of misbelief expect or count on for help apart from God Almighty. The second commandment bids us not to take in idleness or in vain the name of our Lord God, so that we affirm nothing in His name but what is true, that we swear to nothing in His name but what is proper, and that we mention not His name but worshipfully. The third commandment is that we hold and hallow our holy day, Sunday, and other days in the year which are ordained to Holiness through Holy Church; on which days all people both learned and unlearned ought to give themselves willingly to God's service, to hear and say it according to their station in worship of God Almighty and of His good holy things, not then to be tempted to tarry with the world nor live in pleasure or lust, which the flesh yearns for, but willingly to serve God in cleanliness of life. The fourth commandment bids us to worship our father and mother, not only the fleshly father and mother that beget us and foster us forth in the world, but [also] our spiritual father who has raised us and teaches us to live for the salvation of our souls, and our spiritual mother, that is, Holy Church, to be obedient to it and protect its rights, for it is mother to all who live Christian lives and also of each man who is worshipful to worship after its fashion. The fifth commandment bids us to slay no man, that is to say, neither in a bodily nor in a spiritual manner, for we slay men insofar as we abandon or backbite or falsely defame or try to confuse those who do not deserve it or withdraw livelihood from those who have need, if we have means to help them. The sixth commandment forbids us to sin or to dally in a fleshly manner with any woman, whether a sister or a stranger, wedded or unwed, or have any fleshly knowledge or deed with any other than the sacrament of matrimony excuses and the law and the learning of Holy Church teaches. The seventh bids us not to steal, in which we are forbidden to rob and take revenge and to take illegitimately or withhold or hide or conceal other men's goods without the knowledge and consent of the rightful owner. The eighth commandment bids us not to bear false witness against our fellow Christian; in which we are forbidden all manner of belittling, false conspiracy and false swearing, through which our fellow Christians may lose their property, faith, favor, or fame, or anything else, whether it be in spiritual or bodily goods. The ninth commandment is that we not yearn for our neighbor's house; in which we are forbidden all illegitimate covetise of land or of shelter or of anything else that may not be lifted or raised from the ground, as a thing that is steadfast and may not be moved. The tenth commandment and the last is that we not yearn for the wife of our neighbor or of our fellow Christian, or his maiden or his knave, or his ox or his ass. In which we are forbidden to yearn for or to take anything that may be moved of other men's goods, such as robes or riches, or other property that we have no good title or right to; for if we take or get anything any other way than the law and the learning of Holy Church teaches, we may not be absolved of the trespass unless we make restitution however we can to those whom we harmed by withholding their goods. And in case we have through false oaths (as in assizes or other inquests) knowingly or wilfully caused our fellow Christians to lose their patrimony or their heritage, or falsely to be disseized of land or of shelter, or false divorce to be made, or any man to be damned, despite all that we may do for the person yet may we not be absolved of the trespass but by our bishop or by someone who has his power, for such a case is regularly reserved to [the bishop] himself. These ten commandments that I have now enumerated are included in two announced in the Gospel. The one is that we love God over all things; the other is that we love our fellow Christian wholly in our heart as we do ourselves, for we must love God wholly in our hearts, with all our might, with all our thought, with word and with deed. We must also love our fellow Christians in the same way we love ourselves, that is, that they fare well in body and soul and come to that same bliss that we aim for; and whosoever well heeds these two truly fulfills all the ten commandments.

III   *The Seven Sacraments of Holy Church*

The third thing of the six that I mentioned at first is the seven sacraments which Holy Church administers, through prelates and other priests who have the power; of which seven, the first five each Christian ought lawfully to take according to his age and [the other] two lie in the will of those who receive them. The first sacrament of the seven is our baptism which we take when we first become Christian. In which bath are washed away the original sin which we are born with and all other sins which we are filled with before we take it, and the truth of Holy Church is taken through it, without which no sinful man's soul may be saved. And four things are part of this sacrament in order that it be taken rightly as Holy Church teaches. One is correctly saying and reciting the words that he must say who administers this sacrament, which are these: "I baptise thee in the name of the Father and the Son and the Holy Ghost." Another is that it be done only with water, for no other liquid is lawful for this purpose. The third is that he who administers this sacrament give it knowingly and willingly. And the fourth is that he who takes it be not previously baptised by a learned or an unlearned person; for if the priest be unsure whether the person taking it has been baptised or not, then he is to say the words in this manner: "If thou be not baptised, I baptise thee in the name of the Father and the Son and the Holy Ghost." The second sacrament is confirmation, which the bishop administers to those who are baptised, which gives, through his power, to those who receive it the grace and the gift of the Holy Ghost to make them more stalwart than they were before to stand against the fiend and deadly sin; which none has the power to do but the bishop alone who has the status and the place of Christ's Apostles. The third sacrament is called penance, that is, our truly considering our sin without a will or a thought to turn again to it. And this sacrament must have three things. One is sorrow in our heart that we have sinned. Another is open oral confession as to how we have sinned. [The third is] the proper amends for our sin [;] these three, together with a good will to forsake our sin, cleanse us and wash us of all sin. The fourth is the sacrament of the altar, Christ's own body in likeness of bread, as whole as He took it [His flesh] of the blessed maiden [Mary, His mother]; which [sacrament] each man and woman who is of age ought to receive once a year, that is to say, at Easter, according to the practice of Holy Church, when they are cleansed of sin through penance, on pain of excommunication from Holy Church, unless [the church] forbear it for a reasonable cause which ought to be known to them who are to give it; for he who takes it worthily takes his salvation, and whoever takes it unworthily takes his damnation. The fifth sacrament is the last anointing with oil that is hallowed and handled by priests, which sacrament ought only to be given to those who he knows are of reasonable age and whom he sees to be certainly in peril of death, to lighten and allay their sickness if God wishes that they turn again to health, and to forgive venial sins and to lessen pain if they die. Orders is Holy Church's sixth sacrament, which gives power to those who rightfully take it to serve in Holy Church according to their condition and to those who take the order of priest to sing mass and to administer the sacraments of Holy Church, which are appropriate to people according to their condition and their degree. The seventh sacrament is matrimony, that is, a lawful fastening of man and woman with the assent of them both, to live together without any dissolution [of the bond] while their lives last, in remedy of sin and getting of grace, if it be taken with good intent and cleanness of life.

IV   *These are the Seven Corporal [and the Seven Spiritual] Works of Mercy*

The fourth thing of the six to know God Almighty, which it behoves us to fulfill as much as we can, are the seven deeds of mercy toward our fellow Christian, which God is to review on the dreadful day of doom to learn how we have fulfilled them here in this life, as Saint Matthew states in his Gospel. Of which the first is to feed those who are hungry. The second is to give to those who are thirsty. The third is to clothe those who are without clothes, or naked. The fourth is to harbor those who are houseless. The fifth is to visit those who lie in sickness. The sixth is to help those who are in prison. The seventh is to bury the dead who are in need of it. These are the seven bodily deeds of mercy which each man ought to perform who has the power to do so. There are also seven spiritual deeds of mercy which we ought to perform for those who have need of us. One is to give counsel and guidance to those who desire it. Another is to chastise those who do evil things. The third is to solace those who are sorrowful and comfort them. The fourth is to pray for those who are sinful. The fifth is to be long-suffering when men mistreat us. The sixth is gladly to forgive when men have grieved us. The seventh, to teach when men ask us to teach them, if we know more than they do. These are very useful to our neighbors and wonderfully rewarding to those who perform them; for he shall have mercy who is merciful, and a man without mercy shall miss mercy. . . .

V   *The Seven Spiritual Virtues*

The fifth thing of the six to know God Almighty are the seven virtues which Holy Writ teaches; of which seven, the first three of the principal habits teach us how to reach God Almighty; and the [other] four teach us so to live that it be both favorable to God and to man. The first virtue is faith, by which we believe only in God who made all things, with all the other virtues I mentioned before. And this is necessary to all who live Christian lives, for faith is the beginning of all good deeds; for neither is faith worth [anything] without good works, nor can works without faith satisfy God Almighty. The second good habit or virtue is hope, that is, a secure expectation of spiritual good, that through God's goodness and our good deeds we shall come to that bliss that never ends, not alone in trust of God's goodness, not alone in trust of our good deeds, but in trust of them both when they are together; for we are neither to fall so far into despair that we do not trust to have that bliss if we do well, nor are we to come so far into over-hope as to trust so much in God's goodness that we hope to have that bliss without good deeds. The third virtue or habit is charity, which is a dear love that we owe to God Almighty for Himself and to our fellow Christian for God Almighty; for the one may not be loved without the other, as Saint John the Evangelist says in his epistle. "That commandment," he says, "we have of God that whosoever loves God loves his fellow Christian; for he that loves not his brother whom he may see, how should he love God whom he does not see?" The fourth virtue or habit is righteousness, that is, to yield to all what we owe them, to do to each man what we ought to do, to worship those who are worthy, to help the poor who are needy, to do no guile or wrong to any man, but to do what is right to each man. The fifth virtue or habit is prudence, which guides us to beware of the perils of the world, because it teaches us to know good and evil, and always to distinguish one from the other, and to leave evil and take to good, and of two good things to choose the better. The sixth virtue is strength or stalwartness, not only of body but of heart and will, equally to suffer welfare and woe, wealth or misery as they occur, and that our heart not be too proud to do good nor overly humble to avoid evil, but stiffly to stand against our foes, whether they be bodily or spiritual, so that no heavy trial make us fall or be false in our faith toward God Almighty. The seventh virtue and the last is moderation, which keeps us from outrage and holds us in balance, prevents full liking and lust of the flesh and dissuades us from yearnings of worldly goods and keeps [us] in cleanliness of body and soul. For moderation is a measure of all that we do, if we live reasonably, as the law teaches.

VI *The Sixth Thing and the Last*

The sixth thing, and the last of those I first touched, is the seven chief or deadly sins that each man and woman ought to know [in order] to flee and despise [them], for people cannot flee them unless they know of them. Pride, and Envy, Wrath, and Gluttony, Covetise, and Sloth, and Lechery. And they are called the seven chief sins because all others come from them; and they are called deadly sins for they spiritually slay each man's and woman's soul which is caught in all or in any of them. Which is why the wise man bids in his book [that we] seek to flee sin as from the face of the adder. For as the venom of the adder slays man's body, so the venom of sin slays man's soul. The first of these seven sins is called pride, that is, a pleasurable exaltation of a man's heart because of office or of high state or other nobility that he either has by nature or by grace or he hopes that he has more than another. And of this wicked sin come some separate species, boasting and vaunting and disobedience, spite and hypocrisy and pretentiousness, and others that are often seen among proud men. The second deadly sin is called envy, that is, a sorrow and a distress of the welfare, and a joy of the ill fortune of our fellow Christian, of which sin many species spring and spread. One is hatred to speak or hear anything spoken that may be of benefit to those whom they hate. Another, false judging or condemnation of their deeds and an attempt to turn to evil something done as good. The third is backbiting—to say behind them what we will not avow or say before them. Whereas not only he that speaks the evil, but [also] he that hears it spoken, is to blame; for were there no hearer there would be no backbiter. The third deadly sin or chief sin is wrath, that is, a wicked stirring or boiling of heart by which a man wishes to wreak himself or wickedly to avenge himself upon his fellow Christian. And from this wicked sin comes striving and cursing with many false oaths and many foul words, slander to undo a man's good reputation, fighting and felony, and often manslaughter, and many more that do not have to be named. The fourth deadly sin men call guttony, that is, an unreasonable liking or love of tasting or consuming meat or drink; and this trespass men do in several ways. One is to eat or drink over-early or over-late or over-often when necessity does not demand it. Another is to live over-delicately. The third is to eat or drink over-much. The fourth is to eat or drink over-hastily. The fifth is to compass and cast to determine how we can get delicious meats or drinks to fulfill the likings and lusts of the flesh other than we may properly lead our life with. The fifth deadly sin is called covetise, that is, an improper desire or yearning to have any manner of good that we ought not to have. And this is done principally in two ways. One is improperly to get anything that our liking or love lights upon, as by sacrilege or simony, falsehood or usury, or other blandishment, which those worldly men are wont to practice who cast their countenance so to covet that they do not notice whether it be rightful or wrongful, so long as they get what their heart yearns for. Another is improperly to hold what has been obtained, that is, when we will not do to God Almighty or to Holy Church or to our fellow Christian what we ought to do by debt and by law, but only hold what we have for ease of ourselves, whereas not only he who improperly gets, but [also] he who improperly holds, falls into sin. The sixth deadly sin is sloth or laziness, that is, a heartfelt anger or annoyance on our part toward any spiritual good that we ought to do. And of this wicked sin come several species. One is tardiness or delay [so as] to perform very desultorily or to neglect any good deeds that we are to do that may turn us to help or save our souls. Another is a dullness or heaviness of heart that prevents us from loving our Lord God Almighty or from any liking to take part in His service. The third is excessive idleness, which makes [one] loath to begin any good deeds and easily causes us to leave off when something is begun, and whereas we are by nature born to labor, as the fowl is by nature bred to fly, it holds us forever in ease against our nature; for idleness is an enemy to a Christian man's soul, stepmother and obstacle against good habits and a clear guide, and the way to all kinds of vices. The seventh deadly sin is called lechery, that is, a foul liking or lust of the flesh; and of this foul sin come many several species. One is fornication, a fleshly sin between a single man and a single woman; and because it is against the law and the permission and the teaching of Holy Church, it is a deadly sin to them that perform it. Another is adultery, and that is unfaithfulness to a spouse, whether it be bodily or spiritual, which is more grievous and greater than the other. The third is incest, that is, when a man sins in a carnal sense with any of his brothers or sisters or any other of his spiritual or bodily affinity, whoever it be. Many other species spring of this sin, which is overly known in this world by those who lead their lives as their flesh yearns.

These are the six things that I have spoken of which especially make up the law of Holy Church, which we are beholden to know and be acquainted with if we are to know God Almighty and come to His bliss. And to give you a better will to know them, our Father the bishop grants of his grace forty days of pardon to all who know them and also ratifies those granted by others, so much does he desire the salvation of your souls; for if you with understanding know these six things, through them you will know God Almighty, whom, as Saint John says in his Gospel, to know with understanding such as He is, is endless life and everlasting bliss. To which bliss may He bring us, our Lord God Almighty! Amen! Amen! Amen! *Per dominum nostrum Jhesum Christum qui cum deo patri et spiritu sancto vivit et regnat omnipotens deus in secula seculorum. Amen! Amen! Amen!* [Through our Lord Jesus Christ who lives with God the Father and the Holy Spirit and rules eternally as God Omnipotent. Amen! Amen! Amen!]

❧ THE SYMBOLISM OF CHURCHES AND CHURCH ORNAMENTS

William Durandus

Symbolism was of the essence of medieval Christianity. It one believes that this life is only an interlude—a time of trial that will determine how he spends eternity—and that it is the invisible things of the spirit that really matter, then the signs and omens of this spiritual world will take on a significance far greater than that of the everyday world of the senses. In 400 B.C., Plato taught that the senses reveal only pale reflections of true reality, which is "form" or "idea." Starting with Saint Augustine in the fourth century after Christ, almost every important Christian thinker accepted this doctrine and identified "true reality" with God. Plato had also taught that it was possible to lift one's mind, by a kind of rational love, from the reflections and imitations to the original; and in this, too, all medieval thought was platonic. It fitted perfectly with the teachings of Jesus about the transitoriness of earthly pleasures and with his own indifference to his cruel frustrations and death. "Things are not what they seem," this doctrine proclaimed. "There is a deeper truth, visible to those who have eyes to see." To understand a symbol is to see it as it really is: not a piece of wood, but a cross; not a dove, but the Holy Spirit; and so on. To understand the world symbolically is to see it as a veil of illusion, through which the symbols shine as beacons of enlightenment leading to the realities beyond. The Church was the custodian of the accumulated insights of this kind, and they were enshrined in the symbols with which all reli-

gious observances were surrounded, each with its hidden but perfectly definite meaning.

William Durandus (1237–1296) was the author of the Rationale Divinorum Officiorum *(1286), a treatise in eight books on the laws, ceremonies, customs, and mystical interpretation of the Roman Catholic liturgy. Book I, which was translated separately in 1843 under the title* The Symbolism of Churches and Church Ornaments, *and from which the following selections are taken, treats of the church, altar, pictures, bells, churchyard, etc. Book II treats of the ministers; Book III, of vestments; Book IV, of the Mass; Book V, of the canonical hours; Books VI and VII, of the astronomical calendar, the method of finding Easter, etc. Together, the eight books form the most complete medieval treatise of its kind and are the standard authority for thirteenth-century ritual and symbolism.*

THE PROEME

1   All things, as many as pertain to offices and matters ecclesiastical, be full of divine significations and mysteries, and overflow with a celestial sweetness; if so be that a man be diligent in his study of them, and know how to draw 'honey from the rock, and oil from the hardest stone.' But who 'knoweth the ordinances of heaven, or can fix the reasons thereof upon the earth?' For he that prieth into their majesty, is overwhelmed by the glory of them. Of a truth 'the well is deep, and I have nothing to draw with': unless He giveth it unto me Who 'giveth to all men liberally, and upbraideth not': so that 'while I journey through the mountains' I may 'draw water with joy out of the wells of salvation.' Wherefore, albeit of the things handed down from our forefathers, capable we are not to explain all, yet if among them there be anything which is done without reason, it should forthwith be put away. 'Wherefore I, William, by the alone tender mercy of God, Bishop of the Holy Church which is in Mende,' will knock diligently at the door, if so be that 'the key of David' will open unto me: that the King may 'bring me in to His treasury,' and show unto me the heavenly pattern which was showed unto Moses in the Mount: so that I may learn those things which pertain to rites ecclesiastical, whereof they teach and what they signify: and that I may be able plainly to reveal and make manifest the reasons of them, by His help, 'Who hath ordained strength out of the mouth of babes and sucklings': 'Whose spirit bloweth where it listeth,' dividing to 'each severally as it will' to the praise and glory of the Trinity. . . .

6   Furthermore, the symbolism which existeth in things and offices ecclesiastical, is often not seen, both because figures have departed, and now it is the time of truth;

William Durandus, *The Symbolism of Churches and Church Ornaments*, trans. J. M. Neale and B. Webb (3d ed., London: Gibbings and Co., 1906), pp. 1–6, 10–11, 17–18, 39, 42–44, 67–69, 142–144, 149.

and also because we ought not to judaise. But, albeit those types of which the truth is made manifest have departed, yet even to this time manifold truth is concealed, which we see not; wherefore the Church useth figures. For so by white vestments we understand the beauty in which our souls shall be arrayed, or the glory of our immortality, which we cannot manifestly behold: and in the Mass, by the oblation on the altar, the Passion of Christ is represented, that it be held in the memory more faithfully and more firmly.

7   Furthermore, of the things which be commanded in the law, some be moral, and others mystical. They be moral which inform the morals, and are to be understood in the simple tenour of the words: 'Love God: honour thy father: thou shalt do no murder,' and such like. Mystical be such as are typical: where something is set forth beyond the literal meaning. Of these, some be sacramental, and some ceremonial. Sacramental be such as may be accounted for, why thus they were ordered: such as circumcision, and the observance of the Sabbath, and the like. Ceremonial be they for which no reason can be given. Such be, 'Thou shalt not plough with an ox and an ass together': 'Thou shalt not wear a garment of linen and woollen mixed.'

8   Now in things that are moral commands, the law hath received no change: but in things sacramental and ceremonial its outward form is altered: yet not one of the mystical significations is done away: for the law is not done away. Though the 'priesthood being changed, there is made of necessity a change likewise of the law.'

9   Now, in Holy Scriptures, there be divers senses: as historic, allegoric, tropologic, and anagogic. Whence, according to Boethius, all divine authority ariseth from a sense either historical or allegorical or from both. And according to S. Hierom, we ought to study Holy Scriptures in three ways:—firstly, according to the letter; secondly, after the allegory, that is, the spiritual meaning; thirdly, according to the blessedness of the future.

History is *things signified by words:* as when a plain relation is made how certain events took place: as when the children of Israel, after their deliverance from Egypt, made a tabernacle to the Lord. . . .

10   Allegory is when one thing is said and another meant: as when by one deed another is intended: which other thing, if it be visible, the whole is simply an allegory, if invisible and heavenly, an *anagoge.* Also an allegory is when one state of things is described by another: as when the patience of Christ, and the sacraments of the Church are set forth by mystical words or deeds. As in that place: 'There shall come forth a rod of the stem of Jesse, and a branch shall grow out of his roots': which is in plain language, the Virgin Mary shall be born of the family of David, who was the son of Jesse. Truth is also set forth by mystic deeds: as the children of Israel's freedom from Egyptian slavery, wrought by the blood of a lamb, signifieth that the Church is freed by the Passion of Christ from demoniacal servitude. The word allegory is derived from the Greek *allon,* which means *foreign,* and *gore,* which is *sense;* that is, a *foreign sense.*

11   *Tropology* is an injunction unto morality: or a moral speech, either with a symbolical or an obvious bearing, devised to evince and instruct our behaviour. *Symbolical;* as where he saith, 'Let thy garments be always white: and let the oil of thy head never fail.' That is, let all thy works be pure, and charity never fail from thy

mind. And again, it is fit that David should slay the Goliath within us: that is, that humbleness may subdue our pride. *Obvious* as in that saying, 'Deal thy bread to the hungry.' And in that text: 'Let us not love in word, neither in tongue: but in deed and truth.' Now tropology hath his name from *tropos*, a turning, and *logos*, which is a discourse.

12   Anagogue is so called from *ana*, which is upwards, and *goge*, a leading: as it were an upward leading. Whence the anagogic sense is that which leadeth from the visible to the invisible: as light, made the first day, signifieth a thing invisible, namely the angelic nature which was made in the beginning. *Anagoge*, therefore, is that sense which leadeth the mind upwards to heavenly things: that is to the Trinity and the orders of angels, and speaketh concerning future rewards, and the future life which is in the heaven: and it useth both obvious and mystical expressions; obvious, as in that saying, 'Blessed are the pure in heart: for they shall see God': mystical, as that, 'Blessed are they that have made white their robes: that they may have right unto the tree of life, and enter in through the gate into the city.' Which signifieth, blessed are they who make pure their thoughts, that they may have a right to see 'God, who is the way, the truth, and the life': and after the example of the fathers, enter into the kingdom of heaven.

In like manner, Jerusalem is understood historically of that earthly city whither pilgrims journey; allegorically, of the Church Militant; tropologically, of every faithful soul; anagogically, of the celestial Jerusalem, which is our country. . . .

CHAPTER I: OF A CHURCH AND ITS PARTS

1   First of all, let us consider a church and its parts. The word church hath two meanings: the one, a material building, wherein the divine offices are celebrated: the other, a spiritual fabric, which is the collection of the faithful. The Church, *that is* the people forming it, is assembled by its ministers, and collected together into one place by 'Him who maketh men to be of one mind in an house.' For as the material church is constructed from the joining together of various stones, so is the spiritual Church by that of various men.

2   The Greek *ecclesia* is in Latin translated by *convocatio*, because it calleth men to itself: the which title doth better befit the spiritual than the material church.

The matter typifieth the spiritual Church: as shall be explained when we treat of its consecration. Again, the Church is called Catholic, that is universal, because it hath been set up in, or spread over, all the world, because the whole multitude of the faithful ought to be in one congregation, or because in the Church is laid up the doctrine necessary for the instruction of all. . . .

14   The arrangement of a material church resembleth that of the human body: the chancel, or place where the altar is, representeth the head: the transepts, the hands and arms, and the remainder—towards the west—the rest of the body. The sacrifice of the altar denoteth the vows of the heart. Furthermore, according to Richard de Sancto Victore, the arrangement of a church typifieth the three states in the Church: of virgins, of the continent, of the married. The sanctuary is smaller than the chancel, and this than the nave: because the virgins are fewer in number than the continent, and these than the married. And the sanctuary is more holy than the chancel: and the chancel than the nave: because the order of virgins is more worthy than that of the continent and the continent more worthy than the married.

15   Furthermore, the church consisteth of four walls, that is, is built on the doctrine of the Four Evangelists; and hath length, breadth, and height: the height representeth courage, the length fortitude, which patiently endureth till it attaineth its heavenly home; the breadth is charity, which, with long suffering, loveth its friends in God, and its foes for God; and again, its height is the hope of future retribution, which despiseth prosperity and adversity, hoping 'to see the goodness of the Lord in the land of the living.'

16   Again, in the temple of God, the foundation is faith which is conversant with unseen things: the roof, charity, 'which covereth a multitude of sins.' The door, obedience, of which the Lord saith, 'If thou wilt enter into life, keep the commandments.' The pavement, humility, of which the Psalmist saith, 'My soul cleaveth to the pavement.'

17   The four side-walls, the four cardinal virtues, justice, fortitude, temperance, prudence. Hence the Apocalypse saith, 'The city lieth four-square.' The windows are hospitality with cheerfulness, and tenderness with charity. Concerning this house saith the Lord, 'We will come unto him, and make our abode with him.' But some churches are built in the shape of a cross, to signify, that we are crucified to the world, and should tread in the steps of the Crucified, according to that saying, 'If any man will come after Me, let him deny himself and take up his cross and follow Me.' Some also are built in the form of a circle: to signify that the Church hath been extended throughout the circle of the world, as saith the Psalmist: 'And their words unto the end of the world.' Or because from the circle of this world, we reach forth to that crown of eternity which shall encircle our brows.

CHAPTER III: OF PICTURES AND IMAGES

1   Pictures and ornaments in churches are the lessons and the Scriptures of the laity. Whence Gregory: It is one thing to adore a picture, and another by means of a picture historically to learn what should be adored. For what writing supplieth to him which can read, that doth a picture supply to him which is unlearned, and can only look. Because they who are uninstructed thus see what they ought to follow: and *things* are read, though letters be unknown. . . .

6   The image of the Saviour is more commonly represented in churches three ways: as sitting on His throne, or hanging on His cross, or lying on the bosom of His Mother. And because John Baptist pointed to Him, saying, 'Behold the Lamb of God,' therefore some represented Christ under the form of a lamb. But because the light passeth away, and because Christ is very man, therefore, saith Adrian, Pope, He must be represented in the form of a man. A holy lamb must not be depicted on the cross, as a principal object: but there is no let when Christ hath been represented as a man, to paint a lamb in a lower or less prominent part of the picture: since He is the true

Lamb which 'taketh away the sins of the world.' In these and divers other manners is the image of the Saviour painted on account of diversity of significations.

7   Represented in the cradle, the artist commemorateth His nativity: on the bosom of His Mother, His childhood: the painting or carving His cross signifieth His Passion (and sometimes the sun and moon are represented on the cross itself, as suffering an eclipse): when depicted on a flight of steps, His ascension is signified: when on a state or lofty throne, we be taught His present power: as if He said, 'All things are given to Me in heaven and in earth': according to that saying, 'I saw the Lord sitting upon His throne': that is, reigning over the angels: as the text, 'Which sitteth upon the cherubim.' Sometimes He is represented as He was seen of Moses and Aaron, Nadab and Abihu, on the mountain: when 'under His feet was as it were a paved work of sapphire stones, and as the body of heaven in His clearness': and as 'they shall see,' as saith S. Luke, 'the Son of Man coming in the clouds with power and great glory.' Wherefore sometimes He is represented surrounded by the seven angels that serve Him, and stand by His throne, each being portrayed with six wings, according to the vision of Isaiah, 'And by it stood the seraphim: each one had six wings: with twain he covered his face, and with twain he covered his feet, and with twain he did fly.'

CHAPTER IV: OF BELLS

3   You must know that bells, by the sound of which the people assembleth together to the church to hear, and the clergy to preach, 'in the morning the mercy of God and His power by night,' do signify the silver trumpets, by which under the Old Law the people were called together unto sacrifice. . . . For just as the watchmen in a camp rouse one another by trumpets, so do the ministers of the Church excite each other by the sound of bells to watch the livelong night against the plots of the devil. Wherefore our brazen bells are more sonorous than the trumpets of the Old Law, because then God was known in Judea only, but now in the whole earth. They be also more durable: for they signify that the preaching of the New Testament will be more lasting than the trumpets and sacrifices of the Old Law, namely, even unto the end of the world.

4   Again bells do signify preachers, who ought after the likeness of a bell to exhort the faithful unto faith: the which was typified in that the Lord commanded Moses to make a vestment for the high priest, having seventy-two bells to sound when the high priest entered into the Holy of Holies. Also the cavity of the bell denoteth the mouth of the preacher, according to the saying of the Apostle, 'I am become as sounding brass or a tinkling cymbal.'

5   The hardness of the metal signifieth fortitude in the mind of the preacher: whence saith the Lord, 'Behold I have made thy face strong against their faces.' The clapper or iron, which by striking on either side maketh the sound, doth denote the tongue of the teacher, the which with the adornment of learning doth cause both Testaments to resound.

6   Wherefore a prelate which hath not the skill of preaching will be like unto a bell without a clapper: according to that saying of Gregory, 'A priest, if he knoweth not how to preach nor what voice of exhortation he can deliver, is a dumb preacher,

and also as a dumb dog which cannot bark.' The striking the bell denoteth that a preacher ought first of all to strike at the vices in himself for correction, and then advance to blame those of others: lest indeed, contrary to the teaching of the Apostle, 'when he hath preached to others, he himself should be a castaway.' Which also the Psalm doth testify, 'But unto the ungodly, saith God: why dost thou preach my laws, and takest my covenant in thy mouth?' Because truly by the example of his own suffering he often gaineth access to those whom by the learning of his discourse he cannot move. The link by which the clapper is joined or bound unto the bell is moderation: by which, namely, by the authority of Scripture, the tongue of the preacher who wisheth to draw men's hearts is ruled.

CHAPTER IX: OF THE SACRAMENTS OF THE CHURCH

1   With respect to the sacraments of the Church, it is to be noted, that according to Gregory, there is a *sacrament* in any celebration when an outward act is so performed as that we receive inwardly some degree of the thing signified; the which is to be received holily and worthily. Also a *mystery* is that which the Holy Ghost worketh secretly, and invisibly, so as to sanctify by His operation, and bless by His sanctification. A mystery is said to exist in sacraments; a ministry only in ornaments. . . .

4   Some of the sacraments be of necessity only; some of dignity and necessity; some of order and necessity; some of dignity and choice; and some of choice only. The sacrament of necessity only is baptism, which when administered by anyone, so it be in the form of the Church, and in the greatest extremity profiteth unto salvation. And it is said to be 'of necessity,' because without it no one can be saved, if it be neglected through contempt. Of this sacrament we shall speak in the sixth book, under the head of Holy Saturday. The sacrament of dignity and necessity is confirmation: of dignity because it is conferred by the bishop alone; of necessity, because he who neglecteth it through contempt of it, cannot be saved. Of this also we shall speak under the head just specified.

5   The sacraments of order and dignity are Penance, the Eucharist, and Extreme Unction. Of order; because they ought only to be administered by such as are rightly ordained according to the Church's power of the keys; except in necessity, in which one may *confess* even unto a layman: of necessity; since such as neglect them through contempt of them cannot be saved. About penance, see the sixth book, upon the fifth day of Holy Week, the *Caena Domini:* about the Eucharist, we shall speak in the fourth book, upon the Canon; about Extreme Unction we have spoken in the preceding chapter.

6   But the sacrament of dignity and choice is Orders: of dignity; because conferred by bishops alone, and because no one is admitted thereunto save a worthy person and in a worthy way: of choice; because anyone may be saved without it. Of this we shall speak in the preface to the second book.

7   The sacrament of choice only is matrimony; and it is said to be of choice, because anyone may be saved without it. Indeed a man seeking to marry is not inclined to tend towards the kingdom of heaven.

৺৩ THE CHRONICLE OF JOCELIN OF BRAKELOND

The paradox of medieval monasticism (and to some extent, of the medie-
val Church in general) was that although it institutionalized otherworld-
liness, it never succeeded for any length of time in escaping from this
world. The very reputation of a monastery or a monastic order for aus-
terity and sanctity drew donations from high and low alike, with the
result that St. Benedict's rule of poverty for the individual *monk would*
be foiled by the accumulation of wealth by the monastic community.
This wealth, most of it in land, inevitably carried political and eco-
nomic rights and obligations, so that the great monastic foundations
came to play a key role as manorial landlords, feudal overlords, royal
vassals, and patrons of growing towns.

All these roles can be traced in the Chronicle of Jocelin of Brakelond,
in which a monk and chaplain of Bury St. Edmund, probably the most
famous (and cerainly the wealthiest) abbey in medieval England, relates
the career of its hardheaded and capable abbot, Samson. Nothing is
known of Jocelin beyond the few details which he himself supplies in
his chronicle, such as his becoming a monk in 1173, and the various
offices which he held within the monastery. The Chronicle *is confined*
almost entirely to events that Jocelin knew firsthand, and as an observer
he was shrewd and relatively objective. Even his admiration for Abbot
Samson, obviously the hero of the account, is never uncritical.

The Chronicle *deals with Bury St. Edmund from the late 1170s to about*
1203. It then breaks off abruptly, a number of years before the death
of Samson or that of Jocelin himself. Jocelin's account coincides with
the reigns of Henry II, Richard the Lionhearted, and John of Magna
Carta fame, but he is little concerned with national or international
events as such.

. . . As concerned the choice of an abbot, assuming the King gave us free election, divers men spoke in divers ways—some publicly, some privately; and "so many men, so many opinions."

One said of another, "That brother is a good monk, a likely person; he is well conversant with the Rule and custom of the house; although he may not be so perfect a

The Chronicle of Jocelin of Brakelond: A Picture of Monastic Life in the Days of Abbot Samson, ed. E. Clarke (London: De la More Press, 1903), pp. 17–20, 24–28, 31–35, 39–50, 82, 85–88, 96–99.

philosopher as certain others, he would make a very good abbot. Abbot Ording was not a learned man, and yet he was a good abbot, and governed this house wisely: we read, too, in the fable, that it had been better for the frogs to have chosen a log for a king, upon which they might rely, than a serpent, who venomously hissed, and after his hisses devoured his subjects."

Another would answer, "How may this be? How can an unlearned man deliver a sermon in chapter, or to the people on festivals? How can he who does not understand the Scriptures attain the knowledge of 'binding and loosing'? seeing that the cure of souls is the art of arts and science of sciences. God forbid that a dumb image should be set up in the Church of St. Edmund, where many learned and studious men are well known to be."

Also said one of another, "That brother is a good clerk, eloquent and careful, strict in the Rule; he has much loved the convent, and has undergone many hardships in respect of the possessions of the church: he is worthy to be made abbot." Another answered, "From good clerks, Good Lord, deliver us: that it may please Thee to preserve us from the barrators * of Norfolk, we beseech Thee to hear us, good Lord." Moreover, one said of another, "That brother is a good manager, which is proved from his department, and from the offices which he has well served, and by the buildings and reparations which he has performed. He is able to travail for and defend the house, and is, moreover, something of a clerk, although 'much learning has not made him mad': he is worthy to be made abbot." Another answered, "God forbid that a man who can neither read nor chant, nor perform Divine service—a wicked and unjust man, and a grinder of the faces of the poor—should be abbot."

Also said one of another, "That brother is a kind man, affable and amiable, peaceful and well-regulated, open-hearted and liberal, a learned man and an eloquent, a proper man enough in looks and deportment, and beloved by many, indoors as well as out; and such a man might, with God's permission, become abbot to the great honour of the church." The other answered, "It is no honour, but rather a burden, to have a man who is too nice in his meat and drink; who thinks it a virtue to sleep long; who is expert in spending much, and yet gets little; who is snoring when others are awake; who always is desirous to be in plenty, nor yet cares for the debts which increase from day to day, nor considers the means of discharging expenses; hating anxiety and trouble; caring for nought so long as one day comes and another goes; a man cherishing and fostering flatterers and liars; a man who is one thing in name and another in deed. From such a prelate defend us, O Lord!"

Also said a certain one of his fellow, "That man is almost wiser than all of us put together, both in secular and ecclesiastical matters; a wonderful counsellor, strict in rule, learned and eloquent, and of proper stature; such a prelate would do honour to our church."

The other answered, "True, if he were of known and approved reputation. His character is questionable: report may lie, or it may not. And although the man you mean is wise, of lowly carriage in chapter, devout in psalmody, strict in the cloister whilst he is in the cloister, yet it is mere outward show with him. What if he do excel in any office? He is too scornful, lightly esteems the monks, is closely intimate with

* [Legal sharks. (*Ed.*)]

secular persons; and should he be angry, scarcely returns an answer with a good grace to any brother, or to one even asking a question of him."

I heard in like manner one brother disparaged by some, because he was slow of speech; of whom it was said that he had paste or malt in his mouth when he was called upon to speak. And as for myself, being at that time a youth, "I understood as a youth, I spoke as a youth", and said I never could consent that any one should be made abbot unless he knew somewhat of dialectics, and knew how to discern truth from falsehood. Again, a certain person, who in his own eyes seemed very wise, said, "May the almighty Lord bestow on us a foolish and simple shepherd, so that it should be the more needful for him to get help from us!". . .

One year and three months having elapsed since the death of Abbot Hugh, the King commanded by his letters that our prior and twelve of the convent, in whose mouth the judgment of our body might agree, should appear on a certain day before him, to make choice of an abbot. On the morrow, after the receipt of the letters, we all of us met in chapter for the purpose of discussing so important a matter. In the first place the letters of our lord the King were read to the convent; next we besought and charged the prior, at the peril of his soul, that he would, according to his conscience, name twelve who were to accompany him, from whose life and conversation it might be depended upon that they would not swerve from the right; who, acceding to our charge, by the dictation of the Holy Ghost named six from one side and six from the other side of the choir, and without gainsaying satisfied us on this point. From the right-hand choir were named—Geoffrey of Fordham, Benedict, Master Dennis, Master Samson the sub-sacrist, Hugh the third prior, and Master Hermer, at that time a novice; from the left-hand side—William the sacrist, Andrew, Peter de Broc, Roger the cellarer, Master Ambrose, Master Walter the physician.

But one said, "What shall be done if these thirteen cannot agree before our lord the King in the choice of an abbot?" A certain one answered that that would be to us and to our church a perpetual shame. Therefore, many were desirous that the choice should be made at home before the rest departed, so that by this forecast there should be no disagreement in the presence of the King. But that seemed a foolish and inconsistent thing to do, without the King's assent; for as yet it was by no means a settled thing that we should be able to obtain a free election from the King.

Then said Samson the sub-sacrist, speaking by the spirit of God, "Let there be a middle-course, so that from either side peril may be avoided. Let four confessors be chosen from the convent, together with two of the senior priors of the convent, men of good reputation, who, in the presence of the holy relics, shall lay their hands upon the Gospels, and choose amongst themselves three men of the convent most fit for this office, according to the rule of St. Benedict, and put their names into writing. Let them close up that writing with a seal, and so being closed up, let it be committed to us who are about to go to the court. When we shall have come before the King, and it shall appear that we are to have a free election, then, and not till then, shall the seal be broken, and so shall we be sure as to the three who are to be nominated before the King. And let it be agreed amongst us, that in case our lord the King shall not grant to us one of ourselves, then the seal shall be brought back intact, and delivered to the six under oath, so that this secret of theirs shall remain for ever concealed, at the peril of their souls." In this counsel we all acquiesced, and four confessors were then named; namely, Eustace, Gilbert of Alveth, Hugh the third prior, Anthony, and two other old men, Thurstan and Ruald. Which being done, we went forth chanting "Verba mea," and the aforesaid six remained behind, having the rule of St. Benedict in their hands; and they fulfilled that business as it had been pre-ordained.

Now, whilst these six were treating of their matter, we were thinking differently of different candidates, all of us taking it for granted that Samson would be one of the three, considering his travails and perils of death in his journey to Rome for the advancement of our church, and how he was badly treated and put in irons and imprisoned by Hugh the abbot, merely for speaking for the common weal; for he could not be induced to flatter, although he might be forced to hold his tongue.

After some delay, the convent being summoned returned to chapter; and the old men said they had done as they were commanded. Then the prior asked, "How shall it be if our lord the King will not receive any of those three who are nominated in the writing?" And it was answered that whomsoever our lord the King should be willing to accept should be adopted, provided he were a professed monk of our house. It was further added, that if those thirteen brethren should see anything that ought to be amended by another writing, they should so amend it by common assent or counsel.

Samson the sub-sacrist, sitting at the feet of the prior, said, "It will be profitable for the church if we all swear by the word of truth that upon whomsoever the lot of election shall fall, he should treat the convent according to reason, nor change the chief officers without the assent of the convent, nor surcharge the sacrist, nor admit any one to be a monk without assent of the convent." And to this we all of us assented, holding up our right hands in token of assent. It was, moreover, provided, that if our lord the King should desire to make a stranger our abbot, such person should not be adopted by the thirteen, unless upon counsel of the brethren remaining at home.

Upon the morrow, therefore, those thirteen took their way to court. Last of all was Samson, the purveyor of their charges, because he was sub-sacrist, carrying about his neck a little box, in which were contained the letters of the convent—as if he alone was the servant of them all—and without an esquire, bearing his frock in his arms, and going out of the court, he followed his fellows at a distance. . . .

At last the prior and the twelve that were with him, after many fatigues and delays, stood before the King at Waltham, the manor of the Bishop of Winchester, upon the second Sunday in Lent. The King graciously received them; and, saying that he wished to act in accordance with the will of God and the honour of our church, commanded the brethren by prolocutors—namely, Richard the Bishop of Winchester, and Geoffrey the chancellor, afterwards Archbishop of York—that they should nominate three members of our convent.

The prior and brethren retiring as if to confer thereupon, drew forth the sealed writing and opened it, and found the names writtened in this order—Samson, subsacrista; Roger, celerarius; Hugo, tercius prior. Hereupon those brethren who were of higher standing blushed with shame; they also marvelled that this same Hugh should be at once elector and elected. But, inasmuch as they could not alter what was done, by mutual arrangement they changed the order of the names; first naming Hugh, because he was third prior; secondly, Roger the cellarer; thirdly, Samson, thus literally making the last first and the first last.

The King, first inquiring whether they were born in his realm, and in whose lordship, said he knew them not, directing that with those three, some other three of the convent should be nominated. This being assented to, William the sacrist said, "Our prior ought to be nominated because he is our head," which was directly allowed. The prior said, "William the sacrist is a good man"; the like was said of Dennis, and that was settled. These being nominated before the King without any delay, the King marvelled, saying, "These men have been speedy in their work; God is with them."

Next the King commanded that, for the honour of his kingdom, they should name three persons of other houses. On hearing this, the brethren were afraid, suspecting some craft. At last, upon conference, it was resolved that they should name three, but upon this understanding, that they would not receive any one of those three, unless by assent of the convent at home. And they named these three—Master Nicholas of Waringford, afterwards (for a season) Abbot of Malmesbury; Bertrand, Prior of St. Faith's, afterwards Abbot of Chertsey; and Master H. of St. Neot's, a monk of Bec, a man highly religious, and very circumspect in spiritual as well as temporal affairs.

This being done, the King thanked them, and ordered that three should be struck off of the nine; and forthwith the three strangers were struck off, namely, the Prior of St. Faith's, afterwards Abbot of Chertsey, Nicholas, a monk of St. Albans, afterwards Abbot of Malmesbury, and the Prior of St. Neot's. William the sacrist voluntarily retired, two of the five were struck out by command of the King, and, ultimately, one out of the remaining three. There then remained but two, the prior and Samson.

Then at length the before-named prolocutors of our lord the King were called to the council of the brethren: and Dennis, speaking as one for all, began by commending the persons of the prior and Samson, saying, that each of them was learned, each was good, each was of meritorious life and good character. But always in the corner of his discourse he gave prominence to Samson, multiplying words in his praise, saying that he was a man strict in life, severe in reforming excesses, and ready to work hard; heedful, moreover, in secular matters, and approved in various offices. The Bishop of Winchester replied, "We see what it is you wish to say; from your address we gather that your prior seems to you to have been somewhat remiss, and that, in fact, you wish to have him who is called Samson." Dennis answered, "Either of them is good, but, by God's help, we desire to have the best." To whom the bishop, "Of two good men the better should be chosen. Speak out at once; is it your wish to have Samson?" Whereupon several, in fact the majority, answered clearly, "We do wish Samson." No one gainsaid this, though some studiously held their peace, being fearful of offending either one or the other.

Samson was then named to the King, and after a brief consultation with those about him, the King called all in, and said, "You present to me Samson—I know him not; had you presented to me your prior, I should have accepted him, because I know and am well acquainted with him; but now I will do as you desire me. Take heed to yourselves; by the very eyes of God, if you have done ill, I shall call you to severe account." And he inquired of the prior, whether he assented to this choice and agreed thereto;

who replied that he was well content it should be so, and that Samson was worthy of a much greater dignity.

Then the elect, falling down at the King's feet and kissing them, hastily arose, and forthwith went towards the altar, erect in gait, and with unmoved countenance, singing "Miserere mei Deus," together with his brethren.

The King, observing this, said to the bystanders, "By the eyes of God, this abbot-elect thinks himself worthy to govern an abbey!". . . .

While these things were taking place I was the prior's chaplain, and within four months was made the abbot's chaplain, noting many things, and committing them to memory. On the morrow of his feast the abbot called to him the prior and some few besides, as if seeking advice from others, though he himself knew what he would do. He said that a new seal should be made with a mitred effigy of him, although his predecessors had not the like; but for a time he used the seal of our prior, subscribing at the end of all letters, that he had no seal of his own and therefore he used for the time that of the prior.

Afterwards, setting his household in order, he appointed divers servants to various duties, saying that he had decided to have twenty-six horses in his courtyard, and that a child must first creep and then stand upright and walk. He enjoined this to his servants beyond all things, that they should take heed that in his new state he be not dishonoured by a lack of meat and drink, but rather that they in all things should anxiously provide for the hospitality of the house. In ordering and appointing these and all other things, he fully relied upon God's providence and his own understanding, and judged it beneath him to require counsel at another's hand as if he were not able to look after his own affairs.

The monks marvelled, the knights were discontented, accusing him of arrogance, and, in some measure censuring him at the King's court, saying that he refused to govern according to the advice of his own freemen. As for him, he removed from his own private counsel the heads of the abbey, lay as well as clerical; indeed, all those without whose advice and assistance the abbey, as it seemed, could not be governed. By reason of this circumstance, Ranulf de Glanville, Justiciary of England, at first held him in distrust, and was less gracious to him than was fitting, until it was made clear, by good evidence, that the abbot had been acting with due caution and prudence in respect of indoor as well as external matters.

A general court having been summoned, all the barons, knights and freemen appeared to do homage on the fourth day of Easter; when, behold, Thomas of Hastings, with a great multitude of knights, came introducing Henry his nephew, not yet a knight, claiming the stewardship with its perquisites, according to the tenor of his charter. To whom the abbot replied, "I do not refuse Henry his right, nor do I wish so to do. If he were competent to serve me in his own person, I would assign him necessaries for ten men and eight horses in my own court-lodge, according to the tenor of his charter. If you present to me a steward, his deputy, who is competent and able to perform the duty, I will receive him in the same manner as my predecessor retained him at the time of his decease, namely, with four horses and their appurtenances. And if this does not content you, I shall carry the plaint before the King or his chief justice." Hereupon the business was deferred.

Ultimately there was presented to him a simple and foolish steward, Gilbert by name, of whom, before he received him into his household, he spoke to his friends as follows: "If there be a default in the administration of the King's justice through the unskilfulness of the steward, he will be in mercy of the King, and not I, for this, that he claims the office by hereditary right; and therefore I had much rather receive him for the present than a sharper witted man to deceive me. By God's assistance I trust I shall be my own steward."

After receipt of the homages, the abbot sued for an aid from the knights, who promised each twenty shillings; but immediately they took counsel together and withheld twelve pounds in respect of twelve knights, alleging that those twelve ought to assist the other forty in keeping their castle-guards, and for their escuages, as well as in respect of the abbot's aid. The abbot, hearing this, waxed wroth, and said to his intimate friends that if he lived long enough he would give them turn for turn and wrong for wrong.

THE NEW ABBOT'S REFORMS

After these things the abbot caused inquisition to be made throughout each manor, concerning the annual quit rents from the freemen, and the names of the labourers and their tenements, and the services due from each; and he reduced all into writing. Likewise he repaired those old halls and unroofed houses round which hovered kites and crows. He built new chapels, and likewise inner chambers and upper stories in many places where there never had been any dwelling-house at all, but only barns. He also enclosed many parks, which he replenished with beasts of chase, keeping a huntsman with dogs; and, upon the visit of any person of quality, sat with his monks in some walk of the wood, and sometimes saw the coursing of the dogs; but I never saw him take part in the sport.

He cleared much land, and brought it into tillage, in all things looking forward to the benefit likely to accrue to the abbey; but I wish he had been equally careful in assigning the manors of the convent. Nevertheless, he, for a time, kept our manors of Bradfield and Rougham in hand, making up the deficiencies of the rents by the expenditure of forty pounds. These he afterwards reassigned to us when he heard that dissatisfaction was expressed in the convent, on account of his keeping our manors in his own hand. Likewise in managing these manors, as well as in all other matters, he appointed keepers who were far more careful than their predecessors—some monks, some laymen, to look after us and our lands more carefully.

He also held the eight hundreds in his own hand, and, after the death of Robert of Cockfield, he took in hand the hundred of Cosford, all which he committed to the keeping of those servants who were of his own table; referring matters of greater moment to his own decision, and deciding by means of others upon matters of lesser import—indeed, wringing everything to his own profit.

Moreover, by his command, a general survey was made throughout the hundreds of the leets and suits, of hidages and foddercorn, of hen-rents, and of other dues and rents and issues, which, for the greater part, had ever been concealed by the farmers. He reduced it all to writing, so that within four years from the time of his election, there was not one who could defraud him of the rents of the abbey to the value of a single penny, whereas he himself had not received from his predecessors any writing touching the management of the abbey, except one small schedule, wherein were the names of the knights of St. Edmund and the names of the manors, and what rent was due on each farm. This book he called his kalendar, wherein also were entered the debts he had satisfied; and this same book he almost daily perused, as if in the same he were beholding the face of his honesty in a glass.

The first day that he held a chapter, he confirmed to us, under his new seal, sixty shillings from Southrey, which his predecessors had unjustly received from Edmund, surnamed the golden monk, for the liberty of holding the same vill to farm all the days of his life. He also proposed, as a general rule, that from thenceforth no one should pledge the ornaments of the church without the assent of the convent, as had been the custom heretofore, nor that any charter should be sealed with the convent seal, unless in chapter in the presence of the convent. He appointed Hugh as sub-sacrist, ordering that William the sacrist should not have anything to do with the sacristy, either in the matter of receipt or disbursement, unless by his consent. After this, but not on the same day, he transferred the former keepers of the offerings to other offices; lastly, he deposed the same William: wherefore those who liked William said, "Behold the abbot! Lo, here is the wolf of whom it was dreamed! See how he rages!"

And some of them would have entered into a conspiracy against the abbot. When this was disclosed to him, he, not caring to be altogether silent, nor yet to disquiet the convent, entered the chapter-house on the morrow, and pulled out a little bag full of cancelled deeds, the seals yet hanging thereto, consisting of the securities, partly of his predecessor, partly of the prior, partly of the sacrist, partly of the chamberlain, and other officials, whereof the total was three thousand and fifty-two pounds and one mark without alloy, besides the interest that had accrued thereupon, the amount of which could never be ascertained. All these he had arranged for within one year after his election, and within twelve years entirely discharged. "Behold," said he, "the good management of William, our sacrist; look at the multitude of securities signed with his seal, whereby he has pledged silken copes, dalmatics, censers of silver and books ornamented with gold, without the knowledge of the convent, all which I have re-deemed and have restored to you."

He likewise added many other things, showing why he had deposed the said William: howbeit he suppressed the real cause, not wishing to put him to open shame. And when he put Samson the precentor in his place, a person approved by us, and above all objection, everything was quiet again. Furthermore, the abbot commanded that the houses of the sacrist in the cemetery should be entirely plucked up, as though they were not worthy to stand upon the earth, by reason of the frequent wine-bibbings, and certain other acts not to be named, which he, with grief and indignation, had witnessed while he was sub-sacrist. So completely did he obliterate the whole that, within a year, upon the spot where a noble dwelling had stood, we saw beans growing, and where casks of wine had lain, nettles abounding.

After the end of Easter, the abbot went over every one of his and our manors, as well as over those we had confirmed to the farmers in fee, requiring from all of them aid and acknowledgment, according to the law of the land. Thus every day he was increasing in secular knowledge, and was turning his attention to the learning and method of ordering outdoor affairs. Now when he had come to Warkton, where he slept at night, there came to him a voice saying, "Samson, arise up quickly"; and, again, "Get up without delay." Getting up astonished, he looked around him, and perceived a light in a necessary house, namely, a candle ready to fall down upon the straw, which Reiner the monk had carelessly left there. When the abbot had put it out, going through the house, he perceived the door (which was the sole entrance) so fastened that it could only be opened by a key—likewise the windows fastened: so that if a fire had arisen, he, and all with him, who slept upon that floor, had surely perished, for there was no place whence they might get out or escape.

At that time, wheresoever the abbot went, there came about him Jews as well as Christians, demanding debts, and worrying and importuning him so that he could not sleep. Thereupon he became pale and thin, and was constantly repeating, "My heart will never rest until I know the extent of my debts." The feast of St. Michael being come, he took all his manors into his own hand, with but small store of live or dead stock; he freely forgave Walter of Hatfield nineteen pounds arrears, that he might absolutely take back four manors which Hugh the abbot had confirmed to him, namely, Hargrave and Saxham and Chevington and Stapleford; Harlow, indeed, the abbot deferred to take to himself on the present occasion.

Once on a time, as we passed through the forest in returning from London, I inquired in the hearing of my lord abbot, from an old woman passing by, whose was this wood, and of what town, who was the lord, and who was the keeper? She answered that the wood belonged to the abbot of St. Edmund, as part of the town of Harlow, and that the name of the keeper was Arnald. When I inquired further, how Arnald conducted himself towards the men of the town, she answered, that he was a devil incarnate, an enemy of God, and one to flay the poor alive; but now, she added, he is afraid of the new abbot of St. Edmund, whom he believes to be prudent and vigilant, and therefore he treats the men gently. On hearing this, the abbot was delighted, and deferred taking to the manor for a season.

At that time there came unexpectedly the news of the death of the wife of Herlewin of Rungton, who had a charter to hold the same town for her life; and the abbot said, "Yesterday, I would have given sixty marks to have freed the manor from this incumbrance, but now God has freed it." And as he was going thither without delay, that he might take that town into his own hand, and on the morrow was going to Tillener, a part of that manor, there came a certain knight offering thirty marks for the tenure of that carucate of land, with the appurtenances, by the old rent-service, to wit, four pounds, whereto the abbot could not agree; and he had therefrom in that year twenty-five pounds, and the second year twenty pounds.

These and such like things induced him to hold everything in his own keeping; as it is written elsewhere, "Caesar was all in all." In the first place, far from being inert, he commenced building barns and byres, above all things solicitous to dress the land for tillage, and watchful in preserving the woods, in respect whereof, either in giving or diminishing, he confessed himself to be a very miser. There was but one manor, and that was Thorpe, which by his charter he confirmed to one of English birth, a villein, whose honesty he trusted the more, as he was a good husbandman, and could not speak French. . . .

Whilst there was war throughout England, during the captivity of King Richard, the abbot, with his whole convent, solemnly excommunicated all movers of the war and disturbers of the public peace, not fearing the Earl John, the King's brother, nor any other, so that he was styled the "stout-hearted abbot." After this he went to the siege of Windsor, where he appeared in armour with certain other abbots of England, having his own standard, and retaining many knights at heavy charges, being more remarkable there for his counsel than for his piety. But we cloister folk thought this act rather perilous, fearing lest in consequence some future abbot might be compelled to attend in person upon any warlike expedition. On the conclusion of a truce he went into Germany, and there visited the King with many gifts. . . .

There was a general court summoned for the hundred of Risbridge, to hear the plaint and trial of the Earl of Clare, at Witham. He, indeed, accompanied by many barons and knights, including the Earl Alberic and many others, stated that his bailiffs had given him to understand that they were accustomed to receive yearly for his use five shillings from the hundred and the bailiffs of the hundred, and that this was now unjustly detained; and he alleged that the land of Alfric, the son of Withgar, who had in ancient time been lord of that hundred, had been granted to his predecessors at the conquest of England. But the abbot, taking thought for his own interest, without stirring from his place, answered, "It is a strange thing, my lord earl; your case fails you. King Edward the Confessor gave, and by his charter confirmed, to St. Edmund, this entire hundred; and of those five shillings there is no mention made therein. You must tell us for what service, or for what reason, you demand those five shillings." And the earl, after advising with his attendants, replied that it was his office to carry the standard of St. Edmund in battle, and for that cause the five shillings were due to him. The abbot answered, "Of a truth it seems a mean thing that such a man as the Earl of Clare, should receive such a petty gift for such a service. To the Abbot of St. Edmund, it is but a slight grievance to give five shillings. The Earl Roger Bigot holds himself as seised, and asserts that he is seised, of the office of bearing the standard of St. Edmund; indeed, he actually did bear it when the earl of Leicester was taken and the Flemings destroyed. Thomas of Mendham also claims this as his right. When, therefore, you shall have proved against these your right, I will with great pleasure pay you the five shillings you now seek to recover of me." The earl upon this said that he would talk the matter over with the Earl Roger, his kinsman, and so the matter was put off even to this day.

On the death of Robert of Cockfield, there came Adam, his son, and with him many of his relations, the Earl Roger Bigot, and many other great men, and made suit to the abbot for the tenements of the aforesaid Adam, and especially for the half hundred of Cosford, to be held by the annual payment of one hundred shillings, just as if it had been his hereditary right; indeed, they all said that his father and his grandfather had held it for fourscore years past and more.

When the abbot got an opportunity of speaking, putting his two fingers up to his two eyes, he said, "May I be deprived of these eyes on that day, nay, in that hour, wherein I grant to any one a hundred to be held in hereditary right, unless indeed the King, who is able to take away from me the abbey and my life with it, should force me to do so."

Explaining to them the reason of that saying, he averred, "If any one were to hold a hundred as an inheritance, and he should make forfeit to the King in any wise, so that he ought to lose his inheritance, forthwith will the Sheriff of Suffolk and the King's bailiffs have seisin of the hundred, and exercise their own power within our liberties; and if they should have the ward of the hundred, the liberty of the eight hundreds and a half will be endangered."

And then addressing himself to Adam, he said, "If you, who claim an inheritance in this hundred, should take to wife any free woman who should hold but one acre of land of the King in chief, the King, after your death, would possess himself of all that your tenement, together with the wardship of your son, if he be under age; and thus the King's bailiffs would enter upon the hundred of St. Edmund, to the prejudice of the abbot. Besides all this, your father acknowledged to me that he claimed nothing by right of inheritance in the hundred; but because his service was satisfactory to me, I permitted him to hold it all the days of his life, according as he deserved of me."

Upon the abbot saying thus much, money was offered; but he could not be persuaded by words or money. At last it was settled between them thus: Adam disclaimed the right which he had by word of mouth claimed in the hundred, and the abbot confirmed to him all his other lands; but touching our town of Cockfield, no mention was made of that, nor indeed is it believed that he had a charter thereof; Semer and Groton he was to hold for the term of his life. . . .

The two counties of Norfolk and Suffolk were put in the "mercy" of the King by the justices in eyre for some default, and fifty marks were put upon Norfolk, and thirty upon Suffolk. And when a certain portion of that common amerciament was assessed upon the lands of St. Edmund, and was sharply demanded, the abbot, without any delay, went to our lord the King. We found him at Clarendon; and when the charter of King Edward, which discharges all the lands of St. Edmund from all gelds and scots, had been shown to him, the King commanded by his writ that six knights of the county of Norfolk and six of Suffolk should be summoned to consider before the barons of the exchequer, whether the lordships of St. Edmund ought to be quit from common amerciament. To save trouble and expense, only six knights were chosen, and these for the reason that they had lands in either county; namely, Hubert of Briseword, W. Fitz-Hervey, and William of Francheville, and three others, who went to London with us, and on behalf of the two counties gave their verdict in favour of the liberty of our church. And thereupon the justices then sitting enrolled their verdict.

The abbot Samson entered into a contest with his knights—himself against all, and all of them against him. He had stated to them that they ought to perform the service of fifty individual knights in escuages, in aids, and the like, because, as they themselves said, they held so many knights' fees. The point in dispute was, why ten of those fifty knights were to be without performing service, or by what reason or by whose authority the forty should receive the help of those ten knights. But they all answered with one voice, that such had ever been the custom, that is to say, that ten of them should assist the other forty, and that they could not thereupon—nor ought they thereupon—to answer, nor yet to implead.

When they were summoned in the King's court to answer hereupon, some, by arrangement, excused themselves from appearing, the others cunningly appeared, saying that they ought not to answer without their peers. On another occasion, those presented themselves who had first absented themselves, saying in like manner, that they ought not to answer without their peers who were joined with them in the same plaint. And when they had several times thus mocked the abbot, and had involved him in great and grievous expenses, the abbot complained of this to Hubert, the archbishop, then justiciary, who replied in open court that each knight ought to plead singly, and in respect of his own tenure, and said straight out that the abbot was clever enough and able enough to prove the rights of his church against all and every one of them. Then the earl, Roger Bigot, first of all freely confessed that, in law, he owed to his superior lord the abbot his service of three entire knights' fees, in reliefs as well as in escuages and aids; but, so far as concerned his performing castle-guard at the castle of Norwich, he said nothing.

Next came two of these knights, then three, and again more, until nearly all of them had come, and, by the earl's example, acknowledged the same service. Because such acknowledgment thereupon made in the court of St. Edmund was not sufficient in law, the abbot took all of them to London at his own charges, with the wives and women who were inherited of the lands so held, that they should make the acknowledgment in the King's court, and they all received separate charters of the concord thus made. Alberic de Vere and William of Hastings and two others were in the King's service beyond sea when this was done, and therefore the plaint concerning them was stayed. Alberic de Vere was the last who held out against the abbot; but as it was, the abbot seized and sold his cattle, wherefore it behoved him to come into court, and answer, as did his fellows. Taking advice upon it, he at length acknowledged to the abbot and St. Edmund their right.

The knights, therefore, being all defeated, a great profit would have accrued to the abbot from this victory unless he had been inclined to spare some of them; for so often as twenty shillings are charged upon a fee, there will remain twelve pounds to the abbot, and if more or less are assessed, more or less will remain over as a surplus to him, according to the strict apportionment.

⤳ THE FIRST CRUSADE

Ekkehard of Aurach

Were the Crusades a Christian Holy War, or the last of the barbarian invasions, or the ultimate effort of the restless Normans who only decades earlier had conquered England in the north and Sicily in the south? What-

ever interpretation historians accept, they agree that by the time the crusading spirit abated some 200 years later western Europe, which had been a backwater in the eleventh century, had reached the cultural level of its Moslem and Byzantine foes.

Ekkehard, the author of the chronicle below, was abbot of the south German monastery of Aurach (or Aura). Although he was not a participant in the original movement of 1096, he did go to the Holy Land with the so-called German Crusade of 1101. The chronicle was composed about 1115, after Ekkehard's return to Germany. For the early narrative, Ekkehard relied on manuscript chronicles which scholars have identified, but he probably also talked to participants.

As a historian Ekkehard leaves much to be desired. He was careless, a confusing narrator, deficient in the most elementary knowledge of geography, and certainly very credulous. Midway between an illiterate country priest and a brilliant intellectual like Abélard, Ekkehard provides insight into the social ideas and values of his time. The chronicle is therefore less significant for its fund of facts—which is not always very accurate—than for reflecting the climate of opinion of the early twelfth century. Indeed, despite its apparent simplemindedness, Ekkehard's view of the crusade, and of the Moslems and Byzantines (whose very name was to become a synonym for "wily"), helped to create western stereotypes that persisted for centuries.

Here begins, in the name of Christ, a book I call *The Jerusalemiad* for it describes the oppression, the liberation, and the renewal of the Church in Jerusalem.

CHAPTER I: PROLOGUE

My spirit burns, O reverend father, to describe to you, in some way, the reasons for the military expedition to Jerusalem which was ordained for our times not so much by man as by God. From almost all parts of the world they came, but particularly from the kingdoms of the West; and I hope that my account of this campaign will satisfy your authority and the whole community of Saints Stephen and Vitus that is subject to your mighty rule. Indeed, I do not think it right that I, who am devoted to this kind of work and who have ever served you as well as I could in such serious

Ekkehardi, Abbatis Uraugiensis, Hiersolymita, Recueil des Historiens des Croisades: Historiens occidentaux (Paris: Imprimerie nationale, 1895), Vol. V, 11–40. Translated from the Latin by Howard W. Clarke for this volume.

matters as editing the accounts of various chronicles from the beginning of time down to our own dreary days, should now fail your kindness in this smaller matter, for to do so would amount to my stinting my sacrifice to the Lord. Furthermore, I am almost compelled to this work by the necessity to refute certain imprudent (or rather, impudent) writers who, ever pleased with their own persistent errors, dare to rebuke with their rash tongues this recent effort which was so needed by our aging and almost perishing world, while in the darkness of their own hearts they are, like Epicureans, embracing the broad path of pleasure rather than the narrow path of divine servitude and claiming that it is advisable to seek the things of this world and foolish to scorn them, as they confuse, alas, light with darkness, good with bad, and life with death. What has seduced them and prompts them in their boldness is a kind of vicious perversion of values, found everywhere but particularly in these areas, by which wisdom is despised, all virtue is scorned, religion is hated, and humility is debased, while slyness wins precedence, vice corrupts love, cruelty intimidates reverence, and pride commands honor. We, on the other hand, trust only in the Lord and look toward future, not present, rewards, and though we are but humble spectators we can nonetheless be devoted partisans; so let us praise those other men of our time, glorious men who have conquered kingdoms of the world and who, abandoning their wives and their children, their kingdoms and their wealth, have taken their lives in their hands as they fought with the zeal of armies for the Lord their God. With bravery these men entered the service of their Heavenly King, and their zeal was fired by the frequent reports they received of how the savage Turks in their subject territories had for some years been oppressing the Sepulcher of the Lord and desolating with unimaginable disasters all the churches of the East. These men decided to come to the aid of the Eastern Church and many of them hastened toward Jerusalem by various routes and under various and obscure leaders. The first group, estimated at fifteen thousand, followed a monk named Peter the Hermit and proceeded peacefully through Germany and then through Bavaria and Hungary, as many as could going by boat down the Danube or else by foot through Alamannia [Swabia, in southwestern Germany]; others, amounting to twelve thousand, were led through Saxony and Bohemia by a preacher named Volkmar; while still others were led through eastern France by a preacher named Gottschalk. But more of this later.

CHAPTER II: HOW THE TURKS OBTAINED THE EASTERN PROVINCES

At the time when Henry IV was Emperor of Rome and Alexius Emperor of Constantinople, then, according to the prophecy of the evangelists, everywhere nation rose against nation, kingdom against kingdom, and there were great earthquakes throughout the land and pestilence and hunger, and in the sky terrible signs and portents. Because at this time the trumpet of the evangelists was heralding to all peoples the coming of the Just Judge, the Universal Church considered that now the entire world was far and wide evidencing those signs foretold by the prophets. Jerusalem was then held by the Saracens and was in servitude to Babylon [Old Cairo], which is now the capital of the kingdom of Egypt; so in Jerusalem the Christian religion was very insecure and maintained itself only by payment of a daily tribute. Bethlehem, the home of the Bread of Angels, was turned into an enclosure to keep cattle, and for a number of years all the practices of the Universal Church were subjected to the ridicule of the pagans. When a most unfortunate war broke out among the Eastern Christians, between Greeks and Armenians, the Armenians, who were weaker in resources and numbers, recruited their warlike neighbors from Persia. These neighbors were Turks and they were fighters of great renown. When the Armenians were satisfied that the disturbance had been put down, they sent the Turks back to their own territories. The Turks, however, had been much attracted by the abundance and fertility of the lands they had seen, and so, after some years vast masses of these pagans decided to leave the north and come down from Khorassan, a land which is said to have too many people and not enough food to support them. These Turks were grouped under four sultans (sultan is the title they use for their leaders) and in Persia they had been obliged to worship only one Persian emperor almost as if he were a god. Now these Turks poured through Armenia and then spread through Cappadocia and all the Romania [Byzantium] and Syria.

CHAPTER III: AT FIRST THEY STORM AND CAPTURE NICAEA

At first the Turks stormed and captured Nicaea, once the firmest citadel of the Catholic faith, and put to death the Christians they captured there. They left a man named Soloman, one of their leaders, with a garrison to guard the city and they set out to devastate utterly all the neighboring regions, all the way to the march or bay of the sea, which is called Saint George's Arm. They spared not a single Christian life, not a church, not a monastery, nay, not even the statues of the saints. We have visited there and seen—and one can still see—in the half-ruined chapels the statues of Our Savior, of His Glorious Mother, and of the Saints with noses and ears, hands and feet, chopped off; and these statues seem to symbolize the grief of the ruined churches and to witness by their ever fresh wounds the wand of divine judgment that watches over them. O Constantinople, noblest of cities, these wounds are the swords that have redeemed you—not the infinite wiliness of your king, not the immense number of your citizens, not the frequency of your market days or the vast masses of your gold. It was not your many fleets or your mercenary Varangians [Scandinavians in Byzantine service], Petchenegs [an Asiatic nomadic people occupying southern Russia], or Turks that defended you; your only protection was the location of the aforementioned swamp —indeed, only the Creator's work fortified your city. Antioch, that was once so powerful, also succumbed to the same furious attacks, and, to make a long story short, soon all of Syria and Palestine surrendered.

CHAPTER IV: JERUSALEM BURDENED BY A DOUBLE YOKE

And so the land of the Second Promise was subjugated, and Jerusalem, the Mother of Our Redemption and Our Faith, was oppressed by a double yoke of captivity. Yet there was some slight consolation for the Christians in that the Saracens, who had been oppressing them and who were much worse than the Turks, were now being equally punished. After the Sultan was installed in Jerusalem along with a large force of soldiers, those monasteries which were outside the city were destroyed to rebuild the city wall (which can still be seen today) and certain other buildings; but the Sepulcher of Our Lord was left untouched in return for tribute paid by the Christians. That most famous Temple of Our Lord, which is, as I judge, comparable to no other human structure, was reserved for the sacrilegious religion of the pagans, and was always held by them in such veneration that they never entered it without taking off their shoes and washing their feet. However, all these years, both under Saracens and Turks, they never permitted any Christians (whom they considered very unclean) to enter the main part of the temple.

CHAPTER V: THE EMPEROR ALEXIUS BEGS AID FROM POPE URBAN

Now that the conquering Turks had completed their military efforts and transplanted themselves from their dry and hungry homes into this rich and fertile land, they turned from the sweat of arms to the delights and indulgences of victory. Only one who has experienced them can bring himself to believe what torments the surviving Christians suffered in their servitude, what crosses they bore, what miseries they endured; but we can easily refer to the countless delegations and letters (even we have seen them) by which the Church at Jerusalem called sadly for aid from the Universal Church. Alexius, whom we have mentioned as Emperor of Constantinople, sent many letters to Pope Urban regarding these barbarous depredations that were taking place throughout the greater part of his empire. In these letters he regretted that he was not able to defend the eastern churches and he begged that, if possible, the entire West, where the Christian faith was everywhere professed, be called to his aid. He promised that he would personally provide everything necessary on land and sea for those who would come to fight.

CHAPTER VI: A GENERAL COUNCIL IS CALLED, AT WHICH AN EXPEDITION IS ANNOUNCED

At this the Pope and the entire Church was aroused, and in the year of Our Lord 1096, His Holiness ordered a General Council to be convened in Clermont, Spain. His Holiness himself attended, after making a difficult journey from Italy, and to the many peoples assembled there and to the delegates of various kingdoms he described with much eloquence and detail the events we have here recorded. Soon thousands of men were weeping openly and in various tongues lifting their laments to the sky, when their glorious leader promised them remission of all their sins if, renouncing all that they possessed, they would with one heart and one mind follow Christ, take up the cross, and bring help to their suffering fellow Christians. This solemn promise stirred their spirits, and on the spot around one hundred thousand men were recruited for the army of God. They came from Aquitaine [southwestern France] and from Normandy, from England, Scotland, and Ireland, from Brittany, Galicia [northwestern Spain], Gascony, France, Flanders, Lorraine, and other Christian countries whose names are now no longer current. They wore on their cloaks the sign of the cross, which this "cross-bearing" army carried before it as a reminder of its sacrifice, trusting in this as the great Constantine once trusted that the vision of the cross revealed to him would enable him to triumph over the enemies of Christ. By a great and wondrous dispensation of God, so many limbs of Christ's Body, though they differed in languages, tribes, and nations, suddenly joined to form one body united in the love of Christ. And all of them accepted Christ as their King, though each nation had its own leader: Godfrey of Lorraine, his brothers Baldwin and Eustace, Robert of Flanders, Robert of Normandy, Count Raymond of Saint Giles, Hugh, brother of Philip, King of France, and other warriors of the same energy, nobility, and bravery. Over all of these His Holiness placed Bishop Adhemar, a man of great sanctity and wisdom, to whom he gave the power to bind and to loose, the right of the Roman see inherited from Saint Peter, to be exercised in his name. He then gave his apostolic blessing to this army branded with the sign of heavenly soldiery and, after all had agreed on the departure time [August 15, 1096] for the first expedition, he returned to Italy accompanied by a large company of men who would take part in this expedition.

CHAPTER VII: THE NUMBER OF CRUSADERS GROWS

The delegates then returned, each to his own country, and soon reports of what had happened spread far and wide and aroused the entire world. In fact, strange though it may sound, so swift was the speed with which this report flew that it passed the ocean's limit and soon made the seas themselves overflow with fleets from the islands which were joining the army of the Heavenly King. For, as we have learned from very reliable sources, the ocean poured out on to our shores peoples so unknown to us that our coastal dwellers or our sailors could not even recognize their languages, much less their habits and their customs. Still others came who used nothing for food except bread and water, and there were some who used silver instead of iron for all their utensils. Each day, and from all parts of the world, the number of Crusaders increased, and, as we have said above, the whole world was shaken and excited—indeed, transformed.

CHAPTER VIII: FRANCE WAS THEN AFFLICTED BY HUNGER AND SICKNESS

It was easy at this time to persuade the people of western France to leave their fields. For some years Gaul had been afflicted, sometimes by civil disturbances, other times by hunger and sickness. Finally, the plague, which began near Nivalensem [present-day Nivelles, in Belgium], where they had begun the Church of Saint Gertrude, had terrorized the citizenry even to despair of their lives. Their disease was something like this: the patient was assailed by an invisible fire that attacked some part of his body and burned with an incurable and torturing pain as long as he retained sensation in that part of his body. His suffering did not end until he either lost his life or his afflicted limbs; and many today who are bereft of hands or feet bear witness to this disease. From other nations not included in the papal edict came groups of people and individuals who announced that they had been summoned to the Promised Land by prophets who had recently risen among them or by revelations or signs in the sky, and still others said that they had been compelled to make their solemn pledges by a variety of unusual events. A great number of these men set out burdened with their wives, children, and households.

CHAPTER IX: THE CRUSADE NOT PREACHED AMONG THE ALAMANNI BECAUSE OF THE SCHISM

This trumpet call to arms sounded but weakly among the eastern Franks, the Saxons and Thuringians, the Bavarians and the Alamanni [Swabians], the chief reason being the schism which has prevailed between kingdom and clergy from the time of Pope Alexander to today and which, alas, made us as hated and despised by the Romans as they are by us. This is the reason why almost all the Teutons, at the beginning, were unaware of the reason for this expedition and assumed that they were witnessing some sort of mass delirium as they saw passing through their territories so many legions of cavalry, so many companies of infantry, so many bands of farmers, women, and little children, all of whom were abandoning their native lands and the security of the past for the insecurity of the future, heading for a Promised Land beset by uncertainties, looking back on what they had, looking forward to what they would acquire. But although our German nation is much more stubborn than other nations, still, through God's mercy, they learned of the whole matter from the crowds of pilgrims passing through, and their Teutonic passion finally was swayed by the announcement of the rewards promised to the Crusaders.

CHAPTER X: VARIOUS PORTENTS INCITE THE TEUTONS TO THIS SACRED WAR

In addition, the sign which I have mentioned above was seen in the sky and various other portents appeared, both on land and in the air, stirring up the hearts of many who had previously been reluctant to join a campaign of this sort. I think it would be very useful to describe some of these at this point, though it would take too much space to include them all. First, from September 30 to October 14, 1097, we saw a comet gleaming in the noonday sky that looked like a sword; two years later, on February 24, 1099, we sighted another star in the east that moved quickly in long leaps across the sky. We also have witnesses to confirm that we saw bloody clouds that arose in the west as well as in the east and rushed together in mid-sky, as well as fiery splendors that came up in the northern sky around midnight and many smaller fires that flew through the heavens. A few years before this, late one afternoon an aged man named Siggerus saw two horsemen attacking one another in the sky. They fought together for some time until the one who was carrying a cross, with which he seemed to strike the other, emerged the victor. At the same time another preacher G. (who has now consecrated himself to Christ with us as a professed monk) was walking in a forest with two companions at midday when suddenly he saw a wondrously long sword lifted aloft by a gust of wind. Where it came from he did not know, but he heard it crash through the air and he saw the gleam of its metal until it disappeared from his sight high in the sky. Some men who were out in pastures guarding horses reported that they saw a kind of city appear in the sky and that toward it hastened various groups of men, on foot and on horseback, from various directions. Several displayed the sign of the cross divinely figured on their brows or on their clothes or on some other part of their bodies, and they believed by this brand that they were enrolled in the army of the Lord. Others, then, feeling a sudden change of heart or inspired by this nocturnal vision, decided to dispose of their fields and their household property and sew on their clothes this sign of consecration. And to all these incredibly large masses of people who now rushed to their churches, the church assigned, with its blessing and in a special rite, swords, walking sticks, and knapsacks. Finally, how can I describe such occurrences as that of a woman who was pregnant for two straight years and finally was delivered of a son who could speak; or the small baby born with a double set of limbs; or the two-headed baby; or the lambs born with two heads; or the foals born with teeth even larger than their dams', of a size that nature ordinarily grants only to three-year-old horses?

CHAPTER XI: FALSE PROPHETS AND DECEIVERS IN SHEEP'S CLOTHING

With these signs and others like them, all of God's creation was urged to serve in the army of its Creator. But our enemy was ever active, he who watches while others sleep, and he set about to sow tares over the good seed and to raise false prophets under the appearance of religious zeal to infiltrate the army of the Lord with false brethren and dishonorable women; and the flocks of Christ were so corrupted by the lies and hypocrisy of some and the nefarious pollutions of others that, as the Good Shepherd once prophesied, even the elect were led into error. They were the source of a rumor invented about Charlemagne, according to which he had been raised from the dead; and they told of others, too, who had come back to life; and also of a goose that misled its own mistress, and other nonsense of this sort. But just as deceivers are known by their fruits and revealed as wolves masquerading in sheep's clothing, so we may ask of those deceivers who are still among us from which port did they sail, as they promised, across the sea, and in what areas and in what battles did they slay hosts of infidels with small forces, and which pagan fortress did they capture, and, finally, at which part of Jerusalem's walls did they pitch their camps? To questions like these they would have no answers; and so they must be compelled to do penance for the offerings they have falsely collected from the faithful, for the people they have deceived and killed for the sake of plunder, and, in particular, for their own apostasies.

CHAPTER XII: THE PREACHERS VOLKMAR AND GOTTSCHALK

Now, to take up where we left off, the people following Volkmar through Bohemia came to Nitra, a city in Hungary. Here a disturbance broke out in which many were put to the sword and many others thrown into captivity. The very few who survived still maintain that what saved them from imminent death was the sign of the cross that appeared above them in the heavens. Gottschalk, who was not a true but a false servant of God, then entered Hungary via East Noricum with his army, but not without some losses. Here, masking his true intentions under the guise of religion, he established an armed camp on a hill, fortified it with a garrison, and with his remaining men began to devastate the Hungarian countryside. Of course the Hungarians at once captured his camp and killed and incarcerated many of his followers: the rest of the flock was scattered, and this Gottschalk, who was a hireling, not a shepherd, fled in disgrace. Still another warlord arose in those same days, a man named Emich, who was a count living in the area around the Rhine River. Although he once had a notorious reputation as a petty tyrant, he claimed now to be a second Saul called to the cause of religion by divine revelations. He won to his service almost twelve thousand recruits and led them down through the cities of the Rhine, the Main, and the Danube, where they occupied themselves with massacring or driving into the bosom of the Church that cursed race of Jews wherever they could be found—a practice in which they displayed their Christian zeal. By the time Emich's army had arrived at the Hungarian border, their ranks were swelled by countless numbers of men and women; but they were forbidden by the small garrison there to enter that kingdom, which is circled partly by forests, partly by swamps. A report had reached the ears of the Hungarian King Coloman warning him that the Germans made no distinction between killing pagans and killing Hungarians. The Germans then laid siege to the town of Wiesselburg for six weeks and suffered many hardships there. Whatever Hungarian land any of them seized in the name of his king was shaken by foolish civil disorders. And so they made a final attack, broke through the walls and drove the townspeople in flight. The Hungarian armed forces then began to burn their own fields, when, by the wondrous will of almighty God, the victorious German army turned its back, abandoned its equipment and fled, its booty left behind and its soldiers scarcely saving their own lives. This is what happens to people of our nation who act with the zeal of God but not with His wisdom, for they had begun to persecute their fellow Christians in a campaign that Christ had provided for the liberation of Christians. Now they had spilled their brothers' blood and they were driven back by the mercy of God; and in this way the Hungarians were freed. This is the reason why certain of our more credulous brethren, who did not know the facts of the situation, were scandalized and, acting like excessively hasty judges, decided that this entire undertaking was vain and frivolous.

CHAPTER XIII: CHRIST'S TRUE ARMY, WITH GODFREY AT ITS HEAD, RECEIVES
AN UNFRIENDLY RECEPTION FROM ALEXIUS, EMPEROR OF CONSTANTINOPLE

Now that a blast like this had blown the chaff from the Lord's threshing floor, we
saw the grains of wheat emerging in their weight and substance. For we saw Godfrey
and other men I have named above, the leaders of the Lord's true army, each of
whom with its followers, because of their disciplined camps and their examples of
humility and charity (as true disciples of Christ), won safe conduct and assistance
from the leaders of the nations through which they passed. Finally, by various and
difficult journeys they crossed Bulgaria and came to the fortifications of Constantinople.
We have read a book about Jerusalem that describes very carefully the series of
events that began at this point and continued through three years of suffering endured
by God's people until its happy conclusion in the capture of Jerusalem. Of these many
events we will relate but a few here; in particular, those thoroughly false favors by
which Emperor Alexius won the friendship of these great heroes and how, after he
had extorted promises from them not to do harm to his kingdom and while their
first cohorts were awaiting the arrival of the others, he would have treacherously put
them to death if it had not been for their wise leader Godfrey who kept careful watch
over the herds of the Lord. Evidence for this treachery is the suburbs of the city
which Godfrey then destroyed and the bridge which he took by storm. Why say
more? For a space of about two months the army received new recruits every day
until it finally numbered, apart from an incredible crowd of women and children,
three hundred thousand fighting men. Formerly, the cohorts that had followed Peter
the Hermit, that had finally been transported into Asia at Alexius' order, had been
ridiculed by the pagans.

CHAPTER XIV: NICAEA AND ANTIOCH TAKEN BY THE FRANKS

After they had broken camp, the Franks moved on the city of Nicaea which they took
by storm after its leader Soloman had fled. They then handed the captured city over
to the garrisons of the emperor, in this way honoring their pledge to return to the
emperor whatever captured cities had belonged to him while they, for their part, could
be assured of arms and assistance from the emperor to aid them in taking these cities.
They then proceeded through the kingdom of Constantine, a particularly rich and
fertile land, and came to the city of Marash. A letter sent by a certain Robert, who
accompanied the Crusaders, reports that Christ administered to His forces with such
an abundance of supplies that sheep could be bought for pennies, cattle for slightly
more. "Moreover," he writes, "as often as Saracen kings and princes rose against us,
they were, by the will of God, easily crushed and defeated. But either because our
progress had been too easily achieved or because some amongst us had grown proud,
God crossed our path with Antioch, a city impregnable to human forces. There for
nine months He kept us so occupied with a siege and so humiliated our proud
warriors that all their swollen pride abated. When they had been so humiliated that

scarcely a hundred good horses could be found in the entire army, God opened to them the abundance of His blessing and mercy, brought them into the city, and surrendered to them the Turks and all their possessions. Since they were now holding the city which they had won by their own resources (so they thought), and since they were not giving worthy glory to God, Who had provided them with all these things, they were in turn harassed by such a horde of Saracens that not one of this vast army dared to go out of the city. Moreover, famine had become so serious in the city that some could hardly restrain themselves from cannibalism. It would take too long to describe the miseries that afflicted the city of Antioch. Finally, God, looking down upon His people whom He had so long punished, consoled them with His kindness and showed them, as a kind of satisfaction for their tribulations and as a pledge of their victory, the Lance by which He had been wounded on the cross and which had not been seen since the time of the Apostles. In this way He so strengthened their hearts that He inspired even those crippled by sickness and hunger to take arms and fight manfully against their enemies."

CHAPTER XV: SARACEN CITIES OF ALBARA AND MAARAT AL-NUMAN
CAPTURED BY THE FRANKS

The enemy was now overcome, but hunger and exhaustion were weakening the army at Antioch and the leaders quarreled amongst themselves. The Franks then set out into Syria, captured the Saracen cities of Albara and Maarat al-Numan, and won control of the castles in this area. While they were delaying there, there was such famine in the army that the rotting bodies of the Saracens were eaten by Christian people. When they then moved on, following God's will, into the Syrian interior, they had with them the hand of their Almighty Father, generous, merciful, victorious. For the people of the region through which they were now proceeding sent delegates to them from their towns and castles with many gifts and declared themselves ready to give up their towns and serve them. But since their army was not large and since they were hastening with one mind to Jerusalem, they accepted the guarantees of these delegations and made them tribute-paying subjects, although just one of the many cities which lay along the coast had more men than were in the Christian army. When the knights at Antioch, Laodicae, and Edessa heard that the hand of God was with them, many left the army that had remained there and followed the Crusaders to Tyre. And so, with God as their fellow traveler and fellow worker, the Franks went all the way to Jerusalem. They made no immediate effort to besiege the city, particularly because of a lack of water, and in a council meeting the bishops and leaders said that they should walk barefoot around the city in order that He who had entered this city for us in humility might now observe the humility of these witnesses to Him before His enemies and might open the gate. The Lord was pleased by this show of humility and eight days later [July 15, 1099] gave the city to the Franks, on the very same date on which the early Church was driven from the city, for this is the date celebrated by many of the faithful in commemoration of the dispersion of the Apostles.

CHAPTER XVI: THE ARABS CAPTURE JERUSALEM IN THE SAME YEAR
AND STRONGLY FORTIFY IT

While describing all of this I must not neglect to mention that while the Crusaders were delayed in besieging Antioch, all the nations of the East were struck by terror and sent out their agents from every part of the earth, some to seek peace, some to seek war. The ambassadors of the Arabian king appeared at a meeting of the leaders and promised among other things that if Antioch were taken they would drive the Turks out of Jerusalem and control it as friends and brothers to all Saracens [Moslems]. For, as we have already recounted, the Turks had a while before seized Judaea and all of Palestine from the Saracens. For this reason a number of selected knights were sent to Babylon [Old Cairo] under a safe-conduct pledge; there the Arabs were so astonished by their size, valor, clothing, and bearing—their general elegance—that they acknowledged the Franks (the name they apply to all western peoples) to be more than mortal, that is, gods, and admitted that it was not surprising that warriors like them should presume to subject the world to their will. In accordance with this plan, then, the Arab king laid siege to Jerusalem, and when the city sent him ambassadors he declared himself allied with the Franks and threatened that if they did not surrender their city to him then, he would have them surrendered to the swords of the Franks. And so, by this trickery, the Moslem Arabs seized the city, which was terrified not of him but of the Franks; and when he had driven out the Turks and their followers he fortified the city as well as he could with equipment and soldiers against the coming of the Christians. This is how it happened that Jerusalem was captured twice in one year, first by the Saracens, then by the Franks.

CHAPTER XVII: THE FRANKS WIN A SPLENDID VICTORY OVER THE MOSLEMS
AT ASCALON

If anyone wants to know what happened to the Crusaders' enemies in Jerusalem, he should read what is written in the portico of the Temple of Soloman: "The victors rode in Saracen blood up to the knees of their horses." When arrangements had been made for some of the Franks to control the city, and others because of their love for their country and their families wanted to return home, a report came that the king of the Arabs had arrived in Ascalon with a large multitude of his Moslems and was intending to capture the Franks who were in Jerusalem and capture the city of Antioch. Those were his words, but the Lord had decided otherwise. So, when the Crusaders in Jerusalem learned for certain that the Arab army was at Ascalon, they left their baggage and their sick with a garrison in Jerusalem and they hastened to meet the pagans. When they sighted the countless numbers of the enemy army, they bent their knees and called upon God to attend them in their present battle as He had always attended them in their past necessities and to crush the forces of the pagans and the devil and thereby extend the kingdom of Christ and the Church all the way from sea to sea. At once God answered their calls and was with them, providing such power and valor that whoever saw them rushing against the enemy would consider slow a thirsty stag racing for a stream of fresh water. It was indeed remarkable, when one considers that the Christian army had no more than five thousand horsemen and fifteen thousand foot soldiers, whereas their opponents could have had a hundred thousand horsemen and four hundred thousand infantry; how God appeared miraculously among His servants and, before the two armies clashed, turned this multitude to flight. He also seized all their weapons so that if they wanted to renew the fight they would have no arms to rely on. As for booty, it was impossible to count the loot when the treasure of the Arab king was captured. Moreover, over a hundred thousand Moors fell to the sword, and the panic among them was so great that around two thousand of them were suffocated in a pile-up at the gate of the city. We have no count of those who perished in the sea; the thickets also entrapped many of them. Indeed, all of creation was fighting on the side of the Christians, and were it not that many of them were preoccupied with looting the enemy camp, there would have been but few of the enemy's vast numbers to bring back the news of the battle.

CHAPTER XVIII: CAMELS, SHEEP, AND CATTLE FOLLOW THE ARMY RETURNING TO JERUSALEM

On the day before the battle took place, the army had captured many thousands of camels, sheep, and cattle. The leaders ordered their followers to release them as they marched to the fight, when, strange to relate, these same animals formed into herds and accompanied the army, hurrying when the army hurried, standing when the army stood. Also, the clouds protected the Christians from the heat of the sun and cooled them. After celebrating their victory, the army returned to Jerusalem, where they left Godfrey in charge, and then Count Raymond of Saint-Giles, Robert, Duke of Normandy, and Robert, Count of Flanders, returned to Laodicea. There they found a fleet from Pisa and Bohemund with his men. A large number of Crusaders, in addition to those who had settled at Antioch with Bohemund or had left Edessa with Baldwin, had remained at Tyre and had dispersed throughout the surrounding country-side; now they held a meeting there. When the Archbishop of Pisa had reconciled the quarreling leaders, a very great number decided to return to their homeland; but Godfrey, as we have said, took command of the people who had remained at Jerusalem.

CHAPTER XIX: GLORIOUS DEEDS OF GODFREY

Godfrey was a splendid leader, incomparable in his services to his religion, and though supported by but a small band of followers, he set about to achieve great things for the Lord. He pursued the surviving remnants of the heathen wherever they were, he established garrisons at opportune places, he rebuilt Jaffa which had been long destroyed, and restored the port there which had also been desolated, he restored the churches and clergy as well as he could, he set up religious communities in other places, and he very piously gave many gifts to monasteries as well as to the Crusaders' guest house which had always been in Jerusalem. To assure commerce he established very peaceful relations with Ascalon and Damascus. He honored the soldiers of our Teutonic race above all other warriors, and with his customary tact and urbanity he commended their fierceness to his Gallic horsemen. The resultant ill will between these peoples he was able to mollify by his skilled knowledge of their two languages.

CHAPTER XX: A CONVENTION OF PILGRIMS AT JERUSALEM; GODFREY DIES OF DISEASE

In the year 1100 when Godfrey was defender of the Church at Jerusalem, he called to a great convention at Jerusalem all Christian pilgrims who were in the East, and especially those who had settled in Antioch or in Syria or in Edessa or in Palestine, and announced to them that on the Feast of Our Lord's Nativity as many bishops as possible would be consecrated for the adjacent regions. Thus were the mystical verses of the prophets transformed into visible history: "Rise and shine, Jerusalem," and "Rejoice with Jerusalem," and "Celebrate a feast of God, all ye that love her," etc. [Isaiah 51:17 and 66:10]. In the following summer, as the weather grew warm, the atmosphere throughout Palestine was tainted by rotting corpses. There are also those who say that the springs were poisoned by the barbarians or that the wells were polluted by the gore of dead bodies. The pestilence that resulted killed many of our men who were fighting under this foreign sky, among them Godfrey himself, whose death was lamented in the tears of the whole Catholic Church. All too soon had this disease taken him from God's people, whom he had tended with a father's solicitude and cherished with a mother's affection. After only one year in charge of God's people, he was overcome by sickness and on July 18, 1100, full of faith and good works, he ended his life in Christ. Apart from all his other virtues, he had been so gentle in his dealings with the local peoples as well as with his fellow Crusaders that it would be hard to say if his death was more lamented by the Franks than by the Syrians or Greeks. A mausoleum of Parian marble was built for him before Mount Calvary in the Church of the Holy Sepulcher.

CHAPTER XXI: GODFREY IS SUCCEEDED BY HIS BROTHER BALDWIN, LEADER OF EDESSA, WHO IS CROWNED BY THE PAPAL LEGATE

At this time Baldwin, Count of Edessa (though called Rohas and thought to be Rages, a city of the Medes), a famous city and part of Armenia, where he had settled and taken over the control of that nation, suffered the loss of Thoros, his aged Armenian associate, a very faithful Christian who had brought him to Edessa from Antioch as his defender and, after he had zealously waged many battles, had even adopted him as his son and heir. The great city of Edessa had been attacked again and again since antiquity, but had never surrendered to the pagans, the reasons being that its walls were superhumanly strong, there was also a raging stream within the walls, and the site of the city was strengthened by an abundance of people and foodstuffs. It is not the purpose of this work now to recount how often Baldwin with a small band destroyed a vast horde of barbarians, or how, himself defeated, he still won out, or how, when one army was defeated, he brought another one from the siege at Antioch, or how, finally, he escaped from the wiles of his treacherous Turkish ally, a certain Balduc, then captured him and put him to death. Anyone wanting to describe all these events would sooner run out of time than material. Well, when Baldwin heard of the death of his brother Godfrey, he entrusted his people and his city to his cousin Baldwin of Le Bourg and with around three hundred men he set out for Jerusalem. He tricked a force of a thousand pagans trying to ambush him, then met and defeated them, and triumphantly entered Jerusalem laden with spoils. Praised and requested by all to be their leader, he consented and shortly thereafter laid his head upon the tomb of the Holy Sepulcher of Our Lord and consecrated himself to its perpetual service. Then, to strike the pagans with even greater fear of Christians, Baldwin received the royal blessing and was crowned King of Jerusalem by the legate of the Apostolic See. Next he captured the coastal cities of Arsuf and Caesarea and killed the Saracens who inhabited them; then he extended his own kingdom at the expense of the Arab king.

CHAPTER XXII: A NEW ARMY OF TEUTONS, LOMBARDS, AND AQUITAINIANS

In the same year, 1101, an acquaintance of ours saw a star resembling a rather large city that appeared to fly from west to east. Also, a vast army of flying insects, which looked somewhat like butterflies, flew for three straight days from what seemed to be the area of Saxony into Bavaria. Soon they were followed by a great popular movement, comparable in numbers almost to the earlier crusade, which was begun by the remaining nations of the West after they had heard of the unexpected successes enjoyed by those who had gone to Jerusalem. All those now set out whom lack of courage, faith, reason, or strength had previously dissuaded. The first contingent was Lombards, numbering about fifty thousand, and led by the bishops of Milan and Pavia; the next came from various German provinces; and the last was Aquitainians, numbering thirty thousand armed men in addition to civilians and led by William IX, Duke of Aquitaine.

CHAPTER XXIII: THIS ARMY BADLY RECEIVED BY EMPEROR ALEXIUS

The Lombards passed through Carinthia with the permission of Henry, Duke of Carinthia, and crossed through Hungary, but their number began to dwindle as they wintered in the cities of Bulgaria. At last they arrived in Constantinople and were transported over to the Asian side of the Bosphorus (that favor, at least, the cursed Alexius hastily provided for all foreigners), but once across they were exposed to the arrows of the pagans. For the Turks, discovering the slow progress of the Lombards, harassed them with hit and run attacks, a tactic which, as far as the Teutonic army (which came the same way to Constantinople at the beginning of June) could discover, had never been used against previous armies. The result was that there was not a single survivor who returned from Byzantium. From the time the Crusaders entered Belgrade, the first city of Bulgaria, until they reached Constantinople, Alexius' messengers, who were always peaceably disposed toward us [Ekkehard was an eyewitness to the events in this and the following chapter] kept approaching us and, after riding ahead of us or beside us, disappeared like vanishing sparks. An army of their soldiers, whom they call Petechenegs, attacked us, now from the rear, now from the side, now—in conventional battle line—from the front, and at night broke into our camp. For twenty days these soldiers were always near us, always harassing us, until we took up a position and were joined by the squadron of Duke Guelph, the army of William, and various other forces that were arriving each day. In fifteen days the total reached 100,000 men. From all of these forces Alexius, as was his custom, took the leaders of the individual squadrons and named them his "sons." Then, after general handshaking and pledging of agreements, Alexius distributed gifts, as he had to the previous armies, and gave orders that the poor pilgrims outside the city be assisted and that they be given an opportunity to acquire provisions. Because of his obsessive suspiciousness he permitted entrance to each city, camp, or fort throughout his empire to very few people, and to them only secretly and after payment of a bribe. For this reason, when William IX and his army were forbidden passage through the middle of Adrianople, where the royal road leads, the Aquitainians, swollen with scornful pride and shouting slogans, burned the suburbs and invaded the city. While they were encountering bitter resistance to their attack, they discovered that the Petcheneg army, which, as always, had been sent ahead on the emperor's orders to observe their line of march, was attacking them from the rear. In the ensuing conflict they killed many, lost many, and at last proceeded along the road that had been long forbidden them.

CHAPTER XXIV: ALEXIUS FAVORS THE TURKS RATHER THAN THE CHRISTIANS

Therefore, all that vast number of people was preparing to march through Byzantium and was buying provisions necessary for the deserted regions ahead of them, while we were being ferried across that arm of the sea named after Saint George, as much under compulsion as voluntarily. We, uncertain, were awaiting the outcome of daily meetings of our leaders and their daily interviews with the emperor when all of a sudden the rumor arose that this hated emperor favored the side of the Turks rather than that of the Christians, and that he was spying on us and sending frequent messages to the Turks encouraging them against us. "This," they said, "is that wicked Alexius who used the help of some German mercenaries to unseat his master Nicephorus and usurp his throne, and who then condemned to death and exile those who had conspired with him in his crime. This is the man who now says that he is as much concerned about Franks fighting with Turks as he would be with dogs fighting amongst themselves." When some of the Crusaders tried to hire ships, they heard that the emperor had set ambushes for them even at sea and had recently sunk many ships by this criminal act. Therefore they all cursed and anathematized him and all called him not an emperor but a traitor. For one who has experienced this, it is unbearable to recall and horrible to recount how great the tribulation was in our German group, which was smaller than all the others, when father was separated from son, brother from brother, and friend from friend, not by death but—more bitterly —by life, as one entrusted himself to the sea and the other to the land. Some, after paying their money to hire boats and spending one or two nights at sea, gathered their equipment and leaped ashore with great losses. They then hired back at a higher price the horses that they had recently given up and by avoiding one death they hastened to another. For a long time we too were much troubled by the same indecision until we joined those who dared to entrust themselves to the sea and, with divine clemency governing our miseries, we reached the port of Jaffa after six weeks. Blessed be Jesus Christ in all things!

CHAPTER XXV: THE ARMY IS HARASSED BY THE TURKS NEAR KHORASSAN

Next, when the general had accepted three hundred men from Turcopolis to lead his legions along a suitable way, the whole army turned against Nicomedea and then moving south into Byzantium marched toward the land of Khorassan, which is the homeland of the Turks. But the deceitful Alexius had laid waste all the areas of Byzantium which adjoined the public road, and as long as he did not dare bring aid to our people long besieged in Antioch, as he had sworn to do, he was suspected from then on as much by the Franks as by the Turks. In addition, this army proposed to make a name for itself among the heathen, just as it had done in the past; but, as events turned out, this was not the pleasure of divine destiny. For within a few days these same pagans whetted their swords which, as we said above, had been dulled by the blood of the Lombards that was still fresh on their blades. Inspired by that success, they now presumed to withstand this infinite mass of warriors. Some four thousand Turks, themselves specially chosen, equipped with the fastest horses, arms, and weapons, and highly trained in archery came out to test their own luck or the courage of an unknown army, which they did rather by reconnaissance than by open conflict. Their tactics were to attack first the people at the edges of the army, as if to rob them, then to capture or kill, and then to break through their lines and destroy their supplies by fire or some other means, and sometimes even to harass the army all day with fire and smoke as it proceeded by wagon and cart, and sometimes at night to break into this or that part of the camp and spread panic among all the inhabitants. Not once in all this did they face us like soldiers with battle line drawn up and front ranks exposed; but instead they yielded to resistance, fled when pursued, and then returned to follow us again. If I try with my pen to do full justice to those miseries which were more miserable than all other miseries, I will at once exceed the limit of possibility if I describe the numbers of noble men who perished ignobly, of rich men who perished in need, of brave men who perished without striking a blow, in situations where the servant could not assist his master, riches could not help the wealthy man, nor was the brave man permitted to fight. Moreover, the terrain in which the machinations of the traitorous Alexius incarcerated too many of God's people was narrow, trackless, and uninhabited, known to the enemy, unknown to our men.

CHAPTER XXVI: ALMOST THE ENTIRE CHRISTIAN ARMY PERISHES

Why do I delay? For about twenty-one days our men were exposed like targets to the Turkish arrows and were offered up like lambs to the daily slaughter. At last, in desperation, they took to the woods and thereby hastened the slow but certain death awaiting them. Flight, however, was of use to only a few, except that it protracted the final fate of all. For, alas! alas! of God's countless people we believe that not a thousand men survived, whom we afterwards saw, flesh scarcely clinging to their bones, at Rhodes, Paphos, and other ports, and a few even at Jaffa. Among the survivors were Count Bernhard of Bavaria and Count Henry of Ratisbon, both of whom died at Jerusalem, and Duke Guelph of Bavaria, who returned to Paphos where he died and was buried. The story of their martyrdom is too long to be described within the limits of this brief work, but of our Germans they reported that Thiemo, Archbishop of Salzburg, was captured, that the Dowager Margravine Ida of Austria was killed, and the two noble Brunos, both canons, died of hunger and thirst. The survivors reported from among the French leaders were William, Raymond, Stephen, and some others.

CHAPTER XXVII: BALDWIN URGES HIS MEN TO FIGHT AGAINST THE ARABS, WHOM HE PUTS TO FLIGHT

While these things were going on, the Christians in Judaea knew no relief, but were subjected to daily robbery from Damascus and Ascalon as well as attacks from the Arabs. In mid-May of 1102, Baldwin drew up a battle line against an Arab army encamped not far from Ramleh. A few days before, his men had by the grace of God won a great deal of booty from the Arabs with but a small band, so now he urged them not to yield to the masses of their enemy. "Let us live," he said, "by their destruction, or let us risk death. Here is the war, my brave soldiers, that we have long desired, the war for which we have renounced country, parents, and peace. It is an honorable thing to fight for Christ's birthplace against foreign marauders who have invaded the Holy Land, and it is a glorious thing to die in certainty of victory over such enemies. Their native land offers them flight, our exile here offers us victory. Let us therefore confirm the charges of the Arabs that the Franks do not fear death, that as Christ's Crusaders we are willing to conquer in Christ or die for Christ." After he had said these words and aroused their spirits, by the wondrous will of Almighty God the vast masses of Saracens fell back before only one or two legions of our men; as a result, our troops did not even venture to join with them in battle, but after spending some days in the same location they returned ashamed of having accomplished nothing.

CHAPTER XXVIII: A NEW ARMY OF ARABS

Again, at the beginning of September, 1101, when the report of the coming of the Christians whom I have described above had terrified the kingdoms of the Arabs, they made plans and preparations for our destruction, that is, for the destruction of all of us who were then in Judaea or in any of their territories. They sent letters to Damascus, Tripoli, Jebail, and other heathen communities and made a mutual assistance pact against the name of Christianity. They sent out an army of forty thousand from Egypt to take Jaffa first; then it encamped not far from Ascalon after acquiring additional forces from that city. Baldwin, who was aware of this, called together his own troops from all sides, that is from Jerusalem, Nicopolis (Emmaus), Mount Tabor, Hebron, Caesarea, and Assur, and ordered them to Jaffa, where there was still a large number of Crusaders.

CHAPTER XXIX: COUNTLESS CHRISTIANS PERISH OF THE PLAGUE; SPEECH OF ARNULF OF ROHES TO THE SOLDIERS ABOUT TO FIGHT

We saw so many people dying these days (I barely escaped death myself) that up to three hundred corpses were counted day after day as they were brought out of Jerusalem, and at Jaffa a great field was filled with graves within a few days. Finally, on September 6, 1101, a meeting of all Christians was called for nine A.M. outside the city of Jaffa. During this meeting a piece of the Cross of Christ appeared before King Baldwin. The year before, the Syrians had shown this fragment to Duke Godfrey after it had long been hidden in the earth. At the order of King Baldwin, Arnulf Malecorne of Rohes, a venerable and learned churchman, delivered the following speech in the midst of the meeting. " 'Blessed is the nation whose God is the Lord; and the people whom He hath chosen for His own inheritance.' [Psalm XXXIII.12] You, O dearest brethren, are that blessed people, that holy people, you are that people who are heirs of Christ, the people who will gain all because they have abandoned all, country, parents, and property to bear a daily cross in Christ's footsteps. For Christ's sake you have given up your bodies to suffering. You only think you have been fighting; in reality, Christ has taken the blood you have willingly shed for Him, and, through the precious lives of your brethren in arms, He has deigned to cleanse the place of His sanctification and has willed through your devoted servitude to liberate Jerusalem, the city of His death, from its long years of subjection to a vile race. 'This,' says the Lord, 'is my rest for ever: here will I dwell; for I have desired it.' [Psalm CXXXI.14] This is the hope that has been given us by divine promise, but now opposing it are these letters we took by the will of God from pagan ambassadors we captured the day before yesterday. In these letters they invoke the demons of the prophecies and call for our death in battle this year, for the total destruction of Jerusalem, and, worst of all abominations, for the piecemeal demolishment of the Glorious Sepulcher of Our Lord and its removal by camels to the remotest corner of the sea where it can be submerged beyond recovery by the Christians. Realize, then, my Christian brethren, what must be done, and consider carefully what end the presumption of these pagans will take." At once wild shouting prevented him from speaking further, and all cried as if with one voice, "The crisis is now! We must decide promptly to fight bravely for Christ and His laws and our own or else perish miserably. We must either die gloriously and live eternally or else retreat in disgrace and win a brief and shameful life at the price of eternal death. But no one can live, either now or hereafter, who does not choose to fight against the profane and blasphemous boldness of the pagans." At once before the Cross of our Redemption the Crusaders unanimously humbled themselves to make a confession of their sins, and, after forgiveness had been pronounced by the Apostolic Delegate who happened to be present and they had received his blessing, they called upon the assistance of the Lord and returned in high spirits to camp. The next morning they came out of camp, seven thousand infantry and a thousand horsemen, and with great joy they faced their immense danger.

CHAPTER XXX: THE ENEMY ARE TURNED TO FLIGHT

When the pagans' encampment was seen, our men, strange though it may seem, began to glow with such confidence that each one was sure he alone could destroy whole legions. Thus it happened that after attacking at a run for a mile they broke ranks and carelessly infiltrated among the enemy so that the first cohort was attacked on the flank and totally destroyed. Baldwin was so upset by this that he led his cavalry against the enemy with such violence that the pagans, although they had been assured of victory by the responses from their idols and hence resisted more bitterly than ever before, melted before him like wax before fire. The venerable Abbot Gerhard, who was then carrying the Cross of Christ at the side of King Baldwin, reported to me that he had never seen a storm of snow or rain to compare with the density of spears and arrows directed at King Baldwin; but after seeing the precious wood of the Cross, not one of the enemy trusted his weapons but they all took refuge in flight.

CHAPTER XXXI: JAFFA BESIEGED BY LAND AND SEA

And so, after this victory granted them by God (Who saves both many and few), our men were seizing the camp and booty of the enemy, when a messenger arrived from the people of Jaffa to report that the city was besieged both by land and by sea. At once our men, laden down with booty after setting fire to the rest of the enemy property, rushed as quickly as possible to aid our people who were caught within the blocked gates of the city, besieged on land by cavalry and on sea by forty-two warships. After a number of attacks by the enemy and after suffering a great deal from disease and privation, they made us complete with great joy the Feast of the Nativity which we had begun with sorrow on that very day. For on the following day thirty ships brought us a great supply of grain and all sorts of foodstuffs along with some twelve thousand Crusader brethren. While the enemy fleet was attempting to attack and human aid could not be brought from the city, by the wondrous power of God the king ordered the Holy Cross to be uplifted from the opposite side and it so effectively checked the ships that by no skill or effort of rowing could a single ship be moved from its place, much to the wonderment of the pagans as well as the Christians.

CHAPTER XXXII: THE MIRCLE OF THE DIVINELY LIGHTED LAMPS

I must not pass over in silence something that we learned happened on Mount Olivet to the venerable preacher Heriman. What follows are his words: "On the day of the most holy Sabbath, Holy Saturday, according to the consolation afforded us out of the Lord's ancient mercy, we celebrated the baptismal service and in our devotion we waited until evening for a light to be shown us from heaven. We offered up our customary prayers, but because of our sins we were totally disappointed of our heavenly gift which in the days of old Christians were accustomed to receive even in the presence of the pagans. So we abstained from all joyful prayers and spent the night before Easter Sunday in grieving and lamenting. Early in the morning we marched barefoot from the Holy Sepulcher of Our Lord chanting litanies and entered the Temple of the Lord, in the place where, according to scripture [I Kings 9:3], Solomon was promised that all would be heard who prayed there with a devout heart. There we wept and prayed that Christ would not desert us and thereby incur blasphemy on His name among the pagans. We had not yet all left that famous edifice when suddenly we heard shouts of praise from those who had remained. We entered the church and rejoiced greatly to see two lamps that had been lit by the hand of God. Need I say more? We began at the baptismal service at which we had left off and with most joyous devotion we completed the entire labor of our service that was due to the Lord right up to the completion of Mass. After we had left, other lamps were divinely lighted during the Mass of the Syrian Christians, who are accustomed always after we leave to chant psalms in the same manner. As many as sixteen lamps of this kind were seen to be lighted before vespers and during the vesper prayers. Thus it happened that there were few people to be found in Jerusalem, Christians or pagans, who would not testify that they had witnessed evidence of the power of Christ.

CHAPTER XXXIII: BALDWIN MAKES ASCALON A TRIBUTARY STATE; MORE ABOUT THE TREACHERY OF EMPEROR ALEXIUS

Five years later [1104–1105] King Baldwin made the city of Ascalon [Ekkehard's error for Accon] a tributary state after a long siege. He accomplished this by surrounding the city by land with a small army and by sea with a very large fleet. Some months later fifty thousand Saracens suddenly attacked the city but were repulsed by divine power and only four thousand of Baldwin's men, with the loss of one Emir, the second in command after the Arab king, who was captured, and another Emir who was killed with the other Moslems. Thus was the favor of Christ prospering his Crusaders in Antioch, Syria, Palestine, and throughout Asia, and everywhere eliminating, by their efforts, the vileness of barbarism. But the jealous Emperor Alexius, that covert persecutor of the Church, gave vent to the vicious poison of his treachery that he had long been concealing, and very secretly made an agreement with the Turks, who now had little or no hope of ruling in the East, and—O vicious crime—betrayed to the sons of the tyrant Soloman the city of Nicaea, that ancient bastion of our faith, which, as we described above, had been won back by the profuse shedding of Christian blood. [Ekkehard is wrong; Nicaea remained under Byzantine rule until 1330.] By frequent messages he encouraged the Egyptian king against us and set up garrisons on land and sea to keep Crusaders from crossing his empire. The people of Antioch captured many fleets of warships that Alexius had sent to fight against them and to disconcert him they cut off the noses and thumbs of his men, filled a small boat with them, and sent this load of flesh to the emperor, himself the killer of many thousands of men. Bohemund, who was released by divine providence from three years of captivity, sailed to Italy where he had warships built and then went on to southern France where he began to collect as large an army as he could by every means possible to lead against the tyrannical Alexius. On the night of December 23–24, 1105, so large a fire was seen to blaze among the stars in the west that it would have been thought to be a ray of the sun if it had been seen in the east. At this time, too, some victorious Crusaders returning from Jerusalem reported that Accaron had been taken by our men. In reporting on the state of the Church in Jerusalem they also recounted several other successes which could afford us great rejoicing. They also informed us that King Baldwin had married the widow of King Conrad and daughter of Roger, Duke of Sicily, thus adding to his command a large fleet of Sicilians and Normans. These ships he could use in his sea attack on the city of Ascalon, which was again hostile to Christianity. King Baldwin again took this city by a land siege and made it tributary to him.

CHAPTER XXXIV: THE LORD LOOKS UPON SION

Shortly thereafter, when the Lord, after hiding His face for a little while [Isaiah 54:8], had looked again upon Sion, which He had long ago chosen for His habitation, throughout the whole world the seed of joy began to be spread, deservedly, into the souls of the faithful (these souls are the true daughters of Jerusalem) and, watered by prayers, bore good fruit far and wide. Prophecies that had long been forgotten were now repeated in the hearts, tongues, and voices of men everywhere. "Lo," they said, "in our age, to whom has come the end of time, the Lord has looked upon Sion and will be seen there in His glory. He has taken pity on Jerusalem, the city of His sanctification, the city of His repose. Rejoice all you who were mourning for her." [Psalm 102:16–19; Isaiah 66:10]. This and a thousand other prophecies like it may be applied, by analogy, to our motherly Jerusalem which is above us; yet, when the weaker members of our faith were nourished by the milk of the consolation I have been describing here, they urged one another by word and deed to brave all dangers in return for the opportunity to see and experience the great joy available to them. We have heard tell of a man who claims that in a vision he heard the hymn "Laetatus sum" with an "Alleluia," and that he himself joined in with the voices of the singers. As a result of this he was so eager to take part in this same crusade that his spirit had no rest until after many tribulations he could make his adoration in person and tread the same ground once trod by the feet of the Lord.

CHAPTER XXXV: PRAISE AND DEFENSE OF CHRIST'S CRUSADERS

It should be a cause not for surprise but for devotion that after removing the stumbling blocks of the pagans' hearts (which are harder than stone) from the way of the Lord, the Catholic Church journeyed with one heart along a new way of penitence to the source of its being, to the cradle of its earliest institution, and to the special home of the True Bread. It is certain that along this same way it has long exposed its precious members, like sheep being slaughtered, not only to death but also to the mockeries of the pagans. Few are the confessors of Christ who have survived to testify—and it is a pitiable story to record—that they took not a step among the idolators without suffering, much less receiving food and shelter. Who can adequately describe the countless and unheard of torments they suffered in return for the gold extorted from them? A bitter death was their reward, their cross was their life. But, if we may now return to our own times when we may say what we know and describe what we see, although the way to the Holy Land has been made smooth, it is still possible for those hurrying to an absolution of their sins to win the rewards of martyrdom by suffering the perils of robbers, rivers, the sea, solitude, hunger, thirst, storms, sickness, and a thousand other discomforts of a pilgrimage that are hardly believable to one who has not undergone them. A proof of our words are the many headless bodies of those who took up the Cross of Christ that are strewn along this way. Attacked by pagan robbers, they drank from the chalice of Christ amidst the prayers of those for whom they were making their pilgrimage and were stretched out on the ground in the form of a cross pointing east. Therefore, those who are caught in the chains of worldly pleasure should cease their erring ways and should hasten, with Simon, to take up the labor of carrying the cross behind Christ. Why should they continue to hasten along a road that is nowhere recommended by God's laws? But if they are unable to better themselves and follow the demanding ways of the Lord, then at least let them cease with poisoned tongues to disparage those who can. For what can we believe except that they were truly martyrs, those who lost all and for whom all was lost. They by their suffering crucified themselves to those things of this world, signing themselves with the sign of the cross; and of the many who left very few returned in triumph, victors over the forces of death.

CHAPTER XXXVI: THE CONDITION OF THE CHURCH AT JERUSALEM

Those who live in the Land of the Second Promise still suffer daily martyrdom, arbitrary exile, absence of loved ones, material want, attacks, robberies, constant fear of barbarian treachery, and endless wars with the kingdoms of the Persians and the Arabs. And yet, day by day, the Daughter of Sion, the Church of Jerusalem, raises them out of the dust and does not cease to sing a new song to her beloved by which he has worked miracles: "In the multitude of the sorrows in my heart, thy comfortings have delighted my soul." [Psalm 94:19] For amidst these trials, the holy places are being cleansed of the pagans' inveterate foulness, destroyed churches are being rebuilt, bishoprics and religious communities are being established in places that never had them, cities and forts are being built, ports and markets that were once deserted are now doing a thriving business, and farmers, shepherds, and vineyard keepers are able to work, and, what surpasses all temporal benefits, the heavenly fire at Easter is providing its annual blessing to mankind. There has also come into our hands a copy of that letter we believe has been disseminated throughout the world which men say the Archangel Gabriel has received from Our Saviour Himself for delivery to the Church at Jerusalem and through it to all churches. This letter threatens deceivers with many terrors but it does not deny the usual consolations of divine mercy to those who change their ways. Therefore, so great is the glory that has risen over Jerusalem through the multitudinous mercies of Our Lord that the tribes of all the earth, remembering the salvation that once came into the world from Mount Sion, should now rejoice with their ancient mother as they have so long, like dutiful children, grieved over her. Let them now drink deeply of the milk of her consolation, coming to her from the rising of the sun and its setting, from the north and from the south, and let them, free from doubt, profess in every way the name of Our Lord Jesus Christ, Who, by His Incarnation, has consecrated this place even more (if, as a faithful Christian, I may say this) than the Garden of Eden by His miracles, His passion, His resurrection, and His ascension. May all things announce and glorify His name and His mercy for ever and ever. Amen.

The Inquisition

From the time that Christianity became an official religion, heresy (that is, deviation from accepted religious doctrine or practice) was punished as a crime. No special courts for this purpose were created until the thirteenth century, a time when the Catholic Church was meeting serious competition from heretical and even non-Christian sects that defied the established church. In the face of this threat, the Inquisition, responsible directly to the papacy and staffed by Dominican monks, was set up as the chief institution to root out heresy.

Bernard Gui (ca. 1261–1331) is the source of the first three selections. Gui, a Dominican who later became a bishop, was Inquisitor in the area of Toulouse in southern France from 1307 to 1324. In 1323 he completed the compilation of his Manual of the Inquisitor, a vast collection of Inquisition lore, for the benefit of his successor. In writing his Manual, Gui not only relied on his vast professional experience, but also incorporated information from a number of earlier manuals and from legal documents in the archives of the Inquisition at Toulouse.

The first selection gives some idea of the Inquisition's self-defined task; the second (an account of the so-called Order of the Apostles) provides a concise history of a fairly typical medieval heresy from inception to near-extinction. The third selection, on the interrogation of sorcerers, raises the knotty problem of the relationship of witchcraft to heresy.

There is no question that the two are indeed related. Both heretics and witches were considered deviants from orthodoxy and were prosecuted as such. It is also undeniable that the Inquisition took the lead in rooting out witchcraft, much as it had sought to extirpate heresy. Yet at the time of Bernard Gui the Inquisition was sceptical about the supernatural abilities of sorcerers and the like. The belief in the reality of witches' powers, and with it an elaborate mythology of devil worship, came to be sponsored by the Inquisition only in the fifteenth century —a new attitude made into official policy by a papal bull of 1484.

What was this phenomenon of witchcraft and witch-hunting in western Europe? Some scholars accept the view that witchcraft really was an organized "old religion," an ancient fertility cult that competed with Christianity until it was stamped out by the great persecutions of the sixteenth and seventeenth centuries. Others, pointing to the lesson of mass delusions in our own day, stress the significance of social dislocation and the consequent unbalanced state of mind of the witch-hunters. In any case, the witch persecutions reached incredible proportions in the sixteenth and seventeenth centuries, before finally dying out in the eighteenth. Catholics and Protestants were indistinguishable in their witch-burning zeal. Estimates of the number of victims range from 300,000 to 9,000,000. It is in this context that the last selection, dealing with the seventeenth-century witch persecution in Bamberg, Germany, should be considered.

৺ঌ MANUAL OF THE INQUISITOR

Bernard Gui

INSTRUCTIONS OR GENERAL INFORMATION

Whoever is to appear for a hearing or for interrogation, whether it be of his own free will or after having been cited or called to answer to a suspicion, imputation, con-

Bernard Gui, *Practica Inquisitionis Heretice Pravitatis*, ed. G. Mollat (Paris: H. Champion, 1926), Vol. I, 2–9; Vol. II, 2–25, 50–55, 66–84, 102–108. Translated from the Latin by Peter Amann for this volume.

tention, or accusation of the crime of heresy or of having abetted or harbored heretics . . . should begin by heeding the well-meaning request and discreet admonition of the inquisitor or his substitute, and swear upon God's holy evangelists to speak the whole truth and nothing but the truth with regard to acts of heresy or acts related to it that fall in whatever form within the jurisdiction of the Inquisition, whether the accused was personally involved in such acts or is merely testifying concerning the activities of persons living or dead.

Once the oath has been sworn and accepted, he [the accused] will be required and exhorted to volunteer the truth concerning anything he may know, or may have known or heard, with regard to the act of heresy. If he asks for a delay or for a moment of reflection so as to answer more thoughtfully, if this is deemed expedient the inquisitor may grant the request, particularly if it seems to have been made in good faith and not through constraint. Otherwise the accused is to answer without delay for his own acts.

After this, the public notary will write down the day of his appearance: *In such and such a month of such and such a year, the named such and such, born in such and such a town or village or such and such a diocese, having presented himself, or been cited or called in judgment before the churchman named such. Inquisitor of Heresy for the Kingdom of France by delegation from the Apostolic See, after swearing to speak the whole truth and nothing but the truth upon God's holy evangelists, concerning any act or crime of heresy and related acts, whether they mainly concerned himself or whether other persons, living or dead, were involved, has stated and confessed, etc.*

It should be noted that were anyone to speak clearly and openly against the faith, employing the heretics' own customary arguments and authorities, he would easily be convicted of heresy by the educated who are faithful to the Church, since the act of defending error would itself be considered heretical. Yet as the present heretics attempt and seek to disguise their errors rather than to confess them openly, the men instructed in the knowledge of the Scriptures cannot convict them, because of the heretics' semantic tricks and cunning thoughts. The learned men tend to be confounded by the heretics, who, glorying in it, are thus strengthened by deceiving the wise and eluding their hands by the trickery of foxy, crooked, and tortuous answers.

It is indeed all too difficult to get the heretics to reveal themselves when they hide their errors, instead of frankly confessing them, or when reliable and adequate testimony against them is lacking. In such a case all kinds of problems confront the inquisitor. On one hand, his conscience would torment him should he inflict punishment without having obtained a confession or a conviction of heresy; on the other hand, his anxiety is enhanced by having repeatedly experienced the falseness, cunning, and malice of such people. If because of their fox-like cunning the latter escape punishment, they increase still further in strength, numbers, and cunning at the expense of the Faith. Also, laymen of staunch faith find it a scandalous matter if an inquisitorial trial, once begun, is abandoned for some kind of lack of method. When they see the learned thus deceived by common and vile persons, the faith of the faithful is in some degree weakened; for they believe that we always have at our disposal luminous and certain arguments that cannot be refuted, and they expect us to be able to vanquish [the heretics] in such a way that even laymen can clearly follow the arguments. It is therefore inexpedient in the presence of laymen to debate matters of faith with heretics who are so astute.

Let us note, furthermore, that a single remedy does not fit all maladies and that treatment should be varied with each case. Thus an identical method of interrogation, inquiry, and examination is not suitable for the divers sects of heretics. . . . Hence the inquisitor, prudent physician of souls that he is, will proceed cautiously in his inquiry and interrogation. He should take into account the persons whom he is questioning and those associated with him in the proceedings, keeping in mind their status, condition, situation, illnesses, as well as any local circumstances. He will not ask everyone all of the questions that we shall list. Toward some let him not always be mild, but restrained only by discretion; let him circumvent the cunning of the heretic, so that with God's help and the skill of an obstetrician, he may deliver the slippery serpent from the sinkhole and abyss of errors.

Indeed, no single and infallible rule can be suggested. Were this possible, the sons of darkness would have ample opportunity to await the constant application of a uniform method, evading all snares more readily by being on guard against them. There are times when the wise inquisitor will take advantage of the witnesses' statements, at other times of the accusers' contentions; sometimes [he will profit] from the lessons of experience, at other times from the sharpness of his own intellect; yet again by questioning or interrogating, as the Lord may dictate.

In order to set down the procedure for interrogation, in the pages that follow we shall successively furnish some details regarding five sects—that is to say, the Manicheans [usually known as Albigenses], the Waldensians or Poor Men of Lyon, the Pseudo-Apostles, those commonly called the Beguines [also known as Spiritual Franciscans] and the converted Jews who have reverted to the Jewish vomit, as well as the sorcerers, soothsayers, and demon-worshippers who are a plague greatly injuring the purity of the Faith—first dealing in general terms with the substance of each sect's error, then with the [proper] form and mode of interrogation, as will appear later. . . .

The Sect of Those Claiming to Belong to the Order of Apostles

The aim of the following pages is to provide people now and in times to come with information on the origins, founders, and errors of the sect of those who call themselves the Order of Apostles, claiming to lead an apostolic life and to observe evangelical poverty.

It was in the year 1260 that one Gerardo Segarelli of Parma in Lombardy appeared, bringing evil upon himself and many others. Simulating a life of perfection, he advocated a new way of living; by means of false humility, by his depraved inventions and private talks, he attracted a few disciples and followers. In secret meetings he gradually and surreptitiously infected them with a pestilential germ, preaching (what follows will clearly demonstrate this) against the entire position of the Holy Roman Church, against the prelates and the whole clergy, monks of all orders, and even against the condition of the laity. Under the cloak of a false and lying saintliness he inculcated the new doctrine in the minds of his listeners.

Ostentatiously displaying his intention to observe and follow the way and conduct of the Apostles and, like the Apostles, to preach and teach the people a new way, he ignored the fact that old paths are surer and healthier. That is why he named his disciples and followers "Apostles," thus seeking to designate those who, in imitation of the first Apostles of Our Lord Jesus Christ, throughout their lifetime recognized no other authority than God himself. Not so much because of his authority, which was non-existent, but because of his great audacity, he was able to impose this name "Apostles" upon this sect. Its members were to wander throughout the world, begging like paupers, living on alms, and preaching to the peoples everywhere: "Repent, for the Kingdom of God is at hand," and other such phrases which at first impressed listeners, particularly the simple-minded. He also originated numerous errors which he transmitted to his adherents, not openly and publicly but secretly, to form the basis of their belief and teaching.

In the beginning the Apostles wore their hair long and dressed in a white, alb-like tunic [a priestly vestment worn during Mass] and a white cape with high collar. I have seen several who hid this costume under a roomy coat. Shunning in their life and ways the usual habits of the faithful, at times they wore sandals, at other times they went barefoot. In such a garb they outwardly imitated the perfect apostolic life, and in this way presented their evangelical doctrine to their listeners and the populace. In fact, their life was inwardly corrupt, while their outward behavior was abominably shameless. As to the doctrine they professed in their secret gatherings, it was as heretical as it was unwholesome.

At the start this plague remained largely hidden under cover of religion, and no one sought to arrest the progress of these wolves in sheep's clothing. Thus simple-minded people, holding such fraudulent sanctity in awe, began to favor them and support them with alms. Consequently the followers of the sect multiplied considerably and steeped themselves in evil for about twenty years. Then their pestilential doctrine could not be hidden any longer: gradually it came to light and to the attention of Catholics. It was then that a few among the latter became suspicious of the sectarians, accusing them of heresy.

At the end of some twenty years, the evil repute of the sect calling itself the Order of Apostles reached the ears of the Lord Pope Honorius IV, who condemned it as pernicious, rejecting its way of life. The text of this decision may be found in an apostolic letter on the subject addressed to all prelates of the Church [in 1286]. As Honorius IV had done before him, Nicholas IV addressed a similar letter to all prelates of the Church in 1290, the third year of his pontificate.

Following these apostolic letters, the pernicious sect declined and gradually came to be shunned by the faithful. Nonetheless, as it had become widespread in different parts of the world, it could not be entirely extirpated during the times of Popes Honorius and Nicholas IV, because of the favor it enjoyed among simple-minded people as well as because of the negligence of the hierarchy. And as there was no hand to root out the shoot, the sons of Belial increased and multiplied, headed by the aforementioned Gerardo, chief heretic and leader in iniquity, who was still alive at that period.

As their error and heresy became increasingly widespread in the course of years, the Inquisitors of Heresy delegated by the Holy See began to search them out to take steps against them. Until the time of Boniface VIII, Gerardo succeeded in holding out and in recruiting disciples and even teachers to propagate his errors. Finally, barely forty years after his beginnings, Gerardo, thanks to the studious zeal of the Inquisitors of the

Order of Preachers [that is, the Dominicans], was caught in the act of heresy, condemned, and burned as a heretic during the pontificate of the same Boniface. The verdict was rendered by Brother Manfred of Parma, Inquisitor of the Order of Preachers, at the episcopal palace of that city, on July 18 of the year 1301. A number of his sectarians were also arrested. A few were converted and made to do penance for their sins after they had confessed the errors of the sect and abjured them in court. Others were punished according to their deserts, though many escaped, going into hiding or setting out for other provinces.

After the elimination and execution of the chief heretic Gerardo, one of his disciples, Dolcino, an illegitimate son of a priest from the diocese of Novara, took the former's place in the magistracy of error and false doctrine. He became leader and standard-bearer to this whole sect and congregation, which is not apostolic as is falsely claimed. Rather, these people are really apostates heaping error upon error (as may be learned in the pages that follow, where these errors have been gathered together in summary form so that, being made more familiar, the faithful may find them easier to avoid).

The sect of the said Dolcino embraced several thousand persons of both sexes, particularly in Italy, Tuscany, and neighboring regions. Transmitting to them a pestiferous doctrine and moved, not indeed by the spirit of prophecy but by fanaticism and madness, he made numerous predictions, claiming and faking the gift of divine revelation and understanding of the prophets. All this, as has been recognized, was nothing but falsehood, lie, snare, and delusion both on his part and that of the sorceress and heretic Margarita, his accomplice in crime and error as will be shown hereafter.

Dolcino has written three letters addressed to all Christian faithful in general, but in particular to his adherents. In these letters he raves wildly about the Holy Scriptures. Though at first he simulates his faith in the Roman Church, the letters themselves expose his perfidy. I have two of them at hand and have extracted the following summary, omitting for the sake of brevity those points which seem irrelevant.

The first letter is dated in the month of August of the year of Our Lord, 1300. Dolcino contends, first of all, that his congregation is spiritual in nature, characterized by a way of life that is truly apostolic and hence named accordingly. It is characterized by special poverty and admits only internal obedience, while rejecting external authority. This sect, he asserts, has lately been specially chosen by God, who has sent it for the salvation of souls. He who heads the congregation (that is, himself, who is named Brother Dolcino) has also been specially chosen by God. He has received revelation about present and future events that will affect the righteous as well as the evildoers. His mission is to explain the prophecies and interpret the writings in the Old and New Testaments to this generation.

Many commoners, nobles and tyrants, the secular clergy, all monks (notably the Preachers, the Friars Minor, and others) who persecute him and his followers are, so he says, not merely his personal opponents but the devil's ministers. . . . That is why, he adds, he—Dolcino—hides and flees before his persecutors as his predecessors before him, until the time when his opponents shall have been exterminated. Then he and his followers will appear in public, as he says, and openly preach to all. All his persecutors, he says, will soon vanish, together with the prelates of the Church who will be destroyed. Those who by chance do survive will come to join his sect, so that eventually he and his followers will prevail over all.

He distinguishes four ages in the condition of the saints, each one characterized by its own way of life. The fathers, patriarchs, and prophets of the Old Testament, as well as the other just men who lived before Christ, belong to the first age. In that state, he says, marriage was a good and laudable institution required for the multiplication of the human race. Yet later the descendants departed from the spirituality and goodness of their ancestors until Christ appeared to cure their ills, accompanied by his Apostles, disciples, and those who imitated them.

This was the second age of the saints, calling for a new way of life. They came as the perfect remedy for the infirmity of those who had preceded them, demonstrating their true faith by miracles, humility, patience, poverty, chastity, and other examples of virtuous life, in contrast to their predecessors. In this second state, virginity and chastity were preferable to marriage, as was poverty to riches. It was better to live without property than to possess the wealth of the world. This age lasted until the time of the sainted Pope Sylvester and the Emperor Constantine, yet by then there was already a falling off from the original perfection.

The third age began with Saint Sylvester in the time of Constantine, when generally increasing numbers of gentiles and others were becoming converted to the Christian faith. As they were newly converted, their love of God and of their neighbors had not yet cooled. Hence it was better for the blessed Pope Sylvester and his successors to accept and possess worldly goods and wealth. In order to maintain and safeguard the peoples, it was better to rule than not to rule. Yet as the peoples' love of God began to cool, the best of all ways of life was that of the blessed Benedict, as it was more rigorous about worldly goods and more removed from worldly rule. At that period, Dolcino concedes, the way of life of the good priests living monastically was laudable. Yet the number of good priests was declining, while that of the monks increased. Later, priests and monks cooled almost entirely in their love for God and their neighbors, and they almost completely abandoned their former condition. The best way of life at that time was that of Saint Francis and Saint Dominic [the early thirteenth-century founders of the Franciscan and Dominican orders, respectively], who in matters of worldly possessions and power were stricter than the blessed Benedict had been.

Now that their love for God and their neighbors has cooled, and all the prelates, clerics, and monks are neglecting the ways of their predecessors, it would be better to return to the apostolic way of life than to embrace any other. This apostolic way of life, Dolcino affirmed, was what God had ordained for the present times. This was the way of life inaugurated by Brother Gerardo Segarelli of Parma, that great friend of God, which would endure to the end of the world, bearing fruit on the day of the last judgment. Such was the fourth and last age, characterized by a way of life truly apostolic, different from that of the saints Francis and Dominic, who owned [monastic] houses to which they took the alms they received. We, on the other hand, have no domicile and must not even carry our alms with us. That is why our way of life is the greatest and ultimate remedy for everyone.

According to Dolcino, from the time of Christ to the end of the world, the Church is to go through four different stages. During the first the Church was destined to be, and indeed was, good, virgin, chaste, and persecuted; this is how it was down to the blessed Pope Sylvester and the Emperor Constantine. During the second phase the Church was destined to be, and indeed was, rich and respected while persevering in virtue and chastity. This is how it was while priests, monks, and various religious followed the examples of Saint Sylvester, Saint Benedict, Saint Dominic, and Saint Francis. In the course of the third phase the Church was destined to be, and indeed is at present, depraved, rich, and laden with honors. This is the prevailing situation, Dolcino claims, at the time he wrote these prophecies. This situation would last until churchmen, monks, and religious of all orders perished miserably. This was to happen soon, that is to say, within three years of his prediction. In the course of the fourth state the Church was destined to be, and indeed had already begun to be, good, poor, persecuted, and reformed by reverting to a pure apostolic life. This reform, begun by Brother Gerardo of Parma, whom Dolcino calls the great friend of God, would continue and increase in perfection, bearing fruit until the end of the world. . . .

From the middle to the end of the letter, he deals with future events to take place within three years. He asserts that all ecclesiastical prelates and other churchmen from the greatest to the least, all those in monasteries and cloisters, all monks and nuns, all brothers and sisters of the Orders of Preachers, Minors, and Cistercians, having already abandoned the way of life of their predecessors, already belong to the third age of the Church described earlier. . . . All these would be exterminated by the sword of God wielded by a new emperor and by new kings instituted by him. All were to be exterminated and would vanish from the earth. This new emperor, he asserts in the same place, shall be Frederick, presently King of Sicily and son of the late Peter, King of Aragon. Frederick will be made emperor and create new kings. He shall fight against Pope Boniface and shall kill him, together with others destined to be killed. To support his prediction Dolcino points to many passages of the Old and New Testaments, interpreting them from his own heart and his own perverse intellect. . . .

Dolcino had a paramour by the name of Margarita, who accompanied him and lived with him. He claimed to deal chastely and honorably with her as with a sister in Christ. When she was noted to be pregnant, he and his followers claimed she was pregnant by the Holy Spirit. Dolcino's disciples and adherents who called themselves Apostles also live, as has often been noted, in the company of such paramours with whom they slept, falsely and hypocritically asserting that they were untroubled by temptations of the flesh. . . .

The Lord Pope Clement V ordered proceedings against the said Dolcino and his adherents, as may be gathered from apostolic letters addressed to the Inquisitors of Heresy, to the Archbishop of Milan, and to the bishops of the Lombard region under his jurisdiction. Therefore, by apostolic mandate, a crusade with a grant of indulgence [for sins committed] was preached against the said Dolcino. Several times the inquisitors raised an army against him without being able to overcome him, so large had the number of adherents who were believers, or who harbored him, sympathized with him or defended him, grown in the Lombard region. Finally the inquisitors of Lombardy, in concert with the Bishop of Vercelli, preached a crusade with a grant of full indulgence, organizing an important expeditionary force against the above-mentioned heresi-arch Dolcino. The latter, having not only revived ancient errors but invented new and perverse dogmas, had infected many people whom he bound to himself; with these numerous disciples and adherents he had withdrawn into the mountains of Novara.

It so happened that many who were in these mountains perished from hunger and the intense cold, losing their lives while steeped in error. Thus, after climbing the mountains, the army of the faithful was able to capture Dolcino with about forty of his followers. Of the four hundred dead who were counted, some had been slain, others had died of hunger and exposure. Margarita, the heretic and sorceress who had been his accomplice in crime and error, was taken with Dolcino. This capture took place on Holy Thursday during Holy Week at the beginning of the year 1308 of the Incarnation of Our Lord. The judicial execution of the culprits was ordered and carried out by the secular arm: the said Margarita was cut to pieces before the eyes of Dolcino; then the latter was also cut into pieces. Their bones and limbs were burned. Some of their accomplices were likewise burned. Such was the deserved punishment for their crimes.

Although he himself had been destroyed, Dolcino's perverse dogmas did not die with him. Hence the Inquisitors of Heresy in Italy, Tuscany, and elsewhere began proceedings for heresy against all disciples and adherents of the said sect of Gerardo and Dolcino, seeking them out, pursuing them, arresting them, imprisoning them, and striking them with canonical penalties as determined by law. After Dolcino's death many persons of both sexes returned to the unity of the Catholic faith. Acknowledging and confessing their errors, they adjured the sect and heresy in court, promising to obey the prescriptions of the inquisitors and the Church. Penance proportionate to the nature of their errors was publicly imposed upon them.

Many others who refused to be converted were handed over to the secular courts. Some managed to go into hiding. Others fled to various parts of the world and to various kingdoms where they were not known. There, surreptitiously and in hiding, they could propagate the erroneous doctrines of their sect among the simple-minded, simulating piety and the false appearance of sanctity. Hence anywhere, no matter in what province or kingdom, should such individuals be found organizing secret conventicles, differing in their life and manners from the common habits of the faithful, secretly or openly spreading doctrines identical or similar to those mentioned earlier, preaching when they are not authorized, and indeed are forbidden to do so publicly, wearing the garb or some similar costume of the people calling themselves Apostles (for they often change their clothes and sometimes even their names) ; wherever such individuals be discovered, particularly if they admit belonging to the sect or doctrine of the said Gerardo or Dolcino, or if they praise or recommend in some manner the life or doctrine of the said Gerardo and Dolcino, prelates and inquisitors upon whom this is incumbent should proceed against these people as heretics. The same applies to their faithful, to those who shelter them, abet them, or defend them.

Believing Catholics, zealous in their faith, should act toward them as toward all those reputed heretics or those tainted with heresy. They will shun intercourse with them, and whenever they learn of their presence, will unmask, discover and denounce them to prelates, churchmen, and inquisitors. Prelates, priests, and preachers of God's word will publicly exhort and admonish the laity about this subject from the pulpit. . . .

What Sorcerers, Soothsayers and Demon-worshippers Are

The pestilential phenomena of sorcerers, soothsayers, and demon-worshippers take on as numerous and varied forms in the different provinces and regions as there are inventions and false and vain delusions by which these superstitious people invoke demons of error and their doctrines.

Interrogation of Sorcerers, Soothsayers and Demon-worshippers   The sorcerer, soothsayer, or demon-worshipper should be asked the nature and number of the spells, divinations, or invocations he knows and who instructed him in them.

Also, one must stoop to details and consider the status and condition of the persons involved: the interrogations should not be the same for all and should differ for men and women. The accused may be asked the following questions: What does he know? What has he learned? In what practices has he engaged in connection with bewitched children in order to break the spell?

Also, in connection with lost or damned souls.

Also, in connection with thieves to be unmasked.

Also, in connection with marital discord.

Also, in connection with making the sterile fruitful.

Also, in connection with substances prescribed by sorcerers to be swallowed, such as hairs, nail parings, and other things.

Also, in connection with the condition of the souls of the dead.

Also, in connection with the prediction of events to come.

Also, in connection with the fairies who bring good luck or, they say, are abroad at night.

Also, in connection with enchantments and spells by means of incantations, fruits, plants, ropes, etc.

Also, whom has he taught? From whom has he acquired this knowledge? Who has instructed him?

Also, what does he know about curing illnesses by means of spells and incantations?

Also, what does he know about gathering herbs, while kneeling toward the east and reciting the Lord's Prayer?

Also, what about these pilgrimages, masses, offerings of candles, and distribution of alms that sorcerers demand?

Also, how does one go about solving thefts and understanding occult things?

Also, the inquiry should deal particularly with all superstitious practices implying irreverence and insult to the sacraments of the Church, particularly the sacraments of the Body of Christ, as well as toward divine service and sacred places.

Also, the inquiry should bear on the practice of secreting the Eucharist and stealing the chrism or sacred oil from churches.

Also, that of baptizing wax or other figures. He should be asked how these are baptized, to what use they are put, and what advantages accrue from them.

Also, the accused will be questioned about the lead figures that sorcerers make: the way they are made and their use.

Also, he will be asked from whom he obtained all this knowledge.

Also, how long it has been since he began such practices.

Also, what and how many persons have consulted him, particularly for the current year.

Also, has he ever been forbidden to engage in such practices? Who forbade him? Has he promised not to engage in such practices and not to employ them henceforth?

Also, has he relapsed despite such a promise and recantation?

Also, did he believe that what the others taught him really existed?

Also, what good, gift, or compensation has he received for his services?

The Manner of Recanting the Pestilential Error of Spells, Divinations, and Invocations of Demons, Particularly When They Are Heretically Opposed to the Truth and Respect for the Sacrament of the Eucharist, of Baptism or of Other Sacraments, or Where Sacrifices or Immolations Are Offered to the Demon, or Where Some Other Formal Offense against the Faith Is Involved   I, such and such from such and such a place in such and such a diocese, appearing in judgment before you, such and such, Inquisitor, wholly renounce any error and heresy contrary to the Catholic faith of our Lord Jesus Christ. I renounce specifically and especially any baptism of images or of other senseless things, as well as any re-baptism of persons already normally and legitimately baptized.

Also, I renounce any sorcery or evil spells in the making of which the Holy Body of Christ, the chrism or the blessed and holy oil are required.

Also, I renounce any divination or invocation of demons, particularly when this implies adoration or reverence, doing homage, offering a sacrifice, or killing a victim. . . .

Also, I renounce the art of making figures of lead or wax or some other substance in order to obtain illicit and harmful effects.

Also, I generally renounce all forbidden sorceries, particularly those intended to produce illicit and harmful effects.

Also, I promise and swear to do all within my power to pursue, to denounce, and to reveal to the inquisitors and prelates, him or them engaging in the above said practices, whenever and wherever they may be.

Also, I swear and promise to observe and to profess the Catholic faith. . . .

◅ THE WITCH-PERSECUTION AT BAMBERG

. . . On Wednesday, June 28, 1628, was examined without torture Johannes Junius, Mayor at Bamberg, on the charge of witchcraft: how and in what fashion he had fallen into that vice. Is fifty-five years old, and was born at Niederwaysich in the Wetterau. Says he is wholly innocent, knows nothing of the crime, has never in his

"The Witch-Persecutions," *Translations and Reprints from the Original Sources of European History* ed. G. L. Burr (New York: Longmans, Green & Co., 1903), Vol. III, No. 4, 23–28.

life renounced God; says that he is wronged before God and the world, would like to hear of a single human being who has seen him at such gatherings [as the witch-sabbaths].

Confrontation of Dr. Georg Adam Haan. Tells him to his face he will stake his life on it, that he saw him, Junius, a year and a half ago at a witch-gathering in the electoral council-room, where they ate and drank. Accused denies the same wholly.

Confronted with Hopffens Elsse. Tells him likewise that he was on Haupts-moor at a witch-dance; but first the holy wafer was desecrated. Junius denies. Hereupon he was told that his accomplices had confessed against him and was given time for thought.

On Friday, June 30, 1628, the aforesaid Junius was again without torture exhorted to confess, but again confessed nothing, whereupon, . . . since he would confess nothing, he was put to the torture, and first the

Thumb-screws were applied. Says he has never denied God his Saviour nor suffered himself to be otherwise baptized; [1] will again stake his life on it; feels no pain in the thumb-screws.

Leg-screws. Will confess absolutely nothing knows nothing about it. He has never renounced God; will never do such a thing; has never been guilty of this vice; feels likewise no pain.

Is stripped and examined; on his right side is found a bluish mark, like a clover leaf, is thrice pricked therein, but feels no pain and no blood flows out.

Strappado. He has never renounced God; God will not forsake him; if he were such a wretch he would not let himself be so tortured; God must show some token of his innocence. He knows nothing about witchcraft. . . .

On July 5, the above named Junius is without torture, but with urgent persuasions, exhorted to confess, and at last begins and confesses:

When in the year 1624 his law-suit at Rothweil cost him some six hundred florins, he had gone out, in the month of August, into his orchard at Friedrichsbronnen; and, as he sat there in thought, there had come to him a woman like a grass-maid, who had asked him why he sat there so sorrowful; he had answered that he was not despondent, but she had led him by seductive speeches to yield him to her will. . . . And thereafter this wench had changed into the form of a goat, which bleated and said, "Now you see with whom you have had to do. You must be mine or I will forthwith break your neck." Thereupon he had been frightened, and trembled all over for fear. Then the transformed spirit had seized him by the throat and demanded that he should renounce God Almighty, whereupon Junius said, "God forbid," and thereupon the spirit vanquished through the power of these words. Yet it came straightway back, brought more people with it, and persistently demanded of him that he renounce God in Heaven and all the heavenly host, by which terrible threatening he was obliged to speak this formula: "I renounce God in Heaven and his host, and will henceforward recognize the Devil as my God."

After the renunciation he was so far persuaded by those present and by the evil spirit that he suffered himself to be otherwise baptized in the evil spirit's name.

---

[1] *"Otherwise baptized" is the usual phrase for the rite, a parody of baptism, by which the Devil was believed to initiate his followers.*

The Morhauptin had given him a ducat as dower-gold, which afterward became only a potsherd.

He was then named Krix. His paramour he had to call Vixen. Those present had congratulated him in Beelzebub's name and said that they were now all alike. At this baptism of his there were among others the aforesaid Christiana Morhauptin, the young Geiserlin, Paul Glaser, [and others]. After this they had dispersed.

At this time his paramour had promised to provide him with money, and from time to time to take him to other witch-gatherings. . . . Whenever he wished to ride forth [to the witch-sabbath] a black dog had come before his bed, which said to him that he must go with him, whereupon he had seated himself upon the dog and the dog had raised himself in the Devil's name and so had fared forth.

About two years ago he was taken to the electoral council-room, at the left hand as one goes in. Above at a table were seated the Chancellor, the Mayor Neydekher, Dr. Georg Haan, [and many others]. Since his eyes were not good, he could not recognize more persons.

More time for consideration was now given him. On July 7, the aforesaid Junius was again examined, to know what further had occurred to him to confess. He confesses that about two months ago, on the day after an execution was held, he was at a witch-dance at the Black Cross, where Beelzebub had shown himself to them all and said expressly to their faces that they must all be burned together on this spot, and had ridiculed and taunted those present. . . .

Of crimes. His paramour had immediately after his seduction demanded that he should make away with his younger son Hans Georg, and had given him for this purpose a gray powder; this, however, being too hard for him, he had made away with his horse, a brown, instead.

His paramour had also often spurred him on to kill his daughter, . . . and because he would not do this he had been maltreated with blows by the evil spirit.

Once at the suggestion of his paramour he had taken the holy wafer out of his mouth and given it to her. . . .

A week before his arrest as he was going to St. Martin's church the Devil met him on the way, in the form of a goat, and told him that he would soon be imprisoned, but that he should not trouble himself—he would soon set him free. Besides this, by his soul's salvation, he knew nothing further; but what he had spoken was the pure truth; on that he would stake his life. On August 6, 1628, there was read to the aforesaid Junius this his confession, which he then wholly ratified and confirmed, and was willing to stake his life upon it. And afterward he voluntarily confirmed the same before the court.

[So ended the trial of Junius, and he was accordingly burned at the stake. But it so happens that there is also preserved in Bamberg a letter, in quivering hand, secretly written by him to his daughter while in the midst of his trial (July 24, 1628):]

Many hundred thousand good-nights, dearly beloved daughter Veronica. Innocent have I come into prison, innocent have I been tortured, innocent must I die. For whoever comes into the witch prison must become a witch or be tortured until he invents something out of his head and—God pity him—bethinks him of something. I will tell you how it has gone with me. When I was the first time put to the torture,

Dr. Braun, Dr. Kötzendörffer, and two strange doctors were there. Then Dr. Braun asks me, "Kinsman, how come you here?" I answer, "Through falsehood, through misfortune." "Hear, you," he says, "you are a witch; will you confess it voluntarily? If not, we'll bring in witnesses and the executioner for you." I said "I am no witch, I have a pure conscience in the matter; if there are a thousand witnesses, I am not anxious, but I'll gladly hear the witnesses." Now the chancellor's son was set before me . . . and afterward Hoppfen Elsse. She had seen me dance on Haupts-moor. . . . I answered: "I have never renounced God, and will never do it—God graciously keep me from it. I'll rather bear whatever I must." And then came also—God in highest Heaven have mercy—the executioner, and put the thumb-screws on me, both hands bound together, so that the blood ran out at the nails and everywhere, so that for four weeks I could not use my hands, as you can see from the writing. . . . Thereafter they first stripped me, bound my hands behind me, and drew me up in the torture.[1] Then I thought heaven and earth were at an end; eight times did they draw me up and let me fall again, so that I suffered terrible agony. . . .

And this happened on Friday, June 30, and with God's help I had to bear the torture. . . . When at last the executioner led me back into the prison, he said to me: "Sir, I beg you, for God's sake confess something, whether it be true or not. Invent something, for you cannot endure the torture which you will be put to; and, even if you bear it all, yet you will not escape, not even if you were an earl, but one torture will follow after another until you say you are a witch. Not before that," he said, "will they let you go, as you may see by all their trials, for one is just like another.". . .

And so I begged, since I was in wretched plight, to be given one day for thought and a priest. The priest was refused me, but the time for thought was given. Now, my dear child, see in what hazard I stood and still stand. I must say that I am a witch, though I am not,—must now renounce God, though I have never done it before. Day and night I was deeply troubled, but at last there came to me a new idea. I would not be anxious, but, since I had been given no priest with whom I could take counsel, I would myself think of something and say it. It were surely better that I just say it with mouth and words, even though I had not really done it; and afterwards I would confess it to the priest, and let those answer for it who compel me to do it. . . . And so I made my confession, as follows; but it was all a lie.

Now follows, dear child, what I confessed in order to escape the great anguish and bitter torture, which it was impossible for me longer to bear.

[Here follows his confession, substantially as it is given in the minutes of his trial. But he adds:]

Then I had to tell what people I had seen [at the witch-sabbath]. I said that I had not recognized them. "You old rascal, I must set the executioner at you. Say— was not the Chancellor there?" So I said yes. "Who besides?" I had not recognized

---

[1] *This torture of the strappado, which was that in most common use by the courts, consisted of a rope, attached to the hands of the prisoner (bound behind his back) and carried over a pulley at the ceiling. By this he was drawn up and left hanging. To increase the pain, weights were attached to his feet or he was suddenly jerked up and let drop.*

anybody. So he said: "Take one street after another; begin at the market, go out on one street and back on the next." I had to name several persons there. Then came the long street. I knew nobody. Had to name eight persons there. Then the Zinkenwert —one person more. Then over the upper bridge to the Georgthor, on both sides. Knew nobody again. Did I know nobody in the castle—whoever it might be, I should speak without fear. And thus continuously they asked me on all the streets, though I could not and would not say more. So they gave me to the executioner, told him to strip me, shave me all over, and put me to the torture. "The rascal knows one on the market-place, is with him daily, and yet won't name him." By that they meant Dietmeyer: so I had to name him too.

Then I had to tell what crimes I had committed. I said nothing. . . . "Draw the rascal up!" So I said that I was to kill my children, but I had killed a horse instead. It did not help. I had also taken a sacred wafer, and had desecrated it. When I had said this, they left me in peace.

Now, dear child, here you have all my confession, for which I must die. And they are sheer lies and made-up things, so help me God. For all this I was forced to say through fear of the torture which was threatened beyond what I had already endured. For they never leave off with the torture till one confesses something; be he never so good, he must be a witch. Nobody escapes, though he were an earl. . . .

Dear child, keep this letter secret so that people do not find it, else I shall be tortured most piteously and the jailers will be beheaded. So strictly is it forbidden. . . . Dear child, pay this man a dollar. . . . I have taken several days to write this: my hands are both lame. I am in a sad plight. . . .

Good night, for your father Johannes Junius will never see you more. July 24, 1628.

[And on the margin of the letter he adds:]

Dear child, six have confessed against me at once: the Chancellor, his son, Neudecker, Zaner, Hoffmaisters Ursel, and Hoppfen Elsse—all false, through compulsion, as they have all told me, and begged my forgiveness in God's name before they were executed. . . . They know nothing but good of me. They were forced to say it, just as I myself was. . . .

Church and State

St. Paul had said that although things spiritual were under the jurisdiction of God, temporal life was properly in the hands of the sovereign. Yet by the eleventh century the papacy was questioning whether the state was a separate or a subordinate realm. The tone for the succeeding five centuries was set in Gregory VII's Dictatus Papae *(ca. 1090),* which proclaimed the universal, eternal, unerring, and supreme majesty of the pope. Until Gregory's stand against separate secular authority, the Church had admin-

istered the rites of salvation but in matters of form the king, with total
jurisdiction, had appointed, transferred, and deposed his bishops, and the
national pattern of worship had usually reflected the king's practices.

In 1075, only two years after his elevation, Pope Gregory excommunicated
five of the advisers of the Holy Roman Emperor Henry IV over the issue
of lay investiture—the appointment and installation of clerics by the
sovereign. In the ensuing contest of wills all manner of charges were
hurled and parried, until Gregory detected Henry's fear of rebellion and
promptly absolved the Emperor's subjects from allegiance to him. The
outcome is documented in a series of letters and decrees between the two
combatants.

The Norman King of England, Henry I, fell heir to a situation equally
ripe for strife. His brother, from whom he inherited the crown, had
insulted and robbed the Church, so offending the beloved Bishop Anselm
that Anselm considered excommunication. Henry hoped for peace, but
in quietly retaining the rights of lay investiture he alienated the Bishop,
who then refused to serve as a royal appointee. But Henry's father,
William the Conqueror, had maintained close relations with the Church
and Henry gained a tenuous truce by promising at his coronation to follow
his father's example rather than his brother's. Still, the fuse sputtered
for seven years, until in 1107 the "Compromise of Bec" ended the danger
of explosion. The king was granted the right to create bishops; the Church
was to perform the ceremony of investing the bishop with the ring and
staff of office. From this period of tension came the anonymous York
Tractates (ca. 1101), an early elaboration of the royal position. The fourth
tractate, from which an excerpt is included here, presents the theme of
monarchical semi-divinity which by the seventeenth century blossomed into
the theory of the divine right of kings.

The issues of lay investiture and taxation of the clergy by the king
impelled the disputants to claim total sovereignty for king or pope.
The York Tractates theorized in favor of royal absolutism, but not until
1301 did the Church produce its theoretical foundation for papal
supremacy. Various popes had issued fiats—the Dictatus Papae, Clericis
Laicos, and Unam Sanctam—but, however powerful, they were only
assertions, not arguments for papal absolutism. Aegidius Romanus presented a systematic treatment of the question of why the pope was all-
powerful in his De Ecclesiastica Potestate ("On the Sovereign Power
of the Church"). Aegidius was Bishop of Bourges and the confidant of
Boniface VIII. He writes of the singular authority resting in the pope,
from whom every lesser governing body received its lawful powers to
function. His central concept, the doctrine of "plenitude of power"

is used here with reference to the Church, but it has remained most influential in a political sense, having been adapted in later centuries by kings and even twentieth-century dictators who never heard of the author.

The final reading in this series on state-church relations is the anonymous Disputatio inter Clericum et Militem *("Debate between a Clergyman and a Knight"), a vastly popular pamphlet that circulated throughout Europe in the later Middle Ages. It is in favor of royal power and French in origin; its setting is the court of Philip IV about the year 1300. In this dialogue between priest and knight, the knight scoffs with lively persiflage at the pretensions of the cleric's claims to supreme authority. Not surprisingly, it became popular among the many groups that found the Church increasingly corrupt. The anticlerical note is self-assured, no longer defensive, and combined with a strident nationalism and a sarcastic social analysis of the Church's wealth. By the fifteenth century the Church, seeming irrelevant, disinterested, and remote, lost touch with many of its votaries. What appeared as a symptom of the increasing estrangement between Church and people in the* Disputatio *was to become a factor in the success of the Reformation in the sixteenth century.*

✌§ PAPAL ASSERTIONS

Gregory VII

1   That the Roman church was established by God alone.

2   That the Roman pontiff alone is rightly called universal.

3   That he alone has the power to depose and reinstate bishops.

4   That his legate, even if he be of lower ecclesiastical rank, presides over bishops in council, and has the power to give sentence of deposition against them.

5   That the pope has the power to depose those who are absent [*i.e.,* without giving them a hearing].

6   That, among other things, we ought not to remain in the same house with those whom he has excommunicated.

7   That he alone has the right, according to the necessity of the occasion, to make new laws, to create new bishoprics, to make a monastery of a chapter of canons, and *vice versa,* and either to divide a rich bishopric or to unite several poor ones.

8   That he alone may use the imperial insignia.

9   That all princes shall kiss the foot of the pope alone.

10   That his name alone is to be recited in the churches.

Gregory VII, "*Dictatus Papae*," *A Source Book for Mediaeval History,* ed. Oliver J. Thatcher and Edgar H. MacNeal (New York: Charles Scribner's Sons, 1905), pp. 136–138.

11   That the name applied to him belongs to him alone.

12   That he has the power to depose emperors.

13   That he has the right to transfer bishops from one see to another when it becomes necessary.

14   That he has the right to ordain as a cleric anyone from any part of the church whatsoever.

15   That anyone ordained by him may rule [as bishop] over another church, but cannot serve [as priest] in it, and that such a cleric may not receive a higher rank from any other bishop.

16   That no general synod may be called without his order.

17   That no action of a synod and no book shall be regarded as canonical without his authority.

18   That his decree can be annulled by no one, and that he can annul the decrees of anyone.

19   That he can be judged by no one.

20   That no one shall dare to condemn a person who has appealed to the apostolic seat.

21   That the important cases of any church whatsoever shall be referred to the Roman church [that is, to the pope].

22   That the Roman church has never erred and will never err to all eternity, according to the testimony of the holy scriptures.

23   That the Roman pontiff who has been canonically ordained is made holy by the merits of St. Peter, according to the testimony of St. Ennodius, bishop of Pavia, which is confirmed by many of the holy fathers, as is shown by the decrees of the blessed pope Symmachus.

24   That by his command or permission subjects may accuse their rulers.

25   That he can depose and reinstate bishops without the calling of a synod.

26   That no one can be regarded as catholic who does not agree with the Roman church.

27   That he has the power to absolve subjects from their oath of fidelity to wicked rulers.

≈§ LETTERS OF GREGORY VII AND HENRY IV

Letter of Gregory VII to Henry IV, December, 1075

Gregory, bishop, servant of the servants of God, to Henry, the king, greeting and apostolic benediction—that is, if he shall prove obedient to the apostolic see as a Christian king should.

"Letters of Gregory VII and Henry IV," *A Source Book for Mediaeval History*, ed. Oliver J. Thatcher and Edgar H. McNeal (New York: Charles Scribner's Sons, 1905), pp. 147–160.

We have sent you our apostolic benediction with some hesitation, knowing that we must render account to God, the severe judge, for all our acts as pope. Now it is reported that you have knowingly associated with men who have been excommunicated by the pope and the synod. If this is true, you know that you cannot receive the blessing either of God or of the pope until you have driven them from you and have compelled them to do penance, and have yourself sought absolution and forgiveness for your transgressions with due penance and reparation. Therefore, if you realize your guilt in this matter, we counsel you to confess straightway to some pious bishop, who shall absolve you with our permission, enjoining upon you suitable penance for this fault, and who shall faithfully report to us by letter, with your permission, the character of the penance prescribed.

We wonder, moreover, that you should continue to assure us by letter and messengers of your devotion and humility; that you should call yourself our son and the son of the holy mother church, obedient in the faith, sincere in love, diligent in devotion, and that you should commend yourself to us with all zeal of love and reverence— whereas in fact you are constantly disobeying the canonical and apostolic decrees in important matters of the faith. For, to say nothing of the rest, in the case of Milan, concerning which you gave us your promise through your mother and through our fellow-bishops whom we sent to you, the event has shown how far you intended to carry out your promise [that is, not at all] and with what purpose you made it. And now, to inflict wound upon wound, contrary to the apostolic decrees you have bestowed the churches of Fermo and Spoleto—if indeed a church can be bestowed by a layman —upon certain persons quite unknown to us; for it is not lawful to ordain men before they have been known and proved.

Since you confess yourself a son of the church, you should treat with more honor the head of the church, that is, St. Peter, the prince of the apostles. If you are one of the sheep of the Lord, you have been intrusted to him by divine authority, for Christ said to him: "Peter, feed my sheep" [John 21:16]; and again: "And I will give unto thee the keys of the kingdom of Heaven; and whatsoever thou shalt bind on earth shall be bound in heaven; and whatsoever thou shalt loose on earth shall be loosed in heaven" [Matt. 16:19]. And since we, although an unworthy sinner, exercise his authority by divine will, the words which you address to us are in reality addressed directly to him. And although we only read or hear the words, he sees the heart from which the words proceed. Therefore your highness should be very careful that no insincerity be found in your words and messages to us; and that you show due reverence, not to us indeed, but to omnipotent God, in those things which especially make for the advance of the Christian faith and the well-being of the church. For our Lord said to the apostles and to their successors: "He that heareth you heareth me; and he that despiseth you despiseth me" [Luke 10:16]. For no one will disregard our admonitions if he believes that the decrees of the pope have the same authority as the words of the apostle himself. For if our Lord commanded the apostles out of reverence for the seat of Moses to observe the sayings of the scribes and Pharisees who occupied that seat, then surely the faithful ought to receive with all reverence the apostolic and evangelical doctrine through those who are chosen to the ministry of preaching.

Now in the synod held at the apostolic seat to which the divine will has called us (at which some of your subjects also were present) we, seeing that the Christian religion had been weakened by many attacks and that the chief and proper motive, that of saving souls, had for a long time been neglected and slighted, were alarmed at the evident danger of the destruction of the flock of the Lord, and had recourse to the decrees and the doctrine of the holy fathers; we decreed nothing new, nothing of our invention [that is, against simony and the marriage of the clergy]; but we decided that the error should be abandoned and the single primitive rule of ecclesiastical discipline and the familiar way of the saints should be again sought out and followed. For we know that no other door to salvation and eternal life lies open to the sheep of Christ than that which was pointed out by him who said: "I am the door, by me if any man enter in he shall be saved, and find pasture" [John 10:9]; and this, we learn from the gospels and from the sacred writings, was preached by the apostles and observed by the holy fathers. And we have decided that this decree—which some, placing human above divine honor, have called an unendurable weight and an immense burden, but which we call by its proper name, that is, the truth and light necessary to salvation—is to be received and observed not only by you and your subjects, but also by all princes and peoples of the earth who confess and worship Christ; for it is greatly desired by us, and would be most fitting for you, that, as you are greater than others in glory, in honor, and in virtue, so you should be more distinguished in devotion to Christ.

Nevertheless, that this decree may not seem to you beyond measure grievous and unjust, we have commanded you by your faithful ambassadors to send to us the wisest and most pious men whom you can find in your kingdom, so that if they can show or instruct us in any way how we can temper the sentence promulgated by the holy fathers without offence to the eternal King or danger to our souls, we may consider their advice. But, even if we had not warned you in so friendly a manner, it would have been only right on your part, before you violated the apostolic decrees, to have asked justice of us in a reasonable manner in any matter in which we had injured or affected your honor. But it is evident in what you have since done and decreed how little you care for our warnings or for the observance of justice.

But since we hope that, while the long-suffering patience of God still invites you to repent, you may become wiser and your heart may be turned to obey the commands of God, we warn you with fatherly love that, knowing the rule of Christ to be over you, you should consider how dangerous it is to place your honor above his, and that you should not interfere with the liberty of the church which he has deigned to join to himself by heavenly union, but rather with faithful devotion you should offer your assistance to the increasing of this liberty to omnipotent God and St. Peter, through whom also your glory may be amplified. You ought to recognize what you undoubtedly owe to them for giving you victory over your enemies, that as they have gladdened you with great prosperity, so they should see that you are thereby rendered more devout. And in order that the fear of God, in whose hands is all power and all rule, may affect your heart more than these our warnings, you should recall what happened to Saul when, after winning the victory which he gained by the will of the prophet, he glorified himself in his triumph and did not obey the warnings of the prophet, and how God reproved him; and, on the other hand, what grace king David acquired by reason of his humility, as well as his other virtues.

Finally, in regard to those matters in your letter which we have not yet touched upon, we will not give a definite answer until your ambassadors, Rapoto, Adelbert, and Wodescalc, and those whom we have sent with them, shall return to us and shall make known more fully your intention in regard to the matters which we committed to them to be discussed with you. Given at Rome, the 6th of the Ides of January, the 14th indiction.

The Deposition of Gregory VII by Henry IV, January 24, 1076

Henry, king not by usurpation, but by the holy ordination of God, to Hildebrand, not pope, but false monk.

This is the salutation which you deserve, for you have never held any office in the church without making it a source of confusion and a curse to Christian men instead of an honor and a blessing. To mention only the most obvious cases out of many, you have not only dared to touch the Lord's anointed, the archbishops, bishops, and priests; but you have scorned them and abused them, as if they were ignorant servants not fit to know what their master was doing. This you have done to gain favor with the vulgar crowd. You have declared that the bishops know nothing and that you know everything; but if you have such great wisdom you have used it not to build but to destroy. Therefore we believe that St. Gregory, whose name you have presumed to take, had you in mind when he said: "The heart of the prelate is puffed up by the abundance of subjects, and he thinks himself more powerful than all others." All this we have endured because of our respect for the papal office, but you have mistaken our humility for fear, and have dared to make an attack upon the royal and imperial authority which we received from God. You have even threatened to take it away, as if we had received it from you, and as if the empire and kingdom were in your disposal and not in the disposal of God. Our Lord Jesus Christ has called us to the government of the empire, but he never called you to the rule of the church. This is the way you have gained advancement in the church: through craft you have obtained wealth; through wealth you have obtained favor; through favor, the power of the sword; and through the power of the sword, the papal seat, which is the seat of peace; and then from the seat of peace you have expelled peace. For you have incited subjects to rebel against their prelates by teaching them to despise the bishops, their rightful rulers. You have given to laymen the authority over priests, whereby they condemn and depose those whom the bishops have put over them to teach them. You have attacked me, who, unworthy as I am, have yet been anointed to rule among the anointed of God, and who, according to the teaching of the fathers, can be judged by no one save God alone, and can be deposed for no crime except infidelity. For the holy fathers in the time of the apostate Julian did not presume to pronounce sentence of deposition against him, but left him to be judged and condemned by God. St. Peter himself said: "Fear God, honor the king" [1 Pet. 2:17]. But you, who fear not God, have dishonored me, whom He hath established. St. Paul, who said that even an angel from heaven should be accursed who taught any other than the true doctrine, did not make an exception in your favor, to permit you to teach false doctrines. For he says: "But though we, or an angel from heaven, preach any other gospel unto you than that which we have preached unto you, let him be accursed" [Gal. 1:8]. Come down, then, from that apostolic seat which you have obtained by violence; for you have been declared accursed by St. Paul for your false doctrines and have been condemned by us and our bishops for your evil rule. Let another ascend the throne of St. Peter, one who will not use religion as a cloak of violence, but will teach the life-giving doctrine of that prince of the apostles. I, Henry, king by the grace of God, with all my bishops, say unto you: "Come down, come down, and be accursed through all the ages."

Letter of the Bishops to Gregory VII, January 24, 1076

Siegfried, archibishop of Mainz, Udo, bishop of Trier, William, bishop of Utrecht, etc. [a list of names of bishops, twenty-six in all], to brother Hildebrand.

At first when you made yourself pope we thought it better to ignore the illegality of your action and to submit to your rule, in the hope that you would redeem your bad beginning by a just and righteous government of the church, although we realized even then the enormity of the sin which you had committed. But now the lamentable condition of the whole church shows us only too well how we were deceived in you; your violent entrance into office was but the first in a series of wicked deeds and unjust decrees. Our Lord and Redeemer has said, in more places than we can well enumerate here, that love and gentleness are the marks of his disciples, but you are known for your pride, your ambition, and your love of strife. You have introduced worldliness into the church; you have desired a great name rather than a reputation for holiness; you have made a schism in the church and offended its members, who before your time were living together in peace and charity. Your mad acts have kindled the flame of discord which now rages in the churches of Italy, Germany, France, and Spain. The bishops have been deprived of their divine authority, which rests upon the grace of the Holy Spirit received through ordination, and the whole administration of ecclesiastical matters you have given to rash and ignorant laymen. There is nowhere in the church to-day a bishop or a priest who does not hold his office through abject acquiescence in your ambitious schemes. The order of bishops, to whom the government of the church was intrusted by the Lord, you have thrown into confusion, and you have disturbed that excellent coördination of the members of Christ which Paul in so many places commends and inculcates, while the name of Christ has almost disappeared from the earth; and all this through those decrees in which you glory. Who among men is not filled with astonishment and indignation at your claims to sole authority, by which you would deprive your fellow-bishops of their coördinate rights and powers? For you assert that you have the authority to try any one of our parishioners for any sin which may have reached your ears even by chance report, and that no one of us has the power to loose or to bind such a sinner, but that it belongs to you alone or to your legate. Who that knows the scriptures does not perceive the madness of this claim? Since, therefore, it is now apparent that the church of God is in danger of destruction through your presumption, we have come to the conclusion that this state of things can no longer be endured, and we have determined to break our silence and to make public the reasons why you are unfit and have always been unfit to rule the church as pope. These are the reasons: In the first place, in the reign of emperor Henry [III] of blessed memory, you bound yourself by oath never to accept the papacy or to permit anyone else to accept it during the life of that emperor or of his son without the consent of the emperor. There are many bishops still living who can bear witness to that oath. On another occasion, when certain cardinals were aiming to secure the office, you took an oath never to accept the papacy, on condition that they should all take the same oath. You know yourself how faithfully you have kept these oaths! In the second place, it was agreed in a synod held in the time of pope Nicholas [II] and attended by 125 bishops, that no one, under penalty of excommunication, should ever accept the papacy who had not received the election of the cardinals, the approbation of the people, and the consent of the emperor. You yourself proposed and promoted that decree and signed it with your own hand. In the third place, you have filled the whole church with the stench of scandal, by associating on too intimate terms with a woman who was not a member of your family [the countess Matilda]. We do not wish to base any serious charge on this last accusation; we refer to it because it outrages our sense of propriety. And yet the complaint is very generally made that all the judgments and acts of the papacy are passed on by the women about the pope, and that the whole church is governed by this new female conclave. And finally, no amount of complaint is adequate to express the insults and outrages you have heaped upon the bishops, calling them sons of harlots and other vile names. Therefore, since your pontificate was begun in perjury and crime, since your innovations have placed the church of God in the gravest peril, since your life and conduct are stained with infamy; we now renounce our obedience, which indeed was never legally promised to you. You have declared publicly that you do not consider us to be bishops; we reply that no one of us shall ever hold you to be the pope.

The First Deposition and Excommunication of Henry IV by Gregory VII, 1076

St. Peter, prince of the apostles, incline thine ear unto me, I beseech thee, and hear me, thy servant, whom thou hast nourished from mine infancy and hast delivered from mine enemies that hate me for my fidelity to thee. Thou art my witness, as are also my mistress, the mother of God, and St. Paul thy brother, and all the other saints, that thy holy Roman church called me to its government against my own will, and that I did not gain thy throne by violence; that I would rather have ended my days in exile than have obtained thy place by fraud or for worldly ambition. It is not by my efforts, but by thy grace, that I am set to rule over the Christian world which was specially intrusted to thee by Christ. It is by thy grace and as thy representative that God has given to me the power to bind and to loose in heaven and in earth. Confident of my integrity and authority, I now declare in the name of omnipotent God, the Father, Son, and Holy Spirit, that Henry, son of the emperor Henry, is deprived of his kingdom of Germany and Italy; I do this by thy authority and in defence of the honor of thy church, because he has rebelled against it. He who attempts to destroy the honor of the church should be deprived of such honor as he may have held. He has refused to obey as a Christian should, he has not returned to God from whom he had wandered, he has had dealings with excommunicated persons, he has done many iniquities, he has despised the warnings which, as thou art witness, I sent to him for his salvation, he has cut himself off from thy church, and has attempted to rend it asunder; therefore, by thy authority, I place him under the curse. It is in thy name that I curse him, that all people may know that thou art Peter, and upon thy rock the Son of the living God has built his church, and the gates of hell shall not prevail against it.

The Agreement at Oppenheim, October, 1076

Promise of king Henry to pope Hildebrand, also called Gregory.

In accordance with the advice of my subjects, I hereby promise to show henceforth fitting reverence and obedience to the apostolic office and to you, pope Gregory. I further promise to make suitable reparation for any loss of honor which you or your office may have suffered through me. And since I have been accused of certain grave crimes, I will either clear myself by presenting proof of my inocence or by undergoing the ordeal, or else I will do such penance as you may decide to be adequate for my fault.

Edict Annulling the Decrees Against Pope Gregory

Henry, by the grace of God king, to the archbishops, bishops, margraves, counts, and to his subjects of every rank and dignity, greeting and good will. Our faithful subjects have convinced us that in our recent controversy with pope Gregory we were led astray by certain evil counsellors. Therefore we now make known to all, that we have repented of our former actions and have determined henceforth to obey him in everything, as our predecessors were wont to do before us, and to make full reparation for any injury which we may have inflicted upon him or his office. We command all of you to follow our example and to offer satisfaction to St. Peter and to his vicar, pope Gregory, for any fault you may have committed, and to seek absolution from him, if any of you are under his ban.

Letter of Gregory VII to the German Princes Concerning the Penance of Henry IV at Canossa, ca. January 28, 1077

Gregory, bishop, servant of the servants of God, to all the archbishops, bishops, dukes, counts, and other princes of the German kingdom, defenders of the Christian faith, greeting and apostolic benediction.

Since you have made common cause with us and shared our perils in the recent controversy, we have thought it only right that you should be informed of the recent course of events, how king Henry came to Italy to do penance, and how we were led to grant him absolution.

According to the agreement made with your representatives we had come to Lombardy and were there awaiting those whom you were to send to escort us into your land. But after the time set was already passed, we received word that it was at that time impossible to send an escort, because of many obstacles that stood in the way, and we were greatly exercised at this and in grave doubt as to what we ought to do. In the meantime we learned that the king was approaching. Now before he entered Italy he had sent to us and had offered to make complete satisfaction for his fault, promising to reform and henceforth to obey us in all things, provided we would give him our absolution and blessing. We hesitated for some time, taking occasion in the course of the negotiations to reprove him sharply for his former sins. Finally he came in person to Canossa, where we were staying, bringing with him only a small retinue and manifesting no hostile intentions. Once arrived, he presented himself at the gate of the castle, barefoot and clad only in wretched woollen garments, beseeching us with tears to grant him absolution and forgiveness. This he continued to do for three days, until all those about us were moved to compassion at his plight and interceded for him with tears and prayers. Indeed, they marvelled at our hardness of heart, some even complaining that our action savored rather of heartless tyranny than of chastening severity. At length his persistent declarations of repentance and the supplications of all who were there with us overcame our reluctance, and we removed the excommunication from him and received him again into the bosom of the holy mother church. But first he took the oath which we have subjoined to this letter, the abbot of Cluny, the countess Matilda, the countess Adelaide, and many other ecclesiastic and secular princes going surety for him. Now that this arrangement has been reached to the common advantage of the church and the empire, we purpose coming to visit you in your own land as soon as possible. For, as you will perceive from the conditions stated in the oath, the matter is not to be regarded as settled until we have held consultation with you. Therefore we urge you to maintain that fidelity and love of justice which first prompted your action. We have not bound ourself to anything, except that we assured the king that he might depend upon us to aid him in everything that looked to his salvation and honor.

The Oath of King Henry

I, Henry, king, promise to satisfy the grievances which my archibishops, bishops, dukes, counts, and other princes of Germany or their followers may have against me, within the time set by pope Gregory and in accordance with his conditions. If I am prevented by any sufficient cause from doing this within that time, I will do it as soon after that as I may. Further, if pope Gregory shall desire to visit Germany or any other land, on his journey thither, his sojourn there, and his return thence, he shall not be molested or placed in danger of captivity by me or by anyone whom I can control. This shall apply to his escort and retinue and to all who come and go in his service. Moreover, I will never enter into any plan for hindering or molesting him, but will aid him in good faith and to the best of my ability if anyone else opposes him.

◆§ THE YORK TRACTATES

By divine authority and also by institution of the holy fathers, kings are ordained in the church of God and consecrated at the holy altar with sacred unction and benediction, that they may have authority to rule the Christian people, . . . which is the holy church of God. Is the church of God anything else than a congregation of believing Christians living together in one faith, hope, and charity in the house of God?

"York Tractates," *Medieval Political Ideas*, ed. Ewart Lewis (New York: Alfred A. Knopf, Inc., 1954), Vol. II, 563–566.

Therefore kings receive in their consecration authority to rule this church, that they may rule it, and confirm it in judgment and justice, and administer it according to the discipline of Christian law; for they reign in the church, which is the kingdom of God, and reign there together with Christ, for this purpose: that they may rule, protect, and defend it. . . . Moreover, the episcopal order is instituted and consecrated with sacred unction and benediction for this purpose: that it may rule the holy church according to the form of doctrine given it by God Himself. Therefore the blessed Pope Gelasius says as follows: 'There are two powers by which this world is principally ruled: the sacerdotal authority and the royal power' [*Decretum,* c. 6, di. 96]. By 'this world' he means the holy church, which is a wayfarer in this world. In this world, therefore, the sacerdotal authority and the royal power have the principate in sacred government.

Now some men divide this principate in the following way, saying that the priest has the principate of ruling souls, but the king that of ruling bodies, as if souls could be ruled without bodies and bodies without souls, which can by no means be done. For if bodies are well ruled it is necessary that souls also be well ruled, and *vice versa,* because both are ruled for the same purpose: that in the resurrection both may be saved together. However, if the king had only the principate of ruling the bodies of Christians, would he not have the principate of ruling the temple of God, which is holy? For the apostle says, 'Do you not know that your bodies are temples of the Holy Spirit?' [I Corinthians 6:19]. . . . For, as the blessed Ambrose says, 'This is the reason why the bodies of Christians are sanctified in baptism and consecrated with sacred unction, and after unction garbed in a mystic vestment, that they may acquire both regal and sacerdotal dignity.' Since these things are so, it is evident that the king has the principate of ruling those who have the sacerdotal dignity. Therefore, the king ought not to be excluded from the government of the holy church: that is, of the Christian people; because thus the kingdom of the church would be divided and made desolate. . . . And the bodies of Christians also would be badly ruled, if the regal power were separated from the church. Thus the holy fathers and the apostolic pontiffs, understanding this through divine providence, consecrated kings for the protection of the holy church and the defence of the catholic faith, because if gentiles and heretics had not been coerced by regal power, they would have brought the church and the catholic faith to confusion and nothingness. But Christian kings have repelled the gentiles from the church and have condemned heretics and eradicated their perverted doctrines deep within the bosom of the church; for they reigned together with Christ—or rather, in the kingdom of Christ they administered the Christian laws. For these things could not be done by sacerdotal power alone, and therefore the kingly power was necessary to the sacerdotal, that it might protect and defend it, and that the peace and security of the church might remain inviolate. In this, therefore, these two persons, namely the priest and the king, seem to represent Christ and bear his image.

For, as the blessed Augustine asserts in the first book of his *De Consensu Evangelistarum,* [ch. 3, sec. 5]: 'Our Lord Jesus Christ, the one true King and true Priest, has shown among our forefathers these two persons, each commended as having borne His likeness: the one for our rule, the other for our expiation.' And also we read in the Old Testament that these two persons were consecrated with the unction of holy oil and sanctified by divine blessing to this end: that they should bear the likeness and office of Christ in ruling His people and should present His image in the sacrament. Therefore, king and priest have a common unction of holy oil and spirit of sanctification and virtue of benediction, and the common name of God and Christ, and something in common to which that name deservedly applies. . . . The priest prefigured one nature of Christ: that is, Christ as Man; the king prefigured the other: that is, Christ as God. The latter, the higher nature by which He is equal to God the Father; the former, the lower nature by which He is less than the Father. . . .

Now we come to the New Testament, because in it also priests and kings are sanctified with the holy oil and consecrated with the chrism and the divine blessing. I think that what was said above of the Old Testament can be said also of the New, since they have more certainly and more truly been made sharers of the divine grace and the divine nature. For both priests and kings are one with God and His Christ; they are very Gods and Christs by the adoption of the Spirit, and in them also speaks Christ and the Holy Spirit; and in them He fulfills and performs His office; in them He hallows and reigns over and rules His people. Whence each is in the Spirit both Christ and God, and each in his office is the figure and image of Christ and God. The priest, of the Priest; the king, of the King. The priest, of His lower office and nature: that is, of His humanity; the king, of the higher: that is, if His divinity. For Christ, God and Man, is the true and highest King and Priest. He is King, but from the eternity of His divinity, not made, not created, not below or diverse from the Father, but equal and one with the Father. But He is Priest from His assumption of humanity, made according to the order of Melchisedech and created, therefore, lower than the father. . . . Hence, therefore, it appears that the royal power in Christ is greater than the sacerdotal power, and higher, in proportion as His divinity is greater and higher than His humanity. Wherefore, also, some think that likewise among men the royal power is greater and higher than the priestly, and the king greater and higher than the priest, as an imitation and emulation of the better and higher nature or power of Christ. Wherefore, they say, it is not contrary to the justice of God if the sacerdotal dignity is instituted through the regal and subjected to it, because even so it was done in Christ: He was made Priest through His own royal power and through His priesthood was subjected to the Father, to Whom through His kingship He was equal. But if anyone says that a priest is also a king—for everyone who rules can rightly be called a king— it would still seem better that the lesser king be instituted through the higher king. And those who hold this opinion can say that in the language of the holy benediction the king is called 'prince above all.'

Yet, although king and priest have certain common charismata of privileges and the same grace, they also have their own diverse offices. For though in ruling they seem to have a common grace, yet in certain respects it is applied differently to priests and kings, and each has a different grace in carrying out his ministry.

But if the priest is instituted through the king, he is not instituted through the power of man but through the power of God. Whence also the king is God and Christ, but through grace, so that, whatever he does, he does it not simply as man, but as made God and through grace. Or rather, He Who by His nature is God and Christ does this through His vicar, through whom He fulfills His office.

But now let us see what the king confers on the man who is to be created bishop by the prerogative of the pastoral staff. I think that he does not confer on him the order or right of priesthood, but what pertains to his right and reign: namely, the control of earthly things, and the guardianship of the church, and the power of ruling the people of God, which is the temple of the living God and the holy church, bride of our Lord Christ. . . .

ON THE SOVEREIGN POWER OF THE CHURCH

Aegidius Romanus

What Plenitude of Power Is, and That in the Supreme Pontiff There Truly Resides a Plenitude of Power

Since in many chapters we have spoken of plenitude of power, in this chapter we wish to explain what plenitude of power is. We shall also show that this plenitude of power is in the Supreme Pontiff, so that his power . . . is without number, weight, and measure.

Now, many explanations of plenitude of power can be given, but for the present let it suffice to show only this: that plenitude of power is in some agent when that agent can do without a second cause anything that he can do with a second cause. For if an agent does not have such power, it follows that he does not have full power, since he does not have the power in which all power is contained. Therefore, in so far as the Supreme Pontiff has the power in which all power is contained, we say that he has full power. And, since we can descend to the government of men through analysis of those natural phenomena which we can see in the government of the world, we shall say that in no agent in the sky is there plenitude of power, nor in any second agent, because the sky cannot do without a second cause what it can do with a second cause: for instance, if the sky and a lion cooperate in the generation of a lion, the sky could not, without a lion, produce a lion, nor could the sky without a horse produce a horse. Now in God Himself there is plenitude of power, since He can do without a second cause anything that He can do with a second cause. Therefore the power of all agents is contained in the first agent: namely, in God. For in the production of the world He produced a man without a preceding man and a horse without a preceding horse; now, however, He produces a horse through the mediation of a horse, but if He wished, and when He wished, He could do so without semen; and He produces a cow through the mediation of a cow, but He could make a cow without a cow; for He could make a calf from a tree-trunk, or from nothing; and even as He wished, so the thing would happen. And although He can do all things, yet He so administers things that He allows them to follow their own courses. Yet

Aegidius Romanus, *"De Ecclesiastica Potestate," Medieval Political Ideas,* ed. Ewart Lewis (New York: Alfred A. Knopf, Inc., 1954), Vol. II, 382–384, 574–579.

God sometimes performs a miracle, or miracles, acting outside the common course of nature and not according to the common laws of nature which He has imposed on it.

So the Supreme Pontiff also, to the extent of the power which is in the church, has plenitude of power and can without a second cause do anything that he can do with a second cause: for instance, in the case of the election of a bishop, how the election of a bishop ought to be held and how the electors should be weighed in regard to zeal and merit and number—that is, how many and what sort of electors there ought to be so that the candidate may be deemed rightly elected—depends on the institution of the Supreme Pontiff; therefore such an election depends on the Supreme Pontiff's decreeing and ordaining the method of election, even as the production of natural things depends on God as a primary cause, Who lays down His laws for natural things, how they shall act and how they shall produce their effects. The election of a prelate depends also on the agreement of the canons as on a second cause, even as the production of natural things depends on natural things themselves under one first agent: namely, under God. Truly, therefore, to the extent of the power which is in the church, there resides a plenitude of power in the Supreme Pontiff, since he can do without a second cause what he can do with a second cause. For he could provide for any church without election by the chapter; and in so doing he would not act in accordance with the common laws which he has imposed but in accordance with his own plenitude of power. For, as we have said, the election of a prelate is made by a primary cause, the Supreme Pontiff, who decrees how the election shall be made, and by a second cause, namely, by the election carried out by the electors according to the form given them. Yet the Supreme Pontiff could, without a second cause of this sort (that is, without election by the electors) provide any church with a prelate. And what has been said about the election of a prelate holds true for other ecclesiastical matters, because the Supreme Pontiff can act without other agents as the one who has plenitude of power, in whom all the power of the church is recognized to reside.

Yet the Supreme Pontiff ought to observe that God, Who has all power (not merely conditionally, in respect of this or that, but absolutely), nevertheless, in order that His works of wisdom may not be in vain, nearly always acts according to the laws which He has laid down for things, and nearly always observes the laws, producing the effects of second agents through the mediation of second agents. For He burns through the mediation of fire, as He cools through the mediation of water, because, according to the laws He has laid down for things, it cannot be that what is in the fire shall not be burned and what is in cold water shall not be cooled; and also, according to these laws, it cannot be said that he who walks in water shall not wet his feet. Sometimes, however, though rarely, He brings it about, in disregard of the common laws, that what is in the fire shall not be burned and that someone may walk in water with dry feet.

So, likewise, the Supreme Pontiff, because he has the authority to decree how the church ought to be governed, ought to govern the church in accordance with these laws, and ought to permit chapters to carry out their elections, and prelates to perform their duties, and other officers of the church to do their work in accordance with the form given them. Yet, for a reasonable cause, he can disregard these common laws and act without other agents, because the power of all agents is contained in him, so that in him is all the power of all the agents in the church; and therefore it is said that in him there is a plenitude of power. . . .

From the order of the universe we can clearly show that the church was established over peoples and kingdoms. For, according to Dionysius [Pseudo-Dionysius], *De Angelica Hierarchia,* [ch. 10], the law of divinity is to subdue the lowest to the highest through the intermediate. Therefore, this requires an order of the universe, that the lowest may be subdued to the highest through the intermediate. For if the lowest were immediately under the highest, as the intermediate are, the universe would not be rightly ordained: which, especially in regard to powers and authorities, is an inadmissible conclusion. And this is evident from the saying of the apostle in Romans 13:[1], when, after saying that there is no power except from God, he immediately adds, 'Moreover, the powers that be are ordained of God.' If, therefore, there are two swords, the one spiritual and the other temporal (as is apparent from the saying of the Gospel [Luke 22:38], 'Behold, here are two swords,' to which the Lord at once adds, 'It is enough,' because these two swords suffice in the church), these two swords, these two authorities and powers, are necessarily from God; because, as has been said, there is no power except from God. It follows, moreover, that they must needs be ordained; because, as we stated, the powers that are from God must be ordained. Now they would not be ordained unless one sword were subjected through the other and placed under the other; because, as Dionysius said, the law of divinity which God gave to all created things . . . requires this: that all be not immediately subjected to the supreme, but the lowest through the intermediate, and the lower through the higher. Therefore the temporal sword, as inferior, is to be subjected through the spiritual sword as through the higher, and the one is to be subordinated to the other as the lower to the higher.

But someone might say that kings and princes ought to be subjected in spiritual and not temporal matters, and that therefore this doctrine ought to be understood to mean that kings and princes are spiritually but not temporally under the church. And he might also argue that the church has received temporals themselves from the temporal lordship, as in the case of the donation and grant which Constantine made to the church. But anyone who says this does not grasp the force of the argument. For if kings and princes were only spiritually subject to the church, sword would not be under sword, temporals would not be under spirituals, there would be no order of powers, the lowest would not be subjected to the highest through the intermediate. Therefore, if these powers are ordained, the temporal sword must be under the spiritual, kingdoms must be under the vicar of Christ, and, as a matter of right— though some may act contrarily as a matter of fact—the vicar of Christ must have dominion over temporals themselves.

Among the wise there can be no doubt that the sacerdotal power precedes the royal and earthly power in dignity and nobility. We can demonstrate this in four ways: first, from the giving of tithes; second, from benediction and sanctification; third, from the origin of the authority itself; fourth, from the government of things.

The first proof proceeds as follows. By divine law and divine institution we are all bound to give tithes, so that every earthly power, as earthly and temporal, is bound to give tithes to the spiritual power. Moreover, such tithes are given in recognition of servitude, as each recognizes himself to be the servant of God. Therefore, even as inferiors pay tribute to a superior in recognition of the fact that what they have, they have and possess from their superiors, so also we have received from God what we have and possess according to the saying in I Corinthians 4:[7], 'What have you that you have not received from Him?' It is fitting, therefore, that we pay tribute for all our possessions to God Himself. For God, as other sciences tell us, is rich through Himself; but others are rich from loans. For God has lent use what we have. Wherefore it is not strange nor unreasonable that on this account we are taxpayers and tributaries to God Himself.

Therefore, the earthly and temporal power, as earthly, that is, as receiving the fruits of the earth, and as temporal, that is, as having temporal goods, is tributary and tax-payer to the ecclesiastical power and, recognizing that this power stands in the place of God, ought to give tithes in recognition of its own servitude. Therefore every earthly power is under the ecclesiastical power, and especially under the supreme pontiff, who stands at the apex of the church in the ecclesiastical hierarchy, and to whom all (both kings, as supreme [I Peter 2:13], and everyone else) ought to be subject.

The second proof is based upon benediction and sanctification; and this is the argument used by Hugh [of St. Victor], who says in *De Sacramentis*, bk. 2, pt. 2, [ch. 4], that in the church of God the sacerdotal dignity consecrates and blesses the royal power. If, therefore, as the apostle says in Hebrews 7:[7], he that blesses is greater than he that is blessed, it is established beyond doubt that the earthly power, which receives blessing from the spiritual, is rightly esteemed inferior.

The third proof is based upon the institution of the power itself. And this argument also Hugh mentions in the same passage, saying, 'Moreover, that the spiritual power is greater in dignity than the earthly power is manifestly shown in that ancient people of the Old Testament, among whom the priesthood was first instituted by God, but afterwards the royal power was ordained at God's command through the priesthood.' Therefore the royal power ought to recognize the superiority of the sacerdotal dignity, as that through which at God's command it was instituted. And if it be said that not every royal power was instituted through the priesthood, we shall say that any royal power not instituted through the priesthood either is not righteous, and therefore is brigandage rather than authority, or is united with the priesthood, or is successor to a power instituted through the priesthood. For when there were kingdoms of the gentiles, under the law of nature, all such kingdoms were obtained through invasion and usurpation. Thus Nimrod, who, as we read in Genesis 10:[8–10], was the first king, reigning in Babylon, made himself king through violence and usurpation, whence it is said there that he began to be mighty in the land; therefore he acquired the kingship through civil power and not through justice. But according to Augustine, *De Civitate Dei,* [bk. 4, ch. 4], kingdoms without justice are great bands of robbers. Moreover, although such rulers are called kings, they are not kings, but thieves and robbers.

Therefore a kingship not instituted through the priesthood either was not a kingship but brigandage or was joined to the priesthood. For before Saul was instituted through Samuel, as through a priest of God, and set up as king, Melchisedech was king of Salem [Genesis 14:18]. But Melchisedech was a priest as well as a king. Whence it is said [Hebrews 7:1] that he was priest of the most high God. Therefore in this case the kingship was not independent of the priesthood but united with the priesthood, so that the priesthood was more principal than the kingship. But modern kingships are the successors of kingships instituted through the priesthood, so that before these kingships existed there were kingships instituted through the priesthood. And because the earlier facts are examples and mirrors of later facts, all later kingships ought to be traced back to the first kingship, which was instituted through the priesthood at God's command. . . .

Therefore let kings recognize that they were instituted through the priesthood. And therefore, if we diligently examine the origin and institution of royal power, the fact that it was instituted through the priesthood leads to the conclusion that the royal power ought to be under the sacerdotal power and especially under the power of the highest priest.

The fourth proof is based on the government of things. Therefore, if we wish to see which power is under which power, we ought to notice the government of the whole machinery of the world. Now in the government of the universe we see that every corporal substance is governed through a spiritual. Inferior bodies, indeed, are ruled through superior bodies, and the grosser through the more subtle and the less potent through the more potent. Yet every corporal substance is ruled through a spiritual substance, and all spiritual substance through the highest spirit: namely, through God. Whence Augustine says in *De Trinitate,* bk. 3, ch. 4, [sec. 9], that 'certain grosser and inferior bodies are ruled by the subtler and more potent in a certain order; moreover, all bodies are ruled through spirit, and the whole creation through its Creator.' And what we see in the order and government of the universe we ought to copy in the government of the commonwealth and in the government of the whole Christian people. For that same God Who is universal ruler of the whole machinery of the world is special governor of His church and those who believe in Him.

Therefore, if the whole universe, of which God has general care, is so well ordained because inferior bodies are under superior bodies and all bodies are under the spiritual substance, and moreover the spiritual substance itself is under the highest spirit, namely, under God, it is altogether absurd to say that the Christian people and the very church which God has chosen for Himself, without stain or blemish, is not well ordained, and that it is not thus entirely joined and united into a whole, and that the order of the universe, which, as Augustine says in the *Enchiridion,* [ch. 10], is a most beautiful order and wonderful beauty—that that wonderful beauty, that most beautiful order, does not shine forth in the church. Wherefore, even as in the universe itself inferior bodies are ruled through superior bodies and the less potent by the more potent, so in the Christian people and among believers the inferior temporal lords are ruled through their superiors and the less potent through the more potent. And even as in the universe itself every corporal substance is ruled through a spiritual substance, since the heavens themselves, which are supreme among corporal things, and which have influence over all bodies, are governed through spiritual substances, namely, through the intelligences that move them, so among believers all temporal lords and every earthly power ought to be ruled and governed through the spiritual and ecclesiastical power, and especially through the supreme pontiff, who holds the apex and the highest rank in the church and in the spiritual power. Moreover, the supreme pontiff is to be judged by God alone. For . . . it is he who judges all and is judged by no one: that is, by no mere man but by God alone.

Therefore, if the earthly power deviates, it will be judged by the spiritual power as by its superior; but if the spiritual power, and especially the power of the supreme pontiff, deviates, it can be judged by God alone. Whence, after saying in *De Sacramentis,* bk. 2, pt. 2, [ch. 4], that the earthly power is judged by the spiritual power, Hugh adds that it, however, was first instituted by God and when it deviates can be judged by God alone. . . .

And if anyone should say that the whole earthly power ought to be under the spiritual in regard to the articles of faith but not in regard to temporal and earthly power, his argument would have no weight, because he who says this does not grasp the force of our reasoning, since bodies, as bodies, are under spirits, even as the movers of bodies, and especially the movers of the superior bodies, are themselves ruled through moving spirits and through the intelligences which move the spheres; so temporal powers, as temporal, and especially the supreme temporal powers, can be judged through the spiritual power and especially through the power of the supreme pontiff, who is the supreme and most sublime spiritual power in the church; inferior temporal lords, if they are at fault, can be judged through temporal lords, but those superior temporal lords can themselves be judged through the spiritual power, since among temporal lords they have no superiors. But the spiritual power, and especially the power of the supreme priest, can be judged by no one but God alone, since no man is superior to it.

ᴇᴦ A DEBATE BETWEEN A CLERIC AND A KNIGHT

The clerk opened the discussion in the following words: I marvel, good Sir, in how few days the times are changed, justice is buried, laws are overturned, and rights are trampled under foot.

Knight   Those are big words, and I am a layman, and though I learned a few letters as a boy I never got deep enough to understand words so high. And therefore, reverend Clerk, you must use a plainer style if you want to talk with me.

Clerk   In my time I have seen the church held in great honour among all kings, princes, and nobles; but now I see it wretched. The church has been made a prey for you all; many things are exacted from us, none given to us; if we do not give up our property it is stolen from us; our rights are trampled under foot; our liberties are violated.

Knight   It is hard for me to believe that the king, whose council is composed of clerics, is acting unjustly toward you or that your right is perishing.

"Disputatio inter Clericum et Militem," Medieval Political Ideas, ed. Ewart Lewis (New York: Alfred A. Knopf, Inc., 1954), Vol. II, 567–574.

Clerk   But indeed we are enduring countless injuries, against all right.

Knight   I should like to know what you call 'right.'

Clerk   By 'right' I mean the decrees of the fathers and the statutes of the Roman pontiffs.

Knight   What they decree, if they decree concerning temporals, may be rights for you; but not for us. For no one can make decrees about things over which he certainly has no lordship. Thus the king of the French cannot make decrees in regard to the Empire, nor the Empire in regard to the kingdom of France. And even as earthly princes cannot decree anything in regard to spirituals, over which they have received no power, so neither can you decree anything in regard to their temporals, over which you have no authority. Thus whatever you have decreed about temporals, over which you have not received power from God, is a waste of time. So I had to laugh recently when I heard that Lord Boniface VIII had just decreed that he is and ought to be over all governments and kingdoms, and thus he can easily acquire a right for himself over anything whatever, since all he has to do is to write and everything will be his as soon as he has written; and thus everything will belong to you, when to decree is nothing more than to wish to have for one's self. Therefore to wish will be the same as to have a right; therefore one need only write, 'I wish this to be mine,' when he wants to have my castle, or my country-house, or my field, or my money and treasure. You can't help seeing, wise Clerk, to what absurdity this argument brings you.

Clerk   You argue cleverly enough, Lord Knight, and slyly produce these arguments against us. . . . But if you want to be a Christian and a true Catholic, you will not deny that Christ is Lord of all things. . . . And who will doubt the validity of the decrees of Him Who, it is certain, is Lord of all things?

Knight   I certainly do not resist divine authority or lordship, since I am and wish to be a Christian. And therefore, if you will show me by various Scriptures that supreme pontiffs are lords over all temporals, then kings and princes must certainly be subject to supreme pontiffs in temporals as well as in spirituals.

Clerk   That can easily be shown from what has been said. For our faith holds that the apostle Peter was instituted plenary vicar of Jesus Christ for himself and his successors. If, therefore, you do not deny that Christ, Who is Lord of heaven and earth, can decree in regard to your temporals, you cannot without blushing deny the same authority to the plenary vicar of Christ.

Knight   I have heard holy and most devout men distinguish two periods in Christ, one of humility and the other of authority: of humility up to His passion, of authority after His resurrection, when He said, 'All power is given to me in heaven and on earth' (Matthew 28:[18]). Now Peter was constituted vicar of Christ for the state of humility, not for the state of glory and majesty. For he was not made vicar of Christ for those things that Christ does now in glory, but to imitate those things that Christ did when He was humble on earth, because those are necessary to us. Therefore He committed to His vicar that power which He exercised as mortal man, not that which He received when glorified. And I shall prove this to you by the testimony of those same Scriptures which you quote. For Christ Himself said to Pilate, 'My kingdom is not of this world' [John 18:36], and that He did not come to be ministered unto, but to minister [Matthew 20:28]. This testimony is plain enough to confound anyone who resists it and to break a neck, however stiff. And this likewise: 'A certain man from the crowd said to Jesus, "Master, say to my brother that he should divide the inheritance with me," And He said to him, "O man, who made Me a judge and divider over you?"' (Luke 12: [13, 14]). Therefore you hear clearly that Christ was constituted neither judge nor divider in temporals; therefore in that state of ministry which He accepted, He neither had temporal kingship nor strove after it. Rather, when they ate the multiplied bread, He fled; and in the commission made to Peter He gave him not the keys of the kingdom of earth but the keys of the kingdom of heaven. And it is certain that the priests of the Hebrews were subject to kings and deposed by kings— and may you escape such a fate! And that you may know that the vicar of Christ was given a spiritual kingship and not a temporal kingship or lordship, listen to this equally clear testimony from Paul himself. For he says, 'Every high priest taken from among men is ordained for men in those things that pertain to God,' not to govern an earthly lordship, but 'that he may offer gifts and sacrifices for sins' [Hebrews 5:1]. You see, therefore, that the pontiff is set above others in regard to the things that concern God, since Paul writes to Timothy, 'Let no one warring for God involve himself in secular affairs' [II Timothy 2:4]. . . .

Clerk   Do you deny, O Knight, that the church has cognizance of sins?

Knight   Far be it from me; for that would be to deny penance and confession.

Clerk   Any injustice is sin, and he who has cognizance of sin has cognizance of the just and unjust. Since, therefore, justice and injustice are characteristics of temporal affairs, it follows that the church should be judge in temporal cases.

Knight   That argument is a sophistry, and its emptiness and weakness ought to be refuted by a similar argument. Hanging robbers and other condemned criminals is a matter of the just and unjust, and of sin too. Therefore by reason of sin the pope ought also to judge concerning blood. But that argument is a feather blown into the air by a light reason. Now it remains to show you, Lord Clerk, how your cognizance of the just and the unjust is related to the judgment of temporal affairs according to human laws, which have settled such matters. But anyone can see what laws these are, and what persons should judge. Therefore it is plain that he who has the right to establish laws, and who has the function of interpreting, explaining, and guarding them, and of making them heavier or milder when it seems expedient, should be the judge and have cognizance of the just and the unjust in accordance with the laws. Therefore, if you exercise a competitive or concurrent jurisdiction by your cognizance of the just and the unjust, you are ploughing with an ox and an ass, contrary to your Scripture; and when the prince says, 'This is just,' the pontiff will say, 'This is unjust.'. . . And I will show you where, according to Paul, your cognizance ought to begin, because the prince by his own right has cognizance of the just and the unjust; and let everyone heed his decision, that it many be maintained, and obey him as it is commanded (Deuteronomy 17:[10, 11]). If, however, anyone, swelling with pride, does not obey his command, and if the prince whose was the office of judging does not have power to resist or coerce him, then your jurisdiction begins; because then your admonition comes into play, as the apostle Paul says in the Epistle to Titus, 3:[1]: 'Admonish them to be subject and submissive to princes and powers.' And in the Epistle to the Romans, [13:1]: 'Let every soul be subject to the higher powers.' Also where evil deeds and crimes are manifest, as looting, robbery, and the like, and there is no one willing or able to correct them. For I do not deny that in such cases you should and can exercise your authority, but not in regard to the just and the unjust, because of this you have no cognizance and you ought not to put your finger into it. And when the situation is manifest, through the decision of the law or when there is obvious crime, so that no cognizance is necessary, then that matter and form can belong to you; otherwise, if you wish to take cognizance of the aforesaid cases through their connection with sin, nothing will remain but that the courts of princes be closed, and the laws and decrees of princes be silent, and yours alone resound. . . .

Clerk   Ought not temporals to serve spirituals? Therefore temporals ought to be subject to spirituals, and the spiritual power ought to rule the temporal power.

Knight   Truly temporals ought to serve spirituals in the proper way, since they are considered necessary to minister to those who maintain the worship of God. For every people holds this principle as if innate and instinctive, and nature itself has decreed this by natural right: that whatever is necessary should be provided for those who minister to the Creator and celebrate divine things, and the necessities of life should be supplied to them as their honest due. . . . But if you want to know what sort of lordship He offers to His ministers, listen to the words of Christ and His apostle Paul. For Christ said to His disciples when they were sent out to preach, 'The labourer is worthy of his hire' [Matthew 10:10]. And Paul says of himself and the other apostles, 'Who ever goes to war at his own wages?' [I Corinthians 9:7]. . . . Behold to what Christ and His apostle Paul compare you. To labourers and wage-earners. Are labourers and wage-earners in any way lords of things? You see that temporals are granted you not for lordship but for the sustenance of life and for the expenses of spiritual ministry. . . .

When you argue further that the supreme pontiff is superior in all things, you run into a bad joke. For if, when the pope is created, he is created lord of all things, by like reason to create a bishop will be to create the lord of his territory, and my priest will be lord of my castle, and of me too. . . . Therefore stop talking this nonsense which everybody laughs at and which has been settled by so many texts of Scripture and logical proofs. For we say that in the Old Law priests were not adored by kings, but kings and princes were adored by priests and prophets, and they were summoned to the kings and commanded to do what pleased the kings, and when they were occasionally at fault in the public administration of temporals they were reproved, as is told in the third book of Kings, [I Kings], chapters 1 and 4.

Clerk   I marvel at what you say: that a king has censured a pontiff in regard to the administration of temporals.

Knight   You excite a sleeping dog, and force me to say more than I had intended.

Clerk   Let the dog be excited, and let him bark.

Knight   Since you do not know how to use the usefulness and patience of princes, I am afraid that after a just bark you will find yourself bitten.

Clerk   What do kings and princes have to do with the administration of our temporals? Let them have their own, and leave ours to us.

Knight   It is our interest in every way. Is it not our interest to worry over the safety of our souls above all things? Is it not our interest to carry out the due rites for our dead fathers, and also to demand such rites? And were not your temporals given you by our fathers, and plentifully provided, for this purpose: that you might entirely expend them in divine worship? But certainly you do nothing with them but apply to your own needs all that with which you ought to fill the bellies of the poor through benefactions and works of charity. Is it not necessary that through holy works of this sort the dead may be freed and the living saved? When you spend these endowments as if they were your own and consume them extravagantly in defiance of the givers' intention and also, in a sense, waste them by misuse, do you not wrong the living and the dead, and damnably steal from them? Should not the wage be taken away from the soldier who refuses to earn it? And certainly a vassal who does not fulfill his service deservedly loses his fief. And, to silence you on this question and because it is up to us to worry over this and find a remedy, listen to the very strong and very clear chapter of the Holy Scriptures. For we read of King Joash (II Chronicles 24:[2]), 'And he did that which was right in the sight of the Lord, all the days of Jehoiada the priest.' And of the same king we read in the twelfth chapter of the fourth book of Kings [II Kings 12:7, 8]: 'King Joash called Jehoiada the high priest, and the other priests, and said to them, "Why repair ye not the breaches of the temple? Therefore take no more money from the people, according to your ordination, but give it up for the restoration of the temple." And the priests were forbidden to take any more money from the people.' You see, therefore, that the Lord praised King Joash, who took care that the oblations should be expended for divine worship according to the intention of the givers: that is, for the restoration of the temple. . . .

Clerk   King Joash did not take goods for himself but for the use of the church; today, however, you take our goods and spend them not for religious uses but for military tumults and warring armies. Thus the example which you cite contradicts your actions and is only a pretext for your violence.

Knight   You always hurt yourself by kicking against the prick of kings. Do you complain when your nephews and kinsmen and other dishonest persons sometimes take away with them some of the goods of the church? But you find it altogether intolerable and injurious when the king gently seeks and graciously accepts something from you for the sake of your safety and for the defence of the church and of your property.

Clerk   O poor me! You take away my skin and my flesh too and call it safety!

Knight   Don't get excited but listen patiently; consider how your neighbours lack goods of their own and cast their eyes on yours. If there were no royal authority, what sort of tranquillity would you have? Would not needy and extravagant nobles when they had used up their own resources turn to yours? Therefore the king's arm is your buttress; the king's peace is your peace; the king's safety is your safety. If this failed, your wealth would be stolen from you or you would lose it through the requirements of your sins, and when your neighbours lay in wait for your wealth, now demanding, now threatening, and laying waste your property, you would be forced to serve them all. Then, when you saw your property ruined, how eager you would be to redeem it and how you would wish that the king's arm should be restored! You see, therefore, that when you hand over a little to the king, you are paying for your own safety, since he saves all your property from being lost. But as you have always been ungrateful for benefits, so you complain of your advantages. But if the king were dead and a hostile army invaded the kingdom, would you not all be ruined by looting and pillaging, and would you not, terrified and awestruck, deserting your homes, flee the barbaric ferocity which you would know to be implacable? And would you not lose all—you who now complain at the smallest sums? But if kings and princes are bound to defend you at their own expense and peril, and to expose themselves freely to death for you, while you rest in the shade, feast splendidly, drink merrily, lie on luxurious beds, sleep quietly, and amuse yourselves with sweet instruments, then you are indeed the only lords, and kings and princes are your slaves. And others also risk their lives and fortunes for you. If churchmen are allowed to rest in peace, it is not much to ask that they contribute their wealth in lieu of their persons. You say that this is hard; but you will not be silent until you have been convinced in the accustomed way, and refuted by the Divine Scriptures which you cannot resist. . . .

Clerk   If things once given to God can be taken back, then cannot all vows be broken?

Knight   This is not taking back things given to God but applying them to the uses for which they were given. For what has been given to God was thereby dedicated to pious uses. But what could be more holy than the safety of the Christian people, and what more precious to God than to keep enemies, robbers, and murderers away from the Christian people, and to buy peace for Christian subjects? Therefore, when the goods of the church are spent for such purposes, they are, in fact, restored to the uses to which they were dedicated. . . .

⤷ OPERA

Jean Gerson

> The late medieval Church reached its zenith and fell to its nadir within a century. The cause of the fall was over-extension in the arena of secular politics. Boniface VIII, the last pope in the tradition of Gregory VII and Innocent III, fought Edward I of England and Philip IV of France over the issues of ultimate sovereignty and state taxation of the clergy. In Philip the papacy took on a determined king with the will to use arms, laws, imprisonment, and humiliation to gain his ends. Boniface died while under surveillance, shortly before the beginning of the sixty-nine-year "Babylonian Captivity" (1309–1378) and the puppet papacy at Avignon, France. Not even the end of the period of French control could free the papacy from its problems, for then began the Great Schism, with three popes simultaneously making claim to Peter's throne.

The very adversities of the Church stimulated programs for reform during the fourteenth century. One advocate of reform was Jean Gerson (1363–1429), Chancellor of the University of Paris. Gerson, the central figure of the conciliar movement, championed the expansion of the papal council in the belief that as the entire Church shared in the process of salvation, so should its policies be considered and promulgated by the entire clergy, the pope being more a chairman than an absolute monarch. Though Gerson's challenging views failed to be accepted after the last Council at Basel (1449), they set off similar movements of thought in politics. Gerson reflected the growth of representative government; he sought a system of estates representation in the Church; his inquiries into divisible sovereignty and popular responsibility anticipated limited monarchy; and, though he joined in the condemnations of Hus's theological individualism, he tried to prune the Church of nonessentials in doctrine and practice, refocusing attention on matters of faith. Gerson certainly would have viewed the current liberal movement within the Catholic Church with keen interest, perhaps with the pride of delayed vindication.

TREATISE ON THE UNITY OF THE CHURCH (1409)

Consideration II

The essential unity of the church continues always in her relation to Christ her Bridegroom. For 'Christ is the Head of the church' [Ephesians 5:23], in Whom we are all one, according to the apostle, even if He has no vicar: that is, when His vicar is bodily or civilly dead or when there is no probability that Christians will ever show obedience to him or to his successors. Then the church, by divine and natural law, to which no positive law rightly understood offers any obstacle, can assemble herself in order to procure for herself, at a general council representing her, one certain vicar; and she can do this not only by the authority of the lord cardinals, but also by the assistance and aid of any prince or other Christian. For the mystical body of the church, most perfectly established by Christ, does not have less right and strength for the procuring of her own union than has any civil, mystical, or true natural body; for there is no provision in immediate and immutable divine or natural law that the church cannot congregate herself and unite herself without a pope or without any particular rank or college, in which death or error can, in a particular instance, occur. . . .

Jean Gerson, *"Opera," Medieval Political Ideas,* ed. Ewart Lewis (New York: Alfred A. Knopf, Inc., 1954), Vol. II, 403–415.

ON THE DEPOSITION OF A POPE *(ca.* 1415)

Consideration X

The vicarious spouse of the church is, in particular cases, removable from the church, either by her direct action or through the general council which represents her or by persons appointed by her for this purpose, regardless of whether or not the vicar himself consents to his abdication.

. . . Surely God gave the church no rank, no degree of dignity, no kind of ministry except for her edification and common utility. This appears in Ephesians 4:[11–12] and Corinthians 6 [I Corinthians 12:4–30]. Surely He gave these things for the peace of her 'in whose borders he made peace,' as the Psalmist says [Psalms 147:14]. And love brings this about; wherefore love is described by the apostle as 'the end of law' [I Timothy 1:5]. And on love Christ based the pastoral office: 'If thou lovest Me,' said Christ to Peter, 'feed My sheep' [John 21:17]. And who does not see that there could be many cases, some of which are involved in the present situation, in which the church would be not edified but destroyed, not united but scattered, not fed but devoured, if he who had been duly and canonically ordained the vicarious spouse of the church would not yield voluntarily, or would not be ejected against his will? And let no one wonder at what we say, as if it contradicted the commandment, 'Touch not My anointed' [Psalms 105:15]. In the same way it would be right for any individual, in case of violence attempted by a true pope against his chastity or life, to repel force with force, instigated by blameless self-defence, and thus he would have a lawful right to lay violent hands upon the pope or throw him into the sea. Why should it not likewise be lawful on occasion for the whole church to do the same, in her own defence and in the cautious repression of attempted violence?

Consideration XI

The vicarious spouse of the church is in particular cases removable by a general council held without his consent or against his will.

Let us say first that regularly by divine law a general council ought not to be held if the pope does not call or approve it, if there is one and if there is no legitimate allegation against him. But general rules often undergo exceptions, even as in grammar, so also in morals, in which, especially, particular cases occur in infinitely variable ways: to which exceptions is ordained the higher law, the interpreter of the others, which Aristotle calls *epieikeia* in V *Ethics,* [ch. 10], and another, more divine, which he calls *gnome* in VI *Ethics,* [ch. 1]. Now this law always has place in the interpretation of other particular laws, where the reason and end of their institution is seen to fail. Now the end of all laws, not only human but also divine, is love, which works unity. If there is a case, therefore, in which the observation of any law would dissipate unity and be an obstacle to the public welfare, who, using reason, would say that it ought to hold? Doubtless no one would wish this to be done in his own case; how much more would all the community reasonably shun it!

But if anyone should ask by what authority a council of this sort is supported, or what authority it uses, seeing that it is, as it seems, headless without the pope, it should be answered that it uses the authority of Christ its Head and indefeasible Spouse; besides this, the authority of His laws both divine and natural, which grant this licence either to necessity or to manifest charity or to religious piety. For this we have a text, Mark 2:23, concerning the excuse of the disciples who wished to pluck grain on the sabbath and who were excused by the law of necessity, confirmed by the example of David, who ate consecrated bread.

Consideration XII

The vicarious spouse of the church is in particular cases removable by the church or the general council, not by advice or recommendation or pronouncement but authoritatively, judicially, and juridically.

Let us presuppose that jurisdiction is the same as the declaration of the law or the authority to declare the law: or, jurisdiction is the immediate faculty of declaring the law. Customarily the term jurisdiction is limited to coercive jurisdiction, which is laid upon or declared upon another even against his will. From this definition first follows the truth of this consideration, how the church or council has on occasion the immediate faculty or authority or power to declare the law even against one who was rightly raised and chosen to be pope. Yet we do not wish to deny that the supreme pontiff has the regitive and authoritative power in respect of all men, as much as Christ wished and thought fit to give him for its exercise: not for his own sake, but rather for the utility of the church. Such authority the rest of the church does not have, unless in a certain unitive and elective way. In terms of this analysis, it is true that the keys were not given to one, but to a unity. It does not, however, follow from this analysis that the whole church or council, in the absence of the pope, especially if he is unworthy, cannot exercise authoritative jurisdiction, as a certain divine and indeviable right to subdue or correct or restrain him, lest he harm not only the church, but himself, like a madman or like a man led astray by drunkenness, the worst of evil passions. For, as Aristotle teaches in V *Politics,* to the whole community belongs the correction or the total disestablishment of the prince, if he persists without amending his ways. And this power cannot be removed or alienated from the free community which can do as it wills about its own affairs, nor can it be suspended through appropriation or by any law. How much the more does the church have this power! . . .

CONVERSATIONS (1415)

Part III, Second Direction

A general council, although it cannot nor ought to withdraw or diminish the plenitude of papal power entrusted by Christ to Peter and to his successors, but to thank God for this, Who granted it, and to revere and esteem it, can nevertheless limit the use of that power by definite laws and statutes for the edification of the church. This the present council has done in many respects, but especially in this, that it has established a law in regard to the election of a future pope and in regard to his electors: that no pope to come can depose the most reverend father Lord Angelo Corario, on account of the praiseworthiness of his spontaneous yielding, from the cardinalate and the power of a legate granted to him by this council, nor attack nor punish him in any way for any past deeds whatever; this was done rightly and by indulgent condescension, that an example for posterity should be given to one voluntarily yielding when either a pious utility or urgent necessity of the church demands this.

It is expedient, moreover, now, before the election of the supreme pontiff, that many things be thus done concerning the general state of the church, in which supreme pontiffs have turned the use of their plenitude of power too often to abuse, as because they did not wish to hold a general council, nor to relinquish the ordaining rights to lesser prelates, and because they deviated from the statutes of the general councils, now by breaking them, now by changing them, now by interpreting them at their pleasure, now by granting privileges and exceptions, openly and without manifest reason or utility.

Whence, in the use of dispensations, the granting of privileges, the innovation of decretals, it is not fitting that the use of the papal power be so restrained that in every such case recourse would be made to the general council, on account of the difficulty and infrequency of convoking it—such as did not exist in the case of the primitive church, when, as Jerome says, all things were done by common consensus. So also it is not expedient that such relaxation be made as would take away and weaken at random the strength and vigour of general councils in their decrees.

Here we may consider Aristotle's teaching about the three kinds of polity: namely, the regal and monarchical, in which one man rules well, of which tyranny is the opposite; another, aristocracy, where the few and good dominate, of which oligarchy is the opposite; and third, timocracy, in which the people rules well, which has democracy as its opposite.

Now, better than any one of these polities would be a polity composed from the regal and the aristocratic, as in the kingdom of France, where the king has instituted a parlement, by which he does not refuse to be judged. But the best and most healthy polity of all would be that which would include this threefold good: the monarchy, the aristocracy, and the timocracy.

Now the general council is a polity so composed, having its direction more from the special assistance of the Holy Spirit and the promise of Jesus Christ than from nature or from human skill alone. . . .

Now what is a general council? It has been described elsewhere, and I repeat: 'The general council is an assemblage, made by a lawful authority, to some place, from every hierarchic degree of the whole catholic church, at which no faithful person who demands to hear is excluded, for healthfully discussing and ordaining those things which concern the due regimen of the same church in faith and morals.' It could be deduced from this definition, together with the preceding statements, in what way the plenitude of papel power was granted by Christ in those things which are supernatural. In others also, which natural, canonical, and civil laws assign to it, as to a monarch, the papal power stands supreme and is concorded with the power of the council, which has been spoken of: because the papal power is included in the council, although this power is in the pope in one way, in the council in another way. Even as the keys were given to Peter in one way, and in another way to the church. Whence the council has, in many things which concern the pope, the authority to advise and recommend; the pope, the authority to exercise and execute. For the council could not of itself either absolve in the court of conscience, or ordain priests, or make the Body of Christ, or conquer the infidels with an armed hand; and so of many things; but it pertains to it to advise or recommend about things of this sort; and he who denies its dictate contumaciously denies the Holy Spirit, whose it is to direct the council itself in advising and recommending. Example in man, where the reason has the power to advise and recommend; the will, the exercise and execution. . . .

CHURCH AUTHORITY AND THE ORIGIN OF RIGHT AND LAW (*ca.* 1416)

Consideration I

Ecclesiastical power is the power which was supernaturally and specially granted by Christ to his apostles and disciples and to their legitimate successors, to the end of time, for the building of the church militant, according to the evangelic laws, for the sake of securing eternal felicity. . . .

'Church' is used as an abbreviation, when we speak here of the power of the church: namely, for those who by a kind of special sign are dedicated to the divine service, from the lowest rank . . . up to the highest, with which the pope is adorned. . . .

Consideration VI

Ecclesiastical power can and ought to be considered in three ways. In one way, formally and abstractly and irrespectively in itself. In another way, materially or respectively, as it is assigned to particular persons by legitimate right, which is commonly done by consecration and election. . . . In the third way, it is considered in respect of exercise or execution. . . . This consideration is useful in distinguishing and resolving the various ways in which theologians and canonists speak of ecclesiastical power, since ignorance or inadvertence about this distinction is a frequent cause of error. . . .

Consideration VII

Ecclesiastical power, considered in itself formally and abstractly, is itself invariable and remains the same from the beginning of the nascent church up to the end. The church, indeed, when it is considered in its essential and permanent parts, which are the papacy, the cardinalate, the patriarchate, the archiepiscopate, the episcopate, and the priesthood, has the quality of being integrated from all these, so that, if one of these powers were utterly removed, the church would no longer remain as it was perfectly instituted by Christ seminally and as in a certain germ of itself: for instance, if one imagines the papacy cut off from the remaining inferior powers, that which remains will not be called a church. For this reason, to ask whether the papal authority is greater than the church, or *vice versa,* is the same as asking: is not the whole greater than the part, or is the part less than the whole? Thence it follows that if a general council represents the universal church sufficiently and completely, it is necessary that it include the papal authority, whether there be a pope, or whether he has ceased to be, through natural or civil death. So we may say of the power of the Roman church, or the sacred college, so of the episcopal power, so of the priesthood, which is the power of the pastors, who in the church are lesser prelates. But if anyone wished curiously to inquire how such an abstraction of the ecclesiastical power can be made, and whether it is something real, universal, specific, and quidditative, beyond all operation of the intellect—as one inquires concerning animality and humanity—we send them to the *Metaphysics.* Therefore we grant that, as Aristotle says, 'Abstraction is not lying,' although we shall have denied that these universals are real—even as mathematicians do not lie, whether points really exist or not. Whence we say, as is sufficient for us, that universality is in the operation and abstraction which the intellect makes from the exterior cognition of individual things by seeing how those things agree with one another or differ, essentially or accidentally; for instance, that any man agrees in essence with another in that he is a rational animal; because the attendant intellect, by a virtue innate in itself, abstracts this likeness, which is not outside of, nor singularly in, single men, and denudes it from place, from time, and from all the confusion of general accidents, and this remains the universal and absolute concept of man in the mind, which, however, originates from singular things outside. So we can think in regard to the ecclesiastical power, when it is considered in itself formally and absolutely. For all priests agree in priesthood, and bishops in episcopacy, and so on for the rest of the powers. . . .

Consideration VIII

Ecclesiastical power, considered respectively and, in a sense, materially, as assigned to particular subjects, can be called variable and removable in many instances. This is demonstrated daily, when changes are made through a new consecration or a new election or institution of ministers. Consequently, we can say the same thing in regard to the papel power, which is mutable and removable by natural death, as is obvious, or by civil death, namely, by deposition, at least in regard to his plenitude of jurisdiction. . . . Whence, as the pope can renounce the papacy and give a bill of divorcement to his bride, the church, even without guilt on her part, though he should not do this without cause, so the church can dismiss her vicarious spouse and give him a bill of divorcement, without guilt on his part but not without cause. . . .

Consideration IX

If ecclesiastical power is considered in respect of its use or execution, it is mutable and variable in many ways. This consideration, together with the two preceding, at once solves the question whether ecclesiastical power is immediately from God or mediately from men. If we consider ecclesiastical power in the first way, it should be conceded without a doubt that it was and is immediately from God, from Christ as Man, so that it was instituted by no other. Nor could an assembly of all mankind, excluding Christ, have instituted a power of this sort, though it could institute for itself an imperial power over all regal power, the power of dukes, counts, and barons, and any other purely secular power. Moreover, it could not institute for itself a priesthood nor a papacy, such as the church has; and in the same way it could not abolish them, since it could not change the law of Christ. . . . If, however, ecclesiastical power is considered in the second way, then in the beginning of the nascent church it was granted immediately by God both to Peter and to the apostles and disciples, on whom Christ immediately conferred the priesthood over His true and His mystic body. . . . And thus, consequently, it is probable that, even as Christ immediately conferred this power originally on his apostles and disciples, assigning it to them and not to others, so also He immediately granted its use, act, or exercise, since he who gives the form gives also the consequence of the form. Let us say, finally, regardless of these facts, that the successors of Peter and of the other apostles by canon law, were and are (short of a miracle or new revelation) instituted mediately by men, by consecration, election, or some other kind of institution. Likewise they received and receive the use and exercise of power mediately through human ministry or grant. And, perhaps, in regard to the use and exercise of ecclesiastical power, after the immediate grant of both the power and its use made by Christ to the apostles and disciples themselves, it so happened that because of the increasing number of believers they defined and restricted the use of power in order to avoid schism and to establish an example for the future; and this was done through Peter, the supreme pontiff, by the consent of the whole primitive church or general council; so that everyone could no longer exercise this power upon whomever he wished; but this restriction of the use of power was made with due consideration for the primary ordination of Christ, whereby He wished His church to be ruled principally under and by one monarch, as there is one faith, one baptism, and one church by the unity of both its primary and its vicarious head; for this is the best kind of rule, particularly in spirituals, to conserve the unity of the faith, to which all men are bound. . . .

Consideration X

Ecclesiastical power in its plenitude is formally and subjectively in the Roman pontiff alone. . . . In defining this we can say that the plenitude of ecclesiastical power is the power of order and of jurisdiction which was supernaturally given by Christ to Peter, as His direct and first king, for himself and for his successors to the end of time, for the sake of the edification of the church militant to the achievement of eternal felicity.

In this definition the term 'supernaturally' is used to distinguish it from the powers or jurisdictions which might belong to the successors of Peter as a result of human civil and political laws, or as a result of that dictate of natural law that gives to him who is supreme in any polity the enjoyment, above other men, of many honours and privileges, or from the special grant or concession of princes and other secular rulers, or, finally, from the favourable concession of the church itself or the general council, such as a perfect community may naturally give its head. There is good reason for such concessions . . . since it is easier to have recourse to the pope and his court than to the general council itself. This is the cause that originally brings about the institution of kings and the assignment to them of the power of making and interpreting laws. Now, some men, not noticing this distinction, have thought that all things that now belong to the supreme pontiffs belong to them as a result of Christ's primary institution and immutable divine law; but this is false. . . .

Consideration XI

Ecclesiastical power in its fulness is in the church as in its end, and as in that which regulates the application and use of this sort of plenitude of ecclesiastical power, either directly or through a general council sufficiently representing it. It is clear, at any rate, that the plenitude of ecclesiastical power was given to Peter by Christ for the building of His church, as our definition sets forth, in conformity with the statement of the apostle. For this reason Augustine says, with certain others, that 'the keys of the church were given not to one, but to a unity, and that they were given to the church.' And this can fittingly be understood in the way which the consideration sets forth, because 'the keys of the church were given for the sake of the church and its unity as for the sake of an end.' Also this plenitude of ecclesiastical power can be said to be in the church or the council not only formally as in its end but also in two other ways: in respect of its assignment to particular persons, and in respect of the regulation of its use, if perchance it should be liable to be turned into abuse.

It is certain that the plenitude of ecclesiastical power is in the church in these three ways, and in the general council as its representative. And indeed, concerning the first and second ways, there is no difficulty. Likewise not concerning the third, if we consider the definition of the plenitude of ecclesiastical power, where it was set forth that it was given for the building of the church. Since, therefore, the supreme pontiff, who has it subjectively, is open to sin and may wish to turn this power into destruction of the church, and likewise the sacred college, which is given to him and which co-assists him as a sort of aristocratic community, is not confirmed in grace or faith: there remains one inobliquable and indeviable rule from the best legislator, Christ, according to which abuse of this sort of power can be repressed, limited, and moderated. Now this rule is either the church or a general council. Whence, since the middle course of virtue may not otherwise be had than as a wise man shall judge, the final recourse for this wisdom is made to the church, where there is indeviable wisdom, or to a general council. On this are founded those many things which have been decreed and done through this sacred council: for instance, that the pope can be judged and deposed by the council. For he is subjected to it in the regulation of his power in regard to its use; and it can say to him, 'Why do you do so?'. . . .

We can add to this consideration that the plenitude of ecclesiastical power, if it be considered in its breadth, is itself not in the pope alone, unless in a certain way, as being in his own way the source and origin of power. For this breadth of power embraces in itself other ecclesiastical powers collectively from the highest to the lowest. And the plenitude of ecclesiastical power of the pope is among them as an integral part in the whole, and thus it is not greater than or superior to the power of the whole church, as a part is not greater than the whole. If, on the other hand, this plenitude is considered in its height, then without any doubt the plenitude of ecclesiastic power of the pope is greater than and superior to the rest; but now that which is the rest can by no compact constitute a general council, according to what was said earlier, that a general council, as such, necessarily includes the papal authority, whether a pope exists or not; for if there is a pope and he is willing to do his duty in convoking a council, certainly it ought to be authorized by him. If, however, he pertinaciously refuses, to the destruction of the church, then action should be taken as if there were no pope; and the power of assembling itself remains in the church itself, and that of providing for itself, and that of ordaining concerning papal power, in the second and third ways, in respect to its allocation and its use; the situation corresponds to that of a chapter and a dean, or a university and its rector.

But the principal difficulty occurs here: what, if the pope is dead or ejected, can this council do? It can, therefore, first constitute one pope for itself in the accustomed way through the election of the lord cardinals; or in another way through consensus; or through the way of the Holy Spirit, if there is a reasonable hope that thus all can be brought to agree upon one candidate; or perchance through the awaiting of a divine miracle, as in the election of Matthew. And concerning this power of the council, that it can make one head for itself, there is no difficulty.

There are many other powers which, if the pope is dead or ejected, the council can exercise either directly or through some organ on behalf of all, such as have often been practised in this council, in regard to various decisions and decrees involving the exercise of coercive jurisdiction: for instance, the summoning and deposition of the pope, excommunication and interdict, the relaxation of rules, the giving of absolution. . . . For we find in the councils of the past, in the time of the apostles and later, that even when there was a living pope it was the council and not the pope that spoke. . . . Finally, in the third place, there are other powers which cannot be exercised except by a determinate subject . . . , and here we can distinguish between those that cannot be exercised except by a pope and cannot in any way be delegated to anyone else, and those that can be delegated, by someone incompetent to exercise them, to someone else who is competent . . . [as a pastor who is not a priest can tell a priest to perform the mass in his curacy]. In the same way, therefore, the council can commit to priests the performance of such things as cannot be done, or at any rate not licitly, either by the council directly or by priests lacking the commission and licence of the council.

In this context, we must raise the question whether there is any power peculiar to the pope, so that he can do something of which no other ecclesiastical power is factually or legally capable. And it seems, *prima facie,* that there is no such power, in accordance with the preponderant opinion of the doctors, who say that the power of the order is equal in all priests. And as for the power of jurisdiction, whatever may be said, it appears that in default of the pope the council can grant it. . . .

But this line of thought seems to lead to the scandalous and improper conclusion that the church could be well ruled to the end of time without a pope. . . . We answer that, although the general council can do such things at any given time, since the precept that there must be a pope is an affirmative precept whose obligation extends for all time but not at every time, nevertheless the general council neither ought to nor could tolerate the lack of a head for ever, so long as the law stands. Yet, through one bishop acting as its vicar, or through several simultaneously or successively, it can supply the lack of a head when urged by necessity or persuaded by evident utility; and in this sense there is said to be a supplementary plenitude of power in the church. . . .

ও§ *Part Three*

Medieval Intellectual Life

✥ THE STORY OF MY MISFORTUNES

Peter Abélard

The life of Peter Abélard (1079–1142) spans one of the most dynamic periods of European history. It was the period of the Hildebrandine reform, of the First Crusade, of the founding of the first universities, of the beginnings of the cult of courtly love, and of the development and perfection of Gothic architecture. Abélard's Historia Calamitatum *("The Story of My Misfortunes"), a vivid autobiography, takes the reader directly into the struggles of the most controversial figure of his day.*

While still in his twenties, Abélard became the greatest dialectician in Europe. The spirit of competition that appears on every page of his work was the source both of his genius and of the animosity that he seemed to bring out in everyone who knew him; everyone, that is, except Héloïse, the brilliant and sensitive student with whom he had a lifelong love affair, celebrated in letters that have come down to us.

But Abélard was much more than a writer on logic and theology. He was above all a teacher, *and one who gave a lasting direction to the development of education. He opened philosophical schools of his own— first at Melun, then at Corbeil, then at Paris. Next he turned to theology, and wrote an explosive book called* Sic et Non *("Yes and No") in which he lined up quotations from the Church Fathers on both sides of 150 different issues, in order to show that such problems could be resolved only by reason, not by authority. A book on ethics called* Scito Teipsum *("Know Thyself") was similarly revolutionary. When Abélard was charged with heresy by the formidable St. Bernard of Clairvaux, first at Soissons in 1121 and then at Sens twenty years later, his response each time was to open a new school in which to promulgate his doctrines. By the time the University of Paris received its charter, half a century after Abélard's death, Abélard's main point had been conceded: "that nothing could be believed unless it could first be understood."*

During Abélard's lifetime, however, his opponents were usually able to silence him. Three times he retired to monasteries, yet only once— in the last—to find peace. At St. Gildas in western France, where he was abbot from 1125 to 1129 and where the Historia *(Chapters XIII and XV) was apparently written, he was harassed to an extent that would be funny if it were not tragic. These chapters must be set alongside Bede's* History *(see page 115) and the* Chronicle of Jocelin *(see page 143) to give a balanced picture of medieval monasticism. He tells us this story of a life of persecution and misunderstanding, as he says in his Foreword, "so that, in comparing your sorrows with mine, you may discover that yours are in truth nought. . . ."*

CHAPTER I

Know, then, that I am come from a certain town which was built on the way into lesser Brittany, distant some eight miles, as I think, eastward from the city of Nantes, and in its own tongue called Palets. Such is the nature of that country, or, it may be, of them who dwell there—for in truth they are quick in fancy—that my mind bent itself easily to the study of letters. Yet more, I had a father who had won some smattering of letters before he had girded on the soldier's belt. And so it came about that long afterwards his love thereof was so strong that he saw to it that each son of his should be taught in letters even earlier than in the management of arms. Thus indeed did it come to pass. And because I was his first born, and for that reason the more dear to him, he sought with double diligence to have me wisely taught. For my part, the more I went forward in the study of letters, and ever more easily, the greater became the ardour of my devotion to them, until in truth I was so enthralled by my passion for learning that, gladly leaving to my brothers the pomp of glory in arms, the right of heritage and all the honours that should have been mine as the eldest born, I fled utterly from the court of Mars that I might win learning in the bosom of Minerva. And since I found the armory of logical reasoning more to my liking than the other forms of philosophy, I exchanged all other weapons for these, and to the prizes of victory in war I preferred the battle of minds in disputation. Thenceforth, journeying through many provinces, and debating as I went, going whithersoever I heard that the study of my chosen art most flourished, I became such an one as the Peripatetics.

CHAPTER II

I came at length to Paris, where above all in those days the art of dialectics was most flourishing, and there did I meet William of Champeaux, my teacher, a man most distinguished in his science both by his renown and by his true merit. With him I remained for some time, at first indeed well liked of him; but later I brought him great grief, because I undertook to refute certain of his opinions, not infrequently attacking him in disputation, and now and then in these debates I was adjudged victor. Now this, to those among my fellow students who were ranked foremost, seemed all the more insufferable because of my youth and the brief duration of my studies.

Peter Abélard, *The Story of My Misfortunes*, trans. H. A. Bellows (New York: The Free Press of Glencoe, 1958), pp. 1–22, 29–36, 59–63, 73–76, 78. Copyright T. A. Boyd, 1922.

Out of this sprang the beginning of my misfortunes, which have followed me even to the present day; the more widely my fame was spread abroad, the more bitter was the envy that was kindled against me. It was given out that I, presuming on my gifts far beyond the warranty of my youth, was aspiring despite my tender years to the leadership of a school; nay, more, that I was making ready the very place in which I would undertake this task, the place being none other than the castle of Melun, at that time a royal seat. My teacher himself had some foreknowledge of this, and tried to remove my school as far as possible from his own. Working in secret, he sought in every way he could before I left his following to bring to nought the school I had planned and the place I had chosen for it. Since, however, in that very place he had many rivals, and some of them men of influence among the great ones of the land, relying on their aid I won to the fulfillment of my wish; the support of many was secured for me by reason of his own unconcealed envy. From this small inception of my school, my fame in the art of dialectics began to spread abroad, so that little by little the renown, not alone of those who had been my fellow students, but of our very teacher himself, grew dim and was like to die out altogether. Thus it came about that, still more confident in myself, I moved my school as soon as I well might to the castle of Corbeil, which is hard by the city of Paris, for there I knew there would be given more frequent chance for my assaults in our battle of disputation.

No long time thereafter I was smitten with a grievous illness, brought upon me by my immoderate zeal for study. This illness forced me to turn homeward to my native province, and thus for some years I was as if cut off from France. And yet, for that very reason, I was sought out all the more eagerly by those whose hearts were troubled by the lore of dialectics. But after a few years had passed, and I was whole again from my sickness, I learned that my teacher, that same William Archdeacon of Paris, had changed his former garb and joined an order of the regular clergy. This he had done, or so men said, in order that he might be deemed more deeply religious, and so might be elevated to a loftier rank in the prelacy, a thing which, in truth, very soon came to pass, for he was made bishop of Châlons. Nevertheless, the garb he had donned by reason of his conversion did nought to keep him away either from the city of Paris or from his wonted study of philosophy; and in the very monastery wherein he had shut himself up for the sake of religion he straightway set to teaching again after the same fashion as before.

To him did I return, for I was eager to learn more of rhetoric from his lips; and in the course of our many arguments on various matters, I compelled him by most potent reasoning first to alter his former opinion on the subject of the universals, and finally to abandon it altogether. Now, the basis of this old concept of his regarding the reality of universal ideas was that the same quality formed the essence alike of the abstract whole and of the individuals which were its parts: in other words, that there could be no essential differences among these individuals, all being alike save for such variety as might grow out of the many accidents of existence. Thereafter, however, he corrected this opinion, no longer maintaining that the same quality was the essence of all things, but that, rather, it manifested itself in them through diverse ways. This problem of universals is ever the most vexed one among logicians, to such a degree, indeed, that even Porphyry, writing in his "Isagoge" regarding universals, dared not attempt a final pronouncement thereon, saying rather: "This is the deepest of all problems of its kind." Wherefore it followed that when William had first revised and then finally abandoned altogether his views on this one subject, his lecturing sank into such a state of negligent reasoning that it could scarce be called lecturing on the science of dialectics at all; it was as if all his science had been bound up in this one question of the nature of universals.

Thus it came about that my teaching won such strength and authority that even those who before had clung most vehemently to my former master, and most bitterly attacked my doctrines, now flocked to my school. The very man who had succeeded to my master's chair in the Paris school offered me his post, in order that he might put himself under my tutelage along with all the rest, and this in the very place where of old his master and mine had reigned. And when, in so short a time, my master saw me directing the study of dialectics there, it is not easy to find words to tell with what envy he was consumed or with what pain he was tormented. He could not long, in truth, bear the anguish of what he felt to be his wrongs, and shrewdly he attacked me that he might drive me forth. And because there was nought in my conduct whereby he could come at me openly, he tried to steal away the school by launching the vilest calumnies against him who had yielded his post to me, and by putting in his place a certain rival of mine. So then I returned to Melun, and set up my school there as before; and the more openly his envy pursued me, the greater was the authority it conferred upon me. Even so held the poet: "Jealousy aims at the peaks; the winds storm the loftiest summits." (Ovid: "Remedy for Love," I, 369.)

Not long thereafter, when William became aware of the fact that almost all his students were holding grave doubts as to his religion, and were whispering earnestly among themselves about his conversion, deeming that he had by no means abandoned this world, he withdrew himself and his brotherhood, together with his students, to a certain estate far distant from the city. Forthwith I returned from Melun to Paris, hoping for peace from him in the future. But since, as I have said, he had caused my place to be occupied by a rival of mine, I pitched the camp, as it were, of my school outside the city on Mont Ste. Geneviève. Thus I was as one laying siege to him who had taken possession of my post. No sooner had my master heard of this than he brazenly returned post haste to the city, bringing back with him such students as he could, and reinstating his brotherhood in their former monastery, much as if he would free his soldiery, whom he had deserted, from my blockade. In truth, though, if it was his purpose to bring them succour, he did nought but hurt them. Before that time my rival had indeed had a certain number of students, of one sort and another, chiefly by reason of his lectures on Priscian, in which he was considered of great authority. After our master had returned, however, he lost nearly all of these followers, and thus was compelled to give up the direction of the school. Not long thereafter, apparently despairing further of worldly fame, he was converted to the monastic life.

Following the return of our master to the city, the combats in disputation which my scholars waged both with him himself and with his pupils, and the successes which fortune gave to us, and above all to me, in these wars, you have long since learned of through your own experience. The boast of Ajax, though I speak it more temperately, I still am bold enough to make:

". . . if fain you would learn now
How victory crowned the battle, by him was
  I never vanquished."

  (Ovid, "Metamorphoses," XIII, 89.)

But even were I to be silent, the fact proclaims itself, and its outcome reveals the truth regarding it.

While these things were happening, it became needful for me again to repair to my old home, by reason of my dear mother, Lucia, for after the conversion of my father, Berengarius, to the monastic life, she so ordered her affairs as to do likewise. When all this had been completed, I returned to France, above all in order that I might study theology, since now my oft-mentioned teacher, William, was active in the episcopate of Châlons. In this field of learning Anselm of Laon, who was his teacher therein, had for long years enjoyed the greatest renown.

CHAPTER III

I sought out, therefore, this same venerable man, whose fame, in truth, was more the result of long-established custom than of the potency of his own talent or intellect. If any one came to him impelled by doubt on any subject, he went away more doubtful still. He was wonderful, indeed, in the eyes of these who only listened to him, but those who asked him questions perforce held him as nought. He had a miraculous flow of words, but they were contemptible in meaning and quite void of reason. When he kindled a fire, he filled his house with smoke and illumined it not at all. He was a tree which seemed noble to those who gazed upon its leaves from afar, but to those who came nearer and examined it more closely was revealed its barrenness. When, therefore, I had come to this tree that I might pluck the fruit thereof, I discovered that it was indeed the fig tree which Our Lord cursed (Matthew xxi, 19; Mark xi, 13), or that ancient oak to which Lucan likened Pompey, saying:

". . . he stands, the shade of a name once mighty,
Like to the towering oak in the midst of the fruitful field."

  (Lucan, "Pharsalia," IV, 135.)

It was not long before I made this discovery, and stretched myself lazily in the shade of that same tree. I went to his lectures less and less often, a thing which some among his eminent followers took sorely to heart, because they interpreted it as a mark of contempt for so illustrious a teacher. Thenceforth they secretly sought to influence him against me, and by their vile insinuations made me hated of him. It chanced, moreover, that one day, after the exposition of certain texts, we scholars were jesting among ourselves, and one of them, seeking to draw me out, asked me what I thought of the lectures on the Books of Scripture. I, who had as yet studied only the sciences, replied that following such lectures seemed to me most useful in so far as the salvation of the soul was concerned, but that it appeared quite extraordinary to me that educated persons should not be able to understand the sacred books simply by studying them themselves, together with the glosses thereon, and without the aid of any teacher. Most of those who were present mocked at me, and asked whether I myself could do as I had said, or whether I would dare to undertake it. I answered that if they wished, I was ready to try it. Forthwith they cried out and jeered all the more. "Well and good," said they; "we agree to the test. Pick out and give us an exposition of some doubtful passage in the Scriptures, so that we can put this boast of yours to the proof." And they all chose that most obscure prophecy of Ezekiel.

I accepted the challenge, and invited them to attend a lecture on the very next day. Whereupon they undertook to give me good advice, saying that I should by no means make undue haste in so important a matter, but that I ought to devote a much longer space to working out my exposition and offsetting my inexperience by diligent toil. To this I replied indignantly that it was my wont to win success, not by routine, but by ability. I added that I would abandon the test altogether unless they would agree not to put off their attendance at my lecture. In truth at this first lecture of mine only a few were present, for it seemed quite absurd to all of them that I, hitherto so inexperienced in discussing the Scriptures, should attempt the thing so hastily. However, this lecture gave such satisfaction to all those who heard it that they spread its praises abroad with notable enthusiasm, and thus compelled me to continue my interpretation of the sacred text. When word of this was bruited about, those who had stayed away from the first lecture came eagerly, some to the second and more to the third, and all of them were eager to write down the glosses which I had begun on the first day, so as to have them from the very beginning.

CHAPTER IV

Now this venerable man of whom I have spoken was acutely smitten with envy, and straightway incited, as I have already mentioned, by the insinuations of sundry persons, began to persecute me for my lecturing on the Scriptures no less bitterly than my former master, William, had done for my work in philosophy. At that time there were in this old man's school two who were considered far to excel all the others: Alberic of Rheims and Lotulphe the Lombard. The better opinion these two held of themselves, the more they were incensed against me. Chiefly at their suggestion, as it afterwards transpired, yonder venerable coward had the impudence to forbid me to carry on any further in his school the work of preparing glosses which I had thus begun. The pretext he alleged was that if by chance in the course of this work I should write anything containing blunders—as was likely enough in view of my lack of training—the thing might be imputed to him. When this came to the ears of his scholars, they were filled with indignation at so undisguised a manifestation of spite, the like of which had never been directed against any one before. The more obvious this rancour became, the more it redounded to my honour, and his persecution did nought save to make me more famous.

CHAPTER V

And so, after a few days, I returned to Paris, and there for several years I peacefully directed the school which formerly had been destined for me, nay, even offered to me, but from which I had been driven out. At the very outset of my work there, I set about completing the glosses on Ezekiel which I had begun at Laon. These proved so satisfactory to all who read them that they came to believe me no less adept in lecturing on theology than I had proved myself to be in the field of philosophy. Thus my school was notably increased in size by reason of my lectures on subjects of both these kinds, and the amount of financial profit as well as glory which it brought me cannot be concealed from you, for the matter was widely talked of. But prosperity always puffs up the foolish, and worldly comfort enervates the soul, rendering it an easy prey to carnal temptations. Thus I, who by this time had come to regard myself as the only philosopher remaining in the whole world, and had ceased to fear any further disturbance of my peace, began to loosen the rein on my desires, although hitherto I had always lived in the utmost continence. And the greater progress I made in my lecturing on philosophy or theology, the more I departed alike from the practice of the philosophers and the spirit of the divines in the uncleanness of my life. For it is well known, methinks, that philosophers, and still more those who have devoted their lives to arousing the love of sacred study, have been strong above all else in the beauty of chastity.

Thus did it come to pass that while I was utterly absorbed in pride and sensuality, divine grace, the cure for both diseases, was forced upon me, even though I, forsooth, would fain have shunned it. First was I punished for my sensuality, and then for my pride. For my sensuality I lost those things whereby I practiced it; for my pride, engendered in me by my knowledge of letters—and it is even as the Apostle said: "Knowledge puffeth itself up" (I Cor. viii, 1)—I knew the humiliation of seeing burned the very book in which I most gloried. And now it is my desire that you should know the stories of these two happenings, understanding them more truly from learning the very facts than from hearing what is spoken of them, and in the order in which they came about. Because I had ever held in abhorrence the foulness of prostitutes, because I had diligently kept myself from all excesses and from association with the women of noble birth who attended the school, because I knew so little of the common talk of ordinary people, perverse and subtly flattering chance gave birth to an occasion for casting me lightly down from the heights of my own exaltation. Nay, in such case not even divine goodness could redeem one who, having been so proud, was brought to such shame, were it not for the blessed gift of grace.

CHAPTER VI

Now there dwelt in that same city of Paris a certain young girl named Héloïse, the niece of a canon who was called Fulbert. Her uncle's love for her was equalled only by his desire that she should have the best education which he could possibly procure for her. Of no mean beauty, she stood out above all by reason of her abundant knowledge of letters. Now this virtue is rare among women, and for that very reason it doubly graced the maiden, and made her the most worthy of renown in the entire kingdom. It was this young girl whom I, after carefully considering all those qualities which are wont to attract lovers, determined to unite with myself in the bonds of love, and indeed the thing seemed to me very easy to be done. So distinguished was my name, and I possessed such advantages of youth and comeliness, that no matter what woman I might favour with my love, I dreaded rejection of none. Then, too, I believed that I could win the maiden's consent all the more easily by reason of her knowledge of letters and her zeal therefor; so, even if we were parted, we might yet be together in thought with the aid of written messages. Perchance, too, we might be able to write more boldly than we could speak, and thus at all times could we live in joyous intimacy.

Thus, utterly aflame with my passion for this maiden, I sought to discover means whereby I might have daily and familiar speech with her, thereby the more easily to win her consent. For this purpose I persuaded the girl's uncle, with the aid of some of his friends, to take me into his household—for he dwelt hard by my school—in return for the payment of a small sum. My pretext for this was that the care of my own household was a serious handicap to my studies, and likewise burdened me with an expense far greater than I could afford. Now, he was a man keen in avarice, and likewise he was most desirous for his niece that her study of letters should ever go forward, so, for these two reasons, I easily won his consent to the fulfillment of my wish, for he was fairly agape for my money, and at the same time believed that his niece would vastly benefit by my teaching. More even than this, by his own earnest entreaties he fell in with my desires beyond anything I had dared to hope, opening the way for my love; for he entrusted her wholly to my guidance, begging me to give her instruction whensoever I might be free from the duties of my school, no matter whether by day or by night, and to punish her sternly if ever I should find her negligent of her tasks. In all this the man's simplicity was nothing short of astounding to me; I should not have been more smitten with wonder if he had entrusted a tender lamb to the care of a ravenous wolf. When he had thus given her into my charge, not alone to be taught but even to be disciplined, what had he done save to give free scope to my desires, and to offer me every opportunity, even if I had not sought it, to bend her to my will with threats and blows if I failed to do so with caresses? There were, however, two things which particularly served to allay any foul suspicion: his own love for his niece, and my former reputation for continence.

Why should I say more? We were united first in the dwelling that sheltered our love, and then in the hearts that burned with it. Under the pretext of study we spent our hours in the happiness of love, and learning held out to us the secret opportunities that our passion craved. Our speech was more of love than of the books which lay open before us; our kisses far outnumbered our reasoned words. Our hands sought less the book than each other's bosoms; love drew our eyes together far more than the lesson drew them to the pages of our text. In order that there might be no suspicion, there were, indeed, sometimes blows, but love gave them, not anger; they were the marks, not of wrath, but of a tenderness surpassing the most fragrant balm in sweetness. What followed? No degree in love's progress was left untried by our passion, and if love itself could imagine any wonder as yet unknown, we discovered it. And our inexperience of such delights made us all the more ardent in our pursuit of them, so that our thirst for one another was still unquenched.

In measure as this passionate rapture absorbed me more and more, I devoted ever less time to philosophy and to the work of the school. Indeed it became loathsome to me to go to the school or to linger there; the labour, moreover, was very burdensome, since my nights were vigils of love and my days of study. My lecturing became utterly careless and lukewarm; I did nothing because of inspiration, but everything merely as a matter of habit. I had become nothing more than a reciter of my former discoveries, and though I still wrote poems, they dealt with love, not with the secrets of philosophy. Of these songs you yourself well know how some have become widely known and have been sung in many lands, chiefly, methinks, by those who delighted in the things of this world. As for the sorrow, the groans, the lamentations of my students when they perceived the preoccupation, nay, rather the chaos, of my mind, it is hard even to imagine them.

A thing so manifest could deceive only a few, no one, methinks, save him whose shame it chiefly bespoke, the girl's uncle, Fulbert. The truth was often enough hinted to him, and by many persons, but he could not believe it, partly, as I have said, by reason of his boundless love for his niece, and partly because of the well-known continence of my previous life. Indeed we do not easily suspect shame in those whom we most cherish, nor can there be the blot of foul suspicion on devoted love. Of this St. Jerome in his epistle to Sabinianus (Epist. 48) says: "We are wont to be the last to know the evils of our own households, and to be ignorant of the sins of our children and our wives, though our neighbours sing them aloud." But no matter how slow a matter may be in disclosing itself, it is sure to come forth at last, nor is it easy to hide from one what is known to all. So, after the lapse of several months, did it happen with us. Oh, how great was the uncle's grief when he learned the truth, and how bitter was the sorrow of the lovers when we were forced to part! With what shame was I overwhelmed, with what contrition smitten because of the blow which had fallen on her I loved, and what a tempest of misery burst over her by reason of my disgrace! Each grieved most, not for himself, but for the other. Each sought to allay, not his own sufferings, but those of the one he loved. The very sundering of our bodies served but to link our souls closer together; the plenitude of the love which was denied to us inflamed us more than ever. Once the first wildness of shame had passed, it left us more shameless than before, and as shame died within us the cause of it seemed to us ever more desirable. And so it chanced with us as, in the stories that the poets tell, it once happened with Mars and Venus when they were caught together.

It was not long after this that Héloïse found that she was pregnant, and of this she wrote to me in the utmost exultation, at the same time asking me to consider what had best be done. Accordingly, on a night when her uncle was absent, we carried out the plan we had determined on, and I stole her secretly away from her uncle's house, sending her without delay to my own country. She remained there with my sister until she gave birth to a son, whom she named Astrolabe. Meanwhile her uncle, after his return, was almost mad with grief; only one who had then seen him could rightly guess the burning agony of his sorrow and the bitterness of his shame. What steps to take against me, or what snares to set for me, he did not know. If he should kill me or do me some bodily hurt, he feared greatly lest his dear-loved niece should be made to suffer for it among my kinsfolk. He had no power to seize me and imprison me somewhere against my will, though I make no doubt he would have done so quickly enough had he been able or dared, for I had taken measures to guard against any such attempt.

At length, however, in pity for his boundless grief, and bitterly blaming myself for the suffering which my love had brought upon him through the baseness of the deception I had practiced, I went to him to entreat his forgiveness, promising to make any amends that he himself might decree. I pointed out that what had happened could not seem incredible to any one who had ever felt the power of love, or who remembered how, from the very beginning of the human race, women had cast down even the noblest men to utter ruin. And in order to make amends even beyond his extremest hope, I offered to marry her whom I had seduced, provided only the thing could be kept secret, so that I might suffer no loss of reputation thereby. To this he gladly assented, pledging his own faith and that of his kindred, and sealing with kisses the pact which I had sought of him—and all this that he might the more easily betray me.

CHAPTER VII

. . . So, after our little son was born, we left him in my sister's care, and secretly returned to Paris. A few days later, in the early morning, having kept our nocturnal vigil of prayer unknown to all in a certain church, we were united there in the benediction of wedlock, her uncle and a few friends of his and mine being present. We departed forthwith stealthily and by separate ways, nor thereafter did we see each other save rarely and in private, thus striving our utmost to conceal what we had done. But her uncle and those of his household, seeking solace for their disgrace, began to divulge the story of our marriage, and thereby to violate the pledge they had given me on this point. Héloïse, on the contrary, denounced her own kin and swore that they were speaking the most absolute lies. Her uncle, aroused to fury thereby visited her repeatedly with punishments. No sooner had I learned this than I sent her to a convent of nuns at Argenteuil, not far from Paris, where she herself had been brought up and educated as a young girl. I had them make ready for her all the garments of a nun, suitable for the life of a convent, excepting only the veil, and these I bade her put on.

When her uncle and his kinsmen heard of this, they were convinced that now I had completely played them false and had rid myself forever of Héloïse by forcing her to become a nun. Violently incensed, they laid a plot against me, and one night, while I, all unsuspecting, was asleep in a secret room in my lodgings, they broke in with the help of one of my servants, whom they had bribed. There they had vengeance on me with a most cruel and most shameful punishment, such as astounded the whole world, for they cut off those parts of my body with which I had done that which was the cause of their sorrow. This done, straightway they fled, but two of them were captured, and suffered the loss of their eyes and their genital organs. One of these two was the aforesaid servant, who, even while he was still in my service, had been led by his avarice to betray me.

CHAPTER VIII

When morning came the whole city was assembled before my dwelling. It is difficult, nay, impossible, for words of mine to describe the amazement which bewildered them, the lamentations they uttered, the uproar with which they harassed me, or the grief with which they increased my own suffering. Chiefly the clerics, and above all my scholars, tortured me with their intolerable lamentations and outcries, so that I suffered more intensely from their compassion than from the pain of my wound. In truth I felt the disgrace more than the hurt to my body, and was more afflicted with shame than with pain. My incessant thought was of the renown in which I had so much delighted, now brought low, nay, utterly blotted out, so swiftly by an evil chance. I saw, too, how justly God had punished me in that very part of my body whereby I had sinned. I perceived that there was indeed justice in my betrayal by him whom I had myself already betrayed; and then I thought how eagerly my rivals would seize upon this manifestation of justice, how this disgrace would bring bitter and enduring grief to my kindred and my friends, and how the tale of this amazing outrage would spread to the very ends of the earth.

What path lay open to me thereafter? How could I ever again hold up my head among men, when every finger should be pointed at me in scorn, every tongue speak my blistering shame, and when I should be a monstrous spectacle to all eyes? I was overwhelmed by the remembrance that, according to the dread letter of the law, God holds eunuchs in such abomination that men thus maimed are forbidden to enter a church, even as the unclean and filthy; nay, even beasts in such plight were not acceptable as sacrifices. Thus in Leviticus (xxii, 24) is it said: "Ye shall not offer unto the Lord that which hath its stones bruised, or crushed, or broken, or cut." And in Deuteronomy (xxiii, 1), "He that is wounded in the stones, or hath his privy member cut off, shall not enter into the congregation of the Lord."

I must confess that in my misery it was the overwhelming sense of my disgrace rather than any ardour for conversion to the religious life that drove me to seek the seclusion of the monastic cloister. Héloïse had already, at my bidding, taken the veil and entered a convent. Thus it was that we both put on the sacred garb, I in the abbey of St. Denis, and she in the convent of Argenteuil, of which I have already spoken. She, I remember well, when her fond friends sought vainly to deter her from submitting her fresh youth to the heavy and almost intolerable yoke of monastic life, sobbing and weeping replied in the words of Cornelia:

". . . O husband most noble,
Who ne'er shouldst have shared my couch! Has fortune such power
To smite so lofty a head? Why then was I wedded
Only to bring thee to woe? Receive now my sorrow,
The price I so gladly pay."

(Lucan, "Pharsalia," viii, 94.)

With these words on her lips did she go forthwith to the altar, and lifted therefrom the veil, which had been blessed by the bishop, and before them all she took the vows of the religious life. For my part, scarcely had I recovered from my wound when clerics sought me in great numbers, endlessly beseeching both my abbot and me myself that now, since I was done with learning for the sake of gain or renown, I should turn to it for the sole love of God. They bade me care diligently for the talent which God had committed to my keeping (Matthew, xxv, 15), since surely He would demand it back from me with interest. It was their plea that, inasmuch as of old I had laboured chiefly in behalf of the rich, I should now devote myself to the teaching of the poor. Therein above all should I perceive how it was the hand of God that had touched me, when I should devote my life to the study of letters in freedom from the snares of the flesh and withdrawn from the tumultuous life of this world. Thus, in truth, should I become a philosopher less of this world than of God.

The abbey, however, to which I had betaken myself was utterly worldly and in its life quite scandalous. The abbot himself was as far below his fellows in his way of living and in the foulness of his reputation as he was above them in priestly rank. This intolerable state of things I often and vehemently denounced, sometimes in private talk and sometimes publicly, but the only result was that I made myself detested of them all. They gladly laid hold of the daily eagerness of my students to hear me as an excuse whereby they might be rid of me; and finally, at the insistent urging of the students themselves, and with the hearty consent of the abbot and the rest of the brotherhood, I departed thence to a certain hut, there to teach in my wonted way. To this place such a throng of students flocked that the neighbourhood could not afford shelter for them, nor the earth sufficient sustenance.

Here, as befitted my profession, I devoted myself chiefly to lectures on theology, but I did not wholly abandon the teaching of the secular arts, to which I was more accustomed, and which was particularly demanded of me. I used the latter, however, as a hook, luring my students by the bait of learning to the study of the true philosophy, even as the Ecclesiastical History tells of Origen, the greatest of all Christian philosophers. Since apparently the Lord had gifted me with no less persuasiveness in expounding the Scriptures than in lecturing on secular subjects, the number of my students in these two courses began to increase greatly, and the attendance at all the other schools was correspondingly diminished. Thus I aroused the envy and hatred of the other teachers. Those who sought to belittle me in every possible way took advantage of my absence to bring two principal charges against me: first, that it was contrary to the monastic profession to be concerned with the study of secular books; and, second, that I had presumed to teach theology without ever having been taught therein myself. This they did in order that my teaching of every kind might be prohibited, and to this end they continually stirred up bishops, archbishops, abbots and whatever other dignitaries of the Church they could reach.

CHAPTER IX

It so happened that at the outset I devoted myself to analysing the basis of our faith through illustrations based on human understanding, and I wrote for my students a certain tract on the unity and trinity of God. This I did because they were always seeking for rational and philosophical explanations, asking rather for reasons they could understand than for mere words, saying that it was futile to utter words which the intellect could not possibly follow, that nothing could be believed unless it could first be understood, and that it was absurd for any one to preach to others a thing which neither he himself nor those whom he sought to teach could comprehend. Our Lord Himself maintained this same thing when He said: "They are blind leaders of the blind" (Matthew, xv, 14). . . .

CHAPTER XII

And so I dwelt in this place, my body indeed hidden away, but my fame spreading throughout the whole world, till its echo reverberated mightily—echo, that fancy of the poet's, which has so great a voice, and nought beside. My former rivals, seeing that they themselves were now powerless to do me hurt, stirred up against me certain new apostles in whom the world put great faith. One of these (Norbert of Prémontré) took pride in his position as canon of a regular order; the other (Bernard of Clairvaux) made it his boast that he had revived the true monastic life. These two ran hither and yon preaching and shamelessly slandering me in every way they could, so that in time they succeeded in drawing down on my head the scorn of many among those having authority, among both the clergy and the laity. They spread abroad such sinister reports of my faith as well as of my life that they turned even my best friends against me, and those who still retained something of their former regard for me were fain to disguise it in every possible way by reason of their fear of these two men.

God is my witness that whensoever I learned of the convening of a new assemblage of the clergy, I believed that it was done for the express purpose of my condemnation. Stunned by this fear like one smitten with a thunderbolt, I daily expected to be dragged before their councils or assemblies as a heretic or one guilty of impiety. Though I seem to compare a flea with a lion, or an ant with an elephant, in very truth my rivals persecuted me no less bitterly than the heretics of old hounded St. Athanasius. Often, God knows, I sank so deep in despair that I was ready to leave the world of Christendom and go forth among the heathen, paying them a stipulated tribute in order that I might live quietly a Christian life among the enemies of Christ. It seemed to me that such people might indeed be kindly disposed toward me, particularly as they would doubtless suspect me of being no good Christian, imputing my flight to some crime I had committed, and would therefore believe that I might perhaps be won over to their form of worship.

CHAPTER XIII

While I was thus afflicted with so great perturbation of the spirit, and when the only way of escape seemed to be for me to seek refuge with Christ among the enemies of Christ, there came a chance whereby I thought I could for a while avoid the plottings of my enemies. But thereby I fell among Christians and monks who were far more savage than heathens and more evil of life. The thing came about in this wise. There was in lesser Brittany, in the bishopric of Vannes, a certain abbey of St. Gildas at Ruits, then mourning the death of its shepherd. To this abbey the elective choice of the brethren called me, with the approval of the prince of that land, and I easily secured permission to accept the post from my own abbot and brethren. Thus did the hatred of the French drive me westward, even as that of the Romans drove Jerome toward the East. Never, God knows, would I have agreed to this thing had it not been for my longing for any possible means of escape from the sufferings which I had borne so constantly.

The land was barbarous and its speech was unknown to me; as for the monks, their vile and untameable way of life was notorious almost everywhere. The people of the region, too, were uncivilized and lawless. Thus, like one who in terror of the sword that threatens him dashes headlong over a precipice, and to shun one death for a moment rushes to another, I knowingly sought this new danger in order to escape from the former one. And there, amid the dreadful roar of the waves of the sea, where the land's end left me no further refuge in flight, often in my prayers did I repeat over and over again: "From the end of the earth will I cry unto Thee, when my heart is overwhelmed" (Ps. lxi, 2).

No one, methinks, could fail to understand how persistently that undisciplined body of monks, the direction of which I had thus undertaken, tortured my heart day and night, or how constantly I was compelled to think of the danger alike to my body and to my soul. I held it for certain that if I should try to force them to live according to the principles they had themselves professed, I should not survive. And yet, if I did not do this to the utmost of my ability, I saw that my damnation was assured. Moreover, a certain lord who was exceedingly powerful in that region had some time previously brought the abbey under his control, taking advantage of the state of disorder within the monastery to seize all the lands adjacent thereto for his own use, and he ground down the monks with taxes heavier than those which were extorted from the Jews themselves.

The monks pressed me to supply them with their daily necessities, but they held no property in common which I might administer in their behalf, and each one, with such resources as he possessed, supported himself and his concubines, as well as his sons and daughters. They took delight in harassing me on this matter, and they stole and carried off whatsoever they could lay their hands on, to the end that my failure to maintain order might make me either give up trying to enforce discipline or else abandon my post altogether. Since the entire region was equally savage, lawless and disorganized, there was not a single man to whom I could turn for aid, for the habits of all alike were foreign to me. Outside the monastery the lord and his henchmen ceaselessly hounded me, and within its walls the brethren were forever plotting against me, so that it seemed as if the Apostle had had me and none other in mind when he said: "Without were fightings, within were fears" (II Cor. vii, 5). . . . .

CHAPTER XV

Reflecting often upon all these things, I determined to make provision for [the] sisters and to undertake their care in every way I could. Furthermore, in order that they might have the greater reverence for me, I arranged to watch over them in person. And since now the persecution carried on by my sons was greater and more incessant than that which I formerly suffered at the hands of my brethren, I returned frequently to the nuns, fleeing the rage of the tempest as to a haven of peace. There, indeed, could I draw breath for a little in quiet, and among them my labours were fruitful, as they never were among the monks. All this was of the utmost benefit to me in body and soul, and it was equally essential for them by reason of their weakness.

But now has Satan beset me to such an extent that I no longer know where I may find rest, or even so much as live. I am driven hither and yon, a fugitive and a vagabond, even as the accursed Cain (Gen. iv, 14). I have already said that "without were fightings, within were fears" (II Cor. vii, 5), and these torture me ceaselessly, the fears being indeed without as well as within, and the fightings wheresoever there are fears. Nay, the persecution carried on by my sons rages against me more perilously and continuously than that of my open enemies, for my sons I have always with me, and I am ever exposed to their treacheries. The violence of my enemies I see in the danger to my body if I leave the cloister; but within it I am compelled incessantly to endure the crafty machinations as well as the open violence of those monks who are called my sons, and who are entrusted to me as their abbot, which is to say their father.

Oh, how often have they tried to kill me with poison, even as the monks sought to slay St. Benedict! Methinks the same reason which led the saint to abandon his wicked sons might encourage me to follow the example of so great a father, lest, in thus exposing myself to certain peril, I might be deemed a rash tempter of God rather than a lover of Him, nay, lest it might even be judged that I had thereby taken my own life. When I had safeguarded myself to the best of my ability, so far as my food and drink were concerned, against their daily plottings, they sought to destroy me in the very ceremony of the altar by putting poison in the chalice. One day, when I had gone to Nantes to visit the count, who was then sick, and while I was sojourning awhile in the house of one of my brothers in the flesh, they arranged to poison me, with the connivance of one of my attendants, believing that I would take no precautions to escape such a plot. But divine providence so ordered matters that I had no desire for the food which was set before me; one of the monks whom I had brought with me ate thereof, not knowing that which had been done, and straightway fell dead. As for the attendant who had dared to undertake this crime, he fled in terror alike of his own conscience and of the clear evidence of his guilt.

After this, as their wickedness was manifest to every one, I began openly in every way I could to avoid the danger with which their plots threatened me, even to the extent of leaving the abbey and dwelling with a few others apart in little cells. If the monks knew beforehand that I was going anywhere on a journey, they bribed bandits to waylay me on the road and kill me. And while I was struggling in the midst of these dangers, it chanced one day that the hand of the Lord smote me a heavy blow, for I fell from my horse, breaking a bone in my neck, the injury causing me greater pain and weakness than my former wound.

Using excommunication as my weapon to coerce the untamed rebelliousness of the monks, I forced certain ones among them whom I particularly feared to promise me publicly, pledging their faith or swearing upon the sacrament, that they would thereafter depart from the abbey and no longer trouble me in any way. Shamelessly and openly did they violate the pledges they had given and their sacramental oaths, but finally they were compelled to give this and many other promises under oath, in the presence of the count and the bishops, by the authority of the Pontiff of Rome, Innocent, who sent his own legate for this special purpose. And yet even this did not bring me peace. For when I returned to the abbey after the expulsion of those whom I have just mentioned, and entrusted myself to the remaining brethren, of whom I felt less suspicion, I found them even worse than the others. I barely succeeded in escaping them, with the aid of a certain nobleman of the district, for they were planning, not to poison me indeed, but to cut my throat with a sword. Even to the present time I stand face to face with this danger, fearing the sword which threatens my neck so that I can scarcely draw a free breath between one meal and the next. Even so do we read of him who, reckoning the power and heaped-up wealth of the tyrant Dionysius as a great blessing, beheld the sword secretly hanging by a hair above his head, and so learned what kind of happiness comes as the result of wordly power (Cicer. 5, Tusc.). Thus did I too learn by constant experience, I who had been exalted from the condition of a poor monk to the dignity of an abbot, that my wretchedness increased with my wealth; and I would that the ambition of those who voluntarily seek such power might be curbed by my example.

And now, most dear brother in Christ and comrade closest to me in the intimacy of speech, it should suffice for your sorrows and the hardships you have endured that I have written this story of my own misfortunes, amid which I have toiled almost from the cradle. . . .

Inspired by those records and examples, we should endure our persecutions all the more steadfastly the more bitterly they harm us. We should not doubt that even if they are not according to our deserts, at least they serve for the purifying of our souls. And since all things are done in accordance with the divine ordering, let every one of true faith console himself amid all his afflictions with the thought that the great goodness of God permits nothing to be done without reason, and brings to a good end whatsoever may seem to happen wrongfully. Wherefore rightly do all men say: "Thy will be done." And great is the consolation to all lovers of God in the word of the Apostle when he says: "We know that all things work together for good to them that love God" (Rom. viii, 28). The wise man of old had this in mind when he said in his Proverbs: "There shall no evil happen to the just" (Prov. xii, 21). By this he clearly shows that whosoever grows wrathful for any reason against his sufferings has therein departed from the way of the just, because he may not doubt that these things have happened to him by divine dispensation. Even such are those who yield to their own rather than to the divine purpose, and with hidden desires resist the spirit which echoes in the words, "Thy will be done," thus placing their own will ahead of the will of God. Farewell.

The Universities

The university—or studium generale, *as it was called during the first several hundred years of its existence—is one of the most ancient Western institutions with an unbroken history. During the earlier Middle Ages both monastic and cathedral schools had provided some advanced training, as had individual teachers like Peter Abélard. Universities as such were not organized before the middle of the twelfth century, when groups of students (as at Bologna, Italy) or of instructors (as at Paris) formed protective associations to defend their corporate interests. Sooner or later these guilds gained recognition from the secular and clerical authorities. Originally the prestige of a university—whether or not it was considered a genuine* studium generale, *awarding degrees recognized throughout Europe—was a matter not of imperial or papal charters, but of the university's reputation for excellence. Oxford never obtained a papal charter; Paris, the most prestigious university in Europe, did not receive written sanction until after its fame had been acquired.*

The Commendation of the Clerk *is the work of an anonymous German cleric who probably had attended the University of Paris. It was written about the middle of the fourteenth century, some 200 years after the first universities had been organized. By that time the university had not only been established as an institution but had been diffused throughout most of Europe. The anonymous clerk is concerned with the purpose, organization, and administration of higher education. In contrast to this, the two other documents, dating from the fifteenth and the early seventeenth centuries, deal with the ever-present problem of the student's special duties and privileges.*

৶ COMMENDATION OF THE CLERK

DIFFERENT KINDS OF SCHOOL HOUSES

There are four kinds of school houses, because there are schools of artists, medicine, jurists and theologians. For so they are distinguished by our venerable mother, the university of Paris, which assigns distinct places as auditoriums to these four faculties and dispenses distinct costumes to their representatives. For the artists cultivate the

University Records and Life in the Middle Ages, ed. and trans. L. Thorndike (New York: Columbia University Press, 1944), pp. 213–231.

liberal arts near the river Seine in the street of Straw, at whose ends straw is sold. And they go forth in black round copes of noble brunet or of fine perse lined with fur, frequenting the chairs of ordinary lectures at daybreak. Moreover, they are called artists from the seven liberal arts and others comprehended under these, whose exercise is only for those of subtle genius, since gross and rude natures cannot attain the fine points of these arts. Their costume befits lords of liberal philosophy, because it is the nature of black to collect the sight. For they must collect their powers of internal vision who seek to inspect intelligently such subtle volumes on nature and to speculate profoundly both as to the different principles and the varied derivatives of the whole machine of the universe. The round cut of their copes denotes the gyration of the created orb, which they seem to enclose by the capacity of their brain, measuring the qualities of the stars, the varied movement of the winds, the natures too of animals and plants, the virtues of minerals, and the origination of every meteorological phenomenon. Whence too the tassel of the beret with which the philosopher crowns his head is a sign of the capacity of his brain and the breadth of his mind. Moreover, the flower in his bonnet signifies decorum of morals and treasures of companions of liberal sciences. Since he is not a perfect philosopher whom every human virtue does not adorn with good morals. The gold on the fingers with which masters of art were adorned of old signifies wisdom of mind, and the gem set in the gold connotes the excellence of the sage to common men, because the sage is naturally lord of the rude populace. Time past once bestowed on the lords of philosophy round scarfs, likewise in front a *patula* also lined with fur, which were made of scarlet flaming with the best red color. And the roundness of the scarf had the same significance as the spherical cope. But this flaming fervor suggested that they above all other men were fervent to increase human knowledge of the world's marvels. For true philosophers care nothing for external utility, but all their labor is to this end, that they may learn the truth as to origins and things originated. And because of unity as to this goal the latitude of all liberal sciences is called one faculty of artists.

Next the medical men dwelling in the houses of their habitations elucidate their aphorisms venerably to their auditors. And these rejoice in ordinary copes of brunet somewhat brighter than the artists and more nearly red like the color of thick rouge. And in the closeness of this color to true brunet is figured the connection between these faculties, since he is a poor physician who knows no logic or who has no recourse to natural philosophy. Rouge too, since it is black declining towards red, signifies the disturbance of disease combined with the fixing of hope on the physician. For unless one was sick, one would not want a physician, nor would the patient seek medical advice, if he did not hope to be aided thereby.

After these the erudite among the jurists flourish, for whom at Paris the street Chnobernelli is set aside, which also is called the street of asses. These rejoice in scholastic copes of scarlet and of a fiery red, since the red color signifies an inflamed mind. For these are afire concerning the tranquility of mankind and involve themselves in innumerable questions to settle matters of lawsuits and to repress the countless efforts of litigators. Or this color, like that of the inside of the *patula,* is bestowed on them because they are solicitous concerning public affairs and human morals.

The highest chairs of all the schools are happily scattered through monastic cloisters and the Sorbonne and other blessed colleges to lecture on books of theology and expound the marvels of divine Scripture. The reverend masters of theological profundity are clad in copes of their Order, if they are regular clergy, or in any simple garb or humble color, if they are secular clergy, to denote the humble and innocent preaching of this science. And as the medical men are derived from physical scientists, so the canonists spring from the theologians, because the sacred canons are often the conclusions of divine utterances, as is clear to one who carefully studies the decrees of the fathers.

Another division may be made between schools, as when it is said that some schools are authentic, others illegitimate. An authentic school is one whose studies are laudably founded on apostolic privileges and imperial liberties, as in the case of the schools of Paris, Bologna, Padua and Oxford. An illegitimate school is one of slight reputation lacking privileges from princes of the world, such as in Germany are the schools of Erfurt, Vienna, and so on. And the difference between them is indeed great, since in the authentic schools knights are dubbed and lords of sciences crowned, so that they enjoy both special costumes and liberties and are revered with marked reverence no less by princes lay and clerical than by the people, and such are laudably entitled masters and lords of the sciences. But in the illegitimate schools although masters are nourished actually, they lack a privileged title, whence it follows that the name of master is equivocal in many respects. For one man is a master in title and reality, another in reality but not in title, a third in title but not in reality, a fourth neither in title nor reality but in name only. The master in title and reality is most properly called master, since he has the holdings of the sciences and with this enjoys a title acquired by outstanding merit and privileged by the liberties of princes. For title is derived from titan, which is the sun, because, as the sun adorns the corporeal orb with its light, so the true title laudably adorns the one to whom it is applied. But a master is so called as thrice great, set above others in mental capacity, reasoning power and moral conduct, of which if he lacks one he is not a good master. How moreover a true master obtains his title will be made clear below. The master in reality but not in title is he who has the treasure of science and the heritage of virtue but does not have a privileged title. And he is like a noble, strong and praiseworthy in arms, who has not yet been knighted. But the master in title and not in reality is he who by prayers or price simonaically receives a title he does not deserve, lacking the knowledge for so high a title. He is like a timid man who never has been or will go to war but accepts the title of knight so that he may appear in silk at church and adorn his fingers with gold. Moreover, he is master neither in reality nor in title who neither is acquainted with the sciences nor has acquired the title in privileged schools but on some occasion has taken the name of master, perhaps as notary to a lord or pleader in the law courts.

PERSONS AND ASSOCIATION OF PERSONS IN THE HOUSE

In the illegitimate school house of the artists there are at least four kinds of persons necessary, to wit, master, disciple, pedagogue and monitor. The master is the paterfamilias and lord of the school house whom the particular persons associated in the same house are bound reverently to obey. But the disciple is the son and heir of the master, to whom the father venerably dispenses the treasure of his mind or at least tries to. The pedagogue is the guide of the schoolboy and his vice-master in the house. Moreover, we call him the monitor who notes the faults of the scholars and reports their offenses to the master. Between the said four persons there are three associations, to wit, of master with disciples as of father with heirs, of master with assistant masters and monitor as of lord with servants, and the association of these servants with the sons of the venerable master. For in this divine house we do not have the association of man and wife as in the domestic house; nevertheless there is no master without mistress, nor poet without muse. For the lawful mate of the philosopher is that leading lady of all delights in this life, Philosophy herself, who the Lord ordering is mistress of all virtues. Since taking the name of philosophy literally, it extends to all wisdom possessed by the human species whether acquired from man or God. For philosophy is, so to speak, loved wisdom, wherefore the artist is a philosopher, the medical man too is a sort of natural philosopher, who starts from the branches of things of nature leaving their roots to the natural scientist. The jurist is a philosopher from a sort of moral philosophy, since juridical erudition is subordinated to moral science, as Johannes Monachi comments on the sixth of the Decretals. The theologian is a philosopher from divine philosophy. But since the artists deal with all the interests of the aforesaid philosophers, for example, about the generation of man and his nature and parts, as is clear in the books of Aristotle on the generation of animals—and in this coincide with students of medicine—and also deal with human morals and the rule of households and cities bidding men live virtuously, as is evident to one perusing the ethical and economic and political books of illustrious Aristotle—and in this coincide with the jurists—and similarly dispute concerning God and the number and natures of the intelligences, as is clear in the books of metaphysics—and in this coincide with the theologians—therefore the artist is called the true philosopher by the very name and *par excellence.*

Returning therefore to what we were saying, we assert that the true wife of each philosopher is his philosophy from which he begets books like himself according to the forms and cast of his mind, and that his disciples are in a fashion his sons. His household consists of the assistant masters and custodians of the schools, who, according to the master's command, instruct the scholars and keep them from things illicit. And assistants are more opportune in unlicensed schools of artists than in others, because their hordes are younger and more heterogeneous and so require more tutors in acquiring both morals and knowledge. In authentic schools of artists, however, only three persons are needed except for the janitors who keep the keys to the schools and the *predones* or bedells who announce the lectures of the masters and disputations to the community. For in the authentic school there is master, bachelor and disciples. Moreover, what the master or disciple is has been stated before, but the bachelor is an arch-scholar who gives cursory lectures in the place of the master and who goes about the classes of the doctors arguing and responding, but has not yet received the laureate of doctoral knighthood, yet is close to the degree of master. . . .

REQUIREMENTS OF THE MASTER IN ARTS

We ought to begin with the discipline of masters in arts as from the venerable mother, without whose essential preliminary regime no one by human effort is raised to the chairs of other faculties. Wherefore anyone who derides the faculty of arts either is a clodhopper, because he knows no letters, or hates the womb in which he was formed, curses the breasts which he sucked, denies his daily bread, refuses the air which he otherwise breathes, and shamefully blasphemes as to be shunned that which is necessary to him. We say therefore that a master in arts occupying a chair in authentic schools and especially in Paris, where this faculty of old possessed singular prerogatives, should combine in himself eight praiseworthy traits: of which the first is that he instruct himself by study, the second that he continue his lectures fruitfully, the third that he proceed systematically, the fourth that he love the truth rather than strive for singularity, the fifth that he shall not snarl at the catholic faith, the sixth that he live a moral life, the seventh that he provide for the necessities of life, and the eighth that he shun influenced promotions as simony.

The reason for the first requirement is that he who lectures without preparation does not speak as well as if he had prepared, wherefore doctors who refuse to study in order to seem more ingenious rather take away their scholars' talents than bestow any on them.

The reason for the second is that a lecturer who does not continue thins out his auditorium and renders the minds of his hearers ungrateful. Wherefore let the doctor postpone his leisure or outside occupations, otherwise he will empty his classroom rather than make it fecund. Nor does he fruitfully continue, although he does not interrupt his lectures who tries to recover what has been spent, striving to turn the sea back into the Danube. But no more does he continue fertilely who does not cover the texts in the allotted time, so that they may be completed in due season in accordance with the university statutes.

The reason for the third requirement is because there is an order in the books of any science according to the order of the things comprised in it. Moreover, the best arrangement is to begin with the easier points and those better known to us and so proceed to those which are more difficult and occult. Wherefore that teaching is not best arranged which proceeds from things which are first in the order of nature to those which follow them, as Plato did, but rather the Aristotelian method is to be followed going from posteriors according to nature to priors.

The reason for the fourth requirement is that he who tries to be singular in everything strives rather to be *sui generis* * than to be judged accurate. And so working against the minds of all he is detested by all rather than praised. For no one has sufficient ability to solve all questions, but it is the part of the true speculator to borrow many ideas from others and discover some by himself.

The reason for the fifth requirement is that he who snarls at the catholic faith dishonors God his Creator, prefers his own fancies to divine miracles, reveals arcana of

* [Unique, "original." (*Ed.*)]

God which he completely ignores, and indeed makes stupid assertions and casts prudence to the winds. Perhaps you will tell me that divine miracles do not concern you when you are discussing natural questions. And what do I say? You certainly are discussing miracles of God when you revolve his creatures in your mind. Has not the prince of this machine of the universe established everything with marvelous wisdom? And if He founded particular things for us in an accustomed course, by his omnipotence he can work marvels with any of them beyond its nature.

The reason for the sixth requirement is that the philosopher who lacks good morals is not a lawful philosopher but rather a counterfeit. For the law of philosophy is to live virtuously, act purely, and reason truly in particular matters. Wherefore a speculator living in iniquity or working impurity or not knowing the truth is entitled *errophilus* * rather than philosopher, for he repudiates philosophy disgracefully and wickedly.

The reason for the seventh requirement is because it is shameful to lower the reverence of so high a name to become in torn tabard a laughing stock in public squares, or for such honorable intellect to beg its bread. It is more laudable for the arch-scholar in the lowest grade to suffer the woes of Codrus than disgracefully to beg in the van of so great a militia.

The eighth requirement is based on this reason, that a master promoting an unworthy scholar to the summit of mastership, corrupted by prayer or price, dishonors the loftiness of such a name, bridles an ass instead of a bear, crowns an ape in place of a man, and honors a clodhopper as a knight. He is an unhappy and ungrateful soldier of wisdom who from favor advances a fool to solemn mastership as if a wise man. Since he detracts from his own honor who gives his honor to aliens, and those are alien from the honor of an honest man who are unworthy of that honor. For just as timidity does not deserve to receive knighthood, but everyone who is truly knighted is of proven bravery, so ignorance wins no venerable mastership, while for laudable experience of the sciences any arch-scholar is made a revered master. . . .

CONCERNING THE PRINCIPAL OF A BOYS' SCHOOL

Now let us see how a master of arts in schools which are not authentic but unlicensed should conduct himself with regard to the scholars and arch-scholars. And first concerning schools where often not a master in arts presides but a teacher of boys is named without title, who however sometimes is really a master although he lacks the title, sometimes indeed in our days is neither a master in fact nor in title but a vainglorious leader. The true teacher of boys ought to consider carefully the different individualities of his pupils, for they come at seven, as the age of infancy is most often reckoned, to receive the first rudiments. In such novices four things are to be considered, to wit, the state of the weather, a normal body, the physical constitution, and the mental capacity. I say that the state of the weather must be noted, because tender limbs are easily struck with cold or penetrated by heat. Wherefore it is advisable to

---

* ["Lover of error." "Philosopher," literally, means "a lover of wisdom." (*Ed.*)]

start young children in school about the middle of springtime, and to be on the safe side it is well to have two classrooms for boys in the same building, one to wit adapted to resist the summer heat and with its windows facing north, which may receive the throng of scholars in summer with the air somewhat cooled off, the other carefully enclosed, which in winter time can be heated with burning coals according to the custom of the region, and this method is observed in many northern regions. Others build their schools on a slope with a subterranean depression well-walled with planks of fir-wood or of pine, which in summertime resists the heat and as winter grows severe shuts out the cold. Also different clothing should be worn, so that in winter for example the boys should be clad in heavy clothing and lighter in summer.

Also from the time a boy begins his schooling the soundness of his members should be watched with respect to continuous as well as discrete quantity and also the disposition of parts of the body. Moreover, I say continuous quantity so that none of his organs may exceed or fall short of its appropriate size and that neither hand nor foot nor head may be bent or crooked. And I say discrete quantity lest forsooth any one of them be substantially lacking, as when boys are found without arms or feet, or lest the number be superfluous, as the sexual parts are in hermaphrodites, or as in the case of monsters with two heads and one trunk, or those with too many fingers or toes and the like. I say also the disposition of parts of the body, because hunchbacks and those with clubfeet or one eye or infected with major diseases such as epileptics, lepers and the like, are not to be endowed with the nobility of letters, since those with noticeable physical defects neither adorn professorial chairs nor become the divine priesthood, in order to avoid scandal. But neither are they advantageously admitted in schools, because the boys wantonly laugh at them and disturb their peace of mind. Besides, those who have contagious diseases may infect the other scholars.

Moreover, the physical constitution is to be noted in schoolboys, since there is not one measure of scholastic discipline for all constitutions, just as there is not the same portion of food and drink for all. For those of sanguine temperament are gentle and pacific amid the turmoils of their associations and with capacity for learning, who seem to pick things up quickly as if it were play and without any great effort. But wantonness often seduces these. The choleric are somewhat less capable but retain more tenaciously and firmly. These as if in a fury disturb the others by various movements, for they jump about like young goats and are seldom found in the same place, wherefore they are deluded by inconstancy, unless God has given them the love of discipline. The phlegmatic indeed are sluggish and sleepy and of slower receptivity and ready forgetfulness because of the abundant humidity in them, wherefore they should be stirred up with some frequency, so that their brains may be warmed up. Those who are melancholy with stony hardness acquire with the greatest labor but retain with indelible memory, and their obtuseness is overcome by diligent study. The first therefore should be aided with due correction to repress their wantonness. The second lot should be threatened by the monitors and custodians so that their restlessness may be quieted. The third and fourth groups are to be fortified by reviews, which help them by frequent repetition of the lessons, for they aid themselves who help others, and he who teaches another instructs himself.

But the mental capacity of boys in the process of learning is quickly ascertained. For in the same kind of composition some are found bright, others brighter, and others brightest of all. So also some are dull, others duller, and others so dull that their mind is despaired of. And this variety comes from the latitude of degrees of the elements which no scientist or even physician can precisely measure, various aspects of the stars contributing to these differences and their quasi innumerable influences on the conception, formation and birth of children, which somehow spread occult affections in human bodies by which human talents are rendered more or less gross or subtle, since, as the art of physiognomy bears witness, the mind follows the body in its dispositions. Therefore let the teacher of boys so direct them that he corrects the timid by words, masters the frivolous with rods, and bestows upon each according to his exigencies the gifts of letters. Nor should the scholars be always kept intent upon their books and writing tablets, but they should be given an occasional recess and set at suitable games, so that their spirits may be raised and their blood stirred by the pleasure of play. For thus the boys' minds which before were fatigued by the tedium of classes are refined and refreshed.

ON GRADUAL ADVANCEMENT IN THE ORDER OF THE SCIENCES

Now descending to particulars let us say that when the seven year olds have first begun to study grammar and have learned the letters of the alphabet and how to write them correctly together in syllables and to put the syllables together into words, it is opportune that they note the meaning etymologically, that is both the significations of the words and the properties of the parts, which the perspicacity of the moderns calls modes of signifying, dwelling upon them for some time, and when they have got the gist of these, let them work at dyasynthetical constructions of speech. Nor is it a bad plan to teach these together, since either profits by the accompaniment of the other. Meanwhile moreover texts of a moral character and of poetical deduction should be combined, in which is acquired both fruit of virtues and fertility of good morals, while traces of rhetorical polish are found in the same. This course of study develops from the first year in school at seven until the end of the scholar's fourteenth year. For then the light of reason begins to gleam in him, and then is the time to propound the involutions of dialectic to the brighter and better pupils together with examples of fine rhetoric, likewise occasionally mixing in something from the easier introductory works of the other sciences. For it is customary in the education of schoolboys to combine the practice of music with the milk of grammar, and also the art of the algorism * which serves practical arithmetic. Similarly treatises on the celestial spheres introductory to astronomy concur with dialectical and rhetorical dissertations. Next from the twenty-first year the scholastic angels generally attack more solid subjects such as embracing natural science in its latitude, hearing metaphysics, and speculating over Euclid's propositions until the end of the third seven year period of education. And thus in his twenty-eighth year the arch-scholar is fitted for the chair of the master. But these three seven year periods of schooling might be reduced to five year periods in the

* [The Arabic or decimal system of numeration. (Ed.)]

case of very bright pupils. Nevertheless it is difficult for any human mind thoroughly to master so many, so great, and such subjects in these spaces of years. And he to whom is given from above so great mental capacity will do well to set for himself far ampler measures. But for him who turns to the sacred page or who seeks canon law it is enough to have the trivium in order to comprehend the eloquence of divine scriptures. And such an one when he has heard the secular arts should also attend the classes in theology and frequent the chairs of the jurists until he has acquired a sufficient hold on these subjects. But the more proficient he is in the arts, the more praiseworthy he will be as a theologian, because it is for the theologian alone to dispute concerning anything and to know the universe, so that he may be able to declare the more clearly the invisibles of God through those things which are visible. For the sacred scriptures make mention of all the things of the universe. The medical man should have knowledge at least of the trivium and natural science and astronomy. Perhaps a little of the last will do, but if he knew it thoroughly, he would be a more circumspect practitioner.

SOLVING SOME DOUBTS AS TO WHAT HAS BEEN SAID

The question arises from what has been said whether it is permissible for a Christian clergyman to study secular arts. And it seems not. For it is read concerning Saint Jerome that when he read Cicero he was chastised by an angel because he a Christian was absorbed in the figments of the pagans. Besides reason convinces us that a Christian should not sweat over the books of the Gentiles, because their arguments are contrary to the catholic faith. For Aristotle has reasoned in the eighth book of the *Physics* and the first book of *De Celo et Mundo* that the world is eternal and that there was no first man and will be no last. But that is expressly contrary to what is believed concerning creation, as is clear in the *Book of Genesis* of Moses. Again Averroes, Third *De Anima*,* proves that there is an individual rational soul in all men, which is apportioned to each of them like one sailor to many boats. And this indeed manifestly denies eternal life in the paradise of delights and unceasing punishment for those who are condemned to the pains of Tartarus by the just judgment of God. Wherefore it follows that it is not right that Christian boys be educated in these vanities, because what we are accustomed to the more readily affects and governs our minds. With this too agrees what some write concerning the prodigal son, comparing him who ate the husks for the pigs and was fain to fill his belly with these to those who pore over the books of the Gentiles and fill their minds with the same. So too Origen by the insects and frogs with which the Egyptians were afflicted understands the idle garrulity and sophistical arguments of the dialecticians. Jerome moreover writing to Damasus of the prodigal son says: "We see priests of God, laying aside Gospels and prophets, read comedies, sing the amatory words of bucolic verse, clasp Virgil in their hands, and make a criminal pleasure of what for boys is a hard requirement." And again, "Does not he seem to us enmeshed in vanity of sense and obscurity of mind who is twisted night and day in

---

* [That is, the commentary by Averros (an Arabian philosopher of the twelfth century) on Book III of Aristotle's *De Anima,* or *On the Soul. (Ed.)*]

the art of dialectic, or who as an investigator of nature lifts his eyes across the skies and beyond the depth of earth and the abyss is plunged into empty space, who gets excited over iambics, who distinguishes and stores away in his studious heart such an underbrush of metres?" So from these statements it would seem to some, that the works of Gentile philosophers should not be read by us, nor should we linger over the verses of the poets.

ARGUING TO THE CONTRARY

Nonetheless it is argued to the contrary: since in the books of secular science on nature it is doubtful to no one that useful things are found, why should we be prohibited from reading what is useful? For there are truths in them which are gifts of God. Whence Isidore in his book on the supreme good says: "Philosophers state much in the world as to measurement of the course of the seasons and the stars and the discussion of the elements, and yet they derived this only from God." And if in their utterances they sometimes make mistakes, we may read these in order to avoid them. Wherefore Ambrose on Luke: "We read some things lest they be neglected, others lest we be ignorant, but others not to hold them but to repudiate them." We are exhorted to the same end by what Bede writes on the *Book of Kings* saying: "He disturbs and weakens the wit of readers who thinks they should be forbidden to read secular works of any sort." In which if aught useful is found, it is lawful for them to make it theirs. Otherwise Moses and Daniel would not have been allowed to be trained in the wisdom and letters of the Egyptians and Chaldeans, whose superstitions and pleasures they at the same time abhorred. Nor would the master of the Gentiles himself, forsooth Paul, have included some verses of the poets in his writings or speeches, if they ought not to be read. To the same conclusion leads what Gratian asserts in the *Decretum* saying: It is read that the Lord bade the children of Israel to despoil the Egyptians of their gold and silver, thus pointing the moral that whether we find the gold of wisdom or the silver of eloquence in the poets, we should turn it to the use of salubrious erudition. In Leviticus too we are ordered to offer first-fruits of honey, that is, the sweetness of human eloquence to the Lord. The magi also offered three gifts to the Lord, by which some would understand three parts of philosophy. These are the words of Gratian. And he understands by the three parts of philosophy the philosophy of speech which consists of the trivium, and real philosophy which concerns the quadrivium and other sciences comprehended under the quadrivium, as I have deduced above. Then the third part of philosophy is moral philosophy, which in general is called ethics, having three principal divisions as set forth above. Corroborative too of our thesis is this which Jerome writes on the Epistle to Titus. If anyone, he says, knows the art of grammar or dialectic, so that he is able to speak correctly and to distinguish between truth and false, we do not blame him. Geometry moreover and arithmetic and music have truth in their science. But it is not the science of piety. The science of piety is to know how to read the scriptures, to understand the prophets, to believe in the gospel, not to ignore the apostles. But the learning of the grammarians can profit life, provided it is utilized for higher ends. And so it is with all the other sciences of the Gentiles and the Chaldeans which are called liberal.

SOLVING THE SAID QUESTION

Moreover in order to solve the said question we must carefully weigh the ends for the sake of which we labor in these and other sciences. For some men study just to know and so delight in this, that they contribute nothing further in the way of happiness or utility to themselves or others. And those who thus read secular studies are detestable, because they do not fructify to life eternal. To whom Isidore says in his book on the supreme good: "The philosophers of the Gentiles, not seeking God as they ought, fell upon prevaricating angels, and the devil became their mediator to death, as Christ is ours to life." And again: "Therefore are prohibited to Christians the figments . . . of idle stories, because they excite the mind to lustful thoughts." And later he says: "Some are more pleased to ponder the sayings of the Gentiles because of their sounding and ornate speech than holy scripture for its lowly eloquence. But what profits it to progress in worldly doctrines and stagnate in things divine, to follow blind figments and shun celestial mysteries? Such books are to be avoided and discarded for love of holy scriptures." To finish what he has to say:

Some study worldly sciences primarily in order to know, and their goal is vainglory. To whom Isidore says: "Love of human or mundane science does nothing else than to extol a man with praises. For the greater are his studies of literature, the more his soul is inflated with arrogance and swells with pride." Lo! they admit almost nothing of divine truth, nay they deride it with the teeth of canine snarling, and what they know to be true, because it is not their invention, their pride will not admit. To whom again Isidore says: "The philosophers of the world indeed knew God, but because the humility of Christ displeased them, they left the true way for a byway." And so dimming the glory of God they inclined toward a lie and leaving the right way fell into tortuous error.

There are also a third set studying the sciences to make money and their master is avarice. Who, if they possessed worldly goods to begin with, would rarely thumb or study the volumes of the scriptures. So moreover the liberal arts in our times are not loved except as they lead on to the possession of other sciences. For the mere artist, unless he is equipped with other sciences, is almost found among us as a beggar. Noticing which, the poet says:

> Art thirsts, the Decretals are fat,
> The law itself is proud, Moses plays the pontiff,
> Medicine sneaks in the chamber door.

A fourth group study for edification to comprehend matters of faith and understand those things which lead to human happiness. And so it is licit for us to read mundane sciences, as is proved by the reasons and authorities cited in opposition to the question above. For the subtlety of all sciences has left its traces in divine eloquence, wherefore

Cassiodorus in his exposition of the Psalter says: All splendor of rhetorical eloquence, every mode of poetical locution, each varied refinement of pronunciation takes its exordium from the divine scriptures. And with this agrees what Ambrose says on the Epistle to the Colossians. Every reason, he says, of supernal science or of terrestrial creature is in Him who is their head and author, so that one who knows Him need search no farther. Because this is perfect virtue and wisdom, and whatever is sought elsewhere is found here in perfection.

A fifth group study the sciences not merely to be edified but that they may edify others, and their master is charity and love of their neighbor. To these it is indeed permitted to know the sciences of the Gentiles, in order that they may be able to decry their evil sayings and convert what they find useful in them to the use of sacred erudition as happy men. Wherefore Jerome on the Epistle to Titus says: How anyone exposes himself to ridicule who tries to write against the *mathematici* * without knowledge of *mathesis* † and to dispute against the philosophers without knowing their systems! Therefore let them learn the doctrine of the Chaldeans in the same spirit in which Moses learned all the wisdom of the Egyptians. And again he says: If sometimes we are forced to recall secular letters and discuss some of those matters which we once abandoned, it is not of our free will but so to speak of the gravest necessity in order that we may prove that those things which were predicted by the holy prophets many centuries ago are contained in the literature alike of the Greeks, Latins and other Gentiles. From this may be seen to what intent the fathers of divine scriptures forbade the liberal arts of Gentile masters and to what extent they commended the same. Since one should not cling to those arts so fondly as to desert the delights of the Faith. . . .

* [Mathematicians. (*Ed.*)]
† [Mathematics. (*Ed.*)]

✑§ STUDENT LIFE

STUDENT LIFE AT OLD HEIDELBERG

No master or student shall presume to visit the public and ordinary gaming houses, especially on days of lectures and above all where the laity meet, under penalty of half a florin and the taking of this into account by the university in making promotions.

No one shall presume by day or night to engage in gaming or to sit or tarry by night or otherwise for any time in a brothel or house of prostitution, under penalty of a florin and under penalty that such persons shall be posted by the university as public procurers and as such to be punished according to statutes previously enacted against such.

University Records and Life in the Middle Ages, ed. and trans. L. Thorndike (New York: Columbia University Press, 1944), pp. 332–333, 390–393.

Concerning dances at Lent or other time of year not being held by students in public and their not going about in unseemly fashion, wearing masks, and not engaging in jousts, the rector at that time always ought and has power to provide under heavy penalties.

All students are required to attend each week at least some lectures. Otherwise, besides statutes previously promulgated against such, which we wish to remain in their strength, the university intends to provide against these as it may see fit, and the rector at the time shall be required to take measures against them in accordance with his office.

If anyone is unwilling to give testimony on oath concerning the excesses of the students or for other reason, when he is required to do so by the rector, or if anyone who has been arrested shall run away, the rector may and should denounce him to the university for expulsion. . . .

STUDENT LIFE: PAST AND PRESENT

Depart therefore from the classrooms, ye inept and unfit who have your brains in your heels and measure all virtue by strength of body . . . "Five hours of sleep for the traveler, six for the student, eight for the merchant, and eleven for all rogues," or, "Five for the student, six for the merchant, seven for the people, eight for the sluggard."

Nor are they to be excused who while they themselves snore and wallow in bed, order their servants to perform the vicarious task of writing and listening in the auditorium. . . . You sons of Venus who, as Luca de Penna says, affect rooms overlooking the street to see the girls across the way or those who pass by, or who often appear in church principally on this account, that you may see the ladies! . . . although in many places the virgins are too gentle and tame and amiable and affable and tractable, and either give ready ear to the students or entice and anticipate in the matter of attentions. At Cologne and Tübingen, says Heinrich Hornmann in his *Commentary on the Line of Love,* chapter four on kissing, it is thought a great sin if a youth who meets a girl does not kiss and hug her. For public decency and the sanctity of the laws do not allow such prodigality of kisses.

Jacob Butrigarius and Baldus write that it is enough to prove a woman a prostitute if students visit her by day and night, without proving the commission of any sexual act, since, when a student talks with such an one, it is not to be presumed that he is repeating the Lord's Prayer. And the same Baldus says that the leaser of a house to a student cannot evict him because he has brought prostitutes there and therefore injured the property, since this should have been presumed as a common occurrence. Such abuses prevail in Italy and other kingdoms of lascivious Venus: our Germany and Suevia are by the grace of God incapable of such petulance.

A student who sells his books unless forced to do so by inevitable necessity becomes infamous *ipso facto,* like a soldier who has lost his arms in battle. . . .

And because these literary studies closely concern the honor of God and public utility, students may study even on feast days and in church: and Peter Rebuff affirms that he has seen many doctors intent on their books in church while vespers were being celebrated. He adds, however, that it would be more seemly and devout to pray in church and dismiss all other thoughts rather than to study . . . and he justly praises Jean Boerius, royal advocate in the parlement of Mombeliard, who on feast days never held consultations except with the poor.

It is also permissible for a student to expel from the house a smith who disturbs his studies. And so at Mombeliard Peter Rebuff compelled a certain weaver who filled the neighborhood with songs and shoutings almost without cessation to change his lodgings, when, despite an injunction of the magistrates, he continued to make a terrible noise.

Matthias Colerus evoked the same law at Jena against a certain cooper, who lived next door to him and used to get up at midnight and make so much noise in putting hoops on wine casks that the priest of Themis passed many sleepless nights and imperiled his health. But, having complained to the wine gild, an order was issued by the senate of Jena that it should compel the cooper either to leave that habitation and seek another or cease his labors in that neighborhood.

. . . And let the student be diligent in his first year, more diligent in the second, most diligent in the third, and even more diligent in the fourth, as Baldus says of the appellant. . . .

But let not the student try to teach himself before he has learned much, or he will learn late and badly. Nor without a guide and teacher should he enter a way which he has never known. . . .

And the spoken word of the professor has some occult virtue that penetrates deeper into the mind of the hearer and makes a greater impression upon the memory than private reading. . . .

Wherefore Caccialupus inveighs severely against those hard-necked students who disdain the lecture hall and master's voice, saying that they do not deserve to be called scholars or to enjoy the privileges of scholars, nay rather should be punished as deceivers. And Peter Rebuff writes that it is a sure sign of a good scholar when he listens readily to all lectures, especially until he is endowed with knowledge: that on the contrary those are foolish students who are willing to attend only one or two lectures a day, for such will not acquire much subject matter but only enough for a couple of lectures. Once at Toulouse there was marvelous competition in occupying the benches of the lecture hall, since students would go to the university at the third hour after midnight or thereabouts to get the best seats. Sometimes they would send servants to keep the places, whom the other students would sometimes drive out, and so dire controversies arose between them and the masters of the servants when they finally arrived. Wherefore, the rule was made that vacant places should be reserved for their first occupants, and that no one else might take a place against the will of its original occupant, but with the proviso that an infrequent auditor should forfeit his place after a fortnight's absence.

Far be, moreover, from our student that profane Italian custom, by which the students fill the auditorium more with petulant clamor, murmurs and tumult than with their presence and attention, and often are accustomed to injure the professor's feelings shamefully by loud laughter, whistling and disorder, and not merely to make a disturbance from the platform. . . .

But no wise man would advise that all students everywhere and without discrimination be strictly required to attend all public lectures. And we have seen students of long standing who were already imbued with much learning take nothing more ill than to be asked in public assembly, as if they were novices and tyros, What lectures have they attended? What ones have they not attended? Why not? Where do they live? Where do they eat? How much do they drink? etc. . . .

At Paris the faculty of canon law passed the following legislation as to attending lectures: We decree that no one shall be regarded as a student of the faculty of canon law and enjoy the privileges and immunities of the university, unless he shall have attended classes at least twice or thrice a week and listened to lectures after the manner of scholars.

In Spain a student does not enjoy the privileges of scholars unless he hears two lectures daily, as may be seen in the Constitutions of Spaniards in the Agreement made with the university of Salamanca, 1492 A.D.

Eobanus Hessus had an audience of fifteen hundred when he lectured on the poets at Erfurt, says Herman Kirchner. And John Corrasius taught law at Toulouse to such a throng of auditors that sometimes four thousand students listened to the professor's voice.

⤷ OPUS MAJUS

Roger Bacon

The life and writings of Roger Bacon (ca. 1214–ca. 1294) illustrate both the heights and the depths of which the thirteenth century was capable. Trained at Oxford and at Paris, Bacon devoted over twenty years to the study of languages and science, while transmitting his own insatiable curiosity to a generation of Oxford students. After he entered the Franciscan Order in 1247, the suspicion of heresy that hounded so many of the great thinkers of the age (including even St. Thomas) began to be attached to his own far-ranging researches. His superiors forced him to stop teaching and writing, and for many years made him a virtual prisoner in the Franciscan House in Paris. Fortunately, Guy Fulcodi, a brilliant Parisian lawyer who became Pope Clement IV in 1265, heard of Bacon and directed him to start writing again. The Opus Majus ("longer work") resulted, and was soon followed by an Opus Minus ("shorter work") and an Opus Tertium ("third work"). (Bacon's inventiveness did not extend to titles.) But after the death of Clement IV Bacon was tried for heresy, in 1278, condemned, and imprisoned until just before his death fourteen years later.

The aim of Bacon's Opus Majus *was ambitious: to show the unity of all knowledge and its relation to the destiny of man as revealed in the Holy Scriptures. The* Opus Majus *is thus a kind of summation, a* summa *corresponding to that of Bacon's great Dominican contemporary, St. Thomas Aquinas. St. Thomas, however, stressed deductive rigor and completeness; Roger Bacon covered a far wider range of subject matter: mathematics, languages, astronomy, astrology, geography, history, optics. He unified these subject by a conception of "experimental method" that was not to bear fruit until four centuries later, when another Englishman, Francis Bacon, once more proposed a unification of the sciences on the basis of a common method.*

Still, Roger Bacon was a thoroughly medieval man, as the selections given here—from Parts II, VI, and VII of his Opus Majus—*will indicate. Their central theme is unity: of science and theology, of observation and mystical intuition, of knowledge and virtue. But there is also much evidence of the audacious questing for new knowledge that alarmed Bacon's superiors and that made him a model for the legendary Doctor Faustus, who sold his soul to the Devil in exchange for the secret of life. Any facile generalization about the Middle Ages as a period in which curiosity and love of learning were stifled by religion must come to terms with Friar Bacon of Oxford.*

PART TWO

Chapter I

Accordingly after the four general causes of all human error have been banished to the lower regions and have been completely removed from this plea, I wish to show in this second part that there is one wisdom that is perfect and that this is contained in the Scriptures. From the roots of this wisdom all truth has sprung. I say, therefore, that one science is the mistress of the others, namely, theology, to which the remaining sciences are vitally necessary, and without which it cannot reach its end. The excellence of these sciences theology claims for her own law, whose nod and authority the rest of the sciences obey. Or better, there is only one perfect wisdom, which is contained wholly in the Scriptures, and is to be unfolded by canon law and philosophy. I make this statement since the exposition of divine truth is made through those sciences. For it is itself unfolded as it were in the palm with these sciences, and yet it gathers within its own grasp all wisdom; since all wisdom has been given by one God, to one world, for one purpose. Therefore this wisdom from its own triple arrangement will obtain

The Opus Majus of Roger Bacon, trans. R. B. Burke (2 vols.; New York: Russell and Russell, 1962), pp. 36–37, 50–51, 583–588, 615–620, 626–634.

unity. But the way of salvation is single, although there are many steps; but wisdom is the way to salvation. For every consideration of a man that does not belong to his salvation is full of blindness, and leads down to the darkness of hell; for which reason many sages famous in this world have been condemned, because they did not have the true wisdom, but an apparent and a false one, whence reckoning themselves wise they became fools according to the Scripture. But Augustine, speaking concerning the Scriptures, says in the second book on Christian Doctrine, if elsewhere there is truth, it is found here; if there is a hurtful thing, it is here condemned. And he wishes the Christian to perceive that, wherever he may have found the truth, it belongs to his Lord, as was said in the beginning. And the truth of Jesus Christ is the wisdom of the Scriptures. Therefore there is no truth elsewhere except that which is contained in that science. Ambrose on the Epistle to the Colossians says, "All knowledge of the science above and of the creation beneath is in Him who is the head and author, so that he who knows Him should seek nothing beyond, because He is the perfect virtue and wisdom." Whatsoever is sought elsewhere is found here in perfection. Since therefore the Scriptures give us this wisdom which is Christ, it is clear that all virtue is here included. But if wisdom elsewhere is so called and is opposed to this, it will be in error, it will have only the name of wisdom; even though it be not called opposing, it is yet different. But difference, although elsewhere it does not produce opposition, does so here, as is shown on Gospel authority, "He who is not with me is against me." So also is it true of this wisdom that what is not connected with it is proved to be against it, and for this reason to be shunned by the Christian. . . .

Chapter VIII

Moreover, all sacred writers and wise men of old in their expositions take a literal sense from the natures of things and from their properties, in order that they may bring out spiritual meanings through convenient adaptations and similitudes. This Augustine declares in the second book on Christian Doctrine, taking an example from the word of the Lord speaking to his Apostles, "Be wise as serpents and harmless as doves." For the Lord meant by this, that like the serpent which exposes its whole body in defense of its head, the Apostles and apostolic men should give themselves and their all for Christ their head and for his Faith. For this reason every creature in itself or in its own likeness or in the universal or in the particular, from the highest part of heaven even to the end of it is placed in the Scripture, even as God has made the creatures and the Scripture, so has he willed to place in the Scripture the things themselves that were made for the understanding of its literal as well as its spiritual sense. But the whole purpose of philosophy is to evolve the natures and properties of things, wherefore the power of all philosophy is contained in the sacred writings; and this is especially clear, since the Scriptures far more certainly, better, and more truly comprehend the creatures than philosophical labor would know how to define them. In place of an infinite number of examples let that of the rainbow make this matter clear. The philosopher Aristotle disturbs us by his own obscurities, nor can we get any clear understanding of the subject through him; nor is this surprising, since Avicenna, his particular imitator, the leading philosopher after him, according to the statement of the commentator on Aristotle's chapter on the rainbow in the third book of the Meteorologics, confesses that he himself did not clearly understand the nature of the rainbow. The reason of this is because the philosophers were ignorant of the final cause of the rainbow; and in their ignorance of the end they are ignorant of those things which pertain to the end, because the end imposes a necessity upon those things that are ordained for the end, as Aristotle maintains in the second book of the Physics. In fact, the final cause of the rainbow is the dissipation of the aqueous vapor, as is clear from the book of Genesis, whence always on the appearance of the rainbow there is a resolution of the clouds into an infinite number of drops, and the aqueous vapors disappear both in the air and in the sea and land; since one part of the rainbow falls into the spheres of water and earth. The disappearance of the aqueous vapor cannot take place through the rainbow except by reason of the solar rays that cause it, for through various reflections and refractions an infinite number of rays are assembled, and the assemblage of the rays is the cause of the resolution and disappearance of the waters, and therefore, the rainbow is produced by multiple reflections. For the rays cannot assemble except through refraction and reflection, as will be shown later in its proper place. From the Scriptural statement therefore of Genesis, "I will place my bow in the clouds of Heaven, that there may no more be a deluge over the earth," we learn the final cause of the rainbow itself, from which the efficient cause and the way in which the rainbow is produced can be investigated. The manner of its production was not clearly understood by the philosophers as their books show us. And such is the case in regard to every creature. For it is impossible for a man to know the ultimate truth of the creature as it is employed in the Scripture unless he shall have been especially illumined by God. For creatures are employed there because of the need of bringing out the truths of grace and glory, concerning which the philosophers were ignorant, and therefore did not attain the ultimate power of knowledge in regard to creatures, as the sacred Scripture contains it in its own vitals. Hence the whole excellence of philosophy lies in the literal sense when philosophy has been adorned with the sacred mysteries of grace and glory, crowned as it were by certain very noble pictures and colors. . . .

PART SIX

Chapter I

Having laid down fundamental principles of the wisdom of the Latins so far as they are found in language, mathematics, and optics, I now wish to unfold the principles of experimental science, since without experience nothing can be sufficiently known. For there are two modes of acquiring knowledge, namely, by reasoning and experience. Reasoning draws a conclusion and makes us grant the conclusion, but does not make the conclusion certain, nor does it remove doubt so that the mind may rest on the intuition of truth, unless the mind discovers it by the path of experience; since many have the arguments relating to what can be known, but because they lack experience they neglect the arguments, and neither avoid what is harmful nor follow what is good. For if a man who has never seen fire should prove by adequate reasoning that fire burns and injures things and destroys them, his mind would not be satisfied thereby, nor would he avoid fire, until he placed his hand or some combustible substance in the fire, so that he might prove by experience that which reasoning taught. But when he has had actual experience of combustion his mind is made certain and rests in the full light of truth. Therefore reasoning does not suffice, but experience does.

This is also evident in mathematics, where proof is most convincing. But the mind of one who has the most convincing proof in regard to the equilateral triangle will never cleave to the conclusion without experience, nor will he heed it, but will disregard it until experience is offered him by the intersection of two circles, from either intersection of which two lines may be drawn to the extremities of the given line; but then the man accepts the conclusion without any question. Aristotle's statement, then, that proof is reasoning that causes us to know is to be understood with the proviso that the proof is accompanied by its appropriate experience, and is not to be understood of the bare proof. His statement also in the first book of the Metaphysics that those who understand the reason and the cause are wiser than those who have empiric knowledge of a fact, is spoken of such as know only the bare truth without the cause. But I am here speaking of the man who knows the reason and the cause through experience. These men are perfect in their wisdom, as Aristotle maintains in the sixth book of the Ethics, whose simple statements must be accepted as if they offered proof, as he states in the same place.

He therefore who wishes to rejoice without doubt in regard to the truths underlying phenomena must know how to devote himself to experiment. For authors write many statements, and people believe them through reasoning which they formulate without experience. Their reasoning is wholly false. For it is generally believed that the diamond cannot be broken except by goat's blood, and philosophers and theologians misuse this idea. But fracture by means of blood of this kind has never been verified, although the effort has been made; and without that blood it can be broken easily. For I have seen this with my own eyes, and this is necessary, because gems cannot be carved except by fragments of this stone. Similarly it is generally believed that the castors employed by physicians are the testicles of the male animal. But this is not true, because the beaver has these under its breast, and both the male and female produce testicles of this kind. Besides these castors the male beaver has its testicles in their natural place; and therefore what is subjoined is a dreadful lie, namely, that when the hunters pursue the beaver, he himself knowing what they are seeking cuts out with his teeth these glands. Moreover, it is generally believed that hot water freezes more quickly than cold water in vessels, and the argument in support of this is advanced that contrary is excited by contrary, just like enemies meeting each other. But it is certain that cold water freezes more quickly for any one who makes the experiment. People attribute this to Aristotle in the second book of the Meteorologics; but he certainly does not make this statement, but he does make one like it, by which they have been deceived, namely, that if cold water and hot water are poured on a cold place, as upon ice, the hot water freezes more quickly, and this is true. But if hot water and cold are placed in two vessels, the cold will freeze more quickly. Therefore all things must be verified by experience.

But experience is of two kinds; one is gained through our external senses, and in this way we gain our experience of those things that are in the heavens by instruments made for this purpose, and of those things here below by means attested by our vision.

Things that do not belong in our part of the world we know through other scientists who have had experience of them. As, for example, Aristotle on the authority of Alexander sent two thousand men through different parts of the world to gain experimental knowledge of all things that are on the surface of the earth, as Pliny bears witness in his Natural History. This experience is both human and philosophical, as far as man can act in accordance with the grace given him; but this experience does not suffice him, because it does not give full attestation in regard to things corporeal owing to its difficulty, and does not touch at all on things spiritual. It is necessary, therefore, that the intellect of man should be otherwise aided, and for this reason the holy patriarchs and prophets, who first gave sciences to the world, received illumination within and were not dependent on sense alone. The same is true of many believers since the time of Christ. For the grace of faith illuminates greatly, as also do divine inspirations, not only in things spiritual, but in things corporeal and in the sciences of philosophy; as Ptolemy states in the Centilogium, namely, that there are two roads by which we arrive at the knowledge of facts, one through the experience of philosophy, the other through divine inspiration, which is far the better way, as he says.

Moreover, there are seven stages of this internal knowledge, the first of which is reached through illuminations relating purely to the sciences. The second consists in the virtues. For the evil man is ignorant, as Aristotle says in the second book of the Ethics. Moreover, Algazel says in his Logic that the soul disfigured by sins is like a rusty mirror, in which the species of objects cannot be seen clearly; but the soul adorned with virtues is like a well-polished mirror, in which the forms of objects are clearly seen. For this reason true philosophers have labored more in morals for the honor of virtue, concluding in their own case that they cannot perceive the causes of things unless they have souls free from sins. Such is the statement of Augustine in regard to Socrates in the eighth book of the City of God, chapter III. Wherefore the Scripture says, "in a malevolent soul, etc." For it is not possible that the soul should rest in the light of truth while it is stained with sins, but like a parrot or magpie it will repeat the words of another which it has learned by long practice. The proof of this is that the beauty of truth known in its splendor attracts men to the love of it, but the proof of love is the display of a work of love. Therefore he who acts contrary to the truth must necessarily be ignorant of it, although he may know how to compose very elegant phrases, and quote the opinions of other people, like an animal that imitates the words of human beings, and like an ape that relies on the aid of men to perform its part, although it does not understand their reason. Virtue, therefore, clarifies the mind, so that a man comprehends more easily not only moral but scientific truths. I have proved this carefully in the case of many pure young men, who because of innocency of soul have attained greater proficiency than can be stated, when they have had sane advice in regard to their study. Of this number is the bearer of this present treatise, whose fundamental knowledge very few of the Latins have acquired. For since he is quite young, about twenty years of age, and very poor, nor has he been able to have teachers, nor has he spent one year in learning his great store of knowledge, nor is he a man of great genius nor of a very retentive memory, there can be no other cause except the grace of God, which owing to the purity of his soul has granted to him those things that it has as a rule refused to show to all other students. For as a spotless virgin he has departed from me, nor have I found in him any kind of mortal sin, although I have examined him carefully, and he has, therefore, a soul so bright and clear that with very little instruction he has learned more than can be estimated. And I have striven to aid in bringing it about that these two young men should be useful vessels in God's Church, to the end that they may reform by the grace of God the whole course of study of the Latins.

The third stage consists in the seven gifts of the Holy Spirit, which Isaiah enumerates. The fourth consists in the beatitudes, which the Lord defines in the Gospels. The fifth consists in the spiritual senses. The sixth consists in fruits, of which is the peace of God which passes all understanding. The seventh consists in raptures and their states according to the different ways in which people are caught up to see many things of which it is not lawful for a man to speak. And he who has had diligent training in these experiences or in several of them is able to assure himself and others not only in regard to things spiritual, but also in regard to all human sciences. Therefore since all the divisions of speculative philosophy proceed by arguments, which are either based on a point from authority or on the other points of argumentation except this division which I am now examining, we find necessary the science that is called experimental. I wish to explain it, as it is useful not only to philosophy, but to the knowledge of God, and for the direction of the whole world, just as in the preceding divisions I showed the relationship of the languages and sciences to their end, which is the divine wisdom by which all things are disposed.

Chapter II

Since this Experimental Science is wholly unknown to the rank and file of students, I am therefore unable to convince people of its utility unless at the same time I disclose its excellence and its proper signification. This science alone, therefore, knows how to test perfectly what can be done by nature, what by the effort of art, what by trickery, what the incantations, conjurations, invocations, deprecations, sacrifices, that belong to magic, mean and dream of, and what is in them, so that all falsity may be removed and the truth alone of art and nature may be retained. This science alone teaches us how to view the mad acts of magicians, that they may be not ratified but shunned, just as logic considers sophistical reasoning.

This science has three leading characteristics with respect to other sciences. The first is that it investigates by experiment the notable conclusions of all those sciences. For the other sciences know how to discover their principles by experiments, but their conclusions are reached by reasoning drawn from the principles discovered. But if they should have a particular and complete experience of their own conclusions, they must have it with the aid of this noble science. For it is true that mathematics has general experiments as regards its conclusions in its figures and calculations, which also are applied to all sciences and to this kind of experiment, because no science can be known without mathematics. But if we give our attention to particular and complete experiments and such as are attested wholly by the proper method, we must employ the principles of this science which is called experimental. . . .

The Second Prerogative of Experimental Science This mistress of the speculative sciences alone is able to give us important truths within the confines of the other sciences, which those sciences can learn in no other way. Hence these truths are not connected with the discussion of principles but are wholly outside of these, although they are within the confines of these sciences, since they are neither conclusions nor principles. Clear examples in regard to these matters can be given; but in what follows the man without experience must not seek a reason in order that he may first understand, for he will never have this reason except after experiment. Hence in the first place there should be readiness to believe, until in the second place experiment follows, so that in the third reasoning may function. For if a man is without experience that a magnet attracts iron, and has not heard from others that it attracts, he will never discover this fact before an experiment. Therefore in the beginning he must believe those who have made the experiment, or who have reliable information from experimenters, nor should he reject the truth, because he is ignorant of it, and because he does not arrive at it by reasoning. I shall state, then, those things that I hold to have been proved by experiment.

Example I. Mathematical science can easily produce the spherical astrolabe, on which all astronomical phenomena necessary for man may be described, according to precise longitudes and latitudes. The device of Ptolemy in the eighth book of the Almagest is used with reference to circles as well as stars, as I have stated, by means of a certain similitude, but the subject is not fully explained by that device, for more work is necessary. But that this body so made should move naturally with the daily motion is not within the power of mathematical science. But the trained experimenter can consider the ways of this motion, aroused to consider them by many things which follow the celestial motion, as, for example, the three elements which rotate circularly through the celestial influence, as Alpetragius states in his book on Celestial Motions, and Averroës in the first book on the Heavens and the World; so also comets, the seas and flowing streams, marrows and brains and the substances composing diseases. Plants also in their parts open and close in accordance with the motion of the sun. And many like things are found which, according to a local motion of the whole or of parts, are moved by the motion of the sun. The scientist, therefore, is aroused by the consideration of things of this kind, a consideration similar in import to that in which he is interested, in order that at length he may arrive at his goal. This instrument would be worth the treasure of a king, and would supersede all other astronomical instruments and clocks, and would be a most wonderful instrument of science. But few would know how in a clear and useful manner to conceive of such a miracle and of similar ones within the confines of mathematical science.

Example II. Another example can be given in the field of medicine in regard to the prolongation of human life, for which the medical art has nothing to offer except the regimen of health. But a far longer extension of life is possible. At the beginning of the world there was a great prolongation of life, but now it has been shortened unduly. Many have thought that the reason for this prolongation and shortening of life is found in the influence of the heavens. For they considered that the arrangement of the heavens was best at the beginning, and that as the world grows old all things decay.

They think that the stars were created in more advantageous positions, in which stars have their dignities, which are called house, exaltation, triplicity, face, and boundary; and in a better relationship of these to one another in accordance with the diversity of aspects or the invisible projection of rays. They also think that they have gradually receded from this position, and that in accordance with this recession they impose a shortened span of life up to some fixed boundary, at which there will be a state of rest. But this idea has many contradictions and difficulties, of which I must now speak.

Whether this shall prove to be true or not, another reason must be given, which is ready at hand for us and is plain, which cannot be contradicted, and which we know by experience. Therefore in regard to this we must strive, that the wonderful and ineffable utility and splendor of experimental science may appear and the pathway may be opened to the greatest secret of secrets, which Aristotle has hidden in his book on the Regimen of Life. For although the regimen of health should be observed in food and drink, in sleep and in wakefulness, in motion and in rest, in evacuation and retention, in the nature of the air and in the passions of the mind, so that these matters should be properly cared for from infancy, no one wishes to take thought in regard to them, not even physicians, since we see that scarcely one physician in a thousand will give this matter even slight attention. Very rarely does it happen that any one pays sufficient heed to the rules of health. No one does so in his youth, but sometimes one in three thousand thinks of these matters when he is old and approaching death, for at that time he fears for himself and thinks of his health. But he cannot then apply a remedy because of his weakened powers and senses and his lack of experience. Therefore fathers are weakened and beget weak sons with a liability to premature death. Then by neglect of the rules of health the sons weaken themselves, and thus the son's son has a doubly weakened constitution, and in his turn weakens himself by a disregard of these rules. Thus a weakened constitution passes from father to sons, until a final shortening of life has been reached, as is the case in these days.

Not only is there this accidental cause, but there is also another, consisting in the disregard of morals. For sins weaken the powers of the soul, so that it is incompetent for the natural control of the body; and therefore the powers of the body are weakened and life is shortened. This weakening passes from father to son, and so on. Therefore owing to these two natural causes the longevity of man of necessity has not retained its natural course from the beginning; but for these two reasons the longevity of man has been shortened contrary to nature. Moreover, it has been proved that this excessive shortening of the span of life has been retarded in many cases, and longevity prolonged for many years by secret experiments. Many authors write on this topic. Wherefore this excessive shortening of life must be accidental with a possible remedy.

Since I have shown that the cause of a shortening of life of this kind is accidental, and therefore that a remedy is possible, I now return to this example which I have decided to give in the field of medicine, in which the power of medical art fails. But the experimental art supplies the defect of medicine in this particular. For the art of medicine can give only the proper rules of health for all ages. For although noted authors have spoken inadequately concerning the proper regimen of the aged, it has been possible, however, for medicine to give such a regimen. This regimen consists in the proper use of food and drink, of motion and rest, of sleep and wakefulness, of elimination and retention, of the air, and in the control of the passions of the mind. But if from birth a man followed a proper regimen to the end of his life, he would reach the limit of life set by God and nature, in accordance with the possibility of a proper regimen. But since it is impossible for this regimen to be followed by any one, and since few, nay, scarcely any one at all, from youth pay any heed to this regimen, and very few old people observe it as it is possible, therefore the accidents of old age of necessity come before old age and senility, namely, in the period of the prime of life, which is the age of human beauty and strength. In these times this period of life does not continue beyond forty-five or fifty years.

All these accidents of old age and senility are white hair, pallor, wrinkling of the skin, excess of mucus, foul phlegm, inflammation of the eyes, and general injury to the organs of sense, diminution of blood and of the spirits, weakness in motion and breathing and in the whole body, failure in both the animal and natural powers of the soul, sleeplessness, anger and disquietude of mind, and forgetfulness, of which the royal Hali says that old age is the home of forgetfulness; and Plato that it is the mother of lethargy. Because of the lack of a proper regimen of health all these accidents and many more come to men in the prime of life, that is, either in greater or lesser degree, in accordance with the better or worse control they have exercised over themselves in the matter of their health, and in accordance with a better and stronger constitution and a better or worse control exercised over their morals. But the medical art does not furnish remedies against this corruption that comes from lack of control and failure in regimen, just as all physicians expert in their own art know, although medical authors confess that remedies are possible, but they do not teach them. For these remedies have always been hidden not only from physicians, but from the whole rank and file of scientists, and have been revealed only to the most noted, whom Aristotle mentions in the first book of the Topics in the division of the probable. Not only are remedies possible against the conditions of old age coming at the time of one's prime and before the time of old age, but also if the regimen of old age should be completed, the conditions of old age and senility can still be retarded, so that they do not arrive at their ordinary time, and when they do come they can be mitigated and moderated, so that both by retarding and mitigating them life may be prolonged beyond the limit, which according to the full regimen of health depends on the six articles mentioned. And there is another farther limit, which has been set by God and nature, in accordance with the property of the remedies retarding the accidents of old age and senility and mitigating their evil. The first limit can be passed but the second cannot be. . . .

Example III. In the third place, the dignity of this science can be exemplified in alchemy. For that whole art is scarcely so perfected that the greater metals may be produced from the lighter ones, as gold from lead, and silver from copper. But that art never suffices to show the natural and artificial grades of gold and the modes of its grades. For experimental science has brought both to light, since it has discovered both the four natural grades and their seventeen modes and the artificial ones. By experiment it can be produced beyond twenty-four. Thus the vessel in which the liquor was contained, by means of which the ploughman became the messenger of the king, had a purity of gold far beyond the twenty-four, as its test and worth showed. But when those twenty-four degrees are found in a mass of gold, the gold is the best that can be produced by nature. But when there are twenty-four degrees of gold and one part of silver or one degree, the gold is inferior to the former, and thus the diminution of the degrees of the gold goes as far as sixteen, so that there are eight grades of gold with an admixture of silver. But the mineral power in the belly of the earth is not able sometimes to digest matter into the nature of gold, and does what it can by digesting it into the form of silver. And that I am not led astray in this matter by my imagination is proved by the fact that men are found in several parts of the world who are clever at producing those sixteen modes, and have discovered pieces and masses of gold in those seventeen modes. They then made a mixture of silver and air with gold in the aforesaid modes, so that they might have seventeen lumps of gold made artificially, by means of which they might learn the natural modes of gold. Since this art is not known to the majority of those who are eager for gold, many frauds consequently are perpetrated in this world. The art of alchemy not only omits these modes, but this gold of twenty-four degrees is very rarely found, and with the greatest difficulty. There have always been a few who during their life have known this secret of alchemy; and this science does not go beyond that. But experimental science by means of Aristotle's Secrets of Secrets knows how to produce gold not only of twenty-four degrees but of thirty and forty degrees and of as many degrees as we desire. For this reason Aristotle said to Alexander, "I wish to disclose the greatest secret"; and it really is the greatest secret, for not only would it procure an advantage for the state and for every one his desire because of the sufficiency of gold, but what is infinitely more, it would prolong life. For that medicine which would remove all the impurities and corruptions of a baser metal, so that it should become silver and purest gold, is thought by scientists to be able to remove the corruptions of the human body to such an extent that it would prolong life for many ages. This is the tempered body of elements, of which I spoke above.

The Third Prerogative or the Dignity of the Experimental Art   But there is a third dignity of this science. It arises from those properties through which it has no connection with the other sciences, but by its own power investigates the secrets of nature. This consists in two things; namely, in the knowledge of the future, the past, and the present, and in wonderful works by which it excels in the power of forming judgments the ordinary astronomy dealing with judgments. For Ptolemy in the book introductory to the Almagest says that there is a more certain road than that through the ordinary astronomy, and this is the pathway of experiment, which follows the course of nature, to which many of the philosophers who are believers are turning, just like Aristotle and a host of the authors of judgments formed from the stars, as he himself says, and as we know by proper practice, which cannot be gainsaid. This science was discovered as a complete remedy for human ignorance and inadvertence; for it is difficult to get accurate astronomical instruments, and it is more difficult to get verified tables, especially those in which the motion of the planets is equalized. The use, moreover, of these tables is difficult, but still more difficult is the use of the instruments. But this science has discovered the definitions and the means by which it can answer easily every question, as far as the power of a single branch of philosophy can do so, and by which it can show us the forms of the celestial forces, and the influences of the heavenly bodies on this world without the difficulty of the ordinary astronomy. This part of the science relating to judgments has four principal divisions or secret sciences.

Moreover, certain bear witness that activities of this science which display philosophy consist in changing the character of a region, so that the habits of its people are changed. One of such witnesses was Aristotle himself, the most learned of philosophers. When Alexander asked him in regard to the nations which he had discovered, whether he should exterminate them because of the ferocity of their character, or should permit them to live, he replied in the book of Secrets, "If you can alter the air of those nations, permit them to live; if you cannot, then kill them." For he maintained that the air of these nations could be changed advantageously, so that the complexions of their bodies would be changed, and then their minds influenced by their complexions would choose good morals in accordance with the freedom of the will. This is one of the secrets.

Moreover, certain assert that change is effected by the sun. There is, as an illustration, the example of Aristotle when he said to Alexander, "Give a hot drink from the seed of a plant to whomsoever you wish, and he will obey you for the rest of your life." Some maintain that an army may be stupefied and put to flight. Of this number is Aristotle, who says to Alexander, "Take such a stone, and every army will flee from you." They bear witness that these statements and innumerable others of this kind are true, not meaning that violence is done to the freedom of the will, since Aristotle, who maintains this view, says in the Ethics that the will cannot be coerced. The body, moreover, can be changed by the influence of things, and the minds of people are then aroused and influenced to desire voluntarily that to which they are directed; just as we see in the book of Medicine that through potions and many medicines people can be changed in body and in the passions of the soul and in the inclination of the will.

There are, moreover, other inventions belonging more to nature which do not have as their object a marvelous change in the will, and they are diversified in character. Some of these possess an excellence of wisdom with other advantages, as, for example, perpetual baths most suitable for human use that do not require any artificial renewal; and ever-burning lamps. For we see many things that cannot be impaired by fire, nay, that are purified by fire, like the skin of the salamander and many other things of this kind, which also can be so prepared that they are externally luminous of themselves, and retain the power of fire, and give forth flame and light. Moreover, against foes of the state they have discovered important arts, so that without a sword or any weapon requiring physical contact they could destroy all who offer resistance. There are many kinds of these inventions. Some of these are perceived by no one of the senses, or by smell alone, and of these inventions Aristotle's book explains that of altering the air, but not those of which I spoke above. These last are of a different character, since they act by means of an infection. There are others also that change some one of the senses, and they are diversified in accordance with all the senses.

Certain of these work a change by contact only and thus destroy life. For malta, which is a kind of bitumen and is plentiful in this world, when cast upon an armed man burns him up. The Romans suffered severe loss of life from this in their conquests, as Pliny states in the second book of the Natural History, and as the histories attest. Similarly yellow petroleum, that is, oil springing from the rock, burns up whatever it meets if it is properly prepared. For a consuming fire is produced by this which can be extinguished with difficulty; for water cannot put it out. Certain inventions disturb the hearing to such a degree that, if they are set off suddenly at night with sufficient skill, neither city nor army can endure them. No clap of thunder could compare with such noises. Certain of these strike such terror to the sight that the coruscations of the clouds disturb it incomparably less. Gideon is thought to have employed inventions similar to these in the camp of the Midianites. We have an example of this in that toy of children which is made in many parts of the world, namely, an instrument as large as the human thumb. From the force of the salt called saltpeter so horrible a sound is produced at the bursting of so small a thing, namely, a small piece of parchment, that we perceive it exceeds the roar of sharp thunder, and the flash exceeds the greatest brilliancy of the lightning accompanying the thunder.

There are also very many things that slay every poisonous animal by the gentlest touch, and if a circle is made around these animals with things of this kind the animals cannot get out, but die, although they are not touched. But if a man is bitten by a poisonous animal, by the application of the powder of such things he can be healed, as Bede states in his Ecclesiastical History and as we know by experience. And thus there are innumerable things that have strange virtues, whose potencies we are ignorant of solely from our neglect of experiment.

But there are other inventions which do not possess such advantage for the state, but are to be looked upon as miracles of nature, such as experiments with the magnet, not only on iron, but on gold and other metals. Moreover, if the experiment on iron were not known, it would be viewed as a great miracle. And surely in respect to the action of the magnet on iron there are phenomena unknown to those who use the magnet which show in a wonderful way the dissolutions of nature. Just as also from these the faithful experimenter knows how to experiment on the mutual attraction of other things, as, for example, the stone that passes to the acid, and bitumen that ignites from fire placed at a distance from it, as Pliny states in the second book of the Natural History; and certain other things that are mutually attracted although locally separated. This is truly wonderful beyond all that I have seen and heard. For after I saw this, there has been nothing difficult for my intellect to believe, provided it had a trustworthy authority. And that this fact may not be hidden from your Reverence, this phenomenon occurs in the parts of plants divided and locally separated. For if a sapling of one year's growth is taken, which springs forth beside the roots of the hazel, and is divided longitudinally, and the divided parts separated by the space of a palm or four fingers, and one person holds on one side the extremities of the two parts, and another similarly on the other side, always with an equal and gentle grasp, so that the parts are kept opposite each other in the same position they had before the division, within the space of half a mile the parts of the twig begin to approach each other gradually, but with greater force at the end of the experiment, so that at length they meet and are united. The ends, however, remain apart, because they are prevented from meeting owing to the force exerted by those holding the parts. This is a very wonderful thing. For this reason magicians perform this experiment, repeating different incantations, and they believe that the phenomenon is caused by virtue of the incantations. I have disregarded the incantations and have discovered the wonderful action of nature, which is similar to that of the magnet on iron. For just as the one attracts the other because of the similar nature of the iron and the magnet, so do the parts in this case. Hence the natural force, which is similar in both parts of the twig, causes them to unite. If they were arranged in the required way, they would meet at the extremities just as in the middle and more quickly, as, for example, if the ends were minutely pierced and threads passed through the ends, so that they could be suspended in the air without hindrance. This is true not only of hazel saplings but of many others, as in the case of willows and perhaps in that of all saplings if they were arranged in the required manner. But since in such matters the mind thinks more aptly than the pen writes, I forbear for the present. I am here merely writing down the statements of scientists and noting their achievements. The genius of these men I admire more than I understand.

Concluding thus the subject of this science experimental without restriction, I shall now show its advantage to theology, as I have done similarly in the case of the other sciences. Since I have now shown the intrinsic nature of this science, it is evident to all that next to moral philosophy this science is the most useful, and it is so in the first place to theology itself in its unrestricted sense because of the literal and spiritual meaning in which it consists. For I showed above that the literal meaning consists in expressing the truth in regard to created things by means of their definitions and descriptions, and I likewise showed that reasoning does not arrive at this truth, but that experiment does. Wherefore this science next to moral philosophy will present the literal truth of Scripture most effectively, so that through suitable adaptations and similitudes the spiritual sense may be derived, owing to the peculiar nature of the sacred Scripture and in accordance with the methods employed by the sacred writers and by all sages.

Then this science as regards the commonwealth of believers is useful, as we saw in its special knowledge of the future, present, and past, and in its display of wonderful works on behalf of Church and state, so that all useful activities are promoted and the opposite are hindered both in the few and in the multitude, as was explained. And if we proceed to the conversion of unbelievers, it is evidently of service in two main ways with numerous subdivisions, since a plea for the faith can be effectively made through this science, not by arguments but by works, which is the more effective way. For to the man who denies the truth of the faith because he cannot understand it I shall state the mutual attraction of things in nature, just as I described it. Likewise I shall tell him that a jar may be broken without human force, and the wine contained in it remain motionless and without flow for three days; and that gold and silver in a pouch, and a sword in its scabbard may be consumed without injury to their containers, as Seneca states in the book of Natural Questions. I shall tell him, moreover, that the birds called kingfisher in the depth of winter compel the stormy sea to be calm and restrain itself until they have laid their eggs and brought forth their young, as Basil and Ambrose in the Hexaemeron and philosophers and poets state. For these facts and similar ones ought to influence a man and urge him to accept the divine verities. Since if in the vilest creatures verities are found by which the pride of the human intellect ought to be subdued so that it may believe them although it does not understand them, conviction should follow, or injury will be done to infallible truth, since a man ought rather to humble his mind to the glorious truths of God. Surely there is no comparison.

But there is still another very useful way; since the formation of judgments, as I have said, is a function of this science, in regard to what can happen by nature or be effected in art, and what not. This science, moreover, knows how to separate the illusions of magic and to detect all their errors in incantations, invocations, conjurations, sacrifices, and cults. But unbelievers busy themselves in these mad acts and trust in them, and have believed that the Christians used such means in working their miracles. Wherefore this science is of the greatest advantage in persuading men to accept the faith, since this branch alone of philosophy happens to proceed in this way, because this is the only branch that considers matters of this kind, and is able to overcome all falsehood and superstition and error of unbelievers in regard to magic, such as incantations and the like already mentioned. How far, moreover, it may serve to reprobate obstinate unbelievers is already shown by the violent means that have just been touched upon, and therefore I pass on.

We must consider, however, that although other sciences do many wonders, as in the case of practical geometry, which produces mirrors that burn up every opposing object, and so too in the other sciences, yet all things of such wonderful utility in the state belong chiefly to this science. For this science has the same relation to the other sciences as the science of navigation to the carpenter's art and the military art to that of the engineer. For this science teaches how wonderful instruments may be made, and uses them when made, and also considers all secret things owing to the advantages they may possess for the state and for individuals; and it directs other sciences as its handmaids, and therefore the whole power of speculative science is attributed especially to this science. And now the wonderful advantage derived from these three sciences in this world on behalf of the Church of God against the enemies of the faith is manifest, who should be destroyed rather by the discoveries of science than by the warlike arms of combatants. Antichrist will use these means freely and effectively, in order that he may crush and confound the power of this world; and by these means tyrants in times past brought the world under their sway. This has been shown by examples without end.

But I now cite the one example of Alexander the Great in place of all other examples that might be cited, who when he set out from Greece to conquer the world had only 32,000 foot soldiers and 4500 horsemen, as Orosius states to Augustine in his book Ormesta Mundi, bringing war with so small a force upon the whole world. It is uncertain which is the more wonderful, that he conquered or that he ventured the attack. In his first battle with King Darius he overcame 600,000 Persians with a loss in his army of 120 horsemen and nine foot soldiers. In the second battle he conquered 400,000 men, and of his own army 130 foot soldiers and 150 horsemen fell. After this he easily subdued the rest of the world, which had become terrified. But Orosius says that he conquered not less by skill than by the valor of the Macedonians. Nor is it to be wondered at, since Aristotle was with him in these wars, as we read in the life of Aristotle. Seneca, moreover, states in the Natural Questions that Alexander conquered the world under the guidance of Aristotle and Callisthenes, who were his teachers in all knowledge. But Aristotle was his chief teacher; and it is easily apparent from what has been said how by the paths of knowledge Aristotle was able to hand over the world to Alexander. Moreover, the Church should consider the employment of these inventions against unbelievers and rebels, in order that it may spare Christian blood, and especially should it do so because of future perils in the times of Antichrist, which with the grace of God it would be easy to meet, if prelates and princes promoted study and investigated the secrets of nature and of art.

৶৯ SUMMA THEOLOGICA

Thomas Aquinas

St. Thomas (1225–1274) was the youngest son of Landulf, Count of Aquino near Naples. Despite the opposition of his family he entered the Dominican Order in 1243, just twenty-seven years after its founding by St. Dominic, and played a leading part in the establishment of Dominican houses of studies in France, Italy, and Germany. He was a pupil and colleague of St. Albert ("the Great") at the universities of Paris and Cologne, and carried out brilliantly his master's project of incorporating the basic insights of Greek philosophy, especially those of Aristotle, within the Christian world view.

Like the other philosophers of the Middle Ages, St. Thomas insisted that it was necessary to accept the Christian faith in order to pursue truth properly. His reasons for this belief are discussed in the selections below. St. Thomas makes a fundamental distinction between philosophy and theology, or "sacred doctrine." Philosophy is based not on faith but on "natural reason," reason is severely limited in its ability to know God and, therefore, the ultimate principles and meaning of our existence, but it can nevertheless grasp fully those objects with which it is naturally fitted to deal. There is thus a proper realm of secular knowledge, and here the ancient Greeks, despite their total ignorance of Christianity, managed to discover the basic truths. In this area, St. Thomas thought, we are and will always remain their students.

But this secular knowledge takes on a new significance in the wider context of the Christian drama of the fall, redemption, and ultimate salvation of man as revealed in the Holy Scriptures. The task of theology is to articulate this total outlook. As its title indicates, this is what is attempted by the Summa Theologica *(1267–1273), the longest and best known of St. Thomas' many writings, from which the following selections are taken.*

The Summa *is divided into three parts: the first on God, the second on the movement of rational creatures toward God, and the third on Christ as the way to God. Our selections are from Part 1 and from the first section of Part 2. Each part is divided into a large number of questions, and each of these questions into several articles. Each article consists of (1) one or more objections to the position St. Thomas considers the true one, followed by (2) a piece of evidence (a quotation from some authority, or a counter-argument) that conflicts with these objections and thus creates a problem, (3) his own solution (beginning, "I answer that") to the problem, and finally (4) the specific answers to the objections, based on the doctrine worked out in his solution. Note that an issue is never settled by appeal to authority—even to the authority of the Scriptures—despite the fact that this is a book of theology. In fact, there are often authorities on both sides of an issue, and one is left to figure out for himself what to do about it. In his choice of method, St. Thomas repeats the lesson of Peter Abélard's* Sic et Non.

PART ONE

Question I: The Nature and Domain of Sacred Doctrine

First Article: Whether, besides the philosophical sciences, any further doctrine is required?

We proceed thus to the First Article:—

Objection 1. It seems that, besides the philosophical sciences, we have no need of any further knowledge. For man should not seek to know what is above reason: *Seek not the things that are too high for thee* (*Ecclus.* iii. 22). But whatever is not above reason is sufficiently considered in the philosophical sciences. Therefore any other knowledge besides the philosophical sciences is superfluous.

Obj. 2. Further, knowledge can be concerned only with being, for nothing can be known, save the true, which is convertible with being. But everything that is, is considered in the philosophical sciences—even God Himself; so that there is a part of philosophy called theology, or the divine science, as is clear from Aristotle. Therefore, besides the philosophical sciences, there is no need of any further knowledge.

On the contrary, It is written (*2. Tim.* iii. 16): *All Scripture inspired of God is profitable to teach, to reprove, to correct, to instruct in justice.* Now Scripture, inspired of God, is not a part of the philosophical sciences discovered by human reason.

Introduction to Saint Thomas Aquinas, ed. Anton C. Pegis (New York: Random House, 1948), pp. 3–5, 20–27, 66–68, 616–625, 635–638, 640–642, 646–656.

Therefore it is useful that besides the philosophical sciences there should be another science—*i.e.*, inspired of God.

I answer that, It was necessary for man's salvation that there should be a knowledge revealed by God, besides the philosophical sciences investigated by human reason. First, because man is directed to God as to an end that surpasses the grasp of his reason: *The eye hath not seen, O God, besides Thee, what things Thou hast prepared for them that wait for Thee* (*Isa.* lxiv. 4). But the end must first be known by men who are to direct their thoughts and actions to the end. Hence it was necessary for the salvation of man that certain truths which exceed human reason should be made known to him by divine revelation. Even as regards those truths about God which human reason can investigate, it was necessary that man be taught by a divine revelation. For the truth about God, such as reason can know it, would only be known by a few, and that after a long time, and with the admixture of many errors; whereas man's whole salvation, which is in God, depends upon the knowledge of this truth. Therefore, in order that the salvation of men might be brought about more fitly and more surely, it was necessary that they be taught divine truths by divine revelation. It was therefore necessary that, besides the philosophical sciences investigated by reason, there should be a sacred science by way of revelation.

Reply Obj. 1. Although those things which are beyond man's knowledge may not be sought for by man through his reason, nevertheless, what is revealed by God must be accepted through faith. Hence the sacred text continues, *For many things are shown to thee above the understanding of man* (*Ecclus.* iii. 25). And in such things sacred science consists.

Reply Obj. 2. Sciences are diversified according to the diverse nature of their knowable objects. For the astronomer and the physicist both prove the same conclusion—that the earth, for instance, is round: the astronomer by means of mathematics (*i.e.*, abstracting from matter), but the physicist by means of matter itself. Hence there is no reason why those things which are treated by the philosophical sciences, so far as they can be known by the light of natural reason, may not also be treated by another science so far as they are known by the light of the divine revelation. Hence the theology included in sacred doctrine differs in genus from that theology which is part of philosophy. . . .

Question II: The Existence of God

First Article: Whether the existence of God is self-evident?
We proceed thus to the First Article:—

Objection 1. It seems that the existence of God is self-evident. For those things are said to be self-evident to us the knowledge of which exists naturally in us, as we can see in regard to first principles. But as Damascene says, *the knowledge of God is naturally implanted in all.* Therefore the existence of God is self-evident.

Obj. 2. Further, those things are said to be self-evident which are known as soon as the terms are known, which the Philosopher * says is true of the first principles of demonstration. Thus, when the nature of a whole and of a part is known, it is at

* [Whenever St. Thomas speaks simply of "the Philosopher," he means Aristotle. This extraodinary compliment indicates the respect in which Aristotle's writings were held. (*Ed.*)]

once recognized that every whole is greater than its part. But as soon as the signification of the name *God* is understood, it is at once seen that God exists. For by this name is signified that thing than which nothing greater can be conceived. But that which exists actually and mentally is greater than that which exists only mentally. Therefore, since as soon as the name *God* is understood it exists mentally, it also follows that it exists actually. Therefore the proposition *God exists* is self-evident.

Obj. 3. Further, the existence of truth is self-evident. For whoever denies the existence of truth grants that truth does not exist: and, if truth does not exist, then the proposition *Truth does not exist* is true: and if there is anything true there must be truth. But God is truth itself: *I am the way, the truth, and the life (Jo.* xiv. 6). Therefore *God exists* is self-evident.

On the contrary, No one can mentally admit the opposite of what is self-evident, as the Philosopher states concerning the first principles of demonstration. But the opposite of the proposition *God is* can be mentally admitted: *The fool said in his heart, There is no God (Ps.* lii. 1). Therefore, that God exists is not self-evident.

I answer that, A thing can be self-evident in either of two ways: on the one hand, self-evident in itself, though not to us; on the other, self-evident in itself, and to us. A proposition is self-evident because the predicate is included in the essence of the subject: *e.g., Man is an animal,* for animal is contained in the essence of man. If, therefore, the essence of the predicate and subject be known to all, the proposition will be self-evident to all; as is clear with regard to the first principles of demonstration, the terms of which are certain common notions that no one is ignorant of, such as being and non-being, whole and part, and the like. If, however, there are some to whom the essence of the predicate and subject is unknown, the proposition will be self-evident in itself, but not to those who do not know the meaning of the predicate and subject of the proposition. Therefore, it happens, as Boethius says, that there are some notions of the mind which are common and self-evident only to the learned, as that incorporeal substances are not in space. Therefore I say that this proposition, *God exists,* of itself is self-evident, for the predicate is the same as the subject, because God is His own existence as will be hereafter shown. Now because we do not know the essence of God, the proposition is not self-evident to us, but needs to be demonstrated by things that are more known to us, though less known in their nature—namely, by His effects.

Reply Obj. 1. To know that God exists in a general and confused way is implanted in us by nature, inasmuch as God is man's beatitude. For man naturally desires happiness, and what is naturally desired by man is naturally known by him. This, however, is not to know absolutely that God exists; just as to know that someone is approaching is not the same as to know that Peter is approaching, even though it is Peter who is approaching; for there are many who imagine that man's perfect good, which is happiness, consists in riches, and others in pleasures, and others in something else.

Reply Obj. 2. Perhaps not everyone who hears this name *God* understands it to signify something than which nothing greater can be thought, seeing that some have believed God to be a body. Yet, granted that everyone understands that by this name *God* is signified something than which nothing greater can be thought, nevertheless, it does not therefore follow that he understands that what the name signifies exists actually, but only that it exists mentally. Nor can it be argued that it actually exists, unless it be admitted that there actually exists something than which nothing greater can be thought; and this precisely is not admitted by those who hold that God does not exist.

Reply Obj. 3. The existence of truth in general is self-evident, but the existence of a Primal Truth is not self-evident to us.

Second Article: Whether it can be demonstrated that God exists?
We proceed thus to the Second Article:—

Objection 1. It seems that the existence of God cannot be demonstrated. For it is an article of faith that God exists. But what is of faith cannot be demonstrated, because a demonstration produces scientific knowledge, whereas faith is of the unseen, as is clear from the Apostle (*Heb.* xi. 1). Therefore it cannot be demonstrated that God exists.

Obj. 2. Further, essence is the middle term of demonstration. But we cannot know in what God's essence consists, but solely in what it does not consist, as Damascene says. Therefore we cannot demonstrate that God exists.

Obj. 3. Further, if the existence of God were demonstrated, this could only be from His effects. But His effects are not proportioned to Him, since He is infinite and His effects are finite, and between the finite and infinite there is no proportion. Therefore, since a cause cannot be demonstrated by an effect not proportioned to it, it seems that the existence of God cannot be demonstrated.

On the contrary, The Apostle * says: *The invisible things of Him are clearly seen, being understood by the things that are made* (*Rom.* i. 20). But this would not be unless the existence of God could be demonstrated through the things that are made; for the first thing we must know of anything is, whether it exists.

I answer that, Demonstration can be made in two ways: One is through the cause, and is called *propter quid,* and this is to argue from what is prior absolutely. The other is through the effect, and is called a demonstration *quia;* this is to argue from what is prior relatively only to us. When an effect is better known to us than its cause, from the effect we proceed to the knowledge of the cause. And from every effect the existence of its proper cause can be demonstrated, so long as its effects are better known to us; because, since every effect depends upon its cause, if the effect exists, the cause must pre-exist. Hence the existence of God, in so far as it is not self-evident to us, can be demonstrated from those of His effects which are known to us.

Reply Obj. 1. The existence of God and other like truths about God, which can be known by natural reason, are not articles of faith, but are preambles to the articles; for faith presupposes natural knowledge, even as grace presupposes nature and perfection the perfectible. Nevertheless, there is nothing to prevent a man, who cannot grasp a proof, from accepting, as a matter of faith, something which in itself is capable of being scientifically known and demonstrated.

Reply Obj. 2. When the existence of a cause is demonstrated from an effect, this effect takes the place of the definition of the cause in proving the cause's existence. This is especially the case in regard to God, because, in order to prove the existence

---

* ["The Apostle" always means St. Paul. (*Ed.*)]

of anything, it is necessary to accept as a middle term the meaning of the name, and not its essence, for the question of its essence follows on the question of its existence. Now the names given to God are derived from His effects, as will be later shown. Consequently, in demonstrating the existence of God from His effects, we may take for the middle term the meaning of the name *God.*

Reply Obj. 3. From effects not proportioned to the cause no perfect knowledge of that cause can be obtained. Yet from every effect the existence of the cause can be clearly demonstrated, and so we can demonstrate the existence of God from His effects; though from them we cannot know God perfectly as He is in His essence.

Third Article: Whether God Exists?
We proceed thus to the Third Article:—

Objection 1. It seems that God does not exist; because if one of two contraries be infinite, the other would be altogether destroyed. But the name *God* means that He is infinite goodness. If, therefore, God existed, there would be no evil discoverable; but there is evil in the world. Therefore God does not exist.

Obj. 2. Further, it is superfluous to suppose that what can be accounted for by a few principles has been produced by many. But it seems that everything we see in the world can be accounted for by other principles, supposing God did not exist. For all natural things can be reduced to one principle, which is nature; and all voluntary things can be reduced to one principle, which is human reason, or will. Therefore there is no need to suppose God's existence.

On the contrary, It is said in the person of God: *I am Who am* (*Exod.* iii. 14).

I answer that, The existence of God can be proved in five ways.

The first and more manifest way is the argument from motion. It is certain, and evident to our senses, that in the world some things are in motion. Now whatever is moved is moved by another, for nothing can be moved except it is in potentiality to that towards which it is moved; whereas a thing moves inasmuch as it is in act. For motion is nothing else than the reduction of something from potentiality to actuality. But nothing can be reduced from potentiality to actuality, except by something in a state of actuality. Thus that which is actually hot, as fire, makes wood, which is potentially hot, to be actually hot, and thereby moves and changes it. Now it is not possible that the same thing should be at once in actuality and potentiality in the same respect but only in different respects. For what is actually hot cannot simultaneously be potentially hot; but it is simultaneously potentially cold. It is therefore impossible that in the same respect and in the same way a thing should be both mover and moved, *i.e.,* that it should move itself. Therefore, whatever is moved must be moved by another. If that by which it is moved be itself moved, then this also must needs be moved by another, and that by another again. But this cannot go on to infinity, because then there would be no first mover, and, consequently, no other mover, seeing that subsequent movers move only inasmuch as they are moved by the first mover; as the staff moves only because it is moved by the hand. Therefore it is necessary to arrive at a first mover, moved by no other; and this everyone understands to be God.

The second way is from the nature of efficient cause. In the world of sensible things we find there is an order of efficient causes. There is no case known (neither is it, indeed, possible) in which a thing is found to be the efficient cause of itself; for so it would be prior to itself, which is impossible. Now in efficient causes it is not possible to go on to infinity, because in all efficient causes following in order, the first is the cause of the intermediate cause, and the intermediate is the cause of the ultimate cause, whether the intermediate cause be several, or one only. Now to take away the cause is to take away the effect. Therefore, if there be no first cause among efficient causes, there will be no ultimate, nor any intermediate, cause. But if in efficient causes it is possible to go on to infinity, there will be no first efficient cause, neither will there be an ultimate effect, nor any intermediate efficient causes; all of which is plainly false. Therefore it is necessary to admit a first efficient cause, to which everyone gives the name of God.

The third way is taken from possibility and necessity, and runs thus. We find in nature things that are possible to be and not to be, since they are found to be generated, and to be corrupted, and consequently, it is possible for them to be and not to be. But it is impossible for these always to exist, for that which can not-be at some time is not. Therefore, if everything can not-be, then at one time there was nothing in existence. Now if this were true, even now there would be nothing in existence, because that which does not exist begins to exist only through something already existing. Therefore, if at one time nothing was in existence, it would have been impossible for anything to have begun to exist; and thus even now nothing would be in existence—which is absurd. Therefore, not all beings are merely possible, but there must exist something the existence of which is necessary. But every necessary thing either has its necessity caused by another, or not. Now it is impossible to go on to infinity in necessary things which have their necessity caused by another, as has been already proved in regard to efficient causes. Therefore we cannot but admit the existence of some being having of itself its own necessity, and not receiving it from another, but rather causing in others their necessity. This all men speak of as God.

The fourth way is taken from the gradation to be found in things. Among beings there are some more and some less good, true, noble, and the like. But *more* and *less* are predicted of different things according as they resemble in their different ways something which is the maximum, as a thing is said to be hotter according as it more nearly resembles that which is hottest; so that there is something which is truest, something best, something noblest, and, consequently, something which is most being, for those things that are greatest in truth are greatest in being, as it is written in *Metaph.* ii.* Now the maximum in any genus is the cause of all in that genus, as fire, which is the maximum of heat, is the cause of all hot things, as is said in the same book. Therefore there must also be something which is to all beings the cause of their being, goodness, and every other perfection; and this we call God.

The fifth way is taken from the governance of the world. We see that things which lack knowledge, such as natural bodies, act for an end, and this is evident from their acting always, or nearly always, in the same way, so as to obtain the best result. Hence

---

* [Whenever St. Thomas refers to a book by its title like this, without indicating the author, it is always a work by Aristotle (or the Bible). (*Ed.*)]

it is plain that they achieve their end, not fortuitously, but designedly. Now whatever lacks knowledge cannot move towards an end, unless it be directed by some being endowed with knowledge and intelligence; as the arrow is directed by the archer. Therefore some intelligent being exists by whom all natural things are directed to their end; and this being we call God.

Reply Obj. 1. As Augustine says: *Since God is the highest good, He would not allow any evil to exist in His works, unless His omnipotence and goodness were such as to bring good even out of evil.* This is part of the infinite goodness of God, that He should allow evil to exist, and out of it produce good.

Reply Obj. 2. Since nature works for a determinate end under the direction of a higher agent, whatever is done by nature must be traced back to God as to its first cause. So likewise whatever is done voluntarily must be traced back to some higher cause other than human reason and will, since these can change and fail; for all things that are changeable and capable of defect must be traced back to an immovable and self-necessary first principle, as has been shown. . . .

Question XI: The Unity of God

Third Article: Whether God is one?

We proceed thus to the Third Article:—

Objection 1. It seems that God is not one. For it is written, *For there be many gods and many lords* (*1 Cor.* viii. 5).

Obj. 2. Further, *one,* as the principle of number, cannot be predicated of God, since quantity is not predicated of God; likewise, neither can *one* which is convertible with *being* be predicated of God, because it imports privation, and every privation is an imperfection, which cannot apply to God. Therefore God is not one.

On the contrary, It is written, *Hear, O Israel, the Lord our God is one Lord* (*Deut.* vi. 4).

I answer that, It can be shown from three sources that God is one. First from His simplicity. For it is manifest that the reason why any singular thing is *this particular thing* is because it cannot be communicated to many, since that whereby Socrates is a man can be communicated to many, whereas what makes him this particular man is communicable only to one. Therefore, if Socrates were a man by what makes him to be this particular man, as there cannot be many Socrateses, so there could not in that way be many men. Now this belongs to God alone; for God Himself is His own nature, as was shown above.* Therefore, in the very same way God is God and this God. It is impossible therefore that there should be many gods.

Secondly, this is proved from the infinity of His perfection. For it was shown above that God comprehends in Himself the whole perfection of being. If, then, many gods existed, they would necessarily differ from each other. Something therefore, would belong to one which did not belong to another. And if this were a privation, one of them would not be absolutely perfect; but if a perfection, one of them would be without it. So it is impossible for many gods to exist. Hence also the ancient philos-

---

* [St. Thomas often refers to earlier passages in the *Summa*, where he has already demonstrated the point in question, as is done in geometry. We have omitted the specific references, since most of these passages are not included in our selections. (*Ed.*)]

ophers, constrained as it were by truth, when they asserted an infinite principle, asserted likewise that there was only one such principle.

Thirdly, this is shown from the unity of the world. For all things that exist are seen to be ordered to each other since some serve others. But things that are diverse do not come together in the same order unless they are ordered thereto by some one being. For many are reduced into one order by one better than by many: because one is the *per se* cause of one, and many are only the accidental cause of one, inasmuch as they are in some way one. Since, therefore, what is first is most perfect, and is so *per se* and not accidentally, it must be that the first which reduces all into one order should be only one. And this is God.

Reply Obj. 1. Gods are called many by the error of some who worshipped many deities, thinking as they did that the planets and other stars were gods, and also the particular parts of the world. Hence the Apostle adds: *Our God is one,* etc. (*1 Cor.* viii. 6).

Reply Obj. 2. *One* which is the principle of number is not predicated of God, but only of material things. For *one* which is the principle of number belongs to the *genus* of mathematicals, which are material in being, and abstracted from matter only in idea. But *one* which is convertible with being is something metaphysical and does not, in being, depend on matter. And although in God there is no privation, still, according to the mode of our apprehension, He is known to us by way only of privation and remotion. Thus there is no reason why certain privative terms should not be predicated of God, for instance, that He is *incorporeal,* and *infinite;* and in the same way it is said of God that He is *one.* . . .

Question XCI: On the Various Kinds of Law

First Article: Whether there is an eternal law?
We proceed thus to the First Article:—

Objection 1. It would seem that there is no eternal law. For every law is imposed on someone. But there was not someone from eternity on whom a law could be imposed, since God alone was from eternity. Therefore no law is eternal.

Obj. 2. Further, promulgation is essential to law. But promulgation could not be from eternity, because there was no one to whom it could be promulgated from eternity. Therefore no law can be eternal.

Obj. 3. Further, law implies order to an end. But nothing ordained to an end is eternal, for the last end alone is eternal. Therefore no law is eternal.

On the contrary, Augustine says: *That Law which is the Supreme Reason cannot be understood to be otherwise than unchangeable and eternal.*

I answer that, As we have stated above, law is nothing else but a dictate of practical reason emanating from the ruler who governs a perfect community. Now it is evident, granted that the world is ruled by divine providence, as was stated in the First Part, that the whole community of the universe is governed by the divine reason. Therefore the very notion of the government of things in God, the ruler of the universe, has the nature of a law. And since the divine reason's conception of things is not subject to time, but is eternal, according to *Prov.* viii. 23, therefore it is that this kind of law must be called eternal.

Reply Obj. 1. Those things that do not exist in themselves exist in God, inasmuch as they are known and preordained by Him, according to *Rom.* iv. 17: *Who calls those things that are not, as those that are.* Accordingly, the eternal concept of the divine law bears the character of an eternal law in so far as it is ordained by God to the government of things foreknown by Him.

Reply Obj. 2. Promulgation is made by word of mouth or in writing, and in both ways the eternal law is promulgated, because both the divine Word and the writing of the Book of Life are eternal. But the promulgation cannot be from eternity on the part of the creature that hears or reads.

Reply Obj. 3. Law implies order to the end actively, namely, in so far as it directs certain things to the end; but not passively,—that is to say, the law itself is not ordained to the end, except accidentally, in a governor whose end is extrinsic to him, and to which end his law must needs be ordained. But the end of the divine government is God Himself, and His law is not something other than Himself. Therefore the eternal law is not ordained to another end.

Second Article: Whether there is in us a natural law?
We proceed thus to the Second Article:—

Objection 1. It would seem that there is no natural law in us. For man is governed sufficiently by the eternal law, since Augustine says that *the eternal law is that by which it is right that all things should be most orderly.* But nature does not abound in superfluities as neither does she fail in necessaries. Therefore man has no natural law.

Obj. 2. Further, by the law man is directed, in his acts, to the end, as was stated above. But the directing of hmuan acts to their end is not a function of nature, as is the case in irrational creatures, which act for an end solely by their natural appetite; whereas man acts for an end by his reason and will. Therefore man has no natural law.

Obj. 3. Further, the more a man is free, the less is he under the law. But man is freer than all the animals because of his free choice, with which he is endowed in distinction from all other animals. Since, therefore, other animals are not subject to a natural law, neither is man subject to a natural law.

On the contrary, The *Gloss* on *Rom.* ii. 14 (*When the Gentiles, who have not the law, do by nature those things that are of the law*) comments as follows: *Although they have no written law, yet they have the natural law, whereby each one knows, and is conscious of, what is good and what is evil.*

I answer that, As we have stated above, law, being a rule and measure, can be in a person in two ways: in one way, as in him that rules and measures; in another way, as in that which is ruled and measured, since a thing is ruled and measured in so far as it partakes of the rule or measure. Therefore, since all things subject to divine providence are ruled and measured by the eternal law, as was stated above, it is evident that all things partake in some way in the eternal law, in so far as, namely, from its being imprinted on them, they derive their respective inclinations to their proper acts and ends. Now among all others, the rational creature is subject to divine providence in a more excellent way, in so far as it itself partakes of a share of providence, by being provident both for itself and for others. Therefore it has a share of the eternal reason, whereby it has a natural inclination to its proper act and end;

and this participation of the eternal law in the rational creature is called the natural law. Hence the Psalmist, after saying (*Ps.* iv. 6): *Offer up the sacrifice of justice,* as though someone asked what the works of justice are, adds: *Many say, Who showeth us good things?* in answer to which question he says: *The light of Thy countenance, O Lord, is signed upon us.* He thus implies that the light of natural reason, whereby we discern what is good and what is evil, which is the function of the natural law, is nothing else than an imprint on us of the divine light. It is therefore evident that the natural law is nothing else than the rational creature's participation of the eternal law.

Reply Obj. 1. This argument would hold if the natural law were something different from the eternal law; whereas it is nothing but a participation thereof, as we have stated above.

Reply Obj. 2. Every act of reason and will in us is based on that which is according to nature, as was stated above. For every act of reasoning is based on principles that are known naturally, and every act of appetite in respect of the means is derived from the natural appetite in respect of the last end. Accordingly, the first direction of our acts to their end must needs be through the natural law.

Reply Obj. 3. Even irrational animals partake in their own way of the eternal reason, just as the rational creature does. But because the rational creature partakes thereof in an intellectual and rational manner, therefore the participation of the eternal law in the rational creature is properly called a law, since a law is something pertaining to reason, as was stated above. Irrational creatures, however, do not partake thereof in a rational manner, and therefore there is no participation of the eternal law in them, except by way of likeness.

Third Article: Whether there is a human law?
We proceed thus to the Third Article:—

Objection 1. It would seem that there is not a human law. For the natural law is a participation of the eternal law, as was stated above. Now through the eternal law *all things are most orderly,* as Augustine states. Therefore the natural law suffices for the ordering of all human affairs. Consequently there is no need for a human law.

Obj. 2. Further, law has the character of a measure, as was stated above. But human reason is not a measure of things, but *vice versa,* as is stated in *Metaph.* x. Therefore no law can emanate from the human reason.

Obj. 3. Further, a measure should be most certain, as is stated in *Metaph.* x. But the dictates of the human reason in matters of conduct are uncertain, according to *Wis.* ix. 14: *The thoughts of mortal men are fearful, and our counsels uncertain.* Therefore no law can emanate from the human reason.

On the contrary, Augustine distinguishes two kinds of law, the one eternal, the other temporal, which he calls human.

I answer that, As we have stated above, a law is a dictate of the practical reason. Now it is to be observed that the same procedure takes place in the practical and in the speculative reason, for each proceeds from principles to conclusions, as was stated above. Accordingly, we conclude that, just as in the speculative reason, from naturally known indemonstrable principles we draw the conclusions of the various sciences, the knowledge of which is not imparted to us by nature, but acquired by the efforts of reason, so too it is that from the precepts of the natural law, as from common and indemonstrable principles, the human reason needs to proceed to the more particular determination of certain matters. These particular determinations, devised by human reason, are called human laws, provided that the other essential conditions of law be observed, as was stated above. Therefore Tully * says in his *Rhetoric* that *justice has its source in nature; thence certain things came into custom by reason of their utility; afterwards these things which emanated from nature, and were approved by custom, were sanctioned by fear and reverence for the law.*

Reply Obj. 1. The human reason cannot have a full participation of the dictate of the divine reason, but according to its own mode, and imperfectly. Consequently, just as on the part of the speculative reason, by a natural participation of divine wisdom, there is in us the knowledge of certain common principles, but not a proper knowledge of each single truth, such as that contained in the divine wisdom, so, too, on the part of the practical reason, man has a natural participation of the eternal law, according to certain common principles, but not as regards the particular determinations of individual cases, which are, however, contained in the eternal law. Hence the need for human reason to proceed further to sanction them by law.

Reply Obj. 2. Human reason is not, of itself, the rule of things. But the principles impressed on it by nature are the general rules and measures of all things relating to human conduct, of which the natural reason is the rule and measure, although it is not the measure of things that are from nature.

Reply Obj. 3. The practical reason is concerned with operable matters, which are singular and contingent, but not with necessary things, with which the speculative reason is concerned. Therefore human laws cannot have that inerrancy that belongs to the demonstrated conclusions of the sciences. Nor is it necessary for every measure to be altogether unerring and certain, but according as it is possible in its own partcular genus.

Fourth Article: Whether there was any need for a divine law?
We proceed thus to the Fourth Article:—

Objection 1. It would seem that there was no need for a divine law. For, as was stated above, the natural law is a participation in us of the eternal law. But the eternal law is the divine law, as was stated above. Therefore there is no need for a divine law in addition to the natural law and to human laws derived therefrom.

Obj. 2. Further, it is written (*Ecclus.* xv. 14) that *God left man in the hand of his own counsel.* Now counsel is an act of reason, as was stated above. Therefore man was left to the direction of his reason. But a dictate of human reason is a human law, as was stated above. Therefore there is no need for man to be governed also by a divine law.

Obj. 3. Further, human nature is more self-sufficing than irrational creatures. But irrational creatures have no divine law besides the natural inclination impressed on

* ["Tully" is Cicero, who ranked immediately behind Aristotle and Plato in the estimation of medieval Christian philosophers. (*Ed.*)]

them. Much less, therefore, should the rational creature have a divine law in addition to the natural law.

On the contrary, David prayed God to set His law before him, saying (*Ps.* cxviii. 33): *Set before me for a law the way of Thy justifications, O Lord.*

I answer that, Besides the natural and the human law it was necessary for the directing of human conduct to have a divine law. And this for four reasons. First, because it is by law that man is directed how to perform his proper acts in view of his last end. Now if man were ordained to no other end than that which is proportionate to his natural ability, there would be no need for man to have any further direction, on the part of his reason, in addition to the natural law and humanly devised law which is derived from it. But since man is ordained to an end of eternal happiness which exceeds man's natural ability, as we have stated above, therefore it was necessary that, in addition to the natural and the human law, man should be directed to his end by a law given by God.

Secondly, because, by reason of the uncertainty of human judgment, especially on contingent and particular matters, different people form different judgments on human acts; whence also different and contrary laws result. In order, therefore, that man may know without any doubt what he ought to do and what he ought to avoid, it was necessary for man to be directed in his proper acts by a law given by God, for it is certain that such a law cannot err.

Thirdly, because man can make laws in those matters of which he is competent to judge. But man is not competent to judge of interior movements, that are hidden, but only of exterior acts which are observable; and yet for the perfection of virtue it is necessary for man to conduct himself rightly in both kinds of acts. Consequently, human law could not sufficiently curb and direct interior acts, and it was necessary for this purpose that a divine law should supervene.

Fourthly, because, as Augustine says, human law cannot punish or forbid all evil deeds, since, while aiming at doing away with all evils, it would do away with many good things, and would hinder the advance of the common good, which is necessary for human living. In order, therefore, that no evil might remain unforbidden and unpunished, it was necessary for the divine law to supervene, whereby all sins are forbidden.

And these four causes are touched upon in *Ps.* cxviii. 8, where it is said: *The law of the Lord is unspotted, i.e.,* allowing no foulness of sin; *converting souls,* because it directs not only exterior, but also interior, acts; *the testimony of the Lord is faithful,* because of the certainty of what is true and right; *giving wisdom to little ones,* by directing man to an end supernatural and divine.

Reply Obj. 1. By the natural law the eternal law is participated proportionately to the capacity of human nature. But to his supernatural end man needs to be directed in a yet higher way. Hence the additional law given by God, whereby man shares more perfectly in the eternal law.

Reply Obj. 2. Counsel is a kind of inquiry, and hence must proceed from some principles. Nor is it enough for it to proceed from principles imparted by nature, which are the precepts of the natural law, for the reasons given above; but there is need for certain additional principles, namely, the precepts of the divine law.

Reply Obj. 3. Irrational creatures are not ordained to an end higher than that which is proportionate to their natural powers. Consequently the comparison fails.

Fifth Article: Whether there is but one divine law?
We proceed thus to the Fifth Article:—
Objection 1. It would seem that there is but one divine law. For, where there is one king in one kingdom, there is but one law. Now the whole of mankind is compared to God as to one king, according to *Ps.* xlvi. 8: *God is the King of all the earth.* Therefore there is but one divine law.

Obj. 2. Further, every law is directed to the end which the lawgiver intends for those for whom he makes the law. But God intends one and the same thing for all men, since according to *1 Tim.* ii. 4: *He will have all men to be saved, and to come to the knowledge of the truth.* Therefore there is but one divine law.

Obj. 3. Further, the divine law seems to be more akin to the eternal law, which is one, than the natural law, according as the revelation of grace is of a higher order than natural knowlege. But natural law is one for all men. Therefore much more is the divine law but one.

On the contrary, The Apostle says (*Heb.* vii. 12): *The priesthood being translated, it is necessary that a translation also be made of the law.* But the priesthood is twofold, as stated in the same passage, viz., the levitical priesthood, and the priesthood of Christ. Therefore the divine law is twofold, namely, the Old Law and the New Law.

I answer that, As we have stated in the First Part, distinction is the cause of number. Now things may be distinguished in two ways. First, as those things that are altogether specifically different, *e.g.,* a horse and an ox. Secondly, as perfect and imperfect in the same species, *e.g.,* a boy and a man; and in this way the divine law is distinguished into Old and New. Hence the Apostle (*Gal.* iii. 24, 25) compares the state of man under the Old Law to that of a child *under a pedagogue;* but the state under the New Law, to that of a full grown man, who is *no longer under a pedagogue.*

Now the perfection and imperfection of these two laws is to be taken in connection with the three conditions pertaining to law, as was stated above. For, in the first place, it belongs to law to be directed to the common good as to its end, as was stated above. This good may be twofold. It may be a sensible and earthly good, and to this man was directly ordained by the Old Law. Hence it is that, at the very outset of the Law, the people were invited to the earthly kingdom of the Chananaeans (*Exod.* iii. 8, 17). Again it may be an intelligible and heavenly good, and to this, man is ordained by the New Law. Therefore, at the very beginning of His preaching, Christ invited men to the kingdom of heaven, saying (*Matt.* iv. 17): *Do penance, for the kingdom of heaven is at hand.* Hence Augustine says that *promises of temporal goods are contained in the Old Testament, for which reason it is called old; but the promise of eternal life belongs to the New Testament.*

Secondly, it belongs to law to direct human acts according to the order of justice; wherein also the New Law surpasses the Old Law, since it directs our internal acts, according to *Matt.* v. 20: *Unless your justice abound more than that of the Scribes and Pharisees, you shall not enter into the kingdom of heaven.* Hence the saying that *the Old Law restrains the hand, but the New Law controls the soul.*

Thirdly, it belongs to law to induce men to observe its commandments. This the Old Law did by the fear of punishment, but the New Law, by love, which is poured into our hearts by the grace of Christ, bestowed in the New Law, but foreshadowed in the Old. Hence Augustine says that *there is little difference between the Law and the Gospel—fear* [timor] *and love* [amor].

Reply Obj. 1. As the father of a family issues different commands to the children and to the adults, so also the one King, God, in His one kingdom, gave one law to men while they were yet imperfect, and another more perfect law when, by the preceding law, they had been led to a greater capacity for divine things.

Reply Obj. 2. The salvation of man could not be achieved otherwise than through Christ, according to *Acts* iv. 12: *There is no other name* . . . *given to men, whereby we must be saved.* Consequently, the law that brings all to salvation could not be given until after the coming of Christ. But before His coming it was necessary to give to the people, of whom Christ was to be born, a law containing certain rudiments of justice unto salvation, in order to prepare them to receive Him.

Reply Obj. 3. The natural law directs man by way of certain general precepts, common to both the perfect and the imperfect. Hence it is one and the same for all. But the divine law directs man also in certain particular matters, to which the perfect and imperfect do not stand in the same relation. Hence the necessity for the divine law to by twofold, as we have already explained. . . .

Question XCIV: The Natural Law

Second Article: Whether the natural law contains several precepts, or only one?
We proceed thus to the Second Article:—

Objection 1. It would seem that the natural law contains not several precepts, but only one. For law is a kind of precept, as was stated above. If therefore there were many precepts of the natural law, it would follow that there are also many natural laws.

Obj. 2. Further, the natural law is consequent upon human nature. But human nature, as a whole, is one, though, as to its parts, it is manifold. Therefore, either there is but one precept of the law of nature because of the unity of nature as a whole, or there are many by reason of the number of parts of human nature. The result would be that even things relating to the inclination of the concupiscible power would belong to the natural law.

Obj. 3. Further, law is something pertaining to reason, as was stated above. Now reason is but one in man. Therefore there is only one precept of the natural law.

On the contrary, The precepts of the natural law in man stand in relation to operable matters as first principles do to matters of demonstration. But there are several first indemonstrable principles. Therefore there are also several precepts of the natural law.

I answer that, As was stated above, the precepts of the natural law are to the practical reason what the first principles of demonstrations are to the speculative reason, because both are self-evident principles. Now a thing is said to be self-evident in two ways: first, in itself; secondly, in relation to us. Any proposition is said to be self-evident in itself, if its predicate is contained in the notion of the subject; even though it may happen that to one who does not know the definition of the subject, such a proposition is not self-evident. For instance, this proposition, *Man is a rational being,* is, in its very nature, self-evident, since he who says *man,* says *a rational being;* and yet to one who does not know what a man is, this proposition is not self-evident. Hence it is that, as Boethius says, certain axioms or propositions are universally self-evident to all; and such are the propositions whose terms are known to all, as, *Every whole is greater than its part,* and, *Things equal to one and the same are equal to one another.* But some propositions are self-evident only to the wise, who understand the meaning of the terms of such propositions. Thus to one who understands that an angel is not a body, it is self-evident that an angel is not circumscriptively in a place. But this is not evident to the unlearned, for they cannot grasp it.

Now a certain order is to be found in those things that are apprehended by men. For that which first falls under apprehension is *being,* the understanding of which is included in all things whatsoever a man apprehends. Therefore the first indemonstrable principle is that *the same thing cannot be affirmed and denied at the same time,* which is based on the notion of *being* and *not-being:* and on this principle all others are based, as is stated in *Metaph.* iv. Now as *being* is the first thing that falls under the apprehension absolutely, so *good* is the first thing that falls under the apprehension of the practical reason, which is directed to action (since every agent acts for an end, which has the nature of good). Consequently, the first principle in the practical reason is one founded on the nature of good, viz., that *good is that which all things seek after.* Hence this is the first precept of law, that *good is to be done and promoted, and evil is to be avoided.* All other precepts of the natural law are based upon this; so that all the things which the practical reason naturally apprehends as man's good belong to the precepts of the natural law under the form of things to be done or avoided.

Since, however, good has the nature of an end, and evil, the nature of the contrary, hence it is that all those things to which man has a natural inclination are naturally apprehended by reason as being good, and consequently as objects of pursuit, and their contraries as evil, and objects of avoidance. Therefore, the order of the precepts of the natural law is according to the order of natural inclinations. For there is in man, first of all, an inclination to good in accordance with the nature which he has in common with all substances, inasmuch, namely, as every substance seeks the preservation of its own being, according to its nature; and by reason of this inclination, whatever is a means of preserving human life, and of warding off its obstacles, belongs to the natural law. Secondly, there is in man an inclination to things that pertain to him more specially, according to that nature which he has in common with other animals; and in virtue of this inclination, those things are said to belong to the natural law *which nature has taught to all animals,* such as sexual intercourse, the education of offspring and so forth. Thirdly, there is in man an inclination to good according to the nature of his reason, which nature is proper to him. Thus man has a natural inclination to know the truth about God, and to live in society; and in this respect, whatever pertains to this inclination belongs to the natural law: *e.g.,* to shun ignorance, to avoid offending those among whom one has to live, and other such things regarding the above inclination.

Reply Obj. 1. All these precepts of the law of nature have the character of one natural law, inasmuch as they flow from one first precept.

Reply. Obj. 2. All the inclinations of any parts whatsoever of human nature, *e.g.*, of the concupiscible and irascible parts, in so far as they are ruled by reason, belong to the natural law, and are reduced to one first precept, as was stated above. And thus the precepts of the natural law are many in themselves, but they are based on one common foundation.

Reply Obj. 3. Although reason is one in itself, yet it directs all things regarding man; so that whatever can be ruled by reason is contained under the law of reason. . . .

Fourth Article: Whether the natural law is the same in all men?
We proceed thus to the Fourth Article:—

Objection 1. It would seem that the natural law is not the same in all. For it is stated in the *Decretals* that *the natural law is that which is contained in the Law and the Gospel.* But this is not common to all men, because, as it is written (*Rom.* x. 16), *all do not obey the gospel.* Therefore the natural law is not the same in all men.

Obj. 2. Further, *Things which are according to the law are said to be just,* as is stated in *Ethics* v. But it is stated in the same book that nothing is so just for all as not to be subject to change in regard to some men. Therefore even the natural law is not the same in all men.

Obj. 3. Further, as was stated above, to the natural law belongs everything to which a man is inclined according to his nature. Now different men are naturally inclined to different things,—some to the desire of pleasures, others to the desire of honors, and other men to other things. Therefore, there is not one natural law for all.

On the contrary, Isidore says: *The natural law is common to all nations.*

I answer that, As we have stated above, to the natural law belong those things to which a man is inclined naturally; and among these it is proper to man to be inclined to act according to reason. Now it belongs to the reason to proceed from what is common to what is proper, as is stated in *Physics* i. The speculative reason, however, is differently situated, in this matter, from the practical reason. For, since the speculative reason is concerned chiefly with necessary things, which cannot be otherwise than they are, its proper conclusions, like the universal principles, contain the truth without fail. The practical reason, on the other hand, is concerned with contingent matters, which is the domain of human actions; and, consequently, although there is necessity in the common principles, the more we descend towards the particular, the more frequently we encounter defects. Accordingly, then, in speculative matters truth is the same in all men, both as to principles and as to conclusions; although the truth is not known to all as regards the conclusions, but only as regards the principles which are called *common notions.* But in matters of action, truth or practical rectitude is not the same for all as to what is particular, but only as to the common principles; and where there is the same rectitude in relation to particulars, it is not equally known to all.

It is therefore evident that, as regards the common principles whether of speculative or of practical reason, truth or rectitude is the same for all, and is equally known by all. But as to the proper conclusions of the speculative reason, the truth is the same for all, but it is not equally known to all. Thus, it is true for all that the three angles of a triangle are together equal to two right angles, although it is not known to all.

But as to the proper conclusions of the practical reason, neither is the truth or rectitude the same for all, nor, where it is the same, is it equally known by all. Thus, it is right and true for all to act according to reason, and from this principle it follows, as a proper conclusion, that goods entrusted to another should be restored to their owner. Now this is true for the majority of cases. But it may happen in a particular case that it would be injurious, and therefore unreasonable, to restore goods held in trust; for instance, if they are claimed for the purpose of fighting against one's country. And this principle will be found to fail the more, according as we descend further towards the particular, *e.g.,* if one were to say that goods held in trust should be restored with such and such a guarantee, or in such and such a way; because the greater the number of conditions added, the greater the number of ways in which the principle may fail, so that it be not right to restore or not to restore.

Consequently, we must say that the natural law, as to the first common principles, is the same for all, both as to rectitude and as to knowledge. But as to certain more particular aspects, which are conclusions, as it were, of those common principles, it is the same for all in the majority of cases, both as to rectitude and as to knowledge; and yet in some few cases it may fail, both as to rectitude, by reason of certain obstacles (just as natures subject to generation and corruption fail in some few cases because of some obstacle), and as to knowledge, since in some the reason is perverted by passion, or evil habit, or an evil disposition of nature. Thus at one time theft, although it is expressly contrary to the natural law, was not considered wrong among the Germans, as Julius Caesar relates.

Reply Obj. 1. The meaning of the sentence quoted is not that whatever is contained in the Law and the Gospel belongs to the natural law, since they contain many things that are above nature; but that whatever belongs to the natural law is fully contained in them. Therefore Gratian, after saying that *the natural law is what is contained in the Law and the Gospel,* adds at once, by way of example, *by which everyone is commanded to do to others as he would be done by.*

Reply Obj. 2. The saying of the Philosopher is to be understood of things that are naturally just, not as common principles, but as conclusions drawn from them, having recititude in the majority of cases, but failing in a few.

Reply Obj. 3. Just as in man reason rules and commands the other powers, so all the natural inclinations belonging to the other powers must needs be directed according to reason. Therefore it is universally right for all men that all their inclinations should be directed according to reason. . . .

Question XCV: Human Law

First Article: Whether it was useful for laws to be framed by men?

We proceed thus to the First Article:—

Objection 1. It would seem that it was not useful for laws to be framed by men. For the purpose of every law is that man be made good thereby, as was stated above. But men are more to be induced to be good willingly by means of admonitions, than against their will, by means of laws. Therefore there was no need to frame laws.

Obj. 2. Further, as the Philosopher says, *men have recourse to a judge as to animate justice.* But animate justice is better than inanimate justice, which is contained in laws. Therefore it would have been better for the execution of justice to be entrusted to the decision of judges than to frame laws in addition.

Obj. 3. Further, every law is framed for the direction of human actions, as is evident from what has been stated above. But since human actions are about singulars, which are infinite in number, matters pertaining to the direction of human actions cannot be taken into sufficient consideration except by a wise man, who looks into each one of them. Therefore it would have been better for human acts to be directed by the judgment of wise men, than by the framing of laws. Therefore there was no need of human laws.

On the contrary, Isidore says: *Laws were made that in fear thereof human audacity might be held in check, that innocence might be safeguarded in the midst of wickedness, and that the dread of punishment might prevent the wicked from doing harm.* But these things are most necessary to mankind. Therefore it was necessary that human laws should be made.

I answer that, As we have stated above, man has a natural aptitude for virtue; but the perfection of virtue must be acquired by man by means of some kind of training. Thus we observe that a man is helped by diligence in his necessities, for instance, in food and clothing. Certain beginnings of these he has from nature, viz., his reason and his hands; but he has not the full compliment, as other animals have, to whom nature has given sufficiently of clothing and food. Now it is difficult to see how man could suffice for himself in the matter of this training, since the perfection of virtue consists chiefly in withdrawing man from undue pleasures, to which above all man is inclined, and especially the young, who are more capable of being trained. Consequently a man needs to receive this training from another, whereby to arrive at the perfection of virtue. And as to those young people who are inclined to acts of virtue by their good natural disposition, or by custom, or rather by the gift of God, paternal training suffices, which is by admonitions. But since some are found to be dissolute and prone to vice, and not easily amenable to words, it was necessary for such to be restrained from evil by force and fear, in order that, at least, they might desist from evil-doing, and leave others in peace, and that they themselves, by being habituated in this way, might be brought to do willingly what hitherto they did from fear, and thus become virtuous. Now this kind of training, which compels through fear of punishment, is the discipline of laws. Therefore, in order that man might have peace and virtue, it was necessary for laws to be framed; for, as the Philosopher says, *as man is the most noble of animals if he be perfect in virtue, so he is the lowest of all, if he be severed from law and justice.* For man can use his reason to devise means of satisfying his lusts and evil passions, which other animals are unable to do.

Reply Obj. 1. Men who are well disposed are led willingly to virtue by being admonished better than by coercion; but men whose disposition is evil are not led to virtue unless they are compelled.

Reply Obj. 2. As the Philosophers says, *it is better that all things be regulated by law, than left to be decided by judges.* And this for three reasons. First, because it is easier to find a few wise men competent to frame right laws, than to find the many who would be necessary to judge rightly of each single case.—Secondly, because those who make laws consider long beforehand what laws to make, whereas judgment on each single case has to be pronounced as soon as it arises; and it is easier for man to see what is right, by taking many instances into consideration, than by considering one solitary instance.—Thirdly, because lawgivers judge universally and about future events, whereas those who sit in judgment judge of things present, towards which they are affected by love, hatred, or some kind of cupidity; and thus their judgment becomes perverted.

Since, then, the animated justice of the judge is not found in every man, and since it can be bent, therefore it was necessary, whenever possible, for the law to determine how to judge, and for very few matters to be left to the decision of men.

Reply Obj. 3. Certain individual facts which cannot be covered by the law *have necessarily to be committed to judges,* as the Philosopher says in the same passage: *e.g., concerning something that has happened or not happened,* and the like.

Second Article: Whether every human law is derived from the natural law?
We proceed thus to the Second Article:—

Objection 1. It would seem that not every human law is derived from the natural law. For the Philosopher says that *the legal just is that which originally was a matter of indifference.* But those things which arise from the natural law are not matters of indifference. Therefore the enactments of human laws are not all derived from the natural law.

Obj. 2. Further, positive law is divided against natural law, as is stated by Isidore and the Philosopher. But those things which flow as conclusions from the common principles of the natural law belong to the natural law, as was stated above. Therefore that which is established by human law is not derived from the natural law.

Obj. 3. Further, the law of nature is the same for all, since the Philosopher says that *the natural just is that which is equally valid everywhere.* If therefore human laws were derived from the natural law, it would follow that they too are the same for all; which is clearly false.

Obj. 4. Further, it is possible to give a reason for things which are derived from the natural law. But *it is not possible to give the reason for all the legal enactments of the lawgivers,* as the Jurist * says. Therefore not all human laws are derived from the natural law.

On the contrary, Tully says: *Things which emanated from nature, and were approved by custom, were sanctioned by fear and reverence for the laws.*

I answer that, As Augustine says, *that which is not just seems to be no law at all.* Hence the force of a law depends on the extent of its justice. Now in human affairs a thing is said to be just from being right, according to the rule of reason. But the first rule of reason is the law of nature, as is clear from what has been stated above. Consequently, every human law has just so much of the nature of law as it is derived from the law of nature. But if in any point it departs from the law of nature, it is no longer a law but a perversion of law.

But it must be noted that something may be derived from the natural law in two

* ["The Jurist" means Justinian, the Byzantine Emperor (527–565) who caused Roman law to be codified, and thus exerted a widespread influence on the history of civil law in Western Europe. (*Ed.*)]

ways: first, as a conclusion from principles; secondly, by way of a determination of certain common notions. The first way is like to that by which, in the sciences, demonstrated conclusions are drawn from the principles; while the second is likened to that whereby, in the arts, common forms are determined to some particular. Thus, the craftsman needs to determine the common form of a house to the shape of this or that particular house. Some things are therefore derived from the common principles of the natural law by way of conclusions: *e.g.,* that *one must not kill* may be derived as a conclusion from the principle that *one should do harm to no man;* while some are derived therefrom by way of determination: *e.g.,* the law of nature has it that the evil-doer should be punished, but that he be punished in this or that way is a determination of the law of nature.

Accordingly, both modes of derivation are found in the human law. But those things which are derived in the first way are contained in human law, not as emanating therefrom exclusively, but as having some force from the natural law also. But those things which are derived in the second way have no other force than that of human law.

Reply Obj. 1. The Philosopher is speaking of those enactments which are by way of determination or specification of the precepts of the natural law.

Reply Obj. 2. This argument holds for those things that are derived from the natural law by way of conclusion.

Reply Obj. 3. The common principles of the natural law cannot be applied to all men in the same way because of the great variety of human affairs; and hence arises the diversity of positive laws among various people.

Reply Obj. 4. These words of the Jurist are to be understood as referring to the decisions of rulers in determining particular points of the natural law; and to these determinations the judgment of expert and prudent men is related as to its principles, in so far, namely, as they see at once what is the best thing to decide. Hence the Philosopher says that, in such matters, *we ought to pay as much attention to the undemonstrated sayings and opinions of persons who surpass us in experience, age and prudence, as to their demonstrations.*

Question CIX: On the Exterior Principle of Human Acts, Namely, the Grace of God

First Article: Whether without grace man can know any truth?
We proceed thus to the First Article:—

Objection 1. It would seem that without grace man can know no truth. For in *1 Cor.* xii. 3 (*No man can say, the Lord Jesus, but by the Holy Ghost*) the *Gloss* of Ambrose says: *Every truth, by whomsoever spoken, is from the Holy Ghost.* Now the Holy Ghost dwells in us by grace. Therefore we cannot know truth without grace.

Obj. 2. Further, Augustine says that *the most certain sciences are like things lit up by the sun so as to be seen.* Now God Himself is He Who illumines, while *reason is in the mind as sight is in the eye, and the eyes of the mind are the senses of the soul.* Now the bodily senses, however pure, cannot see any visible thing without the sun's light. Therefore the human mind, however perfect, cannot, by reasoning, know any truth without divine light; and this pertains to the aid of grace.

Obj. 3. Further, the human mind can understand truth only by thinking, as is clear from Augustine. But the Apostle says (*2 Cor.* iii. 5): *Not that we are sufficient to think anything of ourselves, as of ourselves; but our sufficiency is from God.* Therefore man cannot, of himself, know truth without the help of grace.

On the contrary, Augustine says *I do not approve having said in the prayer: O God, Who dost wish the sinless alone to know the truth; for it may be answered that many who are not sinless know many truths.* Now man is cleansed from sin by grace, according to *Ps.* i. 12: *Create a clean heart in me, O God, and renew a right spirit within my bowels.* Therefore without grace man of himself can know truth.

I answer that, To know truth is a certain use or act of intellectual light, since, according to the Apostle (*Ephes.* v. 13): *All that is made manifest is light.* Now every use implies some movement, taking movement broadly, so as to call thinking and willing movements, as is clear from the Philosopher. But in corporeal things we see that for movement there is required not merely the form which is the principle of the movement or action, but also the motion of the first mover. Now the first mover in the order of corporeal things is the body of the heavens. Hence no matter how perfectly fire has heat, it would not bring about alteration, except by the motion of the body of the heavens. But it is clear that, just as all corporeal movements are reduced to the motion of the body of the heavens as to the first corporeal mover, so all movements, both corporeal and spiritual, are reduced to the absolutely First Mover, Who is God. And hence no matter how perfect a corporeal or spiritual nature is supposed to be, it cannot proceed to its act unless it be moved by God. Now this motion is according to the plan of His providence, and not by a necessity of nature, as the motion of the body of the heavens. But not only is every motion from God as from the First Mover, but all formal perfection is from Him as from the First Act. Hence the action of the intellect, or of any created being whatsover, depends upon God in two ways: first, inasmuch as it is from Him that it has the form whereby it acts; secondly, inasmuch as it is moved by Him to act.

Now every form bestowed on created things by God has power for a determined act, which it can effect in proportion to its own proper endowment; and beyond this act it is powerless, except by a superadded form, as water can heat only when heated by the fire. And thus, the human understanding has a form, viz., intelligible light itself, which of itself is sufficient for knowing certain intelligible truths, viz., those we can come to know through sensible things. Higher intelligible truths the human intellect cannot know, unless it be perfected by a stronger light, viz., the light of faith or of prophecy, which is called the *light of grace,* inasmuch as it is added to nature.

Hence we must say that for the knowledge of any truth whatsoever man needs divine help in order that the intellect may be moved by God to its act. But he does not need a new illumination added to his natural light in order to know the truth in all things, but only in those that surpass his natural knowledge. And yet at times God miraculously instructs some by His grace in things that can be known by natural reason, even as He sometimes brings about miraculously what nature can do.

Reply Obj. 1. Every truth, by whomsoever spoken, is from the Holy Ghost as bestowing the natural light, and moving us to understand and to speak the truth; but not as dwelling in us by sanctifying grace, or as bestowing any habitual gift superadded to nature. For this takes place only with regard to knowing and speaking certain truths, and especially in regard to such as pertain to faith, of which the Apostle was speaking.

Reply Obj. 2. The material sun sheds its light outside us, but the intelligible Sun, Who is God, shines within us. Hence the natural light bestowed upon the soul is God's illumination, whereby we are illumined to see what pertains to natural knowledge; and for this there is required no further illumination, but only for such things as surpass natural knowledge.

Reply Obj. 3. We always need God's help for every thought, inasmuch as He moves the intellect to act; for to understand anything actually is to think, as is clear from Augustine.

Second Article: Whether man can will or do any good without grace?
We proceed thus to the Second Article:—

Objection 1. It would seem that man can will and do good without grace. For that is in man's power of which he is master. Now man is master of his acts, and especially of his willing, as was stated above. Hence man, of himself, can will and do good without the help of grace.

Obj. 2. Further, any being has more power over what is according to its nature than over what is beyond its nature. Now sin is against nature, as Damascene says; whereas the work of virtue is according to the nature of men, as was stated above. Therefore, since man can sin of himself, much more would it seem that of himself he can will and do good.

Obj. 3. Further, the good of the intellect is truth, as the Philosopher says. Now the intellect can of itself know truth, even as every other thing can perform its natural operation of itself. Therefore, much more can man, of himself, do and will good.

On the contrary, The Apostle says (*Rom.* ix. 16): *It is not of him that willeth,* namely, to will, *nor of him that runneth,* namely, to run, *but of God that showeth mercy.* And Augustine says that *without grace men do nothing good when they either think or will or love or act.*

I answer that, Man's nature may be looked at in two ways: first, in its integrity, as it was in our first parent before sin; secondly, as it is corrupted in us after the sin of our first parent. Now in both states human nature needs the help of God, as First Mover, to do or will any good whatsoever, as was stated above. But in the state of integrity of nature, as regards the sufficiency of operative power, man by his natural endowments could will and do the good proportioned to his nature, which is the good of acquired virtue; but he could not do the good that exceeded his nature, which is the good of infused virtue. But in the state of corrupted nature, man falls short even of what he can do by his nature, so that he is unable to fulfill all of it by his own natural powers. Yet because human nature is not altogether corrupted by sin, namely, so as to be shorn of every good of nature, even in the state of corrupted nature it can, by virtue of its natural endowments, perform some particular good, such as to build dwellings, plant vineyards, and the like; yet it cannot do all the good natural to it, so as to fall short in nothing. In the same way, a sick man can of himself make some movements, yet he cannot be perfectly moved with the movement of one in health, unless by the help of medicine he be cured.

Hence in the state of the integrity of nature, man needs a gratuitous strength superadded to natural strength for one reason, viz., in order to do and will supernatural good; but in the state of corrupted nature he needs it for two reasons, viz., in order to be healed and, furthermore, in order to carry out works of supernatural virtue, which are meritorious. Beyond this, in both states man needs the divine help that he may be moved to act well.

Reply Obj. 1. Man is master of his acts, both of his willing and not willing, because of the deliberation of reason, which can be bent to one side or another. And although he is master of his deliberating or not deliberating, yet this can only be by a previous deliberation; and since this cannot go on to infinity, we must come at length to this, that man's free choice is moved by an extrinsic principle, which is above the human mind, namely, by God, as the Philosopher proves in the chapter on *Good Fortune*. Hence the mind even of an uncorrupted man is not so master of its act that it does not need to be moved by God; and much more needy is the free choice of man weakened by sin, whereby it is hindered from good by the corruption of its nature.

Reply Obj. 2. To sin is nothing else than to fail in the good which belongs to any being according to its nature. Now, as every created thing has its being from another, and, considered in itself, is nothing, so does it need to be conserved by another in the good which pertains to its nature. For it can of itself fail in good, even as of itself it can fall into nonexistence, unless it is conserved by God.

Reply Obj. 3. Man cannot even know truth without divine help, as was stated above. And yet human nature is more corrupted by sin in regard to the desire for good, than in regard to the knowledge of truth.

꒰§ *Part Four*

An Impression of the Age

ᴥ§ PROLOGUE TO THE CANTERBURY TALES

Geoffrey Chaucer

Coming after the readings on the characteristic ideas and institutions of the Middle Ages, and before the presentation of readings dealing with the developments that led to their transformation, this selection provides a chance to savor in a more impressionistic way the quality of medieval life at its height, as portrayed by the fourteenth-century English poet Geoffrey Chaucer. The centrifugal tendencies inherent in the later medieval world would soon tear it apart; at this point, however, there seems for a while to be an uneasy equilibrium. Both the tensions and the unity are evident in the Prologue to Chaucer's Canterbury Tales.*

Chaucer's plan was ambitious: to produce a collection of 120 verse narratives of a variety of types—some amusing, some dramatic, some didactic. Although he never lived to complete it, he succeeded in creating a masterpiece: humorous, wise, vivid, and of the highest poetic art. The Prologue sets the scene for the Tales; *it describes a group of thirty Englishmen of all social classes who have gathered at the Tabard Inn in Southwark, a suburb of London, before setting out on a pilgrimage to the shrine of St. Thomas à Becket at the ancient cathedral town of Canterbury. The pilgrims decide that each of them will tell two stories on the way to Canterbury and two on the return to London, as the Prologue describes; but the Prologue is more interesting for its descriptions of the pilgrims themselves, whose motives for making the pilgrimage are as varied as their personalities and interests. Chaucer avoids any idealization of social types, and presents the characters honestly and openly as they are, not as they themselves or apologists for organized society would present them. The result is an incomparable gallery of fourteenth-century portraits, fascinating and true to life.*

When April with its showers of gentle rain
The soil which March had dried hath pierced again,
And bathed each vein in dew, whose moistening power
Engenders in the bud the springing flower;
When Zephyr also with his balmy breath

Geoffrey Chaucer, *The Prologue to the Canterbury Tales, The Romaunt of the Rose, and Minor Poems*, ed. and rendered into modern English by Walter W. Skeat (London: Chatto and Windus, 1907), pp. 1–39.

Inspires anew in every holt and heath
The tender shoots, what time the vernal sun
His latter half-course in the Ram hath run;
And little song-birds make their melody,
That sleep the livelong night with open eye,
(For nature in their breasts instructs them so):
Then people long on pilgrimage to go,
And palmers seek to visit foreign strands,
To distant shrines, well-known in sundry lands;
And specially, from every county's end
Of England, unto Canterb'ry they wend,
The holy blissful martyr for to seek,
That well had helped them, when with sickness weak.

    It happened in that season, on a day,
In Southwark, at 'The Tabard' as I lay,
Ready upon my pilgrimage to start
To Canterb'ry, with good and zealous heart,
At night there came into that hostelry
Some nine and twenty in a company
Of sundry folk that, as it chanced, did fall
In fellowship, and pilgrims were they all,
And would to Canterb'ry together ride.
The chambers and the stables were full wide,
And well were we provided with the best.
And shortly, when the sun had sunk to rest,
So had I spoken with them every one
That I had joined the genial throng anon,
In readiness at early morn to rise
And thither take our way, in fitting wise.

    But ne'ertheless, while I have time and space,
Ere in this narrative I further pace,
Methinks, it would accord to reason well,
The full description, as I can, to tell
Of each of them, e'en as it seemed to me,
What kind of men there were, of what degree;
And eke in what array that each was in:
And at a Knight well may I first begin.

A Knight there was, and that a worthy man,
Who, from the hour in which he first began
To ride abroad, loved always chivalry,
Truth, honour, bounty, and fair courtesy.
Full worthy was he in his master's war,
And therein had he ridden—none so far—
In Christendom and heathen lands the same,
And always honoured for his worthy name.

At Alexandria's famous siege was he;
And highest at the table oft would be
In Prussia, 'bove all strangers, not a few.
In Russia and in Lithuania too
He travelled, none so oft of his degree.
And in Granáda, at the siege was he
Of Algeciras; and in Belmarye;
At Layas' siege, and that of Attalye,
When they were won; and joined a venturous band
Of troops, upon the Mediterranean strand.
In fifteen hard-fought battles had he been,
And for our faith had fought at Tramissene
Three times within the lists, and slain his foe.
This same thrice-honoured Knight had been alsó
In service under Pálathia's lord
On Turkish soil, against a heathen horde:
And evermore with highest praise did meet.
And though thus honoured, was he still discreet,
And meek in his demeanour as a maid.
No contumelious word he ever said
In all his life, against another wight.
He proved a very perfect, gentle Knight.
But, if I come to speak of his array,
Good were his horses, but himself not gay.
A fustian doublet wore he on his back,
Still by his iron hauberk marked with black;
So lately had he reached his journey's end;
But ready now on pilgrimage to wend.

With him there came his son, a youthful Squire,
A lusty bachelor, with love a-fire,
Whose locks were curled, as if full tightly pressed.
His age at twenty might be nearly guessed.
In stature he appeared of middle length,
Full active were his limbs, and great of strength.
Some deeds had he beheld of chivalry,
In Flanders, in Artois, and Picardy,
And well had borne him, in so little space,
In hope to stand well in his lady's grace.
Embroidered was he, like a daisied mead
All full of springing blossoms white and red.
He singing was, or fluting, all the day;
And was as fresh as is the month of May.
His gown was short, but long the sleeves and wide.
Well could he sit his horse, and fairly ride.
Sweet songs could he compose and well endite,

And joust, and dance, and well pourtray and write.
So hotly loved he that, when day did fail,
He slept no more than doth the nightingale.
He showed him modest, courteous, serviceable,
And carved before his father at the table.

A Yeoman had he, and no more beside
At that time, for it pleased him so to ride;
And clad was he in coat and hood of green.
A sheaf of peacock-arrows bright and keen
Beneath his belt he bore full thriftly;
Well could he dress his tackle yeomanly.
His arrows never drooped with feathers low,
And in his hand he bore a mighty bow.
His hair close-cropped, his face was brown of hue;
And all the art of woodcraft well he knew.
A leathern guard upon his arm he wore,
And by his side a sword and buckler bore;
Upon the other side a dagger bright
Right well equipped, and sharp as spear to smite.
Saint Christopher upon his breast was seen;
A horn he bore; the baldrick was of green;
In sooth, he was a forester, I guess.

A nun was also there, a Prioress
That, when she smiled, full simple was and coy;
Her greatest oath was only "by Saint Loy!"
Her name, I heard, was Madame Eglentyne.
Full well she sang the services divine
With nasal intonation clear and high;
And French she spake with ease and gracefully,
The French of Stratford-at-the-Bow, I mean,
For French of Paris knew she not, I ween.
At meat good manners had she learnt withal;
She from her lips would let no morsel fall,
Nor wet her fingers in her sauce too deep.
Each morsel would she raise, and watch would keep
Lest any falling drop her breast should wet.
Much mindfulness on courtesy she set.
Her upper lip she always wiped so clean,
That in the cup she used no drop was seen
Of grease, whene'er her draught she did complete.
In seemly wise she reached towards her meat;
And certainly she loved all simple sport.
She pleasant seemed, and amiable of port,
And eke took pains to counterfeit the talk

Of court, still stately in her ways and walk,
So to be worthy of due reverence.
But to describe her tender consciénce,
So kind of heart and pitiful was she,
At once she wept if she a mouse should see
Caught in a trap, or from a wound to bleed.
Some little dogs she had, that she would feed
With roasted meat, or milk and finest bread.
But sore she wept if one of them were dead,
Or if it, beaten with a stick, did smart;
And all compassion was and tender heart.
In neatest wise her wimple pleated was;
Her nose was long, her eyes as gray as glass;
Her mouth was small, and soft and red beside;
Her forehead certainly was fair and wide;
Its breadth was near a span, as I surmise,
And truly was she not of under size.
Full costly was her cloak, as I was ware;
Of coral small about her arm she bare
A set of beads; the larger ones were green;
Whereon there hung a brooch of golden sheen,
On which was written first a crownéd A,
And after—*Amor vincit omnia.*

Close by her side another nun had she,
Who was her chaplain; and her priests were three.

A Monk was there, a fair one of his race,
Who rode to visit farms, and loved the chace;
A manly man, to be an abbot able.
Full many a dainty horse had he in stable:
And when he rode, men might his bridle hear
A-jingling in the whistling wind as clear
And eke as loud as doth the chapel-bell
Where that this lord was keeper of the cell.
St. Maurus' rule, or of St. Benedict,
Because that it was old and somewhat strict,
This gentle Monk let olden usage slide,
And took the newer world to be his guide.
He cared not for that text a well-plucked hen
That saith, that "hunters are not holy men;"
Or that "a monk, when he is cloister-less,
Is likened to a fish that's waterless;"
That is to say, a monk out of his cloister.
But that remark he held not worth an oyster;
And *I* said, his opinión was sound.

Why should one study till one's brain turns round,
In cloister always on a book to pore?
Or labour with one's hands, and toil full sore
As Austin bids? How shall the world be served?
Let Austin have his toil for him reserved!
To be a horseman therefore seemed it right;
Greyhounds he had, as swift as bird in flight;
In spurring hard and hunting of the hare
Was all his joy; for no cost would he spare.
I saw his sleeves well-bordered, at the hand,
With fur, and that the finest in the land;
And, for to fix his hood beneath his chin,
He had, all wrought of gold, a curious pin:
A love-knot in the greater end there was.
His head was bald, and shone as any glass,
And eke his face, as if well oiled about.
A lord was he, of persons fat and stout.
His eyes were bright, and rolling in his head,
They glowed as doth a furnace 'neath a lead.
His boots were soft, his horse in good estate;
A prelate seemed he surely, fair and great.
He was not pale, as is a pining ghost.
A fat swan loved he best of any roast.
His palfrey was as brown as is a berry.

A Friar too, a wanton one and merry,
A beggar in his bounds, a goodly man.
In all the 'orders four' is none that can
So charm with talk, in language well conveyed.
And many a marriage had he often made
Of youthful women, at his own expence.
He to his order proved a chief defence.
Acceptable and friendly was he found
With wealthy farmers, everywhere around,
And eke with wealthy women in the town:
For he had power to hear confessión,
He said, much more than any priest could do;
He had his order's licence thereunto.
Full sweetly heard he their confessión,
And pleasant was his absolutión;
An easy penance would he give to such
As to his pittance would contribute much.
For gifts to some poor order thus conveyed
Are signs that shrift is well and truly made.
For if a man would give, he durst proclaim
The man's repentance real, and not in name.

Indeed, some men are known so hard of heart,
They cannot weep, how sorely e'er they smart;
And so, instead of tears or thoughts of prayer,
To begging friars men should silver spare.
His tippet bore beneath it little knives,
And pins, as presents for the fairer wives.
His voice had certainly a pleasant ring;
Well could he play the viol, and could sing.
Romances none could tell so well as he.
His neck was white as is the *fleur-de-lis;*
And strong was he as is a champión.
He knew the taverns well in every town,
And taverners and barmaids bore in mind
Much better than a beggar lame or blind;
For unto such a worthy man as he
'Twas all unfitting his ability
To have acquaintance with the leprous poor.
It naught avails, nor can success assure,
With any such poor creatures talk to hold,
But with the rich, and men that victuals sold.
And chiefly, where some profit might accrue,
He courteous was, and paid men service due.
Was no man in the land so virtuous,
The best of beggars he, of all his house;
And made a yearly payment for the grant,
That ne'er a brother should frequent his haunt.
For though a widow ne'er a shoe did own,
His *In principio* was so sweet in tone,
He drew from her a farthing ere he went.
His earnings far surpassed his other rent.
Moreover, he could romp like any whelp.
When 'love-days' came, he gave efficient help;
Not like a meek recluse he showed him there,
Or scholar poor, with cope all thin and bare,
But rather like a master or a pope.
Of double worsted was his semi-cope,
And, like a new-cast bell, about him stood.
He lisped a little, in engaging mood,
To make his English sweet upon his tongue;
And in his harping, when that he had sung,
His eyes would twinkle in his head aright,
As stars that quiver in the frosty night.
And Hubert was this worthy friar's name.

A Merchant next, with forkéd beard, there came,
In motley clad, and high on horse he sat,

Upon his head a Flemish beaver hat;
His boots were fastened neatly and with care.
He spake each sentence with important air
As well beseemed his profits year by year.
He would, the sea were kept from pirates clear
From Middelburgh to Orwell, as was due.
The just exchange of foreign coins he knew.
This worthy man so well engagements met
That no man knew it, if he fell in debt,
So stately was he in his ways of trade,
So well he bargains and agreements made.
Forsooth, he was a worthy man withal;
Yet cannot I, in truth, his name recall.

A Clerk of Oxford next my notice caught,
That unto logic long had given his thought.
His horse appeared as lean as is a rake,
And he was nowise fat, I undertake;
But looked all hollow, and of sober mien.
Full threadbare was his upper mantle seen;
For he, as yet, no benefice could gain,
Nor would he worldly office entertain.
For rather would he have, beside his bed,
Some twenty books, all clad in black or red,
Of Aristotle and his philosophy,
Than fiddle, costly robes, or psaltery.
But, though amongst philosophers enrolled,
Within his chest he had but little gold;
But all that he might gain from any friend
On learning and on books would he expend,
And duly for the souls of those he prayed
That for his studies gave substantial aid.
To gather learning took he care and heed,
And ne'er a word would utter more than need;
And all was said in form and reverence,
In brief and lively terms, and full of sense.
To moral virtue tended all his speech,
And gladly would he learn, and gladly teach.

A Sergeant at the Law, of prudent mien,
Who at St. Paul's church-porch had often been,
Came after him, full rich in excellence.
Discreet was he, and of great reverence:
Or such he seemed, his words appeared so wise.
He often had been justice in assize,
By patent, and by full commissión;

And, for his knowledge and his high renown,
Of robes and fees received he many a one.
So good conveyancer as he, was none.
All was fee simple that employed his care,
And none could his conveyancing impair.
Was nowhere man so busy as was he,
Yet busier than he was he seemed to be.
He knew each case's points and verdicts all
That since the Conquerer William's time did fall.
Deed or agreement could he draught and make,
And none exception to his words could take;
And every statute could he say by rote.
He rode but homely in a motley coat,
And narrow bars his silken girdle bore;
Of his array I need describe no more.

A Franklin in his company appeared;
White as the daisy was his flowing beard,
And sanguine of complexion was his look.
A sop in wine at early morn he took.
A life of pleasure was he wont to lead,
For he was Epicurus' son, indeed,
Who held th' opinion, that unmixed delight
Was verily felicity outright.
A householder of generous kind was he,
With all St. Julian's hospitality.
His bread, his ale was always of the best;
And no man better store of wine possessed.
Without good roasted meat was ne'er his house,
With fish and flesh, and that so plenteous,
His house abounded with good meat and drink,
And all the dainty things that men could think.
He took the seasons of the year as guide,
And varied meats and suppers did provide.
Fat partridges he kept in coops hard by,
And many a bream and pike in stewponds nigh.
Woe to his cook, unless the meat was drest
With piquant sauce, and ready all the rest.
His standing table in the hall alway
Stood ready covered all the livelong day.
At sessions was he chosen lord and sire;
Full oftentimes he knight was of the shire.
A two-edged dagger and a pouch of silk
Hung at his girdle, that was white as milk.
An auditor and sheriff had he been;
So good a landholder was nowhere seen.

A Haberdasher and a Carpenter, a Weaver, Dyer, and Upholsterer
Were with us eke, clad in one livery
Belonging to a great fraternity.
Full fresh and newly trimmed their clothing was;
The scabbards of their knives not capped with brass,
But all with silver, wrought to please the sight,
Their girdles and their pouches fresh and bright.
Each seemed a burgess, of a worthy mien
In guildhall on a platform to be seen.
And each, for wisdom and for tact, was fit
In council as an alderman to sit.
For wealth enough had they, in yearly rent,
And eke their wives were willing to assent;
For otherwise they surely were to blame.
A fine thing is it to be called 'my dame,'
On eves of feasts to walk in front, elate,
And have a mantle borne in royal state.

A Cook they had amongst them, for the nonce,
To boil the chickens with the marrow-bones,
And flavouring powder mix with galingale.
Right well he knew a draught of London ale,
Well skilled to roast and boil, and broil and fry,
Make savoury chicken-soups, and bake a pie.
Yet pity was it, as it seemed to me,
That on his shin an angry sore had he;
White meat of capons made he with the best.

A Shipman was there, from the distant west;
Dartmouth, for all I know, was his abode.
Upon a cart-horse, as he could, he rode,
In cloak of coarsest serge, that reached his knee.
A dagger, hanging by a cord, had he
About his neck, beneath his arm adown.
The summer's heat had made his hue all brown;
A merry comrade was he, sooth to say.
Full many a wine-cask had he borne away
From Bordeaux harbour, while the vintner slept.
His conscience no too tender scruple kept.
If e'er he fought, and gained the upper hand,
He cast men overboard to swim to land.
But as for reckoning well his times and tides,
His currents, and all dangerous things besides,
His pilotage, his harbour, and his moon,
From Hull to Carthage like him was there none.
With courage wise his plans were undertaken;

With many a tempest had his beard been shaken.
He knew well all the havens, as they were,
From Gothland to the Cape of Finisterre,
And every creek in Britain and in Spain;
His well-found barge was named 'The Maudëlayne.'

A Doctor too of physic joined the rout;
None like him, though we searched the world about,
That is, for physic or for surgery;
For he was grounded in astronomy.
He watched his patient by the planets' hours,
And natural magic lent him special powers.
When favouring planets in th' ascendant rose,
He times auspicious for his patients chose.
He knew the cause of every malady,
Were it of hot or cold, or moist or dry,
Whence came it, of what humour it might be;
An excellent practitioner was he.
The cause perceived, and root of all the harm,
Anon his remedies the sick would charm.
Apothecaries would at once attend,
Electuaries and healing drugs to send;
For each of them brought other profit due;
Their friendship, it appeared, was nothing new.
Old Aesculapius his aid supplies,
And Dioscorides, and Rufus wise,
Hippocrates, Haly, and Galien,
Serapion, Rhasis, and Avicen,
Averroes, Damascene, and Constantine,
Bernard, and Gatisden, and Gilbertine.
As to his diet, moderate was he,
For it comprised no superfluity,
But things digestible, for nourishment.
He little study on the Bible spent.
His robes were all of blue and scarlet bright,
With taffeta well lined, and linen white.
And yet he never went to great expence,
But kept his earnings by the pestilence.
For gold a famous cordial supplies;
And therefore gold was precious in his eyes.

A good Wife was there, who abode near Bath;
But somewhat deaf was she, which seemed a scath.
Such famous skill she had in making cloth,
Ypres and Ghent, she went beyond them both.
In all the parish was no wife, I trow,

That dared before her to the altar go;
Or if there did, so wroth indeed was she,
That, for a while, she lost all charity.
Of finest stuff her head-adornments were,
They weighed in truth ten pounds, so durst I swear,
That, on a Sunday, rose above her head.
Her hose were all of finest scarlet red,
And tightly laced; her shoes were soft and new.
Bold was her face and fair, and red of hue.
A worthy woman's life she long had led;
Five husbands at the church-door did she wed,
Not counting several lovers in her youth,
Of whom no mention need be made, in sooth.
She thrice had visited Jerusalem;
And crossed on horseback many a foreign stream.
At Rome she once had been, and at Boulogne,
At Great St. James's shrine, and at Cologne.
And much she knew of wandering by the way;
Her teeth were wide apart, the sooth to say.
Upon an ambling horse with ease she sat,
Her neckcloth pleated, on her head a hat
As broad as is a buckler or a targe.
An ample skirt about her hips full large,
And on her feet a pair of spurs she wore.
In company laughed much, and gossipped more;
Some remedies of love she knew, perchance,
For of that art she knew how goes the dance.

A good man, of religious orders one,
But poor, came next, the Parson of a town;
But rich was he in holy thought and work.
He was besides a learned man, a clerk,
That Christ's pure gospel truthfully would preach;
His parish-flock devoutly would he teach.
Benign he was, and wondrous diligent,
And in adversity full patiént;
And such he many a time was proved to be.
To curse men for his tithes full loath was he,
But rather would he give, beyond a doubt,
Unto his poor parishoners about
Out of his stipend, and his own beside.
A moderate sum his every want supplied.
His parish wide had houses far asunder,
And yet he never ceased, for rain or thunder,
To visit, if misfortune should befall,
The farthest in his parish, great and small;

Upon his feet, with staff in hand, he went.
This fine example to his sheep he lent,
That first he worked, and afterward he taught;
Out of the gospel that advice he caught;
This apologue he added eke thereto,
That, if gold rust, then what will iron do?
For if a priest be foul, in whom we trust,
No wonder though a layman then should rust;
And shame it is—let priests the warning keep—
To see a shepherd foul, though clean the sheep.
Well ought a priest example fair to give,
By purity, how that his sheep should live.
He never let his benefice to hire
And left his sheep encumbered in the mire,
And ran to London, to St. Paul's, to gain
A chantry, singing for men's souls in pain,
Nor sought in some fraternity to dwell;
But stayed at home, and kept his flock full well,
Lest e'er the wolf should cause it to miscarry;
A shepherd was he, and no mercenary.
And though he holy were and virtuous,
Was ne'er to sinful men contemptuous,
Nor haughty, nor disdainful in his speech,
But wisely and benignly would he teach.
To draw his folk to heaven by kindliness
And good example, was his business.
But if he found a sinner obstinate,
Whoe'er he were, of high or low estate,
Him would he sharply of his sin remind.
A better priest, I trow, could no one find.
Obsequious honour would he ne'er expect,
Nor would pretended holiness affect;
But all that Christ and His apostles taught
He preached, and first himself their lessons wrought.

A Ploughman next, his brother, near him rode,
Who oft of dung had carried many a load.
A faithful workman and a good was he,
Living in peace and perfect charity.
God loved he best with all his honest heart,
At all times, both in joy and sorrow's smart;
And, next to God, his love his neighbour shared.
To thrash, or dike, or delve was he prepared,
For Christ's dear sake, for every helpless wight,
Nor ask for payment, if within his might.
Of yearly tithes he duly paid his score,

Both of his earnings and his slender store.
In smock-frock clad, he rode upon a mare.
   A Miller and a Reeve were also there;
A Sumnour and a Pardoner with those;
A Manciple and I the train did close.

A stout churl was the Miller, for the nonce,
Full big was he of brawn, and eke of bones;
As well was proved; for, wheresoe'er he came,
For wrestling would he gain the prize—a ram.
Short-shouldered was he, broad, and thickly set;
No door, but off its hinges he could get,
Or break it, running at it with his head.
His beard as any sow or fox was red,
And broad therewith, as though it were a spade.
Just on his nose's very tip he had,
A wart, and thereon stood a tuft of hairs,
Red as the bristles of an old sow's ears.
His nostrils, coarse and black, extended wide.
A sword and buckler bore he by his side.
His mouth, like any furnace-hole, was great.
He talked and jested at a noisy rate;
Nor gentle were his jests, nor over-nice.
Well could he steal men's corn, still tolling thrice;
And yet had he a thumb of gold, I'll swear.
A white coat, with a blue hood, did he wear.
A bagpipe could he loudly blow and play,
And therewithal he brought us on our way.

The inns of court supplied a Manciple,
From whom all caterers might learn full well
How to be wise in purchasing their store.
For whether that he paid, or kept a score,
He always in his bargains took such heed,
He got the upper hand, and well could speed.
Now is not this of God a full fair grace,
That this untaught man's wit should so outpace
The wisdom of a heap of learned men?
Of masters had he more than three times ten,
And all expert in law and curious;
Of such there were a dozen in that house,
Fit to be stewards both of land and rent,
To any lord throughout this land's extent,
To make him live within his yearly gain
Esteemed, and free from debt, if not insane,
Or live as cheaply as he could desire;

Men able to have charge of all a shire
In any circumstance that might befall;
Yet could this Manciple outwit them all.

The Reeve, a slender choleric man was he;
His beard was shaved as nigh as it could be.
His hair was closely shorn around his ears,
And, like a priest's, his top had felt the shears.
His legs appeared full long, and yet full lean,
Much like a staff, for ne'er a calf was seen.
A garner could he keep, and eke a bin;
Against his score no auditor could win.
Well knew he, by the drought and by the rain,
The produce of his seed, and of his grain.
His master's dairy, cows, and all his flock,
His horses, swine, his poultry and his stock,
Were wholly placed within this Reeve's control,
Who gave account, by covenant, of the whole,
Since that his master numbered twenty years;
And none could find his reckoning in arrears.
No bailiff was there, herd, or labouring wight,
But well he knew his artfulness and sleight;
They dreaded him like pestilence or death.
His dwelling stood full fair, upon a heath;
Green trees with pleasant shade his house supplied.
He better than his master could provide.
His private store supported him with ease;
He sought by subtle means his lord to please,
And money of his own to lend was fain,
His thanks, a new coat, or a hood to gain.
A good employment had he learnt in youth;
A wright was he, a carpenter, in truth.
This Reeve upon a sturdy cob had got,
That was all dapple-gray, whose name was Scot.
A surcoat long, all coloured blue, he had;
And by his side he bore a rusty blade.
This Reeve, of whom I speak, from Norfolk came,
Beside a town, and Bawdswell is its name.
Tucked up was he, just like a friar, about,
And ever he rode the hindmost of the rout.

A Sumnour was there also, in that place,
Who had, all fiery red, a cherub's face;
So pimpled was he, and his eyes so narrow;
And quick he was, and chirpéd like a sparrow;
His scurfy brows were black, and thin his beard;

To see his face were children oft afeard.
No brimstone, lead, or quicksilver availed,
E'en borax, salve, and cream of tartar failed,
No ointment was so strong, to cleanse or brite,
That e'er could cure him of his tumours white
Or knobby warts that sat upon his cheeks.
Well loved he onions, garlic strong, and leeks,
And fain would drink strong wine, as red as blood.
Then would he cry aloud, in frantic mood;
And when he found himself by wine bemused,
No word but scraps of Latin speech he used.
A few stock phrases had he, two or three,
That once he learnt by heart from some decree;
No wonder, for he heard it all the day.
And eke ye know right well, how that a jay
Can call out 'Wat!' as well as can the pope.
But if one further sought his wits to grope,
He had expended his philosophy.
Aye *"Questio quid juris,"* would he cry.
A good companion was he, and a kind,
A better comrade men could seldom find.
He would permit, for just a quart of wine,
A vicious man to live like any swine
A twelvemonth, and excuse his vice in full.
The feathers from a pigeon could he pull.
And if he found a boon companion near,
Anon he counselled him to have no fear,
In case he trespassed, of th' archdeacon's curse,
Unless a man's soul dwelt within his purse;
For in his purse his punishment should be.
"Purse is th' archdeacon's hell;" so counselled he.
But well I know, he lied in very deed;
Of cursing should each guilty man take heed—
For curse will slay, as absolution saveth—
Beware then of the writ *'significavit.'*
He kept in his control, as him did please,
The younger people of his diocese,
And by his guidance were their counsels led.
A garland had he set upon his head,
As large as one above an alehouse-door;
A bun-like loaf he, for a buckler, bore.

With him there rode a gentle Pardoner,
Of Roncivaux, his friend and his compeer,
That straight had come here from the court of Rome.

Full loud he sang—"Come hither, love! Oh come!"
A droning burden did the Sumnour keep;
No trumpet had a sound so loud and deep.
This Pardoner had hair like yellow wax,
But smooth it hung, as doth a bunch of flax;
In clusters lay his locks about his head,
And over both his shoulders were they spread;
But thin they lay, in portions, one by one;
And hood, for greater comfort, wore he none,
For in his wallet was it well bestowed.
He thought he in the newest fashion rode;
Dishevelled, save his cap, he rode all bare.
Such glaring eyes he had as hath a hare.
A 'vernicle' was sewn upon his cap.
His wallet lay before him in his lap,
Brimful of pardons, come from Rome all hot.
A voice he had as small as hath a goat.
No beard he had, nor was he like to have;
As smooth was he, as any one could shave;
I trow, his cheek and eke his chin were bare.
But of his craft, from Berwick unto Ware,
None other such a Pardoner could be.
Within his bag a pillow-case had he,
Which, as he said, had been Our Lady's veil.
He said, he had a portion of the sail
That once St. Peter had, what time he sought
To walk the sea, ere Jesus Christ him caught.
A copper cross had he, with precious stones
Adorned, and in a glass a porker's bones;
And with these relics, when a hold he got
Of some poor dweller in a country cot,
Within a day he drew more money in
Than e'er the Parson in two months could win.
And thus, with flattery and the tricks he played,
Parson and people too his dupes he made.
But finally, to tell as told should be,
A noble churchman in the church was he.
A lesson or a legend could he read,
But best he sang an offert'ry indeed;
For well he knew, whenever that was sung,
He needs must preach, and smoothly file his tongue
In skilful wise, an ample sum to bring;
Therefore he merrily and loud did sing.
    Now have I told you shortly, in a clause,
The state, th' array, the number, and the cause

Why that assembled was this company
In Southwark, at this gentle hostelry,
Known as 'The Tabard,' close beside 'The Bell.'
But now the time has come for me to tell
How we demeaned ourselves that very night
When we did at that hostelry alight.
Next, to narrate our journey I engage,
And all the remnant of our pilgrimage.
But first I pray you, of your courtesy,
That never shall ye lay the blame on me,
Although I speak herein with openness,
And all their very words and ways express,
Or though I give their speeches faithfully.
For this ye needs must know as well as I,
Whoe'er reports a story-telling man
Must needs rehearse, as nigh as e'er he can,
All words alike that come within his charge,
Although the speaker's style be broad and large;
Or else he tells the tale in words untrue,
Or feigns the thing, or speaks in phrases new.
He may not spare, although he were his brother;
He must report both one word and another.
Christ plainly spake Himself in holy writ;
Yet, well ye know, no homeliness is it.
And Plato saith—whoever him can read—
"The words should aye be cousins to the deed."
I pray you likewise to forgive it me,
Although I set not folks in their degree
In order just, as each should rightly stand.
My wit is short, ye well may understand.

   With pleasant cheer our Host received each one,
And to our supper set us down anon;
And served us all with victuals of the best.
Strong was the wine, and greatly in request.
A seemly man our Host appeared withal,
Fit for a marshal in a city-hall.
A portly man, with shining eyes, was he,
In Cheapside fairer burgess none could be:
Bold of his speech, and wise, and wisely taught,
Of manliness, indeed, he lacked in naught.
Moreover, he was found a cheerful man,
And after supper, to be blithe began,
And spake of mirthfulness 'mongst other things,
When we had truly paid our reckonings;
And thus he said: "My masters, certainly,

Ye are to me right welcome, heartily:
For by my troth, no need have I to lie,
This year have I not seen a company
So merry in this hostelry till now.
Fain would I yield you pleasure, wist I how.
And of a pleasure have I now bethought,
To ease your journey; it shall cost you naught.
    Ye go to Canterb'ry; now God you speed!
The blissful martyr render you your meed!
And well I wot, while travelling by the way,
Ye think to tell some tales of mirth and play;
For truly, mirth or comfort is there none
To ride along the road as dumb as stone;
And therefore I desire some sport to make,
As first I said, that pleasure ye may take.
And if it please you all, with one assent,
With my decision to be well content,
And all consent to do as I shall say,
To-morrow, when ye ride upon your way,
Now, by my father's soul!—for he is dead—
But ye be merry, ye may have my head!
Hold up your hands, nor let me further speak."
    Our counsel was not difficult to seek;
We thought, 'twas not worth while to be too nice,
And all agreed, nor sought for more advice,
And bade him say his verdict and his hest.
    "My masters," quoth he, "hearken what is best;
But take it not, I pray you, in disdain;
This is the point, to speak it short and plain,
That each of you, the journey short to make,
Two tales shall, as we travel, undertake,
As on to Canterb'ry we forward ride;
And, in returning, tell two more beside,
Of strange adventures that did once befall.
And which of you shall bear him best of all,
That is to say, who tells us, as we ride,
Tales that most profit and delight provide,
Shall have a supper at our common cost,
Here in this hostel, sitting by this post,
When that we come again from Canterbury.
And, for to make you all still further merry,
I will myself right gladly with you ride,
E'en at my own expense, and be your guide.
And whoso my decision will withsay
Shall pay for all we spend upon the way.

And if you all agree it shall be so,
Tell me anon, and make no more ado,
And I will be prepared at early morn."
　　This thing was granted, and our oaths were sworn
With full glad heart, whereon we prayed him too
He would himself vouchsafe so for to do,
And be our chief director and our head,
Judge and reporter of the stories said,
And set a supper at a certain price;
And we would all be ruled by his advice,
Both high and low; and so, with one consent,
With his decision were we well content.
And thereupon the wine was fetched anon;
We drank, and to our rest we went, each one,
Without delay or longer tarrying.
　　Amorrow, when the day began to spring,
Uprose our Host, and called us, like a cock,
And gathered us together, in a flock,
And, scarce above a footpace, on we rode,
Till at St. Thomas-Watering we abode;
For there our Host began his horse to stay,
And said: "My masters, hearken as ye may.
Ye know how ye agreed to my decree.
If even-song and matin-song agree,
Let's see now who shall tell the foremost tale.
As ever I hope to drink more wine and ale,
Whoe'er from my decision will dissent
Shall pay for all that by the way is spent.
Now draw the lot, before we journey hence,
And he that hath the shortest shall commence.
Sir Knight, my master and my lord," quoth he,
"Now draw the lot; for such is my decree.
Come near," quoth he, "my lady Prioress;
And ye, sir Clerk, lay by your bashfulness,
And study not; lay hand to, every man."
　　To draw his lot then every wight began,
And shortly, to relate it as it was,
Were it by fate, or chance, or happy case,
The truth is this; the lot fell to the Knight.
Whereat full blithe and glad was every wight;
For tell he must his tale, as reason bade,
By stipulation, and by compact made
As ye have heard. What need ye further know?
And when this good man saw that it was so,
Like one that wise was and obedient

To keep his compact by his free assent,
He said: "Since I must now begin the game,
Why, welcome be the lot, in God's own name!
Now let us ride; and hearken what I say."
    And with that word we rode upon our way;
And therewith he began, with merry cheer,
His tale anon, and said as ye shall hear.

Part Five

Renaissance and Reformation

The Renaissance State

During the fifteenth century fairly efficient and recognizably modern states developed on the Italian peninsula. Venice, Florence, and Milan were the most notable among them. They pioneered in, among other things, professionalized diplomacy, having foreign offices formulating policy on the basis of reports from resident ambassadors. (It should be noted however, that even as late as the early sixteenth century, Italian states still relied on roving envoys in states too remote to justify a resident ambassador.) The diplomatic correspondence, as well as the periodic reports sent by these envoys, provides well-informed and dispassionate accounts—unavailable for earlier periods—of various European countries.

Machiavelli's Report on Germany *is the result of a diplomatic mission in behalf of the Florentine Republic. Though Machiavelli is far better known for* The Prince *(see page 359) and the* Discourses, *written after a revolution had exiled him from his native city, his real career was that of a middle-level Florentine official. In 1508 Machiavelli spent five months in Germany in order to find out whether Maximilian, Holy Roman Emperor as well as ruler of the Habsburg hereditary possessions, was planning to invade Italy and whether he had the means to do so.*

Compared with Machiavelli's effort, the Venetian reports, of which that of Marco Antonio Barbaro is a fair sample, are notable for their professional polish. By the sixteenth century, the tradition had been established that a returning Venetian ambassador should write an extensive report on the country of his embassy. Any information on the customs, geography, politics, etc., that might be of interest to members of the Venetian Senate was included, together with an analysis of the country's foreign policy (this section has been omitted from our selection). The very tradition of writing comprehensive reports in an elegant style led to certain literary conventions. The organization of the report, and even certain descriptive passages, varied little from one ambassador to another. Repetitive sections of the Reports on France *were omitted by the nineteenth-century editor; one of the gaps thus created in Barbaro's text has been filled by relying on the corresponding section of the report of his immediate predecessor, Michele Suriano (1562).*

Although Barbaro wrote his report fifty-six years after that of Machiavelli, Germany and France may still be compared on the basis of the two reports. In the sixteenth century, though the pace was quickening, social and political institutions still evolved so gradually that in the course of this half-century no basic changes in the structure of the two countries occurred.

323

REPORT ON THE AFFAIRS OF GERMANY, 1508

Niccolò Machiavelli

No one can doubt the power of Germany, for she abounds in population, wealth, and troops. As to riches, there is not a community that has not a considerable amount in the public treasury; it is said that Strasburg alone has several millions of florins so placed. This arises from the fact that they have no expenses for which they draw money from the treasury, except to keep up their munitions, which, when once provided, require very little to keep them up. The order established in these matters is really admirable; for they always keep in the public magazines grain, drink, and fuel enough for one year. They also keep a supply of the raw material for their industries, so that in case of siege they can feed the people, and supply those who live by the labor of their hands with the necessary materials for an entire year without any loss.

They spend nothing for soldiers, for they keep all their men armed and exercised, and on holidays these men, instead of amusing themselves with idle play, exercise themselves, some with the gun, some with the pike, and some with one or another kind of arms; for which exercises they have established prizes of honor and other rewards. These are their only expenses, for in other matters they spend very little; and thus every community is rich in public treasure.

The reason why the private citizens are rich is, that they live as if they were poor; they do not build, and spend nothing on dress or costly furniture in their houses. They are satisfied with having plenty of bread and meat, and a stove where they can take refuge from the cold; and those who have no other things are satisfied to do without them, and do not seek after them. They spend two florins in ten years for clothing to put on their backs; all live in this proportion, according to their rank, caring little for what they have not, but only for that which is strictly necessary; and their necessities are much less than ours. With such habits, it is natural that the money does not go out of the country, the people being content with what their country produces. But money is always being brought into the country by those who come to purchase the products of their industry, with which they supply almost all Italy. And the profit which they make is so much the greater, as the larger part of the money which they receive is for the labor of their hands only, and but little is for the raw material employed. And thus they enjoy their rough life and liberty, and for that reason they will not take service to go to war, unless they are exorbitantly paid; and this alone will not satisfy them, unless they are ordered by their communities. And therefore does the Emperor of Germany require much more money than any other sovereign, for the more prosperous the men are, the more unwillingly do they take service for the wars.

It may happen that the cities unite with the princes to favor the enterprises of the Emperor, or that they desire to do so by themselves, which would be quite sufficient. But neither cities nor princes would like the aggrandizement of the Emperor; for

The Historical, Political and Diplomatic Writings of Niccolò Machiavelli, trans. C. E. Detmold (Boston: J. R. Osgood, 1882), Vol. IV, *Report on the Affairs of Germany*, 384–388.

if he ever had any states of his own, or were to become powerful, he would so subdue and abase the princes, and would reduce them to that degree of obedience, that he could avail himself of them at his will, and not when it suited them; as the king of France does nowadays, and as was formerly done by King Louis XI., who by making war upon some of the princes, and killing others, reduced them to the degree of submission in which we see them now. The same would happen to the free cities of Germany, for the Emperor would want to reduce them to such a degree of obedience that he could control them at his pleasure, and obtain from them whatever he might ask, and not what might seem good to them.

The want of union between the free cities and the princes arises from the many contrary dispositions and interests that exist in that country. But reducing these to two principal divisions, it may be said that the Swiss are hostile to all Germany, and the princes to the Emperor. And yet it seems a strange thing to say that the Swiss and the free communities of Germany are inimical to each other, whilst both have one and the same object, namely to save their liberties, and to protect themselves against the princes. But their disunion arises from this, that the Swiss are not only hostile to the princes, the same as the free communities, but they are equally hostile to the gentlemen, for in their country there is no difference of rank; and all, with the exception only of those who sit as magistrates, enjoy without distinction an equal and entire liberty. This example of the Swiss alarms the gentlemen in the free communities, and their whole occupation is to keep up the disunion and enmity between them and the Swiss. These have furthermore for enemies all those men of the communities who make war their trade, owing to a natural jealousy lest these should be more esteemed than themselves. So that you cannot bring ever so few or so many together in one camp without their quarrelling or coming to blows.

As to the enmity of the princes towards the cities and the Swiss, that is so well known as to make any discussion of it unnecessary; the same with regard to the hostility between the Emperor and the princes. It is well to bear in mind that the Emperor, instigated by his hatred of the princes, and unable to lower their pretensions by himself, has sought the support of the free cities; and for the same reasons he has for some time past taken the Swiss into his service, and has to some extent gained their confidence.

Considering now all these differences, and adding those that exist between one prince and another, and one community and another, it will be seen how difficult it is to obtain in the Empire that unanimity which is so necessary for an Emperor to carry out his projects. But what makes the enterprises of Germany vigorous and easy of success is, that there is not in all Germany a prince who would dare to oppose the designs of the Emperor, as used to be the case formerly. And yet it must be borne in mind that it is quite a sufficient impediment for an Emperor not to be aided by the princes in any of his projects; for those who will not make open war upon him will nevertheless dare to refuse him their support, and those who will not dare to refuse him aid and support will yet dare not to fulfil the promises which they may have made to the Emperor, while some who will not even dare this will yet venture to be so slow in the execution of their promises, that their performance will no longer be in time to be of value. All this impedes and deranges the Emperor's plans.

The truth of this was shown when the Emperor wanted to pass into Italy the first time, contrary to the wishes of the Venetians and the French. At the Diet held at that time in Constanz, the cities of Germany promised the Emperor sixteen thousand infantry and three thousand horse; and yet they could never get enough of them together to make five thousand men. The reason of this was, that, so soon as the contingent of one community arrived, that of another went home because they had completed their term of service. Some cities, for the purpose of exemption from service, gave money, which it was not difficult to induce the Emperor to accept. And for this and other reasons the promised number of troops was never brought together, and the enterprise failed in consequence.

The power of Germany certainly resides more in the cities than in the princes; for the latter are of two kinds, temporal and spiritual. The first have been reduced to great weakness, partly through their own acts, each principality being subdivided amongst several princes, in consequence of the laws of inheritance which they observe; and partly because the Emperor has debased their power, by the aid of the cities, as stated above, so that they have become as it were useless friends. As for the ecclesiastical princes, if not reduced by hereditary divisions, yet have they been brought very low by the ambition of their communities, sustained by the favor of the Emperor; so that the Archbishop Electors, and other dignitaries of this sort, have no power or influence in their own large communities. The consequence is that the division existing between them and their cities prevents their aiding the Emperor's undertakings, even if they had the wish to do so.

But we come now to the free and imperial cities, which are the real nerve of the Empire, and have money as well as a good organization. For many reasons they enjoy their liberty with indifference, and have no desire to aggrandize their power; and what they do not desire for themselves they care little for others to have. Moreover, as there are a good many of them, and each one governs herself independently, their resolutions, when they wish to decide upon anything, are slow, and have not the desired efficiency. The following is an instance of it. Not many years since, the Swiss assailed the states of the Emperor Maximilian and Suabia. His Majesty agreed with these communities to repel the enemy, and the free cities obligated themselves to put and keep in the field fourteen thousand men; but they never got the half of that number together, for when the troops of one community arrived, those of another went home. So that the Emperor, despairing of success, made terms with the Swiss, leaving them the city of Basle. Now if such was the conduct of these communities where their own interests were involved, think what they would do to aid the enterprises of others. All these considerations taken together diminish the power of these cities considerably, and render them of little advantage to the Emperor.

Owing to the extensive trade which the Venetians have with the merchants of the German cities, they have understood this better than any one else; but in all matters that they have had to do or to negotiate with the Emperor, they have never swerved from a strictly honorable course. For if they had feared the German power, they would have employed some other means, either in the way of money or by the cession of some place; or if they had believed that that power could have been united, they would never have opposed it; but knowing the impossibility of that, they opposed it courageously, and bided their opportunity.

If, therefore, in one of these cities the affairs that concern a great number of citizens are neglected, by how much greater reason will they be even more neglected in so great an empire. Moreover, these cities know very well that every acquisition made in Italy or elsewhere would only be for the benefit of the princes, and not for their own, inasmuch as the princes can enjoy them personally, which a community cannot do; and whenever the reward is unequal, men do not like to spend equally. Thus the power of these cities is great, but it is such that you cannot avail yourself of it. If those who fear Germany had examined the above-explained causes, and the results which this power has achieved for many years past, they would have seen to what extent it can be depended upon.

۶۶ REPORT ON THE KINGDOM OF FRANCE, 1564

Marco Antonio Barbaro

One of the surest ways of safeguarding states and governing them well, Most Serene Prince, most excellent Lords, is, without a doubt, to acquaint oneself with other governments and their administration. The example of others may help to introduce some useful new institutions at home, increase one's appreciation for one's own [institutions], aid in remedying some flaw, or, lastly, train men in prudence by having them observe political success and failure. This is what our Republic has always done by means of its ambassadors. Having returned from the French court to which your Serenity had sent me as an ambassador, and where I spent these last thirty months in full devotion to my duties, I too am here today in order to fulfill the last task incumbent upon me, a task which strikes me as being as important as it is difficult.

It is indeed the duty of an ambassador to inform his prince of everything noteworthy. Thus I should expound upon the antiquity of the French kingdom, its dignity, the advantages of its location, its size and fertility, the number of its inhabitants, its military establishment on land and sea, its fortresses, war supplies, and generals, as well as upon the different states under the sway of the Most Christian King, the revenues and salt taxes, the ordinary expenditures, the national character, the appearance of the principal cities and of Paris especially, upon the *parlements* [the sovereign courts of justice], the form of the government, and the administration of justice. [I should talk] of the offices of the magistrates and councillors, the succession to the throne, the relation of this monarchy to other states, its superiority or inferiority in this respect, the claims that it advances, the Princes of the Blood, the person (that is to say, the character and behavior) of the king himself, the queen mother, and the King of Navarre. Were I free to do as I wished, I would do all that and more; yet in the fear of boring your Serenity by detailing all aspects of the kingdom, I must concentrate

Relations des Ambassadeurs vénitiens sur les Affaires de France au XVIᵉ siècle, ed. M. N. Tommaseo (Paris: Imprimerie Royale, 1838), Vol. I, 483–491; Vol. II, 3–5, 16–33, 34–37. Translated by Peter Amann for this volume.

on religious affairs, which today are of paramount importance. . . . As to other areas, I might not even be able to equal the eloquent and wise speeches by which my predecessors have instructed you. . . .

I briefly described to your Lordship France's military power which has inspired respect and fear in all other princes and which allowed former kings, and in our own day Francis I and Henry II, to carry out ambitious enterprises. The kingdom is in the fortunate position of being able to promote the union or division of the forces of other states as it sees fit. This is what leads one to believe that France is very powerful by herself, and that this valiant nation is not only capable of defending its own territory on any occasion but also of subduing other countries. All that France would need would be to act with less precipitation and greater prudence and also to improve her armies' organization.

The French are naturally proud, vainglorious, and very daring in warfare. Thus it is difficult to sustain their first onslaught. They must, rather, be beaten in the manner of Fabius, who by his delays triumphed over Hannibal. Titus Livy [a great Roman historian] claimed that at the onset of a battle the French are more than men, while at the end of it they are less than women. This derives, I believe, from the fact that their armies are impetuous but lack order. The French would be invincible if they could regulate this ardor. Their lack of discipline stems, as has often been noted, chiefly from their inability to bear fatigue and discomfort for any length of time. . . .

Enough said on this subject; let us turn to His Majesty's possessions.

If one totals up the king's current possessions, present-day France does not coincide with the territory that Caesar designated by the name of Gaul and which came under the rule of the Romans and [later] of Charlemagne. In ancient times France took in the whole region which, starting in the east had the Rhine and the Alps as boundary, the Mediterranean and the Pyrenees on the south, and the Atlantic Ocean on the west. The king is far from controlling all that. Ancient partitions and various accidents have detached Flanders, Lorraine, the county of Burgundy, and but lately Savoy, which was surrendered by Henry at the Peace of 1559 [between France and Spain]. Francis I lost Flanders after he was captured at Pavia [a crushing defeat of the French by the Spaniards in 1525], granting it to Charles V of glorious memory who had claimed it for his own through the female line of his dynasty.

The provinces which at present belong to the Most Christian King are ten in number: [The Ile de] France, properly speaking, which has lent its name to the whole monarchy and whose capital is Paris; Normandy and Brittany, which border the [Atlantic] Ocean; Guyenne and Languedoc down by the Pyrenees; the Dauphiné on the frontier of Savoy; Burgundy touching Switzerland and Germany; Champaign next to Lorraine; and Picardy adjoining Flanders. His possessions on the Italian side of the Alps include the Marquisate of Saluzzo and five fortresses in Piedmont, which he keeps as though safeguarding them for the Duke of Savoy.

The ordinary revenues of His Majesty are six million gold crowns, drawn from dues, from the hereditary ownership of the king's private domain (which would supply one and a half million were most of it not mortgaged), from a tenth of all clerical income, from salt and income taxes, from subsidies that have been turned into regular taxes, from the sale of offices, from exploitation of the forests, from confiscation of the property of aliens who die in France, and from other sources not all of which I can list. In case of emergency or war, he has recourse to an increase in the income tax or to contributions raised by privileged provinces to safeguard the special status which they enjoy. Finally, the king borrows money at interest, as was done recently, to the point where the current debt amounts to fifteen million gold crowns. Thus relying upon the affection and obedience of his people and the fertility and wealth of his realm, you may see that the king can never run out of money. The clergy pays the largest share, which is only fair, for of the fifteen millions that comprise the income of the whole kingdom, six go to the Church, one and a half to the king himself, the rest to the princes, barons, and the people.

Preceding kings, notably Francis I, spent a great deal. Aside from the ordinary expenses (that is, the expenditures for the upkeep of his court, for the salaries of councillors, governors, officers, and other judicial and administrative agents, for his armed retainers, his archers, fortresses, war supplies, galleys, and pensions), this prince spent considerable sums on buildings, jewels, festivities, and other such things. Though large amounts have been spent on construction, [the money] has been used with little discrimination: of the many palaces carefully constructed for the use of the king and his court that I have seen in France, not one is regular in design and deserving of praise. . . .

[France is] densely populated, having a hundred and forty episcopal cities, aside from innumerable castles and villages. Every area is as inhabited as it can be. . . . The nation is divided into three orders, from which originate the three estates of the realm: the first is the clergy, the second the nobility, the third does not have a special name and being composed of so many different classes one may call it by the general name of "people."

The clergy comprises many persons of the third estate as well as many foreigners who, because of the services they have rendered or because of the king's favor, have acquired ecclesiastical livings; yet the nobility constitutes the most notable part. The younger sons of the great families, getting very little of their family patrimony (almost all of which is handed down to the eldest), embrace the clerical estate to obtain wealth and standing.

Under the heading of nobles are meant those who are exempt from all taxes and who merely owe personal service in time of war. Among them are to be counted the princes and the barons. Among the princes, those of the Blood who are heirs to the crown, are the most outstanding, although [even] among them there are some whose luster is dimmed by poverty. . . . As to the other Princes of the Blood and the barons, it would be too tedious and boring to speak of all of them; they are too numerous. Among the princes, the first in power and wealth is the Duke of Guise; among the barons, the Constable.

The third estate includes the educated (who are called men of the long robe), the merchants, the artisans, the people, and the peasants. Among the men of the robe, whoever becomes [court] president or councillor or is honored by some similar function, is ennobled by his office and is treated as a nobleman during his lifetime. Today the merchants, as they hold the purse strings, are coddled and spoiled; yet they have no prominence or status, for every sort of commerce is looked down upon as unworthy of the aristocracy. The merchants are assigned to the third estate, paying taxes just like the non-nobles and peasants. The latter class receives the harshest treatment, both at the hands of the king and the privileged class. The Emperor Maximilian [of the Holy Roman Empire, 1493–1519] said of the King of France that he was the king of donkeys, because his people bore peaceably all kinds of burdens without complaining.

Each in its own way, all three estates serve the kingdom. That of the people retains four important [categories of] offices in its hands. I don't know whether this is because of some law or ancient custom, or because the nobles feel that these [offices] are beneath their dignity. The first office is that of the great chancellor, who is included in all councils, keeps the royal seal, and without whose consent nothing can be discussed or, once decided, put into execution. The second category is that of the secretaries of state, who, each in his own sphere, take care of business, keep the archives, and are entrusted with the most weighty secrets. The third includes the [court] presidents, councillors, judges, trial lawyers, and all those upon whom civil and criminal law within the realm depends. The fourth comprises the treasurers, tax collectors, district tax receivers, local tax receivers who administer all the revenues and expenditures of the crown. Since the people have access to all these important offices through which reputation and wealth are gained, and since the high office of chancellor and all the innumerable judicial posts are given to educated men and men of the robe, everybody wants some member of his family to acquire a [university] education. That is why the number of students is greater in France than anywhere else. . . . For some time even the princes have been sending their sons to study, particularly the younger ones, not in order to obtain such posts for them, but to get them accepted into the church. Indeed, episcopal sees nowadays are no longer granted to ignoramuses as readily as they once were. Would that God had been willing for such care to have been taken earlier for the good of Christianity!

The government is in the hands of the nobles and prelates. The prelates advise but do not act. The nobles serve as advisers and administrators. Yet often the latter leave the honor and care of deliberating to the prelates in the knowledge that they [the nobles] will be the executives in any case, an arrangement which leaves everyone content. The nobles generally are not rich, for they come to court where everything is expensive and where they ruin themselves by excessive expenses for servants, horses, clothes, and food. By contrast, their simple private lives in their *châteaux* do not require vast outlays—neither liveries, rich clothes, high-priced horses, banquets, nor the other extravagances which court life requires of them. That is why the custom of serving a quarter [year] at a time has been introduced: everyone takes his turn for his three months and the rest of the time exercises restraint and compensates by wise economies for expenses to which his service subjects him. Yet prelates have the same expenses for their wardrobe and their following wherever they are. Food, it is true, is more expensive at court, but in the hope of increasing their wealth and power by living in proximity to the king, the prelates are willing to incur this sacrifice. Even when they seek to remain in their sees in accordance with recent edicts, they would not be left in peace by the court; their presence at court is demanded, particularly if they have served as ambassadors at foreign courts. . . . Yet henceforth this will be changed, for the council recently has debarred bishops from ambassadorships, especially to the Holy See.

The real profession of the nobility, the one most useful to the people and the king, is that of war. . . .

This is what I had to say about the number and nature of the French population and the services which the crown derives from each of the three estates. Each of the three estates, by doing its duty without envying the others, by contributing to the welfare of the country in assisting the king by its advice, its money, and its life, respectively, has made France invincible and feared by all the peoples of the world. Yet as soon as the curse of the new religious sects began to spread, turning clergy against nobles, nobles against each other, and the people against the other orders, everything has been turned topsy-turvy, to the great detriment of the entire nation and especially the king, as I shall show shortly. . . .

Formerly the city of Paris enjoyed an almost democratic liberty. . . . Its population is estimated at 400,000 inhabitants. The university contains fifteen to twenty thousand students, most of them poor, who live in colleges. Each faculty has its own professors who are fairly well paid. The Sorbonne is the faculty of theology, whose professors wield extensive authority in the punishment of heretics.

The *parlement* [sovereign court] of Paris also wields great authority within its sphere, being like a senate made up of a hundred and eighty councillors chosen by His Majesty, and eight presidents, among whom the first president acts as a sort of chief magistrate. The twelve peers of France also hold seats. This is where all general affairs of the realm are dealt with. The *parlement* also hears all cases as the highest court of appeals. The council's authority even impinges upon the laws by moderating, interpreting, and sometimes even rejecting the decisions of His Majesty's privy council. The *parlement* enters the [privy council's] acts in a public register.

The government of the state is entirely in the hands of the nobles, that is to say, of the princes and barons, one of whom the king appoints to be in charge of each province. . . . Justice is in the hands of the men wearing the long robe, all of whom are from the third estate and most of whom are doctors of law. From among these are chosen the magistrates, bailiffs, and town seneschals who are something like mayors.

The title of Constable confers a very illustrious status and the great authority of commanding the land armies. This position is always granted to princes or great lords. The marshals, who were four in number . . . have . . . been reduced to three. Next to the Constable they enjoy the greatest power over the army. The Admiral is the captain-general of the naval forces. The place of the Great Chancellor, who sits in on all councils and keeps the Great Seal, is very eminent and most important. As the king requests his advice on all things, nothing of importance is done without him. The knights of the Order of Saint Michael are men of distinction who usually owe the title to merit alone. Louis XI founded this order in 1469. In time of war there are lieutenants whom the king dispatches on various missions.

Now I shall speak to you of the councils of His Majesty. First, there is the Council of Affairs, where state business and other important questions are transacted. Because of the king's minority, the number of councillors is greater today than previously. They include the Queen Mother, the King of Navarre [a principality in the Pyrenees ruled by a Bourbon prince closely related to the French royal family], all the Princes of the Blood [uncles or brothers of the French king], the Duke of Guise, the Cardinal of Lorraine, the Constable, the Great Chancellor, the Cardinals of Châtillon and Tournon, and others. Then there is the Privy Council in which the above-named persons sit together with several others. If the first council deals with high politics, the second one confines itself to those matters to be settled by the king relying entirely upon his regular powers, in accordance with the established laws of the kingdom. The Great Chancellor is the chairman of this latter council. . . .

Finally, there is also an assembly of the three estates representing the whole realm, which has the authority to temper the powers of the king himself. The functions of the assembly are numerous and very significant, for it deliberates on the means of defraying public expenditures and of raising an army, on the lowering and increasing of taxes, the correction of abuses, the administration of justice, the revenues to be assigned to His Majesty's brothers and sons, the reforms to introduce in the government, the measures to take during the minority of the king; in short, on all that has to do with safeguarding and keeping the peace of the kingdom. Yet this assembly is convoked very rarely. It was [last] called in 1560 in the reign of Francis II to deal with the religious disorders. . . .

Here I should compare the kingdom of France to all the others, for the power of a great prince is made manifest by contrasting it to the power of others, rather than by confining one's study to listing the number and extent of the states under his sway, his wealth, and the strength of his armies. Yet to draw a parallel between the forces of France and those of all the other kingdoms would take far too long and require a separate work. I will therefore confine myself to a comparison of the states of France with those of King Philip II [of Spain].

The Catholic King [Philip II] is a member of the House of Austria [i.e., the Habsburg dynasty]. He has inherited so many lordships, kingdoms, and countries that he has twelve kingdoms in Spain and three in Italy; almost all his possessions are scattered. The Most Christian King [i.e., the French monarch] has a single kingdom, completely unified and very extensive. While the Catholic King's revenues total five millions, his expenditures reach six. Although the Most Christian King has an income of six millions, for the time being he does not even spend all of that. In case of emergency [the Spanish king] has a great deal of trouble in raising money by extraordinary taxation; [the French king] raises as much as he needs by the very same means. Philip II's subjects lead in stubbornness and pride, contrasting with the more obedient French who show far greater willingness to part with their wealth in the service of their ruler. Spain has gold mines in its provinces and in the Indies, whereas France, though it has nothing but iron, is never short of silver brought in [from abroad]. Spain is a barren country, poor in great cities as in rivers, and deprived of the comforts of life. France, [on the other hand], is fertile, covered with cities and castles and abounding in rivers and all kinds of products. The Catholic King is superior to His Most Christian Majesty in naval forces, yet as to land armies, French men-at-arms are greatly superior to Spanish horsemen. French infantry is hardly inferior to that of Spain, while the [French] Gascons are every bit as good. As to commanders, France has always been ahead. Thus the forces of these two great kings are almost evenly matched. As we have seen, even that great Emperor Charles V, a man singled out by good fortune, had won many a victory only to be defeated by France and threatened by dire dangers. This struggle has been marked by continual ups and downs. . . .

✒ A FLORENTINE DIARY FROM 1450 TO 1516

Luca Landucci

Many people have attempted to explain the great outburst of energy—in all fields, but most remarkably in the arts and in politics—which we call the Renaissance. Such factors as the rise of a genuinely urban life, based on manufacturing and commerce, and extremely unstable political conditions, leading to interminable civil and interstate strife, go a long way, at least, toward accounting for the phenomenon. The political aspect is illustrated above in "The Renaissance State." The following selection concentrates on the city: the world of the bourgeois. Luca Landucci was a Florentine apothecary; the diary he kept takes us directly to the level of the common man. It is an almost perfect reflection of the complex of ideas and institutions associated with the Renaissance: Landucci is super-stitious yet cynical, alert yet gullible; his Florence is an amazing hotbed of political intrigue, social misery, and magnificent artistic and commercial activity.

Among the many persons you will encounter in Landucci's diary are Cosimo and Lorenzo de' Medici, wealthy merchants whose family was to take political control of Florence in the next generation; the sculptors Donatello, Verrocchio, and Michelangelo Buonarotti; and Leo X, one of the Medici Popes, whose entrance into Florence is the climax of the book. Disguised under somewhat unfamiliar names are, among others, the painter Andrea del Castagno ("Maestro Andreino degl' Impiccati") and the monk Savonarola ("Fra Girolamo"). Savonarola's fiery zeal for reform recalled that of the Old Testament prophets; taking advantage of political and social turmoil and his own great charismatic qualities, he became for a brief period the most important man in Florence, until he was overthrown by the political-religious reaction Landucci describes.

You will notice that the year began on March 25 and that the zero hour for clocks was 8 P.M. The entries for 1529 were made after Landucci's death by an anonymous writer, probably his son.

I record that on the 15th October, 1450, I, Luca, son of Antonio, son of Luca Landucci, a Florentine citizen, of about fourteen years of age, went to learn book-keeping from a master called Calandra; and, praise God! I succeeded.

And on the 1st January, 1452, I entered the shop of the apothecary Francesco, at the sign of the *Scala,* in the *Mercato Vecchio.*

And on the 1st February, 1453, my father's mother died, and was buried in San Piero Maggiore.

And on the 3rd November, 1454, my father Antonio received his mother's inheritance, of which we possess a document giving the details; he inherited all her property both in Florence and in the country; amongst the rest a house which was left as a legacy to her and Antonio for their lives. Messer Otto Niccolini arranged a compromise, by which the monks of Castello, who had the reversion, were to pay Antonio twenty-three *lire* a year for the rest of his life, taking back the said house, and they paid this sum as long as Antonio lived.

In March, 1458, . . . the lantern of the cupola of *Santa Maria del Fiore* was begun; and the palace of Cosimo de' Medici; and the churches of San Lorenzo and Santo Spirito, and the Badìa on the way to Fiesole; also many houses near the walls in the neighbourhood of San Barnabà and Sant' Ambrogio, and in several other parts.

And at this same time the following noble and valiant men were living: Archbishop Antonino, who had been a monk in the monastery of *San Marco,* and always continued to wear the habit of the Dominican Order, a man who may be called *Beato* (holy); Messer Bartolomeo de' Lapacci, a bishop and preacher excelling all others in our day; Messer Paolo, a doctor, philosopher and astrologer, of holy life; Cosimo, son of Giovanni de' Medici, who was called the great merchant, as he had places of business in every part of the town; and to compare anyone to Cosimo de' Medici was as much as to say that no richer or more prosperous person existed; Donatello, the sculptor, who made the tomb of Messer Leonardo d' Arezzo in Santa Croce; and Desidero the sculptor, who made the tomb of Messer Carlo d' Arezzo, also in Santa Croce. Later came Rossellino, a very small man, but great in sculpture; he made the tomb of the cardinal in San Miniato, which is in the chapel on the left; Maestro Antonio, an organist, who surpassed everyone in his day; Maestro Andreino degl' Impiccati, a painter; Maestro Domenico da Vinegia (Venice), also a painter, was beginning to be spoken of; Maestro Antonio and his brother Piero, called the Pollaiuolo, goldsmiths, sculptors and painters; Maestro Mariano, who taught book-keeping, and also my master Calandra, who taught the same subject, and was a very kind and courteous man.

And on the 4th September, 1462, I left Francesco, son of Francesco, the apothecary, at the sign of the Sun, who gave me, the sixth year, the salary of fifty florins, and I joined company with Spinello, son of Lorenzo, the hope of gaining more causing me to give up the gain which was sure. And we opened an apothecary's shop in the *Mercato Vecchio* (Old Market), at the sign of the King, which had formerly been

Luca Landucci, *A Florentine Diary from 1450 to 1516, continued by an anonymous writer till 1542,* ed. Iodoco del Badia, trans. Alice de Rosen Jervis (London: J. M. Dent & Sons, Ltd., 1927), pp. 1–9, 12–13, 26, 31–32, 37–39, 42–43, 45, 48–51, 53–54, 66, 74, 76, 80, 85, 88–89, 118, 122–123, 129–130, 138–139, 142–143, 169, 209, 213–214, 216–218, 222–223, 225–226, 266–267, 274–275, 279–281, 285, 292–294.

the shop of a second-hand dealer, and had a very low roof. We raised the roof, and spent a fortune although I was unwilling to outlay so much. All was done without stint, one cupboard alone costing 50 gold florins. Seeing that the costs were so great, and that the said Spinello had no money to produce, being very badly off, and considering besides that I had already spent 200 gold florins of my own, whilst he had not yet contributed a penny, although we had agreed to go shares, I thought of withdrawing from the enterprise as soon as possible. And on the 27th July, 1463, we agreed to separate, I telling him that I would leave him everything in the shop as it stood, without considering the cost, but that I must have my share of the profits, namely, 50 gold florins, for the time I had been with him, and he must repay me the money which I had put into it. And no agents were required. He replied that it should be so; but that I must give him a few months' time; and to this I agreed, as he gave me sufficient sureties, amounting to 200 gold florins, paid by his brother Lorenzo and Maestro Lorenzo, son of Maestro Leonardo. I left there on the 10th December, 1463, and began chaffering for the shop of San Pulinari; but we could not come to terms over it; I therefore repaired to Giovanni da Bruscoli, who was opening the shop of the *Agnus-Dei,* and who gave me 36 florins a year, so that I was able to buy the shop of the Tornaquinci, on the 1st September, 1466.

1465.   10th April   A young woman, who was the daughter of Zanobi Gherucci, was tried, for having killed, and then thrown into a well, the little girl of Bernardo della Zecca, a goldsmith, for the sake of stealing a pearl necklace and certain silver ornaments that the child wore round her neck. She was taken away in the executioner's cart, and was beheaded.

17th April   There passed through Florence a son of Don Ferante, King of Naples, on his way to Milan to fetch the daughter of the Duke of Milan to be wedded to his brother. This lad was twelve or thirteen years old; he was made much of, and was lodged at Santa Maria Novella. And afterwards he returned through Florence with the bride, accompanied by many signori and dukes, with a large troop of horse; and besides other things, there were so many damsels and matrons in his train that it was magnificent.

And at this time a man was found coining false money, and he was beheaded.

1st December   There was an election in the *Palagio,* and Niccolo Soderini became *Gonfaloniere.* He reduced the tax on wine to 14 *soldi,* for which the people called down blessings on his head.

12th January   During the night, the Arno began to be in flood, although there had not been a drop of rain; but the snow had melted suddenly, so that the river entered the town and flooded it as far as the *Canto a Monteloro,* and benches from the church of *Santa Croce* floated across to that point.

And the water went into the *Piazza del Grano,* reaching more than half-way up the door of the apothecary's shop, and past the *Palagio del Podestà.* The river overflowed its banks opposite Messer Bongianni's houses, and filled the *Prato* and the *Via della Scala.* Many mules and horses were drowned in their stables, and all the wine-casks went floating about, mostly towards the Arno. This flood had come suddenly.

1466.   24th May   A Saturday and the eve of the *Spirito Santo,* I was wedded to a daughter of Domenico, son of Domenico Pagni, whose name was Salvestra.' She had a dowry of 400 florins, in the state funds, praise God!

5th July   A Sunday evening, I gave her the ring, the contract being made before Ser Giovanni, son of Francesco di Neri. (Should be *6th* July. [Trans.])

27th July   A Sunday evening, I took my wife to *Casa Domenico*. She had as bridal outfit the following:

A pale blue sack-garment, with narrow sleeves, embroidered with pearls.
A purple gown, with sleeves of *brocatello*.
A white under-gown.
Twenty-four kerchiefs of hand-woven linen.
Six linen towels.
Twenty-four *benducci da lato* [shoulder handkerchiefs].
Eight shifts, woven in lozenge-pattern; new.
Twelve coifs.
A girdle of white silk webbing, with silver threads.
Three caps of various kinds.
A green reticule, with silver ornaments.
A pincushion, with pearls.

They were estimated by two dealers at the value of thirty-eight florins *di suggello*.

	Lire			*Lire*	
For fine cotton material, for			For red cotton material, for		
the robe	5	8	the gown		9
For twisted gold fringe, for			For a small gold badge	2	0
the robe	1	15	For silk cords, for the gown		10
For making little rings (or eyes)	2	0	For tress (of silk, silver, or		
For blue silk and a piece			gold), for the robe	1	10
of leather		7	For a [ruby] for the pendant	1	5
For linen material, for the gown		18	For blue silk, for the robe		6
For making the gown, to			For blue selvages, for the		
Lorenzo, tailor	5	12	tassels of the robe		7
For bits of enamel, to put			For ermine, for trimming		
between the pearls of			the gown	8	0
the necklace	2	3	For the fringe, for the gown	2	16
For little hooks, for the gown	1	2	For the fringe of the robe	4	4
For gold ribbon, for the gown	1	13	For silk cords, for the gown		2
For the lining for the gown		15	For ribbon to hem the robe		4
For linen material, for the gown	1	13	For seven twisted gold dangles,		
For cotton, for the gown		2	for the collar	1	12

And I will record my own expenses (for the marriage-gift):

	Lire			*Lire*	
Silk webbing for a girdle, with			For 6 *denari* of pearls	3	8
gold and silver ornaments,			For a piece of ribbon	1	0
in all			For some silk, for the robe		6
For an ounce of pearls, for			For cloth, for the lining of the		
snoods, 6 gold *fiorini*	27	6	robe	1	4

	Lire	
A little jewelled brooch, 3 gold *fiorini*	16	16
A couple of little knives, 2 gold *fiorini*	11	4
A pearl band for the forehead, 10 gold *fiorini* and 5 *soldi*	45	5
A pearl necklace, 120 *fiorini*	40	4
For 6 *denari* (half-ounces) of pearls, 1 *fiorino* 10 *soldi*	6	2
For ornaments (or finishings) for the snoods	1	15
For 6 *denari* (half-ounces) of pearls, 1 *fiorino* 15 *soldi*	6	7
For serge, for the robe	17	15
For fine longcloth, for the robe		12
For 1 ounce of pearls, for the robe, 5 *fiorini* 15 *soldi*	26	0
For 1 ounce of spun gold, for the robe	5	2
For a ribbon to twist in the hair	2	14

	Lire	
For some ornaments, (or finishings) for the robe		9
For sik material, for the collar	1	12
For silver and silk, for the robe		15
For crimson silk material, for the gown, 26 gold *fiorini* 6 *soldi*	151	10
For a clasp, for the collar of the robe	4	17
For brokerage to Tommaso di Currado	12	14
For a diamond, 2 gold *fiorini* and 2 *grossi*	11	15
For a sapphire, 2 gold *fiorini* and a half	13	19
For a ruby, 1 gold *fiorino* and a half	8	8
For a broken ring, loss	1	3
To Lorenzo, tailor	1	0
For setting the stones in the pendant		14

My above-mentioned wife and dear companion, who had not her equal for kindness and virtue, died after living with me for forty-eight years, and never once having given me cause for anger. She had twelve children; and at her death left me four boys and three girls, one of the latter a nun at Foligno, and the two others at home. God be praised!

In my time there have been the following popes, though I do not know the day of their election:

Papa Ugenio, who left Florence about 1440, when I was about four years old.
Pope Niccolaio succeeded him. In Ugenio's time Felice was also elected Pope . . . by a Council . . . and there were . . . (Hiatus in MSS.)
Pope Calisto succeeded Niccolaio.
Pope Pio, a Sienese.
Pope Pagolo. . . .

1471. *26th May* I bought some of the first sugar that came here from Madria; which island had been subdued a few years before by the King of Portugal, and sugar had begun to be grown there; and I had some of the first. . . .

1476. *29th December* We heard that the Duke of Milan had been stabbed and killed by one of his citizens called Giovanni Andrea, who was moved to commit the crime by certain unjust acts of the duke. He was put to death by the populace, out of zeal for the common good. There were several conspirators; and the first who reached the duke was this Giovanni Andrea, who feigned to offer him a letter with one hand whilst he stabbed him with the other. It happened as with Scevola the Roman, when they took life for life. Such men are rarely found. And I believe that they carry out their crimes by divine permission. This was on the day of *Santo Stefano,* in church, during the mass. And when they tried to flee, they could not, because of the crowd of people, and mostly the women who hindered them by spreading out their gowns in such a way that the barons of the duke, and chiefly a certain Ghezzo who stood next to him, caught and slew the said Giovanni Andrea. And three others were taken and hung. Some people said that these three who were caught were quartered by four horses. . . .

And at this Christmas-time, what with terror of the war, the plague, and the papal excommunication, the citizens were in sorry plight. They lived in dread, and no one had any heart to work. The poor creatures could not procure silk or wool, or only very little, so that all classes suffered. . . .

1480.   *27th September*   A certain hermit came to the house of Lorenzo de' Medici at the *Poggio a Caiano;* and the servants declared that he intended to murder Lorenzo, so they took him and sent him to the *Bargello,* and he was put to the rack.

15th October   This hermit died at *Santa Maria Novella,* having been tortured in various ways. It was said that they skinned the soles of his feet, and then burnt them by holding them in the fire till the fat dripped off them; after which they set him upright and made him walk across the great hall; and these things caused his death. Opinions were divided as to whether he were guilty or innocent. . . .

1481.   *22nd August*   We apothecaries arranged that we should not keep our shops open on holidays till 22 in the evening (6 p.m.), as had hitherto been the custom, but that four shops in the whole city (to be chosen by lot) should remain open all day. . . .

1483.   *21st June*   In a tabernacle in Orto Sa' Michele there was placed the figure of San Tommaso beside Jesus, and the Jesus in bronze, which is the most beautiful thing imaginable, and the finest head of the Saviour that has as yet been made; it is by Andrea del Verrocchio.

At this time the Duke of Calabria and Signor Roberto left Ferrara and went into Lombardy, where much damage was being done on all sides, and Signor Gostanzo was poisoned there. . . .

7th September   During these days, for fear of hunger and of the war going on in Lombardy, many families left it, and there passed through Florence on their way into Roman territory 50 to 100 at a time, till they amounted to several thousands. Many also went to Romagna and elsewhere. It was said that there were more than 30 thousand persons altogether. It was a most pitiful sight to see these poor people pass, with a wretched little donkey, and their miserable household possessions: saucepans, frying-pans, etc. One wept to see them barefoot and ragged; and it is the cursed wars which have caused all this. No one went by without receiving some little help from us. . . .

1485.   And up till now my brother Gostanzo had gained 20 *palii* with his Barbary horse *Draghetto,* that is, 20 races from the 8th October, 1481, to the 25th June, 1485; the first was Santa Liperata, the next Sant' Anna, and San Vittorio several. Once when he won San Vittorio he sold the *palio* to the Aretini for 40 gold florins, and then he went to Arezzo and won it back again. And when he went to race at Siena, there was a tie between his horse and one belonging to Lorenzo de' Medici, called *La Lucciola* (Firefly), that of Gostanzo being in reality one head's length in advance of the other.

And the people who were present declared that he had won, and told him to go to the magistrate, and they would bear witness. Gostanzo, however, refused to do this, out of respect for Lorenzo, and as it happened, Lorenzo was proclaimed the winner. Another year, also at Siena, a meaner trick was played him: namely, when Gostanzo's horse was a bowshot in advance, and reached the winning-post, he dismounted and got up on the *palio;* then another horse came up, and they said that Gostanzo's horse had not passed the winning-post, and that the other one had passed it. Therefore the prize was given to the other. A very great injustice, that a rider who had not won the *palio* should receive it! It was most unfortunate, as my brother had such a good horse. He rushed about so much after this Barbary horse that in the end it proved his death. He died on the 12th September, 1485. . . .

And in these days of February and March, soldiers were continually being hired, to send to the Duke (of Calabria), who was fighting against the papal forces; so that everyone in Florence who had taken part against the Church was excommunicated. All intelligent people wondered that anyone should go against the Church, especially as as it had nothing to do with us. However, this mistaken conduct was the result of our sins and of our not fearing God.

1486.   *9th May*   Here in the Piazza de' Tornaquinci, by the house of the Tornabuoni, it happened that a bear of an extraordinary size, bred up in this city, being tormented by some children, seized a little girl of about six years old, a daughter of Giovacchino Berardi, by the throat, and it was with great difficulty that several men freed her, covered with blood and with her throat badly torn. But, thank God! she did not die. . . .

1487.   *30th September*   The relics of San Girolamo, that is to say, a jaw-bone and a bone of the arm, were taken from the altar of the Cross at *Santa Maria del Fiore,* and were set in silver and gold, very richly, at a great cost; and then a fine procession was made, and they were replaced in the said chapel with much reverence. This was done at the cost of the estimable Messer Jacopo Manegli, one of the order, having been elected preacher for Lent in *Santa Maria del Fiore,* preached very enthusiastically over and over again, persuading the people to make a *Monte di Pietà,* and to send away the Jews. As a consequence the boys got incensed against the Jews, and a number of them went to the house of a Jew called Manullino, who was a moneylender at the *Vacca,* wanting to assassinate him and to pillage his premises. The "Eight," however, promptly sent their men to stop the mischief and published proclamations threatening offenders with the gallows. Thus the commotion was soon ended. The next morning, the 13th, the "Eight" sent to Fra Bernardino forbidding him to continue preaching, and despatched him to the *Osservanza di San Miniato.* But even that did not satisfy them, and the morning after, Friday the 14th, the "Eight" sent their men again, some of them actually going in person, and commanded him to leave the neighbourhood entirely. This seemed a bad prognostic to those who were desirous to live a Christian life, as he was considered a saint. And it was not long before misfortunes happened to some of these "Eight": one of them broke his neck by falling from his horse, another this thing, and another that. Amongst the rest, that one who had gone in person to drive Fra Bernardino away from the *Osservanza* died mad in hospital. Thus the matter ended ill. God save us! . . .

1489. *20th August* They finished filling in the foundations on this side, in the *Piazza de' Tornaquinci.* And all this time they were demolishing the houses, a great number of overseers and workmen being employed, so that all the streets round were filled with heaps of stones and rubbish, and with mules and donkeys who were carrying away the rubbish and bringing gravel; making it difficult for anyone to pass along. We shopkeepers were continually annoyed by the dust and the crowds of people who collected to look on, and those who could not pass by with their beasts of burden.

21st August They began to build the walls upon the aforesaid foundations.

And at this time all the following buildings were erected:

The *Osservanza di San Miniato de' Fraita de San Francesco*; the sacristy of *Santo Spirito;* the house of Giulio Gondi; and the church of the *Frati di Sant' Agostino,* outside the *Porta a San Gallo.* And Lorenzo de' Medici began a palace at the *Poggio a Caiano,* on his property, where so much has been beautifully ordered, the *Cascine,* etc. Princely things! At Sarrezana a fortress was built; and many other houses were erected in Florence: in the street which goes to Santa Caterina, and towards the *Porta a Pinti,* and the *Via Nuova de' Servi,* at Cestello, and from the *Porta a Faenza* towards San Barnaba, and towards Sant' Ambrogio, and elsewhere. Men were crazy about building at this time, so that there was a scarcity of master-builders and of materials. . . .

1490. *27th June* I, Luca Landucci, opened my new shop, here opposite the said *palagio* of the Strozzi, and I chose the sign of the *Stelle* (Stars). . . .

22nd December The chapel, that is, the *Capella Maggiore,* of *Santa Maria Novella* was opened. Domenico del Grillandaio had painted it, at the order of Giovanni Tornabuoni. And the choir of carved wood was also made round the chapel. The painting alone cost 1000 gold florins. . . .

1491. *1st May* The coinage was changed: that is, silver coins began to be used; and it was decided that the *grossone* should be worth 16 *quattrini* and a half, like the old silver ones. All the taxes were to be paid in silver, which meant a little increase to the people, as a quarter more had to be paid, when there was need, on the contrary, to relieve them. This increase was made by divine permission, on account of our sins; because the poor are generally worse than the rich and great. Praise be to God! . . .

1492. *8th April* Lorenzo de' Medici died on his estate at Careggi; and it was said that when he heard the news of the effects of the thunderbolt, being so ill, he asked where it had fallen, and on which side; and when he was told, he said: "Alas! I shall die, because it fell towards my house." This may not have been so, but it was commonly reported.

And they brought him to Florence the same night, at 5 in the morning (1 a.m.), and put him in the monastery at *San Marco*; and he remained there the whole of the next day, which was a Monday. And on the 10th April, Tuesday, he was buried at San Lorenzo at about 20 in the evening (4 p.m.). Well may we consider what a transitory thing is human life! This man, in the eyes of the world, was the most illustrious, the richest, the most stately, and the most renowned among men. Everyone declared that he ruled Italy; and in very truth he was possessed of great wisdom, and all his undertakings prospered. He had succeeded in doing what no citizen had been able to do for a long time: namely, in getting his son appointed cardinal; which was not only an honour for his house, but for the whole city. In spite of all this, however, he could not live one hour longer when the end came. Then, O man, man, what hast thou to be proud of? True humility is the fit human attribute, and each time that we grow proud, and esteem ourselves above others, failing to recognise that every spiritual, corporal and temporal good comes from God, we exceed the proper limits of humanity. Everything that exceeds its limits is evil, and those things which should be good, turn to ill. The desirable quality for man is true gentleness and humility, and always to esteem God. Man is naught, if not what God has made him; to whom be praise from all creatures, as is His due. May He pardon me my sins! And may He pardon the sins of the dead man, as I trust He may pardon me and all human beings! . . .

1494. *17th November*   The King of France [Charles VIII] entered Florence at 22 in the evening (6 p.m.) by the Porta a San Friano, and passed through the Piazza (de' Signori), proceeding so slowly that it was already 24 (8 p.m.) before he reached Santa Maria del Fiore. He dismounted at the steps, and walked up to the High Altar, there being so many torches that they made a double row from the door to the altar, leaving a way clear in the middle, along which he went with his barons and all his suite, amidst such tumultuous shouting of *Viva Francia* as was never heard. Only think that all Florence was there, either in the church or outside. Everyone shouted, great and small, old and young, and all from their hearts, without flattery. When he was seen on foot he seemed to the people somewhat less imposing, for he was in fact a very small man. Nevertheless there was no one who did not feel favourably disposed towards him. Therefore it should have been easy to make him understand that our hearts are innocent of guile, and that we are truly devoted to him; so that he ought to feel moved towards us in uncommon measure, and to trust us absolutely. This is really the case, and he will see in the future what the faith of the Florentines signifies. Upon coming out of church, he remounted his horse and rode on to the palace of Piero de' Medici, amidst continued cries of *Viva Francia.* Never was such joy seen before, or so much honour done to anyone, with heartfelt sincerity, as we were in hopes that he would bring us peace and rest. In the end it proved not to be so, as he took Pisa from us and gave it to the Pisans, which he had no right to do, seeing that he could not give what was not his. . . .

6th December (Saturday)   Fra Girolamo preached, and ordered that alms should be given for the *Poveri Vergognosi* in four churches: *Santa Maria del Fiore, Santa Maria Novella, Santa Croce,* and *Santo Spirito;* which were collected on the following day, Sunday. And so much was given that it was impossible to estimate it: gold and silver, woollen and linen materials, silks and pearls and other things; everyone contributed so largely out of love and charity. . . .

14th December (Sunday) . . . The same day Fra Girolamo did his utmost in the pulpit to persuade Florence to adopt a good form of government . . . and he preached much about State matters, and that we ought to love and fear God, and love the common weal; and no one must set himself up proudly above the rest. He always favoured the people and he insisted that no one ought to be put to death, but there must be other forms of punishment; and he continued to preach in this manner every morning. . . .

11 January (Sunday)   Fra Girolamo preached, and spoke much concerning the reforms in the city; and exculpated himself from various accusations, saying that there were devils who disturbed the life of the commune; and that they wrote forged letters, which made it appear as if the *Frate* had given Piero de' Medici hopes of returning, in order to make the people turn against him. But nevertheless all this was untrue; he was entirely for the people and the common weal. He was calumniated by these foxes; but the truth would always prevail. It is the fact that he always encouraged this community of feeling amongst the people. . . .

1495.   1st April   Fra Girolamo preached, and said and testified that the Virgin Mary had revealed to him, that after going through much trouble, the city of Florence was to be the most glorious, the richest, and the most powerful that ever existed; and he promised this absolutely. All these things he spoke as a prophet, and the greater part of the people believed him, especially quiet people without political or party passions. . . .

17th June   Fra Girolamo spoke to the king at Poggibonizi. And it was said that this was the cause of his not coming to Florence; that the *Frate* had begged his favour for the city, and said that it was God's will that he should treat it well, it being entirely his friend. So he really was of great assistance to Florence, and the king listened to him. At this time the *Frate* was held in such esteem and the people were so devoted to him, that there were many men and women who, if he had said, *Entrate nel fuoco* (Go into the fire), would have actually obeyed him. He was considered by many to be a prophet, and he himself claimed to be one. . . .

1497.   18th April   There was a commotion in Florence, which arose in the Piazza de' Signori and in the Piazza del Grano. Some poor women went to the door of the *Palagio* begging for bread, and all over the city ran the cry of *Serra, serra!* (Close everything!); so that everyone took in their wares (from the outside shelves), and some shut up their shops. . . .

18th June   An excommunication came from the Pope excommunicating Fra Girolamo, which was published this morning in Santo Spirito, in Santa Maria Novella, in Santa Croce, in the Badìa, and at the Servi. I heard it read and proclaimed in Santo Spirito, in the chancel, between two lighted tapers, and amidst a number of friars. It was read and proclaimed by Fra Leonardo, their preacher, and the adversary of Fra Girolamo. It declared that the said *Frate* had not obeyed a certain Brief which had been sent as far back as the November of 1496, summoning him on his vow of obedience to go to the Pope; and if he did not choose to obey the excommunication, no one was to give him aid or support, and no one must go and hear him, nor go to any place where he was, on pain of excommunication. . . .

11th February   Fra Girolamo began to preach in *Santa Maria del Fiore,* and the stands (for the boys) were made as before. Many people went there, and it was much talked of, on account of his excommunication; and many did not go, for fear of being excommunicated, saying: *giusta vel ingiusta, temenda est.* I was one of those who did not go. We did not hear much of the plague now; it was in one or two houses, but not more. . . .

1498.   *10th April*   At 9 in the evening (5 p.m.) the *Frate* was carried to the *Bargello* by two men on their crossed hands, because his feet and hands were in irons, and Fra Domenico also; and they seized them and put Fra Girolamo to the rack three times and Fra Domenico four times; and Fra Girolamo said: "Take me down, and I will write you my whole life." You may imagine that it was not without tears that right-minded men who had faith in him, heard that he had been tortured; he who had taught this prayer, *Fac bene bonis et rectis corde*. No, it was not without tears and grief, and urgent prayers to God. . . .

19th April   The protocol of Fra Girolamo, written by his own hand, was read in Council, in the Great Hall; he whom we had held to be a prophet, confessed that he was no prophet, and had not received from God the things which he preached; and he confessed that many things which had occurred during the course of his preaching were contrary to what he had given us to understand. I was present when this protocol was read, and I marvelled, feeling utterly dumbfounded with surprise. My heart was grieved to see such an edifice fall to the ground on account of having been founded on a lie. Florence had been expecting a new Jerusalem, from which would issue just laws and splendour and an example of righteous life, and to see the renovation of the Church, the conversion of unbelievers, and the consolation of the righteous; and I felt that everything was exactly contrary, and had to resign myself with the thought: *In voluntate tua Domine omnia sunt posita.* . . .

22nd May (Wednesday morning)   The sacrifice of the three *Frati* was made. They took them out of the *Palagio* and brought them on to the *ringhiera*, where were assembled the "Eight" and the *Collegi*, the papal envoy, the General of the Dominicans, and many canons, priests and monks of divers Orders, and the Bishop of the *Pagagliotti* who was deputed to degrade the three *Frati*; and here on the *ringhiera* the said ceremony was to be performed. They were robed in all their vestments, which were taken off one by one, with the appropriate words for the degradation, it being constantly affirmed that Fra Girolamo was a heretic and schismatic, and on this account condemned to be burnt; then their faces and hands were shaved, as is customary in this ceremony.

When this was completed, they left the *Frati* in the hands of the "Eight," who immediately made the decision that they should be hung and burnt; and they were led straight on to the platform at the foot of the cross. The first to be executed was Fra Silvestro, who was hung to the post and one arm of the cross, and there not being much drop, he suffered for some time, repeating "Jesu" many times whilst he was hanging, for the rope did not draw tight nor run well. The second was Fra Domenico of Pescia, who also kept saying "Jesu"; and the third was the *Frate* called a heretic, who did not speak aloud, but to himself, and so he was hung. This all happened without a word from one of them, which was considered extraordinary, especially by good and thoughtful people, who were much disappointed, as everyone had been expecting some signs, and desired the glory of God, the beginning of righteous life, the renovation of the Church, and the conversion of unbelievers; hence they were not without bitterness and not one of them made an excuse. Many, in fact, fell from their faith. When all three were hung, Fra Girolamo being in the middle, facing the *Palagio*, the scaffold was separated from the *ringhiera*, and a fire was made on the circular platform round the cross, upon which gunpowder was put and set alight, so that the said fire burst out with a noise of rockets and cracking. In a few hours they were burnt, their legs and arms gradually dropping off; part of their bodies remaining hanging to the chains, a quantity of stones were thrown to make them fall, as there was a fear of the people getting hold of them; and then the hangman and those whose business it was, hacked down the post and burnt it on the ground, bringing a lot of brushwood, and stirring the fire up over the dead bodies, so that the very least piece was consumed. Then they fetched carts, and accompanied by the mace-bearers, carried the last bit of dust to the Arno, by the Ponte Vecchio, in order that no remains should be found. Nevertheless, a few good men had so much faith that they gathered some of the floating ashes together, in fear and secrecy, because it was as much as one's life was worth to say a word, so anxious were the authorities to destroy every relic. . . .

1500.   *24th May*   We apothecaries of Florence assembled, about 40 *maestri* (master-apothecaries), in San Gilio, to resuscitate a *Compania* (Guild) of ours, which had been begun in 1477, but abandoned later; and we appointed certain men who would do what was necessary. . . .

1503.   *24th October*   My son Antonio went to the *Studio* (University) at Bologna to study for his degree of medical doctor. . . .

1504.   *14th May*   The marble giant was taken out of the *Opera* (Office of Works of the Duomo); it was brought out at 24 in the evening (8 p.m.), and they had to break down the wall above the door so that it could come through. During the night stones were thrown at the giant to injure it, therefore it was necessary to keep watch over it. It went very slowly, being bound in an erect position, and suspended so that it did not touch the ground with its feet. There were immensely strong beams, constructed with great skill; and it took four days to reach the Piazza, arriving there on the 18th at 12 in the morning (8 a.m.). It was moved along by more than 40 men. Beneath it there were 14 greased beams, which were changed from hand to hand; and they laboured till the 8th July, 1504, to place it on the *ringhiera,* where the "Judith" had been, which was now removed and placed inside the *Palagio* in the court. The said giant had been made by Michelangelo Buonarroti. . . .

8th September   The giant in the Piazza was finished, and completely uncovered. . . .

1505.   *20th December*   I gave a memorandum and a drawing to Simone del Pollaiuolo, as he was an architect, and it seemed to me that he was fit to carry out my idea; which was, that in that place where now stands San Giovanni Evangelista in Florence, a fine temple with a fine cupola ought to be built, in honour of San Giovanni Vangiolista, and to the glory of God and of our city; giving him this design, according to which all the houses and shops in the Piazza di San Lorenzo, a square of about 100 *braccia* each way, should be taken down to make room for this temple, which would be opposite San Lorenzo and facing the street; and we should have as an advocate in heaven with San Giovanni Battista, one who was the beloved of Christ and his brother, according to the flesh, and not less so in eternal life. I made him understand all my ideas about it, which pleased him very much, and he told me several times that he had never seen a finer invention, and explained how he thought he could lay it before those in authority; he was most impatient. . . .

24th January   A young man was hung; and the doctors and scholars of the *Studio* (University), where there were a great number of doctors and worthy men, requested the "Eight" to allow them to have the body to dissect, and it was granted them. And they did this work in some of their rooms at Santa Croce, and it lasted till the first of February, 1505, their meetings taking place twice a day. The physicians were there, and my son Messer Antonio also, every day, to look on. . . .

15th February   There was a muster in the Piazza of 400 recruits whom the *Gon-faloniere* had assembled, Florentine peasants, and he gave them each a white waistcoat, a pair of stockings half red and half white, a white cap, shoes, and an iron breastplate, and lances, and to some of them muskets. These were called battalions; and they were given a constable who would lead them, and teach them how to use their arms. They were soldiers, but stopped at their own houses, being obliged to appear when needed; and it was ordered that many thousand should be made in this way all through the country, so that we should not need to have any foreigners. This was thought the finest thing that had ever been arranged for Florence. . . .

1506.   *13th November*   In the evening, at about 24 in the evening (8 p.m.), at San Michele Berteldi, it began to be said that an image of Our Lady, which is over a door, had miraculously closed its eyes; the one opposite the door of the *Stufa* (Baths). It seemed as if she did not wish to see the sins that are committed there. Before a day had passed, numbers of candles were lighted, and great veneration was paid to it, so that a wall was built in front of it like a church, and if it had not been unfitting for women to go to this place near the *Stufa,* many women would have gone there; and, in spite of this, many waxen images were brought to it and many votive-offerings. . . .

1507.   *2nd August*   As it pleased God, the house in which I lived, next to the shop (the shop being in the middle of a house), was burnt down, and I lost my rooms, in which were all my things, worth more than 250 gold ducats. I had to buy all my household goods, clothes and furniture afresh, three rooms completely stocked; my son Maestro Antonio alone losing more than 50 or 60 ducats' worth: a red-cloth cloak, a purple tunic, both new, and all his other clothes and silk waistcoats, with all his books which were worth more than 25 ducats. I and my three other sons had nothing left but our shirts; and what was worse, Battista's bed had caught fire whilst he was asleep, and he escaped perfectly naked, and went to borrow a shirt in the neighbourhood. Nothing was saved except what the women had with them in the country, and Messer Antonio who was with them; so that they were not here to see the grief we suffered. But I accept adversity like prosperity, and thus give thanks to the Lord for the one as for the other; and I pray Him to pardon my sins and to send me all which tends to His glory. . . .

1512.   *11th March*   Two hours before dawn a rumour arose in Florence that the Cardinal de' Medici was Pope; and there was much bell-ringing, and bonfires were lighted in many parts of the city, with such joy and commotion, and such persistent cries of *Palle!* that it made everyone get up, even the women, and go to the windows; it began at 8 in the morning (4 a.m.), by someone going about crying through the city that he had been elected; nevertheless no news had come, for on inquiring at the *Palagio de' Signori* and the palace of the Medici, we were told that there was no news yet.

It was quite impossible, however, to do anything but cry *Palle!* the whole day, although nothing was known. . . .

At 2 o'clock that Friday night (10 p.m.) the news came, and it was true that the Cardinal de' Medici had been elected Pope, with the name of Lione X. If there had been bonfires and rejoicings before, they were redoubled now, and in a different spirit; innumerable bundles of brushwood, great branches, baskets, barrels, and whatever each poor man chanced to have in his house; all the smallest streets of the city did their part, without stint and the people not yet being content, ran all over Florence to pull down the wooden roofs above the shops and everywhere, burning up everything. They put the whole city in great danger, and if the "Eight" had not made a proclamation that no more roofs were to be pulled down and that the *Piagnoni* were no longer to be insulted, on pain of the gallows, even the tiled roofs would have been destroyed and the shops looted. And this nuisance lasted all Friday and Saturday, bonfires continuing, and illuminations on the *Palagio,* up on the cupola, on the gates, and everywhere, with so much firing of cannon and continual cries of *Palle! Papa Lione!* that it seemed as if the city were upside-down, and anyone who had seen it from overhead would have said: "Florence is burning down the whole city," for there was such a tumult of shouting, and fires, and smoke, and reports of the cannon, large and small; and on Sunday the same, and on Monday worse than ever. . . .

1514. 25th June There was a hunt in the *Piazza de' Signori*: two lions, and bears, leopards, bulls, buffaloes, stags, and many other wild animals of various kinds, and horses; the lions were brought in after the rest, and chiefly the one that came first did nothing, on account of the great tumult of the crowd; except that certain big dogs approaching him, he seized one with his paw and dropped it dead on the ground, and a second the same, without taking any notice of the other wild beasts; when he was not molested, he stood quite still, and then went away further on. They had made a tortoise and a porcupine, inside of which were men who made them move along on wheels all over the Piazza, and kept thrusting at the animals with their lances. This hunt was thought so much of, that the number of wooden platforms and enclosures made in the Piazza was a thing never before seen, the cost of bringing the timber and of erecting these stands being very great; it seemed incredible that any city in the world could have such a mass of timber. One carpenter paid 40 gold florins for the permission to put up a platform against one of these houses, and there were people who paid three or four *grossoni* (*grossone* = about ⅓ of a florin) for a place on the stands. All the stands and enclosures were crowded, as also the windows and the roofs, such a concourse of people never having been known, for numbers of strangers had come from many different parts. Four cardinals had come from Rome disguised, and many Romans accompanied by a quantity of horsemen. At the end of the evening it was found that many men had been injured and about three killed in fighting with the wild beasts; one had been killed by a buffalo. They had made a beautiful large fountain in the middle of the Piazza, which threw the water up in four jets, and round this fountain was a wood of verdure, with certain dens very convenient for the animals to hide in, and low troughs full of water round the fountain, for them to be able to drink. Everything had been very well arranged, except that someone without the fear of God did an abominable thing in this Piazza, in the presence of 40 thousand women and girls, putting a mare into an enclosure together with the horses; which much displeased decent and well-behaved people, and I believe that it displeased even the ill-behaved people. . . .

1515.   *30th November (the day of Sant' Andrea—a Friday)*   The Pope made his magnificent and triumphal entry into Florence, everything having been prepared at an incredible cost. The grandeur of it was incredible; but I will try to give a few details.

All the chief citizens went in procession to meet him, and amongst others fifty young men, on foot, the richest and most important in the city, dressed in a costume of purple silk, with a collar of miniver, each carrying in his hand a sort of small silvered lance, very beautiful to see; and they were followed by a throng of citizens on horseback. With the Pope came numerous infantry, and amongst them the papal guard, consisting of many German soldiers, in a uniform with which they wore two-edged axes in the French fashion. Besides these, many mounted bowmen and musketeers, all belonging to his guard. And he was carried all through the city by the *Signoria* under a rich *baldacchino* (canopy), and was put down at Santa Maria del Fiore. . . .

And then he came down towards Santa Maria Novella, giving the benediction all the time, preceded by many buglers and fife-players, amidst such a crowd of people that it made one's eyes ache to see them. Perhaps there had never been such a multitude assembled in Florence before. He caused money to be thrown to the people as he passed through the streets, *grossi* and silver coins. So far there was nothing extraordinary; but now we will speak of the things undertaken by the directors of the festivities, which were so huge that some of them remained unfinished for want of time. It is unimaginable that any other city or state in the world could have been capable of making such preparations; their magnitude can be realised when you consider that although several thousand men laboured for more than a month beforehand, workdays and holidays alike, it was not possible to bring the whole to perfection, some few being incomplete; even so, however, the beauty of the work could be seen, and its incalculable cost. To show that this is true, I will describe the sights in order, but my words will express very little, the actuality far exceeding any description.

The first was at the gate of *San Piero Gattolino,* where for the sake of splendour they broke down the wall of the outer gate, and laid the portcullis on the ground, ornamenting the outside of the gate with four enormous pillars, 16 *braccia* in height, all silvered over, with bases and capitals like those of Santo Spirito; besides these there were several pilasters with great architraves and cornices and friezes, as such pillars require, reaching up to certain tabernacles on the face of the gate, with a number of statues in the niches and under the arches, all by the hand of good masters, which could not have been made at another time for hundreds of florins, and all illustrating famous stories, which delighted one's eyes.

The second was at *San Felice in Piazza,* at the entrance to Via Maggio, a most beautiful triumphal arch, which reached right across the street. It had eight round pillars, as large as those of Santo Spirito, with numerous pilasters, and the requisite capitals and cornices, all ornamented without stint. Here also there were many statues by the hand of the chief masters, placed between the arches and in niches, making people pause to consider their meaning and admire their beauty.

The third was at the Ponte a Santa Trinità, and surpassed all the rest in beauty. At the entrance to the bridge, towards Via Maggio, there was a splendid triumphal arch, as wide as the bridge; this had six pillars as tall as those of the last arch and larger, placed with such exquisite symmetry that I considered that Florence had many architects of greater talent than any that can be found in the world. . . .

And so that you may realise that money was not spared, I must tell you that at *Santa Maria Novella* they took down that very fine staircase leading to the *Sala del Papa,* and replaced it by another, up which a man could ride on horseback, as may be seen. And even this was not enough, for they also threw down the gates and walls of the court, displeasing many people, in order to make a number of rooms inside it at a great cost.

They also pulled down the projections of the houses and all the pent-roofs over the shops in the Via Porta Rossa and many other places where they wanted to widen the street. They spoilt the steps of the *Badìa* and the roof over them; in fact they spared nothing, breaking up all without discretion.

And you must know that I have not written the tenth part of what might be said; when you think that we had more than 2 thousand men at work, as it was estimated, for for than a month, belonging to various trades: carpenters, stone-masons, painters, carters, porters, sawyers, etc., and a cost of 70 thousand florins or more was mentioned, all for things of no duration; when a splendid temple might have been built in honour of God and to the glory of the city. Certainly, however, the money that was scattered in this way added to the earnings of the poor workmen. . . .

1529.   *10th October*   The army of the Emperor and the Pope came to the walls of Florence, and gradually encircling the city completely, laid siege to it. And this siege lasted almost a year, and there was such a scarcity that the price of corn rose to 3 *lire* 15 *soldi*—the *Signoria* fixing it at that. (The prices of other things were as follows:)

	Lire	Soldi	Denari		Lire	Soldi	Denari
A pound of Cheese	2	18	0	An Onion		4	0
A couple of Capons	49	0	0	A flask of Wine	2	2	0
A couple of Hens	21	0	0	A pound of Fish	2	2	0
A pound of Salt-meat	2	15	0	A Kid's head	1	5	0
A Kid	25	0	0	A Liver and Lights	1	5	0
A Lamb	18	0	0	A pound of wax Candles	1	16	0
A pound of Ass's flesh or Horse-flesh		10	0	A pound of Honey	1	0	0
A Lettuce		6	0	A Lemon		7	0
Two sour Plums			4	An Orange		6	0
One ripe Plum		1	8	A pound of dried Grapes		12	0
A Pomegranate		6	0	A Herring		7	0
A quarter of a peck of soft Beans		2	0	A pound of crushed Almonds	3	12	0
A bunch of Radishes		1	8	Two Walnuts 1 *quattrino*			
A flask of Oil	7	0	0	A little bunch of Beet		1	0
A pound of Preserves	2	10	0	A little bunch of Cabbage		1	0
A pound of Bologna Sausages	2	18	0				

	Lire	Soldi	Denari		Lire	Soldi	Denari
An ounce of Pepper		16	0	A bunch of fresh			
A couple of Eggs		18	0	Leeks		1	0
A pound of muscatel				A fresh Pumpkin	1	15	0
Pears		12	0	An Apricot		4	0
A pound of Cherries		8	0	A Gander	14	0	0
A pound of Mutton	2	10	0	A pound of Sausage	2	16	0

* * *

1533.   *17th April*   In the year 1529 the custom of wearing hoods began to go out, and by 1532 not a single one was to be seen; caps or hats being worn instead. Also, at this time, men began to cut their hair short, everyone having formerly worn it long, on to their shoulders, without exception; and they now began to wear a beard, which formerly was only worn by two men in Florence, Corbizo and one of the Martigli.

At this time also hose were begun to be made in two pieces, which had formerly been made all in one, and without a seam; now they slashed them up everywhere, and put silk underneath, letting it project at all the slashes. . . .

❧ ON EDUCATION

Juan Luis Vives

Juan Luis Vives, like his friends Desiderius Erasmus and Thomas More, was the perfect example of a certain Renaissance type: the pious, cosmopolitan, critical, humanitarian, many-sided scholar. Vives was born in Valencia, Spain, in 1492. He studied at the University of Paris, and in 1519 was appointed professor of humanities at the University of Louvain, in Belgium. Then he lived for a number of years in England as tutor to Mary Tudor, daughter of Henry VIII, and as a lecturer in philosophy at Oxford University. Eventually he moved to Bruges, in Flanders, where he died in 1540. Aside from numerous special studies in literature and philosophy (e.g., an elaborate commentary on Saint Augustine's City of God), Vives wrote much on the general nature and current condition of scholarship, usually strongly attacking the scholastic philosophers and the uncritical acceptance of Aristotle's authority. His most influential work on education, De Tradendis Disciplinis (1531), concludes with an appendix on the life of the scholar; it is from this appendix that the selections below are drawn. Vives discusses the goals and methods of scholarly life in a critical but enthusiastic manner, incidentally revealing, by his frequent references to

*the great writers of antiquity, the extent to which the revival of interest in
the classical world had spread by the early sixteenth century.*

CHAPTER I: THE AIM OF STUDIES

. . . Erudition involves four factors: natural capacity, judgment, memory, application.
Pray tell me, whence the first three of these come: whence except from God? If praise
is to be given to a learned man, it must be sought in the last-named element. And this
element is the lowest and least of all, and even for that how greatly is a man helped by
having a bodily frame, not heavy, nor stupefied, but of sound health. And are not
these states of the body the gift of God? What then remains in himself for the learned
man to boast about? Well, do you say; He has willed to work? But how many others
would will, if it were, through the goodness of God, permitted to them to do what
it is permitted to you? Amid the praises given to himself, the wise man directs himself
to the contemplation of that holy and divine wisdom, in comparison with the lowest
part of which, as Paul says, all human wisdom is mere foolishness. . . .

If now we must propose some end to each of the actions of our life, so much the
more must this be the case with studies, so that it may be settled whither our labour
tends. We must not always be studying so that we do nothing but study, nor must
the mind, bound by no law and with no useful aim, delight itself in any inane sort of
contemplation and knowledge of things. Socrates said that he had no time to busy
himself with poetic fables, since he did not as yet know himself, and that it was
ridiculous that he who did not know himself should closely investigate other
people's concerns. Much less is the fruit of studies to be estimated by their return
in money. Such an opinion has only been held by debased natures, who are far
removed from any true idea of studies. For nothing is so distant from literature
as either the desire or the anxiety for money; so that wherever this desire settles in a
man of studies, forthwith it drives away the zeal for intellectual research, because study
does not commit itself with full confidence to any souls, except those free and loosed
from that disease. People say: "First get rich; then become philosophical." Nay, rather
it should be said: "We must first philosophise, and afterwards get rich." For if we first
get rich we shall soon no longer wish to busy ourselves with philosophy, and, made
anxious by the possession of wealth, snatched away to a thousand vices, ignorant of
philosophy, we shall be ignorant of the true use of riches. But if once we become
philosophers, then it will be easy, afterwards, to get as rich as it is at all necessary
to be. . . .

Nothing has so sullied the glory of all kinds of knowledge and of all learning, and
debased it, as the frivolity of some smatterers who constantly flatter any people whatsoever especially princes, being particularly drawn to some new rather than some

Vives: On Education; a Translation of the De Tradendis Disciplinis of Juan Luis Vives,
ed. Foster Watson (London: Cambridge University Press, 1913), pp. 275–281, 283–287, 289–
296, 299–304.

longer-known person. But this is precisely what truly learned men will not do. The mass of the people, it is true, do not understand the difference. They suppose that every one is a learned man, who writes or speaks the Latin tongue in some form or other. Yet those who thus act defend themselves by the specious argument that they did not praise the pseudo-learned men for such, as they really were, but for the qualities which they ought to have shown. This gives but a very slight "colour" to their praise, and one which others do not recognise. Hence they accuse the learned man of sycophancy, and attach the stigma to the profession of literature itself and detest it, as if it commended a wicked Prince, and made him out to be a very good Prince. Nay even the Prince himself, imbued with the depraved opinion, believes that he is estimated as his flatterers describe him. Hence he becomes from day to day more and more arrogant and intolerable. When he has begun this kind of life he gets confirmed in it, since he finds he obtains so much praise from it, and seeing that it has all been handed down to posterity in the works of the learned, he thinks it must therefore be fixed for certain. If the learned men had not been accustomed to flatter princes, then the latter would, on the one hand, have esteemed learning higher, and, on the other, they would rejoice immeasurably to be praised by them, i.e. according to the saying of the ancient poet *a laudatis viris*. Then, too, the learned man's upbraiding would have had great weight. Nor, then, would the approval of a learned man be otherwise than the weightiest testimony of a most conscientious authority. So, too, a prince not less than any others would regard it as the amplest reward of his virtue in this life, to receive the approval of the learned man. But now princes do not value it at a hair, since they see they can buy it for a farthing or two, nay even for a bit of bread. When circumstances justify the praise of princes, let the praise be somewhat sparing, and in such a manner, that they feel that they would rather be admonished and stimulated in their actions than have their praises sung, as if their course of life were already ended. If you may hope for any good from it, vices ought to be freely condemned, only let there be no bitterness nor rage. But if you are only causing hatred, and you can do no good, then it is better to abstain from the useless task. Nor ought the faults of the powerful, nor indeed of any man, to be covered over, on the ground of expectation of a reward, or for the sake of any gain, for this is particularly shameful. For it has the effect that the bad go on the more boldly in their wickedness, and moreover, with the consent of learned men, others are encouraged to follow their example.

There are others who do not seek from their studies to obtain money, but glory. This is a little better I confess, but only if in youth and in the young man, it may supply very great goads to noble actions. But when this motive appears later in life, it is the ground and source of many evils, as I have elsewhere shown, because we set all our store on being seen by those looking on, nothing on our conscience, which will judge us, in our actions, more justly than any fellow-man possibly can. And thus we often fall by the hope of glory which we have seized, because he who gave us false credit afterwards perceives his error, or he who judged rightly begins himself to be deceived, although it happens more frequently that mistaken estimates are turned to what is sounder, since time confirms what is true and solid, but shatters and removes false and empty judgments. Therefore let no one have confidence that he will secure glory with posterity through the empty favour of the living and by pretence of noble work. For so soon as the passions which have been stirred up have subsided, judgment enters in their place, and this puts things in more exact proportions. . . . Nay, also, how unfortunate is the fame of those who have done deserving work! The works of Ovid remain, but not those of Chrysippus or Crantor. The works of Vincent of Beauvais have come to us complete; but not so those of Titus Livius, not those of Polybius, not those of Marcus Varro, not even those of Marcus Tullius Cicero! . . .

But, put the case that you have obtained renown, praise, glory; what good will it be to you when you come to die? For then you will perceive none of these things, which are happening here, no more than the horse, when he is proclaimed victor in the Olympian games, or the picture of Apelles, which we study closely with admiration. What is all the renown of his name, to Cicero? or to Aristotle? . . .

This then is the fruit of all studies; this is the goal. Having acquired our knowledge, we must turn it to usefulness, and employ it for the common good. Whence follows immortal reward not in money, not in present favour, or pleasures, which are fleeting and momentary. Do we then live rightly and teach rightly, if we do it for the sake of money? Would we exchange the rich gift of God for so vile and contemptible a reward? Would we exchange it for glory? Wretch that I should be, if I were to chase so eagerly after that which, in spite of such labours and pains, cannot be preserved, and which is so uncertain and fleeting, that no servitude can be compared with it; more wretched still, if I were to buy people's good word in exchange for such an excellent and holy reward, and prefer to be praised by mortal men rather than by the immortal God; by fools, rather than by Wisdom Itself. O how we fish with a golden hook, for merely foul eels!

With bold confidence, therefore, we must study all branches of knowledge for that use, for which they were appointed by God. We ought therefore, not always to be studying, but our study must be attuned to practical usefulness in life. Every study is unlimited in itself, but at some stage we ought to begin to turn it to the use and advantage of other people. For this purpose, practical wisdom is necessary, because practice leads us to the consideration of subjects separate from one another, and practical wisdom rules as the valuer and judge of the circumstances considered as a whole.

CHAPTER II: THE SCHOLAR AND THE WORLD

If the learned man intends to go into the sight and haunts of men, then should he have thought over his preparation for this purpose, as if he were in training for a fight, so that he should not be taken possession of by any of those debased passions which attack and beset us on every side. . . . Let him strengthen his mind at home, with great and strong thoughts, tending to the disdain of honours and dignities. . . .

Let him adorn his own bodily bearing with modesty and self-control. In all his words and deeds let there be gravity and consistency, so that he may be an example to others for a like rationality of life. He will indeed convince greatly by his rhetoric, but most of all by his blamelessness of life. So that all which proceeds from him may be the more exact and pure, let him constantly take thought that he says and does nothing which has not good ground for it, and which may not be followed as an example by right-minded men. For they should be able to think that what he does is a law for their life. But to the evil-minded and envious he should serve as a suggestion to inquiry and an example against false judgments. He must therefore be somewhat cautious in action, slow in judgment, and particularly circumspect in his speech. Through him literature and knowledge will gain a respectful hearing, and many men through their desire for such excellence which they observe in him, will give themselves up to the study of knowledge, because they see such delightful and splendid results in him. . . .

Learned men should show themselves gentle, affable, self-controlled, unvanquished by depraved desires, and should demonstrate how much wisdom can accomplish in the human mind, when it has the sovereignty; and what a great distance there is between the wise man and the fool. It will be sufficient for them if they can be strong and efficacious in the really great and noble matters; not to desire to be esteemed highly in all sorts of occupations, in war, in horsemanship, hunting, fishing, dancing, games, in impudent trifling and raillery. All this is the part of busy-bodies, not of wise men, and learned men become ridiculous who are as zealous in such pursuits, as in that of forming wise judgments. . . .

Learned men should live in unity with one another and deal with everyone courteously. For it is very disgraceful in us, that robbers and lions live in greater harmony amongst themselves than do the learned. Neither unanimity nor benevolence will be lacking in the learned, if they have pursued their studies whole-heartedly and religiously; not for glory or reward, for where the desire of these things prevails it is difficult to preserve the sanctity of society. When a comparison of studies is made, then the name of "vanquished" should not be given to the man, who allows that another has argued better than he. For that word "vanquished" signifies something very different from the fact to which it is in this case applied. For in this sort of battle, those who differ are not enemies. This is a very bitter and inimical word applied to what is a very pleasant contest, one in its nature full of good-will between the opponents. For what greater or closer union can we find than that of the mind of one man who is helped by another man's mind towards practical wisdom or virtue. It is a similar relation to that of the husbandman to his field, so that not undeservedly those who train the minds of others may be termed their parents. As is sight to the eyes, so is insight to the mind. Those who cannot see sufficiently clearly through their eyes, yield their judgment to those who have more distinct vision, and do so ungrudgingly. That man possesses sharper and sounder eyes; this man has a mind of clearer insight by nature, or is better trained by experience, age, and industry. Though, of course, sight-observation receives greater praise than mental vision, according to circumstances, as e.g. when a coin is lost, plenty are to be found able to join in the search.

When a man has come to a mature age, we may describe his speeches by such terms as contests, struggles, fights, victories. Let everyone, I beg, consider how great a benefit it is to be freed from the tyranny of ignorance, which is the heaviest and most shameful of all servitudes. Plato says wisely: That it is as much preferable to be beaten in a disputation than to beat, as it is better to be freed from a great evil than to be the one who liberates. For what more deadly thing can happen to men than to form a false opinion? Though in some cases it may be more glorious to be a liberator, it is certainly more useful to be made free. But we should all gladly be delivered from this great evil of ignorance, if disputations were less theatrical, and there were not so much deference shown to the listeners who surround the disputants. The disputation ought to be rather a friendly discussion than a hostile fight for victory. This should be the case in all kinds of discussions, but particularly in theology, in which subject, impious attacks are made on holy truth, and doubts are started in the minds of listeners, about things which ought to be held as certain, fixed and unshakable. The Demon-Enemy then stirs up these scattered doubts and increases them. Men set their hands to the same work, whilst each one exerts himself for the glory of his intellect, rather than for the assertion of truth. We ought to yield to every truth, not only that which concerns pious and sacred matters, but also in secular affairs, and we ought to obey the precept of the wise man: "In no circumstances, to contradict the word of truth."

Clear and wise judgments are of the greatest use in all studies, when, as Tacitus says, "critics have pronounced their judgments without inflicting injury." For there is nothing more harmful than to confuse the standard of judgments, as in the course of volitions, that a man should not clearly know what sort of actions he approves and what he disapproves. This is an especial danger of our times, when it is most dangerous to speak on almost any subject. So stirred are all men's minds to contentions, and prepared for wordy fighting, that it is not safe to offer observations on any matters even if one is looking at them from another standpoint than that in debate. The tender and weak self-consciousness believes itself to be attacked, as horses afflicted with ulcers instantly are aroused in action, when they hear the scraper or *strigilis*. Nevertheless, very many have offered incitement to the increase of this vice (whilst they bitterly blamed others), not so as to advance the truth, but only for insulting and bringing shame on another's name, either drawn on by hatred or allured by the hope of a false glory, under the impression that by this means they would be regarded as splendid and excellent, just so far as they should manage to show others to be disgraceful. It has happened to them quite otherwise than they expected. For whilst all men praise the intellect of the learned man, when it is pure there is sure blame for the malice of even the most erudite scholar. But, further consider how great a blow all this hatred brings on knowledge. The influence of those men thus hatefully wrangling and, as it were, at enmity to the death, steadily is lost; men of distinguished ability lose courage, and after being made disgusted with all this bitterness, and these perpetual gladiatorial displays, they recoil and shrink from studies. All progress in studies is ruined, and truth is obscured whilst some scholars prefer that letters should remain corrupt rather than be restored to soundness by those men to whom they are unfriendly. How great a crime it is when eloquence, wit and other marvellous gifts of God, given to men by God, for the good of mankind, are converted to its injury, by wrong employment of what is good. Such courses of conduct are not fit for beasts, let alone men. Quintilian, though a heathen, had more religion in him than we Christians. For he said: "It would have been better for us to have been born mutes and to lack all reason, than to convert the gifts of Providence into the injury of men to one another." Of what consequence is it how one person attacks another, whether it is with the sword or with the pen, when the intention is just the same? For the most part, you injure more keenly with speech or with the pen, than with the sword; for you only severely wound the body with the sword, but with language you pierce even the soul. The branches of learning are called humanistic, since they make us human. They have their source in God, to make us good men. He who looks in jealousy on another, in regard to anything with which God has endowed him, does he not impugn the sacred judgment of God and condemn the distribution of His gifts? And yet what ground is there for complaining of God? Has He not dealt profusely in His gifts to you? You see some placed above you, but how many more are there placed less favourably than you? The scholar should be slow in imposing limits, and be far from making rash assertions. When he is going to reprehend anything in others, let him read it over and over again, turn it over in his mind, closely examine it, lest in his condemnation, he affirm anything rashly. If he is commending anything, I would be willing for him to be less circumspect. Let him take care lest he does not sufficiently reflect on what he condemns, so that it shall not happen that the man, to whom he attributes a fault, has greater reason for his view, than he, as a critic, has against him. It would be better to say nothing than that the condemnation should recoil on the judge. But if I expect this practical wisdom, or courtesy, in the learned man, how can I adequately express my feelings with regard to those who twist and distort what has been rightly said, so that they may be thought to be clever controversialists. For if to alter any statement to make it better for some pious and very useful purpose is unlawful in the eyes of many people, it is certainly a great crime to twist it into something worse. . . .

We ought to speak guardedly of the living, of the dead reverently; for the latter are now exempt from envy and have returned to their Judge, and have undergone that judgment which remains for all, particularly with regard to their life and moral conduct. It is indeed permissible to speak with somewhat more freedom of their learning. Those authors by whose writings a scholar has made progress should be quoted with gratitude. "Nor should he wish," says Pliny, "rather to be caught in a theft than in paying back a loan, especially when personal advantage has accrued from the borrowing." Formerly men were so just and generous in rendering everyone his own that not a single word would they snatch from another author. This is evident in Plato, Aristotle, Cicero, Seneca, Plutarch and others. Now, words, meanings, and even whole arguments, sometimes discoveries, and works, are appropriated stealthily. This is absolutely a slavish practice and is the source of many animosities in the learned world. . . .

If anyone has corrected another writer in a word or two, or in many words, he should not demand to be constantly considered more learned on that account, or to have it thought that he has therefore rendered greater service to that particular subject. Many men foolishly make this claim for themselves. If they make an emendation in any great author, they think that they must immediately be held superior to that author, as e.g. if a great man makes a slip through lapse of memory or through thoughtlessness (for Horace declares that Homer sometimes is caught napping). Then, too, sometimes knowledge of the (learned) language falls short, and then those semi-learned men seize hold of any mistake in Latin or Greek, as if it were a very great iniquity. They demand from us a knowledge of Latin and Greek speech, i.e. of foreign and unknown languages, such as scarcely is shown in Cicero or Demosthenes, or in any of those writers, who sucked in their language with their mother's milk, and who had the whole of the people as it were for their schoolmaster, and in those points of usage in their language as to which they were in any doubt, they could consult a neighbouring cobbler or a smith. But if those same keen critics were to offer themselves and their works for judgment, they would, I believe, soon become more gentle in their charges against others. We have not a few examples of this most ungracious severity of judgment, not only in ancient times, but in this latest age, e.g. in Laurentius Valla, Politian, Beroaldus, Mancinellus. Nor has our own time produced a smaller number, even if I now pass by the calumnies of this nature, in those writers of whom I have spoken when I was dealing with the corruptions of grammar. I should not, indeed, deny that it is in the interest of knowledge that great writers should be criticised adversely, if necessary. But the critic does not instantly contribute more or even as much to the subject by his notes as he who composed the work itself. In the writer on any one branch of learning, you should interpret favourably his mistakes in speaking of another branch, e.g. the mistakes made in theology by the writer of history; the mistakes made in history by the metaphysician; as long as he is satisfactory in his own subject. You should still more leniently excuse any errors of language. We ought to welcome a good sentence expressed in French or Spanish, whilst we should not countenance corrupt Latin. . . .

CHAPTER III: THE SCHOLAR'S DIFFICULTIES

. . . Since he who has acquired learning not only wishes to be of use to those who come into his company and to those with whom he lives, but also to those who are distant from him, and to posterity, he will write down the thoughts of his mind in monumental literature to last for a long time to come. First he will know himself, and measure out his strength, in those things in which he is strong, on which he is fitted to write. The most suited of all the products of his thought for transmission to posterity are those which are endowed with sturdy and strong judgment, and those which are best calculated to give inspiration. . . . It is not the business of the same man to collect a mass of material and then to be also responsible for a critical judgment on all matters contained in the collection. Therefore students who read many authors without any intermission, listen to all subjects, write and collect in many directions, almost deprive themselves of a well-balanced judgment, the most excellent of all good things in life. . . . One who intends to become an author must read much, reflect much, write much, correct much, publish very little. The proportion in these activities, unless I am mistaken, expressed numerically, is as follows: Reading = 5; reflection = 4; writing = 3. Emendation brings the last named number to 2, and from these two, actual publication of a scholar should be counted as 1.

This work of writing for publication, which is of great importance, should be approached by a man with his mind pure and restful from all passion, even more so than in anything else you could name, after having first prayed for the peace and grace of God. Let the author remember that the right word is quickly lost, that what he says is only closely listened to by a few, and that what he is about to write may be known to all, and in all ages, and therefore anything which is bad in it will not be innocuous. Let not, therefore, writers take their pen in hand, whilst they are swayed by anger, hatred, fear, or ambition, or any other base emotion. If they cannot suppress their feeling, let them quickly lay down the pen, lest they transfuse into their writing any poison from their mind, i.e. the real source of their work.

After you have written, show the work to those friends, from whom you think that you will receive sound counsel, listen to their opinion with close and patient attention. Think it over again, with balanced mind, so that you may correct those points which seem to need it.

How much better it is to be admonished by a friend privately, than to be blamed publicly by an enemy. Yet there are some discoveries which the author himself could better decide upon and judge than any other man. When first he brings to birth a discovery, let him not be so affected by love of the offspring (of his mind), as yet unseen by others, which may seriously weaken his power of judgment, since we sometimes are strongly drawn to a matter before we have thoroughly investigated it. This is what parents do with their sons, who already love them before they are born. Thus it happens, that later on they cannot form a right judgment on them when they are born. Hence it would be well, as Quintilian advises, that a work be put on one side for a while, so that the author may let the ardour of his new ideas get cooled; and return to his work, as if he were an ordinary reader of someone else's work. Much power of judgment will be added by making such a delay, and he will be better able to make comparisons between his own work and that of others. If all of this suggestion be thoroughly carried out, and still the work continues to seem satisfactory, the author may let good hope arise within him that his work will give satisfaction to others. . . . Authors should be advised to apply practical wisdom to the question, and recognise that it behoves them not to effect an immature birth of their writings. For when anyone has proposed to himself any subject for writing, it is necessary to give an all-round consideration attentively and minutely to all things which have any connexion with it before he passes judgment on it, because over-hasty thoughts do not permit him to concentrate the mind on any one point, and completely divert it from the contemplation of the whole. The writer himself is thus deceived, and he deceives others who have placed their trust in him, and drags them into the same error with himself. Then if anything wrong has been stated, when it is pointed out by any critic, the author stoutly defends himself, lest he should be thought to have made a slip. Hence arise sects, the most fruitful seminary of quarrels. But even if the author spontaneously acknowledges his error, he does not correct it in a straightforward way, but in an ambiguous, confused manner, having regard rather to his good name than to the interest of truth. Hence appears edition after edition, composed and revised over and over again, so that some time afterwards, it is not known which was first, second or third, and which is the real opinion of an author; or what is to stand. And the confusion becomes all the greater whenever the second, third, or the following emendations have not been effected.

Nor does it escape me that there are some works which must be published as early as possible, such as narratives of events which are of importance to many of us living now, as well as those books which are composed by us for the purpose of repressing a noxious crime committed against the community or for rebutting an aspersion. It will be sufficient if these works are carefully thought out and written down by us at once for such matters cannot bear delay. They are not of such a nature that they can be prepared for beforehand, but they must be despatched at the time. There are some books which are made worse, not improved by excessive care; for some minds are of so sudden and lively an impetuosity that their works are all the better as they are just thrown off by the author, rather than if they had been over-elaborated by him.

After his book has been published, whatever points appear to him on reflexion to require correction, let him alter clearly, openly, simply, with an anxiety rather for making the truth clear, than for his own glory. By doing this he will not suffer in estimation. For who is there, so ignorant and inexperienced in human affairs as not to know that the very best and wisest men, with time and study, make better and better progress. Am I not then justified in believing that a man with excellent natural ability to begin with, will have more understanding when he becomes older than when he was young? Certainly that man's mind is slack and wretched, if the next day does not bring him something more than the preceding day. If books are of a dogmatic kind, and have already reached a wide circulation, it is most wise that a book of corrections be added, after the example of St Augustine. Or if additions are made to the text then it is well to arrange a separate edition as we have seen in the case of Boethius Severinus. But if the work contains nothing didactic, and also is not very diffuse, then it will be permissible . . . to thoroughly revise the work and, if it is necessary, to begin it afresh. But if the work is corrected by some other writer, let the author recognise it as a kindness and publicly thank him for it. The truth, for which it behoves us all to stand in battle-array, is not private property, but is common to all. If, therefore, anyone has found any truth, you ought not to by angry, but rather to congratulate him on the happiness of his discovery—a happiness which you can share with him. Without doubt, the state of the matter is this: Those who make a struggle to obtain truth have minds ready for understanding what is discovered by anybody else; but those who struggle for their own discoveries, i.e. for their own name and glory, as if for hearth and home, protect whatsoever is produced by them as their own property. There are always plenty of this kind of people in all branches of knowledge, but especially in those arts which occupy themselves in subjects of discourse, e.g. grammar, poetry, rhetoric, and closely allied subjects in philology. For, firstly the knowledge of words, as Augustine rightly observes, greatly puffs up the writer; and next the works of these writers seem to be more particularly their actual offspring than is the case with the writings of the philosopher or theologian. For the orator, as it were, gives birth to his speech, the poet to his song; whereas it is not the philosopher or theologian but Nature which gives birth to truth. So the true philosopher interprets a contrary opinion to his own, as an injury to Nature, rather than to himself. But he who invents what is false is more annoyed if he is rebutted, than he who asserts the truth. For no man is the father of truth whilst the false is born from the liar himself. So, too, he who affirms what is true, commits his cause to Nature, Time, God. He who asserts the false, takes upon himself the defence of himself. Add to this, words, like the face and bodily form, are external, whilst thought, like health and understanding, is concerned with the internal. But men who are handsome show considerable indignation when their skin and features are mentioned slightlingly, more so than good men show when their goodness is belittled. More easily will the good man think it right and just that he should be called bad, than the good-looking man would allow anyone to consider him plain-looking. In all that is connected with morality, it is a serious mistake to form our taste and judgment to suit outside opinion. But in those matters in which men may become either better or worse by reading books, it is expedient that there should be certain public magistrates for the examination of books. These must be men conspicuous and well-tried amongst the whole people, for their judgment, learning and integrity.

✍ THE PRINCE

Niccolò Machiavelli

Niccolò Machiavelli (1469–1527) himself was anything but a Machiavellian. He spent many years as a conscientious civil servant of his native republic of Florence until the overthrow of the republican regime in 1512 forced him into exile. During his long exclusion— which he bitterly resented—from politics and public service, Machiavelli turned to writing. It was during this period that he produced not only The Prince, *but the* Discourses on the First Ten Books of Livy (*a study of the foundations of republican government*), a History of Florence, *a treatise on the art of war, as well as poetry and biting, racy comedies that are still performed today.*

Machiavelli's The Prince *has been widely read, widely condemned, and widely followed ever since it became known in sixteenth-century Europe. It was ostensibly written as a handbook teaching a ruler how to hold on to power by introducing him to the most valuable historical and contemporary exemplars, and contrasted sharply with the traditional "prince's mirror," which outlined the moral duties of a ruler. Machiavelli brought out into the open what must have been already obvious to the politically sophisticated: that the private morality of the individual did not necessarily apply to the behavior of political leaders or state officials.*

Whether Machiavelli himself endorsed such political amorality is an open question. He was a lifelong republican, and no doubt would have preferred a republic resting on the civic virtue of its citizens. Yet did Italians still have the patriotism necessary for such a foundation? Might a ruthless despot actually be needed to save Italy from dismemberment by France and Spain? Or was Machiavelli, as a disillusioned humanitarian

and patriot, commenting on the unscrupulous conduct of the self-
seeking princes of his day and perhaps even exaggerating and distorting
reality in order to underline the absurdities of absolutism?

NICCOLÒ MACHIAVELLI TO THE MAGNIFICENT LORENZO, SON OF PIERO DE' MEDICI

Those who desire to win the favor of princes generally endeavor to do so by offering them those things which they themselves prize most, or such as they observe the prince to delight in most. Thence it is that princes have very often presented to them horses, arms, cloth of gold, precious stones, and similar ornaments worthy of their greatness. Wishing now myself to offer to your Magnificence some proof of my devotion, I have found nothing amongst all I possess that I hold more dear or esteem more highly than the knowledge of the actions of great men, which I have acquired by long experience of modern affairs, and a continued study of ancient history.

These I have meditated upon for a long time, and examined with great care and diligence; and having now written them out in a small volume, I send this to your Magnificence. And although I judge this work unworthy of you, yet I trust that your kindness of heart may induce you to accept it, considering that I cannot offer you anything better than the means of understanding in the briefest time all that which I have learnt by so many years of study, and with so much trouble and danger to myself.

I have not set off this little work with pompous phrases, nor filled it with high-sounding and magnificent words, nor with any other allurements or extrinsic embellishments with which many are wont to write and adorn their works; for I wished that mine should derive credit only from the truth of the matter, and that the importance of the subject should make it acceptable.

And I hope it may not be accounted presumption if a man of lowly and humble station ventures to discuss and direct the conduct of princes; for as those who wish to delineate countries place themselves low in the plain to observe the form and character of mountains and high places, and for the purpose of studying the nature of the low country place themselves high upon an eminence, so one must be a prince to know well the character of the people, and to understand well the nature of a prince one must be of the people.

May your Magnificence then accept this little gift in the same spirit in which I send it; and if you will read and consider it well, you will recognize in it my desire that you may attain that greatness which fortune and your great qualities promise. And if your Magnificence will turn your eyes from the summit of your greatness towards those low places, you will know how undeservedly I have to bear the great and continued malice of fortune.

Historical, Political and Diplomatic Writings of Niccolò Machiavelli, ed. and trans. C. E. Detmold (Boston: J. R. Osgood & Co., 1882), Vol. II, 3–4, 21–28, 48–62, 73–74, 76, 80–88.

Chapter VII. Of New Principalities That Have Been Acquired by the Aid of Others and by Good Fortune

Those who by good fortune only rise from mere private station to the dignity of princes have but little trouble in achieving that elevation, for they fly there as it were on wings; but their difficulties begin after they have been placed in that high position. Such are those who acquire a state either by means of money, or by the favor of some powerful monarch who bestows it upon them. . . .

Moreover, states that spring up suddenly, like other things in nature that are born and attain their growth rapidly, cannot have those roots and supports that will protect them from destruction by the first unfavorable weather. Unless indeed, as has been said, those who have suddenly become princes are gifted with such ability that they quickly know how to prepare themselves for the preservation of that which fortune has cast into their lap, and afterwards to build up those foundations which others have laid before becoming princes.

In illustration of the one and the other of these two ways of becoming princes, by valor and ability, or by good fortune, I will adduce two examples from the time within our own memory; these are Francesco Sforza and Cesar Borgia. Francesco, by legitimate means and by great natural ability, rose from a private citizen to be Duke of Milan; and having attained that high position by a thousand efforts, it cost him but little trouble afterwards to maintain it. On the other hand, Cesar Borgia, commonly called Duke Valentino, acquired his state by the good fortune of his father, but lost it when no longer sustained by that good fortune; although he employed all the means and did all that a brave and prudent man can do to take root in that state which had been bestowed upon him by the arms and good fortune of another. For, as we have said above, he who does not lay the foundations for his power beforehand may be able by great ability and courage to do so afterwards; but it will be done with great trouble to the builder and with danger to the edifice.

If now we consider the whole course of the Duke Valentino, we shall see that he took pains to lay solid foundations for his future power; which I think it well to discuss. For I should not know what better lesson I could give to a new prince, than to hold up to him the example of the Duke Valentino's conduct. And if the measures which he adopted did not insure his final success, the fault was not his, for his failure was due to the extreme and extraordinary malignity of fortune. Pope Alexander VI. in his efforts to aggrandize his son, the Duke Valentino, encountered many difficulties, immediate and prospective. In the first place he saw that there was no chance of making him master of any state, unless a state of the Church; and he knew that neither the Duke of Milan nor the Venetians would consent to that. Faenza and Rimini were already at that time under the protection of the Venetians; and the armies of Italy, especially those of which he could have availed himself, were in the hands of men who had cause to fear the power of the Pope, namely the Orsini, the Colonna, and their adherents; and therefore he could not rely upon them.

It became necessary therefore for Alexander to disturb the existing order of things, and to disorganize those states, in order to make himself safely master of them. And this it was easy for him to do; for he found the Venetians, influenced by other reasons, favorable to the return of the French into Italy; which not only he did not oppose, but facilitated by dissolving the former marriage of King Louis XII. (so as to enable him to marry Ann of Brittany). The king thereupon entered Italy with the aid of the Venetians and the consent of Alexander; and no sooner was he in Milan than the Pope obtained troops from him to aid in the conquest of the Romagna, which was yielded to him through the influence of the king.

The Duke Valentino having thus acquired the Romagna, and the Colonna being discouraged, he both wished to hold that province, and also to push his possessions still further, but was prevented by two circumstances. The one was that his own troops seemed to him not to be reliable, and the other was the will of the king of France. That is to say, he feared lest the Orsini troops, which he had made use of, might fail him at the critical moment, and not only prevent him from acquiring more, but even take from him that which he had acquired; and that even the king of France might do the same. Of the disposition of the Orsini, the Duke had a proof when, after the capture of Faenza, he attacked Bologna, and saw with what indifference they moved to the assault. And as to the king of France, he knew his mind; for when he wanted to march into Tuscany, after having taken the Duchy of Urbino, King Louis made him desist from that undertaking. The Duke resolved therefore to rely no longer upon the fortune or the arms of others. And the first thing he did was to weaken the Orsini and the Colonna in Rome, by winning over to himself all the gentlemen adherents of those houses, by taking them into his own pay as gentlemen followers, giving them liberal stipends and bestowing honors upon them in proportion to their condition, and giving them appointments and commands; so that in the course of a few months their attachment to their factions was extinguished, and they all became devoted followers of the Duke.

After that, having successfully dispersed the Colonna faction, he watched for an opportunity to crush the Orsini, which soon presented itself, and of which he made the most. For the Orsini, having been slow to perceive that the aggrandizement of the Duke and of the Church would prove the cause of their ruin, convened a meeting at Magione, in the Perugine territory, which gave rise to the revolt of Urbino and the disturbances in the Romagna, and caused infinite dangers to the Duke Valentino, all of which, however, he overcame with the aid of the French. Having thus re-established his reputation, and trusting no longer in the French or any other foreign power, he had recourse to deceit, so as to avoid putting them to the test. And so well did he know how to dissemble and conceal his intentions that the Orsini became reconciled to him, through the agency of the Signor Paolo, whom the Duke had won over to himself by means of all possible good offices, and gifts of money, clothing, and horses. And thus their credulity led them into the hands of the Duke at Sinigaglia.

The chiefs thus destroyed, and their adherents converted into his friends, the Duke had laid sufficiently good foundations for his power, having made himself master of the whole of the Romagna and the Duchy of Urbino, and having attached their entire population to himself, by giving them a foretaste of the new prosperity which they were to enjoy under him. And as this part of the Duke's proceedings is well worthy of notice, and may serve as an example to others, I will dwell upon it more fully.

Having conquered the Romagna, the Duke found it under the control of a number of impotent petty tyrants, who had devoted themselves more to plundering their subjects than to governing them properly, and encouraging discord and disorder amongst them rather than peace and union; so that this province was infested by brigands, torn by quarrels, and given over to every sort of violence. He saw at once that, to restore order amongst the inhabitants and obedience to the sovereign, it was necessary to establish a good and vigorous government there. And for this purpose he appointed as governor of that province Don Ramiro d'Orco, a man of cruelty, but at the same time of great energy, to whom he gave plenary power. In a very short time D'Orco reduced the province to peace and order, thereby gaining for him the highest reputation. After a while the Duke found such excessive exercise of authority no longer necessary or expedient, for he feared that it might render himself odious. He therefore established a civil tribunal in the heart of the province, under an excellent president, where every city should have its own advocate. And having observed that the past rigor of Ramiro had engendered some hatred, he wished to show to the people, for the purpose of removing that feeling from their minds, and to win their entire confidence, that, if any cruelties had been practised, they had not originated with him, but had resulted altogether from the harsh nature of his minister. He therefore took occasion to have Messer Ramiro put to death, and his body, cut into two parts, exposed in the market-place of Cesena one morning, with a block of wood and a bloody cutlass left beside him. The horror of this spectacle caused the people to remain for a time stupefied and satisfied.

But let us return to where we started from. I say, then, that the Duke, feeling himself strong enough now, and in a measure secure from immediate danger, having raised an armed force of his own, and having in great part destroyed those that were near and might have troubled him, wanted now to proceed with his conquest. The only power remaining which he had to fear was the king of France, upon whose support he knew that he could not count, although the king had been late in discovering his error of having allowed the Duke's aggrandizement. The Duke, therefore, began to look for new alliances, and to prevaricate with the French about their entering the kingdom of Naples for the purpose of attacking the Spaniards, who were then engaged in the siege of Gaeta. His intention was to place them in such a position that they would not be able to harm him; and in this he would have succeeded easily if Pope Alexander had lived.

Such was the course of the Duke Valentino with regard to the immediate present, but he had cause for apprehensions as to the future; mainly, lest the new successor to the papal chair should not be friendly to him, and should attempt to take from him what had been given him by Alexander. And this he thought of preventing in several different ways: one, by extirpating the families of those whom he had despoiled, so as to deprive the Pope of all pretext of restoring them to their possessions; secondly, by gaining over to himself all the gentlemen of Rome, so as to be able, through them, to keep the Pope in check; thirdly, by getting the College of Cardinals under his control; and, fourthly, by acquiring so much power before the death of Alexander that he might by himself be able to resist the first attack of his enemies. Of these four things he had accomplished three at the time of Alexander's death; for of the petty tyrants whom he had despoiled he had killed as many as he could lay hands on, and but very few had been able to save themselves; he had won over to himself the gentlemen of Rome, and had secured a large majority in the sacred college; and as to further acquisitions, he contemplated making himself master of Tuscany, having already possession of Perugia and Piombino, and having assumed a protectorate over Pisa. There being no longer occasion to be apprehensive of France, which had been deprived of the kingdom of Naples by the Spaniards, so that both of these powers had to seek his friendship, he suddenly seized Pisa. After this, Lucca and Sienna promptly yielded to him, partly from jealousy of the Florentines and partly from fear. Thus Florence saw no safety from the Duke, and if he had succeeded in taking that city, as he could have done in the very year of Alexander's death, it would have so increased his power and influence that he would have been able to have sustained himself alone, without depending upon the fortune or power of any one else, and relying solely upon his own strength and courage.

But Alexander died five years after the Duke had first unsheathed his sword. He left his son with only his government of the Romagna firmly established, but all his other possessions entirely uncertain, hemmed in between two powerful hostile armies, and himself sick unto death. But such were the Duke's energy and courage, and so well did he know how men are either won or destroyed, and so solid were the foundations which he had in so brief a time laid for his greatness, that if he had not had these two armies upon his back, and had been in health, he would have sustained himself against all difficulties. And that the foundations of his power were well laid may be judged by the fact that the Romagna remained faithful, and waited quietly for him more than a month; and that, although half dead with sickness, yet he was perfectly secure in Rome; and that, although the Baglioni, Vitelli, and Orsini came to Rome at the time, yet they could not raise a party against him. Unable to make a Pope of his own choice, yet he could prevent the election of any one that was not acceptable to him. And had the Duke been in health at the time of Alexander's death, everything would have gone well with him; for he said to me on the day when Julius II. was created Pope, that he had provided for everything that could possibly occur in case of his father's death, except that he never thought that at that moment he should himself be so near dying.

Upon reviewing now all the actions of the Duke, I should not know where to blame him; it seems to me that I should rather hold him up as an example (as I have said) to be imitated by all those who have risen to sovereignty, either by the good fortune or the arms of others. For being endowed with great courage, and having a lofty ambition, he could not have acted otherwise under the circumstances; and the only thing that defeated his designs was the shortness of Alexander's life and his own bodily infirmity.

Whoever, then, in a newly acquired state, finds it necessary to secure himself against his enemies, to gain friends, to conquer by force or by cunning, to make himself feared or beloved by the people, to be followed and revered by the soldiery, to destroy all who could or might injure him, to substitute a new for the old order of things, to be severe and yet gracious, magnanimous, and liberal, to disband a disloyal army and create a new one, to preserve the friendship of kings and princes, so that they may bestow benefits upon him with grace, and fear to injure him,—such a one, I say, cannot find more recent examples than those presented by the conduct of the Duke Valentino. The only thing we can blame him for was the election of Julius II. to the Pontificate, which was a bad selection for him to make; for, as has been said, though he was not able to make a Pope to his own liking, yet he could have prevented, and should never have consented to, the election of one from amongst those cardinals whom he had offended, or who, if he had been elected, would have had occasion to fear him, for either fear or resentment makes men enemies.

Those whom the Duke had offended were, amongst others, the Cardinals San Pietro in Vincola, Colonna, San Giorgio, and Ascanio. All the others, had they come to the pontificate, would have had to fear him, excepting D'Amboise and the Spanish cardinals; the latter because of certain relations and reciprocal obligations, and the former because of his power, he having France for his ally. The Duke then should by all means have had one of the Spanish cardinals made Pope, and failing in that, he should have supported the election of the Cardinal d'Amboise, and not that of the Cardinal San Pietro in Vincola. For whoever thinks that amongst great personages recent benefits will cause old injuries to be forgotten, deceives himself greatly. The Duke, then, in consenting to the election of Julius II. committed an error which proved the cause of his ultimate ruin.

Chapter XIV. Of the Duties of a Prince in Relation to Military Matters

A prince, then, should have no other thought or object so much at heart, and make no other thing so much his especial study, as the art of war and the organization and discipline of his army; for that is the only art that is expected of him who commands. And such is its power, that it not only maintains in their position those who were born princes, but it often enables men born in private station to achieve the rank of princes. And on the other hand, we have seen that princes who thought more of indulgence in pleasure than of arms have thereby lost their states.

Thus the neglect of the art of war is the principal cause of the loss of your state, whilst a proficiency in it often enables you to acquire one. Francesco Sforza, from being skilled in arms, rose from private station to be Duke of Milan; and his descendants, by shunning the labors and fatigue of arms, relapsed into the condition of private citizens.

Amongst the other causes of evil that will befall a prince who is destitute of a proper military force is, that it will make him contemned; which is one of those disgraces against which a prince ought especially to guard, as we shall demonstrate further on. For there is no sort of proportion between one who is well armed and one who is not so; nor is it reasonable that he who is armed should voluntarily obey the unarmed, or that a prince who is without a military force should remain secure amongst his armed subjects. For when there is disdain on the one side and mistrust on the other, it is impossible that the two should work well together. A prince, then, who is not master of the art of war, besides other misfortunes, cannot be respected by his soldiers, nor can he depend upon them. And therefore should the practice of arms ever be uppermost in the prince's thoughts; he should study it in time of peace as much as in actual war, which he can do in two ways, the one by practical exercise, and the other by scientific study. As regards the former, he must not only keep his troops well disciplined and exercised, but he must also frequently follow the chase, whereby his body will become inured to hardships, and he will become familiar with the character of the country, and learn where the mountains rise and the valleys debouch, and how the plains lie; he will learn to know the nature of rivers and of the swamps, to all of which he should give the greatest attention. For this knowledge is valuable in many ways to the prince, who thereby learns to know his own country, and can therefore better understand its defence. Again, by the knowledge of and practical acquaintance with one country, he will with greater facility comprehend the character of others, which it may be necessary for him to understand. For instance, the mountains, valleys, plains, rivers, and swamps of Tuscany bear a certain resemblance to those of other provinces; so that by the knowledge of the character and formation of one country he will readily arrive at that of others. A prince who is wanting in that experience lacks the very first essentials which a commander should possess; for that knowledge teaches him where to find the enemy, to select proper places for intrenchments, to conduct armies, regulate marches, and order battles, and to keep the field with advantage. . . .

As regards the exercise of the mind, the prince should read history, and therein study the actions of eminent men, observe how they bore themselves in war, and examine the causes of their victories and defeats, so that he may imitate the former and avoid the latter. But above all should he follow the example of whatever distinguished man he may have chosen for his model; assuming that some one has been specially praised and held up to him as glorious, whose actions and exploits he should ever bear in mind. . . .

A wise prince then should act in like manner, and should never be idle in times of peace, but should industriously lay up stores of which to avail himself in times of adversity; so that, when Fortune abandons him, he may be prepared to resist her blows.

Chapter XV. Of the Means by Which Men, and Especially Princes, Win Applause, or Incur Censure

It remains now to be seen in what manner a prince should conduct himself towards his subjects and his allies; and knowing that this matter has already been treated by many others, I apprehend that my writing upon it also may be deemed presumptuous, especially as in the discussion of the same I shall differ from the rules laid down by others. But as my aim is to write something that may be useful to him for whom it is intended, it seems to me proper to pursue the real truth of the matter, rather than to indulge in mere speculation on the same; for many have imagined republics and principalities such as have never been known to exist in reality. For the manner in which men live is so different from the way in which they ought to live, that he who leaves the common course for that which he ought to follow will find that it leads him to ruin rather than to safety. For a man who, in all respects, will carry out only his professions of good, will be apt to be ruined amongst so many who are evil. A prince therefore who desires to maintain himself must learn to be not always good, but to be so or not as necessity may require. Leaving aside then the imaginary things concerning princes, and confining ourselves only to the realities, I say that all men when they are spoken of, and more especially princes, from being in a more conspicuous position, are noted for some quality that brings them either praise or censure. Thus one is deemed liberal, another miserly (*misero*) to use a Tuscan expression (for avaricious is he who by rapine desires to gain, and miserly we call him who abstains too much from the enjoyment of his own). One man is esteemed generous, another rapacious; one cruel, another merciful; one faithless, and another faithful; one effeminate and pusillanimous, another ferocious and brave; one affable, another haughty; one lascivious, another chaste; one sincere, the other cunning; one facile, another inflexible; one grave, another frivolous; one religious, another sceptical; and so on.

I am well aware that it would be most praiseworthy for a prince to possess all of the above-named qualities that are esteemed good; but as he cannot have them all, nor entirely observe them, because of his human nature which does not permit it, he should at least be prudent enough to know how to avoid the infamy of those vices that would rob him of his state; and if possible also to guard against such as are likely to endanger it. But if that be not possible, then he may with less hesitation follow his natural inclinations. Nor need he care about incurring censure for such vices, without which the preservation of his state may be difficult. For, all things considered, it will be found that some things that seem like virtue will lead you to ruin if you follow them; whilst others, that apparently are vices, will, if followed, result in your safety and well-being.

Chapter XVI. Of Liberality and Parsimoniousness

To begin with the first of the above-named qualities, I say that it is well for a prince to be deemed liberal; and yet liberality, indulged in so that you will no longer be feared, will prove injurious. For liberality worthily exercised, as it should be, will not be recognized, and may bring upon you the reproach of the very opposite. For if you desire the reputation of being liberal, you must not stop at any degree of sumptuousness; so that a prince will in this way generally consume his entire substance, and may in the end, if he wishes to keep up his reputation for liberality, be obliged to subject his people to extraordinary burdens, and resort to taxation, and employ all sorts of measures that will enable him to procure money. This will soon make him odious with his people; and when he becomes poor, he will be contemned by everybody; so that having by his prodigality injured many and benefited few, he will be the first to suffer every inconvenience, and be exposed to every danger. And when he becomes conscious of this and attempts to retrench, he will at once expose himself to the imputation of being a miser.

A prince then, being unable without injury to himself to practise the virtue of liberality in such manner that it may be generally recognized, should not, when he becomes aware of this and is prudent, mind incurring the charge of parsimoniousness. For after a while, when it is seen that by his prudence and economy he makes his revenues suffice him, and that he is able to provide for his defence in case of war, and engage in enterprises without burdening his people, he will be considered liberal enough by all those from whom he takes nothing, and these are the many; whilst only those to whom he does not give, and which are the few, will look upon him as parsimonious.

In our own times we have not seen any great things accomplished except by those who were regarded as parsimonious; all others have been ruined. Pope Julius II., having been helped by his reputation of liberality to attain the Pontificate, did not afterwards care to keep up that reputation to enable him to engage in war against the king of France; and he carried on ever so many wars without levying any extraordinary taxes. For his long-continued economy enabled him to supply the extraordinary expenses of his wars.

If the present king of Spain had sought the reputation of being liberal, he would not have been able to engage in so many enterprises, nor could he have carried them to a successful issue. A prince, then, who would avoid robbing his own subjects, and be able to defend himself, and who would avoid becoming poor and abject or rapacious, should not mind incurring the reputation of being parsimonious; for that is one of those vices that will enable him to maintain his state. And should it be alleged that Julius Caesar attained the Empire by means of his liberality, and that many others by the same reputation have achieved the highest rank, then I reply, that you are either already a prince, or are in the way of becoming one; in the first case liberality would be injurious to you, but in the second it certainly is necessary to be reputed liberal. Now Caesar was aiming to attain the Empire of Rome; but having achieved it, had he lived and not moderated his expenditures, he would assuredly have ruined the Empire by his prodigality.

And were any one to assert that there have been many princes who have achieved great things with their armies, and who were accounted most liberal, I answer that a prince either spends his own substance and that of his subjects, or that of others. Of the first two he should be very sparing, but in spending that of others he ought not to omit any act of liberality. The prince who in person leads his armies into foreign countries, and supports them by plunder, pillage, and exactions, and thus dispenses the substance of others, should do so with the greatest liberality, as otherwise his soldiers would not follow him. For that which belongs neither to him nor to his own subjects, a prince may spend most lavishly, as was done by Cyrus, Caesar, and Alexander. The spending of other people's substance will not diminish, but rather increase, his reputation; it is only the spending of his own that is injurious to a prince.

And there is nothing that consumes itself so quickly as liberality; for the very act of using it causes it to lose the faculty of being used, and will either impoverish and make you contemned, or it will make you rapacious and odious. And of all the things against which a prince should guard most carefully is the incurring the hatred and contempt of his subjects. Now, liberality will bring upon you either the one or the other; there is therefore more wisdom in submitting to be called parsimonious, which may bring you blame without hatred, than, by aiming to be called liberal, to incur unavoidably the reputation of rapacity, which will bring upon you infamy as well as hatred.

Chapter XVII. Of Cruelty and Clemency, and Whether It Is Better to Be Loved Than Feared

Coming down now to the other aforementioned qualities, I say that every prince ought to desire the reputation of being merciful, and not cruel; at the same time, he should be careful not to misuse that mercy. Cesar Borgia was reputed cruel, yet by his cruelty he reunited the Romagna to his states, and restored that province to order, peace, and loyalty; and if we carefully examine his course, we shall find it to have been really much more merciful than the course of the people of Florence, who, to escape the reputation of cruelty, allowed Pistoja to be destroyed. A prince, therefore, should not mind the ill repute of cruelty, when he can thereby keep his subjects united and loyal; for a few displays of severity will really be more merciful than to allow, by an excess of clemency, disorders to occur, which are apt to result in rapine and murder; for these injure a whole community, whilst the executions ordered by the prince fall only upon a few individuals. And, above all others, the new prince will find it almost impossible to avoid the reputation of cruelty, because new states are generally exposed to many dangers. It was on this account that Virgil made Dido to excuse the severity of her government, because it was still new, saying,—

"Res dura, et regni novitas me talia cogunt
Moliri, et late fines custode tueri." [1]

A prince, however, should be slow to believe and to act; nor should he be too easily alarmed by his own fears, and should proceed moderately and with prudence and humanity, so that an excess of confidence may not make him incautious, nor too much mistrust make him intolerant. This, then, gives rise to the question "whether it be better to be beloved than feared," or "to be feared than beloved." It will naturally be answered that it would be desirable to be both the one and the other; but as it is difficult to be both at the same time, it is much more safe to be feared than to be loved, when you have to choose between the two. For it may be said of men in general that they are ungrateful and fickle, dissemblers, avoiders of danger, and greedy of gain. So long as you shower benefits upon them, they are all yours; they offer you their blood, their substance, their lives, and their children, provided the necessity for it is far off; but when it is near at hand, then they revolt. And the prince who relies upon their words, without having otherwise provided for his security, is ruined; for friendships that are won by rewards, and not by greatness and nobility of soul, although deserved, yet are not real, and cannot be depended upon in time of adversity.

Besides, men have less hesitation in offending one who makes himself beloved than one who makes himself feared; for love holds by a bond of obligation which, as mankind is bad, is broken on every occasion whenever it is for the interest of the obliged party to break it. But fear holds by the apprehension of punishment, which never leaves men. A prince, however, should make himself feared in such a manner that, if he has not won the affections of his people, he shall at least not incur their hatred; for the being feared, and not hated, can go very well together, if the prince abstains from taking the substance of his subjects, and leaves them their women. And if you should be obliged to inflict capital punishment upon any one, then be sure to do so only when there is manifest cause and proper justification for it; and, above all things, abstain from taking people's property, for men will sooner forget the death of their fathers than the loss of their patrimony. Besides, there will never be any lack of reasons for taking people's property; and a prince who once begins to live by rapine will ever find

[1] . . . "My cruel fate,
  And doubts attending an unsettled state,
  Force me to guard my coasts from foreign foes."
                                    Dryden

excuses for seizing other people's property. On the other hand, reasons for taking life are not so easily found, and are more readily exhausted. But when a prince is at the head of his army, with a multitude of soldiers under his command, then it is above all things necessary for him to disregard the reputation of cruelty; for without such severity an army cannot be kept together, nor disposed for any successful feat of arms.

Amongst the many admirable qualities of Hannibal, it is related of him that, having an immense army composed of a very great variety of races of men, which he led to war in foreign countries, no quarrels ever occurred amongst them, nor were there ever any dissensions between them and their chief, either in his good or in his adverse fortunes; which can only be accounted for by his extreme cruelty. This, together with his boundless courage, made him ever venerated and terrible in the eyes of his soldiers; and without that extreme severity all his other virtues would not have sufficed to produce that result.

Inconsiderate writers have, on the one hand, admired his great deeds, and, on the other, condemned the principal cause of the same. And the proof that his other virtues would not have sufficed him may be seen from the case of Scipio, who was one of the most remarkable men, not only of his own time, but in all history. His armies revolted in Spain solely in consequence of his extreme clemency, which allowed his soldiers more license than comports with proper military discipline. This fact was censured in the Roman Senate by Fabius Maximus, who called Scipio the corrupter of the Roman soldiers. The tribe of the Locrians having been wantonly destroyed by one of the lieutenants of Scipio, he neither punished him for that nor for his insolence,—simply because of his own easy nature; so that, when somebody wished to excuse Scipio in the Senate, he said, "that there were many men who knew better how to avoid errors themselves than to punish them in others." This easy nature of Scipio's would in time have dimmed his fame and glory if he had persevered in it under the Empire; but living as he did under the government of the Senate, this dangerous quality of his was not only covered up, but actually redounded to his honor.

To come back now to the question whether it be better to be beloved than feared, I conclude that, as men love of their own free will, but are inspired with fear by the will of the prince, a wise prince should always rely upon himself, and not upon the will of others; but, above all, should he always strive to avoid being hated, as I have already said above.

Chapter XVIII. *In What Manner Princes Should Keep Their Faith*

It must be evident to every one that it is more praiseworthy for a prince always to maintain good faith, and practise integrity rather than craft and deceit. And yet the experience of our own times has shown that those princes have achieved great things who made small account of good faith, and who understood by cunning to circumvent the intelligence of others; and that in the end they got the better of those whose actions were dictated by loyalty and good faith. You must know, therefore, that there are two ways of carrying on a contest; the one by law, and the other by force. The first is practised by men, and the other by animals; and as the first is often insufficient, it becomes necessary to resort to the second.

A prince then should know how to employ the nature of man, and that of the beasts as well. This was figuratively taught by ancient writers, who relate how Achilles and many other princes were given to Chiron the centaur to be nurtured, and how they were trained under his tutorship; which fable means nothing else than that their preceptor combined the qualities of the man and the beast; and that a prince, to succeed, will have to employ both the one and the other nature, as the one without the other cannot produce lasting results.

It being necessary then for a prince to know well how to employ the nature of the beasts, he should be able to assume both that of the fox and that of the lion; for whilst the latter cannot escape the traps laid for him, the former cannot defend himself against the wolves. A prince should be a fox, to know the traps and snares; and a lion, to be able to frighten the wolves; for those who simply hold to the nature of the lion do not understand their business.

A sagacious prince then cannot and should not fulfil his pledges when their observance is contrary to his interest, and when the causes that induced him to pledge his faith no longer exist. If men were all good, then indeed this precept would be bad; but as men are naturally bad, and will not observe their faith towards you, you must, in the same way, not observe yours to them; and no prince ever yet lacked legitimate reasons with which to color his want of good faith. Innumerable modern examples could be given of this; and it could easily be shown how many treaties of peace, and how many engagements, have been made null and void by the faithlessness of princes; and he who has best known how to play the fox has ever been the most successful.

But it is necessary that the prince should know how to color this nature well, and how to be a great hypocrite and dissembler. For men are so simple, and yield so much to immediate necessity, that the deceiver will never lack dupes. I will mention one of the most recent examples. Alexander VI. never did nor ever thought of anything but to deceive, and always found a reason for doing so. No one ever had greater skill in asseverating, or who affirmed his pledges with greater oaths and observed them less, than Pope Alexander; and yet he was always successful in his deceits, because he knew the weakness of men in that particular.

It is not necessary, however, for a prince to possess all the above-mentioned qualities; but it is essential that he should at least seem to have them. I will even venture to say, that to have and to practise them constantly is pernicious, but to seem to have them is useful. For instance, a prince should seem to be merciful, faithful, humane, religious, and upright, and should even be so in reality; but he should have his mind so trained that, when occasion requires it, he may know how to change to the opposite. And it must be understood that a prince, and especially one who has but recently acquired his state, cannot perform all those things which cause men to be esteemed as good; he being often obliged, for the sake of maintaining his state, to act contrary to humanity, charity, and religion. And therefore is it necessary that he should have a versatile mind, capable of changing readily, according as the winds and changes of fortune bid him; and, as has been said above, not to swerve from the good if possible, but to know how to resort to evil if necessity demands it.

A prince then should be very careful never to allow anything to escape his lips that does not abound in the above-named five qualities, so that to see and to hear him he may seem all charity, integrity, and humanity, all uprightness, and all piety. And more than all else is it necessary for a prince to seem to possess the last quality; for mankind in general judge more by what they see and hear than by what they feel, every one being capable of the former, and but few of the latter. Everybody sees what you seem to be, but few really feel what you are; and these few dare not oppose the opinion of the many, who are protected by the majesty of the state; for the actions of all men, and especially those of princes, are judged by the result, where there is no other judge to whom to appeal.

A prince then should look mainly to the successful maintenance of his state. The means which he employs for this will always be accounted honorable, and will be praised by everybody; for the common people are always taken by appearances and by results, and it is the vulgar mass that constitutes the world. But a very few have rank and station, whilst the many have nothing to sustain them. A certain prince of our time, whom it is well not to name, never preached anything but peace and good faith; but if he had always observed either the one or the other, it would in most instances have cost him his reputation or his state.

Chapter XIX. A Prince Must Avoid Being Contemned and Hated

Having thus considered separately the most important of the above-mentioned qualities which a prince should possess, I will now briefly discuss the others under this general maxim: that a prince should endeavor, as has already been said, to avoid everything that would tend to make him odious and contemned. And in proportion as he avoids that will he have performed his part well, and need fear no danger from any other vices. Above all, a prince makes himself odious by rapacity, that is, by taking away from his subjects their property and their women, from which he should carefully abstain. The great mass of men will live quietly and contentedly, provided you do not rob them of their substance and their honor; so that you will have to contend only with the ambition of a few, which is easily restrained in various ways.

A prince becomes despised when he incurs by his acts the reputation of being variable, inconstant, effeminate, pusillanimous, and irresolute; he should therefore guard against this as against a dangerous rock, and should strive to display in all his actions grandeur, courage, gravity, and determination. And in judging the private causes of his subjects, his decisions should be irrevocable. Thus will he maintain himself in such esteem that no one will think of deceiving or betraying him. The prince, who by his habitual conduct gives cause for such an opinion of himself, will acquire so great a reputation that it will be difficult to conspire against him, or to attack him; provided that it be generally known that he is truly excellent, and revered by his subjects. For there are two things which a prince has to fear: the one, attempts against him by his own subjects; and the other, attacks from without by powerful foreigners. Against the latter he will be able to defend himself by good armies and good allies, and whoever has the one will not lack the other. And so long as his external affairs are kept quiet, his internal security will not be disturbed, unless it should be by a conspiracy. And even if he were to be assailed from without, if he has a well-organized army and has lived as he should have done, he will always (unless he should give way himself) be able to withstand any such attacks, as we have related was done by Nabis, tyrant of Sparta. But even when at peace externally, it nevertheless behooves the prince to be on his guard, lest his subjects conspire against him secretly. He will, however, be sufficiently secure against this, if he avoids being hated and despised, and keeps his subjects well satisfied with himself, which should ever be his aim, as I have already explained above. Not to be hated nor contemned by the mass of the people is one of the best safeguards for a prince against conspiracies; for conspirators always believe that the death of the prince will be satisfactory to the people; but when they know that it will rather offend than conciliate the people, they will not venture upon such a course, for the difficulties that surround conspirators are infinite.

Experience proves that, although there have been many conspiracies, yet but few have come to a good end; for he who conspires cannot act alone, nor can he take any associates except such as he believes to be malcontents; and so soon as you divulge your plans to a malcontent, you furnish him the means wherewith to procure satisfaction. For by denouncing it he may hope to derive great advantages for himself, seeing that such a course will insure him those advantages, whilst the other is full of doubts and dangers. He must indeed be a very rare friend of yours, or an inveterate enemy of the prince, to observe good faith and not to betray you.

But to reduce this matter to a few words, I say that on the side of the conspirator there is nothing but fear, jealousy, and apprehension of punishment; whilst the prince has on his side the majesty of sovereignty, the laws, the support of his friends and of the government, which protect him. And if to all this be added the popular good will, it seems impossible that any one should be rash enough to attempt a conspiracy against him. For ordinarily a conspirator has cause for apprehension only before the execution of his evil purpose; but in this case, having the people for his enemies, he has also to fear the consequences after the commission of the crime, and can look nowhere for a refuge. Upon this point I might adduce innumerable examples, but will content myself with only one, which occurred within the memory of our fathers. Messer Annibale Bentivogli, grandfather of the present Messer Annibale, being prince of Bologna, was murdered by the Canneschi, who had conspired against him, and there remained of his family one Messer Giovanni, who was still in his infancy. Immediately after the murder of Messer Annibale, the people rose and killed all the Canneschi. This was the consequence of the popularity which the Bentivogli enjoyed in those days in Bologna, and which went to that extent that after the death of Messer Annibale, when there remained not one of the family in Bologna capable of governing the state, the people received information that there was a Bentivogli in Florence who, until then, had been reputed the son of a blacksmith. They sent a deputation to him at Florence and conferred the government of the city upon him, which he exercised undisturbed until Messer Giovanni came to be of suitable age to assume it himself. I conclude, that a prince need apprehend but little from conspiracies, provided he possess the good will of his people, which is one of the most important points that a prince has to look to.

Amongst the well-organized and well-governed kingdoms of our time is that of France, which has a great many excellent institutions that secure the liberty and safety of the king. The most important of these is the Parliament, and its authority; for the founder of that kingdom knew the ambition and insolence of the nobles, and judged it necessary to put a bit into their mouths with which to curb them. He knew at the same time the hatred of the mass of the people towards the nobles, based upon their fears. Wishing to secure both, and yet unwilling to make this the special care of the king, so as to relieve him of the responsibility to the nobles of seeming to favor the people, and to the people of favoring the nobles, he instituted the Parliament to act as a judge, which might, without reference to the king, keep down the great, and favor the weak. Nor could there be a wiser system, or one that affords more security to the king and his realm.

We may also draw another notable conclusion from this, namely, that princes should devolve all matters of responsibility upon others, and take upon themselves only those of grace. I conclude then anew, that a prince should treat his nobles with respect and consideration, and should avoid at the same time making himself odious to his people. . . .

Chapter XXI. How Princes Should Conduct Themselves to Acquire a Reputation

Nothing makes a prince so much esteemed as the undertaking of great enterprises and the setting a noble example in his own person. We have a striking instance of this in Ferdinand of Aragon, the present king of Spain. He may be called, as it were, a new prince; for, from being king of a feeble state, he has, by his fame and glory, become the first sovereign of Christendom; and if we examine his actions we shall find them all most grand, and some of them extraordinary. In the beginning of his reign he attacked Granada, and it was this undertaking that was the very foundation of his greatness. At first he carried on this war leisurely and without fear of opposition; for he kept the nobles of Castile occupied with this enterprise, and, their minds being thus engaged by war, they gave no attention to the innovations introduced by the king, who thereby acquired a reputation and an influence over the nobles without their being aware of it. The money of the Church and of the people enabled him to support his armies, and by that long war he succeeded in giving a stable foundation to his military establishment, which afterwards brought him so much honor. Besides this, to be able to engage in still greater enterprises, he always availed himself of religion as a pretext, and committed a pious cruelty in spoliating and driving the Moors out of his kingdom, which certainly was a most admirable and extraordinary example. Under the same cloak of religion he attacked Africa, and made a descent upon Italy, and finally assailed France. And thus he was always planning great enterprises, which kept the minds of his subjects in a state of suspense and admiration, and occupied with their results. And these different enterprises followed so quickly one upon the other, that he never gave men a chance deliberately to make any attempt against himself. . . .

A prince should also show himself a lover of virtue, and should honor all who excel in any one of the arts, and should encourage his citizens quietly to pursue their vocations, whether of commerce, agriculture, or any other human industry; so that the one may not abstain from embellishing his possessions for fear of their being taken from him, nor the other from opening new sources of commerce for fear of taxes. But the prince should provide rewards for those who are willing to do these things, and for all who strive to enlarge his city or state. And besides this, he should at suitable periods amuse his people with festivities and spectacles. And as cities are generally divided into guilds and classes, he should keep account of these bodies, and occasionally be present at their assemblies, and should set an example of his affability and magnificence; preserving, however, always the majesty of his dignity, which should never be wanting on any occasion or under any circumstances.

Chapter XXIV. The Reason Why the Princes of Italy Have Lost Their States

A judicious observation of the above-given rules will cause a new prince to be regarded as though he were an hereditary one, and will very soon make him more firm and secure in his state than if he had grown old in its possession. For the actions of a new prince are much more closely observed and scrutinized than those of an hereditary one; and when they are known to be virtuous, they will win the confidence and affections of men much more for the new prince, and make his subjects feel under greater obligations to him, than if he were of the ancient line. For men are ever more taken with the things of the present than with those of the past; and when they find their own good in the present, then they enjoy it and seek none other, and will be ready in every way to defend the new prince, provide he be not wanting to himself in other respects. And thus he will have the double glory of having established a new principality, and of having strengthened and adorned it with good laws, good armies, good allies, and good examples. And in the same way will it be a double shame to an hereditary prince, if through want of prudence and ability he loses his state.

If now we examine the conduct of those princes of Italy who in our day have lost their states, such as the king of Naples, the Duke of Milan, and others, we shall note in them at once a common defect as regards their military forces, for the reasons which we have discussed at length above. And we shall also find that in some instances the people were hostile to the prince; or if he had the good will of the people, he knew not how to conciliate that of the nobles. For unless there be some such defects as these, states are not lost when the prince has energy enough to keep an army in the field. . . .

Those of our princes, therefore, who have lost their dominions after having been established in them for many years, should not blame fortune, but only their own indolence and lack of energy; for in times of quiet they never thought of the possibility of a change (it being a common defect of men in fair weather to take no thought of storms), and afterwards, when adversity overtook them, their first impulse was to fly, and not to defend themselves, hoping that the people, when disgusted with the insolence of the victors, would recall them. . . .

Chapter XXV. Of the Influence of Fortune in Human Affairs, and How It May Be Counteracted

I am well aware that many have held and still hold the opinion, that the affairs of this world are so controlled by Fortune and by the Divine Power that human wisdom and foresight cannot modify them; that, in fact, there is no remedy against the decrees of fate, and that therefore it is not worth while to make any effort; but to yield unconditionally to the power of Fortune. This opinion has been generally accepted in our times, because of the great changes that have taken place, and are still being witnessed every day, and are beyond all human conjecture.

In reflecting upon this at times, I am myself in some measure inclined to that belief; nevertheless, as our free will is not entirely destroyed, I judge that it may be assumed as true that Fortune to the extent of one half is the arbiter of our actions, but that she permits us to direct the other half, or perhaps a little less, ourselves. I compare this to a swollen river, which in its fury overflows the plains, tears up the trees and buildings, and sweeps the earth from one place and deposits it in another. Every one flies before the flood, and yields to its fury, unable to resist it; and notwithstanding this state of things, men do not when the river is in its ordinary condition provide against its overflow by dikes and walls, so that when it rises it may flow either in the channel thus provided for it, or that at any rate its violence may not be entirely unchecked, nor its effects prove so injurious. It is the same with Fortune, who displays her power where there is no organized valor to resist her, and where she knows that there are no dikes or walls to control her.

If now you examine Italy, which is the seat of the changes under consideration, and has occasioned their occurrence, you will see that she is like an open country, without dikes or any other protection against inundations; and that if she had been protected with proper valor and wisdom, as is the case with Germany, Spain, and France, these inundations would either not have caused the great changes which they did, or they would not have occurred at all.

These remarks I deem sufficient as regards resisting fortune in general; but confining myself now more to particular cases, I say that we see a prince fortunate one day, and ruined the next, without his nature or any of his qualities being changed. I believe this results mainly from the causes which have been discussed at length above; namely, that the prince who relies entirely upon fortune will be ruined according as fortune varies. I believe, further, that the prince who conforms his conduct to the spirit of the times will be fortunate; and in the same way will he be unfortunate, if in his actions he disregards the spirit of the times. For we see men proceed in various ways to attain the end they aim at, such as glory and riches: the one with circumspection, the other with rashness; one with violence, another with cunning; one with patience, and another with impetuosity; and all may succeed in their different ways. We also see that, of two men equally prudent, the one will accomplish his designs, whilst the other fails; and in the same way we see two men succeed equally well by two entirely different methods, the one being prudent and the other rash; which is due to nothing else than the character of the times, to which they either conform in their proceedings or not. Whence it comes, as I have said, that two men by entirely different modes of action will achieve the same results; whilst of two others, proceeding precisely in the same way, the one will accomplish his end, and the other not. This also causes the difference of success; for if one man, acting with caution and patience, is also favored by time and circumstances, he will be successful; but if these change, then will he be ruined, unless, indeed, he changes his conduct accordingly. Nor is there any man so sagacious that he will always know how to conform to such change of times and circumstances; for men do not readily deviate from the course to which their nature inclines them; and, moreover, if they have generally been prosperous by following one course, they cannot persuade themselves that it would be well to depart from it. Thus the cautious man, when the moment comes for him to strike a bold blow, will not know how to do it, and thence will he fail; whilst, if he could have changed his nature with the times and circumstances, his usual good fortune would not have abandoned him.

Pope Julius II. was in all his actions most impetuous; and the times and circumstances happened so conformably to that mode of proceeding that he always achieved
happy results. Witness the first attempt he made upon Bologna, when Messer Giovanni
Bentivogli was still living. This attempt gave umbrage to the Venetians, and also to the
kings of Spain and France, who held a conference on the subject. But Pope Julius, with
his habitual boldness and impetuosity, assumed the direction of that expedition in person; which caused the Spaniards and the Venetians to remain quiet in suspense, the
latter from fear, and the others from a desire to recover the entire kingdom of Naples.
On the other hand, the Pope drew the king of France after him; for that king, seeing
that Julius had already started on the expedition, and wishing to gain his friendship for
the purpose of humbling the Venetians, judged that he could not refuse him the assistance of his army without manifest injury to himself.

Pope Julius II., then, achieved by this impetuous movement what no other pontiff
could have accomplished with all possible human prudence. For had he waited to start
from Rome until all his plans were definitely arranged, and everything carefully organized, as every other pontiff would have done, he would certainly never have succeeded;
for the king would have found a thousand excuses, and the others would have caused
him a thousand apprehensions. I will not dwell upon the other actions of Julius II.,
which were all of a similar character, and have all succeeded equally well. The shortness of his life saved him from experiencing any reverses; for if times had supervened
that would have made it necessary for him to proceed with caution and prudence, he
would assuredly have been ruined; for he could never have deviated from the course to
which his nature inclined him.

I conclude, then, inasmuch as Fortune is changeble, that men who persist obstinately
in their own ways will be successful only so long as those ways coincide with those of
Fortune; and whenever these differ, they fail. But, on the whole, I judge impetuosity
to be better than caution; for Fortune is a woman, and if you wish to master her, you
must strike and beat her, and you will see that she allows herself to be more easily vanquished by the rash and the violent than by those who proceed more slowly ond coldly.
And therefore, as a woman, she ever favors youth more than age, for youth is less cautious and more energetic, and commands Fortune with greater audacity.

Chapter XXVI. Exhortation to Deliver Italy from Foreign Barbarians

Reviewing now all I have said in the foregoing discourses, and thinking to myself that,
if the present time should be favorable for Italy to receive and honor a new prince, and
the opportunity were given to a prudent and virtuous man to establish a new form of
government, that would bring honor to himself and happiness to the mass of the Italian people, so many things would combine for the advantage of such a new prince, that,
so far as I know, no previous time was ever more favorable for such a change. And if,
as I have said, it was necessary for the purpose of displaying the virtue of Moses that
the people of Israel should be held in bondage in Egypt; and that the Persians should
be opposed to the Medes, so as to bring to light the greatness and courage of Cyrus;
and that the Athenians should be dispersed for the purpose of illustrating the excellence of Theseus; so at present, for the purpose of making manifest the virtues of one

Italian spirit, it was necessary that Italy should have been brought to her present condition of being in a worse bondage than that of the Jews, more enslaved than the Persians, more scattered than the Athenians, without a head, without order, vanquished and despoiled, lacerated, overrun by her enemies, and subjected to every kind of devastation.

And although, up to the present time, there may have been some one who may have given a gleam of hope that he was ordained by Heaven to redeem Italy, yet have we seen how, in the very zenith of his career, he was so checked by fortune that poor Italy remained as it were lifeless, and waiting to see who might be chosen to heal her wounds, —to put an end to her devastation, to the sacking of Lombardy, to the spoliation and ruinous taxation of the kingdom of Naples and of Tuscany,—and who should heal her sores that have festered so long. You see how she prays God that he may send some one who shall redeem her from this cruelty and barbarous insolence. You see her eagerly disposed to follow any banner, provided there be some one to bear it aloft. But there is no one at present in whom she could place more hope than in your illustrious house, O magnificent Lorenzo! which, with its virtue and fortune, favored by God and the Church, of which it is now the head, could make an effectual beginning of her deliverance. And this will not be difficult for you, if you will first study carefully the lives and actions of the men whom I have named above. And although these men were rare and wonderful, they were nevertheless but men, and the opportunities which they had were far less favorable than the present; nor were their undertakings more just or more easy than this; neither were they more favored by the Almighty than what you are. Here, then, is great justice; for war is just when it is necessary, and a resort to arms is beneficent when there is no hope in anything else. The opportunity is most favorable, and when that is the case there can be no great difficulties, provided you follow the course of those whom I have held up to you as examples. Although in their case extraordinary things, without parallel, were brought about by the hand of God,—the sea divided for their passage, a pillar of cloud pointed their way through the wilderness, the rock poured forth water to assuage their thirst, and it rained manna to appease their hunger,—yet your greatness combines all, and on your own efforts will depend the result. God will not do everything; for that would deprive us of our free will, and of that share of glory which belongs to us.

Nor should we wonder that not one of the Italians whom I have mentioned has been able to accomplish that which it is to be hoped will be done by your illustrious house; for if in so many revolutions in Italy, and in the conduct of so many wars, it would seem that military capacity and valor have become extinct, it is owing to the fact that the old military system was defective, and no one has come forward capable of establishing a new one. And nothing brings a man who has newly risen so much honor as the establishing of new laws and institutions of his own creation; if they have greatness in them and become well established, they will make the prince admired and revered; and there is no lack of opportunity in Italy for the introduction of every kind of reform. The people have great courage, provided it be not wanting in their leaders. Look but at their single combats, and their encounters when there are but a few on either side, and see how superior the Italians have shown themselves in strength, dexterity, and ability. But when it comes to their armies, then these qualities do not appear, because of the incapacity of the chiefs, who cannot enforce obedience from those who are versed in the art of war, and every one believes himself to be so; for up to the present time there have been none so decidedly superior in valor and good fortune that the others yielded him obedience. Thence it comes that in so great a length of time, and in the many wars that have occurred within the past twenty years, the armies, whenever wholly composed of Italians, have given but poor account of themselves. Witness first Taro, then Alessandria, Capua, Genoa, Vaila, Bologna, and Mestri.

If, then, your illustrious house is willing to follow the examples of those distinguished men who have redeemed their countries, you will before anything else, and as the very foundation of every enterprise, have to provide yourself with a national army. And you cannot have more faithful, truer, and better soldiers than the Italians. And whilst each individual is good, they will become still better when they are all united, and know that they are commanded by their own prince, who will honor and support them. It is necessary, therefore, to provide troops of this kind, so as to be able successfully to oppose Italian valor to the attacks of foreigners.

And although the infantry of the Swiss and of the Spaniards is looked upon as terrible, yet both of them have a defect, which will permit a third organization not only to resist them, but confidently hope to vanquish them. For the Spaniards cannot withstand the shock of cavalry, and the Swiss dread infantry, when they encounter it in battle as obstinate as themselves. Whence we have seen, what further experience will prove more fully, that the Spaniards cannot resist the French cavalry, and that the Swiss succumb to the Spanish infantry. And although we have not yet had a full trial of the latter, yet have we had a fair specimen of it in the battle of Ravenna, where the Spanish infantry confronted the line of battle of the Germans, who have adopted the same system as the Swiss; and where the Spaniards with great agility, and protected by their bucklers, rushed under the pikes of the Germans, and were thus able to attack them securely without the Germans being able to prevent it; and had it not been for the cavalry which fell upon the Spaniards, they might have destroyed the entire German infantry.

Knowing, then, the defects of the one and the other of these systems of infantry, you can organize a new one that shall avoid these defects, and shall be able to resist cavalry as well as infantry. And this is to be done, not by a change of arms, but by an entirely different organization and discipline. This is one of the things which, if successfully introduced, will give fame and greatness to a new prince.

You must not, then, allow this opportunity to pass, so that Italy, after waiting so long, may at last see her deliverer appear. Nor can I possibly express with what affection he would be received in all those provinces that have suffered so long from this inundation of foreign foes!—with what thirst for vengeance, with what persistent faith, with what devotion, and with what tears! What door would be closed to him? Who would refuse him obedience? What envy would dare oppose him? What Italian would refuse him homage? This barbarous dominion of the foreigner offends the very nostrils of everybody!

Let your illustrious house, then, assume this task with that courage and hopefulness which every just enterprise inspires; so that under your banner our country may recover its ancient fame, and under your auspices may be verified the words of Petrarca:—

"Virtù contro al furore
Prenderà l' arme, e fia il combatter corto;
Chè l' antico valore
Negli Italici cuor non è ancor morto."

Canz. XVI. v. 93–96.

THE COURTIER

Baldassare Castiglione

During the sixteenth century the culture of Renaissance Italy captivated all Europe. Russian Czars imported Italian architects to build the Kremlin; German artists, such as Dürer, traveled to Italy to learn from the masters; troupes of Italian comedians were retained by fashion-conscious French princes; Italian became the language of aristocratic society even as far afield as England, where Queen Elizabeth prided herself on her mastery of it.

Baldassare Castiglione's Book of the Courtier (1528) reflects the attractiveness of a style of life firmly based on the civilized classical values as the Italians of the sixteenth century interpreted them. Although it was really a treatise on statesmanship, it came to be widely read throughout Europe as a book of polite manners. Basically it is a discussion of courtiership, showing the courtier as another distinctive Renaissance type. Each of the four books making up The Courtier is the record of a single evening's conversation in the court of Urbino in central Italy, to which Castiglione was for some time attached. On each evening one speaker dominates the conversation, presenting his views, which are then discussed and criticized by the others. The following selections are from Book II, in which Duke Frederick leads a discussion on the conduct of a courtier, and from Book IV in which Octavian discusses the chief purpose of the courtier, which is to guide his prince toward virtue. You will notice that Castiglione raises fundamental questions about political ethics in a fashion very different from that of Machiavelli.
The dialogues are not authentic transcriptions of actual conversations, having been carefully composed by Castiglione some time after they took place; but the characters are real, and we can assume that the book in fact represents a distillation of evenings actually spent by this urbane and elegant company.

BOOK TWO

[*Duke Frederick is Speaking.*] Inasmuch . . . as the Count yesternight has so copiously and in such a graceful manner delivered himself upon this subject of the *Courtier*, he has made me in reality conceive no small fear and doubt, that I shall never be able to satisfy, as I ought, this noble audience in what is incumbent on me to discourse of, as he has done: However, that I may share as much as possibly I can of his praise, and be sure not to err, I shall not contradict him in any thing he has advanced.

I am therefore entirely of the same sentiment with that gentleman, in relation to birth, wit, and disposition of person, and gracefulness of aspect in a *Courtier;* but shall beg leave farther to observe, that besides all these, in order to his deservedly acquiring the good esteem of everyone, and the good graces of the prince he serves, it appears to me absolutely necessary for him to know so to frame his whole life and conversation, as that he may gracefully display all his good qualities in general, without incurring the envy of anyone.

And how difficult a matter this is, may be considered from those very few who ever arrive to that perfection, for we are all of us naturally more given to dispraise and ill action, than to commend a good one; and one would really imagine, by the constant practice of a great many, that thro' an innate malice, though fully convinced of the excellency of a thing, they enforce themselves with all their diligence and study to discover in it either an error, or the semblance of one.

It is therefore necessary that our *Courtier* act in every respect with a great deal of circumspection, so that all his words and actions be agreeable to prudence; and not only to take care to have in himself excellent qualities and conditions, but to order and dispose the whole course of his life in such manner, that it may in every respect be correspondent thereto, and no ways disagreeable in itself, but make one body of these good parts; so that every action of his may result and be composed of all virtues, as those of a wise man, in the language of the stoicks, ought to be; and altho' one virtue is ever predominant, they are all of them notwithstanding so chained together, that they all tend to the same end, and all may serve and concur to the same effect.

For which account it is highly necessary that he know how to make the most advantagious use of them, and by comparison, and as it were by contrariety of one, sometimes to make the other more clearly known; like good painters, who with their shades artfully discover the beauties of their lights, and so, on the contrary, mingle their several colours together in such order, that by this variety both become more agreeable, and the admirable disposition of the figures, one contrary to the other, aids them to what is in reality the true intention of painting.

This makes an affability and sweetness of temper wonderful in a gentleman of the army, who has true courage; for as magnanimity is much greater when accompanied with modesty, so does that modesty encrease, and appear to greater advantage, by that courage or greatness of mind.

To do much, therefore, and use few words, and not praise one's self in worthy

Balthasar, Count Castiglione, *The Courtier*, trans. Robert Samber (London: A. Bettesworth, 1724), pp. 12–16, 27–33, 36–37, 60–66, 245–254.

actions, agreeably dissembling them, gives addition to both virtues, in a person who knows how to do all this with discretion: which also may be said of every other good quality.

I would therefore have our *Courtier,* in all his words and actions, make use of certain general rules; which, in my judgment, briefly contain as much as belongs to me to speak.

And for the first, and most important of all; let him by all means (as the Count well observed yesternight) in everything avoid affectation; then let him consider well what the nature of the thing is which he speaks or does, the place where it is done, in whose presence, in what time, the cause why he does it, his age, profession, the end to which it tends, and the means that may bring him to it; and by these considerations let him discreetly apply himself to whatever he has a mind to do or say.

Having thus said, he seemed to pause a little: whereupon Signor *Morello da Ortona* took an occasion to speak; In my opinion, Sir, said he, these rules of yours give but little instruction; and for my part I know just as much now as before you began, tho' indeed I remember I have heard of them from the good fathers when I have been at confession, and I think they call them circumstances.

Here Signor *Frederick,* with a smile, replied; If you remember, said he, the Count, last night, would have the principal profession of a *Courtier* to be that of arms, and spoke very copiously how he should be excellent therein; for which reason we shall rehearse no more of that subject. However, by our rule, in whatever warlike action our *Courtier* is, either by sea or land, he ought prudently to sever himself from the multitude, and do what he has to do with as little company as he can, and in sight of persons of the highest rank and distinction, and, if possible, in the very presence of the king or prince he serves; for in reality it is of great advantage to anyone to be taken notice of in doing of brave and gallant actions. For I am of opinion, as it is an ill thing to hunt after false glory in what really deserves no praise at all; so it is full as bad for a man to defraud himself of that honour which is due to him, and not to seek after that renown which only is the true reward of virtuous actions.

And I remember well some certain persons, who thought they were really men of courage, were yet in this respect but gross headed, and would put their life in as much danger to take a flock of sheep, as in being the foremost to scale the walls of a town; which oversight, to give them the softest term, our *Courtier* will not be guilty of, if he reflects on the cause that induced him to the camp; which ought to be only honour.

And farther, I must beg leave to observe, that if he happen to be one of those concerned in publick exercises, as tilt, tourney, or the like, let him remember the place where he is to be, and accordingly provide a horse and proper accoutrements, no less handsome than sure, in order to engage the eyes of the spectators, with everything that is graceful; as the loadstone attracts the iron. Let him also take particular care never to come with the last in the lists; always remembering that the spectators, especially the ladies, take more notice of the first than the last; for the eye and mind, which at the beginning are taken with that novelty, observe every little matter, and make sure impressions of it; whereas by continuance, they not only are satiated, but quite tired.

For which reason, in old times, there was a famous player, that would always appear the first upon the stage.

Besides, if it happen our *Courtier* should fall into any discourse relating to arms, let him consider well the profession of those he talks with, and frame discourse accordingly; using one manner of speech to men, and another to women: and in case he has a mind to touch upon anything redounding to his own reputation, let him do it covertly, and as it were *en passant,* and with that caution and circumspection as the Count last night very well observed. . . .

But to conclude, all these fine qualities in our *Courtier* will not acquire him the general favour of great men and ladies, if he have not also a genteel and amiable manner in his daily conversation. But of this, I believe, it will be very difficult to prescribe any rules, by reason of that infinity of cases, which occur continually in conversation; and forasmuch as, amongst all men in the world, there are not two that agree together in everything. For which reason, he, who is to converse with so many, must guide himself by his own judgment; and, by knowing the difference of persons, change his stile and manner, according to the temper and disposition of those he is to converse with. And, for my part, I can prescribe no better rules in this case than have been mentioned, and which, Signor *Morello* says, he learned, from a child, of the good friars in confession.

Here *Donna Emilia* smiling said, you would fain get rid of your employment, Signor *Frederick,* but you are not like to escape so; for you must entertain us with discourse 'till bed-time.

But suppose, Madam, said he, I can say no more? We shall now see your wit, replied *Donna Emilia,* and if what I have heard be true, there have been men so very witty and eloquent, that they have not wanted matter in an instant to make a book in the praise of a fly, others in praise of a quartan ague, and others again in honour of baldness; and are you at a loss to speak somewhat for one night of the *Courtier?*

We have already, said Signor *Frederick,* said as much as will very near make two books. But since no excuse will be admitted, I shall talk so long, 'till you, Madam, shall think I have done, if not my duty, at least to the utmost of my power.

I suppose, the conversation, which the *Courtier* ought principally to attend to, with all his care, in order to make himself acceptable, is the very same he may have with his prince; and tho' this term conversation carries along with it an idea of a certain equality, which one would not judge can pass between a master and servant, yet for once we will give it that denomination.

I would therefore have our *Courtier,* besides his daily displaying his good qualities to the world, as we have said he is obliged to do, to turn all his thoughts and force of mind to love, and even (if I may be permitted the expression) to adore the prince he serves above all other things, and in every minute circumstance endeavour to please him.

Here *Pietro de Napoli* could hold no longer; of these sort of *Courtiers,* said he, Signor *Frederick,* you may find a great many now-a-days; for I think, in a few words, you have drawn to the life a very noble flatterer.

You are quite out there, said Signor *Frederick,* for flatterers do not love their lords nor friends; both which I principally require in our *Courtier;* and to please his prince, and obey his commands, may be done without flattery: I mean such as are honourable, and agreeable to reason, or such as of themselves are neither good nor bad; as in play, by giving himself up more to one exercise than another; and to this I would have our *Courtier* conform himself, though naturally he should have no inclination to it; so that whensoever his lord looks upon him, he may think he has somewhat agreeable to discourse him about: which more certainly will be, if he has that good judgment to know what may please his prince, and prudence and understanding to accommodate himself to him, and a deliberate will to make him delighted with that which naturally might displease him.

If he has these good qualities, he will never appear with a sad and melancholy air in his presence, nor so sullen as many, and that one would imagine they had some misunderstanding with their sovereign; which is a thing true, odious and detestable.

Besides this, he will never be guilty of raillery, especially against his superiors; a thing which too often happens in courts, where a certain tempest governs, which carries along with it this unhappy temper, that those who have received the greatest favours from their prince, and are promoted from a low condition to the highest honours, are perpetually complaining, and speak the worst they can of him, which is a thing entirely misbecoming, not only in them, but in those who really have received but ill treatment.

Neither must our *Courtier* use any kind of foolish presumption, nor be guilty of carrying trifling news, nor be so inadvertent as to make use of such expressions which may give offence, instead of pleasure.

He must not be obstinate nor contentious, as some are, who seem to take no other delight and satisfaction, than to be as troublesome as flies; and make profession of spitefully contradicting everybody without distinction; no babler, nor guilty of false reports, nor vain-glorious, nor silly flatterer; but modest, reserved, ever using, especially in publick, that reverence and respect as becomes a servant towards his lord; not doing as too many do, who meeting a prince, how great soever he be, if they have once spoken to him before, approach him with a certain smiling and friendly countenance, as if they were going to caress one of their equals, or do a favour to an inferior.

Seldom or never let him ask anything of his prince for himself; lest his prince, being as it were ashamed to deny him, should grant it him with regret; which is much worse. And if he has occasion to ask any favour for another, let him prudently observe a fit time and season, and desire nothing but what is agreeable to honour and reason; and so frame his petition, as to leave out every minute circumstance which he knows may displease him, and with all his address and dexterity soften every difficulty, so as to engage his lord ever to grant his desires. But in case he be refused, let him by no means surmise he is injured, or give the least sign of discontent; for very often princes, after having denied a request to one who has made his address to them with great instance, think the person who requested it with such importunity, was very eager of obtaining it, and being frustrated, would, for that reason, resent it one time or other, or lessen his esteem for them: on which suspicion they begin to hate such a person, and ever after look on him with no good eye.

And tho' he be of ever so great authority, yet let him never desire to press into the chamber, or other private place where his prince has withdrawn himself, unless he be bidden; for princes, very frequently, when they are in private, love a certain liberty to say and do what they please, and therefore will not be seen or heard of any person that may make observations; which indeed is but reasonable.

Those therefore who speak against princes who make choice of such persons for their bed-chamber, that are qualified for little else but attending about their persons, in my judgment are wrong; for in reality I cannot see why they should not have the same liberty, to refresh and unbend their minds, as we ourselves make use of.

So also, if a minister of state, employed in the more arduous and difficult affairs of the government, happen to be in private with his prince, let him divest himself of his gravity, and defer talking of matters of moment and importance to another time and place, and give himself entirely up to such pleasant conversation, as may be agreeable to his sovereign, that he may not give the least impediment or obstacle to such relaxation: but in this, as in all other things, let him take a special care not to give him the least chagrin or uneasiness.

In relation to favours and preferments, I would rather have our *Courtier* wait till they are offered, than sollicit for them so openly as some do, who are so eager for them, that one would think if they were refused, they could not live a moment longer: and if they happen to fall into any disgrace, or see others in favour, they are in such an agony, that they know not how to dissemble their envy; which infallibly proves a subject of merriment and diversion to everybody, and very frequently gives occasion to the prince to bestow his graces on the next he casts his eye on, on purpose only to mortify them.

On the other hand, if they happen again to be taken into favour, they keep no bounds, but grow so giddy with their good fortune, that they know not what to do for joy; and by the odd motion of their hands and feet, one would imagine they had a mind to have people come about them, and congratulate them on what they had never been used to. Such a one I would by no means have our *Courtier* to be; and though I would have him value his prince's favours, but not so as to make the world think he could not live without them; and when he has gained them, let him not shew himself new or strange, nor wonder at them when they are offered him; nor refuse them after such a manner as some do, who thro' real ignorance do not accept them, and on that account give room for people to believe they are conscious to themselves of their own incapacity: Yet ought a man always to be somewhat more remiss in this respect, than perhaps, according to his rank, he might be, and not accept so easily those honours and high posts that are offered him, but modestly refuse them, with a due sense of their value, and that too, in such a manner, as may give occasion to him who offers them, to do it with greater instance and importunity. For the more one refuses them after this manner, the more seems he to be esteemed by the prince, who offers them; and so much greater is the favour, the greater value he that receives them seems to have for them, and the greater honour he believes he acquires from them.

And these are the true and only favours which make a man esteemed by those, who publickly see him; because, when they are not sollicited, or fought for, everyone presumes, they are the recompence of true virtue, and much more so, when they are accompanied with modesty. . . .

Let our *Courtier,* as opportunity offers, be fluent and eloquent, and, in his discourses on state-affairs, sage and prudent, and have that art and address, as to frame himself according to the customs of the country he lives in. Then, in matters of less moment, let him be pleasant, courteous, and affable, and reason well on every subject, but, above all things, let him direct his intention always to do good; let him never be invidious, nor a detractor, nor be induced to seek favour, or preferment, by over-reaching craft, or subtilty, or by any other ill means whatsover.

I assure you, Sir, said *Calmeta,* all other ways are much longer, and more doubtful that what you discommend; because now-a-days (and I must repeat it) princes and great men love none but such as they make use of.

Do not persist in those unhappy sentiments, said Signor *Frederick;* for that would be too plain an argument, that the great men of our time were all bad and wicked, which is not true, for there are some very good. But if it falls to our *Courtier's* lot to serve one that were vicious and wicked, as soon as he knows it, let him immediately abandon his service, that he may not feel that extreme affliction, all good men suffer, who serve the wicked.

We must pray to God, said *Calmeta,* to help us to good; for when we are once embarqued in their service, we must take them with all their faults; for a gentleman, after he is once entred into a prince's service, for infinite respects is obliged not to leave him. But the misfortune is in the beginning, and *Courtiers,* in this case, are not unlike those wretched fowl, that are hatched in obscure and dismal valleys.

I think, said Signor *Frederick,* duty ought to prevail above all other respects, but yet so as a gentleman leave not his lord in time of battle, or any other adversity, or be thought to do it to follow fortune, or because he seemed then to be deprived of all means of pursuing his private interest and advantage: At all other times, I believe; he may with good reason, and ought to abandon that service, which, amongst all good men, may bring him to shame; for everyone presumes, that he, who serves the good, is good, and he, that serves the wicked, wicked. . . .

I will not descend to those particular things, which are too well known; as that our *Courtier* ought not to profess himself a great eater, or drinker, or intemperate in any respect, or slovenly in his way of living, like some peasants, that smell of the plough a thousand miles off; for such a one is not only, not to be hoped to make a good *Courtier,* but, indeed, can be employed about nothing better, than to keep sheep.

And to conclude, I say, that it by all means behoves our *Courtier* to have a perfect knowledge in what we have said is fit for him; so that everything possible may be easy to him, and all men admire him, and he nobody; but I would by no means here be understood, that he shew a lofty and unmanly carriage, as some do, that do all they can to make people believe, they do not at all wonder at what things other people do, because they presume to do them much better, and by their silence despise them, as things unworthy our notice, and make semblance as if no one were (I do not say their equals, but) capable of understanding their profound knowledge.

A *Courtier* therefore ought to shun this hateful conduct, and with sweet temper and humanity commend the good actions of other men; and tho' he may know, that he excels others in several respects, yet let him take care not to let the world know he thinks so of himself. But because very seldom, or perhaps never, these high perfections are found in human nature, yet should not a man, who finds himself wanting in some respect, lay aside all hopes of arriving at some degree, tho' he cannot reach that height, of excellency, he aspires to: For, in every art and science, there are many worthy places besides the first, and it is seldom seen, but he, who aims at the highest, passes beyond the middle station.

I would then have our *Courtier,* in case he find himself excellent in anything besides arms, to shew his merit after a genteel manner, and that he have that discretion and good judgment, as to know how, with dexterity and address, to invite people to hear and see what in him is most excellent; always taking this caution, not to seem to do it thro' ostentation, but accidentally, and rather to be intreated by others, than to do it of his own choice; and, in everything that he is to do, or speak of, let him always be prepared, and think of it before hand, seeming however to do it *extempore,* and on the sudden.

But those subjects, of which he understands but little, let him only transiently touch upon, without dwelling thereon too much, yet, in such a manner, that he may be thought really to understand more of them than he speaks; as some poets, who have treated summarily of the most abstruse points in philosophy, or other sciences, of which perhaps they knew very little; and, in what he knows himself altogether ignorant of, I would not have him make profession that he knew anything of the matter, or seek to gain any reputation, but, as occasion serves, freely confess he knows nothing of it.

This method, said *Calmeta, Nicoletto* would never have made use of; who, being a most excellent philosopher, and knew no more of the law, than how to fly, tho' a certain *Podestà* of *Padua* had a mind to give him a lesson, would never yield, at the persuasion of several scholars, to deceive the Governour, and confess he knew nothing of it, always saying, that he was not, in this point, of the opinion of *Socrates;* for it is not the part of a philosopher, at any time, to say he knew nothing.

I do not say, answered Signor *Frederick,* that a *Courtier* should of himself, without being asked, go and tell everybody, he knows nothing; for I am no way pleased with that folly of a man's condemning and dispraising himself; and I have often laughed at some people, who, without any necessity, recount voluntarily such things; which, tho' they might have happened, without any fault of theirs, carry, however, along with them some shadow of infamy and disgrace: As did a certain gentleman, whom we all know; who, whenever he heard anyone talk of the action in the *Parmesan,* against King *Charles,* would immediately begin to entertain the company, how he ran away; that a man by his discourse would imagine, he did nothing else: Then he would tell you, how he was foiled at such a famous tournament; and very often, in his discourse, seemed to bring in by head and shoulders, how such a night, as he was going to speak to a lady, he was soundly cudgelled.

Such fooleries as these I would not have our *Courtier* talk of, but my opinion is, that when occasion offers that he should discourse of what he is ignorant of, he should, by all means, seek to avoid it; which if he cannot handsomely do, let him frankly confess his ignorance, rather than run any risque; and thus shall he escape those censures, which many now-a-days deserve; who, I know not by what perverse instinct, or judgment, ever undertake to do those things they know nothing of, and omit what they sufficiently understand.

For a confirmation of this, I know a very excellent master of musick, who, laying by that science, gave himself entirely up to poetry, and believes himself a very great man in that respect, tho' he made everybody laugh at him, and now has even lost his musick. Another, one of the principal painters in the world, neglecting his art, in which he is very excellent, is going to learn philosophy; in which he has such strange conceits, and new chimeras, that, with all his painting, he cannot make any description of them. There are an infinity of such as these.

And some there are, who, knowing themselves excellent in one thing, make their principal profession to be so in another; of which however they are not ignorant; but always, when occasion offers them to shew their skill in what they know they best understand, do it to perfection; which sometimes has that good success, as to make the spectators, who see they have so high a degree of knowledge in what is not their profession, imagine them to be much more excellent in what they do profess: This art, if attended with good judgment, I am no ways displeased with.

I cannot think this an art, said Signor *Pallavicino,* but a real deceit, and I believe it unworthy a good man to deceive at any time.

This, answered the other, is rather an ornament attending the action, than a deceit; and tho' it be a deceit, yet is it no discommendable one. Will you not, for the same reason, say, he that conquers his adversary at foils cheats him? and this is only because he has more art than his companion. Again, if you have a jewel, which, being unset, is very beautiful; and afterwards, when it comes out of the jeweller's hands, appears with greater lustre, will you not, with as good grounds, say, the workman deceives the eye of him that looks upon it? and yet, for this deceit, he deserves to be commended; since, by good judgment and art, a masterly hand adds a grace and ornament to ivory, silver, or precious stones, by setting them in gold. Let us not therefore say, that art (or deceit, if you will have it so) deserves reproach.

Nor is it ill in any man, who knows himself excellent in any one thing, handsomely to take an opportunity to convince the world he is so, and even to cover those particulars which he thinks of little merit; but the whole with a certain discreet dissimulation.

Do you not remember how King *Ferdinand,* without making any semblance he designed to do so, very frequently took occasion to strip himself into his waistcoat? and this, because he knew he was finely shaped; and for the like reason, because he knew he had but indifferent hands, he seldom pulled off his gloves; and yet there were very few, who took notice of this management of his: And, I think, I have somewhere read, that *Julius Caesar* wore his wreath of lawrel on purpose to hide his baldness. But in these things a man must make use of a great deal of prudence and good judgment, lest he overshoot himself; for oftentimes a man, by too much endeavouring to avoid one error, falls into another; and for honour, which he sought after, gains only its reverse.

The most secure way therefore in the world, for a man to live and converse, is ever to govern himself with the golden mean, which is, undeniably, the greatest and strongest shield against envy; which one ought to avoid as much as possible.

I would also have our *Courtier* take care never to incur the censure of being either vainglorious, or (to speak in downright terms) a liar; which too often happens to be the fate of those who do not deserve it; for which reason, in his discourse, let him be always careful not to deviate from the likelihood of truth, nor even to mention, too frequently, those truths, that seem to wear the visage of falsehood; as some do, who never speak but of miracles, and will be thought of such authority, that everything, tho' never so incredible, must be believed, because they say so.

There are other people, again, no less culpable, who, at their first entring into a friendship with anyone, to insinuate themselves into the favour and good opinion of their new friend, make most direful imprecations, that there is not a person in the world whom they love better, and that, for his dear sake, they would sacrifice their lives, and talk many such unreasonable romantick things; and when they part, give demonstrations of the highest sorrow, and can scarce speak a word for tears, and, by being willing to be thought mighty friends, gain the character of base flatterers and liars.

But it would take up too much time to enumerate all the faults and errors in conversation; for which, I think, after what has been said, it will be sufficient to add, that our *Courtier* never want agreeable discourse, with a certain sweetness of utterance, in order to engage the attention of those who hear him, and with pleasant and jocose expressions to make them sometimes laugh, and, without tiresomness or satiety, ever delighted in his company. . . .

BOOK FOUR

[*Octavian is speaking.*] Since, Madam, I wished many other good qualities in the *Courtier,* and that I have promised to treat upon them, I shall freely declare my sentiments; not believing I can speak all that may be said upon this subject, but only so much as may suffice to remove from you, that which was yesterday objected to me, which is, that I so spoke, rather to detract from the praises of the *Court-Lady,* in making you falsely believe, that other excellent qualities might be added to the *Courtier,* and by this artifice prefer him to her, than that he really deserves one should do so.

To accommodate myself therefore to the time, which is later than at other times, when we began our discourse, I shall be very short, and so continuing in the discourse of these noble lords and gentlemen, which I approve and confirm; I say, that of those things which we call good, some there are which simply, and of themselves, are always so, as temperance, fortitude, health, and all other virtues which produce peace and tranquillity in the mind. Others are only relatively good on several respects, and for the end they are applied to, as the laws, liberality, riches, and the like.

I think therefore the *Courtier* (if he be of the perfection that Count *Lewis,* and Signor *Frederick* have described him) may certainly be very good and worthy of all praise; but for all that, he is not simply so, not by himself, but in respect to the end, to which he may be of singular use and benefit.

For certainly if the *Courtier* with his noble birth, gracefulness, pleasantry of behaviour, and experience in so many gallant exercises, should produce no other advantage but only merely to be endued with all these good qualities, I should not think that to acquire such perfections, a man reasonably ought to waste so much time, and take such pains as are necessary for him who is resolved to attain them. But I should rather say, that many of the fine qualities assigned him, as dancing, singing, and play, are vanity and folly, and, in a man of worth and merit, rather to be dispraised than commended.

For these modes and fashions, devices, railleries, and the like, which are proper for the entertainment of the ladies and love, though perhaps others may be of a contrary sentiment, do many times only emasculate our minds, corrupt youth, and lead them insensibly into a libertine way of life: Whence afterwards arise these effects, that the name of *Italy* is become so opprobrious and infamous, that there are very few who have the courage, I do not say to die, but to put themselves in any danger whatsoever. And without doubt there are an infinity of other things, which if we bestow our study and industry upon, would produce much more advantage both in peace and war, than this *Courtiership,* considered precisely as such.

But if the actions of a *Courtier* be directed to that good end they ought to be, and as I intend; I think, in such case, so far are they from being vain and unprofitable, that they are most useful and worthy infinite praise and eulogy.

The end therefore of a perfect *Courtier* (of which hitherto nothing has been said) is, I think, by means of those good qualities these gentlemen have given him, so to gain the good graces of his prince, that he may speak to him, and truly inform him of everything he ought to know, without fear or danger of displeasing him. And when he knows his mind bent to do anything unbecoming his grandeur and high character, to have the courage to inform him of his mistake, and to be so hardy, with due respect, through the credit he has with him, on account of his good qualities to dissuade him from every ill action, and set him in the road of virtue. Thus shall the *Courtier,* if he have that goodness which these gentlemen have assigned him, attended with a promptitude of wit, pleasant temper, prudence, and a knowledge of letters, and so many other good qualities bestowed on him, know how to behave himself in all occurrences, and agreeably give his prince to understand, what honour and advantage will accrue from justice, liberality, magnanimity, affability, and other virtues, fit for a good prince; and on the contrary, what damage and infamy would proceed from the opposite vices. Therefore, in my opinion, as musick, play, and the like, are the flower, this may be said to be the fruit of the *Courtier*'s art.

And because the praise of doing well consists in two points; one of which is choosing out the end to which we direct our actions, and which may be truly good, the other the knowledge of apt means to bring us to that end; certainly the mind of him who thus acts with his prince, will never be anywise deceived, or led away by flatterers, raillers, and impostors; but will be acquainted with both good and bad, and love and hate each accordingly, and of consequence tend to the best and most desirable end.

I am of opinion also, that the qualities and good conditions attributed to the *Courtier* by these gentlemen, may indeed be a very good means to bring this about; and for this reason, because of the great many errors we see now-a-days in most of the princes, are principally ignorance, and the opinion they entertain of themselves.

And the root of these two mischiefs is nothing else (for I am resolved to speak out plain) but downright lying; a vice worthily abhorred of God and man, and more hurtful to princes than any other; inasmuch as they have more scarcity of what they ought to have most abundance of, than of anything else; I mean those who should tell them the truth, and put them in mind of doing good: For enemies are not incited thro' love to do these good offices, but rather take delight to see them live wickedly, without any hopes of amendment; and besides, they dare not blame them openly for fear of being punished themselves.

As for friends, few of them have free admittance to them; and those few, out of respect, are afraid to reprehend their faults with that freedom as they would those of private men; and so very often, to gain their favour, give themselves up entirely to invent what may be subservient to their pleasures, though it be ill consistent with honesty and honour; and thus become vile flatterers, pimps, and parasites, instead of friends; which name, how speciously soever they may pretend to wear, they are a dishonour to, and the highest scandal.

And to turn this privacy to their own base profit and advantage, they frame all their words and actions only to please, and for the most part, open the way with lies and horrid falshoods, which beget in the prince's mind an ignorance not only of outward things, but even of his own self: And this may be said to be the greatest and most enormous lie of all others; because an ignorant mind deceives itself, and is to itself the greatest liar in the world.

Hence it comes to pass, that great men, besides that they never understand the truth of anything, drunk with that licentious liberty which dominion always brings along with it, and the abundance of delights, deep drowned in pleasures, are so much deceived, and their minds so much corrupted, in seeing themselves always obeyed, and as it were adored with so profound veneration, and excessive praise, without ever being reprehended or contradicted; that through this ignorance, they fall into such an extreme persuasion of themselves, that afterwards they will not admit any counsel or advice of others.

And because they fancy, that to know how to rule is a most easy matter, and that to acquit themselves worthily, requires no more than meer force and power; they turn all their thoughts to maintain the power they have, thinking it the true happiness of a man to do what he arbitrarily has a mind to.

On which account some abhor reason and justice, because they think it a certain check upon themselves, and a means that may bring them into servitude, and diminish in them that false satisfaction and pleasure they have in ruling, should they observe it; and that their dominion would not be perfect and entire, if they should be constrained to obey virtue, and their own duty; because they are of opinion, that *He who obeys is not truly a lord.*

Taking then these principles for their rule, and suffering themselves to be transported with a persuasion of themselves, they grow proud, and with imperious looks, austere deportment, with pompous habits glittering with gold and jewels, and by being seldom seen in publick, they think to acquire authority with men, and to be esteemed as gods.

But these, in my opinion, are like those *Colossi* that were made in *Rome* last year, on the feast of the *Piazza d' Agone,* which in the outside looked like great men, and triumphal horses, but were fluffed up in the inside only with rags. But the princes of this kind are so much worse; for the *Colossi,* by their own weight and gravity stood upright, but these by being ill counterpoised and disproportionably set on unequal bases, thro' their own proper weight ruin and overthrow themselves, and from one error run into an infinity of others: Because their ignorance accompanied with this false opinion, that they *can do no wrong;* and that the power they have, proceeds from their own knowledge, induces them by every way, either just or unjust, boldly to possess themselves of the territories and dominions of others, whenever it lies in their power. But did they but deliberate to know and do what they ought, they would rather choose not to reign at all; because then they would perceive what a dangerous matter it would be for subjects, who are to be governed, to be wiser than the princes who are to govern them.

You see that ignorance in musick, dancing, and riding, hurts nobody, and yet he that does not understand musick, is ashamed and afraid to sing in the presence of others; the same may be said of those who cannot dance, or ride: But from the unskillfulness in governing, arise so many evils, deaths, destructions, burnings, and ruines, that this ignorance may be termed the most mortal plague on earth. And yet some princes, the most ignorant in government, are not ashamed to take upon them that weighty charge, I will not say in the presence of four, or half a dozen persons, but in the face of the whole world; inasmuch as their station is so lofty and conspicuous, that all eyes behold them, and therefore not only their great vices, but their most minute faults are taken particular notice of.

Thus it was written that *Cimon* was spoken ill of for loving wine, *Scipio* sleep, *Lucullus* banqueting; but would to heaven the princes of our times would accompany their vices with so many virtues, as they did of old; who, if they erred in some things, refused not the sage advices of those whom they knew able to correct their errors, and even endeavoured, as much as possible, to frame their lives according to the rules of these extraordinary men; as *Epaminodas* did by the advice of *Lysias* the *Pythagorean, Agesilaus* of *Xenophon,* and *Scipio* of *Panetius,* and many others.

But now if a grave philosopher, or any other, should come in the presence of any of our princes, who would shew them, openly and without disguise or mask, this frightful face of true virtue, and instruct them in a good conduct, and what the life of a good prince ought to be; I am assured they would abhor him at the first sight as a *Basilisk,* or else with a loud laughter answer his instructions, as the most sottish and ridiculous thing in the world.

I say then, that since now-a-days princes are so corrupt in their manners, through ignorance, and a false opinion of themselves, and that it is so difficult a matter to give them any notions of truth, and incline them to virtue; and men with lies, and horrid falshoods, flatteries, and such other vicious ways, endeavour to creep into their favour; the *Courtier,* by those noble qualities bestowed on him by Count *Lewis* and Signor *Frederick,* may easily and ought to acquire the good graces of his prince, and in such a manner sooth his mind, that he may always have a free and sure access to his person, in order to discourse with him on every subject, without being troublesome: By which means he may by degrees distill into his mind all virtues, as continency, justice, fortitude, temperance, and make him taste those delicious sweets, which are covered with those little bitters, which at first offer themselves to him who combats vice, which is ever hurtful and displeasing, and attended with blame and infamy; while virtue is ever profitable, pleasant, and merits praise, and engages people to her with the examples of many celebrated generals, to whose immortal honour people of ancient times used to erect statues of brass and marble, and sometimes of gold, and that too in publick places, as encouragements also to others, who, by a noble emulation, might endeavour to arrive themselves at those heights of glory.

Thus may he conduct him through the rough paths of virtue, adorning them, as it were, with shady boughs, and shewing them with variety of beautiful flowers, to alleviate, in some measure, the fatigue of the painful journey, in those who are but yet weak: And sometimes with musick, sometimes with arms and horses, now with poetry, then with love, and by all those other ways these gentlemen have already described, to keep his mind continually employed in honest and honourable pleasures; imprinting notwithstanding, as has been said, ever among these agreeable entertainments, some virtuous quality, and beguiling him with a salutary deceit, as physicians do, who commonly, when they give a bitter medicine to children and such as are of a delicate constitution, sweeten the potion, or gild the pill.

The *Courtier,* then, for this end, making use of the veil of pleasure, in every time, place, and exercise, will attain that end, and merit more recompence and praise, than by any other good work he can perform in the world: For there is no treasure of such universal advantage as a good prince, nor no evil so universally pernicious as an ill one. For which reason, there can be no cruel punishment in the world invented, sufficient to punish those wicked *Courtiers,* who make use of their fine address and good qualities for an ill end; and to insinuate themselves into their prince's favour, that they may corrupt them, and make them leave the way of virtue, to wander in the endless labyrinths of vice: For these shining villains may be said not only to infect, with mortal poison, a cistern where only one man goes to drink, but the publick fountain resorted to by all. . . .

ᴇ§ LIFE OF LEONARDO DA VINCI

Giorgio Vasari

The word "Renaissance," is inevitably associated with the astonishing outburst of creativity in the fine arts which culminated in the master artists of the fifteenth and sixteenth centuries, especially in Italy. Not only did these artists match the excellence of their ancient Greek models, but they set a new standard for the expression of personality through art—particularly through painting. Some of them, like Michelangelo Buonarotti, were gifted in so many areas that it becomes impossible to identify their primary field of accomplishment. Others surpassed even these by attaining a

breathtaking versatility, establishing what has become known as the ideal
of the "universal man" or "universal genius," exemplified by such men as
Thomas Jefferson and Benjamin Franklin in the eighteenth century and
Albert Schweitzer in our own.

The great exemplar of this type of human excellence is Leonardo da Vinci,
whose biography by the sixteenth-century artist and critic Giorgio Vasari is
included virtually complete. What Vasari presents is a portrait of an artist in
many media who is also an engineer, an inventor, and a public figure of
great acclaim, possessed by an almost demonic creative urge that drove him
from one project to another with such breathtaking force that he was seldom
able to complete any. Vasari's own implied criteria for greatness, reflected
in his admiration for Leonardo, are almost as interesting a subject as
Leonardo's remarkable career.

The richest gifts are occasionally seen to be showered, as by celestial influence, on certain human beings, nay, they some times supernaturally and marvellously congregate in one sole person; beauty, grace, and talent being united in such a manner, that to whatever the man thus favoured may turn himself, his every action is so divine as to leave all other men far behind him, and manifestly to prove that he has been specially endowed by the hand of God himself, and has not obtained his pre-eminence by human teaching, or the power of man. This was seen and acknowledged by all men in the case of Leonardo da Vinci, in whom, to say nothing of his beauty of person, which yet was such that it has never been sufficiently extolled, there was a grace beyond expression which was rendered manifest without thought or effort in every act and deed, and who had besides so rare a gift of talent and ability, that to whatever subject he turned his attention, however difficult, he presently made himself absolute master of it. Extraordinary power was in his case conjoined with remarkable facility, a mind of regal boldness and magnanimous daring; his gifts were such that the celebrity of his name extended most widely, and he was held in the highest estimation, not in his own time only, but also, and even to a greater extent, after his death, nay, this he has continued, and will continue to be by all succeeding ages.

Truly admirable, indeed, and divinely endowed was Leonardo da Vinci; this artist was the son of Ser Piero da Vinci; he would without doubt have made great progress in learning and knowledge of the sciences, had he not been so versatile and changeful, but the instability of his character caused him to undertake many things which having commenced he afterwards abandoned. In arithmetic, for example, he made such rapid progress in the short time during which he gave his attention to it, that he often confounded the master who was teaching him, by the perpetual doubts he started, and

Giorgio Vasari, *Lives of the Most Eminent Painters, Sculptors, and Architects,* ed. Mrs. J. Foster (London: Henry G. Bohn, 1914), Vol. II, 366–390.

by the difficulty of the questions he proposed. He also commenced the study of music, and resolved to acquire the art of playing the lute, when, being by nature of an exalted imagination and full of the most graceful vivacity, he sang to that instrument most divinely, improvising at once the verses and the music.

But, though dividing his attention among pursuits so varied, he never abandoned his drawing, and employed himself much in works of relief, that being the occupation which attracted him more than any other. His father, Ser Piero, observing this, and considering the extraordinary character of his son's genius, one day took some of his drawings and showed them to Andrea del Verrocchio, who was a very intimate friend of his, begging him earnestly to tell him whether he thought that Leonardo would be likely to secure success if he devoted himself to the arts of design. Andrea Verrocchio was amazed as he beheld the remarkable commencement made by Leonardo, and advised Ser Piero to see that he attached himself to that calling, whereupon the latter took his measures accordingly, and sent Leonardo to study in the bottega or workshop of Andrea. Thither the boy resorted therefore, with the utmost readiness, and not only gave his attention to one branch of art, but to all the others, of which design made a portion. Endowed with such admirable intelligence, and being also an excellent geometrician, Leonardo not only worked in sculpture (having executed certain heads in terra-cotta, of women smiling, even in his first youth, which are now reproduced in gypsum, and also others of children which might be supposed to have proceeded from the hand of a master); but in architecture likewise he prepared various designs for ground-plans, and the construction of entire buildings: he too it was who, though still but a youth, first suggested the formation of a canal from Pisa to Florence, by means of certain changes to be effected on the river Arno. Leonardo likewise made designs for mills, fulling machines, and other engines, which were to be acted on by means of water; but as he had resolved to make painting his profession, he gave the larger portion of time to drawing from nature. He sometimes formed models of different figures in clay, on which he would arrange fragments of soft drapery dipped in plaster; from these he would then set himself patiently to draw on very fine cambric or linen that had already been used and rendered smooth, these he executed in black and white with the point of the pencil in a most admirable manner, as may be seen by certain specimens from his own hand which I have in my book of drawings. He drew on paper also with so much care and so perfectly, that no one has ever equalled him in this respect: I have a head by him in chiaro-scuro, which is incomparably beautiful. Leonardo was indeed so imbued with power and grace by the hand of God, and was endowed with so marvellous a facility in reproducing his conceptions; his memory also was always so ready and so efficient in the service of his intellect, that in discourse he won all men by his reasonings, and confounded every antagonist, however powerful, by the force of his arguments.

This master was also frequently occupied with the construction of models and the preparation of designs for the removal or the perforation of mountains, to the end that they might thus be easily passed from one plain to another. By means of levers, cranes, and screws, he likewise showed how great weights might be raised or drawn; in what manner ports and havens might be cleansed and kept in order, and how water might be obtained from the lowest deeps. From speculations of this kind he never gave himself rest, and of the results of these labours and meditations there are numberless examples in drawings, &c., dispersed among those who practise our arts: I have myself seen very many of them. Besides all this he wasted not a little time, to the degree of even designing a series of cords, curiously intertwined, but of which any separate strand may be distinguished from one end to the other, the whole forming a complete circle: a very curiously complicated and exceedingly difficult specimen of these coils may be seen engraved; in the midst of it are the following words:—*Leonardus Vinci Academia.* Among these models and drawings there is one, by means of which Leonardo often sought to prove to the different citizens—many of them men of great discernment—who then governed Florence, that the church of San Giovanni in that city could be raised, and steps placed beneath it, without injury to the edifice: he supported his assertions with reasons so persuasive, that while he spoke the undertaking seemed feasible, although every one of his hearers, when he had departed, could see for himself that such a thing was impossible. In conversation Leonardo was indeed so pleasing that he won the hearts of all hearers, and though possessing so small a patrimony only that it might almost be called nothing, while he yet worked very little, he still constantly kept many servants and horses, taking extraordinary delight in the latter: he was indeed fond of all animals, ever treating them with infinite kindness and consideration; as a proof of this it is related, that when he passed places where birds were sold, he would frequently take them from their cages, and having paid the price demanded for them by the sellers, would then let them fly into the air, thus restoring to them the liberty they had lost. Leonardo was in all things so highly favoured by nature, that to whatever he turned his thoughts, mind, and spirit, he gave proof in all of such admirable power and perfection, that whatever he did bore an impress of harmony, truthfulness, goodness, sweetness and grace, wherein no other man could ever equal him.

Leonardo, with his profound intelligence of art, commenced various undertakings, many of which he never completed, because it appeared to him that the hand could never give its due perfection to the object or purpose which he had in his thoughts, or beheld in his imagination; seeing that in his mind he frequently formed the idea of some difficult enterprise, so subtle and so wonderful that, by means of hands, however excellent or able, the full reality could never be worthily executed and entirely realized. His conceptions were varied to infinity; philosophizing over natural objects; among others, he set himself to investigate the properties of plants, to make observations on the heavenly bodies, to follow the movements of the planets, the variations of the moon, and the course of the sun.

Having been placed then by Ser Piero in his childhood with Andrea Verrocchio, as we have said, to learn the art of the painter, that master was engaged on a picture the subject of which was San Giovanni baptizing Jesus Christ; in this Leonardo painted an angel holding some vestments; and although he was but a youth, he completed that figure in such a manner, that the angel of Leonardo was much better than the portion executed by his master, which caused the latter never to touch colours more, so much was he displeased to find that a mere child could do more than himself.

Leonardo received a commission to prepare the cartoon for the hangings of a door which was to be woven in silk and gold in Flanders, thence to be despatched to the king of Portugal; the subject was the sin of our first parents in Paradise: here the artist depicted a meadow in chiaro-scuro, the high lights being in white lead, displaying an immense variety of vegetation and numerous animals, respecting which it may be truly said, that for careful execution and fidelity to nature, they are such that there is no genius in the world, however God-like, which could produce similar objects with equal truth. In the fig-tree, for example, the foreshortening of the leaves, and the disposition of the branches are executed with so much care, that one finds it difficult to conceive how any man could have so much patience; there is besides a palm-tree, in which the roundness of the fan-like leaves is exhibited to such admirable perfection and with so much art, that nothing short of the genius and patience of Leonardo could have effected it: but the work for which the cartoon was prepared was never carried into execution, the drawing therefore remained in Florence, and is now in the fortunate house of the illustrious Ottaviano de'Medici, to whom it was presented, no long time since, by the uncle of Leonardo.

It is related that Ser Piero da Vinci, being at his country house, was there visited by one of the peasants on his estate, who, having cut down a fig-tree on his farm, had made a shield from part of it with his own hands, and then brought it to Ser Piero, begging that he would be pleased to cause the same to be painted for him in Florence. This the latter very willingly promised to do, the countryman having great skill in taking birds and in fishing, and being often very serviceable to Ser Piero in such matters. Having taken the shield with him to Florence therefore, without saying any thing to Leonardo as to whom it was for, he desired the latter to paint something upon it. Accordingly, he one day took it in hand, but finding it crooked, coarse, and badly made, he straightened it at the fire, and giving it to a turner, it was brought back to him smooth and delicately rounded, instead of the rude and shapeless form in which he had received it. He then covered it with gypsum, and having prepared it to his liking, he began to consider what he could paint upon it that might best and most effectually terrify whomsoever might approach it, producing the same effect with that formerly attributed to the head of Medusa. For this purpose therefore, Leonardo carried to one of his rooms, into which no one but himself ever entered, a number of lizards, hedge-hogs, newts, serpents, dragon-flies, locusts, bats, glow-worms, and every other sort of strange animal of similar kind on which he could lay his hands; from this assemblage, variously adapted and joined together, he formed a hideous and appalling monster, breathing poison and flames, and surrounded by an atmosphere of fire; this he caused to issue from a dark and rifted rock, with poison reeking from the cavernous throat, flames darting from the eyes, and vapours rising from the nostrils in such sort that the result was indeed a most fearful and monstrous creature: at this he laboured until the odours arising from all those dead animals filled the room with a mortal fetor, to which the zeal of Leonardo and the love which he bore to art rendered him insensible or indifferent. When this work, which neither the countryman nor Ser Piero any longer inquired for, was completed, Leonardo went to his father and told him that he might send for the shield at this earliest convenience, since so far as he was concerned, the work was finished; Ser Piero went accordingly one morning to the room for the shield, and having knocked at the door, Leonardo opened it to him, telling him nevertheless to wait a little without, and having returned into the room he placed the shield on the easel, and shading the window so that the light falling on the painting was somewhat dimmed, he made Ser Piero step within to look at it. But the latter, not expecting any such thing, drew back, startled at the first glance, not supposing that to be the shield, or believing the monster he beheld to be a painting, he therefore turned to rush out, but Leonardo withheld him, saying:—The shield will serve the purpose for which it has been executed, take it therefore and carry it away, for this is the effect it was designed to produce. The work seemed something more than wonderful to Ser Piero, and he highly commended the fanciful idea of Leonardo, but he afterwards silently bought from a merchant another shield, whereon there was painted a heart transfixed with an arrow, and this he gave to the countryman, who considered himself obliged to him for it to the end of his life. Some time after Ser Piero secretly sold the shield painted by Leonardo to certain merchants for one hundred ducats, and it subsequently fell into the hands of the Duke of Milan, sold to him by the same merchants for three hundred ducats.

No long time after Leonardo painted an admirable picture of Our Lady, which was greatly prized by Pope Clement VII.; among the accessories of this work was a bottle filled with water in which some flowers were placed, and not only were these flowers most vividly natural, but there were dewdrops on the leaves, which were so true to nature that they appeared to be the actual reality. . . .

Leonardo also had a fancy to paint the head of a Medusa in oil, to which he gave a circlet of twining serpents by way of head-dress; the most strange and extravagant invention that could possibly be conceived: but as this was a work requiring time, so it happened to the Medusa as to so many other of his works, it was never finished. . . .

Leonardo was so much pleased when he encountered faces of extraordinary character, or heads, beards or hair of unusual appearance, that he would follow any such, more than commonly attractive, through the whole day, until the figure of the person would become so well impressed on his mind that, having returned home, he would draw him as readily as though he stood before him. Of heads thus obtained there exist many, both masculine and feminine; and I have myself several of them drawn with a pen by his own hand, in the book of drawings so frequently cited. Among these is the head of Amerigo Vespucci, which is a very beautiful one of an old man, done with charcoal, as also that of the Gypsy Captain Scaramuccia, which had been left by Gianbullari to Messer Donato Valdambrini, of Arezzo, Canon of San Lorenzo. A picture representing the Adoration of the Magi was likewise commenced by Leonardo, and is among the best of his works, more especially as regards the heads; it was in the house of Amerigo Benci, opposite the Loggia of the Peruzzi, but like so many of the other works of Leonardo, this also remained unfinished.

On the death of Giovanni Galeazzo, Duke of Milan, in the year 1493, Ludovico Sforza was chosen in the same year to be his successor, when Leonardo was invited with great honour to Milan by the Duke, who delighted greatly in the music of the lute, to the end that the master might play before him; Leonardo therefore took with him a certain instrument which he had himself constructed almost wholly of silver, and in the shape of a horse's head, a new and fanciful form calculated to give more force and sweetness to the sound. Here Leonardo surpassed all the musicians who had assembled to perform before the Duke; he was besides one of the best *improvisatori* in verse existing at that time, and the Duke, enchanted with the admirable conversation of Leonardo, was so charmed by his varied gifts that he delighted beyond measure in his society, and prevailed on him to paint an altar-piece, the subject of which was the Nativity of Christ, which was sent by the Duke as a present to the Emperor. For the Dominican monks of Santa Maria delle Grazie at Milan, he also painted a Last Supper, which is a most beautiful and admirable work; to the heads of the Apostles in this picture the master gave so much beauty and majesty that he was constrained to leave that of Christ unfinished, being convinced that he could not impart to it the divinity which should appertain to and distinguish an image of the Redeemer. But this work, remaining thus in its unfinished state, has been ever held in the highest estimation by the Milanese, and not by them only, but by foreigners also: Leonardo succeeded to perfection in expressing the doubts and anxiety experienced by the Apostles, and the desire felt by them to know by whom their Master is to be betrayed; in the faces of all appear love, terror, anger, or grief and bewilderment, unable as they are to fathom the meaning of their Lord. Nor is the spectator less struck with admiration by the force and truth with which, on the other hand, the master has exhibited the impious determination, hatred, and treachery of Judas. The whole work indeed is executed with inexpressible diligence even in its most minute part, among other things may be mentioned the table-cloth, the texture of which is copied with such exactitude, that the linen-cloth itself could scarcely look more real.

It is related that the Prior of the Monastery was excessively importunate in pressing Leonardo to complete the picture; he could in no way comprehend wherefore the artist should sometimes remain half a day together absorbed in thought before his work, without making any progress that he could see; this seemed to him a strange waste of time, and he would fain have had him work away as he could make the men do who were digging in his garden, never laying the pencil out of his hand. Not content with seeking to hasten Leonardo, the Prior even complained to the Duke, and tormented him to such a degree that the latter was at length compelled to send for Leonardo, whom he courteously entreated to let the work be finished, assuring him nevertheless that he did so because impelled by the importunities of the Prior. Leonardo, knowing the Prince to be intelligent and judicious, determined to explain himself fully on the subject with him, although he had never chosen to do so with the Prior. He therefore discoursed with him at some length respecting art, and made it perfectly manifest to his comprehension, that men of genius are sometimes producing most when they seem to be labouring least, their minds being occupied in the elucidation of their ideas, and in the completion of those conceptions to which they afterwards give form and expression with the hand. He further informed the Duke that there were still wanting to him two heads, one of which, that of the Saviour, he could not hope to find on earth, and had not yet attained the power of presenting it to himself in imagination, with all that perfection of beauty and celestial grace which appeared to him to be demanded for the due representation of the Divinity incarnate. The second head still wanting was that of Judas, which also caused him some anxiety, since he did not think it possible to imagine a form of feature that should properly render the countenance of a man who, after so many benefits received from his master, had possessed a heart so depraved as to be capable of betraying his Lord and the Creator of the world with regard to that second, however, he would make search, and after all—if he could find no better, he need never be at any great loss, for there would always be the head of that troublesome and impertinent Prior. This made the Duke laugh with all his heart, he declared Leonardo to be completely in the right, and the poor Prior, utterly confounded, went away to drive on the digging in his garden, and left Leonardo in peace: the head of Judas was then finished so successfully, that it is indeed the true image of treachery and wickedness; but that of the Redeemer remained, as we have said, incomplete. The admirable excellence of this picture, the beauty of its composition, and the care with which it was executed, awakened in the King of France, a desire to have it removed into his own kingdom, insomuch that he made many attempts to discover architects, who might be able to secure it by defences of wood and iron, that it might be transported without injury. He was not to be deterred by any consideration of the cost that might be incurred, but the painting, being on the wall, his Majesty was compelled to forego his desire, and the Milanese retained their picture. . . .

While still engaged with the paintings of the refectory, Leonardo proposed to the Duke to cast a horse in bronze of colossal size, and to place on it a figure of the Duke, by way of monument to his memory: this he commenced, but finished the model on so large a scale that it never could be completed, and there were many ready to declare (for the judgments of men are various, and are sometimes rendered malignant by envy) that Leonardo had begun it, as he did others of his labours, without intending ever to finish it. The size of the work being such, insuperable difficulties presented themselves, as I have said, when it came to be cast; nay, the casting could not be effected in one piece, and it is very probable that, when this result was known, many were led to form the opinion alluded to above, from the fact that so many of Leonardo's works had failed to receive completion. But of a truth, there is good reason to believe that the very greatness of his most exalted mind, aiming at more than could be effected, was itself an impediment; perpetually seeking to add excellence to excellence, and perfection to perfection; this was, without doubt, the true hindrance, so that, as our Petrarch has it, the work was retarded by desire. All who saw the large model in clay which Leonardo made for this work, declared that they had never seen anything more beautiful or more majestic; this model remained as he had left it until the French, with their King Louis, came to Milan, when they destroyed it totally. A small model of the same work, executed in wax, and which was considered perfect, was also lost, with a book containing studies of the anatomy of the horse, which Leonardo had prepared for his own use. He afterwards gave his attention, and with increased earnestness, to the anatomy of the human frame, a study wherein Messer Marcantonio della Torre, an eminent philosopher, and himself, did mutually assist and encourage each other. Messer Marcantonio was at that time holding lectures in Pavia, and wrote on the same subject; he was one of the first, as I have heard say, who began to apply the doctrines of Galen to the elucidation of medical science, and to diffuse light over the science of anatomy, which, up to that time, had been involved in the almost total darkness of ignorance. In this attempt Marcantonio was wonderfully aided by the genius and labour of Leonardo, who filled a book with drawings in red crayons, outlined with the pen, all copies made with the utmost care from bodies dissected by his own hand. In this book he set forth the entire structure, arrangement, and disposition of the bones, to which he afterwards added all the nerves, in their due order, and next supplied the muscles, of which the first are affixed to the bones, the second give the power of cohesion or holding firmly, and the third impart that of motion. Of each separate part he wrote an explanation in rude characters, written backwards and with the left-hand, so that whoever is not practised in reading cannot understand them, since they are only to be read with a mirror. Of these anatomical drawings of the human form, a great part is now in the possession of Messer Francesco da Melzo, a Milanese gentleman, who, in the time of Leonardo, was a child of remarkable beauty, much beloved by him, and is now a handsome and amiable old man, who sets great store by these drawings, and treasures them as relics, together with the portrait of Leonardo of blessed memory. To all who read these writings it must appear almost incredible that this sublime genius could, at the same time, discourse, as he has done, of art, and of the muscles, nerves, veins, and every other part of the frame, all treated with equal diligence and success. There are, besides, certain other writings of Leonardo, also written with the left-hand, in the possession of N. N., a painter of Milan; they treat of painting, of design generally, and of colouring. This artist came to see me in Florence no long time since; he then had an intention of publishing this work, and took it with him to Rome, there to give this purpose effect, but what was the end of the matter I do not know.

But to return to the labours of Leonardo. During his time the King of France came to Milan, whereupon he (Leonardo) was entreated to prepare something very extraordinary for his reception. He therefore constructed a lion, and this figure, after having made a few steps, opened its breast, which was discovered to be entirely filled full of lilies. While in Milan, Leonardo took the Milanese Salai for his disciple; this was a youth of singular grace and beauty of person, with curled and waving hair, a feature of personal beauty by which Leonardo was always greatly pleased. This Salai he instructed in various matters relating to art, and certain works still in Milan, and said to be by Salai, were retouched by Leonardo himself.

Having returned to Florence, he found that the Servite Monks had commissioned Filippino to paint the altar-piece for the principal chapel in their church of the Nunziata, when he declared that he would himself very willingly have undertaken such a work. This being repeated to Filippino, he, like the amiable man that he was, withdrew himself at once, when the Monks gave the picture to Leonardo. And to the end that he might make progress with it, they took him into their own abode with all his household, supplying the expenses of the whole, and so he kept them attending on him for a long time, but did not make any commencement; at length, however, he prepared a cartoon, with the Madonna, Sant'Anna, and the infant Christ, so admirably depicted that it not only caused astonishment in every artist who saw it, but, when finished, the chamber wherein it stood was crowded for two days by men and women, old and young; a concourse, in short, such as one sees flocking to the most solemn festivals, all hastening to behold the wonders produced by Leonardo, and which awakened amazement in the whole people. Nor was this without good cause, seeing that in the countenance of that Virgin there is all the simplicity and loveliness which can be conceived as giving grace and beauty to the Mother of Christ, the artist proposing to show in her the modesty and humility of the virgin, filled with joy and gladness as she contemplates the beauty of her Son, whom she is tenderly supporting in her lap. And while Our Lady, with eyes modestly bent down, is looking at a little San Giovanni, who is playing with a lamb, Sant'Anna, at the summit of delight, is observing the group with a smile of happiness, rejoicing as she sees that her terrestrial progeny have become divine; all which is entirely worthy of the mind and genius of Leonardo: this cartoon was subsequently taken to France, as will be related hereafter. Leonardo then painted the portrait of Ginevra, the wife of Amerigo Benci, a most beautiful thing, and abandoned the commission entrusted to him by the Servite Monks, who once more confided it to Filippino, but neither could the last-named master complete it, because his death supervened before he had time to do so.

For Francesco del Giocondo, Leonardo undertook to paint the portrait of Mona Lisa, his wife, but, after loitering over it for four years, he finally left it unfinished. This work is now in the possession of the King Francis of France, and is at Fontainebleau. Whoever shall desire to see how far art can imitate nature, may do so to perfection in this head, wherein every peculiarity that could be depicted by the utmost subtlety of the pencil has been faithfully reproduced. The eyes have the lustrous brightness and moisture which is seen in life, and around them are those pale, red, and slightly livid circles, also proper to nature, with the lashes, which can only be copied, as these are, with the greatest difficulty; the eyebrows also are represented with the closest exactitude, where fuller and where more thinly set, with the separate hairs delineated as they issue from the skin, every turn being followed, and all the pores exhibited in a manner that could not be more natural than it is: the nose, with its beautiful and delicately roseate nostrils, might be easily believed to be alive; the mouth, admirable in its outline, has the lips uniting the rose-tints of their colour with that of the face, in the utmost perfection, and the carnation of the cheek does not appear to be painted, but truly of flesh and blood: he who looks earnestly at the pit of the throat cannot but believe that he sees the beating of the pulses, and it may be truly said that this work is painted in a manner well calculated to make the boldest master tremble, and astonishes all who behold it, however well accustomed to the marvels of art. Mona Lisa was exceedingly beautiful, and while Leonardo was painting her portrait, he took the precaution of keeping some one constantly near her, to sing or play on instruments, or to jest and otherwise amuse her, to the end that she might continue cheerful, and so that her face might not exhibit the melancholy expression often imparted by painters to the likenesses they take. In this portrait of Leonardo's, on the contrary, there is so pleasing an expression, and a smile so sweet, that while looking at it one thinks it rather divine than human, and it has ever been esteemed a wonderful work, since life itself could exhibit no other appearance.

The excellent productions of this divine artist had so greatly increased and extended his fame, that all men who delighted in the arts (nay, the whole city of Florence) were anxious that he should leave behind him some memorial of himself, and there was much discussion everywhere in respect to some great and important work to be executed by him, to the end that the commonwealth might have the glory, and the city the ornament, imparted by the genius, grace, and judgment of Leonardo, to all that he did. At that time the great Hall of the council had been constructed anew, the architecture being after designs by Giuliano di San Gullo, Simone Pollaiuoli, called Cronaca, Michelagnolo Buonarroti, and Baccio d'Agnolo, as will be related in the proper place. The building having been completed with great rapidity, as was determined between the Gonfaloniere and the more distinguished citizens, it was then commanded by public decree that Leonardo should depict some fine work therein. The said hall was entrusted, accordingly, to that master by Piero Soderini, then Gonfaloniere of Justice, and he, very willing to undertake the work, commenced a cartoon in the hall of the Pope, an apartment so called, in Santa Maria Novella. Herein he represented the History of Niccolò Piccinino, Captain-General to the Duke Filippo of Milan, in which he depicted a troop of horsemen fighting around a standard, and struggling for the possession thereof; this painting was considered to be a most excellent one, evincing great mastery in the admirable qualities of the composition, as well as in the power with which the whole work is treated. Among other peculiarities of this scene, it is to be remarked that not only are rage, disdain, and the desire for revenge apparent in the men, but in the horses also; two of these animals, with their fore-legs intertwined, are attacking each other with their teeth, no less fiercely than do the cavaliers who are fighting for the standard. One of the combatants has seized the object of their strife with both hands, and is urging his horse to its speed, while he, lending the whole weight of his person to the effort, clings with his utmost strength to the shaft of the banner, and strives to tear it by main force from the hands of four others, who are all labouring to defend it with uplifted swords, which each brandishes in the attempt to divide the shaft with one of his hands, while he grasps the cause of contention with the other. An old soldier, with a red cap on his head, has also seized the standard with one hand, and raising a curved scimitar in the other, is uttering cries of rage, and fiercely dealing a blow, by which he is endeavouring to cut off the hands of two of his opponents, who, grinding their teeth, are struggling in an attitude of fixed determination to defend their banner. On the earth, among the feet of the horses, are two other figures foreshortened, who are obstinately fighting in that position; one has been hurled to the ground, while the other has thrown himself upon him, and, raising his arm to its utmost height, is bringing down his dagger with all his force to the throat of his enemy; the latter, meanwhile, struggling mightily with arms and feet, is defending himself from the impending death. It would be scarcely possible adequately to describe the skill shown by Leonardo in this work, or to do justice to the beauty of design with which he has depicted the warlike habiliments of the soldiers, with their helmets, crests, and other ornaments, infinitely varied as they are; or the wonderful mastery he exhibits in the forms and movements of the horses; these animals were, indeed, more admirably treated by Leonardo than by any other master; the muscular development, the animation of their movements, and their exquisite beauty, are rendered with the utmost fidelity.

It is said that, for the execution of this cartoon, Leonardo caused a most elaborate scaffolding to be constructed, which could be increased in height by being drawn together, or rendered wider by being lowered: it was his intention to paint the picture in oil, on the wall, but he made a composition for the intonaco, or ground, which was so coarse that, after he had painted for a certain time, the work began to sink in such a manner as to induce Leonardo very shortly to abandon it altogether, since he saw that it was becoming spoiled.

Leonardo da Vinci was a man of very high spirit, and was very generous in all his actions: it is related of him that, having once gone to the bank to receive the salary which Piero Soderini caused to be paid to him every month, the cashier was about to give him certain paper packets of pence, but Leonardo refused to receive them, remarking, at the same time, "I am no penny-painter." Not completing the picture, he was charged with having deceived Piero Soderini, and was reproached accordingly; when Leonardo so wrought with his friends, that they collected the sums which he had received and took the money to Piero Soderini with offers of restoration, but Piero would not accept them.

On the exaltation of Pope Leo X. to the chair of St. Peter, Leonardo accompanied the Duke Giuliano de' Medici to Rome: the Pontiff was much inclined to philosophical inquiry, and was more especially addicted to the study of alchemy: Leonardo, therefore, having composed a kind of paste from wax, made of this, while it was still in its half-liquid state, certain figures of animals, entirely hollow and exceedingly slight in texture, which he then filled with air. When he blew into these figures he could make them fly through the air, but when the air within had escaped from them they fell to the earth. One day the vine-dresser of the Belvedere found a very curious lizard, and for this creature Leonardo constructed wings, made from the skins of other lizards, flayed for the purpose; into these wings he put quicksilver, so that when the animal walked, the wings moved also, with a tremulous motion: he then made eyes, horns, and a beard for the creature, which he tamed and kept in a case; he would then show it to the friends who came to visit him, and all who saw it ran away terrified. He more than once, likewise, caused the intestines of a sheep to be cleansed and scraped until they were brought into such a state of tenuity that they could be held within the hollow of the hand, having then placed in a neighbouring chamber a pair of blacksmith's bellows, to which he had made fast one end of the intestines, he would blow into them until he caused them to fill the whole room, which was a very large one, insomuch that whoever might be therein was compelled to take refuge in a corner: he thus showed them transparent and full of wind, remarking that, whereas they had previously been contained within a small compass, they were now filling all space, and this, he would say, was a fit emblem of talent or genius. He made numbers of these follies in various kinds, occupied himself much with mirrors and optical instruments, and made the most singular experiments in seeking oils for painting, and varnishes to preserve the work when executed. About this time he painted a small picture for Messer Baldassare Turini, of Pescia, who was Datary to Pope Leo: the subject of this work was Our Lady, with the Child in her arms, and it was executed by Leonardo with infinite care and art, but whether from the carelessness of those who prepared the ground, or because of his peculiar and fanciful mixtures for colours, varnishes, &c., it is now much deteriorated. In another small picture he painted a little Child, which is graceful and beautiful to a miracle. These paintings are both in Pescia, in the possession of Messer Giulio Turini. It is related that Leonardo, having received a commission for a certain picture from Pope Leo, immediately began to distil oils and herbs for the varnish, whereupon the pontiff remarked, "Alas! the while, this man will assuredly do nothing at all, since he is thinking of the end before he has made a beginning to his work." There was perpetual discord between Michelagnolo Buonarroti and Leonardo, and the competition between them caused Michelagnolo to leave Florence, the Duke Giuliano framing an excuse for him, the pretext for his departure being that he was summoned to Rome by the Pope for the Façade of San Lorenzo. When Leonardo heard of this, he also departed and went to France, where the king, already possessing several of his works, was most kindly disposed towards him, and wished him to paint the cartoon of Sant' Anna, but Leonardo, according to his custom, kept the king a long time waiting with nothing better than words. Finally, having become old, he lay sick for many months, and, finding himself near death, wrought diligently to make himself acquainted with the Catholic ritual, and with the good and holy path of the Christian religion: he then confessed with great penitence and many tears, and although he could not support himself on his feet, yet, being sustained in the arms of his servants and friends, he devoutly received the Holy Sacrament, while thus out of his bed. The king, who was accustomed frequently and affectionately to visit him, came immediately afterwards to his room, and he, causing himself out of reverence to be raised up, sat in his bed describing his malady and the different circumstances connected with it, lamenting, besides, that he had offended God and man, inasmuch as that he had not laboured in art as he ought to have done. He was then seized with a violent paroxysm, the forerunner of death, when the king, rising and supporting his head to give him such assistance and do him such favour as he could, in the hope of alleviating his sufferings, the spirit of Leonardo, which was most divine, conscious that he could attain to no greater honour, departed in the arms of the monarch, being at that time in the seventy-fifth year of his age.

The death of Leonardo caused great sorrow to all who had known him, nor was there ever an artist who did more honour to the art of painting. The radiance of his countenance, which was splendidly beautiful, brought cheerfulness to the heart of the most melancholy, and the power of his word could move the most obstinate to say, "No," or "Yes," as he desired; he possessed so great a degree of physical strength, that he was capable of restraining the most impetuous violence, and was able to bend one of the iron rings used for the knockers of doors, or a horse-shoe, as if it were lead: with the generous liberality of his nature, he extended shelter and hospitality to every friend, rich or poor, provided only that he were distinguished by talent or excellence; the poorest and most insignificant abode was rendered beautiful and honourable by his works; and as the city of Florence received a great gift in the birth of Leonardo, so did it suffer a more than grievous loss at his death. To the art of painting in oil this master contributed the discovery of a certain mode of deepening the shadows, whereby the later artists have been enabled to give great force and relief to their figures. His abilities in statuary were proved by three figures in bronze, which are over the north door of San Giovanni; they were cast by Gio Francesco Rustici, but conducted under the advice of Leonardo, and are, without doubt, the most beautiful castings that have been seen in these later days, whether for design or finish.

We are indebted to Leonardo for a work on the anatomy of the horse, and for another much more valuable, on that of man; wherefore, for the many admirable qualities with which he was so richly endowed, although he laboured much more by his word than in fact and by deed, his name and fame can never be extinguished. . . .

৶ঌ THE JOURNAL OF CAPTAIN NICHOLAS DOWNTON

The man of the Renaissance is celebrated as adventurer, explorer, and builder of empires; the roving aspect of his many-dimensional character has been the source of much romanticizing. Drake and Raleigh are envisioned as swashbucklers—sinking Armadas, carving out empires. This attractive image can ignore the down-to-earth practicality of the typical Renaissance voyager. Ships were a highly expensive investment, not to be risked needlessly; their captains were often dour, God-fearing, cautious men, more interested in profit than adventure: more often like Nicholas Downton than like the vainglorious Raleigh. Nevertheless, in the perilous exploits that Downton saw only as unavoidable necessity, the modern reader finds high adventure—and rightfully so, despite Downton's matter-of-fact account.

Downton's employer, the English East India Company, came late to the Oriental trade; the Portuguese and Dutch had long before claimed valuable islands and coastlines. From 1600 to 1613, the East India Company's captains timidly put agents ashore in the Indies wherever they could find trade. These "factors," as they were called, lived with the natives, establishing their "factories," purchasing as much as would fill the holds of the annual ships from home, endeavoring to keep alive in the face of disease and Portuguese and Dutch agents whose notion of fair competition included assassination. In 1613, Captains Best and Downton secured respect for the Company flag by defeating the Portuguese viceroy's fleet; this victory enabled the English to set up a factory at Surat on the northeast coast of India. A year later Downton, with three ships, returned to purchase cotton and spices. His journal of that voyage reveals the tenuousness of England's first hold on the Indian subcontinent. Downton's narrative indicates both the Indian attitude toward Europeans and his own primitive colonialism. His flattering treatment of the Indian princes and successful undermining of the Portuguese competition are illustrative of the methods by which England built an empire where other nations failed.

The ships employed were the *New Year's Gift,* Admiral, of burthen six hundred and fifty tons: The *Hector,* Vice-Admiral, of five hundred tons: The *Merchant's Hope,*

Nicholas Downton, "Journal," in *Purchas His Pilgrimes* (Glasgow: James MacLehose and Sons, 1905), Vol. IV, 214–228, 230–239, 241–251.

of three hundred tons, and the *Salomon,* of two hundred tons. Master William Edwards was Lieutenant and Cape Merchant, and Commander of the *Hector:* Master Nicholas Ensworth Cape Merchant and Commander of the *Merchant's Hope:* Master Thomas Elkington Cape Merchant, and Commander of the *Salomon:* Master Peter Rogers Minister, Martin Pring, Arthur Spaight, Matthew Molineux and Hugh Bennet, Masters of the four ships, assisted with divers mates.

The first of March 1613, we set sail. . . .

The ninth of September, [1614] we anchored in the Bay of Delisa in Socotora. The next day we went on shore to salute the King, who was ready with his troop to give me entertainment, and told me of the wars at present in India, the Mogol and Kings of Decanie joining to root the Portugals out of the country. The reason whereof was, their taking of a ship which came from Jedda in the Red Sea, wherein was three millions of treasure. He also informed me of Captain Best's two great fights with the Portugals, with other news of those parts. Here I procured what refreshing we could get, and bought of the King Alloes, two thousand seven hundred twenty-two pounds, and on the fourteenth departed.

The second of October, we had sight of land being on the coast of Decany near Dabul. We found great hinderance, till by observation we were taught to stay the ebbs and ply the floods.

The twelfth, we again weighed and plied the floods, and anchored the ebbs till the fourteenth day in the evening, and then anchored two miles and an half short of the bar, where presently came a fleet of frigates being fourteen sail and anchored near us, discovering themselves by their lights being dark: but seeing our readiness by the lights out of our ports, durst come no nearer unto us, so we rid quietly all night.

The fifteenth, early in the morning we weighed with the land-turn, and approaching somewhat near them, they also weighed and stood to the southwards, and we held on our course by the bar towards South Swally, where soon after we arrived after much striving against contrary winds. As soon as I anchored I sent Master Molineux in his pinnasse, and Master Spooner, and Samuell Squire in my gelliwat to sound the depths within the sands. Master Molineux took a channel in which in our former voyage we had but five foot at low water, but now found three fathoms water, and Master Spooner found that where our boats could not pass formerly by reason of shoals, he had now seven and eight foot water. In the afternoon, I seeing people ashore sent my pinnasse to them, supposing some of our merchants had been come from Surat: but found otherwise to be some people of Cogenozan sent down to discover what nation we were; two of which came aboard to me, by whom I understood further of their wars with the Portugals; they besieged Damon and Diu, and that Mocrib Can was general of the Mogol's forces against Damon, and also to my grief, I understood that he was Governour, and as Viceroy not only over Surat, but also over all the country near about it; I esteeming him to be the greatest adversary to our nation, and one that most favoured the Portugals. This was my settled conceit by former experience. I understood of the health of Master Aldworth and the rest, to whom I writ to hasten his presence, and sent it away by Baly Ball, together with the other servants of Cogenozan.

The sixteenth, in the morning early I sent my purser and pinnasse on land to buy such commodities as I supposed might be brought, who about ten a clock without buying anything for our turn, returned with Master Aldworth our chief merchant at Surat, and in his company one Richard Steele who came by land from Aleppo to Surat. Master Aldworth strived to persuade me that Mocrib Can the Nabob was our friend, and that now was the best time by reason of their wars (with the Portugals) for us to obtain good trade and all privileges that in reason we could demand; and for that both he and all the country people did so much rejoice at our coming, therefore of necessity could not but give us royal entertainment, I liking all their hopeful words, yet ever wishing some other in his place, and that Mocrib Can had been further away, of whom I rested still in doubt, that we should have no free trade but according to his accustomed manner; and to see and to be privy to all that ever past, and restrain all others, which then I took to be an injury forced by him to cross us, and not by the direction of the King, which in time, though too late, we were better advised. And notwithstanding the remembrance of his name given him by the King, Mocrib, which is as much as his own bowels, and Can which is as much as great Lord: Yet I was too much deluded by being persuaded that his state in favour of the King stood tottering, and might easily be made subject to any disgrace, by any complaint of things done contrary to the will or humour of the King, which made us somewhat too bold and thereby prejudice to our business when we found him opposite to our wills, and as we thought contrary to reason. I inquiring of the state of our business, and the health of our people, Master Aldworth informed that Paul Canning and divers others were long since dead, and that Thomas Kerridge had long since resided at Court in his room, and that there was no more factors but only himself and William Bedulph at Surat. . . .

The four and twentieth in the morning, Cogenozan came down to the water-side with a great train as their manner is, resting himself in my tent till my landing: unto whom I repaired ashore accompanied with all the merchants and a good guard of halberts, shot, and pike; I having a coach to carry me up from the boat to a place near the tent; and at the instant when I alighted from the coach, he came forth of the tent, addressing himself to meet me, and after salutations returned into the tent and sat down. And before any other conference began he was let to know, that there was a present to be delivered him for the Nabob, which was presently brought in, viz. one case with six knives, two pair of knives, six sword blades, six spanish pikes, one comb-case, one looking-glass, one picture of Mars and Venus, one picture of Paris in judgement, two Muscovy hides, and one great gilded case of bottles full of rich and strong waters. Then for himself I caused a present to be delivered him, which was six knives in single sheaths, four sword blades, two pikes, one comb-case, one looking-glass, one picture of Moses, one case of bottles, in regard of the promise of the Nabob to our people that what Cogenozan should do, he would perform. I therefore moved for the enlarging of our privileges; for the lessening of our custom, especially at Baroch to have a bazaar or market by the waterside, that we might buy beef for the people's eating (in regard that other flesh was not good for them) according to the King's Firma given. His answer was, that if I would assist them against the Portugals, the Nabob would do us all the favour that in his power lyeth; but for the custom of Baroch it was out of his power, for the King had let it to another by rent, and could not be [helpful]. A bazaar we should have, but for bullocks and kine, the King had granted his Firma to the Banians for a mighty sum yearly to save their lives. In sum, we found nothing that he had power to grant us; yet willing to leave me in content, wishing that I would send some of my merchants along with him to the Nabob, that our business on both sides might be considered on, and receive answers accordingly from each other. I sent along with him Master Aldworth, Master Ensworth (who desired to go up because he was not well) Master Dodsworth, Master Mitford and others; which when they had access to the Nabob, two or three days after he would know again their demand, which was as aforesaid. Then he desired to know if we would go with our ships to fight against Damon for him, and then he would do us any favour; but that was answered, that we could in no wise avouch the doing thereof, for that there was peace between our King and the King of Spain. Then he demanded if we would go to the bar and ride there and fight with them that should come to prejudice them. That we could neither covenant to do, for it was a breach of the peace between our two Kings as aforesaid. Then he answered, that if we would do nothing for him, he would do nothing for us. Divers of the principal merchants of the town came to move our merchants that I might give way to the Nabob's reasonable request, and though I did grant for satisfying his mind, yet I might do what I list: and that they all knew the frigates might for all my riding at the bar come in and out on each side [of] me. Answer was returned it was unfit for me to halt, but whatsoever I promised, I must maintain, though it were to the loss of my life, and all under my command: and that I would not be hired to fight with the Portugals, which is contrary to my King's commission (unless they gave me first cause) not for the world; neither would I be withheld from fighting with them if they provoked me, not for his wealth, which difference it seems he took small notice of; but that we refused to fulfill his desire, he was much moved, and in all things crossed our proceedings all that he might: insomuch that he had almost quelled all former conceived hopes of happy commerce in this place. Continually devising what to do, or what course to take, this means failing us, as I see no likelihood to the contrary, I made inquisition of Gengomar and Castelletta, also of Gogo, but could hear small encouragement for transportation to seek better dealing; so with doubts we rested perplexed a long while, yet returning to our business at the ships.

The seven and twentieth, in the morning Nicholas Ufflet going ashore found all the people of Swally departed thence in the night: he demanding the reason, they told him that the Nabob had expressly commanded them so to do, as also the people from the tents. Whereupon he inquiring further thereof, was certified that our merchants were stayed at Surat, and that attempting to pass over the bridge, they were perforce withheld, and received some store of blows by the guard thereto appointed by the Nabob, with whom in company to attend upon them, the gunner's boy and his companion formerly supposed to have been run away, were also well beaten and withheld as the rest.

The one and thirtieth, we began to take in fresh water, because our stay here was so uncertain, not knowing how suddenly our departure might be. This day Thomas Smith the master's boy being swimming about the ship, had most of the outside of his thigh bitten away by a great fish which pulled him under the water, yet he coming up again swam to the ship side, and got up to the bend, where as soon as he was come up, he presently sounded. Then the chirurgion brought him into the gunner's room to see what might be done for his recovery: but the issue of blood had been so great that they could not revive him, but presently died, and towards night was buried ashore.

The second of November towards night Master Aldworth and Master Elkington came down from Surat, where they had left Master Ensworth very sick: they declared unto me their proceedings with the Nabob as formerly, and of their reconciliation, with large promises of future good respect, with free trade throughout all their countries. This hard measure hitherto offered us by the Nabob, I cannot attribute unto any hatred or ill will born to our nation, but his own doubt and fear of us, least I should join with the Portugals against him: which fear was the more increased in him, in that I would not agree to fight against Damon. And this suspicion and doubt was the more increased by a knavish device in the subtle and lying Jesuits, who took occasion by my denial, voluntarily without cause to fight against the Portugals at Damon, or otherwise. They pretended a letter from the Viceroy, to give notice to the Nabob, that unless he made peace with them, that both he and the English his friends should join together and come against Surat; which devilish device did us much hinderance in our business, by the Nabob's continual doubt, which he made of our friendship towards them. And besides unfortunately by their extreme unkind usage Master Aldworth in the midst of his haste, and thinking to qualify their rigorous courses, and yet altogether ignorant of the practice of the Jesuits, in threatening-wise wished them to take heed, that by their ill usage of us, they do not force us to join with the Portugals against them; which proved a kind of confirming the Jesuit's former report from the Viceroy, as altogether making against us. Likewise, he forbade all trade with our people aboard, which at first we likewise thought had proceeded out of his troublesome humour to cross us; but afterwards we were advised the contrary by Thomas Kerridge's letter, who declared that he and all seaport governours, had express commandment from the Mogol, not to suffer any trade with us, till they had made choice of all strange things that we bring, and they to buy them for the King's use, and to send it unto him.

The third, I called a council concerning our business, viz. how far we might proceed in their aid against the Portugals, and examined our commission in that point; also we appointed the merchants for the several places of employment, as well those that were to stay here, as those also that were to proceed on the voyage. The goods that were at Surat of the twelfth voyage came aboard, which was of Indigo sixty bales, and cotton yarn eleven packs. . . .

The sixth of December, the Nabob, Mocrib Can, seemed now to be ashamed, for that he had not since my arrival here shewed me the least taste of courtesy; and therefore being desirous to excuse himself, entreated Master Elkington to accompany aboard the great Banian that brought our tusks, and Lacandas the Banian Merchant of the junk of the King of Cushan, whom he made choice of, and entertained (by reason of his former familiarity with our people) to buy among them such commodities as they had to sell, viz. sword blades, knives, looking-glasses. By them he sent me a present of two corge of coarse bastas, ten fine bastas, ten topseeles, ten cuttonies and three quilts, certifying me that the Nabob was minded to come down to see me within two or three days at the most. At their going ashore I gave them five great shot. They told me that the Nabob heard from Goa, that for certain, the [Portuguese] Viceroy was preparing to come against us, with all the force he could make to fight with us: likewise that the Nabob requested me that I would waft a ship or two of his off the coast for two or three days, being bound for the Red Sea. But I answered, that having once put off from the coast, the wind being adverse, I could not recover it again: but if he would further our dispatch that we might be ready in convenient time, then would I do anything reasonable.

The ninth, the Nabob's son came to the water-side, but would not come aboard; whereupon I went ashore to him, who against my landing sent a horse to fetch me, he willed me to sit down upon the mount with him, which I did. Then he commanded part of his horsemen to shew me some pleasure upon the sands, by warlike chasing each other, after the manner of Decanie, from whence they were: then he desired to hear some ordinance go off, and I gave him eleven shot. He at present would drink no wine, but being departed, he sent for it, and for a fowling piece which he found in the hands of one of our people, both which I sent him with a bowl to drink his wine.

The sixteenth, Master Elkington wrote me that the Nabob told him that the Portugal frigates had burnt Gogo with many gonges, or villages, thereabouts, and ten great ships, one whereof was the *Rehemee,* and one hundred and twenty small vessels: and that he was displeased at me for not shooting at them when they past by us; which did renue his suspicion of our friendship with the Portugals: to all which Master Elkington answered him, yet he could not rest satisfied.

The three and twentieth came two boats more for lead. This day we saw twenty-two frigates, who in the night came to anchor between us and the river's mouth, where they rode most part of the next day.

The four and twentieth, in the morning we saw four boats coming down the river towards us, who seeing the frigates returned, two frigates chasing them up the river: but seeing they could not fetch them up, went ashore and fired two or three poor houses, and took away two or three head of cattle, and so returned back to their company, who in the afternoon went up into the river together. . . .

The six and twentieth, in the morning I sent the *Hope* to the northwards a good way from the rest of the fleet, to see if the Portugals would charge upon her.

The seven and twentieth, early in the morning, the frigates came and made a bravado before our ship, and then before the *Salomon,* which was next unto us, and from her to the *Hope* which rode a great way from us, who drove directly upon her with all their men stowed, not a man to be seen. The master twice hailed them, but they would not speak, whereupon they let fly at them with their bow-pieces, having no other to ply upon them, which made them with some loss to depart: the master doubting, that if he had not shot, they would have boarded him, or mischieved him by fire, they coming upon the advantage both of wind and tide, that none of the rest of the ships could come to the rescue; and in such sort right a head, that hardly can he traverse any piece of ordnance at them. In the afternoon I sent the *Salomon* to accompany the *Hope,* who went to the northwards of her, and made five or six shot at the frigates, who rode at anchor hard by the *Hope*. But we did not perceive any hurt she did them: wherefore I commanded my gunner to shoot a piece to warn them to give over, whereupon the *Salomon* stood in again and came to anchor.

The eight and twentieth, in the morning I went in the pinnasse aboard the *Hope* and *Salomon,* to understand the occasions of their shooting: and the Portugals seeing our boats pass to and again, removed in the afternoon, and rode a little without us to cut off all intercourse. In the meantime, came the former boat which was chased ashore aboard the *Gift,* and brought some letters from Master Elkington. The master sent the bearer with the letters to me in the *Hope,* where having answered Master Elkington's letter, I sent him back again to the *Gift,* to go thence in the night to Surat: but as the gelliwat returned, the frigates chased her, which I perceiving, caused to wave to the gelliwat to return, which they not seeing held on her way. But the frigates held her so close that they were within shot of her, and made one fair shot at her, and had not the *Gift* let slip one cable, and veered another, and plied upon them with her ordnance, it would have gone hard with them: which made them give over the chase not without some damage: and late in the night upon the tide of ebb, I commanded the *Hope* and *Salomon* to set sail and fall nearer to the other ships, and then I went aboard the *Gift*. . . .

The fourteenth of January, we heard of the approach of many frigates, which rode at the bar till next day within night, and then in the dark came from thence, and rode within shot of us all night till the morning, when they weighed and went to the southwards; whom I thought were the Mallabars, that the Nabob promised formerly to send me: and therefore put forth a flag of truce, and sent Master Spooner, one of the master's mates, towards them with the gelliwat, and appointed him to have an eye back to our signs that we would make, if we mistrusted anything. I seeing the gelliwat so near, and no shew of friendship from them in answer of ours, put forth my flag which before was taken in, and shot a piece of ordnance for a sign to my boat to come aboard, which presently upon sight thereof she did, who was not scarce aboard, when our sentinel from top-mast head, descried another fleet of frigates, who afterwards met together at the bar, and went altogether into the river: whereby I perceived they were Portugals, and was glad that our men and boat so well escaped their hands. I thinking these frigates were forerunners of greater forces, caused all the decks to be cleared, and the ordnance freed, and all things else fitting both for the ordnance, shot, and barracades to be in a readiness. . . .

Formerly hearing of the Viceroy's forces to come, we imagined it would not be so great as now by view it seems, therefore high time to enter into best considerations, how by God's help to resist the same. The odds and advantages he had over me, put me to my shifts in casting up all things that made against me, being overtopt by his forces, whom I esteemed furnished with the principal ships and means of India, and people of greatest rank and valour in these parts, in likelihood too hard for us when we should put into the deep water; nay, I know not how to put into deep water, but they always ready to intercept, overcharge, or force me aground irrecoverable on one side or other: my disadvantages so great in putting out, and their smaller vessels I knew might much with fireworks, or otherwise hazard us within at anchor where we rode, where I had hope their great ships through the shoaldness of water, could not or durst not put in. The things with me to give me hope was, my people (though much with death and sickness shortened) all from the highest to the lowest, seem very courageous and comfortable; though (for the most) ignorant, either of the danger, or how to prevent it, yet pleasing to me to see their willingness. My care is not small, how to do my best in maintaining the honour of my country, nor negligent in the memory of the estates and charge of my friends, and employers in this journey; not only for the hazard of this at present committed to my charge, but also all hope of future times, if I should now be overthrown: by reason the enemy in getting the upper hand of me, would make his peace with these people upon what conditions he lust, to the expelling of our nation [from] this country for ever. And what my care was for the safety of my people, I refer to the consideration of such fathers, as are tender over the safety of their obedient children. All this while my whole powers so kept in action, that I found little time to converse, or almost shew myself sensible of the dangers approaching; yea, ever as I could be solitary or free from others; very earnestly craving aid and assistance from the Lord of Hosts, and from that mighty and merciful God, who hath manifold ways formerly delivered me; often I say desiring his Majesty so to guide and direct me, that I might omit nothing which might tend to the safety of my own charge, nor the danger of the enemy: and that God would grant my request, I had a strong confidence; and the same again often quelled by the assembly of my manifold and grievous offences, and but for God's mercy sufficient to drown the world; whereby forced afresh by prayer to pierce the heavens, and fly unto God for aid against both inward and outward assaults. I so resolved by God's assistance what to do, if my assistants the masters of the ships would yield thereunto; knowing if we should receive a foil riding at our anchor, our disgrace will be greater, and our enemies little abashed: but in moving, I might move the Viceroy in greediness and pride, to do himself wrong against the sands; hoping that that might be an occasion whereby God might draw him to shorten his own forces, and so might open the way for our getting out amongst the rest: which would rather have been for a necessity, then any way hopeful: for at present our goods on the way, and daily by some and some expected to come hither, and if once gotten out, unless it had pleased God to make us conquerors, and drive the Viceroy clean away, I could not return into my place, where only (and nowhere else) I could take in my lading: I esteeming the Viceroy to hold his honour in so high regard, that he must have been dead before he would have given way. I also, though helpless, remembered two great advantages the enemy had of me in this war. Ever before my people came to fight, they are first tired, or half spent with the labour of the ship, as heaving at capstain, and getting up our anchors, setting of sails, and other labours, which greatly quells their courages, making them in hot countrys both weary and faint; and then of necessity must become soldiers: whereas the Viceroy his soldiers come fresh to fight, being troubled with no labour, which is done by slaves and inferiour sea-people, which are never accompted companions of soldiers. Secondly, if the Viceroy lose many men in his ships, he may be supplied again out of his fresh supplies, to be fetched from their nearest towns by their frigates, whereas we could not have one man supplied, how many soever we should have slain or disabled.

This present Thursday at night, I having no merchants at all aboard, but all employed in the country (besides those with Master Elkington at the house at Surat) I sent for all my masters to supper, with some mates, where (as the time served) I began speech of our present business, desiring every man to speak freely, how he thought best for us to work, considering to the present straight we seemed to be in; alledging my confidence to be (for all the bragging of these Portugals abounding in force) that God would not suffer their injurious attempts upon us, that have been tender not to wrong them in the East. I have had also a jealous conceit carried over me by the Nabob, and principals of the country, as though I had been confederate with the Portugals, for that I did not shoot at the saucy-governed bragging frigates. I found all the masters to my heart's desire, willing and tractable to whatsoever I should wish; and had some few speeches about our provident mooring, as also of the removing somewhat lower down. But ere long, I let them know my conceit, desiring their free opinion therein: which was, that now our ships were as fit for fight as we could make them, and our danger by night if we rode still (work never so providently) to prevent is not small; therefore I thought fittest in the morning at low water, to send down one ship to ride, as we might have water enough at low water for all our ships: for then none can come to annoy her, which may prepare the Viceroy's mind to some attempt at high water, and as the flood comes, the other three should bear down against the stream (the spring now near the highest) to prove what attempt the Viceroy would give, to attend it, and work accordingly as we shall see reason, in hope that God will put designs into the mind of the Viceroy, that he may commit some error, to the weakening of his own forces; which if he do, then will be fittest time in the dark of the night following, to put out when it shall be unfit for them to come to sail to hinder us. Or if we see reason, we may with the wind work every day to and again with our sails on the flood, to be always ready in action, when the tide is aloft, which may somewhat the courage of the people quell and dismay, though the gallants seem to think otherwise. This no sooner propounded, but liked for the best way, and so we agreed to proceed, and for that I found M. Molineux willing at low water in the morning to fall down with the *Hope,* which was accordingly performed.

The twentieth in the morning, at low water I sent down M. Molineux with the *Hope,* to prepare the enemy to some attempt, when the tide shall be up; which being done, upon the flood we also with the other three ships stood after her. The Viceroy and all the worthy knights about him, supposed I had been flying, hastened also as the stream would permit them, towards the entrance to stop my coming forth; but contrariwise we all anchored short of the *Hope,* not altogether of purpose to leave her destitute of our help, but rather doubting of depth for our ships (so far down) to ride at low water. I was no sooner at anchor, and gone down to my cabin, and set down to write, to give my friends and merchants ashore notice of my purposes and resolution, howsoever it might please God to dispose of me; and that they might know it to be no rashness, but in good discretion to tend upon my best advantages to prejudice my enemies; but presently I had notice, that three ships with most of the frigates were before the wind, running stem-long aboard the *Hope,* and the galleons after them, so far as the sands gave leave. We assayed to weigh our anchor, but time not permitting, we cut cable, and set sail for the *Hope's* rescue, but the enemy's ships were aboard her, and entered their men before we came sufficiently near them; their men being entered with great shew of resolution, but had no quiet abode there, neither could rest in their own ships, nor make them loose from the *Hope,* for our great and small shot; so that when the principal were killed, the rest in great number, for quietness sake, leapt into the sea, where their frigates took many of them up. But first of purpose to have burnt the *Hope* with them, they made preparation to fire their own ships, which was well performed without harm to the *Hope,* (praised be the Lord of heaven) for so soon as the fire was well kindled, the ships of fire were let loose, and drove aground on the sands, where they burned til the flowing water came and quenched them; while daylight lasted, we continued changing of shot in all our ships with the galleons, they being on the outside of a spit of sand, and we on the inside; by which they did little harm to our hulls, but to our ropes and sails overhead. In this conflict besides them which were wounded, we lost five men, by great mischance the *Hope's* main top, top-sail, top-mast, and shrouds came afire, and burnt away, with a great part of the main mast, by the fireworks that were in the said top, the man being slain that had the charge thereof. This mishap kept us from going forth into deep water to try our fortunes with the Viceroy, but were put to our shifts, not knowing how, or by what means to get the said mast cured.

The one and twentieth, I sent to weigh the anchor we had cut the day before. The two and twentieth, I understood that many great men, with five or six hundred horse, and a Portugal Father [Catholic priest] came down to Swally, to send on the morrow the Father with three or four principal Moors, to conclude a peace betwixt them: and the Nabob sent me word that he sought no such thing, and was resolved to make none, but wherein we should be included. He also granted me what timber we should want, which we made use of. Likewise we were promised provisions. The Portugals continued quiet.

The five and twentieth, the Muccadam of Swally came to me, and told me that the former Father had sent to intice him to poison the former well, where hence we had our water, which he would not yield unto, and therefore had put into the well some live Tortoises, who would by their death demonstrate the poisoning thereof, if it should by them be performed. At night came part of the hundred and seventy bales of indigo to the water side, which was presently fetched aboard. Isaac Beg sent me a present of the fruits of his own garden. This day came down the rest of the timber for the *Hope's* mast.

The seven and twentieth, I sent all our boats to sound the swach at low water; chiefly to keep the enemy always ignorant of what I intended: whither was sent by the enemy to prevent them, one galley and five frigates, thinking to cut off our boats, whereof they failed, as of all other things they attempted. . . .

The third of February, there came to the water side twenty-four bales indigo, seven packs white bastas, seven packs black bastas, six packs cotton-yarn, four packs blue bastas, three packs caudikens, one pack crecany, all which were presently fetched aboard: this day also the Viceroy's supplies came in sight, which were two ships of burthen, two junks, and eight or ten of the country boats. The Nabob sent Lacandas to inform me, that these supplies were not for war, but filled full of combustible matter to fire, and so to be let drive with the tide upon our ships in the night; which advise I was glad to understand, and addressed myself also to prevent that, and all other their attempts with smaller ships. The spring now near the highest, and fittest for their assaults, which every tide I expected: and to shew that I was in a readiness to entertain them, as also how little I cared for them (having all the time formerly ridden without the like) I purposed and performed the setting and clearing our watch, morning and evening, with a volley of shot from every ship, and the best piece in my ship directed to the prow of the Viceroy, which I did to daunt the courage of them he must employ, and to try his temper, whether it would make him angry or no: and I still think it proved to good end. It pleased God this day at night, when I had least leisure to mourn, to call to his mercy my only son George Downton, who early the next morning was buried ashore, and the volleys aforesaid, appointed to try the temper of the Viceroy, served also to honour his burial.

This morning also came to me one Mousa Attale, a Malabar captain (with his troop attending) to visit me, expecting some business this day by the Portugals to be attempted; whom I entertained with all kind respect, and by conference made the best use of his company that I might; by drawing from him the description of the principal ports and harbours in his country, and manifesting the desire I had to be acquainted with him, and to entertain love, league, and familiarity between the English and them, with a mutual trade and traffic one with another: the which with great desire he seemed to embrace, willing me to give him some letters of my hand, for their ships to carry to shew to my countrymen, wheresoever they should meet them: which I delivered, as also a letter for him to move their King for the kind usage of our nation, whensoever any of our ships should arrive in any of his harbours, and so after leave taken, he departed, I presenting him with a sword blade, and three or four knives. The master of the *Hope* complained, that besides those presently killed, he had many hurt, bruised, and disabled for service: whereupon I sent him for supply, three men from the *Gift,* four from the *Hector,* and four from the *Salomon.*

The fifth, I received letters from M. Aldworth from Baroch, who writes of their arrival there, and that the day before, nine courses from Baroch, they were set upon by two hundred thieves, Rashpooses, with pikes, small shot, and bows and arrows: and skirmishing a little while with them, they fled, three of them being killed, and more wounded, they having shot Humfrey Elkington through the thigh, and killed one of the horses that Surder Can sent to guard our men; and Master Aldworth's horse likewise received a shot. The Nabob sent me word that the Viceroy would assault this day, and therefore sent Gogenozan to guard the land; who came to the water-side and sent his son Mamod Jehad aboard to see me, with a cavalier, called Kemagee, the son of Leckdarsee, Raspoose of Guigomar, or Castelletto (who maintained war with the Mogore and Portugal together a long time) they entreated leave to see and partake in the fight: who seeing no attempt that day given, stayed aboard all night; and the Raspoose seeing the backwardness of the enemy, went the next day ashore: but the other desirous to see the issue thereof, stayed two or three days longer aboard; and then seeing nothing would be done by the enemy, he departed.

The eight in the forenoon, we received more indigo aboard. In the afternoon all the frigates, with the two junks and two galleys, came driving up with the flood, making shew of some attempt at the instant, either by fire, (which I most doubted) or otherwise: whereupon we all weighed to go nearer to them, who no sooner perceived it, but they altogether made away as fast as they might, and we came to an anchor not far from our former place. This device was nothing but to make us think that those fire-boats should come from the northwards, that we might not mistrust their coming from the northwards: and therefore the next day against night, they assembled both junks, frigates, and galleys all together, a little without the sands, to take away all suspicion of the north from us: which I well perceived, and did always resolve, that that way was the place of most danger for us: And therefore gave a special charge of good looking out both ways, but chiefly that way: which accordingly fell out; for that a little within night we did discern them (between us and a great light to the westward, upon the island of Gogo) creeping to the northwards upon the flood, and then upon the last quarter ebb, about ten of the clock in the dark of the night, before the rising of the moon, there came driving down two fire-boats, being towed by frigates, whom we discovered before they came near us, and plied at them both with our ordnance and small shot, whereby we beat off the frigates that towed them, who durst adventure no further with them, but turned them off, who came driving with the tide a pretty distance from the other. The first drove clear of the *Gift, Hector,* and *Salomon,* and came thwart the *Hope's* hauser, and presently blew up, and with the blow much of their ungracious stuff: but (blessed be God) to no harm to the *Hope,* for that by cutting her cable, she cleared herself. The latter came likewise upon the quarter of the *Hope,* and then flamed up, but did no harm, driving down the ebb, and came foul of us again on the flood, the abundance of fuel continually burning, which our people in our boats towed ashore, and the former sunk down near us by daylight. This day I received a letter from Master Aldworth, who writes of the receipt of a letter from Thomas Kerridge, specifying that Nicholas Whittington is distracted, and out of his right senses, and that he writeth somewhat doubtfully of Richard Steele. . . .

The twelfth, Lacandas came down, informing me from the Nabob (he being so assured by the Jesuits, with whom he always kept fair weather for his better security, if we should be put to the worse) that there were six or eight frigates gone to the northwards, with four or five fire-boats to be let drive among us in the night: and therefore wished carefully to look out, for that it should be when we should least suspect. I allowed of his kindness, was glad of his careful regard, although needing no such admonition, suspecting such practises as well when they were out of sight, and furthest from us, as when they rode hard by us.

The thirteenth, for as much as frigates or other vessels in the offing could not so well discern the place of our ships, in the dark night, for the shadow of the shore, though very low; therefore in the times of their hellish gunpowder practises, they had lights for aim given them ashore, where fittest to come in. Now night by night we saw the like, in the like place as before; therefore esteeming some of their creatures again to give aim for their coming to like practices, though no vessels seen by daylight. And being formerly warned, as aforesaid, to look out for like attempts, in hope to take hold of this fireman, at night I sent William Gurdin ashore with twenty men, shot and pike, to encompass and take the blaser of the said fire, supposing it to be some traitor inhabiting these nearest parts: who in his passage coming near it, it would seem presently out, and again at an instant at another place contrary to their pursuit, and so playing in and out with them so long, that in the end they gave it over, esteeming it some delusion of the devil, not knowing otherwise how to conjecture thereof. This present night the Viceroy set sail from the bar, leaving in the river some twenty of his frigates, which continued the place, shifting to relieve each other sometimes more, and sometimes less, and kept in the Mallabar's frigates, which were there in service for the defence of the Town. . . .

The eighteenth, the Nabob sent Cogearson Allee, the Sabandar, and other merchants of Surat, to entreat my stay for fifteen days, which in no sort I would grant: then they importuned me for ten days, which yet by no means would I yield unto, shewing how great prejudice to my voyage my stay here so long might be. The cause of their request, was their fear lest the Viceroy after my departure should come against Surat with all his forces. Wherefore I considering the weight of this business, and the prejudice it might be to ourselves, and also being unwilling to send them back with denial, seeing them much discontented thereat as a disgrace unto them, and being loath at my departure to give the Nabob any distaste therein, that have done to my uttermost hitherto to give them all content possible; and knowing what future hindrance it might be to our business ashore: and last of all, seeing there was six days' work of the ten to be done in the *Hope,* before we could be possibly ready; I at length (when they were altogether out of hope thereof, and upon departure) condescended to their request, whereat they were exceeding joyful, and departed.

The two and twentieth at night, I received a letter from Surat, informing me of the Nabob's coming to see me the next day.

The three and twentieth, in the morning, came down two elephants and six camels, bringing his tents and other provisions.

The four and twentieth, Master Aldworth came down with the rest of the merchants to finish all business with me.

The five and twentieth in the morning, the Nabob came down with a very great train, and six elephants more, and had been two hours ashore before I knew thereof: which when it was told me, being sorry for my neglect of him, I sent Master Aldworth, Master Elkington, and M. Dodsworth ashore unto him, to hold him in discourse until I came unto him, which was not long after; I purposed to go unto him (as a son unto his father) in my doublet and hose, without any arms or great trains, according to custom, thereby to shew my trust and confidence that I reposed in him: but my friends persuaded me to the contrary, that I should rather go well appointed and attended on with a sufficient guard, to continue the custom. Whereunto I consented (though in conclusion, it repented me that I had not taken mine own course) and went ashore with about one hundred and forty men, of pike and shot, who at my entrance into the Nabob's tent gave me a volly of shot. The Nabob entertained me very kindly, seeming very joyful of my coming ashore to him: we sitting a while under a very fair tent, open on all sides round about, environed with many people, as well of mine, as of his attendants. At length he brought me into a more private room near adjoining, having on his side only Alle Can, a great Persian captain, and the Banian, Henie, for his interpreter; and on my side, Master Aldworth, Master Elkington, and Master Dodsworth: where he conferred both of the estate of his country at present, and also of our affairs. At length I demanded of him if he would go aboard with me to see the ship; whereunto he very willingly consented. Then he presented me with his own sword (accompanied with many good words, telling me that it was the custom of their country, to honour captains with arms, that had deserved well) which as he told me was made in his own house, the hilts thereof being of massie gold, and in lieu thereof I returned him my sute, being sword, dagger, girdle and hangers, by me much esteemed of, and which made a great deal better shew, though of less value. We came both forth of the private tent, and I walked down to the water-side, there staying his coming; whether he sent me a present of ten cuttonee quilts, and twenty topseells; and not long after came the Nabob himself, and then we took boat together and went aboard, where having shewed him the lying of our ordnance, and all our warlike preparation for defence, I presented him with a very fair standing gilt cup with a cover, and certain very fair knives, and a rundlet of muskadine, with some other toys. Then he desired to see our ordnance shoot off, and how far they would carry their shot upon the water, and I gave him three. Then he would have taken leave, but I accompanied him to the shore, and gave him at his departure eleven great shot. At our parting at the water-side, the Nabob gave me four baskets of grapes; he likewise gave the gunners and trumpeters between them two hundred mamudies, and among the ship's company five hundred mamudies, and one hundred books of white bastas, of two mamudies apiece: and then after some compliments we took leave one of the other, and departed. I rowed along the shore for my better getting aboard, the tide running so swiftly, and saw Lacandas the Banian come running towards the boat, being sent of the Nabob to know of me, if he should erect a tomb over my son: I returned him many thanks, and willed Lacandas to tell him that I had already begun it: then I returned aboard, and he went to Surat; and not long after his tents were taken down, and went after him with the rest of his carriages.

The six and twentieth, the Nabob's son and son-in-law (a very ingenious young man) came aboard to take their leaves of me: upon whom I bestowed some knives, and other things which I had left, which could not be much, having still had one great man or other to visit me, who seldom or never went away without some one present or other: so they viewed the ship and departed.

The seventeenth, there came aboard unto me the three sons of Alle Can, the two youngest first, and after them came the eldest, called Guger Can, who as yet had never been aboard: He presented me with two antelops, male and female, whereat I was glad, since I had sent to enquire for some to send home to Sir Thomas Smith, but could not procure any. I presented him with four Spanish pikes with heads, and some other things of my own, and shewed him all the ship, with our warlike preparation for defence, as also all our ordnance; and a little while after he took his leave, and at his departure I gave him eleven shot.

The third of March in the afternoon, upon the tide of ebb, and a small gale came up northerly, to give steering way to our ships, we seeing our friends the Mallabars (which had desired to go with us) not attempting to come forth, we hastened to get up our anchors, and to set sail to proceed on our journey: yet seeing coming in from the westward another fleet of Portugal frigates, I was willing to shew my best, in the view of the country people, to hinder their coming into the river of Surat; which was nothing, for that there was room enough for them to pass by us every way out of the reach of our shot; yet we shot at the nearest of them, without hope to shoot near them, but only to shew our good wills, and for encouragement to our friends on land; as also for those which went alongst the coast (as I esteemed) to give knowledge to the galleons of our coming, that they might report also that we shot at their fellows going to Surat: that they might also expect that we cared the less for their greater strength. In our passage this night, we had divers flaws of unconstant winds, for which we came to anchor for a while. Afterwards seeing it blew steady, though faint, we set sail, continuing our course south by east alongst the shore. At that time the daylight began to discover to us all things near us; we descried between us and the shore our enemy's forces of galleons, and two galleys, all coming to sail presently after they saw us, and stood after us with a faint gale, we standing somewhat without our course with all our sails, partly to gain time to make ourselves in perfect readiness to fight, partly to refresh my people that had taken much pains the night past; as also the further I draw them off the coast, the further they will be from fresh supplies to be sent them. But ere long, the tide of flood being come, and little wind to hold our own, we came to an anchor, while the enemy resting his hopes in the wind, kept longer under sail to his greater disadvantage. But I not taking it for an error in them, but of purpose to do us more harm, it brought me into a new and great doubt, which drew all my powers to devise how to prevent. This was, that now we were at sea, they meant to return to Surat with all their strength, and there to work their wills on our friends and goods, which I had no means to prevent, but by following them; knowing they durst not unarm, nor unfurnish their ships while I was in sight of them. But the time now grew so late, that I doubted by the most haste that I could make, I should hardly get off the coast before the foul weather came; which put me into some hope, that the Viceroy being so great a soldier, and so discreet a gentleman, would not expose himself, his people and ships to such great perils as the hastning winter did threaten. While these things floated in my mind, the tide of flood was spent, and time to work if we make use of the ebb, we (to my great content) saw the Viceroy's fleet standing towards us with a fresh gale of wind. We likewise set sail, and stood away our own course before him all that tide, and so spent the night to the best advantage, partly by sailing, and partly by stopping.

The fifth in the morning, we saw the enemy had gotten but little ground of us: This day also we spent, as before, in riding and sailing, as time served to our best advantage: and for that the *Hector* went best, and the *Hope* (logloaden) worst, I sent to the *Hector* to take in her boat, and to prepare for the *Hope*. I sent to the *Hope* to give directions to hasten to the *Hector,* to be towed, and to the end she should have nothing to hinder her, I had her boat to tow at my stern, and so spent the night working for the best, the wind fresh we had no cause to anchor. This night the Viceroy's ships got much ground of us: by this I was gotten well off from the shore, and also an end to the southwards, and by his working I recovered some assurance to my conceit, that these forces would not this year annoy Surat: and for my business for encountring the enemy, I had by good leisure well considered how to contrive it, and withal I had considered of the cases of either, and the difference between the Viceroy and me, I mean in our several satisfactions and contents: My coming hither was by the authority of my King, and to follow the designs of my employers, which was in merchant's ships fitted for defence, and to endeavour by honest commerce, without striving to injury any, which God hath of his tender mercy and bountiful blessing so assisted me, that we have performed beyond my former conceit, and in most things hitherto God hath granted me my heart's desire: and am now in a good way upon my way with the same: with which without further tempting of God, or presuming of God's continuing mercies in further deliverances, if I by pride swerve from what is just, and before him to be allowed, whose mercies have been free, and without any cause in me for His own Namesake: therefore I hold it fit to proceed soberly, and attend upon the enemy's attempt, yet not in base manner, but in a warlike sort.

On the other side, the unhappy Viceroy, a famous valiant man, therefore now sent by his master the King of Spain with ships (the principal of India) with men (all the gallants and principal braggards of those nearer parts of India) what to do? Not only to disturb or intercept the peaceable and quiet trade of the English with the subjects of the Mogol, a great king in his own country, but to take or burn them: so little regard is had to the effusion of Christian blood; never looking towards the judgements of God, nor remembering that as men do to others, they must expect to be done to. This captain was furnished with abundance of all things the country might yield, and wanted nothing but an upright cause, fit for God to favour. He came to the place where he found what he sought, four poor merchant ships, a few men, and many of them sick and dead; and those braggards measured our minds by their own, thought we would never stand out against so powerful a force, as they esteemed they had; and the conceit of that, set those coxcombs a-madding to be doing mischief, to increase their pride, which they entitle honour. I seeing the difference, and the cause I had to pray to God my only refuge, whom it pleased to grant the request of me His poor and unworthy servant: in consideration whereof, I put forward the business, and as it were, baited my hook, and the fish presently ran thereat as aforesaid.

They came three ships, and thirty or forty frigates, as I imagined; with a veaze laid the *Hope* aboard with the flower of all their gallants, where by the hand of God in their amazed carriage, they received such a blow, as few (and they by their extraordinary chance) escaped with safety, and the three ships burnt. Thus it pleased God to cross their first attempt, and never after, though they beleaguered us round about by sea, with all their sorts of ships for many days together, our people still in action, and half tired with continual labour, some receiving in goods; yet, blessed be God, they could never get the advantage to win from us the value of a louse, unless our bullets which we lent them, his fire-boats failing, and nothing prospering; and once in four and twenty hours, I sent him a defiance for many days together, to try his temper; all which must needs lie heavy on the stomach of a gentleman of so great courage. I esteem now he will hazard much to recover some of his honour formerly lost (but craving pardon for this my digression, I will now return and proceed with my former business).

Wherefore the sixth in the morning betimes, I sent for my master, and let him know that my purpose was, that when the Viceroy should come up near with us, that we would all at once cast about with him, and charge him first on the sudden, to strike an unexpected terror in the hearts of his people, who now . . . brag, seeing us going away before them. And to that end I now went aboard every ship, to give them all directions; and more, that I would cause the *Hector,* with her pinnasse and mine, to take in an hundred fardels of the *Hope's* goods to lighten her, and mend her going: which business (by reason of my pinnasse to help) I stayed to see it done; so that it grew to be midday, near which time, my ship which I left far astern for my better coming aboard, struck sail, whereat (as we imagined) the Viceroy seeing the Admiral strike her sails to fall astern, might take it of purpose to stay for him in contempt, he with his consorts bore up with the shore, and gave over the hope of their fortunes by further following of us: which course I like very well, since he is so patient; for there is nothing under his foot that can make amends for the loss of the worst man's finger I have. Besides, I wish no occasion to fight; for that which I have already paid for, I am already possest on, and I am so far from the humour to fight for honour, unless for the honour of my King or country, that I had rather save the life or lives of one of my poorest people, then kill a thousand enemies. Having now finished with the Viceroy, I set myself to write letters for the dispatch of the *Hope,* yet still thinking to have haled into the bar of Goa, to prove if I could have left some commendations there for the Viceroy at his return: this was my great desire that I long promised, yet so long trifled in dispatch of the *Hope,* that we were shot far past it before we had finished the same.

⊷§ ADDRESS TO THE GERMAN NOBILITY

Martin Luther

Martin Luther (1483–1546), the great instigator of the various rebellions against the supremacy of the Catholic Church which are collectively called the Protestant Reformation, was destined for this role both by temperament and by historical circumstances. Angered by what he considered grave abuses in the papal leadership of the Church, encouraged by social cleavages in German public life which made princes and merchants his comrades-in-arms, and pushed by a Church hierarchy that failed to recognize the seriousness of the tensions in European ecclesiastical and political life, Luther proceeded from an initial protest over the sale of indulgences in Germany to a genuine theological separation from the Church and to leadership of a national movement.

This selection is taken from the "Address to the German Nobility," written early in Luther's career. In it he states with all the force at his command his position regarding the host of abuses that he felt had crept into the Church. The opening section on the "three walls" of the Papists is intended as a refutation of the Church's claim to political and ecclesiastical supremacy. It is followed by a brief section in which Luther suggests some specific major problems that he felt could be cured if Church councils were, as he hoped, called to reform them. The final section is an additional collection of miscellaneous abuses. This work is a gold mine of Luther's attitudes on subjects ranging from beggary and drinking to celibacy— attitudes which have remained strong in those areas of Western civilization where the moral outlook of the Reformation took root.

INTRODUCTION

To His Most Serene and Mighty Imperial Majesty and to the Christian Nobility of the German Nation

Dr. Martinus Luther

The grace and might of God be with you, Most Serene Majesty, most gracious, well-beloved gentlemen!

It is not out of mere arrogance and perversity that I, an individual poor man, have taken upon me to address your lordships. The distress and misery that oppress all the Christian estates, more especially in Germany, have led not only myself, but every one else, to cry aloud and to ask for help, and have now forced me too to cry out and to ask if God would give His Spirit to any one to reach a hand to His wretched people. Councils have often put forward some remedy, but it has adroitly been frustrated, and the evils have become worse, through the cunning of certain men. Their malice and wickedness I will now, by the help of God, expose, so that, being known, they may henceforth cease to be so obstructive and injurious. . . .

THE THREE WALLS OF THE ROMANTISTS

The Romanists have, with great adroitness, drawn three walls round themselves, with which they have hitherto protected themselves, so that no one could reform them, whereby all Christendom has fallen terribly.

Firstly, if pressed by the temporal power, they have affirmed and maintained that the temporal power has no jurisdiction over them, but, on the contrary, that the spiritual power is above the temporal.

Secondly, if it were proposed to admonish them with the Scriptures, they objected that no one may interpret the Scriptures but the Pope.

Thirdly, if they are threatened with a council, they pretend that no one may call a council but the Pope.

Thus they have secretly stolen our three rods, so that they may be unpunished, and intrenched themselves behind these three walls, to act with all the wickedness and

Martin Luther, "Address to the German Nobility," *The Harvard Classics*, ed. Charles W. Eliot (New York: P. F. Collier & Son, 1909), Vol. XXXVI, 276–292, 302–305, 308–309, 311–315, 317–320, 324–325, 329, 333–336, 338–342, 347–352.

malice, which we now witness. And whenever they have been compelled to call a council, they have made it of no avail by binding the princes beforehand with an oath to leave them as they were, and to give moreover to the Pope full power over the procedure of the council, so that it is all one whether we have many councils or no councils, in addition to which they deceive us with false pretences and tricks. So grievously do they tremble for their skin before a true, free council; and thus they have overawed kings and princes, that these believe they would be offending God, if they were not to obey them in all such knavish, deceitful artifices.

Now may God help us, and give us one of those trumpets that overthrew the walls of Jericho, so that we may blow down these walls of straw and paper, and that we may set free our Christian rods for the chastisement of sin, and expose the craft and deceit of the devil, so that we may amend ourselves by punishment and again obtain God's favour.

(a) The First Wall: That the Temporal Power Has No Jurisdiction over the Spiritualty

Let us, in the first place, attack the first wall.

It has been devised that the Pope, bishops, priests, and monks are called the *spiritual estate*, princes, lords, artificers, and peasants are the *temporal estate*. This is an artful lie and hypocritical device, but let no one be made afraid by it, and that for this reason: that all Christians are truly of the spiritual estate, and there is no difference among them, save of office alone. As St. Paul says (1 Cor. xii.), we are all one body, though each member does its own work, to serve the others. This is because we have one baptism, one Gospel, one faith, and are all Christians alike; for baptism, Gospel, and faith, these alone make spiritual and Christian people.

As for the unction by a pope or a bishop, tonsure, ordination, consecration, and clothes differing from those of laymen—all this may make a hypocrite or an anointed puppet, but never a Christian or a spiritual man. Thus we are all consecrated as priests by baptism, as St. Peter says: "Ye are a royal priesthood, a holy nation" (1 Peter ii. 9); and in the book of Revelations: "and hast made us unto our God (by Thy blood) kings and priests" (Rev. v. 10). For, if we had not a higher consecration in us than pope or bishop can give, no priest could ever be made by the consecration of pope or bishop, nor could he say the mass, or preach, or absolve. Therefore the bishop's consecration is just as if in the name of the whole congregation he took one person out of the community, each member of which has equal power, and commanded him to exercise this power for the rest; in the same way as if ten brothers, co-heirs as king's sons, were to choose one from among them to rule over their inheritance, they would all of them still remain kings and have equal power, although one is ordered to govern.

And to put the matter even more plainly, if a little company of pious Christian laymen were taken prisoners and carried away to a desert, and had not among them a priest consecrated by a bishop, and were there to agree to elect one of them, born in wedlock or not, and were to order him to baptise, to celebrate the mass, to absolve, and to preach, this man would as truly be a priest, as if all the bishops and all the popes had consecrated him. That is why in cases of necessity every man can baptise and absolve, which would not be possible if we were not all priests. This great grace and virtue of baptism and of the Christian estate they have quite destroyed and made us forget by their ecclesiastical law. In this way the Christians used to choose their bishops and priests out of the community; these being afterwards confirmed by other bishops, without the pomp that now prevails. So was it that St. Augustine, Ambrose, Cyprian, were bishops.

Since, then, the temporal power is baptised as we are, and has the same faith and Gospel, we must allow it to be priest and bishop, and account its office an office that is proper and useful to the Christian community. For whatever issues from baptism may boast that it has been consecrated priest, bishop, and pope, although it does not beseem every one to exercise these offices. For, since we are all priests alike, no man may put himself forward or take upon himself, without our consent and election, to do that which we have all alike power to do. For, if a thing is common to all, no man may take it to himself without the wish and command of the community. And if it should happen that a man were appointed to one of these offices and deposed for abuses, he would be just what he was before. Therefore a priest should be nothing in Christendom but a functionary; as long as he holds his office, he has precedence of others; if he is deprived of it, he is a peasant or a citizen like the rest. Therefore a priest is verily no longer a priest after deposition. But now they have invented *characteres indelebiles,* and pretend that a priest after deprivation still differs from a simple layman. They even imagine that a priest can never be anything but a priest—that is, that he can never become a layman. All this is nothing but mere talk and ordinance of human invention.

It follows, then, that between laymen and priests, princes and bishops, or, as they call it, between spiritual and temporal persons, the only real difference is one of office and function, and not of estate; for they are all of the same spiritual estate, true priests, bishops, and popes, though their functions are not the same—just as among priests and monks every man has not the same functions. And this, as I said above, St. Paul says (Rom. xii.; 1 Cor. xii.), and St. Peter (1 Peter ii.): "We, being many, are one body in Christ, and severally members one of another." Christ's body is not double or twofold, one temporal, the other spiritual. He is one Head, and He has one body.

We see, then, that just as those that we call spiritual, or priests, bishops, or popes, do not differ from other Christians in any other or higher degree but in that they are to be concerned with the word of God and the sacraments—that being their work and office—in the same way the temporal authorities hold the sword and the rod in their hands to punish the wicked and to protect the good. A cobbler, a smith, a peasant, every man, has the office and function of his calling, and yet all alike are consecrated priests and bishops, and every man should by his office or function be useful and beneficial to the rest, so that various kinds of work may all be united for the further- ance of body and soul, just as the members of the body all serve one another.

Now see what a Christian doctrine is this: that the temporal authority is not above the clergy, and may not punish it. This is as if one were to say the hand may not help, though the eye is in grievous suffering. Is it not unnatural, not to say unchristian, that one member may not help another, or guard it against harm? Nay, the nobler the member, the more the rest are bound to help it. Therefore I say, Forasmuch as the

temporal power has been ordained by God for the punishment of the bad and the protection of the good, therefore we must let it do its duty throughout the whole Christian body, without respect of persons, whether it strikes popes, bishops, priests, monks,
nuns, or whoever it may be. If it were sufficient reason for fettering the temporal power
that it is inferior among the offices of Christianity to the offices of priest or confessor,
or to the spiritual estate—if this were so, then we ought to restrain tailors, cobblers,
masons, carpenters, cooks, cellarmen, peasants, and all secular workmen, from providing the Pope or bishops, priests and monks, with shoes, clothes, houses or victuals, or
from paying them tithes. But if these laymen are allowed to do their work without
restraint, what do the Romanist scribes mean by their laws? They mean that they withdraw themselves from the operation of temporal Christian power, simply in order that
they may be free to do evil, and thus fulfil what St. Peter said: "There shall be false
teachers among you, . . . and in covetousness shall they with feigned words make
merchandise of you" (2 Peter ii. 1, etc.).

Therefore the temporal Christian power must exercise its office without let or hindrance, without considering whom it may strike, whether pope, or bishop, or priest:
whoever is guilty, let him suffer for it.

Whatever the ecclesiastical law has said in opposition to this is merely the invention
of Romanist arrogance. For this is what St. Paul says to all Christians: "Let every
soul" (I presume including the popes) "be subject unto the higher powers; for they
bear not the sword in vain: they serve the Lord therewith, for vengeance on evildoers
and for praise to them that do well" (Rom. xiii. 1–4). Also St. Peter: "Submit yourselves to every ordinance of man for the Lord's sake, . . . for so is the will of God"
(1 Peter ii. 13, 15). He has also foretold that men would come who should despise
government (2 Peter ii.), as has come to pass through ecclesiastical law.

Now, I imagine, the first paper wall is overthrown, inasmuch as the temporal power
has become a member of the Christian body; although its work relates to the body, yet
does it belong to the spiritual estate. Therefore it must do its duty without let or
hindrance upon all members of the whole body, to punish or urge, as guilt may deserve, or need may require, without respect of pope, bishops, or priests, let them threaten
or excommunicate as they will. That is why a guilty priest is deprived of his priesthood
before being given over to the secular arm; whereas this would not be right, if the secular
sword had not authority over him already by Divine ordinance. . . .

(b) The Second Wall: That No One May Interpret the Scriptures But the Pope

The second wall is even more tottering and weak: that they alone pretend to be considered masters of the Scriptures; although they learn nothing of them all their life.
They assume authority, and juggle before us with impudent words, saying that the
Pope cannot err in matters of faith, whether he be evil or good, albeit they cannot
prove it by a single letter. That is why the canon law contains so many heretical and unchristian, nay unnatural, laws; but of these we need not speak now. For whereas they
imagine the Holy Ghost never leaves them, however unlearned and wicked they may
be, they grow bold enough to decree whatever they like. But were this true, where were
the need and use of the Holy Scriptures? Let us burn them, and content ourselves with
the unlearned gentlemen at Rome, in whom the Holy Ghost dwells, who, however, can

dwell in pious souls only. If I had not read it, I could never have believed that the devil should have put forth such follies at Rome and find a following.

But not to fight them with our own words, we will quote the Scriptures. St. Paul says, "If anything be revealed to another that sitteth by, let the first hold his peace" (1 Cor. xiv 30). What would be the use of this commandment, if we were to believe him alone that teaches or has the highest seat? Christ Himself says, "And they shall be all taught of God." (St. John vi. 45). Thus it may come to pass that the Pope and his followers are wicked and not true Christians, and not being taught by God, have no true understanding, whereas a common man may have true understanding. Why should we then not follow him? Has not the Pope often erred? Who could help Christianity, in case the Pope errs, if we do not rather believe another who has the Scriptures for him?

Therefore it is a wickedly devised fable—and they cannot quote a single letter to confirm it—that it is for the Pope alone to interpret the Scriptures or to confirm the interpretation of them. They have assumed the authority of their own selves. And though they say that this authority was given to St. Peter when the keys were given to him, it is plain enough that the keys were not given to St. Peter alone, but to the whole community. Besides, the keys were not ordained for doctrine or authority, but for sin, to bind or loose; and what they claim besides this from the keys is mere invention. But what Christ said to St. Peter: "I have prayed for thee that thy faith fail not" (St. Luke xxii. 32), cannot relate to the Pope, inasmuch as the greater part of the Popes have been without faith, as they are themselves forced to acknowledge; nor did Christ pray for Peter alone, but for all the Apostles and all Christians, as He says, "Neither pray I for these alone, but for them also which shall believe on Me through their word" (St. John xvii.). Is not this plain enough? . . .

(c) The Third Wall: That No One May Call a Council but the Pope

The third wall falls of itself, as soon as the first two have fallen; for if the Pope acts contrary to the Scriptures, we are bound to stand by the Scriptures, to punish and to constrain him, according to Christ's commandment, "Moreover, if thy brother shall trespass against thee, go and tell him his fault between thee and him alone; if he shall hear thee, thou hast gained thy brother. But if he will not hear thee, then take with thee one or two more, that in the mouth of two or three witnesses every word may be established. And if he shall neglect to hear them, tell it unto the Church; but if he neglect to hear the Church, let him be unto thee as a heathen man and a publican" (St. Matt. xviii. 15–17). Here each member is commanded to take care for the other; much more then should we do this, if it is a ruling member of the community that does evil, which by its evil-doing causes great harm and offence to the others. If then I am to accuse him before the Church, I must collect the Church together. Moreover, they can show nothing in the Scriptures giving the Pope sole power to call and confirm councils; they have nothing but their own laws; but these hold good only so long as they are not injurious to Christianity and the laws of God. Therefore, if the Pope deserves punishment, these laws cease to bind us, since Christendom would suffer, if he were not punished by a council. Thus we read (Acts xv.) that the council of the Apostles was not called by St. Peter, but by all the Apostles and the elders. But if the right to call it had lain with St. Peter alone, it would not have been a Christian council, but a heretical *conciliabulum*. Moreover, the most celebrated council of all—that of Nicaea—was neither called nor confirmed by the Bishop of Rome, but by the Emperor Constantine; and after him many other emperors have done the same, and yet the councils called by them were accounted most Christian. But if the Pope alone had the power, they must all have been heretical. Moreover, if I consider the councils that the Pope has called, I do not find that they produced any notable results.

Therefore when need requires, and the Pope is a cause of offence to Christendom, in these cases whoever can best do so, as a faithful member of the whole body, must do what he can to procure a true free council. This no one can do so well as the temporal authorities, especially since they are fellow-Christians, fellow-priests, sharing one spirit and one power in all things, and since they should exercise the office that they have received from God without hindrance, whenever it is necessary and useful that it should be exercised. Would it not be most unnatural, if a fire were to break out in a city, and every one were to keep still and let it burn on and on, whatever might be burnt, simply because they had not the mayor's authority, or because the fire perchance broke out at the mayor's house? Is not every citizen bound in this case to rouse and call in the rest? How much more should this be done in the spiritual city of Christ, if a fire of offence breaks out, either at the Pope's government or wherever it may! The like happens if an enemy attacks a town. The first to rouse up the rest earns glory and thanks. Why then should not he earn glory that descries the coming of our enemies from hell and rouses and summons all Christians?

But as for their boasts of their authority, that no one must oppose it, this is idle talk. No one in Christendom has any authority to do harm, or to forbid others to prevent harm being done. There is no authority in the Church but for reformation. Therefore if the Pope wished to use his power to prevent the calling of a free council, so as to prevent the reformation of the Church, we must not respect him or his power; and if he should begin to excommunicate and fulminate, we must despise this as the doings of a madman, and, trusting in God, excommunicate and repel him as best we may. For this his usurped power is nothing; he does not possess it, and he is at once overthrown by a text from the Scriptures. For St. Paul says to the Corinthians "that God has given us authority for edification, and not for destruction" (2 Cor. x. 8). Who will set this text at nought? It is the power of the devil and of antichrist that prevents what would serve for the reformation of Christendom. Therefore we must not follow it, but oppose it with our body, our goods, and all that we have. And even if a miracle were to happen in favour of the Pope against the temporal power, or if some were to be stricken by a plague, as they sometimes boast has happened, all this is to be held as having been done by the devil in order to injure our faith in God, as was foretold by Christ: "There shall arise false Christs and false prophets, and shall show great signs and wonders, insomuch that, if it were possible, they shall deceive the very elect" (Matt. xxiv. 23); and St. Paul tells the Thessalonians that the coming of antichrist shall be "after the working of Satan with all power and signs and lying wonders" (2 Thess. ii. 9).

Therefore let us hold fast to this: that Christian power can do nothing against Christ, as St. Paul says, "For we can do nothing against Christ, but for Christ" (2 Cor. xiii. 8). But, if it does anything against Christ, it is the power of antichrist and the devil, even if it rained and hailed wonders and plagues. Wonders and plagues prove nothing, especially in these latter evil days, of which false wonders are foretold in all the Scriptures. Therefore we must hold fast to the words of God with an assured faith; then the devil will soon cease his wonders.

And now I hope the false lying spectre will be laid with which the Romanists have long terrified and stupefied our consciences. And it will be seen that, like all the rest of us, they are subject to the temporal sword; that they have no authority to interpret the the Scriptures by force without skill; and that they have no power to prevent a council, or to pledge it in accordance with their pleasure, or to bind it beforehand, and deprive it of its freedom; and that if they do this, they are verily of the fellowship of antichrist and the devil, and have nothing of Christ but the name.

OF THE MATTERS TO BE CONSIDERED IN THE COUNCILS

Let us now consider the matters which should be treated in the councils, and with which popes, cardinals, bishops, and all learned men should occupy themselves day and night, if they love Christ and His Church. . . .

1. It is a distressing and terrible thing to see that the head of Christendom, who boasts of being the vicar of Christ and the successor of St. Peter, lives in a worldly pomp that no king or emperor can equal, so that in him that calls himself most holy and most spiritual there is more worldliness than in the world itself. He wears a triple crown, whereas the mightiest kings only wear one crown. If this resembles the poverty of Christ and St. Peter, it is a new sort of resemblance. They prate of its being heretical to object to this; nay, they will not even hear how unchristian and ungodly it is. But I think that if he should have to pray to God with tears, he would have to lay down his crowns; for God will not endure any arrogance. His office should be nothing else than to weep and pray constantly for Christendom and to be an example of all humility. . . .

A simple mitre would be enough for the Pope: wisdom and sanctity should raise him above the rest; the crown of pride he should leave to antichrist, as his predecessors did some hundreds of years ago. They say, he is the ruler of the world. This is false; for Christ, whose vicegerent and vicar he claims to be, said to Pilate, "My kingdom is not of this world" (John xviii. 36). But no vicegerent can have a wider dominion than his Lord, nor is he a vicegerent of Christ in His glory, but of Christ crucified. . . .

2. What is the use in Christendom of the people called "cardinals"? I will tell you. In Italy and Germany there are many rich convents, endowments, fiefs, and benefices, and as the best way of getting these into the hands of Rome, they created cardinals, and gave them the sees, convents, and prelacies, and thus destroyed the service of God. That is why Italy is almost a desert now: the convents are destroyed, the sees consumed, the revenues of the prelacies and of all the churches drawn to Rome; towns are decayed, the country and the people ruined, because there is no more any worship of God or preaching; why? Because the cardinals must have all the wealth. No Turk could have thus desolated Italy and overthrown the worship of God.

Now that Italy is sucked dry, they come to Germany and begin very quietly; but if we look on quietly Germany will soon be brought into the same state as Italy. We have a few cardinals already. What the Romanists mean thereby the drunken Germans are not to see until they have lost everything—bishoprics, convents, benefices, fiefs, even to their last farthing. Antichrist must take the riches of the earth, as it is written (Dan. xi. 8, 39, 43). They begin by taking off the cream of the bishoprics, convents and fiefs; and as they do not dare to destroy everything as they have done in Italy, they employ such holy cunning to join together ten or twenty prelacies, and take such a portion of each annually that the total amounts to a considerable sum. The priory of Würzburg gives one thousand guilders; those of Bamberg, Mayence, Treves, and others also contribute. In this way they collect one thousand or ten thousand guilders, in order that a cardinal may live at Rome in a state like that of a wealthy monarch. . . .

What has brought us Germans to such a pass that we have to suffer this robbery and this destruction of our property by the Pope? If the kingdom of France has resisted it, why do we Germans suffer ourselves to be fooled and deceived? It would be more endurable if they did nothing but rob us of our property; but they destroy the Church and deprive Christ's flock of their good shepherds, and overthrow the service and word of God. Even if there were no cardinals at all, the Church would not perish, for they do nothing for the good of Christendom; all they do is to traffic in and quarrel about prelacies and bishoprics, which any robber could do as well.

3. If we took away ninety-nine parts of the Pope's Court and only left one hundredth, it would still be large enough to answer questions on matters of belief. Now there is such a swarm of vermin at Rome, all called papal, that Babylon itself never saw the like. There are more than three thousand papal secretaries alone; but who shall count the other office-bearers, since there are so many offices that we can scarcely count them, and all waiting for German benefices, as wolves wait for a flock of sheep? I think Germany now pays more to the Pope than it formerly paid the emperors; nay, some think more than three hundred thousand guilders are sent from Germany to Rome every year, for nothing whatever; and in return we are scoffed at and put to shame. Do we still wonder why princes, noblemen, cities, foundations, convents, and people grow poor? We should rather wonder that we have anything left to eat.

Now that we have got well into our game, let us pause a while and show that the Germans are not such fools as not to perceive or understand this Romish trickery. I do not here complain that God's commandments and Christian justice are despised at Rome; for the state of things in Christendom, especially at Rome, is too bad for us to complain of such high matters. Nor do I even complain that no account is taken of natural or secular justice and reason. The mischief lies still deeper. I complain that they do not observe their own fabricated canon law, though this is in itself rather mere tyranny, avarice, and worldly pomp, than a law. . . .

TWENTY-SEVEN ARTICLES RESPECTING THE REFORMATION OF THE CHRISTIAN ESTATE

Now though I am too lowly to submit articles that could serve for the reformation of these fearful evils, I will yet sing out my fool's song, and will show, as well as my wit will allow, what might and should be done by the temporal authorities or by a general council.

1   Princes, nobles, and cities should promptly forbid their subjects to pay the *annates* to Rome and should even abolish them altogether. For the Pope has broken the compact, and turned the *annates* into robbery for the harm and shame of the German nation; he gives them to his friends; he sells them for large sums of money and founds benefices on them. Therefore he has forfeited his right to them, and deserves punishment. In this way the temporal power should protect the innocent and prevent wrong-doing, as we are taught by St. Paul (Rom. xiii.) and by St. Peter (1 Peter ii.) and even by the canon law (16. q. 7. de Filiis). That is why we say to the Pope and his followers, *Tu ora!* "Thou shalt pray"; to the Emperor and his followers, *Tu Protege!* "Thou shalt protect"; to the commons, *Tu labora!* "Thou shalt work." Not that each man should not pray, protect, and work; for if a man fulfils his duty, that is prayer, protection, and work; but every man must have his proper task. . . .

3   It should be decreed by an imperial law that no episcopal cloak and no confirmation of any appointment shall for the future be obtained from Rome. The order of the most holy and renowned Nicene Council must again be restored, namely that a bishop must be confirmed by the two nearest bishops or by the archbishop. If the Pope cancels the decrees of these and all other councils, what is the good of councils at all? Who has given him the right thus to despise councils and to cancel them? If this is allowed, we had better abolish all bishops, archbishops and primates, and make simple rectors of all of them, so that they would have the Pope alone over them as is indeed the case now; he deprives bishops, archbishops, and primates of all the authority of their office, taking everything to himself, and leaving them only the name and the empty title; more than this, by his exemption he has withdrawn convents, abbots, and prelates from the ordinary authority of the bishops, so that there remains no order in Christendom. The necessary result of this must be, and has been, laxity in punishing and such a liberty to do evil in all the world that I very much fear one might call the Pope "the man of sin" (2 Thess. ii. 3). Who but the Pope is to blame for this absence of all order, of all punishment, of all government, of all discipline, in Christendom? By his own arbitrary power he ties the hands of all his prelates, and takes from them their rods, while all their subjects have their hands unloosed, and obtain licence by gift or purchase. . . .

4   Let it be decreed that no temporal matter shall be submitted to Rome, but all shall be left to the jurisdiction of the temporal authorities. This is part of their own canon law, though they do not obey it. For this should be the Pope's office: that he, the most learned in the Scriptures and the most holy, not in name only, but in fact, should rule in matters concerning the faith and the holy life of Christians; he should make primates and bishops attend to this, and should work and take thought with them to this end, as St. Paul teaches (1 Cor. vi.), severely upbraiding those that occupy themselves with the things of this world. For all countries suffer unbearable damage by this practice of settling such matters at Rome, since it involves great expense; and besides this, the judges at Rome, not knowing the manners, laws, and customs of other countries, frequently pervert the matter according to their own laws and their own opinions, thus causing injustice to all parties. Besides this, we should prohibit in all foundations the grievous extortion of the ecclesiastical judges; they should only be allowed to consider matters concerning faith and good morals; but matters concerning money, prop-

erty, life, and honour should be left to temporal judges. Therefore the temporal authorities should not permit excommunication or expulsion except in matters of faith and righteous living. It is only reasonable that spiritual authorities should have power in spiritual matters; spiritual matters, however, are not money or matters relating to the body, but faith and good works. . . .

7   The Roman See must abolish the papal offices, and diminish that crowd of crawling vermin at Rome, so that the Pope's servants may be supported out of the Pope's own pocket, and that his court may cease to surpass all royal courts in its pomp and extravagance; seeing that all this pomp has not only been of no service to the Christian faith, but has also kept them from study and prayer, so that they themselves know hardly anything concerning matters of faith, as they proved clumsily enough at the last Roman Council, where, among many childishly trifling matters, they decided "that the soul is immortal," and that a priest is bound to pray once every month on pain of losing his benefice. How are men to rule Christendom and to decide matters of faith who, callous and blinded by their greed, wealth, and worldly pomp, have only just decided that the soul is immortal? It is no slight shame to all Christendom that they should deal thus scandalously with the faith at Rome. If they had less wealth and lived in less pomp, they might be better able to study and pray that they might become able and worthy to treat matters of belief, as they were once, when they were content to be bishops, and not kings of kings. . . .

9   The Pope should have no power over the Emperor, except to anoint and crown him at the altar, as a bishop crowns a king; nor should that devilish pomp be allowed that the Emperor should kiss the Pope's feet or sit at his feet, or, as it is said, hold his stirrup or the reins of his mule, when he mounts to ride; much less should he pay homage to the Pope, or swear allegiance, as is impudently demanded by the popes, as if they had a right to it. The chapter *Solite,* in which the papal authority is exalted above the imperial, is not worth a farthing, and so of all those that depend on it or fear it; for it does nothing but pervert God's holy words from their true meaning, according to their own imaginations, as I have proved in a Latin treatise. . . .

11   The custom of kissing the Pope's feet must cease. It is an unchristian, or rather an anti-Christian, example that a poor sinful man should suffer his feet to be kissed by one who is a hundred times better than he. If it is done in honour of his power, why does he not do it to others in honour of their holiness? Compare them together: Christ and the Pope. Christ washed His disciples' feet and dried them, and the disciples never washed His. The Pope, pretending to be higher than Christ, inverts this, and considers it a great favour to let us kiss his feet; whereas, if any one wished to do so, he ought to do his utmost to prevent him, as St. Paul and Barnabas would not suffer themselves to be worshipped as gods by the men at Lystra, saying, "We also are men of like passions with you" (Acts xiv. 14 *seq.*). But our flatterers have brought things to such a pitch that they have set up an idol for us, until no one regards God with such fear or honours Him with such marks of reverence as he does the Pope. This they can suffer, but not that the Pope's glory should be diminished a single hair's-breadth. Now if they were Christians and preferred God's honour to their own, the Pope would never be pleased to have God's honour despised and his own exalted, nor would he allow any to honour him until he found that God's honour was again exalted above his own.

It is of a piece with this revolting pride that the Pope is not satisfied with riding on horseback or in a carriage, but though he be hale and strong, is carried by men like an idol in unheard-of pomp. My friend, how does this Lucifer-like pride agree with the example of Christ, who went on foot, as did also all His Apostles? Where has there been a king who has ridden in such worldly pomp as he does, who professes to be the head of all whose duty it is to despise and flee from all worldly pomp—I mean, of all Christians? Not that this need concern us for his own sake, but that we have good reason to fear God's wrath, if we flatter such pride and do not show our discontent. It is enough that the Pope should be so mad and foolish; but it is too much that we should sanction and approve it. . . .

12 Pilgrimages to Rome must be abolished, or at least no one must be allowed to go from his own wish or his own piety, unless his priest, his town magistrate, or his lord has found that there is sufficient reason for his pilgrimage. This I say, not because pilgrimages are bad in themselves, but because at the present time they lead to mischief; for at Rome a pilgrim sees no good examples, but only offence. They themselves have made a proverb, "The nearer to Rome, the farther from Christ," and accordingly men bring home contempt of God and of God's commandments. It is said, "The first time one goes to Rome, he goes to seek a rogue; the second time he finds him; the third time he brings him home with him." But now they have become so skilful that they can do their three journeys in one, and they have, in fact, brought home from Rome this saying: "It were better never to have seen or heard of Rome."

And even if this were not so, there is something of more importance to be considered; namely, that simple men are thus led into a false delusion and a wrong understanding of God's commandments. For they think that these pilgrimages are precious and good works; but this is not true. It is but a little good work, often a bad, misleading work, for God has not commanded it. But He has commanded that each man should care for his wife and children and whatever concerns the married state, and should, besides, serve and help his neighbour. Now it often happens that one goes on a pilgrimage to Rome, spends fifty or one hundred guilders more or less, which no one has commanded him, while his wife and children, or those dearest to him, are left at home in want and misery; and yet he thinks, poor foolish man, to atone for this disobedience and contempt of God's commandments by his self-willed pilgrimage, while he is in truth misled by idle curiosity or the wiles of the devil. This the popes have encouraged with their false and foolish inventions of *Golden Years,* by which they have incited the people, have torn them away from God's commandments and turned them to their own delusive proceedings, and set up the very thing that they ought to have forbidden. But it brought them money and strengthened their false authority, and therefore it was allowed to continue, though against God's will and the salvation of souls. . . .

13 Now we come to the great crowd that promises much and performs little. Be not angry, my good sirs; I mean well. I have to tell you this bitter and sweet truth: Let no more mendicant monasteries be built! God help us! there are too many as it is. Would to God they were all abolished, or at least made over to two or three orders! It has never done good, it will never do good, to go wandering about over the country. Therefore my advice is that ten, or as many as may be required, be put together and

made into one, which one, sufficiently provided for, need not beg. Oh! it is of much more importance to consider what is necessary for the salvation of the common people, than what St. Francis, or St. Dominic, or St. Augustine, or any other man, laid down, especially since things have not turned out as they expected. They should also be relieved from preaching and confession, unless specially required to do so by bishops, priests, the congregation, or other authority. For their preaching and confession has led to nought but mere hatred and envy between priests and monks, to the great offence and hindrance of the people, so that it well deserves to be put a stop to, since its place may very well be dispensed with. It does not look at all improbable that the Holy Roman See had its own reasons for encouraging all this crowd of monks: the Pope perhaps feared that priests and bishops, growing weary of his tyranny, might become too strong for him, and begin a reformation unendurable to his Holiness. . . .

14 We see also how the priesthood is fallen, and how many a poor priest is encumbered with a woman and children and burdened in his conscience, and no one does anything to help him, though he might very well be helped. Popes and bishops may let that be lost that is being lost, and that be destroyed which is being destroyed, I will save my conscience and open my mouth freely, let it vex popes and bishops or whoever it may be; therefore I say, According to the ordinances of Christ and His Apostles, every town should have a minister or bishop, as St. Paul plainly says (Titus i.), and this minister should not be forced to live without a lawful wife, but should be allowed to have one, as St. Paul writes, saying that "a bishop then must be blameless, the husband of one wife. . . . having his children in subjection with all gravity" (1 Tim. iii.). For with St. Paul a bishop and a presbyter are the same thing, as St. Jerome also confirms. But as for the bishops that we now have, of these the Scriptures know nothing; they were instituted by common Christian ordinance, so that one might rule over many ministers. . . .

My advice is to restore liberty, and to leave every man free to marry or not to marry. . . .

I offer no opinion, one way or the other, whether those who have at present no wife should marry, or remain unmarried. This must be settled by the general order of the Church and by each man's discretion. But I will not conceal my honest counsel, nor withhold comfort from that unhappy crowd who now live in trouble with wife and children, and remain in shame, with a heavy conscience, hearing their wife called a priest's harlot, and the children bastards. And this I say frankly, in virtue of my good right.

There is many a poor priest free from blame in all other respects, except that he has succumbed to human frailty and come to shame with a woman, both minded in their hearts to live together always in conjugal fidelity, if only they could do so with a good conscience, though as it is they live in public shame. I say, these two are surely married before God. I say, moreover, that when two are so minded, and so come to live together, they should save their conscience; let the man take the woman as his lawful wife, and live with her faithfully as her husband, without considering whether the Pope approve or not, or whether it is forbidden by canon law, or temporal. The salvation of your soul is of more importance than their tyrannous, arbitrary, wicked laws, which are not necessary for salvation, nor ordained by God. You should do as the children of Israel did who stole from the Egyptians the wages they had earned, or as a servant steals his well-earned wages from a harsh master; in the same way do you also steal your wife and child from the Pope. . . .

18 One should abolish all saints' days, keeping only Sunday. But if it were desired to keep the festivals of Our Lady and the greater saints, they should all be held on Sundays, or only in the morning with the mass; the rest of the day being a working day. My reason is this: with our present abuses of drinking, gambling, idling, and all manner of sin, we vex God more on holy days than on others. And the matter is just reversed; we have made holy days unholy, and working days holy, and do no service, but great dishonour, to God and His saints with all our holy days. There are some foolish prelates that think they have done a good deed, if they establish a festival to St. Otilia or St. Barbara, and the like, each in his own blind fashion, whilst he would be doing a much better work to turn a saint's day into a working day in honour of a saint.

Besides these spiritual evils, these saints' days inflict bodily injury on the common man in two ways: he loses a day's work, and he spends more than usual, besides weakening his body and making himself unfit for labour, as we see every day, and yet no one tries to improve it. One should not consider whether the Pope instituted these festivals, or whether we require his dispensation or permission. If anything is contrary to God's will and harmful to men in body and soul, not only has every community, council, or government authority to prevent and abolish such wrong without the knowledge or consent of pope or bishop, but it is their duty, as they value their soul's salvation, to prevent it, even though pope and bishop (that should be the first to do so) are unwilling to see it stopped. And first of all we should abolish church wakes, since they are nothing but taverns, fairs, and gaming places, to the greater dishonour of God and the damnation of souls. It is no good to make a talk about their having had a good origin and being good works. Did not God set aside His own law that He had given forth out of heaven when He saw that it was abused, and does He not now reverse every day what He has appointed, and destroy what He has made, on account of the same perverse misuse, as it is written in Psalm xviii. (ver. 26), "With the froward Thou wilt show Thyself froward"? . . .

21 It is one of the most urgent necessities to abolish all begging in Christendom. No one should go about begging among Christians. It would not be hard to do this, if we attempted it with good heart and courage: each town should support its own poor and should not allow strange beggars to come in, whatever they may call themselves, pilgrims or mendicant monks. Every town could feed its own poor; and if it were too small, the people in the neighbouring villages should be called upon to contribute. As it is, they have to support many knaves and vagabonds under the name of beggars. If they did what I propose, they would at least know who were really poor or not. . . .

24 It is high time to take up earnestly and truthfully the cause of the Bohemians, to unite them with ourselves and ourselves with them, so that all mutual accusations, envy, and hatred may cease. I will be the first, in my folly, to give my opinion, with all due deference to those of better understanding.

First of all, we must honestly confess the truth, without attempting self-justification, and own one thing to the Bohemians, namely that John Huss and Jerome of Prague were burnt at Constance in violation of the papal, Christian, and imperial oath and safe-conduct, and that thus God's commandment was broken and the Bohemians excited to great anger. And though they may have deserved such great wrong and disobedience to God on our part, they were not obliged to approve it and think it right. Nay, even now they should run any danger of life and limb rather than own that it is right to break an imperial, papal, Christian safe-conduct and act faithlessly in opposition to it. Therefore, though the Bohemians may be to blame for their impatience, yet the Pope and his followers are most to blame for all the misery, all the error and destruction of souls, that followed this council of Constance.

It is not my intention here to judge John Huss's belief and to defend his errors, although my understanding has not been able to find any error in him, and I would willingly believe that men who violated a safe-conduct and God's commandment (doubtless possessed rather by the evil spirit than by the Spirit of God) were unable to judge well or to condemn with truth. . . .

Besides this, the Emperor and the princes should send to Bohemia several pious, learned bishops and doctors. . . . Those envoys should inquire into the faith of the Bohemians, to ascertain whether it would be possible to unite all their sects into one. . . .

I do not advise that they be forced to abandon the Sacrament in both kinds, for it is neither unchristian nor heretical. They should be allowed to continue in their present way; but the new bishop must see that there be no dissensions about this matter, and they must learn that neither practice is actually wrong, just as there need be no disputes about the priests not wearing the same dress as the laity. In the same way, if they do not wish to submit to the canon laws of the Roman Church, we must not force them, but we must content ourselves with seeing that they live in faith and according to the Scriptures. For Christian life and Christian faith may very well exist without the Pope's unbearable laws; nay, they cannot well exist until there are fewer of those laws or none. Our baptism has freed us and made us subject to God's word alone; why then should we suffer a man to make us the slaves of his words? As St. Paul says, "Stand fast therefore in the liberty wherewith Christ hath made us free, and be not entangled again with the yoke of bondage" (Gal. v. 1). . . .

25 The universities also require a good, sound reformation. I must say this, let it vex whom it may. The fact is that whatever the papacy has ordered or instituted is only designed for the propagation of sin and error. What are the universities, as at present ordered, but, as the book of Maccabees says, "schools of 'Greek fashion' and 'heathenish manners'" (2 Macc. iv. 12, 13), full of dissolute living, where very little is taught of the Holy Scriptures and of the Christian faith, and the blind heathen teacher, Aristotle, rules even further than Christ? Now, my advice would be that the books of Aristotle, the *Physics,* the *Metaphysics, Of the Soul, Ethics,* which have hitherto been considered the best, be altogether abolished, with all others that profess to treat of nature, though nothing can be learned from them, either of natural or of spiritual things. Besides, no one has been able to understand his meaning, and much time has been wasted and many noble souls vexed with much useless labour, study, and expense. I venture to say that any potter has more knowledge of natural things than is to be found in these books. My heart is grieved to see how many of the best Christians this accursed, proud, knavish heathen has fooled and led astray with his false words. God sent him as a plague for our sins.

Does not the wretched man in his best book, *Of the Soul,* teach that the soul dies with the body, though many have tried to save him with vain words, as if we had not the Holy Scriptures to teach us fully of all things of which Aristotle had not the slightest perception? Yet this dead heathen has conquered, and has hindered and almost suppressed the books of the living God; so that, when I see all this misery I cannot but think that the evil spirit has introduced this study.

Then there is the *Ethics,* which is accounted one of the best, though no book is more directly contrary to God's will and the Christian virtues. Oh that such books could be kept out of the reach of all Christians! Let no one object that I say too much, or speak without knowledge. My friend, I know of what I speak. I know Aristotle as well as you or men like you. I have read him with more understanding than St. Thomas or Scotus, which I may say without arrogance, and can prove if need be. It matters not that so many great minds have exercised themselves in these matters for many hundred years. Such objections do not affect me as they might have done once, since it is plain as day that many more errors have existed for many hundred years in the world and the universities.

I would, however, gladly consent that Aristotle's books of Logic, Rhetoric, and Poetry, should be retained, or they might be usefully studied in a condensed form, to practise young people in speaking and preaching; but the notes and comments should be abolished, and, just as Cicero's Rhetoric is read without note or comment, Aristotle's Logic should be read without such long commentaries. But now neither speaking nor preaching is taught out of them, and they are used only for disputation and toilsomeness. Besides this, there are languages—Latin, Greek, and Hebrew—the mathematics, history; which I recommend to men of higher understanding: and other matters, which will come of themselves, if they seriously strive after reform. And truly it is an important matter, for it concerns the teaching and training of Christian youths and of our noble people, in whom Christianity still abides. Therefore I think that pope and emperor could have no better task than the reformation of the universities, just as there is nothing more devilishly mischievous than an unreformed university.

Physicians I would leave to reform their own faculty; lawyers and theologians I take under my charge, and say firstly that it would be right to abolish the canon law entirely, from beginning to end, more especially the decretals. We are taught quite sufficiently in the Bible how we ought to act; all this study only prevents the study of the Scriptures, and for the most part it is tainted with covetousness and pride. . . .

The civil law, too, good God! what a wilderness it is become! It is, indeed, much better, more skilful, and more honest than the canon law, of which nothing is good but the name. Still there is far too much of it. Surely good governors, in addition to the Holy Scriptures, would be law enough. . . .

Our worthy theologians have saved themselves much trouble and labour by leaving the Bible alone and only reading the Sentences. I should have thought that young theologians might begin by studying the Sentences, and that doctors should study the Bible. Now they invert this: the Bible is the first thing they study; this ceases with the Bachelor's degree; the Sentences are the last, and these they keep forever with the Doctor's degree, and this, too, under such sacred obligation that one that is not a priest may read the Bible, but a priest must read the Sentences; so that, as far as I can see, a married man might be a doctor in the Bible, but not in the Sentences. How should we prosper so long as we act so perversely, and degrade the Bible, the holy word of God? Besides this, the Pope orders with many stringent words that his laws be read and used in schools and courts; while the law of the Gospel is but little considered. The result is that in schools and courts the Gospel lies dusty underneath the benches, so that the Pope's mischievous laws may alone be in force.

Since then we hold the name and title of teachers of the Holy Scriptures, we should verily be forced to act according to our title, and to teach the Holy Scriptures and nothing else. Although, indeed, it is a proud, presumptuous title for a man to proclaim himself teacher of the Scriptures, still it could be suffered, if the works confirmed the title. But as it is, under the rule of the Sentences, we find among theologians more human and heathenish fallacies than true holy knowledge of the Scriptures. . . .

We must also lessen the number of theological books, and choose the best, for it is not the number of books that makes the learned man, nor much reading, but good books often read, however few, makes a man learned in the Scriptures and pious. Even the Fathers should only be read for a short time as an introduction to the Scriptures. As it is we read nothing else, and never get from them into the Scriptures, as if one should be gazing at the signposts and never follow the road. These good Fathers wished to lead us into the Scriptures by their writings, whereas we lead ourselves out by them, though the Scriptures are our vineyard, in which we should all work and exercise ourselves. . . .

27 Let this be enough about the faults of the spiritual estate, though many more might be found, if the matter were properly considered; we must now consider the defects of the temporal estates. In the first place, we require a general law and consent of the German nation against profusion and extravagance in dress, which is the cause of so much poverty among the nobles and the people. Surely God has given to us, as to other nations, enough wool, fur, flax, and whatever else is required for the decent clothing of every class; and it cannot be necessary to spend such enormous sums for silk, velvet, cloth of gold, and all other kinds of outlandish stuff. I think that even if the Pope did not rob us Germans with his unbearable taxes, we should be robbed more than enough by these secret thieves, the dealers in silk and velvet. As it is, we see that every man wishes to be every other man's equal, and that this causes and increases pride and envy among us, as we deserve, all which would cease, with many other misfortunes, if our self-will would but let us be gratefully content with what God has given us.

It is similarly necessary to diminish the use of spices, which is one of the ships in which our gold is sent away from Germany. God's mercy has given us more food, and that both precious and good, than is to be found in other countries. I shall probably be accused of making foolish and impossible suggestions, as if I wished to destroy the great business of commerce. But I am only doing my part; if the community does not mend matters, every man should do it himself. I do not see many good manners that have ever come into a land through commerce, and therefore God let the people of Israel dwell far from the sea and not carry on much trade.

But without doubt the greatest misfortune of the Germans is buying on usury. But for this, many a man would have to leave unbought his silk, velvet, cloth of gold, spices, and all other luxuries. The system has not been in force for more than one hundred years, and has already brought poverty, misery, and destruction on almost all princes, foundations, cities, nobles, and heirs. If it continues for another hundred years Germany will be left without a farthing, and we shall be reduced to eating one another. The devil invented this system, and the Pope has done an injury to the whole world by sanctioning it.

My request and my cry therefore is this: Let each man ·consider the destruction of himself and his family, which is no longer at the door, but has entered the house; and let emperors, princes, lords, and corporations see to the condemnation and prohibition of this kind of trade, without considering the opposition of the Pope and all his justice and injustice, nor whether livings or endowments depend upon it. Better a single fief in a city based on a freehold estate or honest interest, than a hundred based on usury; yea, a single endowment on usury is worse and more grievous than twenty based on freehold estate. Truly this usury is a sign and warning that the world has been given over to the devil for its sins, and that we are losing our spiritual and temporal welfare alike; yet we heed it not.

Doubtless we should also find some bridle for the *Fuggers* and similar companies. Is it possible that in a single man's lifetime such great wealth should be collected together, if all were done rightly and according to God's will? I am not skilled in accounts, but I do not understand how it is possible for one hundred guilders to gain twenty in a year, or how one guilder can gain another, and that not out of the soil, or by cattle, seeing that possessions depend not on the wit of men, but on the blessing of God. I commend this to those that are skilled in worldly affairs. I as a theologian blame nothing but the evil appearance, of which St. Paul says, "Abstain from all appearance of evil" (1 Thess. v. 22). All I know is that it were much more godly to encourage agriculture and lessen commerce; and that they do the best who, according to the Scriptures, till the ground to get their living, as we are all commanded in Adam: "Cursed is the ground for thy sake. . . . Thorns also and thistles shall it bring forth to thee. . . . In the sweat of thy face shalt thou eat bread" (Gen. iii. 17–19). There is still much ground that is not ploughed or tilled.

Then there is the excess in eating and drinking, for which we Germans have an ill reputation in foreign countries, as our special vice, and which has become so common, and gained so much the upper hand, that sermons avail nothing. The loss of money caused by it is not the worst; but in its train come murder, adultery, theft, blasphemy, and all vices. The temporal power should do something to prevent it; otherwise it will come to pass, as Christ foretold, that the last day shall come as a thief in the night, and shall find them eating and drinking, marrying and giving in marriage, planting and building, buying and selling (Matt. xxiv. 38; Luke xvii. 26), just as things go on now, and that so strongly that I apprehend lest the day of judgment be at hand, even now when we least expect it.

Lastly, is it not a terrible thing that we Christians should maintain public brothels, though we all vow chastity in our baptism? I well know all that can be said on this matter: that it is not peculiar to one nation, that it would be difficult to demolish it, and that it is better thus than that virgins, or married women, or honourable women should be dishonoured. But should not the spiritual and temporal powers combine to find some means of meeting these difficulties without any such heathen practice? If the people of Israel existed without this scandal, why should not a Christian nation be able to do so? How do so many towns and villages manage to exist without these houses? Why should not great cities be able to do so?

In all, however, that I have said above, my object has been to show how much good temporal authority might do, and what should be the duty of all authorities, so that every man might learn what a terrible thing it is to rule and to have the chief place. What boots it though a ruler be in his own person as holy as St. Peter, if he be not diligent to help his subjects in these matters? His very authority will be his condemnation; for it is the duty of those in authority to seek the good of their subjects. But if those in authority considered how young people might be brought together in marriage, the prospect of marriage would help every man and protect him from temptations.

But as it is every man is induced to become a priest or a monk; and of all these I am afraid not one in a hundred has any other motive but the wish of getting a livelihood and the uncertainty of maintaining a family. Therefore they begin by a dissolute life and sow their wild oats (as they say), but I fear they rather gather in a store of wild oats. I hold the proverb to be true, "Most men become monks and priests in desperation." That is why things are as we see them.

But in order that many sins may be prevented that are becoming too common, I would honestly advise that no boy or girl be allowed to take the vow of chastity or to enter a religious life before the age of thirty years. For this requires a special grace, as St. Paul says. Therefore, unless God specially urge any one to a religious life, he will do well to leave all vows and devotions alone. I say further, If a man has so little faith in God as to fear that he will be unable to maintain himself in the married state, and if this fear is the only thing that makes him become a priest, then I implore him, for his own soul's sake, not to become a priest, but rather to become a peasant, or what he will. For if simple trust in God be necessary to ensure temporal support, tenfold trust in God is necessary to live a religious life. If you do not trust to God for your worldly food, how can you trust to Him for your spiritual food? Alas! this unbelief and want of faith destroys all things, and leads us into all misery, as we see among all conditions of men.

Much might be said concerning all this misery. Young people have no one to look after them, they are left to go on just as they like, and those in authority are of no more use to them than if they did not exist, though this should be the chief care of the Pope, of bishops, lords, and councils. They wish to rule over everything, everywhere, and yet they are of no use. Oh, what a rare sight, for these reasons, will a lord or ruler be in heaven, though he might build a hundred churches to God and raise all the dead!

But this may suffice for the present. For of what concerns the temporal authority and the nobles I have, I think, said enough in my tract on *Good Works*. For their lives and governments leave room enough for improvement; but there is no comparison between spiritual and temporal abuses, as I have there shown. I daresay I have sung a lofty strain, that I have proposed many things that will be thought impossible, and attacked many points too sharply. But what was I to do? I was bound to say this: if I had the power, this is what I would do. I had rather incur the world's anger than God's; they cannot take from me more than my life. I have hitherto made many offers of peace to my adversaries; but, as I see, God has forced me through them to open my mouth wider and wider, and, because they do not keep quiet, to give them enough cause for speaking, barking, shouting, and writing. Well, then, I have another song still to sing concerning them and Rome; if they wish to hear it, I will sing it to them, and sing with all my might. Do you understand, my friend Rome, what I mean?

I have frequently offered to submit my writings for inquiry and examination, but in vain, though I know, if I am in the right, I must be condemned upon earth and justified by Christ alone in heaven. For all the Scriptures teach us that the affairs of Christians and Christendom must be judged by God alone; they have never yet been justified by men in this world, but the opposition has always been too strong. My greatest care and fear is lest my cause be not condemned by men, by which I should know for certain that it does not please God. Therefore let them go freely to work, pope, bishop, priest, monk, or doctor; they are the true people to persecute the truth, as they have always done. May God grant us all a Christian understanding, and especially to the Christian nobility of the German nation true spiritual courage, to do what is best for our unhappy Church. Amen!

At Wittenberg, in the year 1520.

⇜§ ANTIDOTE TO THE COUNCIL OF TRENT
John Calvin

Within three decades of its inception Lutheranism had become quiescent, turning into a staid official religion wherever it had been implanted. Its competitor Calvinism, by contrast, remained an expanding, even revolutionary faith for well over a hundred years. This remarkable dynamism of the Calvinist churches may be traced directly to their French founder, John Calvin (1509–1564), who excelled as an organizer as well as a theologian and polemicist. Calvin headed the theocratic, tightly organized republic of Geneva (not then part of Switzerland), which served as a model for reformed churches from Hungary to New England. To the task of reformulating the individual's relation to God and his church, Calvin brought a scholar's thoroughness and a lawyer's logic. His Institutes of the Christian Religion *is the most important theological work produced during the Protestant Reformation.*

What Calvin's doctrine meant and how it compared with traditional Catholic Christianity may be seen in the selection below, which consists of excerpts from the proceedings of the Council of Trent together with Calvin's commentary. The Council of Trent (1547 to 1573) had been called by the Catholic Church, not to modify religious doctrine as a result of Protestant criticism, but to reaffirm the traditional views, and to remove ambiguities and confusion wherever possible. It was remarkably successful in that its essential definitions of Catholic dogma and practice have been maintained these 400 years. No other Church council made any substantial changes until the Vatican II Council of the 1960s, and even its changes have dealt not so much with doctrine as with Church organization and relations with other Christian and non-Christian groups.

The selections from the Decrees of the Council, alternating with Calvin's comments, are as follows: first, the prefatory discourse of the first session, in which the assembled delegates are directed in their main task; second, a decree of the fourth session, on the Holy Scriptures, which leads Calvin to express some characteristic Protestant opinions; third, a series of decrees and canons on justification (i.e., salvation) from the sixth session, dealing especially with the doctrine of predestination; finally, a series of canons, from the seventh session, on the sacraments and on ecclesiastical benefices (Church holdings).

ADMONITION AND EXHORTATION OF THE LEGATES OF THE APOSTOLIC SEE TO THE FATHERS IN THE COUNCIL OF TRENT

Read in the first session

Reverend Fathers, &c.— . . . To begin with that of which, particularly at the outset, we ought also to be reminded, each one of us ought to place in his view, first of all, what the things are which are expected from this sacred Council. Thereby each will easily understand how great a burden lies upon him. Now, the things expected (to embrace them all summarily) are those contained in the Bull calling the Council, namely, The Extirpation of Heresies, The Restoration of Ecclesiastical Discipline and Reformation of Manners, and, finally, The External Peace of the whole Church. These, therefore, are the things for which it behoves us to care, or which we ought constantly to pray that God would of His goodness grant. . . .

Let us look then for a little to the evils by which the Church is oppressed, and at the same time to our sins. But these who can number? Along with other evils, they are more than the sand of the sea, and cry aloud to heaven. Let us therefore circumscribe the multitude of our sins within those limits within which this Council summoned to cure the worst of evils has circumscribed them. These, as we have mentioned above,

John Calvin, *Tracts Containing Antidote to the Council of Trent* . . . [*et al.*] (Edinburgh: Calvin Translation Society, 1851), Vol. III, 19–20, 22–25, 27–28, 38–41, 65–66, 71–72, 74–77, 92–98, 104–106, 108–112, 116, 125, 147–151, 155–156, 163–165, 167–169, 171–172, 174, 177–179, 185–188.

are three, viz., heresies, decay of discipline, intestine and external war. Here, then, let us see and consider, since the Church has been now for many years vexed with these calamities, in what sources they had their origin—whether we did not in some measure begin—whether we have not fomented them.

First, let us examine the beginning of the Heresies which have everywhere sprung up in this our day. Should we deny that we gave a beginning to them because we ourselves have not been the authors of any heresy, still, inasmuch as perverse opinions concerning faith are a kind of brambles and thorns which have sprung up in the field of the Lord, given to us to cultivate, although these have risen of their own accord, as weeds are sometimes wont to do, yet he who has not cultivated the field as he ought —who has not sown it—who, as the weeds sprung up spontaneously, has not been careful to extirpate them, may be said to have given them a beginning, just as if he had sown them, especially considering that they all derive their origin and increase from the carelessness of the husbandman. Here, then, let those who are husbandmen in the Lord's field examine themselves, let them ask their conscience how they have acted in cultivating and in sowing. Those who have done so, especially in these times in which very few labour in cultivating the field of the Lord, have, we presume, little doubt that to themselves belongs the blame of the heresies which have grown rank in every part of the Church. But enough has been said by way of admonition concerning the evils which belong to the first head.

Let us come to the second, which relates to The Decay of Discipline, and what are called Abuses. Here it is of no use to spend time in inquiring who were the authors of those great evils, since beside ourselves no others can be named.

Let us therefore proceed to the third head, which relates to The Obstacles to the Peace of the Church, such as wars, domestic or foreign. For these long ago disturbed the peace of the Church, and disturb it still. Here we only say, that if war be (as God has shewn by infallible signs) the scourge by which He chastises us, then as we are guilty under the two former heads, in regard to which we cannot excuse ourselves, so we cannot deny that we are the principal cause of those wars. Such scourges, we presume, God sends in order to chastise us as sinners, and set before our eyes the very sins by which we have most grievously offended His majesty. Here let every one who has observed in what way the Church has been vexed by warlike violence, consider with himself what those things are in which the Church thereby suffers loss. Nor does it matter here of what kind of warfare we speak—whether of the intestine wars of our own princes, or the foreign wars of Turks, which of late years have brought great calamities upon us, or of the wars of those who have thrown off obedience to their pastors, and driven them from their sees. What we say applies in general to all kinds of warfare, including that of those who have wielded weapons against us—have banished pastors from their churches—confounded orders—substituted laymen in the room of bishops—plundered the property of the Church, and obstructed the course of the Word of God. Here we say, that if those who claim the name of pastors will but read what is contained in the book on the abuses of pastors, the greater part of them will find it stated, in express terms, that they have themselves committed them. For they will find that our ambition, our avarice, our passions first brought those evils on the people of God. Owing to them pastors were driven from their churches, and churches deprived of the nurture of the Word; the property of churches, which is the property of the poor, was taken from them; the priests' office was conferred on unworthy persons, and given to those differing in no respect from laity except in dress, and not even in this. Which of these things can we deny that we have done in recent years? Wherefore if the Turk, if heretics do the very same against us, what else do we behold than our own flagrant misdeeds, and at the same time see the just judgment of God—a judgment, however, fraught with mercy? For had He chastised us according to our deservings, we should long ago have been as Sodom and as Gomorrah.

But why do we now bring these things to mind? Is it for your confusion? Far from it. It is rather to admonish you as dear fathers and brethren, and first of all admonish ourselves how we may be able to avoid the scourges which now chastise us, and the severer scourges impending, unless we repent, that we may escape the dreadful judgment of God—dreadful indeed to all the impenitent, but especially to those who rule. Those who rule, says Scripture, will be severely judged. We see that judgment now begins at the house of God. While priests are cast out and trampled under feet of men, what else is indicated but the Divine judgment upon us, which our Saviour foretold when He said that His priests are the salt of the earth, but if the salt hath lost its savour, it is good for nothing but to be cast out and trodden under feet of men? All these things we now suffer. If it were for righteousness' sake, like our forefathers, happy were we; but now it is justly, because the salt has lost its savour. We do not at all suffer for righteousness' sake; for in all our afflictions we see the just judgment of God. Would, indeed, that we did see it; for this were the first step of escape from all the judgments and chastisements of God, and of entrance into favour and true glory.

It is this that has made us longer and stricter in calling these things to mind. For unless these things be known, and thoroughly understood, in vain do we enter the Council, in vain do we invoke the Holy Spirit, who always makes His first entrance into the soul of man by condemning the man himself, that He may convict the world of sin. Wherefore, unless that Spirit have first condemned us to ourselves, we may be assured that He has not entered into us, and will not even enter if we refuse to listen to our sins. For the same thing will be said to us which was said to the ancient people by the Prophet Ezekiel, when without acknowledging their sins, they wished to inquire at God through the Prophet. The Prophet speaks thus,—"The children of Israel came to me to inquire at the Lord, and sat before me. But thus saith the Lord, Have you come to inquire at Me? As I live, saith the Lord, I will not answer you." And He adds, "If you judge them, shew them the abominations of their fathers." In these words God shews why he refused to answer them, viz., because they had not yet listened to their own abominations and those of their fathers. Wherefore, seeing the Divine Spirit who then gave responses is the same whom we now invoke, while sitting before the Lord, you see what we have to do to procure a proper answer, and at the same time how necessary it was for us who preside in this sacred assembly to employ our first address in laying open our sins. . . .

This is perhaps the place where, after the example of the same Prophet whose words we have just quoted, we who are priests should not only confess our own sins, but those of the people and the princes, before God and His Church, and implore pardon for all. For Daniel speaks thus,—"When I was yet speaking and praying, and confessing my own sins and the sins of my people"—under the name of people in this place comprehending people of all ranks, as his confession just quoted declares. In this matter he seems plainly to intimate what we who have come hither for the safety of the whole Church, now suffering from so many evils, have to do, namely, with tears to confess our own sins, and also those of the princes and people, as we now do abundantly in the spirit of sorrow, but would do more exuberantly in words, were the princes themselves present to join us with their confession and their tears. But in such matters the sins of the priests, and princes, and people also, are bound together, as the Prophets express it, as with a rope of sins, so that it is difficult to inquire into the sins of one class, without at the same time making manifest the sins of other classes. Hence Ezekiel, accusing all classes in one continued discourse, thus speaks in the name of God among his ancient people. "Their priests have despised My law, and polluted My sanctuary. Their princes in the midst of them, like ravening wolves, in shedding blood, destroying souls, and greedily following after lucre, have made no distinction between sacred and profane. The nations of the earth uttered calumny." Would that these words were applicable to those times only, and did not exhibit an image of our own! Would that when we speak of the corruption of priests, we were able to affirm that princes and people have not given the greatest occasion, the largest materials and sanction to it! But let us now reserve our words for a more reasonable time, and open fountains of common tears. . . .

[CALVIN:] ON THE PREFATORY DISCOURSE BY THE LEGATES IN THE FIRST SESSION, AND OTHER PRELIMINARY MATTERS OF THE COUNCIL

It is well! At length the Romanists confess, that the fearful distraction of the Church at present, which all good men deplore, is in a great measure attributable to themselves. Any one, not very shrewd, on hearing this candid confession, will forthwith conceive good hopes. And the exhortations which follow exhibit no ordinary zeal for the renovation of the Church. Thus, that part in which they declare that none can succour their falling affairs save Christ the only Shepherd that therefore they must implore and listen to Him alone; that all will go prosperously if He guides all their actions and presides over them; that all other counsels, other arts, are but leaky cisterns which let out water; that the wisdom of man does nought but further provoke the anger of God, and increase evils rather than cure them—of all that part, I say—how strongly it breathes of piety! But it is apparent from the acts which followed, that those were vain words given to the winds. Nay, they do not wait till a judgment is formed from their acts. For in regard to the doctrine of salvation, which they have wholly adulterated by their impious and abominable fictions; in regard to the sacraments which they have utterly vitiated, and which they prostitute to a vile and shameless trafficking, they find nothing in themselves to correct. How little aid, then, do they bring to ruined affairs! And truly we can expect nothing from the Tridentines who serve under Neptune but what is of a watery nature, when the business to be undertaken is the Reformation of the Church. But when persecution is to rage against the innocent, and impious tyranny is to be confirmed by the blood of the godly, they at once blaze into flame. Indeed, something resembling this may be seen within the realm of Neptune, when with roaring noise he lashes the waves into foam. Soon, however, it bursts by its own tumescence, and the uproar immediately subsides. They, in like manner, as soon as the smoke has cleared away from their forehead, shew without disguise what the nature of their conduct is to be in regard to the principal head. They are to cling with a death-grasp to all their impieties, while we who desire nothing but the reign of Christ, and maintain the pure doctrine of the Gospel, are to be judged heretics. For thus, before cognisance is taken, they declare all heretical who have dared at this time to move a whit against the received doctrine of the Roman Church. What is this? The whole Christian world was in expectation of a Council in which controverted points might be regularly discussed. These men avow that they sit for no other end than to condemn whatever is not to their mind. Therefore, let no man any longer deceive himself: From their own mouths we hear that this pompous Council is held not for inquiry, but to establish that kind of doctrine, be it what it may, with which monks and sophists have imbued the world; that all rites shall remain by whatever superstition they may have crept in; and all the fetters of conscience be drawn into a tighter knot.

Can any one still be so stupid as to think of seeking any alleviation of our evils from a Council? We complain that the whole doctrine of godliness is adulterated by impious dogmas; that the whole worship of God is vitiated by foul and disgraceful superstitions; that the pure institution of the sacraments has been supplanted by horrible sacrilege; that their use has been converted into a profane trafficking; that poor souls, which ought to have been ruled by the doctrine of Christ, are oppressed by cruel bondage; that nothing is seen in the Christian Church that is not deformed and debased; that the grace of Christ not only lies half-buried, but is partly torn to pieces, partly altogether extinguished. All these complaints, which we have made for many years, and in published books, and which we make in our daily sermons, we are prepared to prove well founded, whenever a freedom of utterance is given. Such is the goodness of our cause, that it does not at all fear the light. And many are the tens of thousands so firmly persuaded of it, that they desired no farther investigation. Still, lest the Christian world might lay aside dissension, and unite in holy concord, a Council is summoned. Ought not its members to have discussed controverted points before they prejudged either themselves or others? They allow nothing of the kind. Nay, should any one have attempted to change one tittle of their customs, they hold him as already condemned.

Behold the specious Reformation, with the promise of which they have hitherto amused the world! The many portentous idolatries by which the Church of God is deformed—the many defilements of superstitions—the many profanations of sacred things—the vast sink of errors must not be touched. There is to be no diminution of the tyrannical yoke of impious laws by which miserable consciences have been ensnared; but all who desire any change are to be judged heretics. Where is that hearing which many were simple enough to promise themselves? If religion had any hold of their minds, nay, if they had any belief of a God, would they so confidently, and, as it were, in jest, skip over matters of so much moment? The glory of God is in question, the everlasting kingdom of Christ, the safety of the whole Church. They are compelled, in compliance so far with the common wishes of the Christian people, to hold a Council. They, however, premise, that they come for the very purpose of cutting off all hope of reform. For these words are the same in effect as if they had plainly and distinctly declared that the future would be no better than the past. And yet in thus acting they exhibit nothing foreign to their character. For in the overthrow of piety and the corruptions of sacred things, which in the present day all good men deplore, there is nothing of which those men who sit as judges do not deserve the blame. Do we wonder, then, if, while they themselves are the accused parties, they proceed forthwith, without touching the cause, to pass sentence in their own favour? It is more than absurd to leave the power of judging to those whose criminality is under discussion. And yet, what do they gain, but just to make all who have eyes aware that they do not in the least repent of their crimes while they pertinaciously defend everything of which we accuse them? They will not succeed, however, in getting a sanction to their impiety, because they are themselves obstinate.

Some one will now ask, What then do they hold forth as the benefits to be derived from a Council? To put an end to wars among Christian princes and give tranquillity to the Church. Folly! For who knows not that the Romanists are bellows which fan the flame of warlike commotions wherever their blast is applied? The only thing remaining, therefore, is to restore lapsed discipline, especially in their own clergy. With what faith they have exerted themselves in this direction is apparent from their acts; for they there, as we shall see, open up a way by which everything which has been allowed in time past is to be allowed in future. But to prevent it being thought that after all this costly show nothing has been done, there will, perhaps, be some reformation in caps and shoes, and other parts of dress. While they in this way mock God and men, they are not ashamed to personate the Prophets, as if the three Legates of Antichrist were the three intercessors of whom Ezekiel speaks, who first threw themselves into the breach to appease the anger of God. They make an humble confession of sins—they mention groans and tears, the signs of repentance. I believe the person employed as their reader on this occasion must have found it difficult to keep from laughing. . . .

SECOND DECREE OF THE FOURTH SESSION

Moreover, the foresaid Holy Council considering that it may confer no small benefit on the Church of God, if from among all the Latin editions of the Sacred Books which are in use, it notifies what one is to be held authentic, it statutes and declares that the ancient Vulgate edition, approved by its long use for so many centuries in the Church itself, be held authentic in public lectures, debates, sermons, and expositions; and that no man is to dare or presume on any pretext to reject it.

Besides, in order to curb petulant minds, the Council decrees that no man trusting to his own wisdom, in matters of faith and discipline pertaining to the edification of Christian doctrine, twisting the Sacred Scripture to his own sense, dare to interpret the Holy Scripture contrary to that sense which holy mother Church, to whom it belongs to judge of the true sense and interpretations of the Holy Scriptures, has held and holds, or even contrary to the unanimous consent of the Fathers, even though these interpretations are never to be published. Let those who contravene be denounced by the ordinaries, and punished with the pains appointed by law. . . .

[CALVIN ON THE FOURTH SESSION]

In condemning all translations except the Vulgate, as the error is more gross, so the edict is more barbarous. The sacred oracles of God were delivered by Moses and the Prophets in Hebrew, and by the Apostles in Greek. That no corner of the world might be left destitute of so great a treasure, the gift of interpretation was added. It came to pass—I know not by what means, but certainly neither by judgment nor right selection—that of the different versions, one became the favourite of the unlearned, or those at least who, not possessing any knowledge of languages, desired some kind of help to their ignorance. Those, on the other hand, who are acquainted with the languages perceive that this version teems with innumerable errors; and this they make manifest by the clearest evidence. On the other hand, the Fathers of Trent contend, that although the learned thus draw the pure liquor from the very fountain, and convict the infallible Vulgate of falsehood, they are not to be listened to. No man possessed of common sense ever presumed to deprive the Church of God of the benefit of learning. The ancients, though unacquainted with the languages, especially with Hebrew, always candidly acknowledge that nothing is better than to consult the original, in order to obtain the true and genuine meaning. I will go further. There is no man of ordinary talent who, on comparing the Vulgate version with some others, does not easily see that many things which were improperly rendered by it are in these happily restored. The Council, however, insists that we shall shut our eyes against the light that we may spontaneously go astray.

Who could have imagined they would be so senseless as thus boldly to despise the judgments of good men, and hesitate not to make themselves odious and detestable to all? Those who were aware that they had nothing useful in view, were yet persuaded that they would make some show of it to the world, and assign to some of their sworn adherents the task of executing a new version. In this instance, however, they use no deceit. They not only order us to be contented with a most defective translation, but insist on our worshipping it, just as if it had come down from heaven; and while the blemishes are conspicuous to all, they prohibit us from desiring any improvement. Behold the men on whose judgment the renovation of the Church depends! . . .

I come to the right of interpreting, which they arrogate to themselves whenever the meaning is doubtful. It is theirs, they say, to give the meaning of Scripture, and we must acquiesce. For everything which they bestow upon the Church they bestow upon themselves. I acknowledge, indeed, that as Scripture came not by the private will of man (2 Pet. i. 21), it is unbecoming to wrest it to the private sense of any man. Nay, in the case of an obscure passage, when it is doubtful what sense ought to be adopted, there is no better way of arriving at the true meaning than for pious doctors to make common inquiry, by engaging in religious discussion. But that is not now the question. They wish, by their tyrannical edict, to deprive the Church of all liberty, and arrogate to themselves a boundless license; for, be the meaning which they affix to Scripture what it may, it must be immediately embraced. Except themselves, moreover, no man will be permitted to prove anything out of Scripture. Would that they were equal to the performance of so great a task. But oxen usurp the reins, or rather asses the lyre. In short, their aim is to make all revere a Scripture hidden in darkness like the mysteries of Ceres, and let none presume to aspire to the understanding of it.

There would be no end were I to collect all the examples which would make it plain to my readers what fetters of iniquitous and intolerable slavery are forged by this decree. I will therefore give a specimen, in the case of only one Council. About the year 800 was held a Council of Nice, which both restored images that had been overthrown under Leo and decreed that they were to be worshipped. That Council, because it supports idolatry, the Papists deem holy and lawful. Hence, according to their axiom, it cannot have erred in the exposition of Scripture. But if such interpreters of sacred things are to be listened to (it is abominable to say they are), the religion of the Egyptians will be preferable to the Christian. To prove from Scripture that churches were properly adorned with images and pictures, the following passages were adduced: —"God created man after His own image and likeness;" "Joshua erected twelve stones;" "No man lighteth a candle and putteth it under a bushel;" whence they inferred that images were to be placed upon altars! Again, "The light of Thy countenance has been stamped upon us;" "As we have heard, so have we also seen;" "O Lord, I have loved the beauty of Thy house;" "Shew me Thy face, for it is lovely." In support of adoration, they wrested the following passages:—"Abraham worshipped the people of the land;" "Jacob set up an inscription, and blessed." Again, "He worshipped the top of the staff of his son Joseph;" "All the rich among the people will deprecate Thy countenance;" "Worship His footstool;" "God is to be admired in His saints." And that nothing might be wanting to crown their effrontery, they appended out of another psalm, "His saints who are on the earth." This they applied to images!

I am aware that the narrative I now give will scarcely seem credible. I was myself amazed when I read it, though our ears should long ago have been trained by them to any absurdities, however enormous. Were I to collect all their interpretations, which even children would laugh at, and not even all, but those which are distinguished by some notable absurdity, I would require to form a volume thrice as large as the Bible.

The sum is, that the spirit of Trent wished, by this decree, that Scripture should only signify to us whatever dreaming monks might choose. For what else do they mean by the Church? Though the Roman bishops, I mean all who serve under the banner and auspices of that Anti-Christian See, were to assemble from every quarter of the world, how, pray, could they, by laying their heads together, frame a proper version for us? Many of them hardly knew the elements of grammar. At least, they will not venture to deny that there is scarcely one in a hundred who has read an entire book of the Prophets, or one of the Apostolical Epistles, or one of the Gospels. They are too much occupied with other cares to have any leisure for sacred literature. The only resource is, to reserve the privilege for the Apostolic See, and say that the interpretation of Scripture must be sought from the holy lips of Paul Farnese! Otherwise, let them shew us a Church which may justly be deemed able to sustain so great a burden. For, how highly soever they may extol the Roman See, they can never persuade some men either that Cephas is its head, or that chaste and holy marriage is the carnal life which is accursed in the sight of God. Both of these have been asserted in Papal responses. They cry out that the whole authority of the Church must fall if it is denied the right of interpreting Scripture—that a door would thus be thrown open to lascivious minds, allowing them to break through every restraint. Nay, in order to cast obloquy upon us, they are wont to charge us with arrogating the interpretation of Scripture to ourselves, in order that there may be no check on our licentiousness. Modesty will not allow me to speak of ourselves as fact would justify; and yet I will most truly declare that we have thrown more light upon the Scriptures than all the doctors who have appeared under the Papacy since its commencement. This praise even they themselves dare not deny us. Still there is none of us who does not willingly submit his lucubrations to the judgment of the Church. Therefore we neither contemn nor impair the authority of the Church; nor do we give loose reins to men to dare what they please. I wish they would shew us such a Church as Scripture itself portrays; we should easily agree as to the respect due to it. But when, falsely assuming the name of Church, they seize upon the spoils of which they have robbed it, what else can we do than protest?

SIXTH SESSION OF THE COUNCIL OF TRENT

Of the Incapability of Nature and the Law to Justify Men

II   The Holy Council declares that to understand the doctrine of Justification properly and purely, it is necessary for every one to acknowledge and confess, that when all had lost their innocence by the transgression of Adam, had become impure, and as the Apostle says, by nature children of wrath, as has been explained in the decree concerning Original Sin, they were so much the servants of sin and under the power of the devil and of death, that not only the Gentiles by the power of nature, but even the Jews by the very letter of the law of Moses, could not be freed therefrom, or rise, notwithstanding that free-will was by no means extinguished in them, though weakened in its powers and under a bias. . . .

Of the Necessity of Preparation in Adults for Justification, and Whence It Is

VI   The Council declares that the commencement of this justification in adults is to be derived from the preventing grace of God through Jesus Christ; that is, from His calling, by which they are called without any existing merits of their own, so that those who, by sins, were alienated from God, are, by His exciting and assisting grace, disposed to turn in order to their own justification, by assenting freely to the same grace, and co-operating with it. Thus, while God touches the heart of man by the illumination of His Spirit, man himself does nothing at all in receiving that inspiration, for he can reject it; and yet he cannot of his own free will, without the grace of God, make a movement towards justification before Him. Hence, in the Sacred Scriptures, when it is said, "Turn ye unto Me, and I will turn unto you," we are reminded of our freedom; and when we reply, "Turn thou us, O Lord, and we shall be turned," we acknowledge that we are prevented by the grace of God. . . .

What Is the Justification of the Ungodly Man, and What Are Its Causes

VIII   This preparation or disposition is followed by justification, which is not the mere forgiveness of sins, but also Sanctification, and the renewal of the inner man, by the voluntary reception of grace and gifts; whence the man from unrighteous becomes righteous, from an enemy becomes a friend, so as to be heir according to the hope of eternal life. The causes of justification are these:—The final cause is the glory of God and Christ, and eternal life: the efficient cause is a merciful God, Who freely washes and sanctifies, sealing and anointing with the Holy Spirit of promise, which is a pledge of our inheritance: The meritorious cause is His beloved, only-begotten Son, our Lord Jesus Christ, Who, when we were enemies, because of the great love wherewith He loved us, by His own most holy passion on the wood of the cross, merited justification, and gave satisfaction to the Father for us: The instrumental cause is the sacrament of baptism, which is the sacrament of faith, without which justification is never obtained: In fine, the only formal cause is the righteousness of God, not that by which He Himself is righteous, but that by which He makes us righteous, *i.e.,* by which He presents us with it, we are renewed in the spirit of our mind, and are not only reputed, but are truly called and are righteous, each one of us receiving His righteousness in ourselves according to the measure which the Holy Spirit imparts to each as He pleases, and according to the proper disposition and co-operation of each. For although no man can be righteous unless the merits of Christ's passion are communicated to him, that takes place in this justification of the ungodly, when, by the merit of the same holy passion, the love of God is diffused by the Holy Spirit in the hearts of those who are justified, and inheres in them. Hence, in justification itself, along with the remission of sins, man receives, through Jesus Christ, in whom he is ingrafted, all these things infused at the same time, viz., faith, hope, and charity; for faith, unless hope and charity are added to it, neither unites perfectly with Christ, nor forms a living member of His body; for which reason it is most truly said that faith without works would be dead and inoperative, and that in Christ Jesus neither circumcision nor uncircumcision availeth anything, but faith which worketh by love. This faith, before the sacrament of baptism, catechumens, in accordance with the tradition of the Apostles, seek from the Church when they seek faith producing eternal life; which life faith cannot produce without hope and charity. Hence also they immediately hear the words of Christ, "If ye would enter into life, keep the commandments." Therefore, receiving true and Christian righteousness as a first robe, instead of that one which Adam lost by his disobedience—lost both for himself and for us—a fair and immaculate robe, presented to them by Jesus Christ, which, on being born again, they are enjoined to preserve, that they may produce it before the tribunal of our Lord Jesus Christ, and have eternal life. . . .

Against the Vain Confidence of Heretics

X   But although it is necessary to believe that sins neither are remitted, nor have ever been remitted, except freely by the Divine mercy through Christ, it is not be said to any one boasting a confidence and certainty of the forgiveness of his sins, that his sins are forgiven, or have been forgiven; seeing this vain confidence, totally remote from piety, may exist in heretics and schismatics, nay, in our own time does exist, and is extolled with great hostility to the Catholic Church. Neither is it to be asserted that it becomes those who are truly justified to determine with themselves, without any kind of doubt, that they are truly justified, and that no man is absolved from sin and justified, save he who assuredly believes that he is acquitted and justified, and that acquittal and justification are obtained by this faith alone; as if any one who does not believe this were doubting the promise of God and the efficacy of the death and resurrection of Christ. For as no pious man ought to doubt of the mercy of God, the merit of Christ, and the virtue and efficacy of the sacraments, so every one, while he beholds his own weakness and disinclination, may be in fear and dread respecting his own gracious state; seeing that no man can know with a certainty of faith, as to which there can be no lurking error, that he has obtained the grace of God. . . .

Canons

IV Whosoever shall say that the free-will of man, moved and excited by God, does not at all co-operate with God when exciting and calling, that thus he may dispose and prepare himself for obtaining the grace of justification, and that he cannot dissent though he wills it, but like something inanimate does nothing at all, and acts passively merely, let him be anathema.

V Whosoever shall say that the free-will of man was lost and extinguished after Adam's sin, or that it is a thing of name merely, or a name without a thing, in short, a figment introduced into the Church by Satan, let him be anathema.

VI Whosoever shall say that it is not in the power of man to make his ways evil, but that God produces bad works as well as good, not permissively only, but properly and of Himself, so that the treachery of Judas is no less His proper work than the calling of Paul, let him be anathema. . . .

IX Whosoever shall say that the wicked is justified by faith alone, in such a sense that nothing else is required in the way of co-operation to obtain the grace of justification, and that it is in no respect necessary that he be prepared and disposed by the movement of his own will, let him be anathema. . . .

XVII Whosoever shall say that the grace of justification falls to none but those predestinated unto life, and that all others who are called are called indeed, but do not receive grace, as being predestinated by the Divine power to evil, let him be anathema.

XVIII Whosoever shall say that the commandments of God are impossible of observance even to a justified man, and to one constituted under grace, let him be anathema. . . .

XX Whosoever shall say that a justified man, however perfect, is not bound to the observance of the commandments of God and the Church, but only to believe as if the Gospel were a naked and absolute promise of eternal life, without the condition of observing the commandments, let him be anathema. . . .

[CALVIN:] ON THE SIXTH SESSION OF THE COUNCIL OF TRENT

The doctrine of man's justification would be easily explained, did not the false opinions by which the minds of men are preoccupied, spread darkness over the clear light. The principal cause of obscurity, however, is, that we are with the greatest difficulty induced to leave the glory of righteousness entire to God alone. For we always desire to be somewhat, and such is our folly, we even think we are. As this pride was innate in man from the first, so it opened a door for Satan to imbue them with many impious and vicious conceits with which we have this day to contend. And in all ages there have been sophists exercising their pen in extolling human righteousness, as they knew it would be popular. When by the singular kindness of God, the impiety of Pelagius was repudiated with the common consent of the ancient Church, they no longer dared to talk so pertly of human merit. They, however, devised a middle way, by which they might not give God the whole in justification, and yet give something.

This is the moderation which the venerable Fathers adopt to correct the errors on justification, which, they say, have arisen in our day. Such indeed is their mode of prefacing, that at the outset they breathe nothing but Christ; but when they come to the subject, far are they from leaving Him what is His own. Nay, their definition at length contains nothing else than the trite dogma of the schools: that men are justified partly by the grace of God and partly by their own works; thus only shewing themselves somewhat more modest than Pelagius was.

This will easily be shewn to be the fact. For under the *second* head, where they treat of Original Sin, they declare that free-will, though impaired in its powers and biassed, is not however extinguished. I will not dispute about a name, but since they contend that liberty has by no means been extinguished, they certainly understand that the human will has still some power left to choose good. For where death is not, there is at least some portion of life. They themselves remove all ambiguity when they call it impaired and biassed. Therefore, if we believe them, Original Sin has weakened us, so that the defect of our will is not pravity but weakness. For if the will were wholly depraved, its health would not only be impaired but lost until it were renewed. The latter, however, is uniformly the doctrine of Scripture. To omit innumerable passages where Paul discourses on the nature of the human race, he does not charge free-will with weakness, but declares all men to be useless, alienated from God, and enslaved to the tyranny of sin; so much so, that he says they are unfit to think a good thought. (Rom. iii. 12; 2 Cor. iii. 5.) We do not however deny, that a will, though bad, remains in man. For the fall of Adam did not take away the will, but made it a slave where it was free. It is not only prone to sin, but is made subject to sin. Of this subject we shall again speak by and bye. . . .

In the *sixth* head, they assert that we are prepared by the grace of God for receiving justification, but they assign to this grace the office of exciting and assisting, we ourselves freely co-operating; in other words, we are here treated with the inanities which the sophists are wont to babble in the schools. But I ask, Is it the same thing to excite a will, and aid it when in itself weak, as to form a new heart in man, so as to make him willing? Let them answer, then, whether creating a new heart, and making a heart of flesh out of a heart of stone, (both of which the Scripture declares that God does in us), is nothing else than to supply what is wanting to a weak will. But if they are not moved by these passages, let them say whether He who makes us to be willing simply assists the will. Paul claims the whole work for God; they ascribe nothing to Him but a little help. But for what do they join man as an associate with God?

Because man, though he might repudiate it, freely accepts the grace of God and the illumination of the Holy Spirit. How greatly do they detract from the work of God as described by the Prophet!—"I will put my law," says he, "in your hearts, and make you to walk in my precepts." Jer. xxxii. 39; Ezek. xxxvi. 27; Heb. viii. 10; x. 16.

Is this the doctrine delivered by Augustine, when he says, "Men labour to find in our will some good thing of our own not given us of God; what they can find I know not?" (Aug. Lib. de Precator. Merit. et Remiss. 2.) Indeed, as he elsewhere says, "Were man left to his own will to remain under the help of God if he chooses, while God does not make him willing, among temptations so numerous and so great, the will would succumb from its own weakness. Succour, therefore, has been brought to the weakness of the human will by divine grace acting irresistibly and inseparably, that thus the will however weak might not fail." (Aug. de Corruptione et Gratia.) But the Neptunian fathers, in a new smithy, forge what was unknown to Augustine, viz., that the reception of grace is not of God, inasmuch as it is by the free movement of our own will we assent to God calling. This is repugnant to Scripture, which makes God the author of a good will. It is one thing for the will to be moved by God to obey if it pleases, and another for it to be formed to be good. Moreover, God promises not to act so that we may be able to will well, but to make us will well. Nay, He goes farther when He says, "I will make you to walk;" as was carefully observed by Augustine. The same thing is affirmed by Paul when he teaches, that "it is God that worketh in us both to will and to do of His good pleasure." The hallucination of these Fathers is in dreaming that we are offered a movement which leaves us an intermediate choice, while they never think of that effectual working by which the heart of man is renewed from pravity to rectitude. But this effectual working of the Holy Spirit is described in the thirty-second chapter of Jeremiah, where he thus speaks in the name of God, "I will put the fear of My name into their hearts, that they decline not from My commandments." In short, their error lies in making no distinction between the grace of Regeneration, which now comes to the succour of our wretchedness, and the first grace which had been given to Adam. This Augustine carefully expounds. "Through Christ the Mediator," he says, "God makes those who were wicked to be good for ever after. The first man had not that grace by which he could never wish to be bad; for the help given him was of that nature that he might abandon it when he would, and remain in it if he would, but it was not such as to make him willing. The grace of the second Adam is more powerful. It makes us will, will so strongly and love so ardently, that by the will of the spirit we overcome the will of the flesh lusting against it." A little farther on he says, "Through this grave of God in receiving good and persevering therein, there is in us a power not only to be able to do what we will, but to will what we are able." (Aug. Lib. ad Bonif. 2, c. 8.) Although the subject is too long to be despatched thus briefly, I feel confident that my statement, though short, will suffice with readers of sense to refute these fancies. . . .

The whole dispute is as to The Cause of Justification. The Fathers of Trent pretend that it is twofold, as if we were justified partly by forgiveness of sins and partly by spiritual regeneration; or, to express their view in other words, as if our righteousness were composed partly of imputation, partly of quality. I maintain that it is one, and simple, and is wholly included in the gratuitous acceptance of God. I besides hold that it is without us, because we are righteous in Christ only. Let them produce evidence from Scripture, if they have any, to convince us of their doctrine. I, while I have the whole Scripture supporting me, will now be satisfied with this one reason, viz., that when mention is made of the righteousness of works, the law and the Gospel place it in the perfect obedience of the law; and as that nowhere appears, they leave us no alternative but to flee to Christ alone, that we may be regarded as righteous in Him, not being so in ourselves. Will they produce to us one passage which declares that begun newness of life is approved by God as righteousness either in whole or in part? But if they are devoid of authority, why may we not be permitted to repudiate the figment of partial justification which they here obtrude? . . . .

In the *tenth* chapter, they inveigh against what they call The Vain Confidence of Heretics. This consists, according to their definition, in our holding it as certain that our sins are forgiven, and resting in this certainty. But if such certainty makes heretics, where will be the happiness which David extols? (Psalm xxxii.) Nay, where will be the peace of which Paul discourses in the fifth chapter to the Romans, if we rest in anything but the good-will of God? How, moreover, have we God propitious, but just because He enters not into judgment with us? They acknowledge that sins are never forgiven for Christ's sake, except freely, but leaving it in suspense to whom and when they are forgiven, they rob all consciences of calm placid confidence. Where, then, is that boldness of which Paul elsewhere speaks, (Eph. iii. 12), that access with confidence to the Father through faith in Christ? Not contented with the term confidence, he furnishes us with boldness, which is certainly something more than certainty. And what shall we say to his own occasional use of the term certainty? (Rom. viii. 37.) This certainty he founds upon nothing but a mere persuasion of the free love of God. Nay, they overthrow all true prayer to God, when they keep pious minds suspended by fear which alone shuts the door of access against us. "He who doubts," says James, (James i. 6), "is like a wave of the sea driven by the wind." Let not such think that they shall obtain anything of the Lord. "Let him who would pray effectually not doubt." Attend to the antithesis between faith and doubt, plainly intimating that faith is destroyed as soon as certainty is taken away. . . . .

[CALVIN:] ANTIDOTE TO THE CANONS OF THE COUNCIL OF TRENT

Canon IV

This was answered above, when I explained how free-will assents to God calling and exciting it. We certainly obey God with our will, but it is with a will which He has formed in us. Those, therefore, who ascribe any proper movement to free-will, apart from the grace of God, do nothing else than rend the Holy Spirit. Paul declares, not that a faculty of willing is given to us, but that the will itself is formed in us, (Phil. ii. 13), so that from none else but God is the assent or obedience of a right will. He acts within, holds our hearts, moves our hearts, and draws us by the inclinations which He has produced in us. So says Augustine. (Lib. de Corrupt. et Grat., c. 14.) What preparation can there be in a heart of iron, until by a wondrous change it begins to be a heart of flesh? This, as the Prophet declares, is entirely the work of God. The will of man will, indeed, dissent from God, so long as it continues contrary, but when it has been framed for obedience, the danger of dissenting is removed. But that the efficacy of divine grace is such, that all opposition is beaten down, and we who were unwilling are made obedient, it is not we who assent, but the Lord by the Prophet, when He promises that He will make us to walk in His precepts; and Christ also, when He says, "Whosoever hath heard of My Father cometh unto Me." (John vi. 45.)

Canon V

Let us not raise a quarrel about a word. But as by free-will they understand a faculty of choice perfectly free and unbiassed to either side, those who affirm that this is merely to use a name without a substance, have the authority of Christ when He says, that they are free whom the Son makes free, and that all others are the slaves of sin. Freedom and slavery are certainly contrary to each other. As to the term itself, let them hear Augustine, who maintains that the human will is not free so long as it is subject to passions which vanquish and enthral it. (Epist. 144, ad Anastas.) Elsewhere he says, "The will being vanquished by the depravity into which it has fallen, nature is without freedom." (Hom. 3, in Joann.) Again, "Man making a bad use of free-will lost both himself and it." Again, "Man received great powers of free-will when he was created, but lost them by sinning. Foolish men consider not that in the term free-will freedom is implied. But if they are the slaves of sin, why do they boast of free-will? For of whom a man is overcome, to the same is he bound a slave." Nay, in another place he openly derides the name. "The will," says he, "is free, not freed—free to righteousness, the slave of sin! Why, then, do they so much inflame miserable men by reminding them of their slavery, but just that they might learn to flee to the deliverer?" (Aug. de Perfect. Justit. Lib. de Verb. Apost. Serm. 3; De Spiritu et Litera, c. 30; De Corrupt. et Grat., c. 13.)

Canon VI

As I abhor paradox, I readily repudiate the saying that the treachery of Judas is as properly the work of God as the calling of Paul. But they never will convince any man that God only acts permissively in the wicked, except it be one who is ignorant of the whole doctrine of Scripture. When it is said that the reprobate are set apart to execute the work of God; that His are the snares, swords, and axes which are directed by His hand; that His hiss arouses them to execute what His hand and counsel have decreed; that Christ was slain by the Jews by the determinate counsel of God, (Isaiah x. 5; Ezek. xvii. 20; xxxii. 2; Psalm xvii. 13; Acts ii. 4, 23), the words are too strong to be evaded by the subterfuge of permission. Augustine interprets better. After quoting the passages of Scripture in which the Father is said to have delivered up the Son, and Christ to have delivered Himself, he immediately adds, "What, then, did Judas do but sin?" Nor can he be justly blamed for saying elsewhere, that "God worketh in the hearts of men to incline their wills as He pleaseth, whether to good, of His mercy, or to evil, according to their deservings, and that by His judgment, sometimes open, sometimes hidden, but always just;" for he immediately adds the qualification, that "the malice is not His." (De Verb. Dom. Serm. 63.) In like manner he had said a little before, "He does not command the wicked by ordering, in which case obedience would be laudable, but by His secret and just judgment He bends their will, already bad by their own depravity, to this misdeed or that." (Aug. de Gr. et Lib. Arb. c. 21.) For there is nothing here but what the Scriptures teach almost in the same words when they speak of *inclining* and *turning, hardening* and *doing.* . . .

Canon IX

This Canon is very far from being canonical; for it joins things which are utterly at variance. They imagine that a man is justified by faith without any movement of his own will, as if it were not with the heart that a man believeth unto righteousness. Between them and us there is this difference, that they persuade themselves that the movement comes from the man himself, whereas we maintain that faith is voluntary, because God draws our wills to Himself. Add, that when we say a man is justified by faith alone, we do not fancy a faith devoid of charity, but we mean that faith alone is the cause of justification. . . .

Canon XVII

The words of Luke are, "All who had been pre-ordained to life believed." (Acts xiii. 48.) He intimates whence it was that in one audience such a difference existed that some believed, and others persisted in their obstinacy. In like manner Paul asserts, that those are called whom God has previously chosen. (Rom. viii. 29.) Are not also the reprobate called? Not effectually. For there is this difference in the calling of God, that He invites all indiscriminately by His word, whereas He inwardly calls the elect alone, as Christ says, "All that the Father hath given Me will come to Me." (John vi. 37.) In short, if any man is ignorant that the Spirit of regeneration is given to none but the regenerate, I know not what part of Scripture he holds.

Canon XVIII

Were Regeneration perfected in this life the observance of the law would be possible. But seeing that believers as long as they live here only perceive the goal at a distance, and with much difficulty keep panting towards it, where is the perfection of obedience, of which those men dream, to be found? But there is no wonder that they prate so boldly of things they know not. War is pleasant to those who never tried it. . . .

Canon XX

While no sane man will strike off the yoke of God from the shoulders of believers, as if they behoved not to keep His Commandments, it must still be understood that assurance of salvation by no means depends on the observance of them. For the words of Paul always hold true, that the difference between the Law and the Gospel lies in this, that the latter does not like the former promise life under the condition of works, but from faith. What can be clearer than the antithesis—"The righteousness of the law is in this wise, The man who doeth these things shall live in them. But the righteousness which is of faith speaketh thus, Whoso believeth," &c. (Rom. x. 5.) To the same effect is this other passage, "If the inheritance were of the law, faith would be made void and the promise abolished. Therefore it is of faith that in respect of grace the promise might be sure to every one that believeth." (Rom. iv. 14.) As to ecclesiastical laws, they must themselves see to them: we acknowledge one Legislator, to whom it belongs to deliver the rule of life, as from Him we have life.

SEVENTH SESSION OF THE COUNCIL OF TRENT

[Canons] of the Sacraments in General

I Whosoever shall say that the Sacraments of the New Law were not all instituted by our Lord Jesus Christ, and are either more or fewer than seven, viz., Baptism, Confirmation, the Eucharist, Penance, Extreme Unction, Orders, and Matrimony, or even that any one of these seven is not truly and properly a Sacrament, let him be anathema. . . .

IV Whosoever shall say that the Sacraments of the New Law are not necessary to salvation, but superfluous, and that without them or a wish for them, men by faith alone obtain the grace of justification, though all are not necessary for each, let him be anathema. . . .

X Whosoever shall say that all Christians have right to administer the word and all the Sacraments, let him be anathema. . . .

XIII Whosoever shall say that the received and approved Rites of the Catholic Church, accustomed to be used in the solemn administration of the Sacraments, may either be despised or omitted, at pleasure, by the minister, without sin, or changed into other new rites, by any pastors of churches, let him be anathema.

Decrees on Residence

The same Holy Council, the same Legates presiding, intending to prosecute the business of Residence and Reformation already commenced, unto the praise of God and increase of the Christian Religion, have thought proper to enact as follows, always without prejudice to the authority of the Apostolic See.

For the government of Cathedral Churches, let no one, unless born of lawful wedlock, and of mature age, gravity of manners, and skill in literature, according to the constitution of Alexander III., which begins, "Whereas in all," promulgated in the Lateran Council, be held qualified.

Let no man, however conspicuous in dignity, rank, or pre-eminence, presume either to accept or hold at the same time more than one Metropolitan or Cathedral Church by title or *in Commendam,* or under any other name, contrary to the ordinances of the Sacred Canons, since he is to be regarded as very happy to whose lot it has fallen to govern one Church well and fruitfully, and with safety to the souls committed to him. Let those who now hold several Churches, contrary to the tenor of the present decree, after choosing the one which they wish to retain, be bound to demit the others within six months, if they are at the free disposal of the Apostolic See, or, if otherwise, within a year. Otherwise let the Churches themselves, the last obtained only excepted, be considered *ipso facto* vacant.

Let inferior Ecclesiastical Benefices, especially those having a cure of souls, be conferred on fit and worthy persons, who may be able to reside on the spot, and discharge the cure in person, according to the constitution of Alexander III. in the Lateran

Council, beginning, "As some," and another of Gregory, published in the General Council of Lyons, beginning, "Although the Canon." Let any collation or provision made otherwise be held null and void, and let the ordinary giving collation know that he will incur the penalties of the constitution of the General Council, beginning, "Too heavy.". . .

Let Ecclesiastical Benefices with cure, which are found perpetually united and annexed to Cathedral, Collegiate, or other Churches, and also Monastries, Benefices, or Colleges, or pious places whatsoever, be visited every year by the Ordinaries of the places, who must be solicitously careful to provide that the cure of souls be laudably performed by fit perpetual vicars, (unless a different arrangement should seem to said Ordinaries to be expedient for the good government of the Churches), to be appointed to the same by them, with a portion (greater or less, at the discretion of said Ordinaries) of the thirds of the fruits to be allocated over a certain subject,— appeals, privileges, exemptions, even with the deputations of judges, and any interdicts of theirs whatsoever being of no force in the matters aforesaid.

Let the Ordinaries of the places be bound to visit all Churches whatsoever, however exempted, once a year with Apostolical authority; and provide, by suitable remedies of law, that those things which need reparation be repaired, and the Churches be by no means defrauded of the cure of souls (if any belongs to them) and other due services; appeals, privileges, customs, even those having the prescription of time immemorial, the deputations of judges and their interdicts being utterly excluded. . . .

[CALVIN:] ANTIDOTE TO THE SEVENTH SESSION

Canon I

They insist that Seven Sacraments were instituted by Christ. Why, then, did they not order Him to institute them? The number Seven which they place under the sanction of an anathema has not only no support from Scripture, but none even from any approved author. This is little. Of the Sacraments which they enumerate we shew that some were temporary, as the anointing of the sick, and others, falsely so called, as matrimony. The arguments by which we evince this are plain and strong. What! will they boast that they have the gift of healing? If anointing is the symbol of that gift, are they not apes when they use it without the reality? Again, what promise is there in this ceremony that has any application to us? If a sacrament consists of spiritual grace and an external sign, where will they find anything of the kind in penance? For giving marriage this name they have no other reason than the gross ignorance of the monks, who reading in the Epistle to the Ephesians (Eph. v. 32) the word *sacrament* used instead of *mystery,* and that concerning the secret union between Christ and His Church, transferred it to marriage. Of all these things our writings contain clear and copious demonstrations, which the good Fathers refute by the one vocable *anathema.* This is to conquer without a contest, or rather to triumph without a victory! . . .

Canon IV

I will readily allow that the use of those things which Christ gave us as helps to salvation is necessary, that is, when an opportunity is given: although believers are always to be reminded that there is no other necessity for any sacrament than that of an instrumental cause, to which the power of God is by no means to be tied down. Every pious person must with his whole heart shudder at the expression that the things are superfluous. But here the worthy Fathers, with their usual stupidity, perceive not that whatever grace is conferred upon us by the Sacraments, is nevertheless to be ascribed to faith. He who separates faith from the Sacraments, does just as if he were to take the soul away from the body. Therefore, as we exclude not the doctrine of the Gospel when we say that we obtain the grace of Christ by faith alone, so neither do we exclude the Sacraments, the nature of which is the same, as they are seals of the Gospel. . . .

Canon X

No sound Christian makes all men equal in the administration of Word and Sacraments, not only because all things ought to be done in the Church decently and in order, but also because, by the special command of Christ, Ministers are ordained for that purpose. Therefore, as a special call is required, no man who is not called may take the honour upon himself. Moreover, where do they find the office of baptizing enjoined on women, as they permit them to do? . . .

Canon XIII

What they mean by the received and approved Rites of the Church every one is aware. Hence by this *caveat* they establish whatever superstitions human presumption has superinduced on the pure ordinances of the Lord. The genuine rite of Baptism is simple, and the administration of the Supper simple, if we look to what the Lord has enjoined. But under how many, and how various and discordant additions has this simplicity been buried? They will say, that if there is any excess, it behoves to be rescinded—only, however, if they think so. But what hope do they give us, when with bacchanalian fury they belch forth their anathemas against whosover permits himself to omit one little ceremony? All the godly complain, or at least regret, that in Baptism more is made of the chrism, the taper, the salt, the spittle in fine, than the washing with water, in which the whole perfection of Baptism consists. They deplore that the Supper has not only been vitiated by impure additions, but converted into a kind of spurious show. According to the Fathers of Trent, nothing can be so monstrous as not to find a place among the approved rites of the Catholic Church. Augustine, even in his time, complained that the Church was burdened with a Jewish bondage, though the rites then in use were scarcely a tenth part of those the observance of which is now more rigidly required than that of any human or divine law. The men of Trent deliberate as to what should be done, and then, without holding out any hope of relief, launch curses and imprecations at all who will not submit to every iota of the usages prescribed!

[CALVIN:] ANTIDOTE TO THE SUBSEQUENT CANONS ON RESIDENCE

I sometimes wonder how it happens that, in such light of the Gospel, they are just as absurd as they were wont to be in the thickest darkness. But I immediately turn to reflect on the admirable judgment of God, by which it is certain that they are so blinded and stupified, that, lost both to sight and feeling, they cast away all shame, and glory unblushingly in their own disgrace. Since the provisions of the Church, which were destined for the maintenance of pastors long ago, have begun to be the revenues of idle men, and those who are maintained at the expense of the Church think that no obligation lies upon them, they profess to have prepared themselves for the correction of this great iniquity. When they enter upon the subject they seem to say something. Where corruption is so rampant, it is, I admit, no small matter that two bishoprics are not to be held by one man. And there are other things of a similar nature, framed to curb the licentiousness which now stalks abroad, although in any reformation which they attempt, they are far, I say not from the primitive and austerer discipline which flourished a thousand years ago, but from any tolerable state of pious and well ordered government. They forbid a Bishop to absent himself from his diocese for more than half a year. The leave is liberal enough which gives six months' vacation out of twelve to those who ought to watch continually over the flock, both day and night. But even here a reservation is added—unless they have a just excuse for absence. When will they be without such excuse? And yet, supposing they most strictly observe what is here prescribed, what benefit will result, unless, perhaps, that they will not be able to carry out of the district all the money which the living yields? If they love the city, they will have their palaces where, away from all noise, they will drink, play, and sleep as usual; if they prefer the country, they will have pleasant retreats in their seats and castles. Thus they will perform their office doing nothing, and yet giving actual residence. . . .

I will spend no more time in exposing their impudence. But as all see that they are worse than hopeless, every one who is wise will in future disregard their decrees, and be in no dubiety about them. It were indeed most desirable that the dissensions by which the Church is now disturbed should be settled by the authority of a pious Council, but as matters are we cannot yet hope for it. Therefore, since Churches are scattered in a dreadful manner, and no hope of gathering them together appears from man, each cannot do better than hasten to rally round the banner which the Son of God holds out to us. This is not a time to keep waiting for one another. As every one sees the light of Scripture beaming forth, let him instantly follow. In regard to the whole body of the Church, we commend it to the care of its Lord. Meanwhile, let us not be either slothful or secure. Let each do his best. Let us contribute whatever in us is of counsel, learning, and abilities, to build up the ruins of the Church. But, in affairs so desperate, let us be sustained and animated by the promise that, as none appears from among men to undertake the office with manly and heroic mind, THE LORD, armed with His own justice and with the weight of His own arm, will Himself alone perform all things.

Menno Simons

To many individuals and groups in sixteenth-century Europe, the revolt against the Catholic Church meant neither Lutheranism nor Calvinism, but simply religious freedom—the freedom to believe and practice what one felt to be the true teaching of Christ, without regard to doctrinal consistency or organizational feasibility. As a result, Luther's revolt triggered the establishment of hundreds of tiny sects, each with its own interpretation—usually radical—of the Scriptures. Sometimes an entire sect was founded on a single sentence in the Old or New Testament, to which, it was held, insufficient attention had previously been paid.

Many historians consider the influence of this "left wing" of the Reformation, especially in England and America, at least as important as that of the larger, more conservative branches. The description "left wing" comes not so much from the socioeconomic doctrines of these people as from their passionate effort to overthrow any social convention or religious practice that might stand in the way of fulfilling true Christian principles as they interpreted them. Their opposition to any authoritarian church caused them to be persecuted by the established churches, both Catholic and Protestant, and their anti-intellectualism earned them the scorn of theologians and other scholars; it is to their great honor that they had the courage to face these consequences.

It is difficult to find a typical representative of this type of Protestantism. The writings of Menno Simons (1496–1561), whose ministry was in Holland and North Germany, are lucid, ardent, intelligent, and influential; his Mennonite Church still flourishes. Our selection consists of snippets from these writings, compiled to give an idea of Simons' fundamental concepts, his appeal, and the image he had of his own group. They have been taken from a volume published by Mennonites in 1936, the 400th anniversary of Simons' renunciation of Catholicism.

[Regeneration]

The new birth consists verily not in water nor in words, but it is the heavenly quickening power of God in our hearts which comes from God and through the preaching of

Menno Simons' Life and Writings: a Quadricentennial Tribute 1536–1936, ed. and trans. H. S. Bender and J. Horsch (Scottdale, Pa.: Mennonite Publishing House, 1944), pp. 68–72, 75–79, 81–82, 86, 88–98, 104–106, 108–109.

the divine word, if we accept the same by faith, touches, pierces, renews and changes our hearts, so that we are converted from unbelief to faith, from unrighteousness to righteousness, from evil to good, from carnality to spirituality, from the earthly to the heavenly, from the evil nature of Adam to the good nature of Jesus Christ. [II:215a]

All who accept by faith this grace in Christ which is preached through the Gospel, and adhere to it from their hearts, are born anew of God, through the power of the Holy Ghost. Their heart and mind is changed and renewed; yea, they are transferred from Adam into Christ. They walk in newness of life, as willing and obedient children, in the grace that is extended to them. They are renewed, I say, have become poor in spirit, meek, merciful, compassionate, peaceable, patient, hungry and thirsty after righteousness, ready to suffer for the truth; they strive steadfastly by good works after eternal life; for they are believing, they are born of God, they are in Christ and Christ in them; they partake of His Spirit and nature and thus live by the power of Christ which is in them, according to the Word of the Lord. This is what it means, according to the Scriptures to believe, to be Christians, to be in Christ and Christ in us. [I:147b]

God does not seek words nor appearance but power and deed. Do you think it sufficient if you know Christ only according to the flesh? Or if you but say that you believe on Him, that you are baptized and are Christians, and that you are purchased by the blood and death of Christ? Ah no! I have told you often and tell you again, you must be born of God and your life changed and converted in such a manner that you are new men in Christ, that Christ be in you and you in Christ, or you can never be Christians, for, If any man be in Christ, he is a new creature. [I:172b]

But, first and above all, if you would be saved, your earthly, carnal, ungodly life must be changed. For all the Scriptures, with all their admonitions, threatening, reproving, miracles, examples, ceremonies and ordinances teach us nothing but repentance and a new life. And if you do not repent, there is nothing in heaven or on earth that can help you, for without true repentance one is comforted in vain. We must be born from above, must be changed and renewed in our hearts and thus be transplanted from the unrighteous and evil nature of Adam into the righteous and good nature of Christ, or we can not be helped in eternity by any means, whether divine or human.

The regeneration of which we write, from which follows the contrite, pious life having the promise, comes alone from the Word of the Lord if it is rightly taught and is through the Holy Spirit rightly received into the heart through faith. [I:169a]

[Holiness of Life]

For true evangelical faith is of such nature that it can not be workless or idle; it ever manifests its powers. For as it is the nature of fire to produce nothing but heat and flame, of the sun nothing but light and heat, the water moisture, and a good tree good fruit after its natural properties, so also true evangelical faith brings forth true evangelical fruit, in accordance with its true, good, evangelical nature. [I:118b]

The true believers show in act and deed that they believe, are born of God and spiritually minded. They lead a pious, unblameable life before all men, they are baptized according to the Lord's command, as a proof and testimony that their sins are taken away through Christ's death and that they desire to walk with Him in newness of life; they break the bread of peace with their beloved brethren, as a proof and testimony that they are one with Christ and with His church and that they have or know no other means of grace and of remission of their sins, neither in heaven nor upon earth, than the innocent body and blood of our Lord Jesus Christ alone, which He once through His eternal Spirit, in obedience to the Father, has offered up and shed upon the cross for us poor sinners. They walk in all love and mercy, they serve their neighbors, etc. In short, they order their lives, in their weakness, according to all the words, commandments, ordinances, spirit, rule, example and measure of Christ, as the Scriptures teach; for they are in Christ and Christ is in them. And therefore they live no longer in the old life of sin after the first earthly Adam (weakness excepted), but in the new life of righteousness which is by faith, after the second and heavenly Adam, Christ; as Paul says, "I do not now live, but Christ liveth in me, and the life which I now live in the flesh, I live by the faith of the Son of God Who loved me and gave Himself for me" (Gal. 2:20). And Christ says, that those who love Him will keep His commandments (John 14:15). [II:262*b*]

Besides we teach the true love and fear of God, the true love of our neighbor, to serve and aid all mankind and to injure none, to crucify the flesh and its desires and lusts, to prune the heart, mouth and the whole body with the knife of the divine word, of all unclean thoughts, unbecoming words and actions. Consider now whether this is not the will of God, the true doctrine of Jesus Christ, the rightful use of the ordinances, and the true life, which is of God, although all the gates of hell may willfully oppose it. [II.244*a*]

Again the thoughts of those who are Christians in fact are pure and chaste, their words are true and seasoned with salt, with them yea is yea and nay nay, and their works are done in the fear of the Lord. Their hearts are heavenly and renewed, their minds peaceful and joyous; they seek righteousness with all their heart. In short, they have through the Spirit and word of God such assurance of their faith, that they will through such faith valiantly overcome all bloodthirsty, cruel tyrants with all their tortures, imprisonments, exiling, spoiling of their property, stocks, stakes, executioners, tormentors and henchmen; and out of a godly zeal, with an innocent, pure heart, with simple yea and nay they are willing to die. The glory of Christ, the sweetness of the Word and the salvation of their souls are dearer to them than all that is under heaven. [I:170*a*]

[A True Brotherhood]

In the fourth place some of them charge and assert that we have our property in common. We reply that this charge is false and altogether without foundation. We do not teach nor practice the doctrine of having all property in common. But we teach and maintain by the word of the Lord that all true believers are members of one body, are baptized by one Spirit into one body (I Cor. 10:18) and have one Lord and one God (Eph. 4:5, 6).

Inasmuch as they are thus one, therefore it is Christian and reasonable that they truly love one another and that the one member be solicitous for the welfare of the other, for both the Scriptures and nature teach it. All Scripture urges charity and love, and it is the one sign by which a true Christian may be known, as the Lord says, "By this shall all men know that ye are My disciples (that is, that ye are Christians) if ye have love one to another" (John 13:35).

Beloved reader, it has not been heard of that an intelligent person clothes and cares for one part of his body and leaves the rest destitute and naked. O no, it is but natural to care for all the members. Thus it must be with those who are the Lord's church or body. All who are born of God, are partakers of the Spirit of the Lord and are called into one body of love, according to the Scriptures, are ready by such love to serve their neighbors, not only with money and goods, but also, according to the example of their Lord and Head, Jesus Christ, in an evangelical manner, with life and blood.

They practiced charity and love as much as they have ability; they suffer no one to be a beggar among them; they distribute to the necessity of the saints, receive the miserable, take the stranger into their houses, console the afflicted, assist the needy, clothe the naked, feed the hungry, do not turn their face from the poor, and do not despise their own suffering members—their own flesh (Isa. 58:7, 8). [II:309a]

To repeat: This love, charity and community we teach and practice, and have for seventeen years taught and practiced in such manner that although we have to a great extent been robbed of our property and are yet robbed, and many a pious, God-fearing father and mother has been put to death by the fire, water, or the sword, and we have no secure place of abode, as is manifest, and besides there are dear times, yet, thanks be to God, none of the pious, nor any of their children who have been committed to us, have been found to beg. [II:309b]

They boast of following the word of God, and of being the true Christian church, and never realize that they have entirely lost the evidence of true Christianity. For although they have plenty of everything and many of their own people fare sumptuously and live in voluptuousness, in superfluous expense, going about in silk and velvet, gold and silver and all kinds of pomp and pride and furnish their houses with all manner of costly ornaments, and have their coffers well filled, yet they suffer many of their poor afflicted members, although they are their fellow believers, have received one baptism and partaken of the same bread with them, to go begging, some of them suffering from the bitterest want, hunger and need, and so many of their aged, sick, lame, blind members are compelled to beg their bread at their doors. [II:310a]

[Ordinances]

For the truly regenerated and spiritually minded conform in all things to the word and ordinances of the Lord; not for the reason that they suppose to merit the propitiation of their sins and eternal life; by no means. For this they depend on nothing except the blood and merits of Christ, relying upon the sure promise of the merciful Father which was graciously given to all believers, which blood alone, I say again, is and ever will be the only and eternally valid means of our reconciliation, and not works, baptism or Lord's Supper, as said above. [I:158a]

Repentance must come before the ordinances, and not the ordinances before repentance. For the ordinances of the New Testament are in themselves quite powerless, vain and useless, if that which they signify, namely the new contrite life is not in evidence as has been said above in treating of baptism. [II:65a]

This is briefly, in all matters that concern the Christian church, my only foundation and sincere conviction, that before God neither baptism, nor the Supper, nor any other outward ordinances avail if partaken without the Spirit of God and the new creature, but that before God only faith, spirit, the new creature or regeneration avail, as Paul plainly teaches, Gal. 5:6. All who by the grace of God have received these from above, will be baptized according to the command of the Lord and rightly partake of the Supper. Yea, with ardent desire they accept all the ordinances and doctrine of Jesus Christ and shall never willfully oppose the holy will and plain testimony of God. [II:349b] . . .

[Baptism]

We are not regenerated because we have been baptized, . . . but we are baptized because we have been regenerated by faith and the Word of God (I Pet. 1:23). Regeneration is not the result of baptism, but baptism the result of regeneration. This can indeed not be controverted by any man, or disproved by the Scriptures. [II:215a]

The Scriptures know of only one remedy, which is Christ with His merits, death and blood. Hence, he who seeks the remission of his sins through baptism, rejects the blood of the Lord and makes water his idol. Therefore let every one have a care, lest he ascribe the honor and glory due to Christ, to the outward ceremonies and visible elements. [I:32a] . . .

Since, then, we do not find in all Scripture a single word by which Christ has ordained the baptism of infants, or that His apostles taught and practiced it, we say and confess rightly that infant baptism is but a human invention, an opinion of men, a perversion of the ordinance of Christ. [I:29b]

To baptize before that which is required for baptism, namely faith, . . . is as if one would place the cart before the horse, to sow before plowing, to build before the lumber is at hand, or to seal the letter before it is written. [II:211b]

Lastly, they appeal to Origen and Augustine and say that these assert that they have obtained infant baptism from the apostles. To this we reply and inquire whether Origen and Augustine have proved it from Scripture. If they have done so, we desire to hear it. But if not, we must hear and believe Christ and His apostles, and not Augustine and Origen. [I:37a]

Again, if the infant baptists assert that infant baptism is not forbidden and that therefore it is right, I reply that it is not expressly forbidden in the Holy Scriptures to bless, as they call it, holy water, candles, palms, goblets, and robes, to hold mass and other ceremonies, yet we say rightfully that it is wrong, first because people put their trust in these things, secondly because it is done without the commandment of God, for He has commanded us not a word thereof, and never should any commandment be observed which is not contained or implied in His holy Word, either in letter or spirit. [II:214*b*]

[*Discipline*]

It is evident that a congregation or church can not continue in the salutary doctrine and in a blameless and pious life without the proper practice of discipline. Even as a city without a wall and gates, or a field without an inclosure or fence, or a house without walls and doors, so is also a church without the true apostolic exclusion or ban. For it would be open to all deceiving spirits, all godless scorners and haughty despisers, all idolatrous and insolent transgressors, yes to all lewd debauchers and adulterers, as is the case with all the great sects of the world which style themselves, although improperly, churches of Christ. In my opinion it is a leading characteristic, an honor and a means of prosperity for a true church to teach with Christian discretion the true apostolic exclusion and to observe it carefully with vigilant love according to the teaching of the holy divine Scriptures. [I:241*b*] . . .

[*The Missionary Calling of the Church*]

To the end we preach as much as opportunity and possibility affords, both in daytime and by night, in houses and in fields, in forests and wildernesses, in this land and abroad, in prison and bonds, in water, fire and the scaffold, on the gallows, and upon the wheel, before lords and princes, orally and by writing at the risk of possessions and life, as we have done these many years without ceasing. [II:10] . . .

[*Nonresistance*]

The regenerated do not go to war nor fight. They are the children of peace who have beaten their swords into plowshares and their spears into pruning hooks and know of no war. They give to Caesar the things that are Caesar's and to God the things that are God's. Their sword is the word of the Spirit which they wield with a good conscience through the Holy Ghost. [I:170*b*]

Since we are to be conformed to the image of Christ (Rom. 8:29), how can we, then, fight our enemies with the sword? Does not the apostle Peter say: "For even hereunto were ye called, because Christ also suffered for us, leaving us an example, that ye should follow His steps; Who did no sin neither was guile found in His mouth; Who, when He was reviled, reviled not again; when He suffered He threatened not; but committed Himself to Him that judgeth righteously" (I Pet. 2:21–23; Matt. 16:24). And this accords with the words of John who says: "He that saith he abideth in Him ought himself also so to walk, even as He walked" (I John 2:6). And Christ Himself says: "Whosoever will come after Me, let him deny himself, and take up his cross and follow Me" (Mark 8:34; Luke 9:23). Again: "My sheep hear My voice . . . and they follow Me" (John 10:27). [II:435*b*]

My dear reader, if the poor ignorant world with an honest heart accepted this our hated and despised doctrine, which is not of us but of Christ, and faithfully obeyed it, they could well change their deadly swords into plowshares and their spears into pruning hooks, level their gates and walls, dismiss their executioners and henchmen. For all who accept our doctrine in its power, will by God's grace not have any ill will to any one upon earth, and not against their most bitter enemies, much less wrong and harm them by deeds and actions; for they are children of the Most High who from their hearts love that which is good and in their weakness avoid that which is evil; nay, hate it and are inimical thereto. [II:103*a*]

O man! man! look upon the irrational creatures and learn wisdom. All roaring lions, all frightful bears, all devouring wolves, live in peace among themselves with their own species. But you, poor, helpless creatures, created in God's own image and called rational beings, are born without teeth, claws, and horns and with a feeble nature, speechless and strengthless, yea neither able to walk nor stand, but have to depend entirely upon maternal care—to teach you that you should be men of peace and not of strife. [I:76*a*]

Peter was commanded to put his sword into the sheath. All Christians are bidden to love their enemies, do good to those who do them evil, and pray for those who abuse and persecute them; to give the cloak also if any one sue them at law for the coat; if they are stricken on the right cheek to turn to him who abuses them the other also. Say, beloved, how can a Christian, according to the Scriptures, consistently retaliate, rebel, war, murder, slay, torture, steal, rob and burn cities and conquer countries? (Matt. 26:52; John 18:10; Matt. 5:12, 39, 40). [II:306*b*]

I am well aware that the tyrants who boast themselves Christians attempt to justify their horrible wars and shedding of blood, and would make a good work of it, by referring us to Moses, Joshua, etc. But they do not reflect that Moses and his successors, with their iron sword, have served out their time, and that Jesus Christ has now given us a new commandment and has girded our loins with another sword.—They do not consider that they use the sword of war, which they wield, contrary to all evangelical Scripture, against their own brethren, namely those of like faith with them who have received the same baptism and have broken the same bread with them and are thus members of the same body. [I:198]

Again, our fortress is Christ, our defence is patience, our sword is the Word of God, and our victory is the sincere, firm, unfeigned faith in Jesus Christ. Spears and swords of iron we leave to those who, alas, consider human blood and swine's blood of well nigh equal value. He that is wise, let him judge what I mean. [I:81*b*]

Captains, knights, soldiers and such like bloody men are offering to sell soul and body for money, and swear with uplifted hand that they will destroy cities and countries, apprehend and kill the citizens and inhabitants and rob them of their possessions, although they have never harmed them nor given them any provocation. O what an accursed, wicked, abominable business! And yet it is said that they protect the country and people and assist in administering justice! [I:137*a*]

[Oaths]

Christ says, "Ye have heard that it has been said to them of old time: Thou shalt not forswear thyself, but shalt perform unto the Lord thine oaths. But I say unto you:

Swear not at all, neither by heaven, for it is God's throne, nor by the earth, for it is His footstool," etc. (Matt. 5:33–35). And you, Micron, say that none but light-minded and false oaths are thereby prohibited, as if Moses had permitted Israel to swear light-mindedly and falsely and that to us under the New Testament only, Christ has forbidden it.

If we have the same liberty as the Israelites in this matter, as you assert . . . then tell me, why did the Lord not say: Ye have heard that it has been said to them of old time: Thou shalt not forswear thyself, and I say unto you: Obey this injunction. But he says: Moses has permitted you to swear rightly; but I say unto you: Swear not at all. [II:409*a*]

The oath is required for no other purpose than to obtain truthful statement and testimony. Can, then, the truth not be told without an oath? Do all tell the truth who are under oath? You will admit that the first question is to be answered in the affirmative and the second in the negative.

Is, then, the oath itself the truth of the testimony, or does the truth depend upon him who swears the oath? Why then do not the authorities require the truth to be told with yea and nay, as ordained of God, rather than with an oath which God has forbidden? For they can notwithstanding punish those who are found false in their yea and nay, the same as those who commit perjury. [II:410*a*]

That yea is yea and nay nay with all true Christians, is fully proved by those who, in our Netherlands, are so tyrannically visited with imprisonment, confiscation and torture, with fire, the stake and the sword, when indeed with one word they could escape all this, if they would misuse their yea and nay. But as they are born of the truth, therefore they walk in the truth, and testify to the truth unto death, as may be abundantly seen in Flanders, Brabant, Holland, West Friesland, etc. [II: 274*b*]

[*Capital Punishment*]

If a criminal would truly repent before his God and be born from above, he would then be a saint and a child of God, a fellow partaker of grace, a spiritual member of the Lord's body, sprinkled with His precious blood and anointed with the Holy Spirit —and for such an one to be hanged on the gallows, executed on the wheel, burned at the stake or in any manner be harmed by another Christian who in Christ Jesus is one heart and soul with him, this I should think strange and out of place, considering the compassionate, merciful, loving disposition, spirit and example of Christ, the meek Lamb, which example He has commanded all His chosen children to follow.

Again, if he remain impenitent and his life be taken, this would be nothing else but to unmercifully cut short his time for repentance of which, in case his life were spared, he might yet avail himself; to tyrannically deliver his soul which was purchased with such a precious treasure unto the devil—never taking into consideration that the Son of Man Who says, "Learn of Me" (Matt. 11:28), "I have given you an example" (John 13:15), "Follow Me" (Matt. 16:24), "He is not come to destroy souls, but to save them" (Matt. 18:11; Luke 19:10). [II:407*b*]

Profane history shows that the Lacedemonians who were heathen did not put their criminals to death but imprisoned them and put them at labor. [II:408*a*]

[*Worldliness*]

It would be more in accordance with evangelical requirements, if he [Gellius] would diligently point such proud and exalted persons to the humility of Christ, that they may learn to deny themselves and to consider their origin and destination, that they may repent of their excessive pomp and vanity, their superfluity and ungodliness, fear God from their hearts, walk in His ways and in true humility of heart serve their neighbors with their riches. [II:17*a*]

This is not a kingdom in which one adorns himself with gold, silver, pearls, silk, velvet and costly finery, as does the proud, haughty world, and also your leaders, giving you liberty to do likewise, under the excuse that it is harmless if your heart is free from it. So even Satan might excuse his pride and pretend the lust of his eye to be pure and good. But this is the kingdom of all humility in which not the outward adorning of the body but the inward adorning of the spirit is desired and sought with great zeal and diligence, with a broken heart and a contrite mind. [I:96*a*]

And whatsoever you do, that do in the name and fear of the Lord Jesus, and do not adorn yourself with gold, silver, pearls and embroidered hair, nor with costly, showy clothes, but dress yourselves in such apparel as becometh women of godliness and is serviceable. [I:148]

[*Religious Tolerance*]

Tell me, kind reader, where have you, in all the days of your life read in the apostolic Scriptures, or heard, that Christ or the apostles called upon the power of the magistracy against those who would not hear their doctrine or obey their words? Yea, reader, I know to a certainty that wherever the government is to perform the ban with the sword, there is not the true knowledge, Spirit, word and church of Christ. [II:71]

Faith is a gift of God, therefore it can not be forced upon any one by worldly authorities or by the sword; alone through the pure doctrine of the holy Word and with humble ardent prayer it must be obtained of the Holy Ghost as a gift of grace. Moreover it is not the will of the Master of the house that the tares should be rooted up as long as the day of reaping is not at hand, as the Scriptural parable teaches and shows with great clearness.

Now if our persecutors are Christians, as they think, and accept the word of God, why do they not heed and follow the word and commandment of Christ? Why do they root up the tares before the time? Why do they not fear, lest they root up the good wheat, and not the tares? Why do they undertake to do the duty of angels who, at the proper time, shall bind the tares in bundles and cast them into the furnace of everlasting fire? [I:199]

Further I say: If the government rightly knew Christ and His kingdom, they would in my opinion, rather choose death, than with their worldly power and sword undertake to settle spiritual matters, which are not subject to the authority of man but to that of the great and Almighty God alone. But now they [the magistrates] are taught by their theologians that they should arrest, imprison, torture and slay those who are not obedient to their doctrine, as may, alas, be seen, in many cities and countries. [II:104]

Beloved rulers and judges, if you take to heart these cited Scriptures, and diligently reflect upon them, you will observe that your office is not your own, but God's office and service; and it is in your place to humble yourselves before His majesty, fear His great and adorable name and rightly and reasonably perform your ordained office; further that you should not so unscrupulously, with your earthly and temporal power, undertake to adjust that which belongs to the jurisdiction and kingdom of Christ, the Prince of all princes, you should not by your iron sword judge and punish that which is reserved solely for the judgment of the Most High, namely the faith and matters pertaining thereto, as also Luther and others maintained in the beginning of his labors, but after they had come to a higher and more exalted station, they have forgotten it all. [II:303]

Say, beloved, where do the Holy Scriptures teach that in Christ's kingdom and church, conscience and faith which stand under the authority of God alone, are to be regulated and ruled by the violence, tyranny, and sword of the magistracy? In what instance have Christ and the apostles ever done, advised or commanded this? For Christ says simply: "Beware of the false prophets," and Paul commands that a heretic is to be shunned after one or two admonitions. John says that we shall not greet or receive into our houses the transgressor who does not bring the doctrine of Christ. But they say not: Down with the heretics, arraign them before the magistrates, imprison them, drive them from cities and countries, cast them into the fire and water, as the Romish have done for many years, and even now is found to a great extent among you who fancy yourselves to adhere to the Word of God. [II:118]

Besides, the proud, carnal, worldly, idolatrous and tyrannical princes who do not know God (I speak of the evil princes) set up their mandates, decrees and laws as authoritative, however much they may be contradictory to God and His blessed Word; just as if the almighty Father, the Creator of all things Who holds heaven and earth in His hands, Who rules all things by the Word of His power, had ordained them to command, rule and according to their own judgment prescribe ordinances not only in the temporal kingdom of this perishable world, but also in the heavenly kingdom of our Lord Jesus Christ. O no, beloved, no. This is not the will of God, but it is an abomination in His sight if mortal man will usurp for himself His authority. [II:238]

I think, beloved brethren, that I have clearly shown that the excuses of the tyrants by which they would avert their tyrannical murdering to be just and right, are heathenish in principle. [I:205]

[Persecution]

He who has purchased me with the blood of His love and has called me unworthily to His service, knows me and knows that I seek neither earthly possessions nor a life of ease, but only the praise of my Lord, my salvation and the salvation of many souls. For this I, my poor, feeble wife and little children have for nearly eighteen years endured extreme anxiety, oppression, affliction, homelessness and persecution and must at all times be in danger of life and great peril. Yea when the ministers of the national churches repose on easy beds and downy pillows, we generally have to hide in secluded corners. When they at weddings and baptismal dinners [held when the rite of baptism was observed] are unbecomingly entertained with pipe and tambour and lute, we must stand in apprehension when the dogs bark, that the catchpolls are at hand.

Whilst they are saluted as doctors, preachers and masters by everyone, we must hear that we are Anabaptists, hedge preachers, seducers and heretics and must be saluted in the devil's name. In short, whilst they are richly rewarded for their service with large incomes and easy times, our recompense and portion must be fire, the sword, and death.

Behold my faithful reader, in such anxiety, poverty, oppression and danger of death have I, a homeless man, to this hour constantly performed the service of my Lord, and I hope through His grace to continue therein to His glory, as long as I remain in this earthly tabernacle. What I and my faithful coworkers have sought or could have sought in these arduous and dangerous labors, is from the works and the fruits apparent to all the well-disposed.

Yea, it has come to this (may God make it better) that where four or five, ten or twenty, have met in the name of the Lord, to speak of the Word of the Lord and to do His work, in whose midst Christ is, who fear God with all their heart and lead a pious, unblameable life before all the world, that if they are caught at a meeting or if accusation is brought against them, they must be delivered up to be burned at the stake, or drowned in the water. But those who met in the name of Belial . . . in public houses of ill fame and the accursed drunken taverns, who live in open disgrace and act wickedly against God's Word, such live in all freedom and peace. [I:78b]

In short, dear reader, if the merciful Lord had not, in His great love, tempered the hearts of some of the rulers and magistrates, but had let them proceed according to the instigations and blood-preaching of their theologians, no pious person would survive. But yet a few are found who, notwithstanding the words and writings of all theologians, tolerate the exiles and for a time show them mercy, for which we will forever give praise to God, the Most High, and also return our thanks in all love to such kind and discreet rulers. [II:104b]

When I was of the world, I spake and did as the world and the world hated me not. —While I served the world, the world rewarded me. All men spake well of me even as their fathers did of the false prophets. But now that I love the world with a godly love, seek from my heart its salvation and blessing, admonish, instruct, and rebuke it with Thy holy Word and point it to the crucified Christ Jesus, the world has become to me a grievous cross and a gall of bitterness. So great is its hatred that not only I myself but also all who show me love, mercy and favor must in some places look for imprisonment and death. O blessed Lord, I am considered by them more unfavorable than a notorious thief and murderer. [I:225b] . . .

The said doctrine of the holy divine Word we have had in the German countries for many years, and have it daily more and more in such power and clearness that it is palpable and evident that it is the finger and work of God. For the haughty become humble, the avaricious liberal, the drunkards sober, the unchaste pure, etc. For the Word of God is accepted of them with such assurance that they do not hesitate to forsake father and mother, husband, wife and children, their possessions and life on account of it, and willingly suffer death. For many are burned at the stake, many drowned, many executed with the sword, many imprisoned, exiled and their property confiscated. Nevertheless all avails nothing with the obdurate persecutors. If it is only said, when a poor innocent one of the sheepfold of the Lord has been slaughtered, "He is an Anabaptist," it is believed sufficient. They do not require what proof and scriptural grounds he had, of what nature his conduct and life was, whether he injured any one or not. Neither do they reflect or consider that it must be a special work and power . . . to cause a man to suffer unspeakable infamy and shame, great persecution and misery and often death, as you may see.

However lamentably we may here be persecuted, oppressed, smitten, robbed, burned at the stake, drowned in the water by the hellish Pharoah and his cruel, unmerciful servants, yet soon shall come the day of our refreshing and all the tears shall be wiped from our eyes and we shall be arrayed in the white silken robes of righteousness, follow the Lamb, and with Abraham, Isaac and Jacob sit down in the kingdom of God and possess the precious, pleasant land of eternal, imperishable joy. Praise God and lift up your heads, ye who suffer for Jesus' sake; the time is near when ye shall hear, "Come ye blessed" and ye shall rejoice with Him for evermore. [I:122b]

✑ OF THE LAWS OF ECCLESIASTICAL POLITY

Richard Hooker

Henry VIII of England, elevating a personal whim to the status of national policy over the issue of divorcing his queen, Catherine, set a pattern for 150 years of religious agitation. At first, England retained Catholic worship while dissolving the monasteries and withdrawing recognition from the pope. During the minority of Henry's son, Edward VI, the boy-king's uncles, influenced by the reform movement on the continent, fostered Lutheranism. Then "Bloody Mary" tried to shepherd England back to Rome. Some religious stability appeared during Elizabeth's reign (1558–1603), although Calvinist-inspired Puritans demanded greater reformation, while Catholics sought a return to Rome. The majority of Englishmen seem to have been content with the moderate, broad-minded Protestantism of the Queen, who refused to "make windows into men's souls." In the middle of the seventeenth century the Elizabethan solution temporarily fell under Puritan assaults. Yet once the crisis had been weathered, the mildly doctrinaire state church, requiring little more than acceptance of the broadest Christian beliefs, was restored.

An Oxford scholar and preacher, Richard Hooker (ca. 1554–1600), attempted the nearly impossible—to define the relation of church and state in terms that would be acceptable to every judicious Englishman. His arguments, not so much systematic as observational, emphasized the collective wisdom of human experience through the ages rather than the duty of conforming to a supposedly rigid will of God. To Hooker, a kindly God permitted more than was forbidden, and more often condoned than punished. Later generations found both his writings and his unwritten implications stimulating. John Locke was to be touched by his tolerance, and Hooker's assumption that man is primarily beneficent was of major importance in the eighteenth-century sentimentalism that influenced Rousseau. Of all the types of Protestantism, Hooker's moderate position proved most adaptable to the modern world, and is by far the most common today.

Concerning rites and ceremonies there may be fault, either in the kind or in the number and multitude of them. The first thing blamed about the kind of ours is, that in many things we have departed from the ancient simplicity of Christ and His Apostles; we have embraced more outward stateliness, we have those orders in the exercise of religion, which they who best pleased God and served Him most devoutly never had. For it is out of doubt that the first state of things was best, that in the prime of Christian religion faith was soundest, the Scriptures of God were then best understood by all men, all parts of godliness did then most abound; and therefore it must needs follow, that customs, laws, and ordinances devised since are not so good for the Church of Christ, but the best way is to cut off later inventions, and to reduce things unto the ancient state wherein at the first they were. Which rule or canon we hold to be either uncertain or at leastwise unsufficient, if not both.

For in case it be certain, hard it cannot be for them to shew us, where we shall find it so exactly set down, that we may say without all controversy, "these were the orders of the Apostles' times, these wholly and only, neither fewer nor more than these." True it is that many things of this nature be alluded unto, yea many things declared, and many things necessarily collected out of the Apostles' writings. But is it necessary that all the orders of the Church which were then in use should be contained in their books? Surely no. For if the tenor of their writings be well observed, it shall unto any man easily appear, that no more of them are there touched than were needful to be spoken of, sometimes by one occasion and sometimes by another. Will they allow then of any other records besides? Well assured I am they are far enough from acknowledging that the Church ought to keep any thing as apostolical, which is not found in the Apostles' writings, in what other records soever it be found. And there-

Richard Hooker, "Of the Laws of Ecclesiastical Polity," *Works*, ed. J. Keble (7th ed.; Oxford: Clarendon Press, 1888), Vol. I, 351–360, 407–415.

fore whereas St. Augustine affirmeth that those things which the whole Church of Christ doth hold, may well be thought to be apostolical although they be not found written; this his judgment they utterly condemn. I will not here stand in defence of St. Augustine's opinion, which is, that such things are indeed apostolical, but yet with this exception, unless the decree of some general council have haply caused them to be received: for of positive laws and orders received throughout the whole Christian world, St. Augustine could imagine no other fountain save these two. But to let pass St. Augustine; they who condemn him herein must needs confess it a very uncertain thing what the orders of the Church were in the Apostles' times, seeing the Scriptures do not mention them all, and other records thereof besides they utterly reject. So that in tying the Church to the orders of the Apostles' times, they tie it to a marvellous uncertain rule; unless they require the observation of no orders but only those which are known to be apostolical by the Apostles' own writings. But then is not this their rule of such sufficiency, that we should use it as a touchstone to try the orders of the Church by for ever.

Our end ought always to be the same; our ways and means thereunto not so. The glory of God and the good of His Church was the thing which the Apostles aimed at, and therefore ought to be the mark whereat we also level. But seeing those rites and orders may be at one time more which at another are less available unto that purpose, what reason is there in these things to urge the state of one only age as a pattern for all to follow? It is not, I am right sure, their meaning, that we should now assemble our people to serve God in close and secret meetings; or that common brooks or rivers should be used for places of baptism; or that the Eucharist should be ministered after meat; or that the custom of church feasting should be renewed; or that all kind of standing provision for the ministry should be utterly taken away, and their estate made again dependent upon the voluntary devotion of men. In these things they easily perceive how unfit that were for the present, which was for the first age convenient enough. The faith, zeal, and godliness of former times is worthily had in honour; but doth this prove that the orders of the Church of Christ must be still the selfsame with theirs, that nothing may be which was not then, or that nothing which then was may lawfully since have ceased? They who recall the Church unto that which was at the first, must necessarily set bounds and limits unto their speeches. If any thing have been received repugnant unto that which was first delivered, the first things in this case must stand, the last give place unto them. But where difference is without repugnancy, that which hath been can be no prejudice to that which is. . . .

Yea, but we have framed ourselves to the customs of the Church of Rome; our orders and ceremonies are papistical. It is espied that our Church founders were not so careful as in this matter they should have been, but contented themselves with such discipline as they took from the Church of Rome. Their error we ought to reform by abolishing all popish orders. There must be no communion nor fellowship with Papists, *neither in doctrine, ceremonies, nor government.* It is not enough that we are divided from the Church of Rome by the single wall of doctrine, retaining as we do part of their ceremonies and almost their whole government; but government or ceremonies or whatsoever it be which is popish, away with it. This is the thing they require in us, the utter relinquishment of all things popish.

Wherein to the end we may answer them according unto their plain direct meaning, and not take advantage of doubtful speech, whereby controversies grow always endless; their main position being this, that "nothing should be placed in the Church but what God in His word hath commanded," they must of necessity hold all for popish which the Church of Rome hath over and besides this. By popish orders, ceremonies, and government, they must therefore mean in every of these so much as the Church of Rome hath embraced without commandment of God's word: so that whatsoever such thing we have, if the Church of Rome hath it also, it goeth under the name of those things that are popish, yea although it be lawful, although agreeable to the word of God. For so they plainly affirm, saying, "Although the forms and ceremonies which they (the Church of Rome) used were not unlawful, and that they contained nothing which is not agreeable to the word of God, yet notwithstanding neither the word of God, nor reason, nor the examples of the eldest churches both Jewish and Christian do permit us to use the same forms and ceremonies, being neither commanded of God, neither such as there may not as good as they, and rather better, be established." The question therefore is, whether we may follow the Church of Rome in those orders, rites, and ceremonies, wherein we do not think them blameable, or else ought to devise others, and to have no conformity with them, no not so much as in these things. In this sense and construction therefore as they affirm, so we deny, that whatsoever is popish we ought to abrogate.

Their arguments to prove that generally all popish orders and ceremonies ought to be clean abolished, are in sum these: "First, whereas we allow the judgment of St. Augustine, that touching those things of this kind which are not commanded or forbidden in the Scripture, we are to observe the custom of the people of God and decree of our forefathers; how can we retain the customs and constitutions of the papists in such things, who were neither the people of God nor our forefathers?" Secondly, "although the forms and ceremonies of the Church of Rome were not unlawful, neither did contain any thing which is not agreeable to the word of God, yet neither the word of God, nor the examples of the eldest churches of God, nor reason, do permit us to use the same, *they being heretics and so near about us,* and their orders being neither commanded of God, nor yet such but that as good or rather better may be established." It is against the word of God to have conformity with the Church of Rome in such things, as appeareth in that "the wisdom of God hath thought it a good way to keep His people from infection of idolatry and superstition, by severing them from idolaters in outward ceremonies, and therefore hath forbidden them to do things which are in themselves very lawful to be done." And further, "whereas the Lord was careful to sever them by ceremonies from other nations, yet was He not so careful to sever them from any as from the Egyptians amongst whom they lived, and from those nations which were next neighbours unto them, because from them was the greatest fear of infection." So that following the course which the wisdom of God doth teach, "it were more safe for us to conform our indifferent ceremonies to the Turks which are far off, than to the papists which are so near.". . .

This in effect is the sum and substance of that which they bring by way of opposition against those orders which we have common with the Church of Rome; these are the reasons wherewith they would prove our ceremonies in that respect worthy of blame. . . .

The ears of the people they have therefore filled with strong clamour: "The Church of England is fraught with popish ceremonies: they that favour the cause of reformation maintain nothing but the sincerity of the Gospel of Jesus Christ: all such as withstand them fight for the laws of his sworn enemy, uphold the filthy relics of Antichrist, and are defenders of that which is popish." These are the notes wherewith are drawn from the hearts of the multitude so many sighs; with these tunes their minds are exasperated against the lawful guides and governors of their souls; these are the voices that fill them with general discontentment, as though the bosom of that famous Church wherein they live were more noisome than any dungeon. But when the authors of so scandalous incantations are examined, and called to account how can they justify such their dealings; when they are urged directly to answer, whether it be lawful for us to use any such ceremonies as the Church of Rome useth, although the same be not commanded in the word of God; being driven to see that the use of some such ceremonies must of necessity be granted lawful, they go about to make us believe that they are just of the same opinion, and that they only think such ceremonies are not to be used when they are unprofitable, or "when as good or better may be established." Which answer is both idle in regard of us, and also repugnant to themselves.

It is in regard of us very vain to make this answer, because they know that what ceremonies we retain common unto the Church of Rome, we therefore retain them, for that we judge them to be profitable, and to be such that others instead of them would be worse. So that when they say that we ought to abrogate such Romish ceremonies as are unprofitable, or else might have other more profitable in their stead, they trifle and they beat the air about nothing which toucheth us; unless they mean that we ought to abrogate all Romish ceremonies which in their judgment have either no use or less use than some other might have. But then must they shew some commission, whereby they are authorized to sit as judges, and we required to take their judgment for good in this case. Otherwise their sentences will not be greatly regarded, when they oppose their *methinketh* unto the orders of the Church of England: as in the question about surplices one of them doth; "If we look to the colour, black methinketh is more decent; if to the form, a garment down to the foot hath a great deal more comeliness in it." If they think that we ought to prove the ceremonies commodious which we have retained, they do in this point very greatly deceive themselves. For in all right and equity, that which the Church hath received and held so long for good, that which public approbation hath ratified, must carry the benefit of presumption with it to be accounted meet and convenient. They which have stood up as yesterday to challenge it of defect, must prove their challenge. If we being defendants do answer, that the ceremonies in question are godly, comely, decent, profitable for the Church; their reply is childish and unorderly, to say, that we demand the thing in question, and shew the poverty of our cause, the goodness whereof we are fain to beg that our adversaries would grant. For on our part this must be the answer, which orderly proceeding doth require. The burden of proving doth rest on them. In them it is frivolous to say, we ought not to use bad ceremonies of the Church of Rome, and presume all such bad as it pleaseth themselves to dislike, unless we can persuade them the contrary. . . .

To leave reformed churches therefore and their actions for Him to judge of, in whose sight they are as they are; and our desire is that they may even in His sight be found such as we ought to endeavour by all means that our own may likewise be; somewhat we are enforced to speak by way of simple declaration concerning the proceedings of the Church of England in these affairs, to the end that men whose minds are free from those partial constructions, whereby the only name of difference from some other churches is thought cause sufficient to condemn ours, may the better discern whether that we have done be reasonable, yea or no. The Church of England being to alter her received laws concerning such orders, rites, and ceremonies, as had been in former times an hinderance unto piety and religious service of God, was to enter into consideration first, that the change of laws, especially concerning matter of religion, must be warily proceeded in. Laws, as all other things human, are many times full of imperfection; and that which is supposed behoveful unto men, proveth oftentimes most pernicious. The wisdom which is learned by tract of time, findeth the laws that have been in former ages established, needful in later to be abrogated. Besides, that which sometime is expedient doth not always so continue: and the number of needless laws unabolished doth weaken the force of them that are necessary. But true withal it is, that alteration though it be from worse to better hath in it inconveniences, and those weighty; unless it be in such laws as have been made upon special occasions, which occasions ceasing, laws of that kind do abrogate themselves. But when we abrogate a law as being ill made, the whole cause for which it was made still remaining, do we not herein revoke our very own deed, and upbraid ourselves with folly, yea, all that were makers of it with oversight and with error? Further, if it be a law which the custom and continual practice of many ages or years hath confirmed in the minds of men, to alter it must needs be troublesome and scandalous. It amazeth them, it causeth them to stand in doubt whether any thing be in itself by nature either good or evil, and not all things rather such as men at this or that time agree to account of them, when they behold even those things disproved, disannulled, rejected, which use had made in a manner natural. What have we to induce men unto the willing obedience and observation of laws, but the weight of so many men's judgment as have with deliberate advice assented thereunto; the weight of that long experience, which the world hath had thereof with consent and good liking? So that to change any such law must needs with the common sort impair and weaken the force of those grounds, whereby all laws are made effectual. . . .

Not to stay longer therefore in speech concerning this point, we will conclude, that as the change of such laws as have been specified is necessary, so the evidence that they are such must be great. If we have neither voice from heaven that so pronounceth of them, neither sentence of men grounded upon such manifest and clear proof, that they in whose hands it is to alter them may likewise infalliby even in heart and conscience judge them so: upon necessity to urge alteration is to trouble and disturb without necessity. As for arbitrary alterations, when laws in themselves not simply bad or unmeet are changed for better and more expedient; if the benefit of that which is newly better devised be but small, since the custom of easiness to alter and change is so evil, no doubt but to bear a tolerable sore is better than to venture on a dangerous remedy. . . .

Touching ceremonies harmless therefore in themselves, and hurtful only in respect of number: was it amiss to decree, that those things which were least needful and newliest come should be the first that were taken away, as in the abrogating of a number of saints' days, and of other the like customs, it appeareth they did; till afterwards the Form of Common Prayer being perfected, Articles of sound Religion and Discipline agreed upon, Catechisms framed for the needful instruction of youth, churches purged of things that indeed were burdensome to the people or to the simple offensive and scandalous, all was brought at the length unto that wherein now we stand? Or was it amiss, that having this way eased the Church as they thought of superfluity, they went not on till they had plucked up even those things also, which had taken a great deal stronger and deeper root; those thing which to abrogate without constraint of manifest harm thereby arising, had been to alter unnecessarily (in their judgments) the ancient received custom of the whole Church, the universal practice of the people of God, and those very decrees of our fathers, which were not only set down by agreement of general councils, but had accordingly been put in use and so continued in use till that very time present?

True it is, that neither councils nor customs, be they never so ancient and so general, can let the Church from taking away that thing which is hurtful to be retained. Where things have been instituted, which being convenient and good at the first, do afterwards in process of time wax otherwise; we make no doubt but they may be altered, yea, though councils or customs general have received them. And therefore it is but a needless kind of opposition which they make who thus dispute, "If in those things which are not expressed in the Scripture, that is to be observed of the Church, which is the custom of the people of God and decree of our forefathers; then how can these things at any time be varied, which heretofore have been once ordained in such sort?" Whereto we say, that things so ordained are to be kept, howbeit not necessarily any longer, than till there grow some urgent cause to ordain the contrary. For there is not any positive law of men, whether it be general or particular; received by formal express consent, as in councils, or by secret approbation, as in customs it cometh to pass; but the same may be taken away if occasion serve. Even as we all know, that many things generally kept heretofore are now in like sort generally unkept and abolished every where.

Notwithstanding till such things be abolished, what exception can there be taken against the judgment of St. Augustine, who saith, "That of things harmless, whatsoever there is which the whole Church doth observe throughout the world, to argue for any man's immunity from observing the same, it were a point of most insolent madness?" And surely odious it must needs have been for one Christian Church to abolish that which all had received and held for the space of many ages, and that without any detriment unto religion so manifest and so great, as might in the eyes of unpartial men appear sufficient to clear them from all blame of rash and inconsiderate proceeding, if in fervour of zeal they had removed such things. Whereas contrariwise, so reasonable moderation herein used hath freed us from being deservedly subject unto that bitter kind of obloquy, whereby as the Church of Rome doth under the colour of love towards those things which be harmless, maintain extremely most hurtful corruptions; so we peradventure might be upbraided, that under colour of hatred towards those things that are corrupt, we are on the other side as extreme even against most harmless ordinances. And as they are obstinate to retain that, which no man of any conscience is able well to defend; so we might be reckoned fierce and violent to tear away that, which if our own mouths did condemn, our consciences would storm and repine thereat. The Romans having banished Tarquinius the Proud, and taken a solemn oath that they never would permit any man more to reign, could not herewith content themselves, or think that tyranny was thoroughly extinguished, till they had driven one of their Consuls to depart the city, against whom they found not in the world what to object, saving only that his name was Tarquin, and that the commonwealth could not seem to have recovered perfect freedom, as long as a man of so dangerous a name was left remaining. For the Church of England to have done the like in casting out of papal tyranny and superstition; to have shewed greater willingness of accepting the very ceremonies of the Turk, Christ's professed enemy, than of the most indifferent things which the Church of Rome approveth; to have left not so much as the names which the Church of Rome doth give unto things innocent; to have ejected whatsoever that Church doth make account of, be it never so harmless in itself, and of never so ancient continuance, without any other crime to charge it with, than only that it hath been the hap thereof to be used by the Church of Rome, and not to be commanded in the word of God: this kind of proceeding might haply have pleased some few men, who having begun such a course themselves must needs be glad to see their example followed by us. But the Almighty which giveth wisdom and inspireth with right understanding whomsoever it pleaseth Him, He foreseeing that which man's wit had never been able to reach unto, namely, what tragedies the attempt of so extreme alteration would raise in some parts of the Christian world, did for the endless good of His Church (as we cannot choose but interpret it) use the bridle of His provident restraining hand, to stay those eager affections in some, and to settle their resolution upon a a course more calm and moderate: lest as in other most ample and heretofore most flourishing dominions it hath since fallen out, so likewise if in ours it had come to pass, that the adverse part being enraged, and betaking itself to such practices as men are commonly wont to embrace, when they behold things brought to desperate extremities, and no hope left to see any other end, than only the utter oppression and clean extinguishment of one side; by this mean Christendom flaming in all parts of greatest importance at once, they all had wanted that comfort of mutual relief, whereby they are now for the time sustained (and not the least by this our Church which they so much impeach) till mutual combustions, bloodsheds, and wastes, (because no other inducement will serve), may enforce them through very faintness, after the experience of so endless miseries, to enter on all sides at the length into some such consultation, as may tend to the best reestablishment of the whole Church of Jesus Christ. To the singular good whereof it cannot but serve as a profitable direction to teach men what is most likely to prove available, when they shall quietly consider the trial that hath been thus long had of both kinds of reformation; as well this moderate kind which the Church of England hath taken, as that other more extreme and rigorous which certain churches elsewhere have better liked. In the meanwhile it may be, that suspense of judgment and exercise of charity were safer and seemlier for Christian men, than the hot pursuit of these controversies, wherein they that are most fervent to dispute be not always the most able to determine. But who are on His side, and who against Him, our Lord in His good time shall reveal.

And sith thus far we have proceeded in opening the things that have been done, let not the principal doers themselves be forgotten. When the ruins of the house of God (that house which consisting of religious souls is most immediately the precious temple of the Holy Ghost) were become, not in His sight alone, but in the eyes of the whole world so exceeding great, that every superstition began even to feel itself too far grown: the first that with us made way to repair the decays thereof by beheading superstition, was King Henry the Eighth. The son and successor of which famous king as we know was Edward the Saint: in whom (for so by the event we may gather) it pleased God righteous and just to let England see what a blessing sin and iniquity would not suffer it to enjoy. Howbeit that which the wise man hath said concerning Enoch (whose days were though many in respect of ours, yet scarce as three to nine in comparison of theirs with whom he lived) the same to that admirable child most worthily may be applied, "Though he departed this world soon, yet fulfilled he much time." But what ensued? That work which the one in such sort had begun, and the other so far proceeded in, was in short space so overthrown, as if almost it had never been: till such time as that God, whose property is to shew His mercies then greatest when they are nearest to be utterly despaired of, caused in the depth of discomfort and darkness a most glorious star to arise, and on her head settled the crown, whom Himself had kept as a lamb from the slaughter of those bloody times; that the experience of His goodness in her own deliverance might cause her merciful disposition to take so much the more delight in saving others, whom the like necessity should press. What in this behalf hath been done towards nations abroad, the parts of Christendom most afflicted can best testify. That which especially concerneth ourselves, in the present matter we treat of, is the state of reformed religion, a thing at her coming to the crown even raised as it were by miracle from the dead; a thing which we so little hoped to see, that even they which beheld it done, scarcely believed their own senses at the first beholding. Yet being then brought to pass, thus many years it hath continued, standing by no other worldly mean but that one only hand which erected it; that hand which as no kind of imminent danger could cause at the first to withhold itself, so neither have the practices so many so bloody following since been ever able to make weary. Nor can we say in this case so justly, that Aaron and Hur, the ecclesiastical and civil states, have sustained the hand which did lift itself to heaven for them, as that heaven itself hath by this hand sustained them, no aid or help having thereunto been ministered for performance of the work of reformation, other than such kind of help or aid as the Angel in the Prophet Zachary speaketh of, saying, "Neither by an army nor strength, but by My Spirit, saith the Lord of Hosts." Which grace and favour of divine assistance having not in one thing or two shewed itself, nor for some few days or years appeared, but in such sort so long continued, our manifold sins and transgressions striving to the contrary; what can we less thereupon conclude, than that God would at leastwise by tract of time teach the world that the thing which He blesseth, defendeth, keepeth so strangely, cannot choose but be of Him? Wherefore, if any refuse to believe us disputing for the verity of religion established, let them believe God Himself thus miraculously working for it, and wish life even for ever and ever unto that glorious and sacred instrument whereby He worketh.